THEIR ANGRY CREED

To Mike
   With my warmest, most
heartfelt thanks for your support
and help with this book

   Herbert Purdy
      11 July 2016

THEIR ANGRY CREED

The shocking history of feminism,
and how it is destroying our way of life.

Herbert Purdy

lps publishing

lpspublishing.co.uk

Contents

'Movements born in hatred very quickly take on the characteristics of the thing they oppose.'

- J. S. Habgood

Introduction

It is almost half-a-century since women's liberationists first laid down their challenge to the world, chanting 'Women demand equality,' and 'I'm a second-class citizen,' and the feminist narrative of the historically victimised woman, needing to strive heroically for her rights in a male-dominated society, is a theme that has become burnt into our social consciousness. The entire paradigm is so politically charged - so politically correct - that no politician of any hue would dare have an all-male cabinet, anymore than a large company would contemplate having an all-male board of directors; and this is causing women to be pushed, promoted, and inserted into every walk of life simply because they are women, which amounts to naked preference, bordering on positive discrimination.

Moral panics about rape and domestic violence are rife, and a plethora of women's help agencies exist to meet the perceived demand for women's aid. Most of them are funded by central government, with ring-fenced budgets, and they feed a constant stream of propaganda about men as potential rapists or wife beaters to the press. Mostly it is patently untrue, but, like all propaganda, it is effective in embedding these false social narratives, which, in a feedback loop, justifies the existence of these agencies and secures their funding. Our universities are now hotbeds of gender politics, where free speech is all but closed down, not least because of the strident demand of millennial women students that they must not have their feelings hurt or be made to feel unsafe. In response, many universities are providing 'safe spaces' for women students, free from their male counterparts; such is the degree to which this hysteria is gripping our campuses.

An alleged pay gap is constantly being promoted by feminist-dominated 'think tanks', politicians, and even heads of state such as the President of the United States, Barack Obama, who couch their message in terms of women being forced to work effectively for nothing from 9th November until the end of the year. This is always portrayed as discrimination, despite the fact that an average woman in her lifetime will undoubtedly earn less than an average man, simply because she is likely to have children, and that causes her to make work-life balance decisions. However, feminist campaigners will not allow these explanations, insisting that women are being actively discriminated against.

Even inadvertent slips of the tongue about women, let alone honest attempts to speak about the changing role and place of women in society, are instantly met with a storm of hysterical protest from prominent feminists, such as female MPs, women's advocacy groups, and women in the media, who allege sexism and misogyny with an anger that seems to know no bounds of reasonable behaviour. Character assassination and premature career termination - even of highly eminent people - await anyone foolhardy enough to speak truth to the power in the land that feminism has now become, and this has created such a climate of fear that it has closed down rational social discourse as effectively as any totalitarian regime of the past. As Kevin Alfred Strom once said, 'To learn who rules over you, simply find out who you are not allowed to criticise.'

However, this book does just that. It is an analytical, sometimes polemical account of the historical development of feminism: its precepts, dogma, and its social outcomes. It is an honest attempt to bring clarity and truth to what is actually happening to our society under this deeply divisive totalitarian ideology, which, like a wrecking ball, is tearing us apart; dividing us along a fault-line of 'gender'. My principal thesis is that despite feminism claiming as its credentials the liberal Enlightenment ideals of freedom and equality of opportunity, it is a masquerade beneath which lies a much darker agenda: one that is being worked out by an ideologically driven elite, and which is anathema to everything Western democracies stand for. In 1970, Germaine Greer said this,

> 'Women's liberation, if it abolishes the patriarchal family, will abolish a necessary substructure of the authoritarian state, and once that withers away Marx will have come true, willy nilly, so let's get on with it.' ('Revolution' *The Female Eunuch* 1970)

Influenced by academics such as Greer, who have colonised our campuses, turning them into madrassas of radical feminist theory, a small but influential cadre of highly politically motivated former Women's Liberationists has succeeded to a remarkable degree in implementing what she was expressing. For more than 40 years, through politics, the media, and other key social institutions, these ideologically-driven women (and, it has to be said, men of the same persuasion) have been at work behind the scenes, gaining control of the levers of social and political power, and inexorably changing social policy, the law, and ordinary people's lives in order to conform us all to their dogma.

Greer looked forward to a time when the patriarchal family - the nuclear family - would be abolished. That time has come. Patriarchal families, cemented together by the institution of marriage, have been the bricks in the wall of our society for centuries, but the entire edifice is now in ruins because of Marxist-inspired feminist revolution. Greer's reference to Marxism (echoed, incidentally, by most of the early women's liberation movers and shakers) can be traced back to the 1848 *Communist Manifesto*, in which Karl Marx and Friedrich Engels openly stated that the aim of the communists was to abolish the 'bourgeois' institution of marriage and create a legalised community of women.

The process is simple. If you remove the interdependence of men and women, you will destroy the institution of lifelong marriage as 'one flesh'. If you destroy that then the fall of the patriarchal family will automatically follow. Then the way is clear for a new social order to be constructed – in Marx's case it was communism – and that is precisely what the Women's Liberationists and their fellow travellers and acolytes, now called 'third wave feminists', continue to seek in what is undoubtedly a sustained campaign to bring about permanent social change. This is what our society looks like after 45 years of feminism:

- Marriage, once the committed union for life of a man and a woman, and the key institution that guaranteed social stability, has been de-constructed, re-defined, and all but destroyed. Today, in what amounts to a tidal wave of divorce, initiated by women three times as often as men, half of all marriages will fail, and their median expectation of lasting is only 11 years, according to the UK Office for National Statistics (ONS)

- Marriage has been replaced by a legally uncommitted union of two 'equal partners' (another Marxist dogma), in which technically illegitimate children are being born wholesale, and which has an even worse prognosis of lasting than marriage

- The social role of the mother has been changed. Once the bearer and nurturer of young children until their emerging viability as 'teens, women now combine career with child-bearing and upbringing, attempting to reconcile an impossible set of roles, and often unable to give their best to any of them – least of all to themselves

- The ready provision of maternity leave and the increasing provision of child care allowances from state funding is manoeuvring mothers into leaving their children's upbringing, in their most crucial formative years, to strangers

- Politically correct child-minders, operating in what amount to state-funded nurseries, are taking over the role of shaping and forming our future generations according to broader societal values, rather than the values of their own families. This is what totalitarian states do
- Under successive interventions from governments of all political hues - joined only by a common acceptance that feminism is a good thing - women have been co-opted into the means of economic production (another communist principle). They have been turned into wage-slaves, just like men have always been, and they emulate precisely the women in socialist-communist states
- In fact, women are now working harder for less, as figures released by the ONS show. Although they are roughly half the workforce, they still only contribute about 28% of all income tax, compared to men's 72%. Women *en masse* are being used as working drones, most of them earning pittances, while their privileged sisters argue about the glass ceiling, the pay gap, and women's representation in the boardroom
- Elite feminists, with their social agendas, have even reworked the idea of what constitutes a normal family. For example, Harriet Harman, as far back as 1990, in a report which she co-authored with Patricia Hewitt, another prominent Labour feminist, said, 'It cannot be assumed that men are bound to be an asset to family life or that the presence of fathers in families is necessarily a means to social cohesion'. This is now widely accepted dogma amongst the political classes

The most effective way to bring about a revolution is to perform a *coup d'etat*: you take out the head of state, and the best way to destroy the family is to do the same to its head - the father. That is the true meaning of the feminists' attack on what they call 'patriarchy', which literally means the 'rule or authority of the father'. Feminists hate patriarchy. Everything they do is designed to overthrow it, because the rule of the father represents the social power of men, and the startling reality is that after just four decades they have largely succeeded in achieving their aim. Today, a father as head of the family – as the leader, provider, and protector of his kin – is laughed at as passé: a total anachronism.

This has resulted in a significant social shift to single parenting - which really means the mother - and which, effectively, creates another aimed-for Marxist-feminist principle – a matriarchal society – one in which women effectively rule everything, and around whom everything revolves. And that is not the end of it. Feminists in power are overseeing the systematic removal of fatherhood from our entire society, not least through the family courts, through which their ideology, disguised as political correctness, works like a virus in its operating system. Every day in Britain and the developed nations across the world, draconian decisions about fathers' access to their children are made that serve only to eliminate fathers from those children's lives. In the weasel-worded name of 'doing what is best for the child', countless thousands of fathers are being separated from their children – often for good.

But what is more, those children are being systematically deprived of the only rightful source of their ultimate protection: their father, to have him replaced by a 'new dad', or, more likely, no dad, and all of this is underpinned by a state apparatus that stands ready to step in and fulfil the role of the father whenever it becomes necessary. The social changes that feminism has brought upon us are deep and damaging – especially to children – and that damage is before us, hidden in plain sight:

- According to Sir Paul Coleridge, retired senior judge of the Family Courts Division, a third of all British children are currently caught up in the family justice system. This amounts to approximately 3.8 million, a figure that is very close to the 3.2 million children who are living in poverty (as estimated by the United Kingdom Department for Work and Pensions). This is the outworking of the new one-parent matriarchies
- Children are being passed like parcels, often between warring ex-spouses, who are pursuing their individual careers, their care and upbringing being parcelled out to whomever has the time or the inclination to care for them
- Former wives are routinely flaunting access granted to fathers, and judges turn blind eyes to it, sitting on their hands when it comes to enforcing their own orders
- Hundreds of thousands of children now live in so-called 'blended families', often thrust against their wills into a jumble of step-parents, half-brothers and sisters and assorted non-blood relatives; and all too often permanently deprived of their natural kin on their father's side of the family
- Approximately one-fifth of children caught up in this mess will lose all contact with their fathers for good, according to NatCen, the research

group funded by the Government's Economic and Social Research Council, and that figure has been put at around a third by the family law department of Mishcon de Reya, a leading family law specialist. This is estimated to represent between 130,000 and 213,000 fathers at any given time

- These children are losing their rightful patriarchal inheritance, which is not only financial but also cultural

No one should be in any doubt that a human tragedy of gigantic proportions is being worked out before our very eyes because of our love affair with feminism and women's rights. Feminism is a form of totalitarianism that is being foisted on all of us in the name of fairness and equality for women, and it is being driven by ideologues across the political spectrum, in government and the institutions. At least those who are on the political left, such as Harriet Harman, are relatively open about their ideology. However, even Conservative politicians declare themselves to be followers of this deeply divisive angry creed. Theresa May, for example, the current British Home Secretary - and a Conservative - is not ashamed to be photographed wearing a T-shirt with the slogan 'this is what a feminist looks like', emblazoned across her front. Under the pretence of fairness and equality, these feminists, and their fellow travellers, present a clear and present danger to us all. They are actively undermining the very basis of our Western civilisation by perpetuating a one-sided struggle for power by women against men, and, collectively, they represent the biggest threat to the stability and social cohesion that our nation has seen since the Second World War.

Feminism has nothing to do with equality, and it is not about fairness. Neither is it egalitarianism, nor is it born of the liberalism of the Enlightenment. Feminists are not interested in equality of opportunity, irrespective of race, colour, creed – or sex – principles that are universally accepted as right. Theirs is the communist-utopian definition of equality qua sameness: parity of numbers disconnected from achievement through merit and ability, and divorced from skills and attributes. And, like in the dystopian communities communism created, feminists are positioning themselves to be a powerful ruling elite who run society for their own benefit.

Elitist feminists are building a gigantic gravy train, for which only they have a ticket, and those who believe feminism is a good thing and that it needs to be upheld and even developed, must remove their rose-tinted spectacles and see it for the parasite it really is that is sapping the strength from our societies. They must wake up to the reality that the Achilles heel of feminism is that it cannot possibly be about equality because it seeks a one-sided solution to a concocted problem that takes no account of the other half of society – men. They must see what feminism is doing to our fathers, sons, husbands, brothers - and, yes, to our mothers, daughters, wives and sisters too.

In this book, I call for a total rejection of all that feminism represents, its dogmas and its false form of equality, and I call for right-minded people to take a stand against it wherever they encounter it, so that we can all begin the process of repairing the damage those who are pushing it are wreaking upon us. I call for the restoration of relationships between men and women that are based on mutual respect and understanding, free from the stridency and competitiveness that feminists have falsely fostered in women. I call for a return to a healed, non-contentious society: one in which the fault line of gender, which feminists have deliberately opened up, is bridged, and then closed for good. I call for a return to a society where the real family - the nuclear family - based on a heterosexual man and a woman living together in a stable marriage, based on a covenant commitment for the procreation of children to be brought up, is supported by the state, the law, and social opinion, and are thus encouraged as well as enabled to ensure that our future generations are fully equipped, fully competent, socially-engaged citizens. Especially, I call for the hearts of the fathers to be restored to the children, and the hearts of the children to be restored to the fathers.

Herbert Purdy

Foreword

Sir Roger Scruton: *Modern Manhood*

(This article is reproduced here, by way of a foreword, by kind permission of Mr Scruton, and City Journal. It was first published in City Journal, New York, in Autumn 1999).

Feminists have harped and harpied on about the position of women in modern societies. But what about the men? The radical changes in sexual mores, patterns of employment, and domestic life have turned their lives upside down. Men now encounter women not as 'the weaker sex' but as equal competitors in the public sphere- the sphere where men used to be in charge. And in the private sphere, where an ancient division of labor once gave guidance to those who crossed its threshold, there is no knowing what strategy will be most effective. Manly gestures - holding open a door for a woman, handing her into an automobile, taking charge of her bags - can spark insulted rejection; displays of wealth, power, or influence are likely to seem ridiculous to a woman who herself has more of them; and the disappearance of female modesty and sexual restraint has made it hard for a man to believe, when a woman yields to his advances, that her doing so is a special tribute to his masculine powers, rather than a day-to-day transaction, in which he, like the last one, is dispensable.

The sexual revolution is not the only cause of men's confusion. Social, political, and legal changes have shrunk the all-male sphere to the vanishing point, redefining every activity in which men once proved that they were indispensable, so that now women can do the job, too - or at any rate appear to do it. Feminists have sniffed out male pride wherever it has grown and ruthlessly uprooted it. Under their pressure, modern culture has downgraded or rejected such masculine virtues as courage, tenacity, and military prowess in favor of more gentle, more 'socially inclusive' habits. The advent of in vitro fertilization and the promise of cloning create the impression that men are not even necessary for human reproduction, while the growth of the single-parent household - in which the mother is the only adult, and the state is too often the only provider - has made fatherless childhood into an increasingly common option. These changes threaten to make manhood redundant, and many children now grow up to acknowledge no source of love, authority, or guidance apart from the mother, whose men come and go like seasonal laborers, drifting through the matriarchal realm with no prospect of a permanent position.

The unhappiness of men flows directly from the collapse of their old social role as protectors and providers. For the feminists, this old social role was a way of confining women to the household, where they would not compete for the benefits available outside. Its destruction, they contend, is therefore a liberation- not of women only, but of men, too, who can now choose whether they wish to assert themselves in the public sphere or whether, on the contrary, they wish to stay at home with the baby (which may very well be someone else's baby). This is the core idea of feminism - that 'gender roles' are not natural but cultural, and that by changing them we can overthrow old power structures and achieve new and more creative ways of being.

The feminist view is orthodoxy throughout the American academy, and it is the premise of all legal and political thinking among the liberal elite, which dissidents oppose at peril of their reputations or careers. Nevertheless, a groundswell of resistance to it is gathering force among anthropologists and sociobiologists. Typical is Lionel Tiger, who three decades ago coined the term 'male bonding' to denote something that all men need, and that few now get. It wasn't social convention that dictated the traditional roles of man and woman, Tiger suggests; instead, the millions of years of evolution that formed our species made us what we are. You can make men pretend to be less dominant and less aggressive; you can make them pretend to accept a subordinate role in domestic life and a dependent position in society. But deep down, in the instinctual flow of life that is manhood itself, they will rebel. The unhappiness of men, Tiger argues, comes from this deep and unconfessed conflict between social pretense and sexual necessity. And when manhood finally breaks out - as it inevitably will - it is in distorted and dangerous forms, like the criminal gangs of the modern city or the swaggering misogyny of the city slicker.

Tiger sees sex as a biological phenomenon, whose deep explanation lies in the theory of sexual selection. Each of us, he believes, acts in obedience to a strategy built in to our genes, which seek their own perpetuity through our sexual behavior. The genes of a woman, who is vulnerable in childbirth and needs support during years of child-rearing thereafter, call for a mate who will protect her and her offspring. The genes of a man require a guarantee that the children he provides for are his own, lest all his labor be (from the genes' point of view) wasted. Hence nature itself, working through our genes, decrees a division of roles between the sexes. It predisposes men to fight for territory, to protect their women, to drive away rivals, and to strive for status and recognition in the public world - the world where men conflict. It predisposes women to be faithful, private, and devoted to the home. Both these dispositions involve the working out of long-term genetic strategies - strategies that it is not for us to change, since we are the effect and not the cause of them.

The feminists, of course, will have none of this. Biology may indeed assign us a sex, in the form of this or that organ. But much more important than our sex, they say, is our 'gender' - and gender is a cultural construct, not a biological fact. The term 'gender' comes from grammar, where it is used to distinguish masculine from feminine nouns. By importing it into the discussion of sex, feminists imply that our sex roles are as man-made and therefore malleable as syntax. Gender includes the rituals, habits, and images through which we represent ourselves to one another as sexual beings. It is not sex but the consciousness of sex. Hitherto, say the feminists, the 'gender identity' of women is something that men have imposed upon them. The time has come for women to forge their own gender identity, to remake their sexuality as a sphere of freedom rather than a sphere of bondage.

Taken to extremes - and feminism takes everything to extremes - the theory reduces sex to a mere appearance, with gender as the reality. If, having forged your true gender identity, you find yourself housed in the wrong kind of body, then it is the body that must change. If you believe yourself to be a woman, then you are a woman, notwithstanding the fact that you have the body of a man. Hence medical practitioners, instead of regarding sex-change operations as a gross violation of the body and indeed a kind of criminal assault, now endorse them, and in England the National Health Service pays for them. Gender, in the feminists' radical conception of it, begins to sound like a dangerous fantasy, rather like the genetic theories of Lysenko, Stalin's favorite biologist, who argued that acquired characteristics could be inherited, so that man could mold his own nature with almost infinite plasticity. Perhaps we should replace the old question that James Thurber put before us at the start of the sexual revolution with a new equivalent: not 'Is Sex Necessary?' but 'Is Gender Possible?'

In a certain measure, however, the feminists are right to distinguish sex from gender and to imply that we are free to revise our images of the masculine and the feminine. After all, the sociobiologists' argument accurately describes the similarities between people and apes, but it ignores the differences. Animals in the wild are slaves of their genes. Human beings in society are not. The whole point of culture is that it makes us something more than creatures of mere biology and sets us on the road to self-realization. Where in sociobiology is the self, its choices and its fulfillment? Surely the sociobiologists are wrong to think that our genes alone determined the traditional sex roles.

But just as surely are the feminists wrong to believe that we are completely liberated from our biological natures and that the traditional sex roles emerged only from a social power struggle in which men were victorious and women enslaved. The traditional roles existed in order to humanize our genes and also to control them. The masculine and feminine were ideals, through which the animal was transfigured into the personal. Sexual morality was an attempt to transform a genetic need into a personal relation. It existed precisely to stop men from scattering their seed through the tribe, and to prevent women from accepting wealth and power, rather than love, as the signal for reproduction. It was the cooperative answer to a deep-seated desire, in both man and woman, for the 'helpmeet' who will make life meaningful.

In other words, men and women are not merely biological organisms. They are also moral beings. Biology sets limits to our behavior but does not dictate it. The arena formed by our instincts merely defines the possibilities among which we must choose if we are to gain the respect, acceptance, and love of one another. Men and women have shaped themselves not merely for the purpose of reproduction but in order to bring dignity and kindness to the relations between them. To this end, they have been in the business of creating and re-creating the masculine and the feminine ever since they realized that the relations between the sexes must be established by negotiation and consent, rather than by force. The difference between traditional morality and modern feminism is that the first wishes to enhance and to humanize the difference between the sexes, while the second wishes to discount or even annihilate it. In that sense, feminism really is against nature.

Yet at the same time, feminism seems an inevitable response to the breakdown of the traditional sexual morality. People readily accepted the traditional roles when honor and decency sustained them. But why should women trust men, now that men are so quick to discard their obligations? Marriage was once permanent and safe; it offered the woman social status and protection, long after she ceased to be sexually attractive. And it provided a sphere in which she was dominant. The sacrifice permanent marriage demanded of men made tolerable to women the male monopoly over the public realm, in which men competed for money and social rewards. The two sexes respected each other's territory and recognized that each must renounce something for their mutual benefit. Now that men in the wake of the sexual revolution feel free to be serially polygamous, women have no secure territory of their own. They have no choice, therefore, but to capture what they can of the territory once monopolized by men.

It was one of the great discoveries of civilization that men do not gain acceptance from women by brashly displaying their manhood in aggressive and violating gestures. But they do gain acceptance by being gentlemen. The gentleman was not a person with feminine gender and masculine sex. He was through and through a man. But he was also gentle - in all the senses of that lucent word. He was not belligerent but courageous, not possessive but protective, not aggressive to other men but bold, even-tempered, and ready to agree on terms. He was animated by a sense of honor—which meant taking responsibility for his actions and shielding those who depended on him. And his most important attribute was loyalty, which implied that he would not deny his obligations merely because he was in a position to profit from doing so. Much of the anger of women toward men has come about because the ideal of the gentleman is now so close to extinction. Popular entertainment has only one image of manhood to put before the young: and it is an image of untrammeled aggression, in which automatic weapons play a major part, and in which gentleness in whatever form appears as a weakness rather than as a strength. How far this is from those epics of courtly love, which set in motion the European attempt to rescue manhood from biology and reshape it as a moral idea, needs no elaboration.

It was not only the upper classes that idealized the relation between the sexes or moralized their social roles. In the working-class community from which my father's family came, the old mutuality was part of the routine of domestic life, encapsulated in recognized displays of masculine and feminine virtue. One such was the Friday-night ritual of the wage packet. My grandfather would come home and place on the kitchen table the unopened envelope containing his wages. My grandmother would pick it up and empty it into her wallet, handing back two shillings for drink. Grandfather would then go to the pub and drink himself into a state of proud self-assertion among his peers. If women came to the pub they would linger in the doorway, communicating by messenger with the smoke-filled rooms inside but respecting the threshold of this masculine arena as though it were guarded by angels. My grandfather's gesture, as he laid down his wage packet on the kitchen table, was imbued with a peculiar grace: it was a recognition of my grandmother's importance as a woman, of her right to his consideration and of her value as the mother of his children. Likewise, her waiting outside the pub until closing time, when he would be too unconscious to suffer the humiliation of it, before transporting him home in a wheelbarrow, was a gesture replete with feminine considerateness. It was her way of recognizing his inviolable sovereignty as a wage earner and a man.

Courtesy, courtliness, and courtship were so many doors into the court of love, where human beings moved as in a pageant. My grandparents were excluded by their proletarian way of life from all other forms of courtliness, which is why this one was so important. It was their opening to an enchantment that they could obtain in no other way. My grandfather had little to recommend him to my grandmother, other than his strength, good looks, and manly deportment. But he respected the woman in her and played the role of gentleman as best he could whenever he escorted her outside the home. Hence my grandmother, who disliked him intensely - for he was ignorant, complacent, and drunk, and stood across the threshold of her life as an immovable obstacle to social advancement - nevertheless loved him passionately as a man. This love could not have lasted, were it not for the mystery of gender. My grandfather's masculinity set him apart in a sovereign sphere of his own, just as my grandmother's femininity protected her from his aggression. All that they knew of virtue they had applied to the task of remaining to some measure mysterious to each other. And in this they succeeded, as they succeeded in little else.

A similar division of spheres occurred throughout society, and in every corner of the globe. But marriage was its pivotal institution, and marriage depended upon fidelity and sexual restraint. Marriages lasted not only because divorce was disapproved of but also because marriage was preceded by an extended period of courtship, in which love and trust could take root before sexual experiment. This period of courtship was also one of display, in which men showed off their manliness and women their femininity. And this is what we mean, or ought to mean, by the 'social construction' of gender. By playacting, the two partners readied themselves for their future roles, learning to admire and cherish the separateness of their natures. The courting man gave glamour to the masculine character, just as the courting woman gave mystery to the feminine. And something of this glamour and mystery remained thereafter, a faint halo of enchantment that caused each to encourage the other in the apartness that they both admired.

The Taming of the Shrew and Romeo and Juliet, Jane Austen and George Eliot, Henry James and Charlotte Brontë, all have matchlessly described all that, as has D. H. Lawrence (in its lower-class version) in his stories. This literature shows what is missing from sociobiology. Marriage does not merely serve the reproductive strategies of our genes; it serves the reproductive need of society. It also serves the individual in his pursuit of a life and fulfillment of his own. Its capacity for ordering and sanctifying erotic love goes beyond anything required by our genes. As our Enlightenment morality rightly insists, we are also free beings, whose experience is through and through qualified by our sense of moral value. We do not respond to one another as animals but as persons - which means that, even in sexual desire, freedom of choice is essential to the aim. The object of desire must be treated, in Kant's famous words, not as a means only, but as an end. Hence true sexual desire is desire for a person, and not for sex, conceived as a generalized commodity. We surround the sexual act with constraints and interdictions that are in no way dictated by the species, precisely so as to focus our thoughts and desires on the free being, rather than the bodily mechanism. In this we are immeasurably superior to our genes, whose attitude to what is happening is, by comparison, mere pornography.

Even when the sacramental view of marriage began to wane, mankind still held erotic feelings apart, as things too intimate for public discussion, which could only be soiled by their display. Chastity, modesty, shame, and passion were part of an artificial but necessary drama. The erotic was idealized, in order that marriage should endure. And marriage, construed as our parents and grandparents construed it, was both a source of personal fulfillment and the principal way in which one generation passed on its social and moral capital to the next. It was that vision of marriage, as a lifelong existential commitment, that lay behind the process of 'gender construction' in the days when men were tamed and women idealized. If marriage is no longer safe, however, girls are bound to look elsewhere for their fulfillment. And elsewhere means the public sphere—for it is a sphere dominated by strangers, with clear rules and procedures, in which you can defend yourself from exploitation.

The advantage of inhabiting this sphere needs no explaining to a girl whose abandoned mother lies grieving upstairs. Nor do her experiences at school or college teach her to trust or respect the male character. Her sex-education classes have taught her that men are to be used and discarded like the condoms that package them. And the feminist ideology has encouraged her to think that only one thing matters—which is to discover and fulfill her true gender identity, while discarding the false gender identity that the 'patriarchal culture' has foisted upon her. Just as boys become men without becoming manly, therefore, so do girls become women without becoming feminine. Modesty and chastity are dismissed as politically incorrect; and in every sphere where they encounter men, women meet them as competitors. The voice that calmed the violence of manhood - namely, the female call for protection -has been consigned to silence.

Just as the feminine virtues existed in order to make men gentle, however, so manliness existed in order to break down the reserve that caused women to withhold their favors until security was in sight. In the world of 'safe sex,' those old habits seem tedious and redundant. In consequence, there has arisen another remarkable phenomenon in America: the litigiousness of women toward the men they have slept with. It seems as though consent, offered so freely and without regard for the preliminaries once assumed to be indispensable, is not really consent and can be withdrawn retroactively. The charges of harassment or even 'date rape' lie always in reserve. The slap in the face that used to curtail importunate advances is now offered after the event, and in a far more deadly form—a form no longer private, intimate, and remediable, but public, regimented, and with the absolute objectivity of law. You might take this as showing that 'safe sex' is really sex at its most dangerous. Maybe marriage is the only safe sex that we know.

When Stalin imposed Lysenko's theories upon the Soviet Union, as the 'scientific' basis of his effort to re-mold human nature and form it into the 'New Soviet Man,' the human economy continued, hidden away beneath the mad imperatives of the Stalinist state. And a black sexual economy persists in modern America, which no feminist policing has yet succeeded in stamping out. Men go on taking charge of things, and women go on deferring to the men. Girls still want to be mothers and to obtain a father for their children; boys still want to impress the other sex with their prowess and their power. The steps from attraction to consummation may be short, but they are steps in which the old roles and the old desires hover at the edge of things. Hence nothing is more interesting to the visiting anthropologist than the antics of American college students: the girl who, in the midst of some foulmouthed feminist diatribe, suddenly begins to blush; or the boy who, walking with his girlfriend, puts out an arm to protect her. The sociobiologists tell us that these gestures are dictated by the species. We should see them, rather, as revelations of the moral sense. They are the sign that there really is a difference between the masculine and the feminine, over and above the difference between the male and the female. Without the masculine and the feminine, indeed, sex loses its meaning. Gender is not just possible, but necessary.

And here, surely, lies our hope for the future. When women forge their own 'gender identity,' in the way the feminists recommend, they become unattractive to men—or attractive only as sex objects, not as individual persons. And when men cease to be gentlemen, they become unattractive to women. Sexual companionship then goes from the world. All that it needs to save young people from this predicament is for old-fashioned moralists to steal unobserved past their feminist guardians and whisper the truth into eager and astonished ears—the truth that gender is indeed a construct, but one that involves both sexes, acting in mutual support, if it is to be built successfully. In my experience, young people hear with great sighs of relief that the sexual revolution may have been a mistake, that women are allowed to be modest, and that men can make a shot at being gentlemen. And this is what we should expect. If we are free beings, then it is because, unlike our genes, we can hear the truth and decide what to do about it.

CHAPTER 1

REVOLUTION!

'Women's revolution is necessarily situationist: we cannot argue that all will be well when the socialists have succeeded in abolishing private property and restoring public ownership of the means of production. We cannot wait that long. Women's liberation, if it abolishes the patriarchal family, will abolish a necessary substructure of the authoritarian state, and once that withers away Marx will have come true, willy nilly, so let's get on with it.'

Germaine Greer, *The Female Eunuch* 1970, 'Revolution'.

Plotting

A remarkable thing happened on 2nd September 2014. Forty-five years after women's liberationists first laid down their challenge to society, Mallory Millett, younger sister of Kate Millett, arguably *the* prime mover and shaker in the early women's movement, finally lifted the lid on feminism. In just 1,200 words of sisterly betrayal, published as an article on FrontPageMag.com, she disclosed to the world what was really going on behind the scenes in the movement that irrevocably changed the world. Her dramatic, seismic story should give any right-minded person deep cause for concern. Here is an extract from *Marxist Feminism's Ruined Lives:*[1]

> During my junior year in high school, the nuns asked about our plans for after we graduated. When I said I was going to attend State University, I noticed their disappointment. I asked my favorite nun, 'Why?' She answered, 'That means you'll leave four years later a communist and an atheist!' What a giggle we girls had over that. 'How ridiculously unsophisticated these nuns are,' we thought. Then I went to the university and four years later walked out a communist and an atheist, just as my sister Katie had six years before me.
>
> Sometime later, I was a young divorcee with a small child. At the urging of my sister, I relocated to NYC after spending years married to an American executive stationed in Southeast Asia. The marriage over, I was making a new life for my daughter and me. Katie said, 'Come to New York. We're making revolution! Some of us are starting the National Organization of Women and you can be part of it.' I hadn't seen her for years. Although she had tormented me when we were youngsters, those memories were faint after my Asian traumas and the break-up of my marriage. I foolishly mistook her for

1

sanctuary in a storm. With so much time and distance between us, I had forgotten her emotional instability.

And so began my period as an unwitting witness to history. I stayed with Kate and her lovable Japanese husband, Fumio, in a dilapidated loft on The Bowery as she finished her first book, a PhD thesis for Columbia University, 'Sexual Politics'. It was 1969. Kate invited me to join her for a gathering at the home of her friend, Lila Karp. They called the assemblage a 'consciousness-raising-group,' a typical communist exercise, something practiced in Maoist China. We gathered at a large table as the chairperson opened the meeting with a back-and-forth recitation, like a Litany, a type of prayer done in [Sic] Catholic Church. But now it was Marxism, the Church of the Left, mimicking religious practice:

'Why are we here today?' she asked.

'To make revolution,' they answered.

'What kind of revolution?' she replied.

'The Cultural Revolution,' they chanted.

'And how do we make Cultural Revolution?' she demanded.

'By destroying the American family!' they answered.

'How do we destroy the family?' she came back.

'By destroying the American Patriarch,' they cried exuberantly.

'And how do we destroy the American Patriarch?' she replied.

'By taking away his power!'

'How do we do that?'

'By destroying monogamy!' they shouted.

'How can we destroy monogamy?'

Their answer left me dumbstruck, breathless, disbelieving my ears. Was I on planet earth? Who were these people?

'By promoting promiscuity, eroticism, prostitution and homosexuality!' they resounded.

They proceeded with a long discussion on how to advance these goals by establishing The National Organization of Women. It was clear they desired nothing less than the utter deconstruction of Western society. The upshot was that the only way to do this was, 'to invade every American institution. Every one must be permeated with 'The Revolution'": The media, the educational system, universities, high schools, K-12, school boards, etc.; then, the judiciary, the legislatures, the executive branches and even the library system.

It fell on my ears as a ludicrous scheme, as if they were a band of highly imaginative children planning a Brinks robbery; a lark trumped up on a snowy night amongst a group of spoiled brats over booze and hashish… I had outgrown the communism of my university days and was clumsily groping my

2

way back to God. How could twelve American women who were the most respectable types imaginable — clean and privileged graduates of esteemed institutions: Columbia, Radcliffe, Smith, Wellesley, Vassar; the uncle of one was Secretary of War under Franklin Roosevelt — plot such a thing? Most had advanced degrees and appeared cogent, bright, reasonable and good. How did these people rationally believe they could succeed with such vicious grandiosity? And why?

I dismissed it as academic-lounge air-castle-building. I continued with my new life in New York while my sister became famous publishing her books, featured on the cover of 'Time Magazine.' 'Time' called her 'the Karl Marx of the Women's Movement.' This was because her book laid out a course in Marxism 101 for women. Her thesis: The family is a den of slavery with the man as the Bourgeoisie and the woman and children as the Proletariat. The only hope for women's 'liberation' (communism's favorite word for leading minions into inextricable slavery - 'liberation,' and much like 'collective' – please run from it, run for your life) was this new 'Women's Movement.' Her books captivated the academic classes and soon 'Women's Studies' courses were installed in colleges in a steady wave across the nation with Kate Millett books as required reading… 'Your sister's books destroyed my sister's life!' I've heard numerous times. 'She was happily married with four kids and after she read those books, walked out on a bewildered man and didn't look back.' The man fell into despairing rack and ruin. The children were stunted, set off their tracks, deeply harmed; the family profoundly dislocated and there was 'no putting Humpty-Dumpty together again.' … when those women at Lila Karp's table in Greenwich Village set their minds to destroying the American Family by talking young women into being outlaws, perpetrators of infanticide, and haters of Western law, men and marriage, they accomplished just what they intended. Their desire — and I witnessed it at subsequent meetings till I got pretty sick of their unbridled hate — was to tear American society apart along with the family and the 'Patriarchal Slave-Master,' the American husband.

Those of us who were old enough at the time to be aware of current events, like Mallory Millett, wrote Women's Liberation off as a ridiculous bunch of bolshie lesbians, a lunatic fringe who were seeking ludicrous things. It is now clear that we were hopelessly wrong. We completely misunderstood what was afoot in those days, and the purpose behind what was going on. This was a cadre of articulate, highly motivated Marxist activists, and they were deadly serious. They were plotting the total subversion of society as we know it.

Sexual politics

Katherine Murray 'Kate' Millett (1934 -) was 35 years old when she sat at that table in her friend's loft apartment in Greenwich Village in 1969. As her sister says, she was working on her doctoral thesis, which she later published as the enormously influential book *Sexual Politics* in which she discoursed extensively on *The Origin of the Family, Private Property and the State* (1884) by Friedrich Engels, the co-creator with Karl Marx of Communism. She was particularly exercised about the failure of the Bolsheviks in the Soviet Union to abolish the family, a core component of communist thinking.

Stating that, 'sex has a frequently neglected political aspect,' her principal thesis was that the relationship between men and women should be seen as a contest for power in a politically opposed gender-based society. 'Who in a patriarchal society has the sexual power over whom?', she asked. Supporting this argument, she alleged that men were basically afraid of being castrated by women's sexual power, which led them to seek to suppress women's sexuality using social control, and all that was wrapped up in a complex system of economic and social power. The sole aim of patriarchy, she averred, was to create a society entirely for men's benefit, and prevent women obtaining true sexual pleasure in their relations with men.

Setting her theory in the context of male literature, Millett cited writers such as D. H. Lawrence, Henry Miller, and Norman Mailer who, she said, portrayed women's sexuality with a basic sense of disgust, their male characters being inherently sexually aggressive towards women. Taking pornography as an example, she argued that men objectify women's bodies, using them only for their own sexual pleasure, and that this male domination could only ever be overturned by a sexual revolution in which the meaning of masculine and feminine would be redefined, and through which male and female roles would be changed, eventually bringing about a society controlled by women, not men. Humanities scholar, Camille Paglia,[2] has described Millett's scholarship as 'deeply flawed,' adding that when Millett achieved prominence, '...American feminism's nose-dive began'.

Kate Millett's views were very much a product of the times - and of the area in which she lived. Greenwich Village, New York, was a hotbed of revolutionary fervour that had been simmering in that district for almost two decades. It was also a seething cauldron of drugs and alternative sexuality. Millett is a lesbian. She was briefly married but divorced after her repeated love affairs with other women, and although she still declares herself bi-sexual, she was forced to 'come out' publicly in November 1970 after being heckled by a lesbian audience at Columbia University.

She is also severely mentally disturbed. Repeatedly throughout her life she has displayed serious anger psychosis and detachment from reality, resulting in incarceration several times in various psychiatric facilities. In one famous incident at the University of California, Berkeley, after the screening of her feminist documentary film *Three Lives*, she totally lost her mental composure and, according to her sister Mallory, started 'babbling and shouting incoherently' at the audience who gradually got up one by one and left. After that she spent five days in a psychotic rage, causing her family to have to apply to a court for her legal commitment under a mental health order. She evaded it by calling on a high-powered lawyer to represent her, and defending herself robustly before the judge.

'Town Bloody Hall'

In direct response to Millett's analysis of his work, Norman Mailer, himself a controversial and outspoken figure, published a rebuttal entitled *The Prisoner of Sex*,[3] which was serialised in *Harper's Magazine* in 1971. That resulted in a sustained, strident attack from Millett and other proto-feminists, which came to a head in a public meeting, chaired by Mailer, and held in Town Hall close to Greenwich Village on 30th April 1971.[4] The event was later described by Mary V. Dearborn, Mailer's biographer, as, 'Surely one of the most singular intellectual events of the time, and a landmark in the emergence of feminism as a major force'. Millett wasn't at the meeting but Germaine Greer, Diana Trilling, Jacqueline Ceballos of the National Organisation for Women (NOW) were, and so was Jill Johnston, described by William Grimes in his 2010 obituary to her in the *New York Times* as, '… a longtime cultural critic for *The Village Voice*,[5] whose daring, experimental prose style mirrored the avant-garde art she covered, and whose book *Lesbian Nation: The Feminist Solution*, spearheaded the lesbian separatist movement of the early 1970s when she began championing the cause of lesbian feminism'. Johnson caused a sensation. Here is just part of what she said:

> All women are lesbians, except those who don't know it naturally. They are but don't know it yet. I am a woman and, therefore, a lesbian. I am a woman who is a lesbian because I am a woman, and a woman who loves herself

naturally who, with other women, is a lesbian. A woman who loves women, loves herself. Naturally, this is the case. A woman is herself is all woman, is a natural-born lesbian, so we don't mind using the name. Like any name it is quite meaningless. It means naturely [Sic]. I am a woman and whatever I am, we are. We affirm being what we are, the way, of course, all men are homosexuals. Being, having a more sense of their homo: their homo-ness, their ecce homo-ness. Their ecce prince and more than master-ness ... to be equal we have to become who we really are. As women we will never be equal women until we love one another. Especially from the White House. The President of the United States last night announced the appointment of a lesbian to his cabinet. We're getting to the bottom of women's lib. We're going down on women's lib... the new thing that's happening is the withdrawal of women to give to each other their own sense of self. Until women see in each other the possibility of a primal commitment, which includes sexual love, they will be denying themselves the love and value they readily accord to men. Thus affirming their second-class status. Until all women are lesbians there will be no true political revolution...

Having exceeded the allotted time of 10 minutes for each contributor, and having refused to relinquish the podium, Mailer tried to restore order and get her to sit down, but she openly defied him. As the pressure from the audience for her to quit increased, she began to engage in sexual activity on stage with a woman who had come up on the platform. They fondled each other, first standing up, then lying down on the floor and rolling around in an overt sexual embrace. Eventually, having run the audience's patience to its limit, and realising she was getting nowhere, she desisted.

Then, Jacqueline Ceballos got up to speak. Here is what she said, reproduced word for word, with interjections from the audience for a fuller flavour:

When Trudi asked me to be on the panellists I have to tell you frankly that I refused. She asked me to think about it overnight and I thought that it would be cowardly of me not to come here because, first of all, NOW is supposed to be fighting within the system for changes, and Norman Mailer really represents the Establishment. Of course, the liberal part of the Establishment, but still he does represent the Establishment.

I'm not interested in fighting with Norman Mailer. I really think that in his article in Harper's Magazine he was sincerely trying to understand, and I guess that's all we can expect from the majority of men. We are too busy doing the work we have to do to fight with the men who disagree with us. And most of us believe that, sooner or later, they'll come along with us anyway because they won't have any choice.

I represent that large, middle class group of women who could have all the comforts and conveniences of life. In fact I did, but I opted out. Instead, I decided to devote my time to fight for equality of women. I'd like to tell you what we do in the National Organisation for Women. This is considered the 'square' organisation of women's liberation, but we're not too square that we still don't frighten off many, many women and men because they are afraid of the whole women's liberation movement.

I don't think it's necessary to argue about whether women are biologically suited to stay home and wash dishes, can take care of men and children all their lives. I don't think that's important. What is important is that the world is changing and that women at last are waking to the fact that they have a right and a duty to enter into the world and change it. And work towards governing the society that governs them.

[Man heckling] We're all people! It's all of us, not just half of humanity!

Ceballos: Yes, that's right ALL of humanity. My goodness, the excitement has already got started.

[Heckler]: It's ALL humanity, not just half of humanity.

Ceballos: Alright, all of humanity. But let me speak!

[Camera cuts to Germaine Greer grinning and blowing kiss to heckler as he leaves.]

I think we are fighting for all of humanity, but I'd like to tell you, one of the reasons why we don't divert our time fighting for the Peace Movement, or the Civil Rights Movement, or changing the environment is because we believe sincerely that the root of everything is women's liberation. We fight on every front. First of all in employment. In spite of the fact that 40 per cent of the women are working in the United States, we all know - and I know that this is a very sophisticated audience - that women are underpaid and overworked; and there is no chance for advancement anywhere.

We now teach women how to fight discrimination against their own companies: how to sue their companies.

[More heckling from the audience]

[Man:] There's a cop outside and I'm going to get you thrown out.

[Woman:] Why don't you get a pay cut!

On the marriage and divorce front, we have been accused, and many women especially have been very worried that we are against marriage as an institution. What we are against is the structure of marriage, and even though the structure is changing, in spite of everything, we intend to direct it in what we think is the right direction. If women are to be married in a society that pushes them towards marriage, they should be paid for the work that they do. We believe that every person getting married should receive a booklet stating all their responsibilities in marriage. We believe that every married couple should take out marriage insurance in case the marriage breaks up, so the woman will not be subjected to receiving and begging for humiliating alimony. We are working for women, or the dependent partners, to have a social security benefit, independent of their husband or their wives' income. Women should receive pensions. And some of us go so far as to say that women should get paid and that they should receive vacations with pay.

As far as women's image is concerned, we are attacking the advertising industry. You know that the woman is portrayed on television, all over in the media, as the stupid or senile creature. She gets an orgasm when she gets a shiny floor. Before marriage, she is encouraged to keep herself deodorised and as pretty as possible in a doll-like way and a plastic way to get the man. Because the man [her emphasis] is going to be her life. Once she gets him, all the advertising is geared to her cleaning her house and taking care of the children. When she gets a little too old for that, she's the bitter shrew, she's the mother-in-law who's coming to taste that coffee, and she's the poor woman who's losing her husband because she's losing her looks and has to use all sorts of ways to get him back… [Norman Mailer interjects about timing] he's telling me my 10 minutes are up. Alright. Thank you.

Mailer, who died in 2007 aged 84, was no reactionary. Indeed, as well as being a towering literary genius, he was something of an *enfant terrible* himself. He too had been part of the Beatnik culture in Greenwich Village where he had co-founded *The Village Voice*. However, it is clear from the film of the proceedings that he was shocked and perplexed, and not a little angry at seeing the unrestrained behaviour of these early women's liberationists, and their open display of defiance mixed with lesbianism that had been laid bare for all to see. His response was both eloquent and incisive:

What I was trying to say in my usual incoherent fashion in the *Prisoner of Sex* was that biology, or physiology if you will, is not destiny - but it is half of it. And if you try to ignore that fact, you then get, at least as far as I can see any perspective on the future, you then get into the most awful totalitarianism of them all, because it's a left totalitarianism.

I think there is something in the human spirit that can't somehow bear the notion of a fascist or right wing totalitarianism because we can all form some romantic dream that we can all fall into some underground cadre and have this venturous [Sic] life at the end where all of us, men and women, are equal and comrades. But, if we get a left-wing totalitarianism, that means the end of all of us because we will have nothing but scrambled minds trying to overcome the incredible shock that the destruction of human liberty came from the left and not the right, and it is this element in women's liberation that terrifies me.

It terrifies me because it is humourless. Because, with the exception of, let's say, Germaine Greer's book on *The Female Eunuch*, there's almost no recognition that the life of a man is also difficult, and that all the horrors that women go through, some of them absolutely determined by men, even more I expect determined by themselves, because we must face the simple fact that it may be that there's a profound reservoir of cowardice in women which hasn't welcomed this miserable, slavish life. But in any case, whether it's their fault or men's fault, what has to be recognised is that there's nothing automatic about female liberty. Every female liberty is going to be achieved every way any other liberty is going to be achieved, which is going to be achieved against the grain, against the paradox of the fact that there's much in human life which forbids liberty.

So I'm not here to say that every woman must have a child, or every woman must have a vaginal orgasm, or any woman must conceive in any way I lay down. Anyone who says that about me just doesn't know how to read my sentences. What I'm trying to say is let's really get hip about this little matter and recognise that the whole question of women's liberation is the deepest question of faith, and we're going to go right to the very elements of existence and eternity before we're through with it. Because the whole question of how much liberty men and women can find with each other, and how much sharing of conditions they can do goes into the centre of everything. And I'd like this discussion to go at that level.

I'm perfectly willing, if you wish me to act the clown, I will take out my modest little Jewish dick and put it on the table. You can all spit at it and laugh at it, and when I walk away you'll find it was a dildo I left there, I hadn't shown you the real one! But if we're going to have a decent discussion, we all got here tonight at great various effort to ourselves, let's have it at the highest level we can. I would ask Jill Johnston something, which is that she put very neatly half of the notion of women's liberation right up front which is women's liberation is two things: it is a profoundly political movement; and it is a profoundly sexual movement, which quite naturally takes on huge lesbian overtones.

That does not mean at all that every woman who is into women's liberation is a lesbian; obviously not. Anyone who would go ahead and say I then said that, is a fool. But what I am saying is it's quite natural for lesbians to centre on woman's liberation, because there's a peculiar difficulty in lesbianism, which homosexuals, although they are much cursed would, I suspect, not have, which is every male is vulnerable to homosexuality because he cannot have it with a woman. He must go to a man to fundamentally feel like a woman, he must go to a man to have something up his anus or in his mouth [interjection from a man in the audience: 'Up your anus!'], not up mine buddy!

With women, the difficulty is that any man who is a superb lover can be about 90 per cent as good to a woman as a lesbian, just doing the things that a lesbian does, and then he's got all the other stuff. So the result is that lesbians do have a tough time and I think it accounts in part for that intense detestation they have of men. And it is around that intense detestation of men that the worst aspects of women's liberation are forming. So the question I would ask Jill Johnston is 'what is she going to do about all of us 90 per cent-ers?'

A good question, the answer to which I hope this book will go some way to providing. Before I do that, however, it is necessary to explain how a number of social factors came together in what amounted to a perfect storm, which allowed Women's Liberation to take root and flourish.

CHAPTER 2

THE SWINGING SIXTIES

'Sexual intercourse began in nineteen sixty-three (which was rather late for me,) between the end of the "Chatterley" ban, and the Beatles' first LP. Up to then there'd only been a sort of bargaining, a wrangle for the ring, a shame that started at sixteen and spread to everything.'

Philip Larkin (1922-1985) *Annus Mirabilis*

A privileged generation

It is widely believed that World War II gave women a new-found freedom and a confidence that they were as good as men, and that this was the reason for the emergence of women's liberation in the post-war period. It is also said that when the men returned from that war they forced women to move back to the kitchen and the cradle and this caused resentment. Nothing could be further from the truth. Two world wars in two generations in the first half of the twentieth century had undoubtedly showed that women were capable of doing men's work whilst the men went off to fight in defence of their country, but both wars saw everyone, men and women alike, rallying magnificently to the defence of their democratic society and their freedom from tyrannical oppression, and that spirit carried over into the peace.

When the men returned, women gladly went back to their hitherto traditional social roles as wives and mothers. So much so that in the decade immediately following the end of World War II there was a massive spike in the birth rate in Britain and America. The biggest baby boom in history was underway. Children were conceived wholesale in love, hope and the commitment to a better future. There were some social hiccups, certainly. Even though the men returned to their peacetime economic roles and, usually, women gave way and went home to be housewives, some women did choose to carry on working in the post-war reconstruction, which was gathering pace, but they came under severe social criticism. Their children were called 'latch-key kids' because they were being left to fend for themselves after school until their mothers returned from work.

The Boomers, as this generation came to be called, were almost certainly the most privileged in modern times, perhaps in history. They were the

11

beneficiaries of a massive amount of planning in the final years of World War II in anticipation of a victorious peace. British Conservative politician R. A. 'Rab' Butler had reformed the education system, passing the Education Act 1944, which created a three tier system of secondary education, graded by an assessment at age 11 called the 'Eleven Plus'. This created a true (and unrepeated) educational meritocracy. The most academically gifted children went to grammar schools irrespective of their social background, opening up the possibility of a university education that their parents would never even have dreamed of. Those with practical aptitudes went to technical schools, becoming draughtsmen, electricians, engineers, etc., and the remainder were prepared with a sound educational basis for work as apprentices, office workers, construction workers, retail assistants, etc. When these children left school, it was not a question of whether they could find work, it was more who they would work for in a job market hungry for talent.

The Boomers' privileges didn't end there either. They were the first truly healthy generation. The National Health Service (NHS), created in 1948, also a product of Conservative planning for peace in the last years of the war, made first-class health care available to everyone 'free at the point of need' and the entire Welfare State, as it came to be called, was completed in 1949 with the introduction of social care 'from cradle to grave'. Doors were being opened for the young, they were being cared for like never before, and they had the world at their feet. I know because I am part of that generation, and the beneficiary of all the opportunities afforded to it.

'Never had it so good'

The 1950s were a time of rapid change. Post-war reconstruction was underway, there was full employment and Britain was buzzing with big ideas. The Festival of Britain, held in 1952 on London's South Bank, was a defiant statement of technological prowess that sowed seeds of optimism for a brighter future. Elizabeth II became Queen in 1952 on the premature death of King George VI, her dearly loved father, who, with his wife, also Queen Elizabeth, had given steadfast moral leadership throughout the worst days of the conflict. The new queen's coronation, broadcast for the first time on television and filmed in colour, provided a welcome day of excitement for a people still living in the grey aftermath of the war years even though Coronation Day itself, even in June, was cold, windy, and wet. Her youth and beauty inspired the entire nation.

Only four days before the coronation, Sir Edmund Hillary conquered

Mount Everest. He was a New Zealander, but that didn't matter, he was part of the British Commonwealth, and the British people claimed his achievement as their own. In the same year, Watson and Crick discovered the structure of DNA at Cambridge.[6] Watson was an American, but again that didn't blunt the sheer Britishness of the breakthrough. Britain was at the leading edge of post-war jet aircraft development, not just for military purposes but also civilian, based on Frank Whittle's 1930 patent on the jet gas turbine. The de Havilland Comet was the first jetliner to go into service in 1952, and it predated the American Boeing 707 by six years. In 1958 the world's first full-scale nuclear power station came online at Calder Hall in Cumberland, and Britain became the first nation in the world to harness nuclear power for electricity.

At the dawn of the 1960s, Britain had thrown off half a century of war and privation. Average weekly wages were double what they had been after the war, and the then Conservative Prime Minister Harold Macmillan said, 'You've never had it so good'. The Boomer generation was about to burst onto the scene and, although the West was locked into the Cold War with the Union of Soviet Socialist Republics (USSR), it never felt like war to these youngsters, whose culture was taking over the developed world. This intensely and vibrantly alive generation, indulged by their parents, and grandparents, was reinventing what it meant to be young. Elvis Presley in the US and Cliff Richard in Britain (neither of them strictly part of the baby boom but certainly its iconic role models) were making a new type of music, and they were accompanied by a glittering array of other still world famous, still forever young, household names such as the Beatles and the Rolling Stones. A new 'pop' culture was emerging, breaking the mould of everything that had gone before, and a heady social revolution was underway, characterised by freedom, optimism, social mobility, and opportunities in abundance, albeit tinged with more than a hint of fear in the new nuclear age.

Not for nothing was the period called 'The Swinging Sixties'. That term also had another meaning. Promiscuity was 'cool,' although not amongst the Boomers, they were too young. Another slightly older generation was into all that. This was the so-called 'Beat' generation, or 'Beatniks' as its followers were called. Born in the late 1930s, they had suffered the privations of war as children, and they were an angry, rebellious generation who eventually caused the Boomers to squander their birthright. I describe this in detail in the next chapter, but suffice to say for now, Bob Dylan, another of the musical icons of the period, was connected to them and he acted like a bridge to the Boomers, across which much of their disaffection and anarchy passed. There is no better expression of this than the lyrics of his most famous song, *The Times, They Are a Changin'*, first released in 1964:

> Come mothers and fathers throughout the land
> And don't criticise what you can't understand
> Your sons and your daughters are beyond your command
> Your old road is rapidly agin'.
> Please get out of the new one if you can't lend your hand
> For the times they are a-changin'.

Sexual revolution

By the time the 1960s were in full swing, to the horror of their parents, their Boomer children really were beyond their command. Released from the traditional standards of behaviour, and fed with the anarchy, rebellion, anti-conformism and sexual freedom of the angry Beat Generation, they had been ripe for the picking - intellectually, politically, and sexually, and the social atmosphere of those times can only be described as foetid. The Cold War with the USSR was already running hot, and almost anyone who was above extreme childhood in those days can remember the Cuban Missile Crisis in 1963. In that tense 13-day international standoff between the US and the USSR, led respectively by President John F. Kennedy and President Nikita Kruschev, the world stood with bated breath in almost constant anticipation, at any hour, of nuclear war.

Then came the series of brutal assassinations of Kennedy himself, his brother Bobby, Malcolm X, then Martin Luther King, leader of the Civil Rights Movement who had inspired the world in his defence of civil rights in his, 'I have a dream...' speech. These events stunned the world, let alone America, and left people numb. President Kennedy had initiated the 'space race' with the USSR in his 1961 speech to Congress where he declared that the United States should set as its goal 'landing a man on the moon and returning him safely to the earth by the end of the decade'. The Vietnam War, which had started in 1955, was escalating, and the body bags containing the boys who had been drafted into that futile campaign for a cause that they didn't fully understand, and had died far too young, were being brought home in large numbers under the glare of a modern media machine. Draft-dodging hippies were incongruously smoking 'pot' (marijuana) and taking LSD (these were astonishing and vivid times in more ways than one), putting flowers down the barrels of soldiers' guns and preaching peace and free love as the answer to all mankind's ills.

The iconic hippy 'love-in,' held in 1969 at Woodstock, New York State, attracted thousands of weird and wonderful people, with equally weird and wonderful ideas, and was a shop window of the most outlandish examples of the 'New Age'. Licentiousness was everywhere, and the young were obsessed by it. Without being too graphic about it, you could almost smell sex on the air, mixed with the fear of imminent nuclear annihilation. Miniskirts and 'hot pants' became the chosen dress for women who were now uncommitted, available - and highly promiscuous. Sexual experience in a woman became sexiness, instead of being something to be condemned as it had been right up to their mothers' generation, and everyone was experiencing a sexual liberation hitherto unheard of. Such was the preoccupation with sex as a pastime that in 1972 - technically not the Swinging Sixties but still very much a part of its culture - British physician Dr Alex Comfort published *The Joy of Sex*, an illustrated manual of how to do 'it'. Dr Comfort, who was 51 years old, and whose name rather incongruously clashes with the sexual contortions his illustrations depicted, controversially adopted the approach used in cookery books at the time, with sections entitled 'starters' and 'main courses', and his book remained at the top of The New York Times bestseller list for 11 weeks, and was in the top five for 70 weeks. Even more controversially, Comfort illustrated oral sex for both sexes for the first time, as well as 'farther out' practices such as sexual bondage and wife swapping, later to be called 'swinging'. However, Comfort's controversial work seemed tame when compared to that of husband and wife academic team, William Masters and Virginia Johnson, who published *Human Sexual Response* and *Human Sexual Inadequacy* in 1966 and 1970, and which eventually became translated into more than 30 languages.

Masters, already a controversial figure in academia through his research into human sexual response, had originally hired Johnson as his research assistant, then involved her in his experiments, engaging in sex with her in laboratory conditions. Eventually, he divorced his wife and married Johnson, but even by today's standards, this was outlandish behaviour, as was their work. Initially, they employed prostitutes for their experiments, but later recruited 382 women and 312 men, all educated and white middle-class. Many of them were married, and their number included married couples; Masters and Johnson allocated them individually to 'assigned partners' for sexual intercourse during which they recorded the couples' physiological responses, paying particular attention to the women's ability to achieve multiple vaginal orgasms, which they recorded with pen recorders. This short extract from their work illustrates the prurient nature of what they were doing:

> While initial stimulative activity tended to be on a mutual basis, in short order control of the specific sexual experience usually was assumed by one partner. The assumption of control was established without verbal communication and frequently with no obvious nonverbal direction, although on one occasion discussion as to procedural strategy continued even as the couple was interacting physically.

Masters and Johnson didn't stop at heterosexual activity; they conducted similar experiments on homosexual couples, both male and female, which shows the amazing degree to which pre-existing mores were changing towards this once taboo subject. This was the social atmosphere at the end of the 1960s period in which the Boomers came of age. Taking their lead from the Beats for their anger and rebelliousness, and from the hippies with their long hair and 'flower power,' they simply threw off all they had inherited. Young men and women became almost androgynous. The women abandoned their chastity and the men their masculinity, taking to wearing their hair long, like women, and dressing in colourful clothing that accentuated their figures, especially their waists. Women's hot pants and mini-skirts were echoed by 'loon' pants and high-heeled shoes, which altered men's posture and caused them to take on a slightly feminine gait. Male deodorants, unheard of in their fathers' generation, became widespread and normal, and men's skin-care products became available. Men were being exhorted to get 'more in touch with their feminine side' and some commentators have suggested this was a significant inadvertent signal that triggered female assertiveness and anger.[7] However, these were by no means the major cause of the changes. No discussion of the Swinging Sixties can pass without understanding the social effects of 'The Pill' and the legalisation of abortion, both of which were seismic, some might say cataclysmic, in their outcomes.

Abortion and the 'Magic Pill'

Throughout the 1960s, calls were being made for abortion to be made legal. Until then, for centuries, the degree of social condemnation of a woman who wanted or needed to terminate an unwanted pregnancy had driven the entire business underground, into the hands of unregulated back street abortionists who were usually local untrained midwives who administered folk-medicine abortifacients. Sometimes they even used mechanical means to procure an abortion, such as knitting needles inserted through the cervix, and, obviously, this was an extremely risky process for the women.

As social mores changed, however, the Abortion Act of 1967 was introduced into the UK, which legalised abortions by licensed practitioners operating under prescribed guidelines. At the time it was stressed that this was not abortion on demand, but this is what it became in practice. This Marxist/Socialist ideal remains a cornerstone of women's liberation/feminist ideology, and underpins the feminist-driven 'Pro-choice' battle against the traditionalists' 'Pro-life' stance, which continues to rage in the US. However, abortion on demand pales into insignificance when compared to the invention of the contraceptive pill. This was arguably the most empowering development for women in the history of mankind. The idea of a 'magic pill' to control women's fertility had been around from the mid nineteenth century, since the days of Marx and Engels, and its introduction during the 1960s was the outcome of a century of increasing activist pressure. It started with Margaret Sanger who, aged 19 years, and having been born into a Roman Catholic family in Corning, New York State, in 1879, witnessed her mother dying at the age of 50 after having successfully given birth to 11 children but experiencing seven miscarriages along the way. Sanger railed at her father at the funeral saying, 'You caused this. Mother is dead from having too many children!'[8]

Sanger became a nurse on the Lower East Side of Manhattan, New York, caring for immigrant women who, in their desperation at having yet another mouth to feed, were seeking $5 back-street abortions. These were often botched affairs, frequently ending up with the women needing medical attention to save their lives, and when Sanger tried to dispense contraceptives to reduce this, she was prevented by state law, even from sending them through the post, which further incensed her and drove her onwards. In 1916, she opened the first ever birth control clinic, and was immediately arrested. Later, in 1921, she founded the American Birth Control League, a precursor of what came to be known as the Planned Parenthood Federation, a cause which she made her life's work.

Sanger dreamed of finding what she called 'a magic pill' to control women's fertility and, after decades of searching, she finally met a biologist, Dr Gregory

Pincus, while on a visit to London in 1953, who had discovered that oestrogen suppressed ovulation in rabbits. Sanger introduced Pincus to 76-year-old Katharine Dexter McCormick, a wealthy benefactor[9] and avid supporter of the birth control movement, and the rest, as they say, is history. McCormick funded the $2,000,000 needed for Pincus to bring his work to completion and, after extended trials in Puerto Rico, where there were no laws banning contraception, he produced a pill, later named *Enovid*, which G. D. Searle brought to the market on 9th May 1960, after gaining US Federal Drug Administration approval. Upon hearing of this, Sanger who was 80 years old at the time is reported to have said, 'It's about time'. She died six years later.

The Pill, as it became popularly known, is now used in its various forms by over 100 million women worldwide, which approximates to around one in three of all women of reproductive age, and there is no doubt that it has saved the lives of countless women. However, what turned the Pill into a society-changing phenomenon was a later relaxation in US law that allowed it to be given to single women. This was soon followed in the UK. Initially, it was only allowed to be prescribed to married women, but, on March 23rd 1972, the US Supreme Court gave a ruling in the case of Eisenstadt v. Baird which said that no state could stand in the way of distributing birth control to a single person. In Britain the matter had been left to the personal conscience of medical practitioners, but, in 1974, free family planning irrespective of age or marital status, including the Pill, was incorporated into the National Health Service by Barbara Castle, the newly appointed Labour Secretary of State for Health, and a Marxist/feminist firebrand. Thus, Margaret Sanger's long sought after 'magic pill', invented for the honourable cause of protecting women's health, became a political instrument in the pursuit of Women's Liberation. Politically powerful feminists used it to fashion society according to their own ideological worldview.

Interestingly, the Pill's power for social control was first seen by the right wing of politics, at least in the UK. Barbara Castle's Conservative predecessor, Sir Keith Joseph, in his famous 'Pills for Proles' speech, advocated better contraception for women in lower social orders on the grounds that too many children were being born to unfit mothers, and it is clear that even he didn't see the full social implications of Sanger's magic pill. In December 2011, Dame Valerie Beral, professor of epidemiology at Oxford University who has spent the last 40 years researching the Pill, said, 'I don't think people thought it would be as revolutionary as it was'.[10]

This is a mighty understatement. The Pill changed the world. By the early 1970s, the ancient promise of courtship, whereby if a woman became pregnant, the father of her child would 'make an honest woman of her' and marry her, became redundant. Overnight, 'shotgun weddings' became a thing of the past, and the Pill, backed up with abortion on demand, released single women from single motherhood by removing the value of their sexual capital. Today, use of the Pill is heavily skewed to women in the 18 to 30 age group, many of whom are neither married nor in stable relationships, and now that women can choose whether to have children on their own and go it alone without the involvement of a father, men as responsible fathers have been rendered redundant. This is the result of the political hijacking of what was undoubtedly a major humanitarian breakthrough.

Jane Falkingham, the director of the ESRC Centre for Population Change (CPC), has said[11] that the Pill changed men's and women's relationships, and contributed to the social change that separated those relationships from their result - children. Christine Northam, a counsellor working for Relate, reinforces this, saying the Pill changed the dynamics of men's and women's relationships: 'It instigated a change in the role of men and women. Men have had to make changes themselves because their roles have changed, and some have found it easier than others to cope with this'.[12] The Pill also removed the biological imperative for women to marry young in order to secure the best of the pick of partners. According to Katz and Golden[13] in their paper *Career and Marriage in the Age of the Pill*, it had a fundamental effect on women's employment opportunities. In 1960, for example, 18.4% of professionals were women, and of those, 4.7% were 'high powered', as they put it. By 1998, the proportion of professional women had doubled to 36.4%, with 25.1% of those being deemed to be high powered, and all this correlates with a massive reduction in the birth rate by around half in the same period. In 1971, for example, 47% of women in England and Wales who were under 25 had babies (369,600 live births), but by 2008 that had fallen to 25% (180,700 live births).[14]

It is widely believed that the Pill has no side effects for women, and that is probably true as far as its medical implications are concerned. However, research is now showing that widespread use of the Pill might be skewing women's responses to men in their relationships. Put bluntly, taking the Pill might be causing women to be attracted to less masculine men.[15] Many women are reporting reduced sexual interest in their chosen partners after they start taking it, and there is also a higher incidence of reports in the last twenty years of panic attacks, depression, bipolar disorder, and anger in women. These symptoms could be the reason why some young women today are showing such pronounced aggression, which opens the intriguing possibility that the Pill is making them more susceptible to feminism's claims and promises.

There is another intriguing social outcome of the Pill. Of all the women born in 1941, 94% had married by the age of 35, whereas, by 1973, only 60% had married by the same age,[16] and, according to the *Introduction to Cohabitation and Marriage in Britain report*,[17] produced by the ESRC Centre for Population Change, University of Southampton, '...in the 1960s in Britain fewer than one in a hundred adults under 50 are estimated to have been cohabiting at any time, compared with one in six currently. Cohabitation has become a normal part of the life course'. However, co-habitation isn't providing the same satisfaction in women as marriage. In the *Evolution of Cohabitation in Britain* study[18] we find that the vast majority of the respondents (90%) disagreed with the proposition that there was 'no point in getting married,' and that, 'it was only a piece of paper'. This suggests a mismatch between social policy and practice, and peoples' aspirations and values. It might well be telling us that the social trend away from marriage as a permanent commitment that meets the needs of women to have a stable framework in which to commit their bodies to childbearing and rearing, which feminists in high places are undoubtedly advocating, is actually going against the grain of ordinary women.

Economic revolution

By the early 1970s, the groovy, licentious love-in that was the Swinging Sixties was over. Both Britain and the United States were on the brink of a very rude awakening indeed: their economies being changed by unstoppable economic forces. Those nations' burgeoning consumer power was proving to be the nemesis of their traditional industrial bases, literally man-power. Two world wars had sustained the *status quo ante* but a century of industrial-scale manufacture was coming to an end, and men's traditional work was under threat. In the eight years from 1961 to 1969, the number of British people actually making things fell by 75 per cent, and in the broader period from 1952 (the time of the Festival of Britain), to the end of the century, manpower-intensive manufacturing fell from 49% of GDP to only 11%. Services became the dominant basis of Western economies and this caused massive industrial unrest, most notably in the docks and in the mines. It was organised labour's last stand, however. The trades unions had played a major role as counterbalances to capitalism, but their power was over. The 1970s were a decade of discontent and disruption in Britain, and it all came to a head in 1978-79, the so-called 'Winter of Discontent,' when a Labour government collapsed under the weight of anger of its own supporters. Men's muscle was no longer a qualifying criterion for work. Women now had ready access to increased economic opportunities as the result of their new-found liberation from the uncertainty of conception and their ability to be free of unwanted pregnancy.

By then, the incessant drumbeat of Women's Liberation had been beating for a decade, especially in the Labour Party, its spiritual home because it shares Marxism as its ideological root. Women had always played a role in industrial output, particularly during the war years, but mainly in support of men on the shop floor who, as the main value-adding component in industry, enjoyed better wages. They didn't do the same work as men, but taking up the Marxist/feminist message about the equality of men and women as equals in the means of production, left-wing feminist politicians started seeking parity of women's pay with that of men. Their claims were based on a comparison of work types, the 'equal pay for equal work' principle, which is a common criterion used to this day in the women's equal pay debate. In 1968, in what was a landmark dispute over equal pay, militant women seat-cover machinists in the Ford Motor Company in Dagenham, UK, famously went on strike for equal pay with men doing work that was graded as more skilled. The strike ended three weeks after it began, largely through the intervention of Barbara Castle, the Labour government's feminist firebrand and Secretary of State for Employment and Productivity, who secured an uplift for the women and commissioned a new Industrial Court, which failed to uphold their claim. Castle then introduced the Equal Pay Act 1970, whose provisions were reinforced in 1973 when Britain joined the European Common Market. Article 19 of the 1957 Treaty of Rome had long prescribed the principle that men and women should receive equal pay for 'equally valued work'.[19]

Social revolution

After a decade or more of further industrial strife accompanied by swift economic decline, Britain elected a Conservative government, led by Margaret Thatcher, who had beaten Heath for the leadership of the party in 1975, running on a mandate of curbing the unions through strong legislation. Despite a few rearguard actions by the stronger unions, the Thatcher government finally prevailed in a last-ditch stand by the miners, who had tried to strangle the country's power grid using secondary picketing, and Britain was once more able to move on to a new era of economic growth and social stability, albeit one that had been irrevocably changed. During the 11 years of Mrs Thatcher's premiership, the old industries withered or were re-engineered (as in the motor industry), while the service sector burgeoned.

Thatcher's election was highly symbolic for another reason. It showed that women with intelligence, tenacity and a strong work ethic could make it to the top. Her ascendancy to power was a beacon to women that they really did have equality of opportunity in a modern world. However, in the feminist movement, it wasn't seen like that. Many people are puzzled why feminists have never hailed Margaret Thatcher as their champion and role model, but the problem is that Mrs Thatcher, although exceptional in her ambition and ability, was very much a conventional wife and mother. She didn't fit the feminist stereotype of the 'liberated' woman, and neither did her politics. Mrs Thatcher was quintessentially a 'small c conservative' and perhaps the most perfect example of the very thing Marxists hate. She was the daughter of a shopkeeper from a provincial town in Lincolnshire, and a fully paid-up member of the petit bourgeoisie - the shopkeepers and traders whom Marx denounced as lackeys of the capitalist bourgeois (represented, incidentally, by the grandees of the Tory party). And what is more, Thatcher was undoubtedly aware of this. She knew that feminism was the antithesis of everything she and her party stood for, and that feminism is Marxism with makeup. As she acidly observed, 'The feminists hate me, don't they? And I don't blame them. For I hate feminism. It is poison.' However, the groundwork of feminism had been done. Everything was in place. The divorce laws had been relaxed, abortion had been made available virtually on demand, and the Pill was now available to single women. The scene was set for cultural Marxism, which is feminism, taking the stage, which it did with a vengeance in the New Labour government of Tony Blair, who was elected by a landslide in 1997. But more of this in a later chapter.

Political opportunism

Just like the Beach Boys, playing in the warm seas off California's golden beaches, who caught a peeling wave and rode it down the line, Women's Liberation/feminism caught the perfect peeling, political, economic, and social wave, and rode it for all it was worth - pulling with it, swirling and spinning in its vortex, the effete, semi-androgynous, idealistic Boomer generation. In what was a perfect storm of social upheaval, feminism as we know it seized its moment, falsely appropriating the dignified rhetoric of equality of opportunity and the just distribution of social benefit for everyone, regardless of race, creed, colour, or sex, which had been ideas in progress for almost 200 years since the Enlightenment, and well before Karl Marx was even born, and installed its own version of equality: socialist equality; sameness; parity of numbers, in everything.

Imbued with Marxism and its antagonism toward marriage, commitment, and the family, the Boomers changed the social paradigm through sheer weight of numbers, and there is no doubt they aided and abetted the development of feminism as the social operating system we have today. Effete and highly feminised, as many of them remain to this day in their fifties and sixties, the male Boomers' primary occupation was chasing readily available (mini) skirt. They took full advantage of the easy sexual availability of women and sought commitment-less relationships, abandoned their social responsibilities, and in the process, also abandoned due respect for women, especially those who wanted a traditional role as homemaker, mother, and selfless wife. The Boomers entered into a Faustian pact with feminism. Little did they realise that there would be a price to pay, and that all of it would rebound on them, and their sons, and their grandsons (and, indeed on their female offspring too) in a storm of divorce and destruction of families. This generation stands guilty of passing a poisoned chalice to its offspring because it abandoned the very thing young people need if they are to become successful adults: the guidance and protection of a wise and steady father. When Margaret Thatcher described feminism as poison, she well knew of its danger.

CHAPTER 3

AN ANGRY GENERATION

'They fuck you up, your mum and dad.'

Opening line of *This Be The Verse* by Philip Arthur Larkin,
CH, CBE, FRSL, English poet, novelist and librarian (1922-1985)

Infiltration

It is important to understand the degree to which Marxism was at work underneath all the turmoil. World War II, the 'hot' war, had ended, and the Cold War with Russia was well under way. The three decades from 1950 to 1970 saw a gigantic ideological and military standoff between America and the West, and the Union of Soviet Socialist Republics (USSR) and its satellite states. Indeed, it is likely that the only thing that prevented one side launching its nuclear missiles at the other was the sinister but appropriately named concept of MAD - Mutually Assured Destruction. This was Communism vs. Capitalism writ large. The nineteenth century political theories of Marx and Engels were being pitched against the eighteenth century capitalist world view.

Both Russia and China had succumbed to communism early in the twentieth century, and both were exercising hegemony in their respective regions. Korea, Vietnam, Laos, Cambodia had also succumbed and Thailand, Malaysia, Indonesia, Burma, and India were potential targets. When Dwight David Eisenhower, former Supreme Allied Commander in Europe during World War II became America's 34th President in 1953, he articulated the 'Domino Effect Theory' that said if one state in a region fell to communism, the rest would fall like dominoes, so he ordered a policy of containment of this ideological epidemic, engaging in proxy wars in Korea where the Soviet Union, China and their communist allies supported the North Koreans, and the US stood firm by the South. This scenario was repeated in Vietnam under Eisenhower's successor, John Fitzgerald Kennedy, 35th President.

However, the battle against Communism wasn't just in far-off places. As early as 1938, an investigative committee called The House Committee on Un-American Activities (HUAC) had been formed by the US House of Representatives to investigate NAZI spies in America. In 1945 it turned its attention to Communist infiltrations, and in 1947 conducted a series of hearings into alleged Communist sympathies in the Hollywood motion picture industry.[20]

The so-called communist witch hunt that took place in 1950s America is most popularly associated with US Senator Joseph Raymond 'Joe' McCarthy, who led a crusade against Communist infiltration into domestic affairs from 1947 until his premature death in 1957, almost certainly of cirrhosis. McCarthy believed passionately that there were large numbers of Soviet spies and communist sympathisers at work within the federal government and the media, and that they were seeking to undermine the country, and he went after them, seeking to root them and their 'fellow-travellers' out. Contrary to popular belief, McCarthy did not lead the HUAC. At the beginning of his second term as a Senator, and due to an increasing weariness in his colleagues of his stridency and bullying tactics, he was appointed to be chairman of the Senate Committee on Government Operations, a backwater committee thought to be a place where he could do no harm. In fact, this committee's jurisdiction extended to the Senate Permanent Subcommittee on Investigations, whose terms of reference allowed him to use it for his own purposes. Eventually, McCarthy was censured by the Senate, and that finally broke him, but it is interesting that at the height of his activity, he enjoyed 50 per cent public support in Gallup Polls, and 'McCarthyism' will forever be remembered.

Commentators have criticised McCarthy,[21] but in the midst of all the anti-communist fervour of the time, neither America nor the world saw the extent to which cultural Marxism was at work under the radar. Allen Ginsberg, the Greenwich Village Beat poet, whose ideas were finding resonance in the emerging Women's Liberation movement, was one of those who were on McCarthy's list of suspected communist subversives, and he and his like capitalised on the social upheaval of the times. The young women whom Mallory Millett witnessed in Lila Karp's loft apartment in 1968 were deeply radicalised Marxists. They were angry, and they were dangerous.

Double tragedy

Whilst the Boomers were still children in the 1950s, the teenagers of the time were from another stable altogether. In a sense, this was a half-generation, a cohort of children who were born from about the mid-1930s up to and including World War II. They were children during the war, then teenagers and twenty-somethings in the 1950s. Unlike the Boomers, all this generation had known was economic privation, uncertainty - and fear. Many of them had lost their fathers in the war, and whilst victory in 1945 assuaged their fear, it did nothing for their privation, which continued until 1954, when rationing came to an end. I call this the Angry Generation.

In Britain, a good number of these children had lost their entire families in the mass bombing raids on London and other major cities such as Coventry. Millions of them had suffered the trauma of evacuation in 1939 and in 1940[22] they were relocated to safer parts of the country away from the bombs, to be temporarily billeted with strangers, some of whom resented them. Some of these surrogate parents were rather less than caring of their charges, sometimes even mistreating them. Back at home, their mothers were recruited into the fire brigade, the ambulance service, Post Office communications, or a variety of types of military service on the home front. They had to work long hours on shift rosters, with barely enough time to be able to visit their children in the countryside. Some of them had gone to work in the factories, or in the fields in the Women's Land Army. And, of course, most of the evacuees' fathers were away abroad in the armed forces. These wartime children undoubtedly suffered from being deprived of their parents' love and care during their vital early years.

Then, when their fathers finally came home after the war, many of them suffered the trauma of broken homes. As we shall see later, there was a considerable spike in divorces in 1946, when some of the men came home after years of being away, they found that their wives who had been left to fend for themselves and their children - worrying, lonely, and trying to make ends meet - had found other comforts. No doubt, many women found they were married to men who had been dramatically changed by the war and they didn't really know them anymore. Post-traumatic stress disorder (PTSD) must have been rife but it simply wasn't recognised in those days. Perhaps love had died in the trauma and separation. Whatever the reasons, the effect on tens of thousands of children must have been devastating. Divorce and the fracturing of families are now well known to induce anger in children, who feel disempowered by what is happening to their basic source of security.

What few people realise is that by an extraordinary twist of fate, this was an almost exact re-run of what had happened a generation earlier, to this Angry Generation's parents. They too had suffered very similar experiences in the aftermath of the Great War of 1914-18, when their parents had also had to answer the call to arms, in their childhood. Born in the Edwardian era, these children's fathers had been among the 8.6 million men from Britain and the

Commonwealth who went to the unspeakable horror of trench warfare in France. Almost a million of those men never came back, and many more were maimed and scarred for life - just shadows of the men they had been. According to figures produced by the UK Central Statistical Office in the 1920s, almost one million men (956,703 - including Americans and Commonwealth nations' troops who had come to Britain's aid in her time of need) were killed in action, had died of their wounds or disease, or were declared missing, presumed dead. A third of these, 338,955, were never even given a decent burial and, to this day, their remains lie in the earth of a foreign field, beneath the countless red poppies that now symbolise theirs, and their comrades', sacrifice.

The effect of this on British society in particular was profound because 886,000 of those men were British. In the decade spanning the Great War, Britain's population went down from 42 million to 38.3 million, partly because of the inevitable dip in births during wartime, partly because of an influenza pandemic that started in 1918 in the field hospitals in France, and went on to kill over 50 million people worldwide, but mostly because the flower of British manhood had been all but wiped out in bloody conflict. Many of these men were already fathers, but many were single men of marriageable age, and this led to a further problem. Taking 25 as the typical age when people marry and settle down, in 1921 there were 329,927 women and only 267,618 men in Britain: a ratio of near enough 1.24 women of marriageable age for every man. Men were 44.7 per cent of the population, and women were 55.3 per cent. That is an almost 11 per cent gap, when it is normally less than one per cent, either way. Many women of that generation never married because they were simply unable to find a husband. I had two spinster aunts like that. They were sisters and inseparable in each other's company all their lives. When one of them died prematurely in her early 50s, the other followed her within two years, such was her loss. I also remember other unmarried, and, of course, childless, middle-aged women living with each other in our street. No one thought it was unusual.

The 'Angries'

This second successive war-crossover generation, who were teenagers and twenty-somethings in the 1950s, became the thirty-somethings in the 1960s, and it was this generation that filled the ranks of the Women's Liberation movement. They carried with them two generations-worth of loss, privation, and uncertainty, and, understandably, no small degree of latent anger and resentment. That anger and resentment had already become clear in the 1950s when, in London, when a group called 'The Cosh Boys' sprang up around Soho; they triggered a violent gang culture called the 'Teddy Boys' or 'Teds' that caught the mood of the times and spread rapidly. The Teds had a distinctly racist flavour to them, and they were present in large numbers at the 1958 Notting Hill Riots. 'Ted' is a reduction of Edward, as in King Edward, from whom the Edwardians gained the epithet, and their dress code, which was precise and prescribed, emulated the slightly flamboyant but precise style of their grandparents and great-grandparents. One can only speculate why the Teds adopted this style, but it seems possible that they were rebelling against the endless austerity that had been the *leitmotif* in their lives. Maybe they had seen photographs of their families from that bygone age? Maybe they saw it through rose-tinted spectacles and were dressing in a way that lent them some grasp of a time when peace and prosperity prevailed? After all, the Edwardian era was known as, 'that period of pleasure between the enormous achievements of the Victorian age, and the abyss of a half-century of war',[23] One thing is sure, the Teds' dress code was bizarrely out of kilter with the austerity of post-war Britain.

It comprised high-waisted 'drain-pipe' trousers cut short to show coloured socks, and long jackets with velvet collars and pocket-flaps. Known as a 'drape', the jacket was worn over a high-necked, loose-collared white shirt known as a 'Mr B' (after the jazz musician Billy Eckstine who pioneered the style), and was often accompanied by a brocade waistcoat. A 'Slim Jim' maverick-style tie completed the outfit, with a thick crepe-soled suede shoe known as 'the brothel creeper', often in bright blue. The Ted's hair was worn long, but heavily greased with a front quiff and combed back on both sides to form a 'DA'- a 'Duck's Arse'. By contrast with this Edwardian persona, the Teds' girlfriends, known as 'Judies', wore their hair in long plaits and dressed in a pencil or hobble skirt (one with a hem cut just below the knee that restricted walking) in true Edwardian fashion. They too had a drape-style jacket. Later, they took to flat shoes worn with rolled-up jeans or a wide hoop skirt, and a ponytail hairstyle following the American style, as seen in the iconic film Grease, which was set in that era in America.

The typical Ted's music was jazz, and skiffle, a folksy, blues-type music made with homemade instruments, probably because of austerity. Every skiffle band either had a single-string bass comprising a box, a piece of string, and a broom handle, or a washboard 'played' with thimbles on the fingers to make a complex percussive sound. Lonnie Donegan famously pioneered this genre of music, and the Teds would dance to it in their brothel creepers, using a slow shuffle known as 'The Creep'. Indeed, a song called *The Creep* came out in 1953. In the late 1950s, when rock and roll came along, the Teds' favourite singers were Bill Haley and The Comets, Eddie Cochran and Elvis Presley, who in his early career dressed like a Ted.

The Teds were the bad boys, but not everyone in that generation was a Ted, or even angry in their anti-social way. The Angry Generation had within it another group of young men for whom increasing post-war plenty was producing no small degree of earning power. Many of them were employed in a trade, earning wages that were many multiples of what their parents had traditionally earned - and they were spending it on themselves. This was the era of the 'Fifteen Guinea Suit', bought easily out of a sizeable pay packet. It was also the era in which the concept of the teenager emerged, with all the yearning angst of youth we know so well today. This was best summed up in the soulful, some might say whining, plea of Marty Wilde's famous song *Why must I be a teenager in love?* which rose to success in 1959, helped no doubt by Wilde's extraordinary boyish brooding pouting good looks.

There was also another expression of British anger in this generation. Another group of angry young men, actually called 'The Angry Young Men', or just 'Angries', were breaking the mould in literature, poetry, and playwriting. This group included John Osborne, Kingsley Amis, Harold Pinter, John Braine, Arnold Wesker, Alan Sillitoe, and Philip Larkin, whose disillusionment with post-war austerity showed through in an outpouring of literary genius. Interestingly, their work, as with much of that of the angry young men of 1950s Britain, became absorbed into mainstream culture. The Royal Shakespeare Company, for example, embraced the work of the Angry Young Men, as did the newly emerging television channel Independent Television (ITV), which showcased their dramas in it's weekly programme *Armchair Theatre*. Even the BBC, pillar of the establishment screened the series the *Wednesday Play*.

Perhaps the most iconic member of this group was playwright John Osborne. He in particular illustrated the anger and disillusionment of the angry young men of those austere times. His play *Look Back in Anger* became an iconic example of what was known as 'kitchen sink realism' in its portrayal of a bankrupted society where lower-class people subsisted in poverty, whilst educated people, who he describes as 'savages', ride high on the hog. Osborne could always be relied upon to make controversial pronouncements with a political slant, hinting at the emerging Socialism that took firm root in his generation, and which later came back with a vengeance in the 1960s.

However, it was poet Philip Larkin who distilled the essence of the Angry Generation in his poem, *This Be The Verse*:

> They fuck you up, your mum and dad.
> They may not mean to, but they do.
> They fill you with the faults they had
> And add some extra, just for you.
> But they were fucked up in their turn
> By fools in old-style hats and coats,
> Who half the time were soppy-stern
> And half at one another's throats.
> Man hands on misery to man.
> It deepens like a coastal shelf.
> Get out as early as you can,
> And don't have any kids yourself.

Larkin and the Angry Young Men were certainly eloquently disillusioned, but on the other side of the Atlantic, things were shaping up very differently indeed. There, an even more disaffected group of the Angry Generation was about to change the world.

Feminism's ground zero

Today, Greenwich Village, Manhattan, is a leafy suburb of very human proportions. It houses the campus of New York University, located just off Washington Park Square between the towering skyscrapers of midtown Manhattan, and those of the Wall Street district, and the Twin Towers' 'Ground Zero' site. It is a peaceful haven in 'the city that never sleeps'; however, back in the 1950s, 60s, and early 1970s, another Ground Zero was located there. Greenwich Village was the crucible of the social rebellion that became known as Women's Liberation, better known today as feminism.

From as early as 1948 groups of the American version of the Angry Generation began to coalesce there. They were known as the 'Beats,' or 'Beatniks', a term derived from the underground world of hustlers, drug addicts, and petty thieves, and slang for 'beaten down' or 'downtrodden'. The

Beats were the quintessence of America's Angry Generation. Born during the 1930s depression era, they had been youngsters during World War II and, like their British counterparts, they too were disaffected and increasingly left-wing. They also had their literary voices. In *Aftermath: The Philosophy of the Beat Generation*, the American novelist, poet, and literary iconoclast, Jean-Louis 'Jack' Kerouac, hailed by the New York Times in 1957 as 'the voice of the new generation,' and probably the founder of the Beat Generation, said this:

> The Beat Generation, that was a vision that we had, John Clellon Holmes and I, and Allen Ginsberg in an even wilder way, in the late Forties, of a generation of crazy, illuminated hipsters suddenly rising and roaming America, serious, bumming and hitchhiking everywhere, ragged, beatific, beautiful in an ugly graceful new way - a vision gleaned from the way we had heard the word 'beat' spoken on street corners on Times Square and in the Village, in other cities in the downtown city night of postwar America - beat, meaning down and out but full of intense conviction. We'd even heard old 1910 Daddy Hipsters of the streets speak the word that way, with a melancholy sneer. It never meant juvenile delinquents, it meant characters of a special spirituality who didn't gang up but were solitary Bartlebies staring out the dead wall window of our civilisation ...[24]

Kerouac, who died in 1969 at the age of 47 of an internal haemorrhage from cirrhosis of the liver caused by a lifetime of heavy drinking, was something of an enigma politically. Falling between two extremes, the right was critical of him for his use of drugs and his sexual licence, and the left was contemptuous of his anti-Catholic, anti-communist stance. In another book, *Desolation Angels*, he wrote, 'When I went to Columbia [University] all they tried to teach us was Marx, as if I cared'. However, his other beatnik collaborators, Allen Ginsberg and William S. Burroughs did care. They picked up the torch he laid down and made it much more political.

Ginsberg had met Kerouac, Burroughs, and other movers and shakers of the beat generation in homosexual circles at Columbia University, and bonded with them instantly. Seeing a new potential for American youth after the strictures of World War II, and despite America already having its own literary geniuses, such as Norman Mailer and John Steinbeck, Burroughs and Ginsberg set about developing a new vision for American literature, and for America's future. Irwin Allen Ginsberg was a Jew, a poet, a Buddhist and a homosexual, whose mother had been an active member of the Communist Party of America and who carried on a lifetime association with communism. In his epic poem *Howl*, he denounced what he saw as the destructive forces of capitalism and conformity, and rejected out of hand the beliefs and behaviours associated with group norms.

Always prominent in non-violent political protests, against everything from the Vietnam war to the war on drugs, he never let an opportunity pass to make his opposition to militarism, conspicuous consumption and sexual repression very plain indeed, and was described by Helen Vendler, professor of English at Harvard University, as tirelessly persistent in protesting against 'imperial politics, and persecution of the powerless'[25], a theme much echoed to this day in the widespread victim culture. In 1948, whilst reading the poetry of William Blake, Ginsberg claimed he had an auditory hallucination, which lasted several days, in which he initially thought he was listening to the voice of God, but later concluded it was the voice of William Blake. He said he was not using drugs at the time but admitted subsequently that he had tried to use them repeatedly since to replicate the experience.

William Seward Burroughs II was the grandson of W. S. Burroughs, founder of the Burroughs Adding Machine Company, which evolved into the mighty Burroughs Corporation. He was a prolific novelist, essayist, and postmodernist, whose work undoubtedly influenced a wide range of popular culture and literature, and he was addicted to morphine, later making a living by selling heroin in Greenwich Village to support his habit. In 1951, during a drunken party in Mexico City, he accidentally shot and killed his wife whilst trying to shoot an apple from her head, like in the William Tell story. He was convicted of manslaughter, and later said that this event was a pivotal moment in his life, and one that provoked his writing, putting it like this:[26]

> I am forced to the appalling conclusion that I would never have become a writer but for Joan's death, and to a realization of the extent to which this event has motivated and formulated my writing. I live with the constant threat of possession, and a constant need to escape from possession, from control. So the death of Joan brought me in contact with the invader, the Ugly Spirit, and maneuvered me into a life long struggle, in which I have had no choice except to write my way out.

In these few words we see expressed Burroughs' high degree of mental instability, as well as an inwardness and sense of the need to resist control by outside forces, which are the primary characteristic of the beat generation. This was altogether a darker, more visceral, more dangerous expression of a highly politicised youth than happened in Britain. It was not just nonconformist, it was anti-conformist, with strong elements of the idealistic utopianism that later became evident in the hippy movement, and which was enormously attractive to the Boomer youth, as Bob Dylan (b. 1941) said years later in 1985:

> I came out of the wilderness and just naturally fell in with the Beat scene, the bohemian, Be Bop crowd, it was all pretty much connected, it was Jack Kerouac, Ginsberg, Corso, Ferlinghetti ... I got in at the tail end of that and it was magic ... it had just as big an impact on me as Elvis Presley.[27]

Pied pipers

By the late 1960s, the young people of the Boomer generation were going up to university, where the talk in the common rooms and the sororities, in the bars, and the political meetings that are the warp and weft of university life, was rich with a toxic mixture of politics, philosophy, pot - and 'Free Love'. Very few people realise that this is a Marxist idea, and the Boomers certainly didn't. They launched into it with all the alacrity of youth, and the entire scene fed their sense of freedom to do anything that was the zeitgeist. Like the children who danced to the tune of the Pied Piper of Hamelin, the Boomers danced to the new Marxist rhetoric, to which was added the existentialist pseudo philosophy peddled by Jean Paul Sartre and his bisexual, paedophile-sympathising lover, Simone de Beauvoir, both of who were leading lights in the Beatnik movement in France. The Boomers bought it all, lock, stock, and barrel, including de Beauvoir's idea, '*On ne naît pas femme: on le devient*' - 'One is not born, but rather becomes, a woman'.[28] In other words, a woman's sex doesn't dictate her social role, society does.

This paved the way for the women's liberationists' attack on patriarchy, which, they claimed, was the agency by which man-shaped society forced women to be wives and mothers, thus oppressing them through sex, which is the standard rhetoric of feminists today. This is the context in which Betty Friedan's 1963 book *The Feminine Mystique*, found traction. Friedan railed against women's alleged 'imprisonment' in 1950s suburban conformity, and she prepared the ground for the social rebellion of women just a handful of years later. Born in 1921, she was of the generation born to the survivors of the Great War, which produced the Angry Generation from which the Beats evolved, and which had spent its youth fighting World War II. There seems little doubt that her book was itself an expression of anger at the constriction of freedom many women must have felt when their men returned from World War II and normal life resumed in the even greater economic miracle of the US in the 1950s.

It was also the context in which Germaine Greer, born in 1939, and therefore one of the youngest of the angry generation who became the rising star of the nascent Women's Liberation Movement. Greer was and remains a Marxist. In her famous book *The Female Eunuch* 1970, she said:[29]

> 'Women's revolution is necessarily situationist: we cannot argue that all will be well when the socialists have succeeded in abolishing private property and restoring public ownership of the means of production. We cannot wait that long. Women's liberation, if it abolishes the patriarchal family, will abolish a necessary substructure of the authoritarian state, and once that withers away Marx will have come true, willy nilly, so let's get on with it.'

No doubt, many young Boomer women looked at their mothers' lives and compared them with their new-found freedom, concluding that their lives were better. No doubt, they thought their mothers were disadvantaged, oppressed, trapped under their fathers' oppressive, domineering, authoritarianism, a throwback to the inevitable authoritarianism and submission that wartime demands of people. No doubt, they looked at their fathers and saw in them an old-fashioned authority derived from military service, which they interpreted as patriarchal control, backed by male privilege. Given the strictures of war, where unquestioning duty is the culture, it is inevitable that this would be men's and women's default stance, and one which they would expect from their children, especially when responding to the unprecedented social changes that were taking place.

Over-authoritarianism is one of the most natural reactions of fathers concerned for the protection of their unworldly children, especially their daughters, during that crucial transition from teenage to adulthood when the rule of the father must give way to the increasing autonomy of the young adult who must tear away. We must not forget that many of these men had suffered too. Most of them had been drafted against their will into the armed forces and sent abroad for years to fight for a cause, and against an enemy they probably feared. Many had suffered the loss of their comrades in arms, as well as the loss of the best years of their youth, and their personal freedom to enjoy those years. Many of them, no doubt, would be strangers to their children when they finally returned, war weary, scarred, and suffering from post-traumatic stress disorder, a condition that was little understood in those days, and which they suppressed beneath the male stoicism that characterised their generation.

In hindsight, it is easy to see how this played to Friedan's frustrations, and Greer's nakedly politically motivated attack on fatherhood, which the women's liberationists adopted with such alacrity. Friedan, being older, would naturally carry authority in what she said, and Greer, young, good looking, sassy, every inch the modern woman, was the role model for women just a few years her junior, in much the same way as feminism flaunts its role models for girls today. These women were rebellious, articulate, vociferous, and they rode the ever-spreading wave of challenge to social norms and the *status quo ante*, which were the spirit of the age. Their message had an easy passage. The young absorbed it without discernment because youth lacks sufficient experience in which to locate its decisions. Youth is incapable of spotting the charlatans who lead it astray with their radical ideas and their axe-grinding agenda.

The Boomer generation of the 1960s was naïve and full of utopian idealism for a better world; a better way for people to live and exist, and that became toxically mixed with left-wing rebelliousness, voiced by damaged people. Like almost all radical women of their time, both Friedan and Greer had experienced stormy marriages, and Greer had a distant father. Both were women who reflected the tensions between women and men, which were already beginning to emerge, as an exponentially rising divorce rate in the 1960s shows. People married young in those days, and the sexual revolution was already taking its toll on them. Disillusionment, disappointment and upset were widespread and under the influence of angry women and their angry creed, women turned on men as the reason for their disappointments.

A bandwagon was rolling that would become a headlong rush of hysterical female discontent, moral indignation about the alleged plight of women, and utter, unrestrained sexual libertinism. As we saw in the Town Hall episode, this was also heavily influenced by militant lesbianism. Under Marxist-inspired Women's Liberation, the Boomer women allowed themselves to be tuned into a strident political class, opposed to men, who they arbitrarily declared were their oppressors. Sex became weaponised and turned into the political construct of 'gender', and the way was paved for women's roles to be changed irrevocably. Marxist-inspired Women's Liberation, later to become the feminist movement we know today, set about re-writing large chunks of the social operating system that dictated how we live, act, think, and relate to one another. And it worked behind the scenes, disrupting society from the inside. Marriage, mores, institutions, and anything that smacked of patriarchy (which in its most literal sense means the rule or authority of the father), came under sustained attack, along with anything that placed even the slightest restriction on the freedom of women to do as they pleased.

CHAPTER 4

MAKING THE PERSONAL POLITICAL

FEMINIST BELIEF:

'What is a lesbian? A lesbian is the rage of all women condensed to the point of explosion...'

Artemis March. The *Radicalesbians* (1970)

Andrea Dworkin

By 1970, Greenwich Village had already attracted another group of social misfits: angry, damaged, lesbian women, of whom Andrea Dworkin (1946-2005) was a prime example. As you would expect with a lesbian, she had a distaste for heterosexual intercourse, seeing it through Kate Millett's distorting prism of sexual politics. In one of her numerous books, Dworkin said this:[30]

> ... the hatred of women is a source of sexual pleasure for men in its own right. Intercourse appears to be the expression of that contempt in pure form, in the form of a sexed hierarchy; it requires no passion or heart because it is power without invention articulating the arrogance of those who do the fucking. Intercourse is the pure, sterile, formal expression of men's contempt for women...

Dworkin is widely believed to be the source of the idea that all sex is rape, although she repeatedly denied ever using the phrase. One thing is sure, she was utterly consumed by the idea that men seek to dominate women through sex, writing repeatedly about how heterosexual intercourse is the expression of male domination, and her denials must be taken in the context of her writings. For Dworkin, intercourse between a man and a woman had little to do with love. She couched it in terms of a 'power relation' in which 'men have social, economic, political power over women,' calling them, 'their women', and exercising control over them in ways that deny their individual creative expression. She even went as far as to suggest that sex was a form of death for a woman:[31]

I have defined heterosexuality as the ritualized behavior built on a polar role definition. Intercourse with men as we know them is increasingly impossible. It requires an aborting of creativity and strength, a refusal of responsibility and freedom: a bitter personal death.

Like Kate Millett and most of the other movers and shakers of early women's liberation, Dworkin was a seriously damaged woman. According to Ariel Levy in his foreword to her 1987 book *Intercourse*, she had been abused as a nine-year-old child by a stranger, and had then gone on to have a series of disastrous relationships with men whilst still at school, including her high-school philosophy teacher, who introduced her to the works of Jean Paul Sartre and Albert Camus. Whilst still at school she turned to prostitution to raise the funds for her frequent trips to Greenwich Village, where she met and befriended the homosexual poet and communist activist Allen Ginsburg, one of the leaders of the rebellious Beat generation who had congregated there. Not only that, according to Alice Shalvi, writing in the online *Jewish Women's Archive*, Dworkin had a difficult relationship with her mother, who was ill most of her life and had repudiated her. She lost her younger brother, a molecular biologist, to cancer at the age of 43 years, and later married a 'violently abusive Dutch political radical' with whom she lived in the Netherlands towards the end of the 1960s. She left him in 1971 after several years of 'living rough, persecuted, harassed, and even threatened with murder by her husband,' and there seems no doubt that this precipitated her move to the cause of women's liberation, about which Shalvi says this:

> A feminist named Ricki Abrams not only gave her asylum but also introduced her to American feminist literature, with which Dworkin was unfamiliar. Together, the two women began to collaborate on what eventually became Dworkin's first major work on male dominance and sexual violence, *Woman Hating* (1974). In it, she opposed all forms of pornography (which both she and her husband had read), because she believed it incited violence against women. The book was also critical of consensual sex between women and men, which she perceived as an act of everyday subjugation in which women were accomplices. In her view, marriage was 'a legal licence to rape.' Her need 'to try and make people understand how destructive and cruel battering is - and how accepted by society,' later led her to publish two essays on the subject: '*A Battered Wife Survives*' (1978) and '*What Battering Really Is*' (1980), both included *Letters From a War Zone* (1989).

It is easy to see how Dworkin's experiences influenced her writing. It is also easy to see the connection between her and modern feminists' preoccupation with pornography and domestic violence. Her anger about her own personal experience is undoubtedly an energy behind feminism today, and that is most visibly expressed in the idea of 'Everyday Sexism,' a clear expression of hostility towards heterosexuality that denies the natural expression of men's basic masculine sexual attraction to women and the erotic delight most women have in receiving it. As Dworkin said in her first book, *Woman Hating: A Radical Look at Sexuality*:[32]

> We want to destroy sexism, that is, polar role definitions of male and female, man and woman. We want to destroy patriarchal power at its source, the family; in its most hideous form, the nation-state. We want to destroy the structure of culture as we know it, its art, its churches, its laws...

Dworkin was an angry revolutionary who made her motives clear in the opening to her 1974 book, *Woman Hating: A Radical Look at Sexuality*, where she openly states that the book itself is a political action with revolution as its goal, and that it has no other purpose. Declaring herself and her work as 'part of a planetary movement,' she clearly intended to restructure society and 'human consciousness' in order to overturn male domination, which she defined as a '...fundamental psychological, political, and cultural reality,' based on the premise that man and woman are 'fictions, caricatures [and] cultural constructs, which are dead ended for male and female both.' This is a regurgitation of the philosophy of Simone de Beauvoir, the bisexual lover of Jean Paul Sartre, to whom I shall be referring later in more detail. Dworkin also defined the idea of men's sexual objectification of women (a concept also derived from de Beauvoir), which she linked with Millett's thesis saying:[33]

> To become the object, she takes herself and transforms herself into a thing: all freedoms are diminished and she is caged, even in the cage docile, sometimes physically maimed, movement is limited: she physically becomes the thing he wants to fuck. It is especially in the acceptance of object status that her humanity is hurt: it is a metaphysical acceptance of lower status in sex and in society; an implicit acceptance of less freedom, less privacy, less integrity. In becoming an object so that he can objectify her so that he can fuck her, she begins a political collaboration with his dominance; and then when he enters her, he confirms for himself and for her what she is: that she is something, not someone; certainly not someone equal.

In common with many feminist writers, such as Charlotte Perkins Gilman (1915), Elizabeth Mann Borghese (1961), Shulamith Firestone (1970), Marge Piercy (1976), and Mary Gentle (1984), whose work I discuss in the chapter Feminism 101, Dworkin aspired to a form of utopian society in which the biological act of procreation would be replaced by other means, and in which families as we know them did not exist. This form of society had been tried as far back as the 18th century by Charles Fourier, who is credited with the first use of the term 'feminism' and was being tried again at the time in the hippy movement that was prevalent during Dworkin's heyday. Again, I shall return to these topics later. This is pure Engelist/Marxist theory, as is her view that:[34]

> The alternative to the nuclear family at the moment is the extended family, or tribe. The growth of tribe is part of the process of destroying particularized roles and fixed erotic identity.

Echoing another of Simone de Beauvoir's views, Dworkin argued that the social taboo against incest should be removed, saying it was 'the worst work of the culture: it teaches us the mechanisms of repressing and internalizing erotic feeling', and that the way to break down the incest taboo was to destroy the nuclear family: the 'primary institution of the culture,' and 'the development of cooperative human community based on the free-flow of natural androgynous eroticism,' thus:[35]

> The nuclear family is the school of values in a sexist, sexually repressed society. One learns what one must know: the roles, rituals, and behaviors appropriate to male-female polarity and the internalized mechanisms of sexual repression.

Summarising, Dworkin's formula goes like this: in order to release sexual repression, you destroy the family, and you do that by removing the male-female polarity, and then the social roles to which women are forced to comply. In this, we see all the elements referred to by Mallory Millett in her vivid description of that consciousness raising group meeting in 1969 in Lila Karp's loft apartment at the beginning of the Women's Liberation Movement. We can also see a deep mental psychosis, which must cause anyone who calls themselves a feminist today to pause and reflect. Dworkin died in 2005 at the age of 58, grossly overweight, and crippled by arthritis in her knees, which were unable to cope with her bulk. She had married a homosexual man,[36] an arrangement whose purpose was widely believed to have been to enable her to gain access to sufficient medical social security at the end of her short and tumultuous life.

Valerie Solanas

Valerie Solanas (1936-1988) was another proto-feminist from the same group as Dworkin and Millett, whose anger ran just as deep. In fact, in Solanas it went very deep, to the point, again, of being serious mental disturbance. In 1968, she attempted to murder Andy Warhol for his refusal to pay her damages for allegedly having lost a script for a play, entitled *Up Your Ass*, which she had written. Convinced that Warhol and Maurice Girodias, Warhol's publisher and owner of Olympia Press, had conspired to steal her work, Solanas first sought out Girodias but couldn't find him, so she went to Warhol's studio and fired three shots at him, missing twice, before turning her gun on Mario Amaya, an art critic who just happened to be there, wounding him too. She then attempted to shoot Warhol's manager, Fred Hughes who was also present, but her gun jammed. After surrendering to the police Solanas was found guilty of the attempted murder of Warhol, but was diagnosed paranoid schizophrenic, spending three years in prison under treatment, including spells in a mental hospital.

Solanas was undoubtedly clinically insane, and it is obvious that her life experience was the precursor to that insanity. It follows the same pattern of her women's liberationist counterparts. Solanas had been abused as a teenager by her drunken grandfather, with whom she went to live after a stormy relationship with her mother, who had divorced her father and remarried. After that, she ran away and became homeless, eventually pulling herself together and gaining a degree in psychology from the University of Maryland, after which she relocated to Berkeley, California. There, between 1959 and 1960, she wrote her infamous *SCUM Manifesto*, which she self-published in 1967 when she moved to Greenwich Village, distributing it at $1 per copy for women and $2 for men. SCUM is an acronym that stands for the 'Society for Cutting Up Men' and the book is a manifesto which is dedicated to overthrowing and eliminating the male sex altogether. This deeply reprehensible book has been reprinted at least 10 times and translated into 13 languages, so popular has it become among feminists to this day, and it features on the reading lists of women's and gender studies' university courses across the world. Characteristically of radical feminists when challenged with their earlier preposterous propositions, Solanas consistently denied the meaning of the acronym, claiming it was just a literary device. However, according to Breanne Fahs writing in 2014,[37] it actually appears in its expanded form in an advert that Solanas placed in *Village Voice*, announcing a series of recruitment meetings for SCUM at the Chelsea Hotel, situated on the edge of Greenwich Village, where she lived at the time. Like Dworkin, Solanas died young, in 1988, aged 52 years, of pneumonia.

Shulamith Firestone

Shulamith ('Shulie') Firestone (1945-2012) was another figure central to the development of early feminism, and she too was deeply troubled. Born in Ottawa, Ontario, Firestone grew up in St Louis, Missouri, graduating in painting from the Washington University (St Louis), then becoming an activist in the anti-Vietnam war and civil rights movements of the time. She moved to New York to co-found New York Radical Women, the first women's liberation group in that city, and then formed *Redstockings*, an organisation whose neologistic name was a play on the term 'blue stocking', applied to intellectual women who were emerging as the driving force behind the women's movement, and intended to indicate a connection between the revolutionary left and academia. *Redstockings'* position was that lesbianism was more of a political identity than a personal one, and that male homosexuality was a deeply misogynistic thing that amounted to a rejection of women. Further, it took the view that feminism was not simply a movement intended to rectify imbalances in the institutional treatment of women, but a true expression of Marxism. Rather than women's subjection being a form of brainwashing by patriarchy, it argued, it was an adaptive accommodation by women to their relative lack of social power.

In 1970, following a period co-editing the influential *Notes From...* series,[38] which tracked the development of the early women's liberation movement (and which is also required gender studies material in universities today), Firestone published *The Dialectic of Sex*, described as a 'Feminist Classic' and widely regarded as the most open statement of what feminism's aims really are. This book is another such 'classic' and remains one of the most widely discussed books of the feminist movement, appearing at the core of gender studies courses in universities around the world to this day. Taking much of her reasoning from Karl Marx and Sigmund Freud, Firestone sought to synthesise a coherent theory of what she called a 'sex-class': the domination of men over women based on biology that gave rise to the conventional family arrangement. This childless young woman, an artist, still only 25 years old, declared that childbirth was 'barbaric' and theorised that advances in medical science would lead to the separation of sex and childbirth for women through the use of 'test-tube' babies. Locating her argument in pure Marxist-Engelist rhetoric, she argued that a woman's subordination was inextricably linked to her role in childbearing, and that the biological family was oppressive to women because it turned sex into a tool of oppression. Firestone argued that women only gave men sexual love in return for an emotional identity, and that this denied them empowerment and creative freedom, whilst ceding all these things to men.

Blending this with Freud's ideas of sexual repression, which she said lay at the heart of 1960s society's malaise, she argued that the only answer must be the full emancipation of women by way of a major structural social change, brought about by a full-blown feminist revolution, and that this was now possible because of improved material conditions in the post World War II period, especially with the invention of the contraceptive pill. Crucially, she argued, this would require the destruction of the nuclear family and with that the expectation for women to marry a man who would provide for her, and her children. In this new world order (and chillingly in the light of modern society), children would be brought up in social arrangements based on rationally constituted, non-permanent bonding arrangements between people who voluntarily undertook their upbringing and whom were not necessarily their biological parents.

My reader might be struck by the degree to which this was a portent of what we now see in society today: the abandonment of marriage as a lifelong institution, which has been replaced by co-habitation in 'partner' arrangements in which no commitment for life is made, the plethora of 'blended families' after commonplace divorce and remarriage, and widespread children's legal illegitimacy, all as advocated by Engels, who observed 'the practical absence of the family among the proletarians'.[39] One might also reflect on the fact that lesbian partnerships are using surrogate sperm to have children, or they are adopting children, and the influence of the Marxist dialectic on Firestone, in which her views are firmly embedded, is shown in the following passage from *The Dialectic of Sex*:

> So that just as to assure elimination of economic classes requires the revolt of
> the underclass (the proletariat) and, in a temporary dictatorship, their seizure

of the means of production, so to assure the elimination of sexual classes requires the revolt of the underclass (women) and the seizure of control of reproduction: not only the full restoration to women of ownership of their own bodies, but also their (temporary) seizure of control of human fertility - the new population biology as well as all the social institutions of child-bearing and child-rearing. And just as the end goal of socialist revolution was not only the elimination of the economic class privilege but of the economic class distinction itself, so the end goal of feminist revolution must be, unlike that of the first feminist movement, not just the elimination of male privilege but of the sex distinction itself: genital differences between human beings would no longer matter culturally. (A reversion to an unobstructed pansexuality Freud's 'polymorphous perversity' - would probably supersede hetero/homo/bi-sexuality.) The reproduction of the species by one sex for the benefit of both would be replaced by (at least the option of) artificial reproduction: children would be born to both sexes equally, or independently of either, however one chooses to look at it; the dependence of the child on the mother (and vice versa) would give way to a greatly shortened dependence on a small group of others in general, and any remaining inferiority to adults in physical strength would be compensated for culturally. The division of labour would be ended by the elimination of labour altogether (through cybernetics). The tyranny of the biological family would be broken.

In a trenchant comment on this passage in his book *Sex Trouble: Essays on Radical Feminism and the War Against Human Nature*, Charles Moore[40] says this:

> What would you call that 275-word paragraph? I call it lunatic gibberish. If you call it 'political analysis,' you're either a radical feminist or mentally ill - two ways of describing the same thing.

After her brief flowering of fame, in her late twenties Shulamith Firestone was diagnosed schizophrenic and lived the remainder of her 67 years painting, reading, and writing in her apartment in East Village, next to Greenwich Village, New York, where, on 17th August 2015 the owner of her building found her body. She had been dead for several days, and had died alone. No one had known of her passing or, it seems, very much cared.

Detachment from reality

Shulamith Firestone was an example of a major strand within the women's liberation movement that displays a distinct detachment from reality. Valerie

Solanas was the same, and so too was Andrea Dworkin. They all represent a clear strand in feminist thinking that had its roots in earlier feminist writers from the turn of the twentieth century. In her 1915 novel, *Herland*, Charlotte Perkins Gilman, a prominent American feminist, depicted an idealised society free from war, conflict and domination, and, of course, composed entirely of women who reproduce asexually by parthenogenesis and didn't have to suffer the rigours of childbirth. Gilman's view, which echoed Betty Friedan, to whom I shall turn anon, was that the domestic environment oppressed women and that the home needed to be socially re-defined and not restricted just to married couples, a view advanced by Charles Fourier, the nineteenth century utopian who first coined the term feminism in 1837, whose life and works I shall cover in depth in the chapter Marxism and 'The Woman Question'. Gilman wanted the home to be more communal and open, so that groups of men and women could live a, 'peaceful and permanent expression of personal life' as single individuals, but having companionship; where groups of men and women shared in, '...a peaceful and permanent expression of life'.[41]

Gilman's thinking was later to emerge in the hippy movement in the 1960s, but it was clearly informed by Marx and Engels. She said that sex and domestic economics went hand in hand, and that a woman effectively sold sex for survival, using her body to please her husband, who, in return, provided financial support for her and her children. She went as far as to say that the housewife was an economic parasite, a theme that was later to emerge in feminism and used to shame women as homemakers. Chillingly, she said the care of children should be carried out by profit-making businesses outside the home, and that the production of food should be prepared and distributed on an industrial basis, again outside the home. It doesn't take much of a stretch of imagination to see the fulfilment of these ideas in the widespread and routine sub-contracting of childcare to working mothers today, who rely extensively on fast food outlets for their offspring's nutrition, which is widely believed to be the source of so much obesity in the young.

Copying August Bebel's ideas (to which I shall also turn in the chapter on Marxism), and indeed Marx himself, Gilman argued for women to be completely economically independent of men, thus allowing coupling without the need for any change in the financial status of the partners, another pronounced fact of modern life and, in an early portent of what Simone de Beauvoir was to say, and feminism was to make a major plank in its argument against patriarchy, Gilman held that young girls were prepared for motherhood by dolls and toys, and conditioned into being female by the way they were dressed. She said that tomboys were 'perfect humans' who ran around using their bodies 'freely and healthily', and describes one of her fictional characters; thus: 'Here she comes, running out of prison and off the pedestal; chains off, crown off, halo off, just a live woman.'

Like Firestone, Solanas, Dworkin, Millett, Friedan, and Ceballos, Gilman was a troubled woman. She was emotionally damaged by relationship and dysfunctional family arrangements. Whilst still an infant, her father had moved out of the family home, abandoning his children. Her mother subsequently showed her no overt affection and banned her from establishing close friendships during her childhood, which meant she was an isolated, impoverished and lonely child. She later married and had a child herself, but suffered a serious postpartum depression that resulted in psychosis and her then husband, following the medical advice of the time, virtually incarcerated her in a room in a summer house for her recuperation.

However, during that period she became seriously psychotic, experiencing hallucinations. After only four years of marriage, she divorced her husband, and, sending her daughter to live with her father and his new wife, and with a remarkable similarity to many of the later women's libbers, immersed herself in several feminist pursuits, and the feminist cause. In 1932, she took her own life by overdosing on chloroform after being diagnosed with breast cancer. Decades later, her flights of feminist fancy returned in feminist theory. Shulamith Firestone, in her 1970 book *The Dialectic of Sex: The Case for Feminist Revolution* (another feminist classic), reflects on women being freed from childbearing and explores the future possibility of technological advances freeing women altogether from their biological role as mothers. In *My Own Utopia* (1961) Elizabeth Mann Borghese described a world in which genderless children matured into women, and some even became men. In 1976, Marge Piercy published *Woman on the Edge of Time*, a science fiction novel and feminist classic in which she explores a utopian future where there is complete gender equality, and even equality of the sex act irrespective of the lovers' gender.

In common with Gilman, and echoing Firestone, in Piercy's world, women no longer give birth. Instead, children are produced by an elaborate machine, and when they are born they get three adoptive 'mothers' who may be male or female. Finally, in Mary Gentle's 1984 book, *Golden Witchbreed*, we see a world in which children begin gender-neutral, do not develop into men and women until puberty, and have no prescribed social roles. This is pure de Beauvoir (as we shall see later), whose ideas by then were established feminist orthodoxy.

Samples of speculative fiction such as these illustrate something very deep about feminism, which strikes deep into its roots. The apparent desperation to be freed from their biologically ordained destiny is such a recurring theme it strongly suggests a form of denial of their own sex's purpose, and we still see it today in many young activist feminists who, childless, undoubtedly have become detached from the reality of life and human existence. It is amazing that women should embrace such an idea, and it smacks heavily of a deep radicalisation that is playing to an innate narcissistic trait in women, which somehow also expresses itself in lesbianism?

Jaqueline Ceballos

Jacqueline Ceballos (née Michot, 1925-), was by no means a major contributor to feminist theory, nor does she appear to be detached from reality but, as the other principal speaker at the Town Hall event, her background is worth mentioning in order to fill out the picture. Ceballos came from a comfortable Southwestern Louisiana family, and was as talented as she was well educated. Moving to her beloved New York to pursue a career as an opera singer she fell in love with and married Alvaro Ceballos, but the couple were forced to leave, moving to Bogota, because of difficulties with Ceballos's citizenship. She had four children to him and showed her obvious inbuilt entrepreneurship, leadership, and independence of spirit by founding Bogota's first opera company, *El Teatro Experimental de la Opera*, which was clearly a consuming passion for her. She even sang the lead role in its opening production.

However, her marriage ended when her husband left her on suspicion of her infidelity with other singers at the opera (which she strenuously denied), and she returned to New York with the assistance of her husband, who helped her to set up an import/export clothing business there. Later, she became the president of the New York chapter of the National Organisation for Women (NOW), founded by Betty Friedan, the author of the seminal feminist book *The Feminine Mystique*. Much later, she founded *Veteran Feminists of America*. I'm afraid there is no other interpretation of what Ceballos was saying in her speech at Town Hall, than that she was clearly a bitter woman and resentful about her experience. Divorced from the man she loved, the father of her children, she undoubtedly must have gone through deep inner examination and upset, as anyone does in a divorce. Heartache is hard to deal with. It goes very deep in any human being, and we can see this in her own words, taken from a personal account of her life on the Veteran Feminists of America web site:[42]

> Everyone was telling me to 'get him back. ...he was a good man, a good husband, a good father'. Some even felt he was right! [About her alleged infidelities] I was miserable. A friend returned from a stateside visit and, hearing my story, handed me 'The Feminine Mystique'. I read it that night, and knew immediately - it wasn't him, it wasn't me, it was society. And society had to change!

So, society has to change because a marriage between two people who couldn't resolve their differences didn't work out? This is such an obvious response to emotional tribulation. In her Town Hall speech, she says she opted out of the conventional life, to pursue the fight for women's liberation, yet that isn't strictly true. Ceballos was doing what many people do in her circumstances, she was rationalising her experience by re-drafting it in terms that put her, and what happened to her, in a different light. Her utterances show her to be a woman who was rationalising and reconstructing her bitter experience and projecting that onto men. We can see that from her attitude to Norman Mailer at the Town Hall meeting, where she is extraordinarily condescending and passively aggressive. Ceballos was making her personal experience political and her politics were of the left. We see this clearly in a message on the Veteran Feminists of America web site, in which she refers to conservatives being in opposition to feminism's precepts:

> We pioneer feminists had set out to make equality of women and men happen, and though there is much yet to be done, we've accomplished a lot. Today we are up against conservatives who want to take away the gains we've won and sadly, often led by women who once fought us, now use the power we've earned for them to support the patriarchal system. Still, I have faith that today's young feminists will pick up the banner and keep us on our march for complete equality worldwide, with liberty and justice for all.

We also see in Ceballos the international aspirations of feminism.

Germaine Greer

To close the loop with the Town Hall event, Germaine Greer (1939-) needs at least passing mention. She, of course, is the most famous of the European feminists, although an Australian by birth. She is also a self-affirmed Marxist, believing that the nuclear family is a bad environment for women and for raising children. As recently as 2008, she described herself in an interview on an Australian community radio station, 3CR, as 'an old anarchist' and reaffirmed her opposition to 'hierarchy and capitalism,' which, she said, were at the centre of her politics.

Greer's version of feminism is somewhat individualistic, but it still contains the basic argument that a patriarchal and woman-hating society has castrated women and created *The Female Eunuch*, the title of her 1970 book that became a worldwide bestseller. She also locates that argument firmly in Marxist theory in her statement about abolishing the patriarchal family, to which I have previously alluded. Echoing the theme of her feminist counterparts, she says that sex for a woman is an 'alienated performance' rather than an expression of an inner desire and that the real means of liberating women is by the development of 'the pleasure principle'. Somewhat high-handedly she says that women must learn to enjoy sex (as though they don't naturally), and goes on to say that all forms of sexual expression are legitimate, thus tacitly endorsing the pronounced lesbian aspects of the feminist movement. No doubt linked to this is her assertion that women should taste their own menstrual flow: 'If you think you are emancipated, you might consider the idea of tasting your menstrual blood - if it makes you sick, you've got a long way to go baby.'

With a master's degree in romantic poetry, Greer says romantic love is a fraud perpetrated by romantic music, fiction, and films, all of which she describes as trash. It seems to be expected then that she would claim that conventional forms of courtship and seduction between men and women amount to a thinly veiled form of rape, articulating this very clearly in her 1974 essay *Seduction is a Four Letter Word* (i.e. 'Rape') where she says, 'probably the commonest form of non-criminal rape is rape by fraud - by phony tenderness or false promises of an enduring relationship…'[43] No doubt the failure of her 1968 marriage, which lasted only three weeks due to her admitted repeated infidelities,[44] reflects in these views.

One of Greer's principle claims, one that is very much still part of current feminist rhetoric, is that women's social values are better than men's. In the introduction to her collection of essays and occasional writings entitled the *Mad Woman's Underclothes* published in 1994, she says this:

> Everything I learn reinforces my conviction that the only corrective to social inequality, cruelty and callousness, is to be found in values which, if we cannot

call them female, can be called sororal. They are the opposite of competitiveness, acquisitiveness and domination, and may be summed up by the word 'co-operation'. In the world of the sisterhood, all deserve care and attention, including the very old, the very young, the imbecile and the outsider. The quality of daily life is what matters, the taste of the food on the table, the light in the room, the peace and wholeness of the moment. Perfect love casteth out fear. The only perfect love to be found on earth is not sexual love, which is riddled with hostility and insecurity, but the wordless commitment of families, which takes as its model mother-love. This is not to say that fathers have no place, for father-love, with its driving for self-improvement and discipline, is also essential to survival, but that uncorrected father-love as it were practised by both parents, is a way to annihilation.

Neil Lyndon, in his hard-hitting anti-feminism book *Sexual Impolitics*[45] responds as follows:

> What a monster! What stupendous and satanic ego in perverted reason and malignant arrogance. Within this passage can be found all the strands of madness which made up the body of hatred and aggression in The Great Terror [Lyndon's term for feminism] and gave it impetus and power in western culture from 1970 to the present... At every turn the reader should ask: is this my own experience? Does sister Greer's picture match my own view of the outer worlds and does it square with the evidence which has come my way?

It seems that Greer's theory that sororal values are the 'opposite of competitiveness, acquisitiveness, and domination,' has its limits for her, however. In 1989 she opposed the election of her transsexual colleague Rachael Padman to fellowship of Newnham College, Cambridge, arguing that Padman had been born a man, and, therefore, should not be admitted to an all-women's college. This resulted in Clare Longrigg of *The Guardian* publishing an article on 25th June 1997, entitled *A Sister with No Fellow Feeling*, which was withdrawn 'on the advice of lawyers', resulting in the following retraction on March 19th, 1998:

RETRACTION:

An article entitled A Sister With No fellow Feeling by Clare Longrigg that appeared on pages 6 and 7 of the tabloid section of the Guardian on 25 June 1997 under the rubric Inside Story fell far below our standards of journalistic accuracy. The article elaborated on an assumption which was incorrect, namely that appearances in the press of stories relating to the appointment to a fellowship at Newnham College of Dr Rachael Padman had been instigated by her colleague Dr Germaine Greer. Dr Greer was accused of 'outing' her colleague for a variety of discreditable motives, all of them without foundation. A number of statements in the article about Newnham College were also incorrect. We apologise to our readers for misinforming them, and to the Principal and Fellows of Newnham College, and we sincerely apologise to Dr Greer. At her request, we have made a donation to the Newnham College Development Fund.

No doubt, Greer had threatened to sue, but there might be some sweet irony in the fact that, despite her intervention, Padman *was* appointed, and Greer resigned.[46] One might also look with some jaundice on her assertion that female values are a counter to cruelty and callousness from her acerbic comment in *The Guardian* in September 2006, about the death of fellow Australian Steve Irwin (known as the 'Crocodile Hunter') who had met sudden death by being stung by a stingray whilst filming wildlife in Australia. Summing it up, she said, 'The animal world has finally taken its revenge on Irwin'. Perfect love indeed!

By way of postscript, it is worth noting that, in common with almost all the leading feminists of her time, Greer had issues with her father. In 1989, she published a semi-autobiographical book entitled *Daddy, We Hardly Knew You*, which took the form of a diary and travelogue about her father, whom she described as, 'Distant, weak, and unaffectionate'.

Juliet Mitchell

Juliet Mitchell (1940-) is another British-residing feminist from the antipodes (she was born in New Zealand) who cannot go without mention because, yet again, she confirms the pattern of the early women's libbers, as strongly left wing, probably lesbian, and at least with issues with men or their fathers. Like Germaine Greer, she is a fully signed-up member of the Angry Generation, and she is also a perfect example of the feminists' colonisation of our universities. In 2010, she was appointed Director of the Expanded Doctoral School in Psychoanalytic Studies at the Psychoanalysis Unit of University College London (UCL), and before that was a fellow of Jesus College, Cambridge, and Professor of Psychoanalysis and Gender Studies at Cambridge University.

Throughout the 1960s, Mitchell was active on the far left of politics, including being on the editorial committee of the influential journal, *New Left Review*, founded in 1960 from a merger of two journals that had emerged out of the political repercussions of the Suez crisis and the Hungarian Revolution of 1956 against Communist annexation. The *New Left Review* was meant to be the organ of a broad New Left: 'The common political focus uniting these two currents was provided by the Campaign for Nuclear Disarmament (CND)', according to its own website. Its aim was to intervene in contemporary political issues, and debated within its pages were topics such as Marxist Humanism, the sense of classlessness, and the communism of Nikita Khrushchev after the communist thaw.

Mitchell has a reputation as an important thinker in the field of socialist feminism, which seeks to integrate feminism, Marxism and Freudian theory, and link it to the idea of women living in intimate proximity to their exploiters. This is the idea behind the modern expression: 'sleeping with the enemy'. She holds the view that psychoanalysis and Freudian thought can be an important tool in the quest for the emancipation of women because it can help women free themselves from the psychological domination that fathers, brothers, and husbands allegedly exercise over them, and she is reported to believe that Marxism can provide non-patriarchal structures for rearing children, disposing of 'the family romance' as she puts it, which will remove the Oedipus complex from a boy's development and liberate girls from the consequences of penis envy and 'castration'. Echoing standard feminist theory, Mitchell contends that the root-cause of women's acceptance of patriarchy is that they are socialised into their gender role in order to become caretakers of their households. Mitchell's family background no doubt informed her views. In a frank interview in May 2008 with anthropologist and historian Alan MacFarlane, Emeritus Professor of Anthropological Science and a Life Fellow of King's College, Cambridge, Mitchell who is a Jewess, explained her early years as follows:

> My father was a geneticist in Canada, where I was conceived, and America; he died when I was eleven and we never lived together; I knew him by letters which were very important to me; my parents were separated and I was brought up by my mother; I had a stepfather and brother when I was five but that broke up; closely after my own father's death my mother married somebody who survived the [concentration] camps.

Betty Friedan

Betty Friedan, also of Jewish descent, was another woman with a chip on her shoulder about men. She died, aged 86, in 2006, after making a career as a novelist, social critic, and *Grande Dame* of feminism. Friedan's 1963 book *The Feminine Mystique* attacks the idea that the cultivation of femininity is the path to personal fulfilment for women, and it became a feminist classic. She also co-founded the National Organisation of Women (NOW) in 1966, with the stated aim of bringing women into the mainstream of American society in full and equal partnership with men, just as Jaqueline Ceballos had said. Friedan's general thesis is that the media, advertisers and even sociologists sold the idea of the 'feminine mystique' to women, causing them to accept a form of female passivity, which also included alleged sexual passivity. She went further, arguing that there was a tacit conspiracy in society that forced women to accept men as the dominant sex and, crucially, she advocated a change from the idea that the primary responsibility for child-upbringing and housework always lay with women on the grounds that women were expected to provide maternal love for their men as well as to their children. She called this the 'housewife syndrome', arguing that women needed to become discontent with it, and aspire to more than suburban domesticity, and seek education and professional training. She argued that these were the best paths to personal happiness and fulfilment for women, not motherhood and being a wife.

Not unexpectedly, bearing in mind the personality patterns of her fellow feminists, Friedan was an enormously flawed woman, and it is obvious she carried a deep, unassuaged anger in her. She was 'famously abrasive… thin-skinned and imperious, subject to screaming fits of temperament,' according to her obituary in The New York Times, where her husband, Carl Friedan, is quoted as saying:[47]

> She changed the course of history almost singlehandedly. It took a driven,
> super aggressive, egocentric, almost lunatic dynamo to rock the world the way
> she did. Unfortunately, she was that same person at home, where that kind of
> conduct doesn't work. She simply never understood this.

Germaine Greer, in her characteristically divisive fashion, had a somewhat different take on Friedan. In her 2006 obituary published in *The Guardian*,[48] UK, she said this:

Betty Friedan 'changed the course of human history almost single-handedly'. Her ex-husband, Carl Friedan, believes this; Betty believed it too. This belief was the key to a good deal of Betty's behaviour; she would become breathless with outrage if she didn't get the deference she thought she deserved. Though her behaviour was often tiresome, I figured that she had a point. Women don't get the respect they deserve unless they are wielding male-shaped power; if they represent women they will be called 'love' and expected to clear up after themselves. Betty wanted to change that forever. She wanted women to be a force to be reckoned with…

There was a longstanding view that Friedan's husband had been a wife beater, and that she had to cover up black eyes on a number of occasions. This came from a statement she once made to the press that he had beaten her, which was sensationalised in the press because it fed the feminist narrative of men as aggressors. Carl Friedan strenuously denied this blackening of his name, and it took some time for his wife to put the record straight. In her autobiography, she finally admitted her part in it all, saying:

> I almost wish I hadn't even written about it, because it's been sensationalized out of context. My husband was not a wife-beater, and I was no passive victim of a wife-beater. We fought a lot, and he was bigger than me.

Emmeline and Christabel Pankhurst

No discussion of feminist activists can take place without factoring in Emmeline and Christabel Pankhurst and their Women's Social and Political Union (WSPU), known more popularly as the 'Suffragettes', and whose activism is widely thought to have won the vote for women. Emmeline Pankhurst, and her daughters Christabel and Sylvia, have become surrounded by a sort of misty-eyed aura of female righteousness, and turned by feminists into heroines of a struggle for downtrodden women in the popular perception. The reality is far different. In fact, these women were radicalised terrorists who displayed the same flawed character traits as their Women's Liberation counterparts many years later, and of the modern so-called 'Third Wave' feminists. They were just as selfish, just as sexually deviant, just as egotistical, and just as full of rage as those women I have been describing so far.

Emmeline Pankhurst, founder of the WSPU, was no oppressed woman. In fact, she was classically bourgeois, marrying radical socialist barrister Dr

Richard Pankhurst, a leading light in the Suffragist movement (of which more later). He was 24 years her senior, and when he died in 1898, Emmeline didn't remarry, but carried on a close and longstanding relationship with a known lesbian composer Ethel Smyth. Christabel, her firebrand eldest daughter, was hardly opportunistically challenged either. She was educated by private governesses until the age of 11, then attended Manchester High School for Girls, after which, as with many of her Women's Liberation counterparts less than a century later, went up to university. (To Owen's College, part of Manchester Victoria University, where she obtained a Bachelor of Laws degree, with honours.) Christabel Pankhurst was almost certainly a lesbian. For example, the *Encyclopaedia of Women's Social Reformers* says this about her:[49]

> Christabel's total rejection of men and her solidarity with her own sex inevitably have aroused debate over her sexuality. Whether she was an active lesbian is not known, but she certainly moved in lesbian groups during her years in her contact with poor working-class women…

The extent to which Christabel, described as 'luminously beautiful,'[50] the subject of 'a rash of crushes across the movement,'[51] and '… unable to give love to the many who adored her,'[52] was intimately involved with a number of her young women followers was only fully revealed in 2000 when Professor Martin Pugh,[53] historian and expert on the women's suffrage movement, discovered some little-known diaries from the period 1908 to 1913, kept by Mary Blathwayt, a Suffragette activist, which he says amounts to a litany of lesbian sexual relationships, rife throughout the Suffragette movement,[54] and which sustained Christabel Pankhurst both physically and emotionally during the Suffragette campaign. Pugh has been challenged by feminist academics[55] who have alleged his book is full of errors, but the evidence is compelling.

Blathwayt, a WSPU courier between London and Paris, was undeniably intimately involved with Christabel. However, it was a brief affair. The real long-term association was with Annie Kenney, a working class girl from Oldham who became besotted with Christabel after hearing her speak at a rally in 1905, becoming Christabel's 'loyal acolyte'[56] and main Suffragette organiser. The two of them had been imprisoned when Christabel deliberately provoked their arrest by spitting in the face of a policeman during a scuffle outside the Free Trade hall in Manchester after they had been ejected for disrupting a meeting addressed by prospective Parliamentary candidate Winston Churchill.

Pugh alleges that the Kenney affair lasted many years, until Christabel became involved with another woman, Grace Roe.

Christabel Pankhurst, who was '... undoubtedly a controversial and compelling figure in her lifetime, accused of excessive ego and arrogance - even megalomania - and frequently remarked upon as being autocratic, cold, and undemonstrative',[57] was an arrogant, angry lesbian woman whose anger was undoubtedly focussed on men. After the spitting incident and a brief term in prison, Christabel (like Lenin, who sought bolt holes across Europe from where he directed the Russian Social Democratic Party) fled to Paris to avoid further arrest, from where she directed the strategy of the WSPU, and from where she demonstrated the same lesbian-rooted hatred of men by issuing a stream of 'virulently animale rhetoric',[58] which revealed her 'unrepentant hostility towards men,'[59] in articles for *The Suffragette*, the magazine of the WSPU. No doubt, the loss of her father at a young age contributed to her rage. Christabel was the eldest child, and firstborn children are known to feel the loss of a parent particularly heavily, whether that loss is through death or divorce. It is probably to do with the loss of their sense of specialness, combined with an automatic assumption of responsibility for their surviving parent. In fact, Christabel's name tells it all. According to Wikipedia,[60] she was so named because of her father's love of the poetry of Samuel Taylor Coleridge and his line, 'The lovely lady Christabel whom her father loves so well'.

The pattern is completed when we see what happened to Christabel after her initial flowering and fame. When she and her mother dissolved the WSPU in November 1917, having been effectively bribed by the government (with a grant of £20,000, a very large sum indeed in those days), to desist from their terrorism, their burning of empty houses and post boxes, and their smashing of shops' plate glass windows, and to turn the WSPU into a recruiting agency for soldiers to go to the trenches, Christabel stood for election as Parliamentary candidate for the constituency of Smethwick in 1918. She lost by a whisker to the Labour Party candidate, but secured the candidature for Westminster Abbey Division under the wartime coalition a year later. However, no by-election was held until 1921, by which time the Conservative Party had chosen its own candidate, and she was dumped.

After that, she went on a speaking tour of Canada and the US, from which she only returned in 1936 to be appointed Dame Commander of the Order of the British Empire, given to her by an obviously gynocentric Stanley Baldwin, a

Conservative Prime Minister who once famously said, 'I would rather trust a woman's instinct than a man's reason.' At the outbreak of World War II she left England again, this time going to California where she became an evangelist and prominent member of the Second Adventist movement, writing her book *Unshackled: The Story of how We Won the Vote*, and books on the second coming of Christ, such as *The Lord cometh!* and *The World's Unrest: Visions of the Dawn*. She never married, but adopted a daughter, Betty, and died alone in her Los Angeles home in 1958 at the age of 77. Her housekeeper found her body still sitting upright in a straight-backed chair.

Making the personal political

These snapshots of the key movers in the early women's movement show that when Norman Mailer said, 'Women's liberation is two things: it is a profoundly political movement; and it is a profoundly sexual movement, which quite naturally takes on huge lesbian overtones,' he had his finger firmly on the pulse. Betty Friedan's legendary anger and sheer chutzpah, Mitchell's obvious anti-male views, Dworkin's detestation of the normal heterosexual act, Solanas's insane hatred of men to the point of wanting to cut them into pieces, Millett's mental derangement, and naked Marxism, shared with Greer, who also expressed unrestrained anarchic views, and Johnson, the unrestrained lesbian and anarchist, and a bigoted, ignorant, defiant creature, high on anything but common sense and full of ludicrous ideas, which she indulged and spread without conscience or responsibility: all of these characteristics point to something very unsavoury in these women. Each of them, without exception, displayed pronounced character flaws and difficult behavioural characteristics, which in some of them was manifested in diagnosed mental illness, and it is a matter of reasonable speculation that their rage led some of them to an early death.

The prime movers of Women's Liberation were decidedly a motley crew, to be frank. In fact, they all make Jaqueline Ceballos look like a normal woman who was just full of anger and hurt, and seeking an explanation for her life's experience anywhere except within herself. All this tells its own story. These women were no role models for women. They all had issues with men, and some of them hated men and everything that men represent. Theirs was not a righteous anger against perceived injustice, it was hysterical and dangerous, and it betrayed a deep meanness of spirit. These women were caught in a spiral of hatred: of repetitive internal narratives that increasingly laid blame on anyone but themselves and led to an unhealthy sense of victimhood, which has now become the default stance of women today, especially young women who are still sold out to feminism. These women completely fail to understand that each of us carries a joint and several responsibility for our relationship failures as well as their successes.

Bad things happen to people. Marriages break down. 'Shit happens', as they say, and the only sane way to deal with it is for the individual to learn to adapt and change, not try to change the world to make his or her pain go away. To attempt the latter is an emotional response, not a rational one, and that is precisely what happened in these women. Like the Suffragettes before them, they were far from being heroines of social change; they were just damaged, dangerous women who wanted to lash out at anything and anyone so they could get what they wanted whilst excusing themselves of their own moral agency. In fact, they made the personal political,[61] a phrase invented by Shulamith Firestone and adopted by the early Women's Liberation movement from 1970 onwards. Erin Pizzey, a passionate woman's activist who became world famous in 1971 when she started one of the first women's refuges in the modern world, in Chiswick, London, which later became the organisation 'Refuge,' and who was persecuted by women's liberationists for daring to speak out against them when they commandeered the women's refuge movement, says this about making the personal political:[62]

> I always hated that slogan. What it really means is you take your personal damage - and one thing that was very obvious in those very early days of the women's movement, how any of the radical leaders of the women's movement themselves, had really disturbed backgrounds and were very, very violent - then you make that political. So if my dad's a shit, then all men are shits. If you say that, you can do almost anything you like. You can go from the personal and make it political. So what happened is a sufficient group of women got together to complain bitterly. You have to remember that the beginning of the feminist movement was a Marxist movement. It was women in the left of politics in Britain who decided that they had had enough of working with men on the left, and were going to have their own 'movement'. So our feminist movement never grew from a grass roots of 'the working class women,' that they were always talking about, there weren't any working class women, it was academics, university lecturers, young women students [that] was the beginning of the women's movement.

Just as activist feminists are today, the Women's Liberationists were educated, middle-class, and indoctrinated in Marxist rhetoric as a framework for their failings - and their feelings. They had within their ranks a significantly higher than normal number of highly driven, highly politicised lesbians and bisexuals who were determined to ensure that normal women were 'liberated' from men, because that was their bent. They were self-deluded, damaged women, and they hated men and the very essence of maleness to such a degree that they rose up in anger and hatred, spurred on by a century-old orthodoxy that gave them a reason to do that. They located their rebellion in the construct of class warfare, using the communist ideology of Karl Marx and Friedrich Engels, which was already being mixed with the quasi-philosophy of existentialism, and this festering amalgam found its expression in the highly emotional, narcissistic, sexually-charged atmosphere of the times.

Liberation: from men

It is axiomatic that lesbians want liberation from men, and it is obvious that they detest maleness. That is why they are lesbians. It is, as they say, something of a no-brainer. They dislike the heterosexual sex act, finding their sexual pleasure in other women, and many of them even find men's ways - their mannerisms, their attitudes, their very smell even - distasteful. It is also obvious that a lesbian would believe that women are the purer, the better, the superior sex, and this is a theme that runs through all modern feminism: everything feminists today say and do reflects this attitude to men. The problem is that this lesbian-inspired feminist hatred of men has become hardwired into our social operating system. It can be seen in the never-ending rhetoric of social institutions such as Women's Aid, Rape Crisis, and a plethora of others of their ilk, which daily peddle a biased creedal message about how men are all potential rapists or wife beaters, and women are always their victims. We hear it echoed and reflected in the media, along with its constant focus on the alleged rape culture and equally alleged and totally overblown violence against women and girls agenda. Men today are being routinely, collectively labelled as oppressors of women in normal social discourse. This narrative is no longer the domain of the lunatic fringe.

And it goes further than that. We see it in the institutionalised attack on men as fathers, who are routinely being deprived of contact with their children after divorce, overwhelmingly initiated by women. We see it in the equally institutionalised bias against men in the criminal justice system that routinely sentences men far more harshly than women for the same offences. We see it in the outrageous disadvantaging of boys in our education system: one that is dominated and run by feminist women who nakedly advantage girls in the classroom and label boys' natural boisterousness as a pathology, sometimes euphemistically labelling it as Attention Deficit Hyperactivity Disorder (ADHT), which is routinely being treated with drugs such as Ritalin to 'calm them down' and conform them to the female order of the classroom. Well, maybe boys *are* suffering from attention deficit? Who can blame them? Especially when in certain social classes most of them have never had a father in their lives, and are endlessly bombarded with negative messages about their maleness. The endless ridicule of men in advertising and TV sitcoms, where they are portrayed as dumb and stupid whilst girls and women are always savvy, sassy and 'together' is just one obvious example. This 'Girl Power' message, which started in the 1990s with the Spice Girls, has remained the predominant message of youth culture ever since. In fact, it has become the default stance of girls, and it is a threat to boys.

We see it in the anti-pornography campaigns such as 'No more Page Three', which seek to blame men for pornography. This is pure Dworkin. Yet at the same time, increasingly, these modern women are using pornography themselves, and it is stating the obvious that liberated women are the primary players in the pornography that excites men. These are liberated women exercising their freedom from hitherto guiding social mores; they are hardly unwilling victims. Pornography is everywhere. From the organised industry it is in California, to the plethora of amateur web sites where ordinary women are uploading their own explicit acts for the world to see. Yet this is all, somehow, men's fault? The sheer hypocrisy of feminists, let alone their totally disjointed thinking, is astonishing. Today, we live in a world in which women and their alleged needs trump everything. A state in which women's natures and alleged better qualities are being trumpeted as the answer to all society's ills. Yet, what people seem unable to see is that the cause of much of society's ills today is so called women's 'liberation'. The entire thing is driven by the ideas of women who, as we have seen, were bigoted, driven deviants. None of them were examples of real womanhood, yet all of them sought to place their perceptions of women and men into the hearts and minds of people in civilised societies. And women in those civilised societies in particular, have made those perceptions their own.

When do we ever hear of men's finer qualities, such as bravery, fortitude, stoicism, patience, protection, provision, love and fatherhood being extolled in society today? Never, is the instant and obvious answer, and this is because of the anti-male militancy of the lesbian-driven, cultural Marxist radicalism that has swamped out culture, and which continues to be promulgated by prominent feminist lesbians such as Julie Bindel and Sandi Toksvig, the latter of whom has recently co-founded the Women's Equality Party. Even as recently as 6th September 2015 Toksvig posed the question, 'Will heterosexuality survive women's liberation?' on the militant feminist website, *Radfem Collective*,[63] where she supports Andrea Dworkin and even goes so far as to say:

> The truth is reconciliation has no place in dealing with men's violence towards women and girls, because the truth with reconciliation is that in reconciling you are saying that you are part of the problem.

So, no compromise there then? We see it in the behind-the-scenes work of women such as Harriet Harman, recently stood-down deputy leader of the British Labour Party, and first ever Minister for Women and Equalities (a ministry of state first created by Tony Blair). Harman is arguably the prime example of militant feminism in action in politics. She had her hands on the levers of power for a very long time and, as I shall go on to show, ensured feminism became deeply embedded in the lives of the British people. She and her like did irreparable damage to people's lives, women included. On the other side of the Atlantic, we see it in the rhetoric of Hillary Clinton and Michelle Obama, and the encouragement and enactment of divisive policy solely aimed at women, which those women encourage. All of them draw their inspiration, their ideas, and their motivation directly from the insane rationalisations of their Women's Liberation mentors, who started what has now become the cult of the woman in society today.

Role models

Feminist activists today fit the same pattern as their forebears. They are still middle-class, opinionated, well educated, young - and damaged - women. They are openly defiant and utterly inaccessible to reason because they are brainwashed in the ideological cult of feminism These women are focussed on men as a breed, for whom they have developed a well-developed creed of contempt, and an equally well-developed desire to overcome patriarchy in every aspect of society. Women who now espouse feminism (and the men who believe in it too) would do well to recognise this. Frankly, feminism is selling us all a pup. Worse, it is selling us a morally corrupt doctrine and a form of dependency culture based on unassuaged, vicariously transmitted, naked rage, toxically mixed with the assertion of false rights for women that have no reference point but Marxism, and no social responsibility. In fact, what is happening through feminism today is just naked selfishness, devoid of any social or personal responsibility to ensure social cohesion.

When we think about the modern feminists' call for role models to help girls achieve their highest potential, and their constant adoration of those 'heroic' women who overcome all apparent anti-female odds to succeed, I wonder how they reconcile that with the true nature of feminism, with its 'matron-saints' and their acolytes-turned-priestesses who were clearly damaged, resentful, bitter, and utterly morally bankrupt women? Feminism's constant referral to the need to have examples of successful women to encourage the young and give them confidence to strike out for themselves is based on a highly dubious moral, ethical, political proposition. It is a giant with feet of clay. What is more, if young women need reinforcement of their ideas from such damaged women, what does that say about women today? Do they have no character? Or ideas of their own? Can they not make decisions for themselves about their lives, their career choices, etc.?

Most of all, what does it say about the lessons being handed down to young women by those corrupted women's liberationists, who clearly were unable to cope with the vicissitudes of life? What does any of it add to women's futures today, and the society of which they will be a part and will shape? What sort of a society are we building from such a cauldron of emotion, division, gender competitiveness, and anger against men: half the human race? These are questions society must face before it is too late.

CHAPTER 5

FEMINISM

FEMINIST BELIEF:

'On ne naît pas femme: on le devient.'
(One is not born, but rather becomes, a woman.)

Simone de Beauvoir. *Le Deuxième Sexe,*
Book 2, Part 4, Chapter 1: 'Childhood'

Feminism 101

One of the most interesting things about feminism is that there is no manual, no central source from which you can get to its core beliefs. Feminism has no central office, or website. In fact, it is an amorphous, often incoherent set of beliefs; barely an ideology, but is capable of shape-shifting, adapting, and applying itself to almost any social situation, wherever the need arises. It is totally opportunistic, in fact. That makes it both difficult to pin down, and even more difficult to counter or contradict. However, there are some core themes, which, because they repeat themselves continually, and show through in social trends, one can identify and describe, thus locating feminism in a set of core tenets, some core beliefs, which build to an ideology. Let me start with the most fundamental of those beliefs: gender identity.

Most people believe that there are immutable differences between men and women: in their moral, psychological, and intellectual makeup that go beyond the simple physiological differences such as their reproductive organs, hormonal balances, physical strength, etc. Most people believe that there are inevitable differences between men and women in the way they perform in society, and that this is the simple order of humanity. In other words, men are men, and women are women. Each sex has its own role to play, each brings different perspectives to living that are complementarity to one another, not opposed or challenging to one another. Feminist theory denies this point blank. It stands implacably, ideologically opposed to the idea that masculine and feminine characteristics at birth are anything other than ambiguous. Carried to its logical conclusion, this means that human beings are essentially androgynous at birth, and that their sexual identity is fashioned by subsequent socialisation.

Of course, they apply this specifically to women, citing Simone de Beauvoir, who once said, 'One is not born, but becomes a woman'.

One of the subtlest, yet most fundamental theories of feminism, is its attempt to draw a philosophical distinction between sex and gender. Sex, they say, is the simple biological difference between the bodies of men and women whose function is solely for the procreation of the species, and that it has nothing to do with our true natures. Boys and girls are to all intents and purposes blank slates upon which are written rules for social conduct, which, because of patriarchy, assumes maleness as the default state. In pursuit of building their case, feminists argue that society is obsessed with gender (an abstract term that is borrowed from grammar to describe the gender of nouns, which has been hijacked and used in a different way to describe their abstract view of one's sex), and argue that biological differences should say nothing about how women are situated in society, or what their social roles should be. They believe that the idea that men and women were created or evolved for fundamentally different purposes is nonsense, and they argue that the sexes' roles and patterns of social behaviour are learned, not innate, and that a man-shaped society imposes social roles on women in their roles as wives, mothers, and, indeed women. Leading feminist theorist Sandra Bartky (b. 1935), Professor Emeritus of Philosophy and Gender Studies at the University of Illinois at Chicago, succinctly sums it up as follows:[64]

> The sex/gender system is that system whereby we are all born bi-sexual, and we are transformed into male and female gender personalities: one destined to command; the other to obey.

This is the first principle of feminism. The second is the flat denial that differences between men and women should be the basis of the arrangement of society, especially in terms of family life. They deny that the generally accepted social arrangement in which children are born and brought up to be functioning adults by a mother and a father who fulfil accepted gender roles is the way it should be. Feminist theory stands implacably opposed to the general perception of the inherently biologically ordered social roles of men and women in the nuclear family, which it says diminishes women and reduces them to mere baby-making machines, whilst men go out and run the world through patriarchy. Feminists such as Bartky argue a third principle: that society is 'man-shaped', that men have created it their way for their own advantage, which is principally so they can dominate women, and that this is a systematic domination, based on a sense of special status routinely claimed by men in what amounts to a hegemony of male domination. Put simply, patriarchy is a system that subjugates women for men's benefit in such things as marriage, motherhood, and the nuclear family, etc., which effectively force women to become slaves of men. They say patriarchy defines all aspects of women's lives as well as all culture, economics, politics, the family, religion, etc.: even ways of thinking, such as the scientific approach which uses only reason and evidence as the means of establishing truth, and fails to take account of intuition, emotion, or 'women's ways of knowing'.

All these are signs of an all-pervading male patriarchy at work as far as feminists are concerned. They believe that men force women to act like women, and to accept male ways of thinking as the norm, thus preventing women becoming truly equal to men. They carry this argument further, alleging that this has been the norm down the ages, in all known societies, which have defaulted to patriarchal control. As evidence of this historical repression of women by men, feminists cite the absence of records of women's intellectual and artistic achievements down the ages. They point out that men have always been the historians and that women's achievements have simply not been recorded by them. Histories of art, for example, contain not one mention of female artists, as though men's achievements and exploits have been the only things that mattered. Some feminists go further and say men have deliberately excluded women from the historical record: that they have deliberately written women out of history. In other words, because the male experience is the dominating paradigm, history is, literally, *his*-story, and that the word should be changed to 'Herstory', in the interests of fair play. This is the degree to which many feminists believe patriarchy has been at work keeping women down, and they go even further, arguing that patriarchy is even damaging to men, who have also been brainwashed by its inherent hegemony into accepting the role of becoming the oppressors of women. Thus, almost everything that feminists say and do is in the name of the eternal struggle against patriarchy. Feminists even complain that the science of sociology has been all about the study of men, and that mainstream sociologists to this day (men, of course) totally ignore these theories (which is true, largely because feminist theories don't actually hold water under scrutiny).

The fourth principle of feminism is the idea of the sisterhood and solidarity of women, united in opposition to patriarchy. Only by seeking unity, it goes, can women regain their rightful position in society. Only by working with each other in a network against the 'old-boys' network, by sharing their experience and common plight, and finding comfort and solace with each other, then rising up in solidarity and power, to throw off men's yoke, can women overcome their persecution, and the deception that causes women to acquiesce passively in the iniquitous social conditions created by men. Using the analogy of unity against oppression, borrowed from revolutionaries down the centuries, the feminist sisterhood implies that all women are potential allies of one another in what amounts to a class war against men and their patriarchal institutions. In this class struggle, all male-supporting institutions need to be torn down. Some particularly hard-line feminists go further, and say that women should not even participate in the male-dominated world and its institutions, and that only a complete separation of the sexes will achieve feminist goals. Others say women should infiltrate the bastions of male domination and work to change them from the inside. Those feminists who are open about their ideology say that the goals of women can only be achieved within a truly socialist society, one that is firmly rooted in Marxism: that socialism and feminism are both sides of the same coin and cannot be separated. They say that patriarchy is synonymous with capitalism and that to overthrow it is to overthrow the ultimate male-created system that has oppressed women, a.k.a. 'workers' for centuries; therefore, only a truly socialist state can bring about the full emancipation of women and all that society needs to become reformed along feminist lines, with socialist men and women working together in solidarity to eliminate capitalist patriarchy.

Female solidarity is linked to a fifth principle: that women have a unique 'female way of knowing' in group consciousness. Only by being in true sisterly solidarity can women come to see how they have been, and remain, truly oppressed by men, and find the answer to the hegemony of men's logic in pursuing truth, allowing women's special ways of understanding to take hold. Only in joint venture, based on common cause, are women able to perceive an essential quality in women *en masse* that men cannot possess, and which equips women to understand what is really going on in the world, stripping the scales from society's eyes. The sixth principle is called 'objectification': the idea that men see women only as sex objects, which they use to diminish and belittle women, thus holding them in subjugation. Objectification is where feminism's lesbian roots have full sway. Carried to its extreme, this is where Kate Millett's argument, that men's objectification of the female body is a means of sexual exploitation, and Dworkin's campaign against pornography and her allegation that, 'All sex is rape', come fully into the equation. Objectification derives from another of Simone de Beauvoir's ideas: that of *self-other*, into which I shall now go in more depth.

Simone de Beauvoir

Simone Lucie Ernestine Marie Bertrand de Beauvoir (1908-1986), more commonly known as Simone de Beauvoir, was a leading member of the French beatniks during the 1950s and 60s, and a Nazi sympathising paedophile bi-sexual whose lover, Jean Paul Sartre, was the principal articulator of existentialism, a branch of philosophy that gained enormous popularity in that time. An intellectually precocious young woman with a very proud and pushing father who would boast, 'Simone thinks like a man,' de Beauvoir first met Sartre whilst studying philosophy at the Sorbonne in Paris, during which she applied for the *Agrégation* in philosophy, a highly competitive postgraduate examination whose purpose was to rank students nationally, becoming the youngest ever student to pass it (although Sartre was awarded first place to her second). Thereafter, she and Sartre developed a life-long relationship, but she chose never to marry, or have children, taking, as did Sartre, many male and female lovers with whom she instigated sexual relationships whilst they were in her charge as a teacher.

De Beauvoir is widely considered to be the matron saint of post-1968 feminism. In 1989, Kate Millett said she did not realise the extent to which she was indebted to her when she wrote her book *Sexual Politics*. However, interestingly, de Beauvoir repeatedly refused to align herself with the early women's liberation movement, for reasons which are unclear. It wasn't until 1972 that she acknowledged her connection with them in an interview in *Le Nouvel Observateur*, when she disclosed having joined a group of Marxist feminists in founding the journal, *Questions féministes*. We can only speculate as to why she did this, although she always described herself as an author and 'midwife' of Sartre's existential ethics, rather than as a philosopher and thinker in her own right (in fact, she was only belatedly acknowledged as feminism's principal philosopher after her death in 1986 at the age of 78, some 20 years or so after the emergence of modern feminism).

Her theories are essentially a reassertion of Sartre's existentialist argument that, 'existence precedes essence', which she uses in her 1949 book *The Second Sex* to develop a feminist narrative. They are also an expression of the powerful anti-bourgeois sentiment that was sweeping through France in the late 1960s, which led to near revolution in 1968. In the chapter *Woman: Myth and Reality*, for example, she argues that men have placed a false aura of mystery around women and that they use this as an excuse not to understand women, or their problems, nor to help them. Existentialism states that there is no such thing as human nature: that the human being does not possess an inherent identity or value, and that one's acts make one what one is. The greatest consideration of the individual, it says, is to act as an independent, responsible, conscious being ('existence'), constructing one's own values, not acting according to roles, labels, stereotypes, definitions, or other preconceived categories conferred on one by society ('essence'). De Beauvoir appropriates this to the man-woman social relationship, arguing that men stereotype women as an excuse to organise things their own way for their own benefit. She says that this is a pattern repeated in societies in which one group that is higher in the hierarchy stereotypes another group lower in that hierarchy, and this shows through also in other categories of identity, such as race, class, and religion, emphasising that this is nowhere truer than in modern society.

She further develops the argument by saying that Sartre's ideas on the duality of men's and women's natures leads to the creation of Self and Other, best summed up in her much quoted statement 'One is not born, but becomes a woman'. In other words, women become Other, the subjects of 'essence' i.e., social conditioning, and denied their 'existence' by men who appropriate to themselves Self, and fail to attribute subjectivity to women, thereby 'objectifying' them: denying them their right to have personal feelings, tastes, and opinions. This objectification of women is what is behind the central idea behind the modern social feminism-defined 'crime' of sexism. All this maps directly onto classic Marxist doctrine. In his writings, Karl Marx talked about the objectification of labour in the capitalist system, which, he claimed, exploited the proletariat and dehumanised the people who ultimately became mere functional objects. He said, '...we have shown that the labourer sinks to the level of a commodity and indeed becomes the most miserable commodity possible'. Herbert Marcuse (1898-1979), famous philosopher of the Frankfurt School (of which more later), so-called 'father of the new left', and a contemporary of de Beauvoir, went much further, suggesting that the preoccupation with sexual stimulation in the 1960s and 1970s was due to the one-dimensional nature of bourgeois life in Europe and the United States, and it served to reinforce political repression of the people by de-sublimating people's political energy, leaving them uncritical and unable to bring about societal change.

True to Marx's communist collaborator, Friedrich Engels, de Beauvoir declared that the housewife's labour creates nothing of any worth and that it is not directly useful to society. The housewife, she says, '...is subordinate, secondary, parasitic', and she is equally scathing about motherhood. And as we saw echoed in many of the later women's liberationists' writings, principally those of Shulamith Firestone, in *The Second Sex*, de Beauvoir refers to babies as 'burdensome', and sucking the life, strength, and happiness out of a woman, inflicting a 'harsh slavery' upon her, about which, '...she feels this individual who menaces the flesh, her freedom, her whole ego.'[65] We can also see echoes of her theories in Betty Friedan's 1966 book *The Feminine Mystique*, some eight years later, and the ideas being expressed by Jacqueline Ceballos on behalf of NOW (National Organisation of Women) at the Town Hall Event in 1971, when de Beauvoir talks about the mother as being 'almost always a discontented woman: sexually she is frigid or unsatisfied; socially she feels herself inferior to man; she has no independent grasp on the world or on the future', and argues that the remedy for this is for marriage as a career choice to be prohibited, and for women to move into the work marketplace, with a concomitant change in the meaning of family in order to facilitate this. All of this has come to pass in our lives. She also said, 'In a properly organised society, children would be largely taken in charge by the community', which we see being implemented in our society today in the widespread farming out of very young children to childcare whilst their mothers pursue their careers, and in widespread 'bureaugamy' (marriage to the state) in which many single mothers exist.

All of modern feminism's precepts can be found in de Beauvoir's writings. The essence of her thrust was that social mores were essentially patriarchal (i.e., derived from fatherly authority) and that these steered girls towards a life in which they would depend on men's financial support in marriage. By contrast, she argued, men were socially programmed to be independent and free to follow a life of social economic utility in their chosen careers. As a result of this programming, de Beauvoir argues, women cannot achieve full freedom and authenticity as long as men maintain a vested interest in keeping these things. She said women needed to set themselves free from this: they must throw off the false imposition of male-inspired gender roles and be liberated from men emotionally, physically, financially, and sexually. These, she said, were the essential prerequisites for women's liberation, and it is hard to imagine anyone currently under the age of 50 with whom such a view would not resonate and appear valid, such is the degree to which feminism has prevailed in changing the general understanding of women's roles. Crucially, she said that the decisive event in the emancipation of women would be a socialist revolution, which came to pass in 1968-70.

Such was the degree of her totalitarian fervour, de Beauvoir completely refused to accept the remotest possibility that women, probably the majority (at least in those days), might actually enjoy motherhood in a settled marital arrangement, and that whilst men are undoubtedly programmed by society to be providers and protectors, they are by no means free and independent themselves if they willingly take on the responsibility of the provision of a home, and for a wife, and children. She was adamant that women must be actually coerced into becoming 'liberated', and the key to understanding how this became the totalitarian ideology of feminism today lies in an interview with Betty Friedan, who asked her opinion about a woman being paid for looking after her own children if she made that choice; de Beauvoir said, 'No, we don't believe that any woman should have this choice. No woman should be authorised to stay at home to bring up her children. Society should be totally different. Women should not have that choice, precisely because if there is such a choice, too many women will make that one. It is a way of forcing women in a certain direction'.[66] De Beauvoir, it seems, was willing to force women to be liberated willy nilly.

Like Jean Paul Sartre, Simone de Beauvoir was a moral degenerate. Bianca Lamblin, a former student of hers, wrote in her book, *Mémoires d'une jeune fille derangée*[67] that de Beauvoir had sexually exploited her when she was underage, and this claim is corroborated by the public record, which shows that in 1939 she was suspended from her teaching job following an accusation that she had seduced another pupil, 17-year-old Nathalie Sorokine. We can obtain further insight into the web of sexual intrigue woven by her and Sartre from her first novel, She Came to Stay, published in 1943, in which she creates a fictional *ménage à trois*, widely regarded as a fictionalised chronicle of her and Sartre's exploitative relationship with the sisters Olga and Wanda Kosakiewicz. Olga was one of de Beauvoir's students in the Rouen secondary school where she taught during the early 1930s. She had rejected Sartre's advances so he turned his attention to her sister Wanda, starting a relationship with her (Olga later married de Beauvoir's other lover, Jaques-Laurent Bost).

It is clear that she remained unrepentant about her abuse of children all of her life, as her 1977 support of a petition to the French Parliament calling for consensual sexual relations between adults and children under 15 to be decriminalised, shows. This coincided with a general move in this direction, echoed in the formation of the Paedophile Information Exchange (PIE) in the United Kingdom as part of a general campaign for the acceptance and understanding of paedophilia that later became affiliated to the National Council for Civil Liberties (NCCL), whose legal officer at the time was Harriet Harman. Harman, of course, went on to become the first Minister for Women in the Blair Labour government in 1997, and the theme was picked up by Andrea Dworkin, another daughter of the beatnik culture of Greenwich Village, of which more later.

Confused logic

The problem with feminism is that it leaves its followers uncritical and unable to see through its confused, confusing, and frequently contradictory rhetoric. In fact, feminism is shot through with simple logical errors that are not that difficult to discern. The most obvious of these is its fundamental belief, that 'one is not born a woman but becomes one'. One cannot escape the simple logic that the entire thrust of this argument is that babies must be born essentially androgynous and are then turned into gendered men and women by sheer social pressure (man-driven, obviously) to act out the social roles of men and women. If you believe that, then that is your business. I suggest it is nonsense. Men and women are fundamentally different from birth.

Nature creates them different, not least in their physique, but in their hormonal balances, and in their brain patterns, as recent medical research has shown. Using Magnetic Resonance Imaging (MRI), Dutch neuroscientist Dick Swaab, has shown there to be 'many hundreds of differences' between male and female brains,[68] and that 'brain gender' is established in the womb at a different stage of development to that of body gender; thus, homosexuality is essentially the result of a change in hormonal balances in the womb, which means lesbians have male-pattern brains, gay men female-pattern brains (hence the 'butchness' of many lesbians and the effeminacy of many gay men). And psychologists have explained brain differences between the sexes in a plethora of papers documenting their research. For example, Professor Simon Baron Cohen shows the female brain to have a strong tendency towards empathising, whereas the male is more oriented towards systemising,[69] an assertion backed up by work he and others did at Cambridge University,[70] in which they showed that male infants showed a stronger interest in physical-mechanical mobiles placed in their view, while the female infants showed a stronger interest in the face. Taking another point of view entirely, this poem[71] explains itself:

> BLESSINGS on the hand of women!
> Angels guard its strength and grace.
> In the palace, cottage, hovel,
> Oh, no matter where the place;
> Would that never storms assailed it,
> Rainbows ever gently curled,
> For the hand that rocks the cradle
> Is the hand that rules the world.
>
> Infancy's the tender fountain,
> Power may with beauty flow,
> Mothers first to guide the streamlets,
> From them souls unresting grow—
> Grow on for the good or evil,
> Sunshine streamed or evil hurled,
> For the hand that rocks the cradle
> Is the hand that rules the world.
>
> Woman, how divine your mission,
> Here upon our natal sod;
> Keep - oh, keep the young heart open
> Always to the breath of God!
> All true trophies of the ages
> Are from mother-love impearled,
> For the hand that rocks the cradle
> Is the hand that rules the world.
>
> Blessings on the hand of women!
> Fathers, sons, and daughters cry,
> And the sacred song is mingled
> With the worship in the sky—
> Mingles where no tempest darkens,
> Rainbows evermore are hurled;
> For the hand that rocks the cradle
> Is the hand that rules the world.

Written in 1890 and therefore a fascinating insight into the status of women in those Victorian days, this poem demonstrates unequivocally the power of the mother in shaping the child and therefore the future adult, particularly the woman. So, how does that reconcile with creating a man-shaped society, I wonder? Surely, given the power of the mother at such a crucial social phase in life, her hand at the cradle would have countered any tendency of fathers to install their male hegemony, wouldn't it? Or did women collaborate in the male hegemony because they were under such pressure from it to conform? Have women in bygone eras been so gullible as to succumb to this, or were they under such coercion from men they had no choice? Were they just automata? This, of course, is the feminist counter argument, but, really, does that sound right?

I suggest that for such a poem to be written shows us that in all classes of society (and don't forget, this was the height of the Industrial Revolution only 40 years or so after Marx and Engels cooked up their communist ideas), women were the primary shapers of children as future citizens, guiding 'the streamlets' from which 'souls unresting grow …for the good or evil, sunshine streamed or evil hurled.' This shows unequivocally that women were the primary creators of society, and to say that they created their own oppression when they had the field to themselves is, frankly, insane. The truth is, society is, and always has been, shaped by women. It is blindingly obvious that women as mothers shape the child to be the adult in those vital early years when the child's social operating system is laid down, and if we are to follow the feminist argument, that 'one is not born a woman but becomes one' to its logical conclusion, it is mothers who have been doing this for as long as socialised humanity has existed. And if we accept that, it follows that women must have also created patriarchy - the very system that allegedly has oppressed them forever.

The next fallacy of 'one is not born a woman but becomes one' fails completely to explain homosexuality, especially lesbianism. Did patriarchal hegemony fail in this case? Why would a man-shaped society (let alone one created by women as I have discussed) seek to socially condition women to be lesbians? Surely that would be against men's best interests, wouldn't it? Now, I can already hear the clamour rising in the distance, that lesbians are the exception that prove the rule: they, of course, have resisted the male hegemonic patriarchy. They were, after all, at the vanguard of the women's liberation movement. Well, fine. Presumably they were able to resist male hegemony as babies and little girls then? Presumably, they had some inbuilt strength, resistance, or knowledge (perhaps female 'knowingness', a latent connection with the sisterhood) that ensured they did not succumb to patriarchy? Or were they just the exceptions whose mothers didn't dress them in pink as babies and give them dolls to nurse and feed? And if all these factors held true in their case, how wasn't the all-pervading, all-powerful, universal man-shaped social conditioning that feminists say exists able to work in their case? Surely the simple truth is that homosexual humans are born like that?

After all, homosexuals themselves claim they are born as they are, not made by social pressures. In fact, many struggle with the pressures that keep them held to the social norms of their sex until they finally have to 'come out'. Far from being androgynous and socially conditioned from birth, most gay, lesbian and transgender people strenuously allege that their sexual orientation is in their nature and that nature will out. This is the essence of their argument fighting social prejudice, isn't it? This alone gives the lie to the 'becomes not born' argument. Lesbian, gay, bisexual, and transgender people (LGBT) frequently say they are only expressing a form of sexuality that is natural to them. In other words, their existence, their sexuality, really does precede their socialised essence, contrary to what Sartre and de Beauvoir assert. By this standard is feminism saying that lesbian feminists are '…not born a lesbian but become one?' If this is true then simple logic demands that lesbianism or male homosexuality could be socially conditioned out of people, who would then become 'straight', to use the commonly accepted term. I'm sorry, but the feminist explanation of social conditioning of women it doesn't wash. Explanations of human behaviour must have universal applicability if they are to be considered valid. They cannot be selectively applied to suit the occasional argument.

There is a third case, which emerges from the last: transexual people: those born with male genitalia and who develop a deeper male voice and male musculature at puberty, but have an inner conviction that they are actually women. Many of these people say they felt like a woman in a man's body even as children and teenagers, and there came a moment in their lives when they needed to make the switch so as to feel normal. Many of them undergo hormone therapy, and surgery to create female genitalia and breasts, such is their conviction they are female. They have a genuine, compelling innate sense of being a woman, so how is it that they could be said to 'become' a woman by social conditioning? Especially when social conditioning is allegedly masculinist and massively stacked against them? These people are brought up as boys and steeped in the social stereotyping of an allegedly male-dominated society with its seemingly all-powerful gender conditioning processes, yet that inner sense still tells them they are a woman. It is so strong they are compelled to switch lifestyles and start living like a woman. This was the case when Germaine Greer sought to block Rachael Padman's promotion in Cambridge. Her doctrines superseded her common sense. And it is also the case with Paris Lees, who published an open letter[72] in *Diva* (an online magazine for lesbians and bi-sexual women), saying this:

> I can't tell you why I am who I am. I don't know if it is psychological or biological, or hormonal, or social, or simply natural human variation. What I do know, however, is that I feel most comfortable expressing myself the way I do, and happiest when other people see me the way I see myself: female. I just am, just as you just are. Just as black people and gay people and left-handed people just are. I am what I am and we are what we are.

This is confirmed by Dick Swaab, the eminent Dutch neuroscientist who gives us compelling evidence that the human brain becomes hardwired in the womb: especially our sexual identity, but also our body integrity, the conviction that parts of our body belong to us - or not (this is called 'body identity disorder'). In the book *We Are Our Brains: A Neurobiography of the Brain, from the Womb to Alzheimer's*,[73] he says this:

> Many hundreds of sex differences have subsequently been identified between the male and female brains… Our description of the first sex differences found in human hypothalami in postmortem brain tissue (Swaab and Fliers, Science 228 [1985] : 1112-15) provoked a hostile reception from feminists. At the time there was widespread denial within the feminist movement of possible biological sex differences in the human brain and behaviour. Speaking about our findings in an interview with the Dutch magazine HP (January 17, 1987), a woman biologist by the name of Joke 't Hart said, 'But if I were to accept that there are differences between the sexes in such fundamental areas as the structure of our brains, I would no longer have a leg to stand on as a feminist.' Whatever the case, I never heard any more of her.

So, if trans-sexuality is just like being left-handed, surely feminists cannot reconcile their basic proposition that a man-shaped society forced these women into their original biologically indicated roles. If that were true, there would be no lesbians, gay men, or transsexuals. The entire proposition that, 'one is not born a woman but becomes one' is counterfeit. It really doesn't hold water. Beneath the feminist rhetoric and quasi reasoning, there is a basic truth: that people *are* born as they are, and they naturally assume their social roles - men, women, boys, girls, lesbian, gay, transgender, bisexual; it is a truly diverse world in which we live.

Objectification

Sexual objectification of women by men, and men by women, is a perfectly normal aspect of human sexuality, yet feminists complain about this biological imperative, naming it as a sort of social/sexual crime. You cannot blame men (or women for that matter), who are humans, for the nature that made them humans. Any sexually mature human being knows that both sexes have sexual fantasies during sex with their partners. This applies in both heterosexual and homosexual encounters. Men have sexual fantasies, during intercourse: often they are about inner sexual gratification, and often they imagine their sexual partner is another person, or a sexual stereotype. Women tend to create a wider sexual imagery in their imagination. They have slut fantasies and imagine themselves in all manner of sexually bizarre scenarios.

Human beings are programmed biologically to procreate and this is how that programming has evolved. Thus, the entire proposition of objectification is false, but that doesn't stop feminists believing it, and seeking to impose their jaundiced views on everyone. Men do objectify women sexually. Women objectify men sexually. Does it matter? No, of course it doesn't. So why are feminists so hung up on men allegedly objectifying women? Why is their focus only on men doing that? You might well ask, although the answer can be inferred from the backgrounds of the women who drove the entire feminist preoccupation with men and sex in the first place. Objectification is only an offence in the feminists' handbook. It only matters if you are using their reasoning, based on the *self-other* theory to judge men. This twisted feminist tenet from the 1950s and 60s was defined by a woman whom, as we have already seen, was herself no saint, and it was carried on by very similar women a couple of decades later. In fact, Simone de Beauvoir was the arch objectifier of both men and women, as well as being a child groomer and a paedophile who openly seduced her own girl pupils, and engaged in *menages a trois* with them and Jean Paul Sartre.

Hegemony

Let me now turn to the meaning of that alleged aspect of patriarchy: its alleged hegemony. Hegemony strictly means 'leadership,' or 'dominance', especially by one country or social group over another, and it must therefore imply agency and active intent. Therefore, people who exercise hegemony must know they are exercising it, surely? And they must have active intent and culpability in its commission; otherwise, why do it? For example, hegemonic countries such as Nazi Germany deliberately invaded half of Europe, and no one could reasonably say that China isn't imposing its culture and political control over Tibet by accident. That gigantic nation has been consciously trying to impose its will on that small, helpless country for decades. Hegemony really has to be a deliberate and definite act, with conscious intent. It is not an accidental or haphazard thing.

Therefore, hegemonic patriarchy must have equally active intent. It must have been actively prosecuted down the ages. If there really is male hegemony, men must have been plotting together down the centuries, seeking to impose their will on women and dominate society. After all, they allegedly wrote women out of history, didn't they? But does that sound right? My experience, admittedly limited to a sample of one man's lifetime, is that I have never come across any of it. I have never been invited to join patriarchy. In fact, the reverse is true. I was raised to respect women by the hand that rocked my cradle. I was socially conditioned to respect women - by women. I was taught to open doors for them, to stand back in a queue and let the woman go first, to relinquish my seat on the bus or train to a woman and to give way to women in general, in honest courtesy, because they were 'the gentler sex' and deserved my respect and honour for their precious role in childbirth and motherhood. Mothers did this to their sons. If there was any hegemony at work, it was a female one.

I simply cannot see how these things could be interpreted as a conscious hegemony of men out to control women. I'm sorry, but nobody is going to tell me that this is hegemony. The sound of it just doesn't ring true. Yet, feminism argues that the outcome of a patriarchal society is male hegemony, which in turn leads to socialisation by gender, a power inequality between men and women, and then social inequality in a self-perpetuating cycle. Described by Mike Donaldson[74] as being 'as slippery as the idea of masculinity itself,' the concept of male hegemony has its provenance in the prison writings of Antonio Gramsci (1891-1937), a founding member of the Italian communist party and its one-time leader, who was imprisoned by the fascist Benito Mussolini. Gramsci, a key member of the so-called Frankfurt School of Socialist Marxism, to which I refer in a later chapter, is regarded as one of the most important Marxist thinkers of the twentieth century and is the originator of the idea of 'Cultural Hegemony', the idea of the domination of a culturally diverse society by a ruling class. Gramsci located his notion of patriarchal hegemony in capitalism and the struggle between the bourgeois and the worker, whom, he argued, identifies with the bourgeois for his or her own good, thus maintaining the *status quo ante*. Hegemony in Gramsci's view is about the winning and holding of power with intent to form or destroy social groups. It is about how ruling classes establish and maintain their hold over society; how they set the terms upon which issues are discussed, and even how events are understood. Crucially, Gramsci said that hegemonic dominance ultimately relies on the 'consented coercion' of the worker, and even more crucially, he advocated 'workers' councils' as being the means by which workers would find solidarity and be enabled to take over control of the means of production that would lead on to a national communist movement. This would involve a process of persuasion of the population through control of the media and through the organisation of social institutions in ways that appear natural, ordinary, and normal, to come to accept the hegemony of oppression. It would also require the collusion of the state to punish non-conformity, thus ensuring enforcement of the hegemonic power.[75]

Feminism nakedly borrows Gramsci's ideas and translates them into male hegemony, which it alleges[76] contains a particular strategy for the subordination of women. In this narrative, male hegemony is both a personal and a collective project for men, based on their hierarchically differentiated, allegedly brutal, violent, pseudo-natural social constructs that are enriched and sustained by cultural connections to the institutions of male dominance. Male patriarchy, the rhetoric goes, is a lived experience for men and an economic-cultural force. Gramsci describes particular groups of men who are 'the weavers of the fabric of hegemony', its 'organising intellectuals', and in support of this, Donaldson (op. cit.) gives examples of priests, journalists, advertisers, politicians, psychiatrists, designers, playwrights, film makers, actors, novelists, musicians, activists, academics, coaches, and sportsmen. These people, he argues, 'regulate and manage gender regimes: articulate experiences, fantasies, and perspectives; reflect on and interpret gender relations'.[77]

Like Marx, Gramsci espoused 'historicism', the idea that assigns significance to context in a historical period. Historicism, of course, stands opposed to empiricism: the belief that knowledge comes only from primary, sensory experience; and from rationalism, the idea that reason is the chief source of knowledge, and both eschew the role of social tradition. Historicism also places great importance on hermeneutics: the theory of textual interpretation (used extensively by biblical scholars to reveal hidden meaning in their corpus of written texts). Gramsci said that Marxism could supersede religion only if it met people's spiritual needs, and that the people would need to think of it as an expression of their own life experience. Here, we see the echoes of the allegations about 'her-story' and the quasi-religious nature of feminist dogma.

The feminist attack on everything that even hints of patriarchy finds its underpinning rationale in Gramsci's notion of cultural hegemony. Feminism truly is a Marxist/Communist nexus that substitutes hatred of patriarchy for hatred of capitalism. These ideas - these two political groupings - are clearly conflated in feminism, and both engender hatred, and the desire to overturn them. Gramsci hated the power of elites in society, and feminism finds its expression in such an elite that sees men as an elite, with power over women who, borrowing from de Beauvoir's ideas, submit to men's power in a version of 'consented coercion'. And the enabler of men's alleged cultural hegemony, their alleged takeover of the means of communication such as the media, academia, and other prominent social institutions, is nakedly being used by an elite of feminists who are deceitfully doing precisely the same in furtherance of their own counter-cultural ideological aims.

Our universities are hotbeds of feminist ideology, and there is a plethora of feminist activist social institutions that daily produce a torrent of feminist propaganda about rape, domestic violence, pay gaps and so on. Feminists have undoubtedly colonised the media, academia, and our major institutions, and there is little doubt that even the state prosecution apparatus, the Crown Prosecution Service, as well as a number of ministries of government, now have feminists controlling them, shaping the legal and political agenda, slanting society always towards their gynocentric, ideological standpoint. The hallmarks of a conscious strategy based on Gramsci's ideas for spreading communism seem inescapable. The feminist sisterhood is clearly linked to Gramsci's ideas of solidarity with the intention of building a national movement so that the downtrodden class (women) could appropriate the means of control of society.

Finally, the degree to which feminists regularly seek to assign significance to the historical context of women's alleged plight and the idea of women's exploits having been written out of history demonstrate an ideological connection between the historicism of Marxism and feminism, as do the rejection of rationalism and empiricism, which is one of the defining aspects of feminist discourse. I leave my reader to reflect on all this, and decide for him or herself what feminism is actually saying. Perhaps to revisit afresh the espousal of a movement that draws on such ideas for its inspiration? And if my reader is a woman, another member with me of the human race, living out to quote Norman Mailer, 'this miserable, slavish life',[78] may I, with the utmost sincerity, suggest that the idea of a hegemonic male patriarchal conspiracy against you doesn't exactly have the ring of realism let alone truth about it?

'Her-story'

What makes even less sense is the idea that men have written women out of history. There is absolutely no evidence that this has been the case. It is simply an argument by assertion, probably better recognised as lying propaganda. The absence of evidence is not evidence of absence. This is an error straight out of the *Logic 101* book of errors. Just because feminists say there must have been women in history whose exploits should have been recorded but weren't, doesn't prove that there were such women, or such exploits. The best that can be said is that there is no evidence of any and those who believe there were have little understanding of the appropriate way to think in order to get to the truth, and probably have lost touch with reality.

Let me explore this a little further in order to make the point more clearly. If someone is found apparently murdered in their own home and there is no sign of a forced entrance anywhere, it is legitimate for the police to say there is no evidence of a forced entry. That is evidence of absence. It is a legitimate basis from which to speculate. The police can make a solid start from evidence like that. Perhaps, the killer had a key or was known to the victim who let the killer into the house, for example? However, the absence of signs of a break-in does not prove that the killer wasn't known to the victim. You cannot draw that conclusion from the absence of such signs. To do so would be folly, and could close a legitimate line of inquiry that might lead to the killer. Believing that the absence of evidence is evidence of absence is, as Rudyard Kipling once said, 'making a trap for fools'.[79]

Or course, it may well be that history has been written by men in the male paradigm, but where is the evidence? There is none, and you cannot make allegations about it without treading into the realm of speculation and supposition, which benefits no one. And in any case, so what? Maybe men were the ones who learned to read and write, and the women had other things to do for the functioning of society? Looking after children and running homes, for example. Maybe women in the past generally just didn't want to engage in historically significant exploits? Maybe they were actually working behind the scenes, operating unobserved and, therefore, unrecorded? Maybe the women of times past were not motivated to write history? Does it matter? Of course, it doesn't, unless you are trying to build a case: a campaign that needs you to create an oppressor narrative about men and portray women as the oppressed. You might equally say that the absence of historical contribution from, say, male peasants, amounted to the suppression of their story, but it is not evidence that they were suppressed or oppressed. Are men to be vilified for the possible choices of women in the past? Is that just? Is it justice? Or is it perhaps just vindictive persecution in the pursuit of a narrative that needs constant feeding and self-justification? One thing we do know from history is that there was precious little recording of events anyway, and today things are different. Nowadays we have a fantastic amount of social commentary going on in books, the media, social media, and so on. In the future, historians will have no difficulty whatever in discerning the fine detail and nuances of the feminist movement, for example, or of the day-to-day minutiae of ordinary people's lives, including those of women. The past can never be like the present, so what is the point in trying to compare the two?

The idea of patriarchy working to expunge women's achievement from the historical record is superficial and brittle. It completely fails to take account of culture, societal development, and differences in people's motivations (let alone those between the sexes). Men and women have different values, different needs, different obligations, and different beliefs according to their natures, their geographical location, their state of education, and the norms of the society in which they live. People's social involvement and contribution differ in a myriad of ways, and that changes in different periods in history. To believe that men have suppressed women's activity and their contribution to the world - worse, have deleted it from the historical record - is really just hysterical nonsense and weak thinking, and it pales into insignificance in the light of feminism's re-writing of history; for example, the story of women's fight to get the vote, a story to which I shall return in due course.

Sisterly solidarity

Feminists talk about the essential sisterhood of women, and it is easy to take that to mean the bonding and rapport that women seem to have with each other naturally. These are undoubtedly female human characteristics, probably the result of aeons of evolutionary programming to be social, possibly because there is safety in numbers. We see that expressed in the herd instinct in animals, and this is what the totalitarian ideology of feminism uses to such powerful effect in its relentless march to power. The sisterhood of feminism is akin to the idea of the communist collective or the 'in group'; a concept found throughout human behaviour, which often translates into bullying. Bullying ideologies always form gangs. They seek to separate 'in group' people from 'out group' people. That is the way they ensure conformity to the central ideology in their followers, and 'toeing the party line', and how they spread the message through marching, group demonstrations, and picking on others, intimidating them into joining the common cause through bullying, or tempting them with the benefits of 'in-group' membership. For some women, the Sisterhood offers empowerment beyond their wildest dreams.

Physical bullying is reprehensible, but ideological bullying is worse. It is what the Nazis practised in the interwar years in order to establish their National Socialist ideas internally before going on to extend their hegemony throughout Europe. They played to the victimhood of the German people who had undoubtedly suffered from the reparations exacted on them through the Treaty of Versailles, following the Allies' victory in World War I. Hitler and his henchmen played to this, offering the German people empowerment and then power over their former enemies, citing the Jews as a scapegoat and focus for national resentment using relentless propaganda, in precisely the same way as feminism seeks to blame men today. The Nazis kept the general populace under their jackboot through fear and intimidation, the weapon of choice of the bully, and through endless brainwashing, and it worked.

We must never forget that the Nazis, although calling themselves socialists, were viscerally opposed to the Marxists in their main opposition in the German political system in the Weimar era. Theirs was the ideology of nationalism and national identity, which stood in stark contrast to the internationalism of the Marxist Socialist parties who were equally active in Germany at the time, seeking to foment a communist uprising. However, the techniques used to ensure that people toed the party line were common to both. Elsewhere, in

Britain for example, the same methods were being used to maintain solidarity in the Marxist-inspired trades union movement. This system prevailed right up to the 1980s, when legislation was finally passed to allow secret ballots in industrial disputes. The pressure to remain in solidarity with their fellow trades unionists often forced otherwise free-thinking men to succumb to the will of their politically motivated trades union leaders who exerted their power through sheer peer pressure, openly brought to bear on dissenters in public meetings. Many of those men needed to keep working to feed their wives and children (for whose welfare they honourably accepted entire responsibility), but were forced into strikes and other industrial action, losing pay and sometimes their livelihood altogether, through what amounted to in-group bullying. Anyone who resisted the mob rule and made their own decisions were bullied by the group and cruelly ostracised ('Sent to Coventry': a form of excommunication). If they failed to toe the party line, they were expelled from the union, which meant they couldn't find work with any employer who operated a 'closed shop' system (which was most of them in those days), a system in which a man had to be a member of the union if he was to be able to be employed. This allowed collective bargaining to take place in a balance of power that served both union leaders and bosses in their respective need for control.

The flaw in feminism is that it has induced women to believe that finding solidarity in the sisterhood is a necessary part of bringing about their liberty and individualism, but 'the sisterhood' is not about liberation. In true totalitarian fashion, it is about coercion, control, and conformity to collectivism: a means of achieving normalisation to a set of standards created by ideologues who seek to mobilise dupes for their political aims, while suppressing individual freedoms and cowing dissenters. The real way to freedom and liberation for any human being is an independent mind and individual personal achievement; and that means not being one of the crowd. This is the opposite of what feminism offers women. Relying on the sisterhood, with its role models in support (moral or otherwise), carries with it a message that you can't make it on your own using your own talent, skills and effort. In fact, the sisterhood is the very thing of which feminism falsely accuses men, but in reverse. Feminists constantly criticise men for being 'one of the boys', of gaining advantage by back door means, yet they encourage women to become part of a sisterhood of solidarity so as to gain the self-same thing. This is yet another egregious double standard that exposes feminism for its duplicity and the dependency culture it is really trying to instil.

Fairness feminism

One woman who is not cowed by the shriek of well-honed feminist dogma is the American 'equity feminist' (her term), Christina Hoff Sommers, a former philosophy professor, and strong critic of late twentieth century feminism. Her two important books on the subject, *Who Stole Feminism?*[80] and *The War Against Boys*,[81] are thorough, balanced, thoughtful pieces of scholarship, packed with examples in support of her claims. In *Who Stole Feminism* (1994), Dr Hoff Sommers exposes a deep concern about a group of feminist zealots, claiming to speak for all women, who were promoting dangerous new agendas that threatened cherished ideals and set women against men in all spheres of life.

These 'ideologically inflamed gender feminists' as she calls them, '... seeking women's advantage only because they are women' have diverted women from the ideals she holds dear as, 'A moderate woman: someone who is not warring with society'. In *The War Against Boys* written some six years later, she identifies the alarming outcome of this, describing how the highly publicised 'girl crisis' has resulted in widespread disadvantaging of boys in education, which has become hostile to boys. In an address she gave at the University of Toledo School of Law as recently as March 14, 2012,[82] Hoff Sommers spoke at length about it all, expanding her views that gender-war eccentrics with a rigid ideology have hijacked public opinion, and have spread man-hatred throughout society. In particular, she singles out university gender studies departments as the principal means by which they have done this, exactly echoing Mallory Millett, whom I quoted at length at the beginning of this book. This is what Hoff Sommers said in her address:

> Pick up any women's studies text book - because I have never seen any exception to what I am about to say - or visit a college women's centre, or look at a syllabus of a typical intro women's studies class, you're likely to find a lot of elaborate theories - I would say conspiracy theories - about the male hegemony, about patriarchy. American college women, as I said, are among the most fortunate in the world, but in women's studies 101 they are taught that they inhabit an oppressive society where women are conditioned to subordination, routinely battered and raped by men, channelled into low-paying jobs, cheated out of almost a quarter of their due income, and that's only if they're not already dead from eating disorders caused by desperate efforts to meet patriarchal standards of beauty.

She quotes Daphne Patai and Noretta Koertge, themselves eminent academics, and their book, *Professing Feminism: Education and Indoctrination in Women's Studies*,[83] in which they talk of 'the sea of propaganda' that overwhelms the contemporary women's studies classroom, where 'sisterly sophistries' are peddled by hard-line feminists who ultimately set the tone in their departments over the heads of the serious scholars. Hoff Sommers says, '…idealistic female students will come into the typical women's studies class and they turn these idealistic young women into relentless grievance collectors'. Tellingly (and, again, reflecting what Mallory Millett said two and a half years later), she expresses the view that parents should think very carefully before sending their daughter to one of the gender-feminised colleges, the most extreme examples of which she names as Wellesley College, Mount Holyoak, Smith Mills and the University of Minnesota, saying they should print an announcement on the first page of their bulletins; thus:[84]

> We will help your daughter discover the extent to which she has been in complicity with patriarchy. We will encourage her to reconstruct herself through dialogue with us. She may become enraged and chronically offended. She will very likely reject the religious and moral codes you raised her with. She may well distance herself from family and friends. She may change her appearance and even her sexual orientation. She may end up hating you (her father) pitying you (her mother). After she has completed her re-education with us, you will certainly be out tens of thousands of dollars and very possibly be out of one daughter as well.

Hoff Sommers is an associate of the Clare Booth Luce Policy Institute, regarded as the home of conservative women leaders, which seeks to advise, train, and guide young conservative women. She is, of course, politically and ideologically at the opposite end of the real politics of feminism, but what she is saying is the key to understanding the essence of gender feminism. Politically and socially at least, she is the American counterpart of Sally Oppenheim, British Conservative Life Peer, albeit a generation behind Oppenheim who, as far back as 1974, articulated the same concerns about the differences between those women who were addressing issues of women's status in society and the radical gender politics of the women's liberationists.

In a debate with Juliet Mitchell, then a professor of Psychoanalysis and Gender Studies at Jesus College, Cambridge, broadcast on the BBC2 television programme *Argument*, Oppenheim opined that every woman wanted equality under the law but most women didn't want radical change in their roles. They wanted elevation of their status, but not to become 'imitation men' as she put it, observing that, even in those days, women's libbers were denigrating feminine characteristics and labelling them as second rate. Arguing that the women's liberation movement didn't speak for women, she went on to castigate it for making them feel second rate because they wanted to be wives and mothers, whilst asserting that those women who choose to pursue a career should, quite rightly, have equal opportunity to do so. Oppenheim criticised the feminists' trivialisation of issues such as the burning of bras and choosing not to wear make-up, none of which, she said, had anything to do with equality of opportunity. What was needed in order to deal with discrimination, she asserted, was to re-educate attitudes and overcome prejudices, not to engage in role re-engineering such as that demanded by the proto-gender feminists of the time, whose ideas she described as 'ridiculous'.

As I observed in the case of The Town Hall, New York, meeting in 1971, hosted by Norman Mailer, here we have a contemporaneous observation of what was going on in the 1970s. Placed in juxtaposition to one another, her view and that of Hoff Sommers, expressed more than 20 years later, are like bookends at each end of an era during which the gender feminists' views held sway and won. They are clear and direct evidence of how the radical gender feminists were the real expression of feminism and remain so to this day. The rhetoric hasn't changed in 40 years.

Oppenheim and Hoff Sommers are from two different generations. Both are passionate, intelligent women operating well within in the mainstream of society, and seeking to assist it in its development by working within it, not against it. Of course, that is what society is all about. That is what politics is all about. These two women, both from the conservative (small 'c') stable, aren't seeking revolution, but evolution of society, through the normal political process. However, that is not what radical feminists want, and radical feminism *is* feminism. So-called equity feminism is a futile attempt at representing women's interests, whilst taking account of men's interests too. It doesn't blame men for inequalities women have experienced, neither does it hate men, nor does it seek a gender war with men. Instead, it seeks the balanced, rational balancing of women's status in a changing world - and it seeks equality of opportunity for all. However, that is not what has happened. The radical gender feminists' approach has prevailed.

They have changed the role of women through revolution and man hatred, and they were able to achieve this by infiltrating the political process, initially riding the widespread sympathy for socialism in the 1960s and 70s, then, after a pause during which the right reasserted itself in the 1980s (in Britain through Margaret Thatcher and in the US through Ronald Reagan) they came back with a vengeance in the Clinton/Blair era, which institutionalised gender politics. The idea articulated by Elizabeth Cady Stanton in 1854: that women ask for no better laws than those made by men for themselves was thrown out of the window, and the real feminism, the radical, revolutionary, role-changing, man-hating feminism, took its place at the centre of our societies.

The real feminism?

I am a great admirer of Christina Hoff Sommers. She is an intelligent, articulate, and brave woman, who stands implacably opposed to 'gender feminism'; however, increasingly, her position is becoming untenable in my respectful submission. When she wrote *Who Stole Feminism?* around twenty years ago the zeitgeist was very different. Her so-called 'equity feminism' idea, seemed like a valid alternative to the radical gender feminism she so castigates, but time has shown that the latter is the real deal that society has bought lock, stock, and barrel, whilst believing it to be the former. As time has passed, we have seen the evidence. The real intent of feminism is to overthrow the basic framework of society, re-define women's roles within it, and change society - all as Marx and Engels intended from the outset. As we shall see later, 'The Woman Question' was always a key element in the development of Marxist revolutionary theory, and so was the creation of 'an openly legalised community of women'. It is there for all to see in the 1848 *Communist Manifesto.*[85]

Feminism in all its forms today is revolutionary. It has achieved what it set out to do, and that is to politicise gender and set women against men. Hoff Sommers herself has said many times that feminism has 'divided society along the fault line of gender', and it stands to reason that you cannot set one half of the human race against the other and not incur serious consequences. The most important thing people need to recognise is that irrespective of how it is labelled, the outworking of feminism among us speaks far more eloquently of its real intent than any weasel words about equality for women ever can. However it is labelled, or thought about, feminism has brought about the breakdown of the institution of marriage and the nuclear family, that stable means by which children are brought up in an individual economic unit by two heterosexual parents who are committed to each other, and to the task of bringing up children to become fully-functioning adults who then go on to build a future stable society.

My reading of Christina Hoff Sommers is that she is a traditional conservative who in a sense sees the danger of feminism, but as a woman of her age, she must hold onto the view that there is a 'good' feminism and a 'bad' one. When it is all boiled down, and the residue is examined, the truth is that all feminism is anathema to her values. In the interim between *Who Stole Feminism?* and *The War Against Boys*, a lot of boiling down has taken place. It is now as plain as the nose on anyone's face that political policy in successive governments of whatever political hue, on both sides of the Atlantic, is marginalising and demeaning men, especially men as fathers. If we look feminism squarely in the face, and judge it by its fruit, we will see it for what it is. The idea of so-called 'equity' or 'fairness' feminism was just a sweetener to cover the taste of the bitter poison that was being poured into our lives. It is high time that feminism is seen for what it really is, and what it is really about. There is no such thing as 'good' feminism.

CHAPTER 6

ON PATRIARCHY

A Chapter in Four Parts

FEMINIST BELIEFS:

Patriarchy: A system of male authority which oppresses women through its social, political and economic institutions. In any of the historical forms that patriarchal society takes, whether it is feudal, capitalist or socialist, a sex/gender system and a system of economic discrimination operate simultaneously. Patriarchy has power from men's greater access to, and mediation of, the resources and rewards of authority structures inside and outside the home.

Feminisms: A Reader[86]

'If we are to correct our unbalanced world, then we need to get rid of patriarchy as a system of social governance. By patriarchy, I mean male supremacy; I mean a society where every avenue of power – especially mainstream institutions of power – is overwhelmingly dominated by men. You don't have to go far to find this, and it isn't a preserve of foreign countries or dictatorial regimes; the UK is patriarchal, just like the rest of the globe. It may look different and take different forms, but it's the same old male supremacy.'

Finn Mackay, Lesbian Feminist[87]

PART I

THE SOCIAL ORIGINS OF PATRIARCHY

'The clan is nothing more than a larger family, with its patriarchal chief as the natural head, and the union of several clans by intermarriage and voluntary connection constitutes the tribe.'

Charles Eastman (1858-1939)[88]

Sons of...

For tens of thousands of years humans were essentially nomadic hunter-gatherers who followed herds of animals on their annual migrations, living off them and deriving everything needed for survival, such as skins for clothing and oil for lighting. Until very recently, the Lapps of the Arctic were such a people. However, following the end of the last glacial period, about 10,000 years ago, people began to settle the land, developing agriculture based on a rich hybrid wheat found in the Fertile Crescent that allowed more nutritional value to be gained from the plant. By about 6,000 years ago (this was the late Stone Age and early Bronze Age), people were becoming more 'civilised', although the concept of true civilisation, exemplified later by the Hellenes, was still a long way off. The men of these social groups were the protectors and hunters and the women were the gatherers, the tillers of the fields, the gleaners of crops, the bearers, and nurturers of the children. They carried the life and death risk of bearing children, whilst the men carried the equally real life and death risk of protecting them and their offspring. These ancient tribes were kin: they were co-sanguineous (of the same blood) relatives and their most pronounced social characteristic was that they self-identified as descendants of a particular progenitor.

Both men and women in a tribe called themselves, 'Sons of...' whomsoever their common progenitor was. For example, we read in the Hebrew Bible (The Old Testament) that as recently as around 1,500 BCE, the tribes of Hebrews called themselves *Bnai Yiśra'el* 'The Sons of Israel' (Israel is more commonly known as Jacob, the grandson of Abraham, another patriarch along with Isaac his father). As populations began to grow and spread, vying for the most productive land became a fact of life. War has only ever really been about land and the need to subjugate the possessors of that land in order to occupy it, and in circumstances such as these it is easy to see how the protection of the discrete social groups would naturally fall to the men of a tribe under the leadership of the senior clan or tribe leader, who would be operating under the nominal authority of the original progenitor. If we accept the Hebrew Bible at least to some extent as a historical account, when a country was invaded by marauding hordes, the men, boys, and old women were frequently put to the sword and the young women and girls either raped or carried off as spoils of war to be given as slaves to the men of the invading race. However, as individual societies developed and found ways of living with others, relative peace for the benefit of all took hold. Clans were the extended families, the tribes that comprised the clans, then nations emerged by the association of tribes that were probably cousin-coupled: their partners being obtained from the families comprising the tribes. Thus, the wider network of developing tribal societies grew into nations in which men and women continued in their social roles. Men remained the protectors and providers, and women continued with the nurturing and home-making, accepting the man as head of the family and taking his name, which passed to the children. Thus, the man became a patriarch in his own right: with sons and daughters who bore his family's name and who looked to him for leadership, wisdom, and moral strength.

This form of patriarchal social leadership goes a long way back into history - probably to the earliest proto-civilisations, although we cannot prove this because there is no historical record. There are other ways of inferring it, however, and the work of Steven Goldberg (b. 1941) who was president of the sociology department at City College New York from 1988 until his retirement, helps us do that. Goldberg is best known for his theory of patriarchy based on biological causes, and he believes the evidence for this is irrefutable. In his book *The Inevitability of Patriarchy*,[89] he points to the ethnography of thousands of known societies that have left a historical record and shown that, overwhelmingly, men have always filled the upper positions of hierarchies in all of them. Even those societies that have been claimed by some anthropologists not to be male hierarchies actually were, and in support of this he cites evidence from those societies' adages and songs in which, he asserts, there is a common theme that, 'Men have to be gotten around'. This is what he says about these third-hand sources:

> These quotations make it clear that not one of these societies even begin to represent an exception. For forty years I have challenged professional

anthropologists and archeologists to risk their reputations by specifying a society lacking any of these [male, hierarchical, social] institutions. None has done so. There are, of course, variations in the manifestation of these… institutions. They are different, for example, in the United States and Saudi Arabia. But all societies, whether Christian or pagan, capital or communal etc. 'Stone-age' or modern industrial etc., exhibit the institutions.

Social leadership by men was a tacit, natural development, born of aeons of natural selection for survival that morphed into men becoming the law-making, law-enforcing agents within developing nations, which not only had to be protected from outside attack, but often from power struggles within.

Every group of people living in common purpose needs leadership; otherwise, it will disintegrate through internecine power struggles. However, its leaders must have a legitimate social basis from which to lead, otherwise the people will not recognise their legitimacy and follow them. Leadership can never be predicated only on position: on the title 'leader' for example. Least of all can it be successfully based on position that is appropriated, misappropriated or obtained by presumption. As French and Raven pointed out in their 1958 article, *The Bases of Social Power*,[90] leaders have the authority to lead conferred on them by those who are led, and the granting of that authority is based on a combination of superior expertise in a particular area, additional experience, or knowledge relevant to the task facing the group. The problem with the feminist construct of patriarchy is that it assumes that men appropriated the leadership, and therefore the control of society by false assumption of power. That is not true. The sheer longevity of this arrangement shows us that it was a humanly effective way of life for both men and women.

So, patriarchy exists and it really means the 'rule of the father,' or, better still, 'the rule of the father of the race,' or even 'the chief of the race'. The etymology of the word is a compound of the Latin *patria*, which means 'lineage' or 'descent,' and the Greek *archon* which means, 'one who has legitimate power'. More crucially, the etymology of patriarch conveys the idea of moral authority (that is, to be concerned with the principles of right and wrong behaviour) and the upholding of those principles in a group or society; it does not have a controlling or coercive element to its meaning. Patriarchy finds its most basic expression in the family, where it is not just a binary relationship between men and women, but a multi-dimensional one that stems from the relationship between a father, a mother, and their children, and how their family unit fits into civilised society, its governance, and its law enforcement. Naturally and historically, therefore, all of this has been the domain of men - simply because they were biologically fitted for the role of protection. Patriarchy, therefore, has a more complex, nuanced meaning than the feminist-alleged hegemonic conspiracy of men to dominate women and hold them down socially, as promulgated by feminist theorists. That interpretation of patriarchy is simply a ploy to justify a case, a 'straw man' argument, one that is put up to be knocked down in order to justify a falsely predicated proposition, and people who believe the feminist rhetoric about it would do well to understand this.

Patriarchy is the way things developed through history. In simple terms, men are pre-disposed physiologically to protect, through their greater musculature, their generally superior strength, and their generally greater height, and this automatically confers a leadership role. (Indeed it has always been the case that tall men command higher social status by their sheer presence, and that helps them succeed, both socially and in their careers.) Men are also programmed to provide, and their ability to do this confers social status too. Goldberg calls this 'Male Status Attainment'. It really is just as simple as that, and it has nothing to do with control, or a desire to control. Quite the reverse: men will sacrifice their health, their safety, their enjoyment of family life and their children, yes, even their lives in the pursuit of their inherent, inherited role. It is all easily explained in terms of psycho-physiological differences between men and women that set limits on the roles and behaviours of each. It is important to clarify the difference between dominance and domination, terms that are used ambiguously these days, mainly by feminist propagandists to justify what they call patriarchy, and to denigrate men and maleness.

At this juncture, it is useful to examine the difference between dominance and domination, because they are not the same thing. In fact, they are two contrasting behaviours that differ in their fundamental psychology, and their outcomes. Domination implies inflexibility, the use of force, commands, threats, dictatorship, etc., whereas dominance is a set of character traits that are aimed at gaining or maintaining the highest status that is possible. Dominance, not domination, is implied in effective leadership, which is about gaining co-operation not coercion, and it is implicit in the desire of men to ascend the career ladder as much as it is about using power and strength in dangerous situations to see off a less dominant aggressor. Dominance in the pursuit of status in a male hierarchy is, clearly, an essentially male characteristic, although some women display it too. Goldberg readily acknowledges that there are some women who manifest dominance behaviour more than some men, but the 'social law of large numbers' as he puts it, guarantees that dominance will be associated with males rather than females.

It is a statistical reality that men usually exhibit more easily released dominance behaviour and that translates into the belief that, 'men are aggressive, and women are passive,' an argument that feminists advance constantly but with negative connotations. He is clear, however, that this behaviour is not the default stance of men; it is simply that in the presence of appropriate environmental stimuli, dominance behaviour is more easily released in the male of the species. Men's social behaviour is conditioned by the inbuilt need to compete for status in the male-dominance hierarchies, where status is the currency that buys a good sexual partner. Women cannot function in such an environment, but men have been given the ability to flourish in these situations through aeons of evolution, and that same process has conditioned women to respond to male status because it implies protection, social elevation, and good survivability for their genes. That is what underpins man's historical role as head of the family, and women's role as head of the household.

Biblical concept

If there is one thing the Hebrew Bible tells us about patriarchy, it is that it is a beneficent concept. Patriarchs in the Bible might have been flawed leaders, but they were generally not tyrants. (Those who did, became the subject of criticism, or were killed by the people.) The rule of the man as head of the family or the tribe was less about being a ruler and judging and more about judgement and leadership. As we saw in the opening to this chapter, patriarchy was the means by which an entire society was able to carry on its life without tearing itself apart through the inevitable internecine struggling within clans and tribes. When that happened it needed the strength and authority of the patriarch, combined with the love and respect his family clan and tribe had for him, to put matters back on the right course. More to the point, patriarchy was never a system of domination or control of women: quite the opposite in fact. The patriarchs of Israel were certainly never anti-female, and the subsequent attitude of Jewish society towards women, even to this day, is evidence of that fact. In the Hebrew Bible, for example, we find a paean to 'The Woman of Noble Character' - here is a modern translation of *Proverbs 31*[91] in which it appears:

A Woman of Excellence

A woman of excellence, who will find? For her worth is far more than precious jewels.

The heart of her husband trusts in her, and gain he will not lack.

She does him good, but not harm all the days of her life.

She seeks wool and flax, and she works with the diligence of her hands.

She is like the ships of a merchant; from far off she brings her food;

And she arises while it is still night, and gives food to her household, and tasks to her servant girls.

She considers a field and buys it, from the fruit of her hand she plants a vineyard.

She girds her waist in strength, and makes her arms strong.

She perceives that her merchandise is good; her lamp does not go out in the night.

Her hands she puts onto the distaff, and her palms hold a spindle.

Her palm she opens to the poor, and her hand she reaches out to the needy.

She does not fear for her house when it snows, for her entire household is clothed in crimson.

She makes for herself coverings; her clothing is fine linen and purple.

Her husband is known at the gates, in his seat among the elders of the land.

Linen garments she makes and sells, and she supplies sashes for the merchants.

Strength and dignity are her clothing, and she laughs at the future.

She opens her mouth with wisdom, and instruction of kindness is upon her tongue.

She looks after the ways of her household, and the bread of idleness she will not eat.

Her children rise and consider her happy, her husband also, and he praises her;

'Many daughters have done excellence, but you surpass all of them'.

Charm is deceit and beauty is vain; but a woman who fears Yahweh shall be praised.

Give to her from the fruit of her hand, and may they praise her works in the city gates.

Now, I am pretty sure that feminists reading this will be boiling over with anger by now, alleging that this passage proves their point entirely. Clearly women were kept in the home by men, and men held this in high regard; thus, they praised it. *An Excellent Woman* perfectly fits their demonised stereotype of a housewife pushed into a historically male-defined, male-constructed role. However, they would do well to reflect that this is a description of a way of life in what was undoubtedly a patriarchal society, but hardly one in which women were dominated or suppressed. It gives us enormous insight into the position of women in ancient societies, and clearly demonstrates that women were not historically put down by a dominating male patriarchy. If this biblical account is anything to go by, women were key contributors to civilised life in ancient society, with markedly obvious independence of action. They had their own money (sufficient to 'buy a field') made from the work of their own hands, and they were able to laugh at the future. That sounds like a spirit-cry of freedom to me. It doesn't sound like oppression, which shows that our view of men and women in the past must be seen in the context of the times.

Patriarchy in antiquity

Much later than the biblical times of Moses, about 1,000 years in fact, we see the same thing in other civilisations. In the fifth century BCE, the Greek historian Herodotus[92] reported observing that Egyptian women sat on local tribunals and bought and sold property. They also inherited and bequeathed property and were able to secure loans, as well as being able to witness legal documents. Egypt, a society that was well established when Moses and the Israelites left it and spent 40 years wandering in the desert, was undoubtedly a patriarchal society, but there is nothing in this historical account that suggests a system of control and domination of women. Then, around 500-400 BCE, it is clear that protective patriarchy was the prevailing ethos in the political system of government by the people, which emerged in ancient Greece around that time. Under *demokratia*, the chief magistrates in the city states were called *archons*, and a significant proportion of those were the male military. However, the term was used variously throughout Greek history in more general senses, ranging from 'club leader' to 'master of the tables' at the common meal held for men and boys in social and religious groups; and, of course, it was later used of kings and queens.

In the Greek system of democracy it is true that women were barred from speaking and voting in the assemblies, the *ekklesia* (although they were entitled to be there), but so too were men under the age of 30. Clearly, maturity was deemed a necessary qualification to have a say in the way things were run, just as it is today. Of course, by today's standards, 30 is hardly maturity, but these were times in which life was 'nasty, brutish, and short'. People typically lived much shorter lives than today (many estimates put it at typically around 40), due largely to war, disease, and the death of women during childbirth, which was commonplace. Therefore, people married in their early teens, shortly after puberty, and children were born in those years. Unmarried women were an exception: a tiny minority, and the strong and fit young men were probably engaged in fighting foreign wars and, therefore, not involved in the daily business of running things, which inevitably fell to the older, mature men who had already proved themselves in defence of the state. Thus, only men who were the acknowledged heads of families were allowed to vote. They were deemed to be doing so on behalf of their families, whose interests were deemed to be synonymous with theirs, unlike today.

Early Christian evidence

Some five hundred years later, during the first century BCE, the Christian *New Testament* gives some fascinating insights into the remarkably prominent role women played in the early Christian churches. The early church assemblies were rich in gender diversity, as Simon Jones points out in his article: *Church for the new millennium: What does the Bible say?*.[93] Using St. Paul's 'hellos', his introductory greetings to his letters to the nascent Christian church assemblies (referred to as *ekklesia* in the original Greek texts, incidentally), Jones shows how gender-diverse society was in those days. He notes a striking number of references to women being leaders in the early church. Dorcas, Lydia, Nympha, Phoebe, Euodia, and Syntyche, all women, seem to have been hosts of the early house churches, and what is more, many of them appeared to be single women and women of substance. Phoebe, who lived in Cenchrae, one of the ports of Corinth and who delivered Paul's letter to the Romans, is described by Paul as being his 'benefactor'. Almost certainly she sponsored his Spanish mission. Priscilla, from the Aventine region, '...the Kensington of ancient Rome' as Jones puts it, appears to be the wealthier partner in her marriage with Aquila.

Yet, Paul was classically patriarchal, and so was the society of the time, but none of this smacks of male domination let alone of female submission. Rather, it shows that women had freedom and status, and were able to be independent within a system of politics engaged in by men. The Bible also shows us that the social welfare of women was a feature of life in these ancient times. Indeed, throughout the Old Testament period (Iron Age times, let us not forget) we see repeated references to the exhortation for communities to support widows and orphans. In *Deuteronomy*, we see an instruction for the distribution of the collective produce of the community to '...the fatherless and the widows who live in your towns may come and eat and be satisfied...'[94] This was a man-led society being concerned for women and children, hardly the agent of women's oppression. In the book of Ruth, from a later period, we see a non-Israelite widow being taken as a wife by her 'kinsman redeemer' Boaz. This system, whereby a man who is the brother of a man who dies leaving a widow is expected to take her as his wife, is patriarchy in action, and it emphasises the social responsibility of men, not their domination and rule.

At the other end of the historical period covered by the Bible, in The New Testament letter of James (a disciple of Jesus), we see him teaching that the outworking of religion is 'to look after orphans and widows in their distress,'[95] and in St Paul's first letter to his protégé Timothy, we see him advising the early Christian churches to care for widows if their family cannot: 'If any woman who is a believer has widows in her care, she should continue to help them and not let the church be burdened with them, so that the church can help those widows who are really in need'.[96] If a woman had no father, brother or husband to care for her, the community of believers was to stand in and see to her needs. Under patriarchy, men had created a social security system for women who were widowed and destitute. These are advanced social ideas designed for the benefit of women, not men. No provision seems to have been made for men in similar circumstances, even old men who couldn't work and were without the means of support weren't catered for, but women whose main support - their husbands - who had been taken away by death, were. Ancient society was not a male privileged one.

Throughout history, systems of social organisation, based originally on men's strength and hunting ability, have provided a solid, practical, and symbolic foundation for civilisation. They have developed through a tacit understanding by both sexes of how hierarchy works and how the rule of law for the protection of women and children in developing societies was achieved - often in the face of threats from outside, or the breakdown of society from within. Patriarchy is simply a system of natural leadership of the weaker sex, by the stronger. Men have always taken the lead because they have the attributes that suit them for that role, and women have acceded to this because their attributes fit them for another role. Throughout history patrimonial patriarchy has been the natural form of society for the good of all, and it has undoubtedly been with the good of women in mind, not their suppression.

Moving tableaux

Social organisation, leading to civilisation, has been a moving tableaux down millennia. As society has evolved, so too have people, changing, adapting, and balancing to take account of the enormous number of shifting factors - not least economic ones - that are the warp and weft of human existence. Patriarchal society hasn't given women roles (or rules for that matter): nature and other factors have. Friedrich Hayek in his landmark book, *The Fatal Conceit: The Errors of Socialism* says this:

> To understand our civilisation, one must appreciate that the extended order resulted not from human design or intention but spontaneously: it arose from unintentionally conforming to certain traditional and largely moral practices, many of which men tend to dislike, whose significance they usually fail to understand, whose validity they cannot prove, and which have nonetheless fairly rapidly spread by means of an evolutionary selection - the comparative increase of population and wealth - of those groups that happened to follow them. The unwitting, reluctant, even painful adoption of these practices kept these groups together, increased their access to valuable information of all sorts, and enabled them to be 'fruitful, and multiply, and replenish the earth, and subdue it' (Genesis 1:28). This process is perhaps the least appreciated facet of human evolution. Socialists take a different view of these matters. They not only differ in their conclusions, they see the facts differently. That socialists are wrong about the facts is crucial to my argument.

Certainly, there have been inequalities of status and opportunity throughout history that demanded adjustment be made, especially when industrialisation came along, and wars happened. Certainly, there was a time when women had a relative disenfranchisement from the developing political process, but so too did men, and, society worked out the necessary changes. Ingrained mindsets and patterns of working often take time to be changed. *'Twas ever thus.* Patriarchy has never been just a binary relationship between men and women for the domination of one over the other. In fact, it has always had a much more embracing dimension than that. In its very essence and meaning, patriarchy is about multi-dimensional, multi-faceted fatherhood. It is also a function of age and experience, and its authority applies to men too. Boys, for example, also come under patriarchal authority. Men, even grown men, cede moral authority to their fathers, especially when they are living in their father's household. Even mature men still seek the moral authority of their father and his guidance and advice, throughout their lives, (girls and women do this too, incidentally).

Yet feminists portray this as female-oppressing power, rather than an expression of care, and they have seen to it that fatherhood is denigrated and marginalised in our society to such a degree that it has almost ceased to have meaning. By demonising patriarchy and defining it simplistically as male domination over women, we have allowed this to happen. The Marxist-feminist view of patriarchy, therefore, is just plain wrong. Men have never sought to dominate women. They have never been in the business of controlling them, or gaining privilege over them. Quite the reverse, in fact. The only mechanism at play in patriarchy is men's inbuilt programming to gain ascendancy in *male* hierarchies - and to protect women in their inherent physical vulnerability because of their weaker physiology and their biological and social role as mothers. Patrimonial patriarchy has existed down the millennia, and it is easy to judge some of its workings by our modern mores and standards of civilisation, but it is hardly the conspiracy of men to disadvantage women that feminism makes it out to be, and attacking it to destroy it is not the answer. The 'rule, or authority of the father,' is an important and vital agent in keeping society together. To suggest otherwise is dangerous nonsense.

PART II

THE EVOLUTION OF PATRIARCHY

'It was all Mrs. Bumble. She would do it,' urged Mr. Bumble; first looking round to ascertain that his wife had left the room. 'That is no excuse,' returned Mr. Brownlow, 'You were present on the occasion of the destruction of these trinkets, and, indeed, are the more guilty of the two, in the eye of the law; for the law supposes that your wife acts under your direction.' 'If the law supposes that,' said Mr. Bumble, squeezing his hat emphatically in both hands, 'the law is a ass - a idiot. If that's the eye of the law, the law is a bachelor; and the worst I wish the law is that his eye may be opened by experience - by experience!'

Charles Dickens *Oliver Twist* (1838)

Couverture

I heard a story a couple of years ago about a man who had been asked to propose the traditional toast, 'To the ladies...' at a formal dinner. When the time came to speak, raising his glass, he said, 'Gentlemen: The ladies - who used to be our superiors and who are now our equals'. Apparently there were gasps from the women and barely concealed chortles of laughter from the men. However, throughout mediaeval British and European history, there is irrefutable evidence of this principle in operation, in the system of 'Couverture', a socially protective system for women that dates back to the early 13th century Common Law of England, but probably goes much further into Anglo-Saxon times. Couverture, which means 'covering', derives from Norman feudal doctrine, was developed after Magna Carta, and honed through centuries of practice by the common people of England, that a man is legally responsible for the welfare of the women in his household, whom he must take under his protection, either as husband, or father. In its most basic expression, it means men must care for women at men's expense.

Couverture has informed the law of marriage in England from its inception. It assumed that, upon marriage, the man became his wife's protector and provider: a role he took on from her father, whose covering was transferred in a continuous system of security for women down generations. To this day, we have the tradition of a father, with bitter sweet emotion (often reciprocated in his daughter), 'giving away' his daughter in marriage in a symbolic representation of historical couverture. However, the responsibilities of men in marriage under couverture continue even in these times of alleged equality. Under couverture, whilst a husband gave up all he owned to his wife upon marriage, his wife could legally keep her property separate from him.

The traditional marriage vows from the Common Book of Prayer stipulates that as the husband places the ring symbolising marriage on his wife's finger, he must say, 'With this ring I thee wed, with my body I thee worship, *and with all my worldly goods I thee endow*[97] [Author's emphasis]. Only the man makes this vow, not the woman, and the divorce courts in Britain, as in the US, to this day maintain this principle in their practice of ensuring a wife has sufficient financial settlement to provide for her needs 'in the style to which she has become accustomed', independent of any financial provision for children. This is further underpinned by Judaism. There is an old rabbinical saying[98] that goes, 'A man is a saint if he says, 'What is mine is yours and what is yours is your own' but that is precisely what is implied when a man marries - even today, where it is reflected in the tragedy of divorce, which all too often renders men financially reduced, while enriching women. On the other hand, a woman can choose whether or not 'to honour and obey' her husband. As a successful lady litigant said to her husband in 1896,[99] 'There is no law which compels me to obey or honour you, but there is a law that you must keep me'.

Even in this age of equality, a man will still be ordered to pay his wife maintenance (a Norman French word of exactly the same spelling, meaning 'the process of preserving someone or something, in an existing state') if the marriage ends. This is so, even if a woman is sufficiently able to sustain herself - albeit not at the same level - after the marriage is ended, and even if she is the agent of the marriage coming to an end. The divorce courts still routinely award 'spousal support', which in the US is called 'alimony', a word whose root is the Latin *alere*, 'to nourish', and which in turn is the root of the word *alimonia*, meaning 'food, support, nourishment, sustenance'. Thus, the principle of couverture is still enforced. Men are still expected to be responsible for a woman's care despite feminism's cry for liberation from them. '*Oh, what a tangled web we weave, when first we practice to deceive!*'

Very few people realise that the law of England has always provided the single adult woman with perfect freedom to act as a legal free agent, just as was the case in ancient Egyptian and Hebrew times. For legal purposes, she was called a *femme sole* (whereas a married woman was called a *femme couverte*). A single unmarried woman was always able to have her own money. She was always able to earn, to make contracts in her own name, and to own her own property. Then, when she married, she switched to a more elevated legal status, whilst preserving all the rights and freedoms she enjoyed as a single woman. There was even a backstop built-in to the system if the husband reneged on his obligations. Upon marriage, it was commonplace for a father to give his daughter a dowry, or a bequest of income from part of his estate, and that remained legally outside her husband's control. Despite the fact that the bulk of woman's property was rarely earned by her (it was usually the result of an inheritance from her father, relatives or even a deceased or former husband), the effect of the entire system was to concentrate property into women's hands. This was all subsequently enshrined in English law in 1870, then later in 1882, with successive Married Women's Property Acts that made a woman's possessions her own by statute utterly beyond the control of her husband or third parties, such as his creditors. Thus, couverture was translated from common law to statute law. The Married Women's Property Acts gave a woman complete power to leave her property in her will upon death, completely free from her husband, even though out of his prosperity he might have given it to her in the first place.

What is more, under couverture, a married woman became exempt from legal liability for many personal misdemeanours, since the law automatically assumed a married woman was acting under the nominal authority of her husband whom, as head of the family, was deemed to be responsible for her actions. Ernest Belfort Bax (1854-1925), a prominent barrister and socialist propagandist, wrote this in *New Age*[100] in 1910:

> No [married] woman can be imprisoned for debt ('contempt of court') no matter what means she may possess, although her husband may be for the non-payment of her debts. Not even can her property be attached for the payment of a debt if settled on her in due form. Neither can she be served with a bankruptcy order unless in relation to a business carried on apart from her husband and in her own name. She is free to leave her husband, and he has no legal power to detain her or compel her to return. He has no control over her personal property. She, on the other hand, can obtain an order for restitution of conjugal rights, by which he is ordered to return, or she can obtain alimony or maintenance, according to her 'station in life'. The husband is responsible for any slander or libel she may commit although he knew nothing of it or even disapproved it. He is liable, that is, for damages and costs, while she escapes with absolute impunity.

Legal couverture didn't just apply to the civil law. Husbands also carried legal responsibility for certain categories of their wives' criminal behaviour too. The principle that all stand equal before the law was waived for married women, as Bax (Ibid.) also points out:

> Let us now turn to the criminal law. A wife enjoys, at present in this country, practical immunity for all offences of which her husband is the victim. Goal and public obloquy are the lot of the husband, as we all know, for similar offences towards the wife. The wife, without forfeiting her right of maintenance, may insult, slander, or libel her husband. The wife is free to neglect every one of her recognised duties, while the husband has no redress. If, on the other hand, the husband neglects her he is at once liable to a police-court separation order with confiscation of property, or wages, for her maintenance. It must be remembered here that everything of which the wife chooses to complain (e.g., coming home late at night) will be held by the Court to constitute neglect, just as everything the wife chooses to call cruelty will be construed as such by a similar chivalrous tribunal. A husband can be arrested and imprisoned for deserting his wife, whereas a wife may desert her husband with impunity... a case is hardly known of a woman being sentenced to imprisonment for bigamy. Men commonly receive seven years for this offence. Similarly, a woman is practically allowed full freedom to commit perjury in the Divorce Court with a view to establishing a case of adultery against her husband. Let the husband but try the same game on and he will find quite another pair of shoes awaiting him. Even if the perjury be committed to exculpate himself – a thing regarded as a matter of course in the wife – the husband is by no means secure from the danger of penal servitude.

Feminists who complain that women have always been oppressed by men would do themselves, and everyone else, a favour if they were to recognise the truth that under couverture and its principles (later enshrined in statute law), women had a fantastic social deal, which imposed enormous, almost unreasonable obligations on men who could not escape carrying a heavy legal responsibility for their wives, and for their children. Couverture was, by any measure, a rigorous system - for men - and it remained in force right into modern times, with important remnants of it living on in divorce law. Women were not prevented from exercising their individual legal rights, neither were they deprived of their own wealth. It is true that married women were not allowed under law to enter into contracts, and that the husband was required to counter sign a woman's application for a credit card, right up until the 1960s,[101] but the feminist interpretation of this as being in some way a conscious demeaning of women is wrong. If we understand this as one of the last vestiges of a social system that placed heavy legal responsibility on a man for his wife and her debts, we can see why it was required. Men had to have a means of ensuring they had some control in the discharge of their heavy legal responsibilities.

In marriage, therefore, a woman was protected by her husband in a variety of ways, in a system that recognised marriage as not just a legal but an honourable ethical contract of covering by a man for his wife. For a woman, marriage has always been, 'an honourable estate'. It was the legal means by which, for 1,000 years (and, as a development of probably 3,000 years or more of social development before it), a woman's safety and wellbeing were assured in a system of care that was passed from her father to her husband. Under couverture, men shouldered enormous responsibility for their wives and families, which brought about the social conditions in which children could be born and brought up in the maximum security possible. Men were, in effect, legally locked into marriage, whilst women remained remarkably free and far from being under the direction of their husbands. In Charles Dickens's novel, *Oliver Twist*, when Dickens's character Mr Bumble is informed, '...the law supposes that your wife acts under your direction,' he replies, acidly: 'If the law supposes that ...the law is a ass - a idiot. If that's the eye of the law, the law is a bachelor; and the worst I wish the law is that his eye may be opened by experience - by experience!'

There is another way of looking at couverture and patriarchy that stands diametrically opposed to the feminist narrative. In fact, it is a touching and honourable thing: steeped in history, and infused with male protectiveness and gallantry. Patriarchy has nothing to do with oppression of women. It did not make a married woman into a whore, as Karl Marx so sordidly described it. It did not turn women into cowed, muted, controlled, timid creatures, as feminists would have us believe today. To be a wife in those days was an honourable thing for a woman. It was a social status that carried with it the ideas of dignity and uprightness. It was far from the picture of the bored and boring housewife of that caricature portrayed by Betty Friedan, which has become the stock in trade of feminist rhetoric today. All of these concepts are twisted inversions of the truth.

Feudalism to modernity

Society, nations, peoples, and statehood have been an emerging, unfolding affair for as long as they have existed. Change can be induced through revolution and an overturning of the *status quo ante*, but violent disruption has proven time and again to set nations back, often irrevocably, because it short circuits the system of social evolution. We need to understand this if we are to see the extent to which feminism is a threat to society: how it is a disruption of our social development, not part of it. This Marxist political ideology is out to tear our society apart, not move it ahead. Societies need to evolve and have time to adapt to the needs of the people who comprise them, not be jolted willy-nilly from one state of being to another, which is what feminists are trying to do.

Nothing proves the benefit of an adaptive evolution better than the change from the feudal system to the modern era, which happened around 1700 CE in Britain. This hinge in history was massive, but it wasn't the destructive revolution experienced by France in 1789 or Russia in 1918. The changes that took place in British society around this time were positive, not destructive, and better seen as metamorphosis: a gradual transition from one state to another. This was a time when the better part of 1,000 years of monarchical patriarchy, which had been enormously successful, morphed and adapted into something new, and it was men who were instrumental in that change. It was men who resisted the overbearing divine right of kings and forced the Magna Carta to be produced, which established the just rule of the people under law, and it was men who formed the first Parliament in 1265 in England, which was the beginning of the democracy we enjoy today.

Men also crafted the feudal system, which was a means of ensuring defence of the realm from the foreign oppressor, as well as being a stable system of social and economic governance. Feudalism, as it is generically known, was really manorialism - hence, the term 'Lord of the Manor'. It was not a political system, but a social framework that involved reciprocal relationships, based on the granting of land in exchange for service, ultimately military service in defence of the realm, and it worked for the best part of 1,000 years. The term Lord comes from the Old English *hlāford* which originated from *hlāfweard* meaning 'bread keeper' or 'loaf-ward', reflecting the Germanic tribal custom of a chieftain providing food for his followers, in much the same model as those social leaders in ancient times whom I described earlier. This was not an outworking of the rule of men, but the role of men who were expected to provide for their families. The lords gave allegiance to the monarch (which means 'one ruler') in a mutual arrangement that guaranteed they would raise armies and support him (or her, as history shows) in the event of enemy attack. In return, the monarch, usually and obviously a man because of men's role, granted ownership of large tracts of land, which locked the lords into the defensive arrangement. In other words, the lords had a vested interest in defending the land, which they owned.

The 'Vassals' were people who gave allegiance to the lord based on a similar mutual obligation: the grant of smaller tracts of land, called 'Manors', which the vassal held as a *fiefdom*, or *fee* (the Middle English equivalent of *feudalis*; hence 'feudal'). The term 'vassal' is also of Middle English origin, from Celtic through Latin (*vassalus*), which means 'retainer', in the same way we use the term today to mean something that keeps another thing in place, and as a payment in advance or a standing charge. Like the lords', the vassal's right to his manorial land was granted in perpetuity as *heritable*: i.e., land which can be passed on to heirs and successors, (to this day, the freehold of a property in Britain subject to local taxation, typically called 'rates' or 'council tax', is called a 'hereditament'- as opposed to a 'tenement', which is a property for which a tenant pays rent in return for his occupation of it.)

Again, this was a national defence commitment lock-in that was extended further down the social spectrum, to the people who either laboured on the farms ('serfs') or were owners of small farms, called smallholdings ('freemen'). A small number of freemen was also known as 'franklin'(originally *franklen, frankleyn,* or *francoleyn*), another Middle English term that derives from the Latin, *francalanus*, meaning 'one who owns *francalia*', a 'territory held without dues'. It was a 'freeholding'. Freemen were hereditary too. Once granted, freeman status could not be taken away. It was passed to their sons, and the land they owned was also hereditable. The serfs occupied the greater majority of the people. They were the lowest social class and bound economically and socially to the lord of the manor by law, in return for their keep, and the benefit of 'the king's peace'- a stable social order under the rule of law. They worked the fields of the manor, dug the lord's mines, felled the trees in his forests, and built roads across his lands. During times of peace they were the backbone of the rural economy, and in times of national threat they provided the manpower for the armies raised to defend the nation by the lord of the manor.

This feudal system remained largely unchanged for centuries, but around 1700 CE things started to change dramatically. The increasing international reach of England that took place under Queen Elizabeth II, through the likes of Sir Walter Raleigh, had started the process. The people still worked on farms owned by the landed gentry, but both commerce, and industry were beginning to take root. Hitherto, the only industry to speak of was cottage industry, where people made things for daily life and spun yarns for clothing (usually the job of the single woman in the household, hence the term 'spinster'). Blacksmiths would shoe horses and make small mechanical devices for the farms; and commerce would be conducted by merchants who operated regionally, but things were changing. Advances in farming practices were taking place, and that demanded increasing mechanisation. Landowners were appointing tenant farmers, and agricultural land was being redistributed from general use by a rural peasantry to larger enclosures with hedges and ditches that needed a more organised method of farming it productively. This unofficial redistribution of the land later became legitimised in law with the passing by Parliament of the General Enclosure Act, 1801, and it sealed the fate of the feudal system.

As the eighteenth century unfolded, factories began to emerge and people flocked to the towns seeking work. Britain's enormous, largely untouched reserves of coal (hitherto, people had burnt wood for heat and cooking), plus increasing access to raw materials such as cotton and pig-iron from her colonies, particularly America, were fuelling the Industrial Revolution. Markets were opening up in India and the Far East. The textiles industry was exploding, using raw cotton imported from America, and from the 1720s onwards, thousands of young adults left their rural homes to move to the centres of production - the towns that later became cities - in the pursuit of work. Wages were pitiful, but this young population was mobile and adaptable to change. Hitherto, land owners and farmers had kept their young workers single, using their economic and social power to restrict early marriage so as to ensure longer productivity. Young couples often had to ask for permission of their master to marry. Now, people were released from these social restrictions and became able to marry and start families sooner. As the marriage registers of the time show, the average age of British brides dropped from almost 27 in the early 1700s to 23 by 1800 CE. Young women are more fertile at this age and can produce far more children, and the 1700s saw the population of Britain double, from around 5.7 million to 8.7 million.

By the time Britain took its massive leap into the machine age, it had its largest population of youngsters ever. As Jane Humphries, Professor of Economic History at Oxford University and Fellow of All Souls College, puts it, 'The country was awash with children' As the century progressed, the Napoleonic Wars meant that a significant proportion of the able-bodied men was away fighting in France. Women, of course, took up many of their jobs, in the cotton mills for example, but skilled adult labour was in such short supply that when his Chancellor of the Exchequer warned Prime Minister William Pitt that businesses were becoming unable to pay their taxes to fund the war, he is on record as saying, 'Then we must yoke up the children to work in the factories!' By 1820, 40% of the population of the United Kingdom was under 15 years of age, and most were sent to work. Between 1796 and 1830, cotton production tripled through the invention of machines that vastly improved the process, such as John Kay's 'Flying Shuttle' (1733), which effectively doubled a weaver's production of cloth, and Richard Arkwright's 'Water Frame' (1769), which used the power of water to produce an even stronger yarn. Then, in 1769, James Watt patented the steam engine, powered by coal, which by now was being mined in enormous quantities, allowing coal mines to proliferate, causing productivity to soar. However, this power quickly became adapted to factory machinery and this sent the Industrial Revolution into overdrive. James Hargreaves produced the 'Spinning Jenny' (1770), which allowed many threads to be spun at once and Samuel Crompton produced his 'Mule' (1779), which combined the benefits of the Spinning Jenny and the Water Frame to produce large amounts of fine, strong yarn, which was being increasingly worked into cloth by Edmund Cartwright's Power Loom (1783).

The enormous creativity and inventiveness of these men had caused an industrial and social explosion. In Lancashire in 1800 CE, there were no cotton weaving machines at all. By 1830, there were 30,000, most of them clustered around Manchester and manned and worked by women and children. However, their creativity wasn't confined just to engineering. Rationalism and science, philosophical debate, publishing, the arts, all began to flourish, and a thirst for knowledge and striving for a better society took hold. This was a time of the Coffee House Movement in England. The 'Penny Universities', as they came to be called, were places where you paid a penny to enter and drank as much coffee as you wanted, whilst you talked, and traded, and mixed with others of a like mind. Many businesses were created at this time and by the last third of the century, the merchant, the handicraft artisan, the journeyman were no longer the main economic agent of the economy. Instead, the industrialist, with his investment in machinery, mechanisation of production, and division of work took over.

The Enlightenment, which started at this time, with its emphasis on reason and science, shaped the milieu, and it spread like wildfire throughout Europe. Mercantilism gave way to capitalism and a new group of economic theorists emerged, not least among whom was the Scottish philosopher Adam Smith (1723-1790). In his 1776 book *An Inquiry into the Nature and Causes of the Wealth of Nations*, Smith pioneered the idea of political economics, and theorised that firms were the answer to the inefficiencies of the pre-existing craft system. By bringing people together and dividing work into specialist tasks, he showed that production could rise by several orders of magnitude, driving down the cost of production, eliminating market transaction costs, and achieving a much higher return on the capital employed in the enterprise. This dramatically increased profit, which generated more capital for further investment.

The nineteenth century saw the second phase of the Industrial Revolution. Division of labour, as advocated by Adam Smith, translated into the creation of formalised operating procedures, with rules for employees to follow; lines of authority developed, and reporting procedures were invented. This was the age of the civil engineer, such as Isambard Kingdom Brunel, who built bridges, railways, and ships. Joseph Bazalgette built the sewerage system in London, which is still in use to this day. These are just two of the many examples of 'superstar engineers' of the time whose fantastic skills shaped our modern world.

Universal enfranchisement

As the industrial era emerged, so too did the change in social order. Capitalists replaced the lords and vassals, the freemen became the middle classes, and the serfs became the working classes, with just as little control over their means of existence as before. They were still selling their labour for a living and, no doubt, this left them with no small degree of resentment in the midst of the wealth that was being created around them. As early as the end of the eighteenth century, the claim for universal suffrage was being made by men. Jeremy Bentham, the proponent of modern utilitarianism, whose axiom was, '…it is the greatest happiness of the greatest number that is the measure of right and wrong' was an ardent campaigner for universal suffrage. He published his *Plan of Parliamentary Reform in the Form of a Catechism, with reasons for each article, with an introduction, shewing the necessity of radical, and the inadequacy of moderate, reform*, as early as 1817, in which he addressed the immensely complicated issue of the ability to vote, irrespective of social status. This was the 'hot potato' issue of the era, expressed in terms of the equality of the ordinary man with the gentry in the post feudal paradigm, and the emergence of democracy and 'liberty, equality, and brotherhood', that cry of the French in 1989, and 'no taxation without representation' that shouted from 'the sons of liberty' in Boston Massachusetts on behalf of the 13 American Colonies in December 1773, which was the trigger for their fight for independence.

Society was changing. Feudalism was under challenge, and like all change, there was considerable resistance to it. We can obtain a real flavour of the tensions in that enormously turbulent period, and the genuine questions being addressed from Jeremy Bentham's papers[102] reveal the extent to which doubts were being expressed about the wisdom of extending the vote universally. Bentham articulated one of the most salient of issues of the time: the degree of education needed for voters to be able to make informed decisions, as follows:

> As to the grounds. First, as to any supposed deficiency in respect of appropriate intellectual aptitude. Among those who, in the shape of landed property, had not so much as 40s. a-year of that day [mediaeval times] - going as far, say as £40 money of the present day - small indeed probably was the number of those who were able to read: how much larger among those who had their 40s. and more? Probably enough, very little. As for the "knights and esquires," some few of them not improbably were in those days able to read: but by not one of them, most certainly, was any book to be found from which any information, tending to the increase of appropriate intellectual aptitude, could be extracted.

Another was the mental capacity of the voter, for example:

> Of absolute universality, if admitted, the effect would be - to admit to the exercise of the franchise in question persons of various descriptions, none of whom would be capable of exercising it to the advantage either of others or of themselves. Idiots, and infants in leading-strings, may serve for examples.

A third was the concern that giving the vote to the common man could lead to the manipulation of the electorate viz.:

> To say that a suffrage ought to be free, what is it but to say—that the will expressed by it ought to be the very will of the person by whom it is so

expressed?—the will of that person and of that person only; his self-formed will - the product of his own judgment, self-formed or derivative as the case may be, - not produced by the knowledge or belief of the existence of any will or wish, considered as entertained by any other person, at whose hands the voter entertains an eventual expectation of receiving good or evil, in any shape: good or evil, according as, by him the said voter, the wishes of such other person, in relation to the matter in question, shall or shall not have been conformed to? In so far as, in the instance of any voter, the vote which is given is, according to this explanation, and in this sense, not free, it is manifestly not genuine: it is spurious:—under the guise and disguise of the expression of the will of the voter, it is the will—not of the voter, but of some other person. In so far as it is given as and for the will of the voter, the giving it, is it anything better than an act of imposture?

This last point refers to the major issue of the 'rotten boroughs', also known as 'pocket boroughs'. The electoral system at the time comprised boroughs (meaning 'a fortified town') declared by Royal Charter since time immemorial, in which the burgesses (the property owning feudal freemen) were required to send two members of Parliament to Westminster to represent the borough. These borough constituencies had stayed the same for centuries, and the system was creaking at the seams. In the seismic social changes that were taking place they were rapidly proving incapable of reflecting the population shifts that were taking place. In some boroughs, the number of electors became so few that the electorate could easily be bribed or intimidated by a single wealthy landowner who still exercised enormous feudal power in the community. In those circumstances, the voting intentions of the freemen electorate who were unwilling to offend their powerful patron became a mere formality, especially as voting was by a show of hands in the local polling station.

Such was the cosy corruption of the system that often only one candidate was nominated by the mayor and the corporation, acting at the behest of the patron, and often that candidature was routinely passed down from father to son. The term 'pocket borough' was pejorative. It meant the borough was in the patron's pocket. However, the corruption of the rotten boroughs wasn't the key issue. Beneath it was disproportionate political representation. Those members of Parliament elected by the property-owning burgesses of the rural boroughs represented only a few constituents, whilst the two elected by the increasing non-property-owning constituents in the rural boroughs represented many. The two-per-borough rule applied to boroughs such as Lancashire, where, for example, Manchester had just suddenly burgeoned, and vast numbers of people were being taxed without sufficient political representation, or representation that understood their needs.

The introduction of The Corn Laws between 1815 and 1846 CE, passed under pressure from rural land owners after the end of the Napoleonic Wars and designed to protect them from the effects of imports of grain from the continent through a tariff, caused food prices to rise steeply, which was hated by the large numbers of poor people in the burgeoning towns. That, combined with massive male unemployment caused by the return of men from the war, brought matters to a head on 16th August 1819, when a mass demonstration of 60-80,000 people took place in St Peter's Field in Manchester, demanding Parliamentary reform of representation. Such was the power of the demonstration that the authorities put it down harshly, using cavalry to disperse the crowd. Fifteen people were killed and between 400 and 700 injured, and such was the shock felt in the country, that the incident came to be known as 'The Peterloo Massacre', in an ironic combination of St Peter's Field and Waterloo, the decisive battle of the Napoleonic Wars from only four years earlier.

Even before this pivotal event, as we saw in Jeremy Bentham's analysis, there were calls afoot in British society for Parliamentary reform. As early as 1792, Charles Earl Grey, MP for Northumberland, whose statue stands proudly at the very centre of Newcastle upon Tyne, one of the key centres of industrial power during the Industrial Revolution and with a proud tradition of the working class, founded an organisation to advocate Parliamentary reform. When he became British Prime Minister in 1830-1834, he promulgated The Representation of the People Act 1832 (better known as 'The Great Reform Act') in Parliament, which instigated the reform of voting rights for ordinary people. Negative feminist rhetoric makes a great play of the fact that the Great Reform Act was deeply misogynistic because its wording specifically referred only to 'male persons'. They point out that patriarchy fought back when John Stuart Mill MP, the dedicated social reformer, attempted to get the term replaced with just 'person' in a second reform bill in 1867, but was defeated in the House of Commons, by 196 votes to 73. Clearly this must have been patriarchy at work, militating against women. But was it? The picture was much more complex than that.

The reform measures actually only applied to those who possessed property valued annually at £10 or more, increasing the proportion of male voters to only about one in six adult males,[103] and all voters to 1 in 24 (in a population of some 14 million at the time). The Great Reform Act and its successor Acts were discriminatory as to class, not gender. It effectively only benefitted the growing middle-class (the 'bourgeoisie,' as Marx called them only a few years later in the 1846 *Communist Manifesto*), it did nothing for the interests of working class people of either sex. It was a step forward in extending the franchise, in moving from feudalism to the modern era, but it was a small step that still relied on retaining the feudal property-ownership qualification.

John Stuart Mill was an interesting character. As towering an intellectual figure as he was, he was very much influenced by his second wife, a radical proto-feminist who undoubtedly was the driving force behind, if not the author of, *The Subjection of Women*[104] (1869), published by Mill shortly before his death at the age of 67 in 1873, and widely seen as his least important work. In a 1901 introduction to Mill's major treatise, the 1859 *On Liberty*,[105] penned by a 'W. L. Courtney, LLD', we find a fascinating insight into Mill's long-standing adulterous relationship with this 'Mrs John Taylor', whom he had met at a dinner party hosted by her husband in 1831, and whom he later married after her husband's death in 1851. This affair was conducted very much against the advice of his friends, who applied pressure on him to desist. In his introduction to *On Liberty*, Courtney writes: 'Opinions were widely divergent as to her merits; but everyone agreed that up to the time of her death... Mill was wholly lost to his friends'. He goes on to comment that Mill's major opus *On Liberty* '...contains the most extraordinary panegyric on a woman that any philosopher has ever penned...', and that, '...the treatise *On Liberty* was written especially under her authority and encouragement, but there are many earlier references to the power which she exercised over his mind'.

Mill himself gives us a flavour of the degree to which this woman exercised power over him in his dedication of his work:

> To the beloved and deplored memory of her who was the inspirer, and in part the author, of all that is best in my writings - the friend and wife whose exalted sense of truth and right was my strongest incitement, and whose approbation was my chief reward - I dedicate this volume. Like all that I have written for many years, it belongs as much to her as to me; but the work as it stands has had, in a very insufficient degree, the inestimable advantage of her revision; some of the most important portions having been reserved for a more careful re-examination, which they are now never destined to receive.

Were I but capable of interpreting to the world one-half the great thoughts and noble feelings which are buried in her grave, I should be the medium of a greater benefit to it than is ever likely to arise from anything that I can write, unprompted and unassisted by her all but unrivalled wisdom.

Harriet Taylor Mill, 'Mrs John Taylor,' later Mrs John Stuart Mill, as well as making her first husband a cuckold for many years, was undoubtedly a modern woman in every sense of the meaning we would apply to that term today. Mrs Thomas Carlyle, the wife of the Scottish essayist, philosopher, and historian, described her thus: 'she is thought to be dangerous'; and Carlyle himself added she was 'worse than dangerous, she was patronising'.

Given the dates, it seems clear that Harriet Taylor Mill was at least influenced by (if not a follower of) Karl Marx and Friedrich Engels, who at that time were formulating their *Communist Manifesto*, first published in 1848. Courtney tells us that Mill directly attributes a specific contribution by her to *On Liberty* in 'The chapter which has had a greater influence on opinion than all the rest, that on the Probable Future of the Labouring Classes, is entirely due to her.' Apparently, this chapter did not exist in the first draft of the book, about which Courtney comments:

> From this it would appear that she gave Mill that tendency to Socialism which, while it lends a progressive spirit to his speculations on politics, at the same time does not manifestly accord with his earlier advocacy of peasant proprietorships. Nor, again, is it, on the face of it, consistent with those doctrines of individual liberty which, aided by the intellectual companionship of his wife, he propounded in a later work. The ideal of individual freedom is not the ideal of Socialism, just as that invocation of governmental aid to which the Socialist resorts is not consistent with the theory of laisser-faire. Yet [On] Liberty was planned by Mill and his wife in concert.

The 1834 Great Reform Act, with all its imperfections, was a start on the road to a more developed society with equality and universal suffrage as its aim, but there was still a long way to go. It did nothing to ease the increasing social pressure, as witness a series of petitions to Parliament (in 1839, 1842, and 1848) by the newly formed Chartist Movement, which was particularly strong in the textile towns of Lancashire and Yorkshire, the East Midlands, the Potteries, and the Black Country, all surrounding Birmingham. The last of the 'Great Petitions', as they came to be called, had 6,000,000 signatures, and demanded full *male* suffrage, secret ballots, the abolition of property-owning qualifications for prospective Parliamentary candidates, payment for MPs, equal electoral districts, and annual elections.

Chartism was very much a working class mass movement, which attracted further repression from the authorities, who were afraid of its power. In a chilling echo of the Peterloo incident, working people had declared themselves *en masse* to be Chartists, and this time they were more organised. After the rejection of the first Great Petition in 1842, a wave of strikes ensued, some of which became violent. In Preston, Lancashire, for example, soldiers opened fire on Chartist crowds. In Halifax, Chartists attacked soldiers who were escorting Chartist prisoners. In the Potteries, 56 Chartists were transported to the colonies for their civil disobedience, and in 1848, when the time came for the last of the Great Petitions to be presented to Parliament, the authorities dispatched Queen Victoria to the Isle of Wight for her safety, calling on the Duke of Wellington to defend London, giving him command of thousands of soldiers and special constables, and banning the proposed Chartist procession to The House of Commons. Wary of provoking another bloodbath, the Chartist leaders complied with the ban, choosing instead to deliver the petition in three cabs led by Feargus O'Connor, the Chartist leader, and others walking alongside him.

The pressure was becoming unstoppable, and it resulted in another two reform acts: in 1867, which extended the vote to skilled urban working class men, increasing the electorate to about 1 in 3; and in 1884, extending the vote to working class men in the countryside. This brought the vote to vote to two out of three men. At this point, in 1866, the call for women to have the same political rights as men emerged. This was supported by Henry Fawcett MP and John Stuart Mill MP, who led the case for *universal* suffrage in the House of Commons. This resulted in the abortive amendment to the second reform bill of 1867 to replace the wording from 'male persons' to just 'person', which was defeated, as we have already seen, and this prompted the formation of the London Society for Women's Suffrage, which spawned a series of similar women's suffrage groups across Britain, 17 of which affiliated into the National Union of Women's Suffrage Societies (NUWSS) in 1897, whose aim was to obtain peaceful and non-confrontational argument for votes for women through education, posters, leaflets, and public meetings. As a sign of the progress these women made, even Queen Victoria endorsed their cause, albeit with caveats when, in 1870, she wrote, 'Let women be what God intended, a helpmate for man, but with totally different duties and vocations'. Women were not being ignored.

As a result of the activism of the NUWSS, the Married Women's Property Act (1870) came into law, which was a clear move to open the way for women's enfranchisement. This act protected women's property in the unlikely and rare event of a divorce. Thus, women could become property owners in their own right and hold that property intact whether they were married, widowed, or divorced. There then followed a string of reforms in rapid succession that ensured not only Parliamentary reform, but legal reforms in which women's legal status, independent of their husbands, was recognised. Women were steadily being reintegrated into a different status in a modern form of society. And this was at the hands of men. This new direction of travel took on further momentum in the early twentieth century when, in 1907, The Qualification of Women (County and Borough Councils) Act was passed, which allowed women to be selected for borough and county councils, and be elected mayors. Then, The Representation of the People Act 1918, which added about 8,000,000 electors to the roll, three-quarters of whom were women (albeit with minimal property qualifications and a different age limit between men and women, of which more in a moment). In the same year, the Qualification of Women Act 1918 provided the right for women to be elected to Parliament even if they hadn't yet reached the age where they could vote.

This is widely regarded as an honourable recognition of the part women had played in the Great War, and the part they were going to play in the peace, and it was the moment when women *as a class* gained access to the *national* political process. At long last, after a century of adjustment to massive social change, universal franchise was becoming a reality, although the First World War forced one final caveat. There had to be a different age qualifications for the right to vote as between women and men. For men it was 21 years of age and for women it was 30 years, provided some minimal property criteria were met. This was not discrimination against women; the reason was the First World War. Even as early as 1908, before the Great War as it was popularly known, there were a million more women in society than men, and the losses in that war exacerbated that situation massively. So many men had been killed in defence of their King and country that society was unbalanced. Had women been given the vote at the same age as men, they would have had a disproportionate and undemocratic level of representation, and in any case, public opinion would not have supported it. It would have been crass and have caused deep civil unrest. Finally, however, the long journey was completed in 1928 with the passing of The Equal Suffrage/Franchise Act, which granted universal suffrage without qualification, to all citizens of the age of majority - men and women alike.

The Suffragettes

The idea that women had to fight to get the vote is nonsense. It is a meme inspired by feminist propaganda that has been successful because of its endless repetition. Like a virus, it has infected the public consciousness to such an extent that it is now considered the truth. It is not the truth. If the truth be known, the Suffragettes were barely a dot at the end of the sentence of the struggle for votes for all people. The real truth starts with the indisputable fact that men of probity, conscience, and influence, acting in honourable and honest response to a broader social inequality, had been speaking out and acting on the issue of universal enfranchisement for almost 100 years. They had doggedly prosecuted the struggle for votes for everyone, using the political system, changing what could be changed in increments (politics is, after all, 'the art of the possible'), ultimately achieving the vote for women in the context of votes for all.

What the feminist narrative neatly omits to mention is that only about half of the men who went to the trenches in the First World War had a national vote,[106] yet they went in their hundreds of thousands to almost certain death or maiming of their young bodies in order to defend a country in which women enjoyed an enormously privileged position. Emmeline Pankhurst, her daughters Christabel and Sylvia, and their followers, well knew that the so-called right to vote for women was a false cause, yet they were prepared to engage in their cynical, selfish behaviour towards men (and boys) who didn't even have what they wanted. From time immemorial, the right to vote in national elections had been granted only to that proportion of the adult male population who owned property over a certain value. This was a fundamental principle of the feudal system. In the period during which heated debate was raging about women's suffrage, only about 3 per cent of the adult male population were qualified to vote in national elections. Yet, the Pankhursts toured the country making speeches exhorting men to fight. This is what Emmeline Pankhurst said to a packed audience in Sun Hall, Liverpool, as reported by the *Evening Post* on 5th June 1916:[107]

> The least that men can do is that every man of fighting age should prepare himself to redeem his word to women, and to make ready to do his best, to save the mothers, the wives and daughters of Great Britain from outrage too horrible even to think of.

The cant of the Suffragettes is only exceeded by the cant of feminists today who allege that men as a class are a danger to women. In those days, it was the other way round. One of the most shameful things the women of the Suffragette movement did was to cynically shame thousands (possibly tens of thousands) of young men and under-age boys into volunteering for the trenches of Flanders by pinning white feathers[108] - a powerful signal of cowardice - on any young man whom they saw was not in uniform. Many soldiers were wrongly accused by the overzealous suffragettes of cowardice, which was reprehensible in the light of what they were shaming these men to do. Wilfrid Owen is widely believed to have referred to this in his deeply moving poem *Dulce et decorum est,* published posthumously in 1920, which contained the most graphic imagery of men being gassed and maimed in defence of Great Britain. The title of Owen's poem is taken from the Roman poet Horace, who wrote *dulce et decorum est pro patria mori* - it is sweet and honourable to die for one's country. This was the message the suffragettes were spreading, and its insensitivity, to choose the softest word, is nauseous. The story of Private Ernest Atkins,[109] who was accosted by one of these vacuous women whilst riding a tram car, illustrates my point perfectly. He smacked the woman across the face with his pay book saying:

> 'Certainly I'll take your feather back to the boys at Passchendaele. I'm in civvies because people think my uniform might be lousy, [full of lice] but if I had it on I wouldn't be half as lousy as you.'

On another occasion, a soldier was asked why he was not in the army and he responded by saying he was German. Apparently, he received a white feather anyway. On yet another, and perhaps most ironically, a seaman - George Samson - who had received the Victoria Cross for gallantry in the Gallipoli campaign, was presented with a white feather whilst on his way to a public reception in his honour.[110]

The Suffragettes were not heroines up at the cutting edge of social change as feminists would have us believe; they were a group of utterly hypocritical, privileged, middle-class fools who wanted the vote on the same terms as it was granted only to equally privileged men. The Pankhursts were women of property - through widowhood and inheritance, under the feudal system - and they wanted a piece of the same action as other property owners. What they were fighting for was privilege through property. In fact, they were party to the maintenance of the *status quo ante*, which people are led to believe they were seeking to overturn. Put bluntly, the Pankhursts were out for themselves in the same way that many vociferous feminists are today, whipping up hysteria in young women in pursuit, for example, of easy and lucrative boardroom posts, exhorting them to break through the 'glass ceiling'. And just like the lie of the glass ceiling, the Suffragettes dealt in lies too. Women were not totally disenfranchised at the turn of the twentieth century. The general idea that they were, as it were, kept chained to the kitchen sink or the crib, held in thrall to their husbands' will, is a historically challenged feminist lie. Nothing could be further from the truth than this revisionist claim suggests.

Women had the right to vote in local politics, and they were able to take part in civic affairs too. They could stand for local political office, such as mayors, and they did. Local government was where the quality of people's lives was managed, and both men and women had a full part to play in that political arena. The key issue was the national vote to elect Members of Parliament, which was still conditional on archaic rules of property ownership derived from feudalism. This was the political arena in which the issue of equalisation of rights for *everyone* was rising to the top of the social agenda. The Industrial Revolution had changed the social order. Working people, who by now included women in their own right, had sought reform and politics had responded by re-shaping society to take account of it all. This was no women's struggle. It was never a simplistic matter of votes for women. It included issues like eradication of slavery, and equal human rights, and how to achieve the greatest good for all citizens. Integrating those things into a changing society had been an ongoing process since the Enlightenment, long before the Suffragettes took up their hysterical cause. They only rode on the back of a trend toward the equalisation of society as a whole - and that trend was driven by men of conscience and intelligence who saw the need for society to grow and adapt as history was unfolding. It was all bound up with the movement from feudalism to modernity in the post-Enlightenment era. The truth is that women got the vote as part of the ongoing drive to enfranchise *every* citizen in the wake of the tumultuous social changes that had happened in the last 200 years, after a period of 700-800 years of social stability. 'Votes for Women' was always going to happen because social and economic change was driving it.

In fact, it is arguable that the Suffragettes actually delayed women getting the vote by their ridiculous antics and questionable ethics. It took the horror of World War I to expose them for what they were, thus making their outrageous claims and appalling behaviour anathema to ordinary people. We gain an interesting insight into this from Ernest Belfort Bax (a Marxist philosopher, incidentally), speaking at a symposium on women's suffrage in February 1911, who said:[111]

> 1. In my opinion there are two most powerful arguments against woman's suffrage. Firstly, the liability of women to hysteria in one or other of the various forms of that abnormal mental condition, a condition which notoriously impairs or destroys the power of judgment. It has been shown that on the average, one woman out of every four or five exhibits symptoms of definite hysteria. If we include those whose temperament is affected by hysteria, but where the actual symptoms are latent, the proportion would of course be larger. Secondly, apart from any question of incapacity for political judgment, and even assuming such relative incapacity not to exist, there remains the fact that woman occupies as such a privileged and exceptional position, not only socially, but before the law and its administration, based ostensibly upon her assumed weakness of will and intellectual power, a weakness which is urged in favour of leniency and exceptional treatment of women in criminal and even in civil proceedings at law, oftentimes by the very same persons who, when it is a question of according women the political rights of men, most strenuously deny the existence of any such relative weakness or inferiority in the female sex. So long, I contend, as women occupy this exceptionally privileged position, even apart from any other consideration, they have no just claim to equality with men in the matter of political rights.

> 2. I believe there is little danger, as things at present stand, of female suffrage becoming law in the lifetime of the present Parliament.

> 3. In my opinion the 'militant methods,' as they are termed, of street hooliganism have failed, as casting ridicule on the movement, and furnishing a sorry sample of the quality of female intelligence, common sense and judgment. How often do we hear the remark: 'And these are the creatures it is proposed to entrust with the destinies of the nation!'

4. The alternative methods I would suggest to those who believe in, and are anxious to obtain, the franchise for women, are the methods adopted by men in every other case, in a community organised politically on democratic lines, and possessing in general the right of free speech, and a free Press, viz.: agitation by means of argument and persuasion rather than by knocking off policemen's helmets, smacking their faces, and breaking post-office windows.

This contemporaneous observation is a powerful insight into the way society viewed the Suffragettes, especially their obvious hysterics, which is a subject to which I shall return in a later chapter. However, it also reveals the extent to which they were actually a highly privileged class in society. Women were so privileged over men that it was considered nonsense to suggest they should fight for equality with men who, without a national vote, were still expected to maintain women in their elevated social status. This was no dominated, downtrodden sex, least of all by men as a class.

PART III

PATRIARCHY AS FATHERLINESS

'That the first kings were fathers of families.'

Sir Robert Filmer (1680) Patriarchy. Chapter 1

The rule of the father

Julia Adams is an associate professor of sociology at Yale University, Arthur F. Thurnau Professor at the University of Michigan, and visiting scholar at the Russell Sage Foundation, New York. She is also a self-identified feminist. However, in her scholarly essay, *The Rule of the Father: patriarchy and patrimonialism in early modern Europe,*[112] she takes issue with the feminist interpretation of patriarchy, arguing for the increased application of the term 'Patrimonialism' in its place. What she says serves to set the narrow feminist narrative in a much broader and more realistic historical milieu. Essentially, Adams says that patriarchy, better thought of as patrimonialism, is all about the accepted notion of the king (or queen) as father or patron of the people. Citing the kings and queens of Europe, she says this:

> Now I would like to press this line of thought further, beginning from the supposition that the category of 'patriarch' itself can be seen as an ongoing cultural and social achievement. The people who first soldered together separate signs like 'father' and 'ruler' had real political imagination. Later propagandists who sought to defend the value of their conjunction – especially in the face of others' efforts to tear them apart – were often astute analysts of the categories of everyday practice and good political tacticians … For example, the opening chapter of Sir Robert Filmer's *Patriarcha* – 'That the first kings were fathers of families' – sets the tone for his ringing defense of patriarchal patrimonialism in an England beleaguered by arguments for 'liberty' by 'usurpers of the right of such fathers'. Whatever their politics, and their enthusiasm for patriarchal privilege (which will doubtless displease most of my readers), these early modern élites were capable of real cultural creativity, of signification as action.

Filmer's *Patriarcha* was written in 1680 and what is interesting about it is that he was speaking to forces in society at the time that were also seeking to challenge the rule of the father, just as feminism is doing today. We can only speculate as to what those forces were, or even why they were at work, but Adams refutes entirely the idea that father-rule has ever been a reflection or even a product of male power and domination:

> The less influential folk who made everyday use of these same homely familial signs and images – whether attracted or repelled by the specific connection between paternity and rule – introduced and embroidered variations of their own. They were all inventors of tradition, paradoxically recreating what Weber called 'the sanctity of immemorial traditions and the legitimacy of those exercising authority under them,' but not by referring them either to capital-N nature or to some rock of 'established belief,' as Weber supposed (Weber 1968: 215). Here I depart both from Weber, Weberianism and from contemporary materialist theorists who see the 'father-ruler' as a simple reflection or production of 'male power' or dominance.

The 'contemporary materialist theorists' to whom Adams refers are, of course, feminist theorists who seek to demonise patriarchy. She takes issue with 'The analogy between father and king [that] has also been a theme of recent feminist political theory,' and points to King James VI of Scotland, also James I of England (1566 - 1625), as follows:

> Indeed he was particularly prolific in print and passionate about his paternal ruling role. Sometimes, he held up kings as nurturant fathers, 'And as the Father of his fatherly duty is bound to care for the nourishing, education and vertuous gouernment of his children; euen so is the king bound to care for all his subjects'. At other moments he stressed the strictures of paternal power: 'Now a Father may dispose of his Inheritance to his children, at his pleasure: yea, euen disinherite the eldest vpon iust occasions, and preferre the youngest, according to his liking: make them beggers, or rich at his pleasure; restraine, or banish out of his presence, as hee findes them giue cause of offence, or restore them in fauour againe with the penitent sinner: So may the King deale with Subiects'. At times he did both in the space of a single text. [Entire passage reproduced *sic erat scriptim*]

Here, again, we see Adams challenging feminist political theory, challenging it with the better interpretation of patriarchy as fatherliness: about love, care and compassion, albeit not necessarily expressed in emotional ways, but more as strength, protection, and leadership, drawn from long-standing monarchical examples. What feminist theory also fails to recognise is that fatherhood is an important signifier not only of family contiguousness, but of family continuity. Adams again (Ibid.):

> … political fatherhood and the vertical genealogies of office that they helped organize created a basis for both the intergenerational continuity in rule and stable relationship between princes and lesser rulers in both absolutist monarchies and estatist republican regimes. The sign of patrilineage knotted horizontal ties as well, not just among monarchs, but among ruling elites of lesser stature… when dependents are granted fiefs or other politico-economic privileges and immunities and become clients and agents of their ruler and now patron, separating themselves from his family-household to form their own households. In this defining and reiterated moment, rulers' agents become potential rulers and patriarchal principals themselves.

At the level of the state, patrilineal patriarchy embodies the process of social continuity. Its purpose is to ensure the security of all members of society within a complex framework of legal power, and that this is passed from one fatherly head of state to another whilst keeping out other, perhaps minority, interests that might seek to gain or usurp power for themselves, or foment internecine tension in the people. Patrilineal patriarchy maintained peace and freedom from destructive war for centuries, and Adams explains the mechanism that made all this work:

> The lateral recognitions of family head to family head – both within what we have come to think of as local and national contexts and apparatuses and over great geographic distances, via international princely marriages – made possible the pervasive elite pacts that undergirded early modern state-formation, of which more anon. What is more, the vertical and horizontal dimensions were interdependent. An individual man could not gain entry to a ruling group without having made an effective claim to honorable lineal descent. Would the members of that group let their daughters marry their sons – or their sons marry their daughters? Conversely, however fictive [Sic] his family lineage, it would be workable if backed up by others' willingness to incorporate him into the circuits of exchange.

All this is far removed from the narrow idea of the arbitrary exercise of social power by men in general over women in general. Far from it being an usurping of power by men from women, patrimonial patriarchy was a system in which women played a very significant and positive role; and one in which they were beneficiaries, not victims. Interestingly, Adams shows how women were an integral part of the entire process:

> Did this pervasive masculinism reduce women to ciphers? I don't think so, although this is a complicated issue, worth lingering on for a bit. It is true that women functioned as objects of exchange and signs of relationships among men – particularly among the élite. This was not their sole role, but it was a constitutive one, without which the interlocked systems of marriage and inheritance would have tottered and collapsed. Of course women also pursued independent projects, just as men did, and they were eminently capable of 'the mystification of manipulation as disinterested empathy,' which Stephen Greenblatt (1980) calls the characteristic Renaissance mode of courtly action, elaborated in and definitive of courtly life. For every real life Iago there was a would-be Marquise de Merteuil. Women were also authorized to perform crucial roles that were defined as both feminine and central in the courtly or manorial theater of power. They gave birth to heirs, and their scripted parts extended to vital supporting performances that dramatized and conferred familial political power.

This is hardly the dominating male hegemony of men over women reducing them to slaves or ciphers, writing them out of history that feminists believe has been the overall state of affairs throughout. What is clear from this analysis is that women historically have espoused 'pervasive masculinism', as Adams puts it. Indeed, some of them had to take on the role of patriarch when the need arose, 'commanding the largest sphere of action', thus (Ibid.):

> When there was a hiccup in the male line, women were called in as the agents or representatives of men, to act on the behalf of the lineage, the ruling group, and their mimetic extensions, including the nation. In these moments - extraordinary and rule-bound - women assumed the mantle of the patriarchs themselves… Most struggled or foundered in the ensuing contradictions, but a few, a very few, surmounted them with discursive élan. Here is Queen Elizabeth I at Tilbury, famously rallying her troops against the invasion of the Spanish Armada: 'I know I have the body but of a weak and feeble woman; but I have the heart and stomach of a king, and of a king of England, too, and think foul scorn that Parma or Spain, or any prince of Europe, should dare to invade the borders of my realm; to which rather than any dishonour shall grow by me, I myself will take up arms, I myself will be your general, judge, and rewarder of every one of your virtues in the field.'

'Again and again,' Adams says, '...in speeches, letters, and diplomatic encounters on the national and international political stage, Elizabeth proved able to use her rhetorical and political skills, not just her symbolic position as a patrilineal patriarch, a king (or prince as she often called herself), but also her sheer femininity, all of which were systematically subordinated and even derided as the opposite and underside of father-rule,' and today in Britain, we have another Queen Elizabeth: Elizabeth II, who has been on the throne of England for more than half a century and who is also deeply respected and loved by her people: men and women alike.

This modern counterpart of Elizabeth I also has 'the body of a weak and feeble woman', but she undoubtedly has the 'heart and stomach of a king, and of a king of England, too'. Although, she is a monarch in a Parliamentary democracy, which is an entirely different proposition from that of her predecessor, Elizabeth II has steadfastly maintained her position as a moral leader of the people of Britain and abroad in her dominions and Commonwealth. She has formed alliances across the world among English-speaking nations as well as those for whom English is not the first language, such as India and Africa, and all of these connections have been mutually beneficial, and mutually sustaining. As Adams (finally) says:

> The pacts transcended faction and strengthened élite networks and institutions in a whole series of medieval and early modern European settings. They set the seal on an enviable degree of political stability – an important foundation for state building – but also opened up systematic vulnerabilities and developmental possibilities. As the élite – or rather élite men and masculinity – was collectively disciplined, state-builders (who included those very men) could put the institutions that they were constructing on an even keel for decades or more.

Queen Elizabeth II has interceded for peace in areas of political conflict, and has succeeded wonderfully, as did the kings of old. She has fulfilled the patriarchal role of monarch with not a hint of any attempt to change that; and she has acted as guide and mentor to no less than 12 prime ministers, one of whom, Margaret Thatcher, was a woman too. Queen Elizabeth II is has done this because she has drawn inspiration from her father George VI, whom she loved, admired, and respected deeply, and who was also loved by his people for his gentle, steady leadership and solidarity with them during World War II.

George VI was a family man, a loving father who doted on his wife and children and rejoiced in his family: and he was a reluctant sovereign. He accepted the call to leadership of his nation after his brother Edward VIII abdicated, and he turned out to be no dominating patriarch. With his wife, also Elizabeth, as his queen, and his two daughters, he did his duty as head of the nation, and head of the leading family of that nation, and he did it with gentle, almost humble strength and fortitude that inspired millions at their worst (and finest) hour. George VI had a speech impediment that plagued him all his life, but he valiantly overcame it in the discharge of his onerous duties, through very difficult times for his people, whom he served with regal humility, as does his daughter to this day.

Even though our present Queen's family has been through its ups and downs, not least in their marriages (in a reflection of the times), all acted out on the public stage, she has remained dignified, steadfast and loyal to her people as an exemplar of kingship and the covenant she made with her people on her coronation, a covenant echoed in her lifelong marriage in which she has also been a true wife and mother. As a very young woman in her early twenties, only a very short time after marrying Prince Philip (a member of the Greek royal dynasty), and suffering from the bereavement of her dearly loved father, Elizabeth took the mantle of monarchy on her shoulders, and the enormous burden of patrimonial leadership of the British people, relying on the deeply ingrained model of monarchy which she inherited from her father, grandfather, great-grandfather, and the long line of monarchs before her - and her people, men, and women alike, recognise her as their patrimonial patriarch, their beneficent Head of State, and as the model for their families too, even in these times when fatherhood has been all but destroyed.

What is more, another queen, Victoria, did the same, barely more than a century earlier. She was monarch during one of the greatest periods of economic and social achievement Britain has ever known: the period known as the Industrial Revolution, in which Karl Marx and Friedrich Engels hatched their plans and provided the ideological inspiration of feminism. Victoria was besotted by her husband, Albert, the Prince Consort who came from a family also connected by blood to many of Europe's ruling monarchs. He and she had nine children, all of whom were, in their turn, married into other European royal dynasties, just as Adams described, giving her the epithet, 'Grandmother of Europe'. Both she and her husband showed total commitment to one another in faithful marriage until his premature death, after which she never remarried. Even as Queen Empress of the British Empire 'upon which the sun never set', Victoria still looked to her husband Albert as her source of strength, guidance, and moral leadership in the myriad decisions about the affairs of state she had to make. Like her successor, Elizabeth II, she was also deeply loved and respected by her people, irrespective of their sex.

Monarchy in all its forms, whether traditional or modern, is the quintessential example of patrimonialism, and its truest expression. It implies not the slightest hint of the historical repression of women by men. It has been a system of father-like beneficence and guardianship of the principles and practices of the people of Britain, and of many countries throughout the world, and has proven highly effective in the development of their societies. During times of danger, and for centuries when it was important to ensure security for the people's chosen way of life, beneficent patrimonialism has succeeded in delivering appropriate, effective leadership and statehood, and it has ensured social development through stability and continuity. Some people resent monarchy; they might hate privilege, and patrilineal descent, but whatever its flaws, patrimonialism has undoubtedly delivered civilisation through its service to those who have acccded to its rule over them. It has achieved this through the exercise of enormous personal discipline and humility on the part of those on whom its mantle has fallen, and it has facilitated the growth of civilisation in relative peace and stability through times of great tension and instability.

Weber on patrimonialism

Patrimonialism is a term first used by Max Weber (1864 –1920) and its emergence at the turn of the twentieth century signals the social shifts of the times. Weber was a German sociologist and political economist who, like Emile Durkheim and Karl Marx, was highly influential in this process in a number of ways. Weber drew his ideas from the spirit of the age, in the post-Enlightenment era in modern Europe, which was also the period of mass industrialisation during which a theory of management had to be developed, and during which immense social change had happened. Weber was highly suspicious of 'Classical Patriarchy', rooted as it was in feudalism and monarchy, etc., that required an automatic acceptance of the authority of the father and the legitimacy of his authority. He also questioned what he called charismatic authority, which, as he put it, rests '…on devotion to the exceptional sanctity, heroism, or exemplary character of a person, and of the normative patterns or order revealed or ordained by him'. Instead, Weber argued for a new understanding of social authority, which he called 'Rational-Legality', the idea that underpins his advocacy of bureaucracy, which means, 'The force of the desk' (probably better thought of as the power of the office, as in someone who holds an office). This was a system from which human-ness was to be eliminated:

> Precision, speed, unambiguity, knowledge of files, continuity, discretion, unity, strict subordination, reduction of friction and of material and personal costs – these are raised to the optimum point in the strictly bureaucratic administration.[113]

Weber passionately believed that this was the most efficient form of organisation, and his ideas prevail to this day. They remain deeply entrenched in our organisational consciousness despite the fact that they were born more than 100 years ago out of forms of industrial organisation that were creaking at the seams after almost 150 years of Industrial Revolution, and which today are largely discredited in favour of more relational, more human, forms of management, not least among which is an understanding of the need for charismatic leadership.

Mirroring the Marxist view, Weber argued that the centrality to the family of the mother-child relationship derived from the traditional authority of the father, which had led to the male-female division of labour in the home. Whereas the charismatic-traditional model of social organisation is more like a manor house run on age-old rules of inherited powers, sacred tradition and the notional separation of roles, and where the mechanics of the household mimic the mechanics of political administration, in the future, Weber said, the discretionary power of the patriarch would give way to the rational-legal exercise of non-emotional power, legitimately conferred by an equally legitimate authority. It would no longer be based on familial or charismatic factors, he said, and this was the key to the process of the ongoing rationalisation of Western society, which would move it away from patriarchal and charismatic authority toward modernity. It was also the key to undermining the family, a cause very dear to the heart of Marx and his co-theorist in Communism, Friedrich Engels, whose views undoubtedly informed the shift in society that was taking place in the early twentieth century, when women were becoming steadily more independent of men, another aim of the communists, as we shall see in a later chapter. This was the social climate in which feminism got its chance to set up patriarchy as the target for its attack, aided by the social turbulence caused by two world wars in the first half of that century, followed by a massive social revolution in the 1960s, which opened the door wide.

The 'Big Lie'

The attack on patriarchy is a 'Big Lie' (*Große Lüge*), a term first coined by Adolf Hitler in his book *Mein Kampf* ('My struggle') in which he outlined his political stance about Jews and his plans for Germany. Written while he was in jail following his failed putsch (the violent attempt to overthrow the government), staged in Munich in 1923, he sought to lay the blame for Germany's economic collapse in the post-war period, and her humiliation in defeat on the Jews. Jeffrey Herf (1947-), professor of modern European history at the University of Maryland, maintains that the Nazis used the Big Lie principle to turn latent anti-Semitism in Germany after the First World War into a narrative of an innocent, besieged nation striking back at 'international Jewry' which, they alleged started the First World War. This is what Hitler said about the 'big lie':[114]

> ... all this was inspired by the principle--which is quite true within itself - that in the big lie there is always a certain force of credibility; because the broad masses of a nation are always more easily corrupted in the deeper strata of their emotional nature than consciously or voluntarily; and thus in the primitive simplicity of their minds they more readily fall victims to the big lie than the small lie, since they themselves often tell small lies in little matters but would be ashamed to resort to large-scale falsehoods. It would never come into their heads to fabricate colossal untruths, and they would not believe that others could have the impudence to distort the truth so infamously. Even though the facts which prove this to be so may be brought clearly to their minds, they will still doubt and waver and will continue to think that there may be some other explanation. For the grossly impudent lie always leaves traces behind it, even after it has been nailed down, a fact which is known to all expert liars in this world and to all who conspire together in the art of lying.

Hitler used the big lie principle when he took over the anti-Semitic German Workers Party in the early 1920s, which he renamed the National Socialist German Worker's Party - hence, NAZI. In fact, the whole party was in itself a big lie. Far from the left wing, socialist implications of its name, it was an extreme right wing party that embraced not just anti-Semitism but elements of fascism and biological racism (an ideology that believed in classifying individuals into different racial categories in a hierarchy of superiority and inferiority). When the Nazis finally gained power in Germany in 1933 with the support of traditional right wing political groupings, Hitler became Chancellor of Germany and set about installing a totalitarian state in which, *inter alia,* Jews and any political opponents were declared 'undesirable', were marginalised, harassed and imprisoned.

By repeating this massively improbable claim in propaganda, cleverly orchestrated by Joseph Goebbels, German Reich Minister of Propaganda from 1933-1945, the NAZIS whipped up a conspiracy theory that gave the alleged underdog, Germany, justification for a 'war of extermination' against the Jews, based on the asserted right to annihilate the Jews in self-defence. Goebbels, with a doctorate in nineteenth century romantic drama and a journalist before becoming politically active, was undoubtedly a master of the art of propaganda. He was a skilled exponent of what we now call spin and was able to turn Germany into a society in which there were no checks on extremism, and it is a matter of history that this led to the extermination of 6,000,000 ordinary, innocent human beings. Human hatred in its blind self-feeding escalation, unchecked by rationality and constantly fed the big lie, can easily reach a state of knowing no boundary of behaviour, and this is what feminists are doing today. They channel every utterance, every angle, every idea through the big lie of patriarchy, and they do it with a bigotry and narrowness of mind that is blind to any possibility that such a thing simply doesn't exist.

A report on Hitler's psychological profile[115] commissioned during World War II by the United States Office of Strategic Services (the forerunner of the CIA), concluded that:

> His primary rules were: never allow the public to cool off; never admit a fault or wrong; never concede that there may be some good in your enemy; never leave room for alternatives; never accept blame; concentrate on one enemy at a time and blame him for everything that goes wrong; people will believe a big lie sooner than a little one; and if you repeat it frequently.

I trust my reader will recognise these signs in the feminist narrative that pours from our social and broadcast media today. It is relentless in the assertion of its 'truth', never allowing the general public to cool off and take stock. We see it in the endless narrative about a so-called 'rape culture' and sexual offences against women, which are alleged to be at epidemic proportions. They are not, as rational examination of the figures reveals. We see it in the complete inability of feminists to accept that women have agency and can legitimately be expected to sensibly take responsibility for not placing themselves in dangerous situations, as any man would. But no, it is all men's fault, men's nature that is at fault. Feminism has one enemy - men and maleness - and it stays firmly fixed on this message to the point now that many, perhaps most, people believe men are the enemy of women. No one challenges this; it is now taken as a given.

As I have said before, the feminism idea of patriarchy is an argument by assertion; it cannot be proven. Feminism is using it and other techniques to constantly brainwash society into believing its big lie, and it is now institutionalised. Most societies of the developed world, but particularly America, Canada, and Britain, have pressure groups intent on spreading feminism's ideology. In Britain, they are deeply embedded in our institutional framework, often granted charitable status despite the fact that their aims are far from philanthropic (which means brotherly love). The US has a plethora of such pressure groups lobbying Congress, as Christina Hoff Sommers says:[116]

> In Washington there is a women's lobby that's working night and day, that is still completely fixated on this idea that women are a subordinate class and all disparities, any statistical distinction between men and women can only be explained by discrimination and every week, they have lawyers, they have 112 organisations in a group called the National Council for Research on Women. These aren't small organisations. These are huge, like the AAUW [American Association of University Women], the National Women's Law Center, The Wellesley Center for Research on Women. They're working night and day. They're nice, but they are ideological and they see discrimination and they have a boilerplate explanation for all disparities. Now, because long ago, fortunately, we outlawed overt discrimination, now they've come up with elaborate theories about unconscious bias and invisible barriers and so forth. These groups are promoting laws. They are fundamentally changing our society in ways that are detrimental.

Looked at rationally, like Nazism, feminism is a mixture of extreme left-wing collectivist, Marxist beliefs mixed with historical distortion and revisionism, and enforced with fascist tactics. We cannot escape the simple logic that feminists are seeking to classify human beings, men, into *untermensch*, an inferior people, and they are also pursuing legitimately questionable views on abortion, another distinctly NAZI (and Communist) policy. Rush Limbaugh, the American TV talk show host from the 1990s first used the term 'FEMINAZI' when referring to the utterances of prominent feminists Gloria Steinem, Susan Sarandon, Christine Lahti, and Camryn Manheim on abortion (by way of balance, it has to be said that Limbaugh is conservative and anti-abortion).

Vladimir Lenin said, 'A lie told often enough becomes the truth,' and Richard Belzer the American comedian, author, and actor says in his book *UFOs, JFK, and Elvis: Conspiracies You Don't Have To Be Crazy To Believe*, 'If you tell a lie that's big enough, and you tell it often enough, people will believe you are telling the truth, even when what you are saying is total crap'. The idea that there has always been a hegemonic, worldwide conspiracy of men to organise society according to their rules and ways of thinking, and subdue women is just that, and all it takes is just a modicum of rational thought to reveal how unlikely it is. For most of history, men have been trying to survive, not rule.

Fathers and feminism

Men in our modern societies are no longer overtly patriarchal because they don't need to be. Society has moved on but the naturalness of the father's rule in the family needs to be preserved. Provision for the family is still a social imperative for men, as is its protection and defence. It is a vital component of our social organisation, where men instinctively seek status, and women cooperate in that for their good and the good of their children. The biological imperative that ordains women to be the bearers of children to men of status cannot be changed, and society as a whole would do well to wake up to the downright stupidity of the proposition that men are superfluous to the family. Fatherhood must not be expunged from our society, as feminism is undoubtedly trying to do. Diminishing and marginalising men, particularly as fathers, is not only delusional, it is evil. Families need fathers. Children need fathers. The state does not make a good father.

Treating men as though they were just a sperm bank and a cash point, institutionally and legally dismissing them from their children's lives after divorce and condemning children to single parenthood is not only unjust; it is insane. Men still need to be responsible for their offspring, and to the women who bear their offspring. A child needs a father's provision as well as being nurtured by its mother. To have it any other way amounts to child abuse. All the current direction of travel of our society will lead to is dystopia, and sooner or later the women who are being duped by feminism must wake up to the reality that this is where their belief in this totalitarian ideology is taking them.

They must come to their senses and realise they are being cheated by feminism in the name of a political ideology that is alien to everything the developed world stands for. Women cannot in all common sense become the sole means by which children are brought up. They cannot fulfil their biological role and still hold down a full-time career, let alone progress that career. Despite the sophistries of feminists, women cannot have their cake and eat it. The feminist rhetoric of the superwoman is patent nonsense. There are only so many hours in the day, and only so much energy any human being has, and motherhood and career need both those things; otherwise, neither will be achieved successfully. We still need men to work full-time, whole of life, to provide for their families, and women still have to fit child bearing into their lives. That is the way life is. That is the way evolution, not men, has formed society over aeons: around the biology of men and women, the male and female of the species. To seek to arrange it any other way, especially for dogmatic political principles, is neither realistic nor workable. In fact, it is ridiculous.

Fatherly patriarchy was both the product of civilisation, and the means by which it came about because it had beneath it an understanding of the inherent need to protect individual societies from attack and annihilation. That has been proved time and again in fearful wars, not least those of the twentieth century, in which men laid down their lives for women and their children in their millions. Not only that, but judging from eight thousand years of human social development, it certainly looks as though mankind has been content with the arrangement. Maybe feminists, with their forty-year-old ideas have discovered something countless billions of people before them didn't know? Somehow I don't really think so. The feminist depiction of patriarchy is a shallow, disingenuous distortion, intended to justify not only a political position but also a personal one. We should not forget the mantra 'make the personal political' of the early feminists, every one of whom had issues with fathers or men. Neither should we forget that those young feminist women today with their distinctly man-hating mindsets are just being hysterical, a theme that runs through feminism from its earliest origins, and a psychology upon which I shall expand in due course.

PART IV

PATRIARCHY TODAY

'The patriarchy requires violence or the subliminal threat of violence in order to maintain itself.'

Gloria Steinem, Feminist

Real patriarchy

One July Sunday morning recently I was in my local park enjoying a coffee and watching the world go by. At the next table there was a couple, a man and wife who looked to be in their mid 30s, and they had their children with them. One of them, a little girl about seven or eight who had been sitting with her parents enjoying a soft drink said, 'Daddy, may I go and play on the swings please?' Her father briefly glanced over to the play area and said, 'Of course darling, just be careful, I'll keep an eye on you and you'll be all right'. The child skipped off, head waving from side to side at each skip, hair tossing in the breeze and arms waving in that childlike, carefree expression of vibrant life, and I briefly felt a warm memory of how she must be feeling: secure, safe, loved.

I reflected that in her reticence born of the inherent vulnerability of the child she instinctively recognised the rule and authority of her father. This was the truest, sweetest expression of patriarchy anyone could possibly imagine, and it was exquisitely beautiful to behold. It is easy to imagine that sweet child growing up secure in her daddy's love for her; and that his 'looking out' for her will continue throughout her life. Their relationship will mature and change, certainly, but he will always be her daddy. He will always 'be there' for her, ever on hand. That will be a given in her life even if she has a family of her own. It is likely she will still look to her father for his manly advice and wisdom - maybe she will seek a firm view on her own moral decisions - how she treats her own children - perhaps she will still call on his strength and support in times of desperate need, remembering the protection he so gently cast over her when she was little. And when he dies, it is easy to imagine that she will feel, as most women do, the deep unassuaged grief at the departure from her life of her bedrock.

Then, a cold shiver came over me, and I realised that the fatherhood in which this sweet child, and millions like her, was basking in, is the very thing feminists wish to destroy. In their deep anger and bitter bigotry, feminists are 'liberating' little girls (and boys for that matter) from the natural loving authority of their father: his inbuilt instinct to care for his children and his wife, and their equally natural instinct to respond to it. Feminism is destroying our children's rights to have their father's tender, loving care, the very thing girls need for their safety in their early years, their later social development, and their effective transition into competent adulthood. In the name of false equality, it is seeking to impose a twisted world view on the majority of women who have had a normal family background, and this, of course, exposes the truly totalitarian nature of this angry creed.

I make no apology for stating yet again that the word patriarchy means 'the rule or authority of the father' - it does not mean the rule of men in general, nor does it mean 'man-shaped society'. Patriarchy is fatherhood: a vital component of the sanguineous family; that central social cell, which, for centuries if not millennia, has been the building block of stable societies. Patriarchy has ensured the protection of women and children, the defence of the realm, and the passing on of private family assets to children without the interference of the state. Patriarchy is not a system designed by men in order to shape society to men's advantage and subjugate women. In its purest and simplest form, patriarchy is fatherliness, born of fatherhood: that is all it is. It is as natural as motherhood. It provides a framework for children in which they can grow up in safety and learn to be balanced adults.

The politics of patriarchy

Patriarchy, that *bête noir* of feminism's quest for equality, is an idea as narrow as it is naïve. Feminists are presumptuously seeking to overturn aeons of evolutionary development, and thousands of years of developing civilisation, in a matter of a few decades. That is how naïve they are, and how lacking in realism. The same lack of realism that Engels and Marx displayed in explaining their reasoning about how society could become communist, a subject to which I turn in the next chapter, and the same detachment from reality we saw in the early movers and shapes of women's liberation. If women are in submission to anything, they are in submission to nature, and no amount of social re-engineering is going to change that.

We cannot get away from the reality that men are different from women, not just in their reproductive organs, their hormonal balance, physical strength, etc., but in their moral, ethical, psychological, and intellectual attributes too.

Men have an outlook on life that women don't have. Men can see things that women can't see - because they are men. They especially know how the male dominance hierarchy in society works because that is how they are programmed to be. It is, of course, the same in reverse. Women have a take on life that benefits men. They can see things men cannot, thus, men and women evolved to be complementary to one another, not competitors engaged in a political struggle for social dominance, a state to which feminism has reduced us. Society can only advance through women and men cooperating with each other in both their joint best interests for the common good.

So why are we now engaged in an energy-sapping gender class war where women are competing with men for social power and advantage? The answer, of course, lies in the revolutionary politics that underpin the feminist drive to wreck society in order to re-shape it according to Marxist rhetoric. Feminists want to overthrow men so they can rule society their way. Their true aim is to install matriarchy, the precise equivalent to the patriarchy they are so adamantly against, where women assume the role they allege men have always had. All this can be found in the ideas of Karl Marx and Friedrich Engels, who believed ancient societies were structured that way, and who postulated communism as a way to return to that state. However, the very fact that civilisation has developed at all shows that what must have been before was, by definition, *un*civilised.

The social systems that predated patriarchy may well have been rather worse for women and children than since its development. In fact, it seems obvious to me that society and civilisation have been brought about because of patrimonial patriarchy, which has been benign and caring, providing the stability to society that has allowed it to adapt to tumultuous change, and above all preserving freedom, often with men's blood. The freedom of speech fought for and delivered by men is a right enjoyed by those who would seek to destroy men's rightful role in society. Men cannot submit to what feminism proposes, and in any case why should they? Men have human rights too. Women's rights end where men's rights begin. Their happiness and their futures are important too. Men have a right to be themselves, unfettered by political chicanery, sexual bullying and the denial of absolute rights such as the right to a home life and a relationship with their children. It is deeply wrong that these things should be denied to them by women whose sole desire is to gain control over them by any means, fair or foul, using what amounts to thought-policing and arbitrary reassignment of their social role. Millions of men have died to resist oppression from outside our nations, and I sincerely hope it will not take another world war, a social war, to resist this one.

Is patriarchy a bad thing?

So, let me ask the obvious question: 'Is patriarchy a bad thing?' It depends on whether you are a feminist or not. If you are not, you need to take a balanced view of the relative roles and rights men and women should have in a balanced society, and compare that to the things I have been discussing, and with the present situation. Let me pose a different question: 'Does patriarchy control and dominate women?' Apart from the obvious answer, which is an emphatic 'No,' I suggest this is a classic example of a begged question: one whose underlying premise is itself questionable; and a prime example of feminist guile. It is only valid to ask it if patriarchy, as defined by feminism, exists, and I believe there is a wealth of evidence to suggest that it does not. Therefore, the question is not only irrelevant, it is deceitful. We need to get beneath the froth of feminism and smell the true flavour of their coffee if we are to avoid becoming embroiled in what they are peddling. I go further and suggest that patriarchy is a good thing.

It is not the mean-spirited, controlling, dominating hegemony of manhood, the lie that feminism constantly portrays. That is a gross calumny on half the human race. The man-shaped society that genuine patriarchy has delivered over millennia hasn't dominated women, or expunged them from history, or held them down in servitude to men. Quite the contrary, it has cared for them and protected them; it has raised women up, putting their interests high above men. Above all, it has provided for women so they could bear the next generation and bring it up in a stable family arrangement, so it could become successful. Patriarchy is a proud, honourable, service-from-strength, which men have exercised for the good of society as a whole, since society started to develop.

Naturally, there have been exceptions: perhaps far too many, particularly in totalitarian regimes (most of them communist, incidentally), but the general thrust has always been men exercising their role as patriarchs - patrimonially - lovingly, and in a fatherly way. I also believe that most women today would agree with this. The vast majority of women who have fathers with whom they are in contact love their fathers from the deepest recesses of their very being. They look up to their father as their first hero and seek from him leadership, strength, wisdom, and guidance throughout their lives (men do that too with their fathers). Most women, if they are lucky enough to have a father who is actively involved in their lives, and far too many women and girls these days do not, will turn to him time and again throughout their lives for sage wisdom, a male perspective on things, and the protection that their mothers simply cannot provide (even a loving, protective, affirming hug from a father makes bad times a lot better), and they are devastated when their fathers die and they lose the first rock upon which they were able to build their lives. Such women, of course, are now becoming something close to being an endangered species.

The generations we have produced in the last 40-50 years under the heel of feminism have produced ever more dysfunctional people, because extremists, acting for their own political ends, have effectively destroyed trust in fatherhood. There is much talk today about how women are disadvantaged by patriarchy and discriminated against, but here is an example that raises an expression of patrimonial patriarchy at work in our society today (at least in the United Kingdom, although there is every reason to believe the same is true in the US) that is actually being used against men, and about which, in a feminist society, we never hear any complaint from feminists.

Martin Mears is the former President of the Law Society of Great Britain and member of its Family Law Committee. In his book, *Institutional Injustice*, he very explicitly describes what he calls, '…old-fashioned paternalism' toward women in the legal system. In Chapter 5, 'Institutional Bias: Ancient, and Modern', he says this:

> The overriding characteristic of the law, created by the coterie [of a few dozen people comprising The Family Division of the High Court] is an institutional bias in favour of wives/mothers and against husbands/fathers. This bias originally derived from old fashioned paternalism. For judges of Lord Denning's generation, women were weak, put-upon creatures ever in need of the active protection of chivalrous courts. This assumption went hand in hand with the notion that traditional male/female roles were part of the natural order of things… In practice, this meant that virtually every one of the courts' frequent reinterpretations of the law represented a diminution in the position of husbands and an aggrandisement in that of wives.

I might have missed something here, but I haven't seen feminists parading outside the Royal Courts of Justice demanding an end to this particular expression of patriarchy. Call me a cynic if you like.

Figment of a febrile feminist imagination

The idea of the hegemony of patriarchy - that underpinning rant of feminists - provides them with justification for their political crusade, and is a straw man argument: one that is put up to be shot down. It is a figment of irrational minds stirred up into a mighty anger through implanted delusions, and sewn into a system of conditioning through the use of propaganda and practices that are tried and tested ways of conditioning people's minds. Feminism sells the pup of a promise that women can in some way be equal to men, which is as much nonsense as the idea of men being equal to women.

Despite the lunatic ravings of unhinged feminist dreamers, and the dubious philosophy of the moral degenerates whose books remain at the core of feminist propaganda today in our universities, and whose ideas we hear and read endlessly in our media and our governments, women will always be the bearers and nurturers of children. Only a febrile feminist imagination could even entertain such a ludicrous proposition that they should not be so. The idea of male domination through patriarchy belongs in the little red book of Marxist feminist dogma, which has been tried around the world and found wanting because they sought to re-engineer the societies which they infected against human nature.

The real truth is that feminism is the ideology of hate, whipped up into a false struggle by a small cadre of fellow-travelling, politically motivated, greedy-for-power women who want to overturn the *status quo ante* so they can create a society in which they and their like can dominate. And it doesn't take much trawling of the reader-responses to feminist news items on the Internet to see the degree to which their demonised version of patriarchy is believed in the febrile imaginations of young women today, who are clearly caught up in the fervour without displaying any understanding of what it is they are actually saying and believing. Here are just the headlines, and opening synopses of articles taken from recent editions of Huffington Post, obtained by simply Googling 'patriarchy', which leave no doubt that there is yet another generation of radicalised young women emerging who are buying into the big lie and are full of the cant about patriarchy, with which I rest my case:

Women's Magazines: Reinforcing patriarchy Using Women to Police Women

Louise Pennington | Posted 25.07.2013 | UK Lifestyle

Read More: Women's Magazines, Britney Spears, Duchess of Cambridge, Capitalism, Feminism, Kerry Katona, patriarchy, Royal Baby, UK Women, UK Media, UK Lifestyle News

I wasn't at all shocked by OK Magazine's newest cover story: 'Kate's Post-Baby Weight Loss Regime'. Body-shaming a woman less than 48 hours after they gave birth is entirely keeping within the normative behaviour of women's magazines. OK Magazine might have been the first of the women's magazines to publish diet tips for the Duchess of Cambridge but they won't be the last.

The Objectification of Women - It Goes Much Further Than Sexy Pictures

Joy Goh-Mah | Posted 09.08.2013 | UK Lifestyle

Read More: UK Media, Objectification of Women, Tomb Raider, Women's Issues, Sexual Objectification, Feminism, patriarchy, UK Lifestyle News

When feminists decry the objectification of women, most people immediately think of the images that saturate our magazines, movies, adverts and the Internet. Yet, while sexual objectification is a huge problem, it is, sadly, only a fraction of the objectification of women that permeates our world, from the moment we enter it.

'Masculinity Defines Men, Rather Than the Reverse' - Why the 'Masculinity' Debate Is So Important

Natalie Gyte | Posted 29.07.2013 | UK Lifestyle

Read More: Diane Abbott, Masculinity, Third Wave Feminism, Gender-Based Violence, Feminism, patriarchy, Crisis in Masculinity, UK Lifestyle News

The truth is that men, through socially defined 'masculinity', have always enjoyed a privileged relationship with social and economic power. Through history, the idea of 'manhood' has been centred in physical strength, toughness, earning, providing, and dominating, creating a paradigm in which we have been collectively socialised to the idea of 'masculinity' within every faculty of our psyche.

Muslim Women Complicit in their Repression?

Sajda Khan | Posted 23.07.2013 | UK Universities & Education

Read More: Muslim World, Rights, Islam, Muslim Women, Repression, Islamophobia, Egalitarian, Prophet Muhammad, Iraq, God, patriarchy, John Stuart Mill, Misogynist, Laura Bush, Qur'An, Colonial, Oppression, Feminists, Afghanistan, UK Universities & Education News

When I was a first year undergraduate student, my psychology lecturer told me that Muslim women were complicit in their own repression and did not know what it was like to be liberated. As a student of humanities and social sciences I gauged that his views were conspicuously grounded in the litany of anecdotal sources cited by the media.

Teenage Pregnancy, Teenage Pregnancy, Patriarchal Hypocrisy and Immaculate Conception

Louise Pennington | Posted 20.07.2013 | UK Lifestyle

Read More: Abortion, Teenage Pregnancy, Candies Foundation, Welfare State, NHS, Patriarchy, Child Care, Teen Pregnancy, Modern Parenting, Health Care, UK Lifestyle News

We already know the causes of teenage pregnancy and [Sic], yet, the UK is following the US's path with parents demanding the right to prevent their children learning about real sexual education. The destruction of the welfare state and universal healthcare is already having serious detrimental effects on families

The Capitalist-patriarchy Hurts Men Too Shocker

Louise Pennington | Posted 13.07.2013 | UK Lifestyle

Read More: Pornography, Rape, Nia, Male Violence, Rape Culture, Homophobia, Racism, Andrea Dworkin, Capitalism, patriarchy, Women's Issues, Women, Men, UK Lifestyle News

Hyper-masculinity is damaging and destructive. It assumes that men are predisposed to violence; that men are nothing more than violent sexual predators incapable of self-control and empathy. The capitalist-patriarchy states that men are inherently violent and that nothing will ever change that.

Lad Culture Is THE Culture

Lauren Hossack | Posted 27.05.2013 | UK Universities & Education

Read More: Lad Culture, Gender Equality, Women, Stereotypes, Men, Masculinity, Society, Femininity, Feminism, patriarchy, UK Universities & Education, Gender, UK Universities & Education News

Let's talk about lads. Specifically, lad culture. Call it what you like, dismiss it as a joke, but it doesn't hide the fact that it's just plain misogyny and sexism, with stereotypical, age-old notions of masculinity at the core.

It's the Official Patronising of Women Day: The Capitalist-Patriarchal Conspiracy of Mother's Day

Louise Pennington | Posted 10.05.2013 | UK Politics

Read More: Andrea Dworkin, Rape, Capitalism, Feminism, Mother's Day, Patriarchy, Women's Issues, Gender Inequality, UK Politics News

Mother's Day, in its present form, is merely another capitalist-patriarchal tool to beat women over the head with. It remains nothing more than a depressing attempt at brain-washing women into believing that 'their' work is valued. Women's work has never been valued. We still do the majority of the childcare and housework whilst in paid employment.

BLOG: 'Why I Won't Support One Billion Rising'
Natalie Gyte | Posted 16.04.2013 | UK Lifestyle
Read More: Rape, Violence Against Women, Women's Issues, One Billion Rising Campaign, Stella Creasy, Third Wave Feminism, Neocolonialism, Feminism, Gender-Based Violence, Patriarchy, One Billion Rising, UK Lifestyle News
The primary problem with One Billion Rising is its refusal to name the root cause of women's inequality; its outright refusal to point the finger at a patriarchal system which cultivates masculinity and which uses the control and subjugation of women's bodies as an outlet for that machoism.

Handmaidens, Feminism and Reclaiming the Internet
Louise Pennington | Posted 09.01.2013 | UK Lifestyle
Read More: Nadine Dorries, Mumsnet, Misogyny, Feminism, Everyday Sexism Project, Patriarchy, Hollaback, Women Under Siege, Sisterhood, Louise Mensch, Women's Room UK, UK Lifestyle News
I care about making spaces safe online for women, so whilst I will never support the policies of Dorries and Mensch, I do think we need to stop belittling and denigrating them. It is possible to criticise their policies without making it personal and supporting patriarchy in silencing women. That is what we do when we fall into denigrating women. We are effectively helping to silence other women's voices. Instead, we need to reclaim the Internet and make it the most subversive weapon we have against patriarchy.

'Patriarchy Is Unrepentant': Sexy A-Levels Blog Closes
The Huffington Post UK | Dina Rickman | Posted 16.08.2012 | UK Universities & Education
Read More: Sexy A Levels, UK News, A Level Results, Feminism, Patriarchy, A Levels, UK Universities & Education News
It's Thursday. It's the second week of August. So it must be time for sexy A-levels? Except the infamous blog, which chronicles the epidemic of new...

Monotheism and the War on Women
Sam Ambreen | Posted 09.09.2012 | UK Politics

Read More: Misogyny, Adam and Eve, Islam, Church of England, Desire, Feminist, Man, Woman, Genesis, God, Sexuality, Patriarchy, Feminism, Abrahamic, Women-Bishops-Amendments, Taliban, Afghanistan Execution, Christianity, Sharia, Monotheism, Original Sin, Judaism, UK Politics News The Church of England is procrastinating whether women deserve equal promotion to senior clergy, initially proposing legislation that would mean it would have enshrined in law the very prejudices against which supporters of female bishops have battled so long.

CHAPTER 7

MARXISM AND 'THE WOMAN QUESTION'

'Socialism is a philosophy of failure, the creed of ignorance, and the gospel of envy, its inherent virtue is the equal sharing of misery.'

Winston Spencer Churchill

The Marxist basis of feminism

As early as the mid-nineteenth century, the issue of women's liberation was already a key component in the theories of Karl Marx (1818-1883) and Friedrich Engels (1820-1895), and their revolutionary aims to change society to Communism. Marx argued that the very essence of the relationship between men and women was between the strong and the weak, and that the victory of human nature over brutality (meaning the animal nature of mankind) was evident in how men's and women's relationships manifested in society. He and Engels argued that, under Communism, women would have a completely different role, and they spelled that out in the *Communist Manifesto*[117] of 1848, where they said this:

> The bourgeois sees in his wife a mere instrument of production. He hears that [under communism] the instruments of production are to be exploited in common, and, naturally, can come to no other conclusion than that the lot of being common to all will likewise fall to women. He has not even a suspicion that the real point aimed at [by communism] is to do away with the status of women as mere instruments of production. Nothing is more ridiculous than the virtuous indignation of our bourgeois at the community of women which, they pretend, is to be openly and officially established by the Communists.
>
> The Communists have no need to introduce a community of women; it has existed almost from time immemorial. Our bourgeois, not content with having wives and daughters of their proletarians at their disposal, not to speak of common prostitutes, take the greatest pleasure in seducing each other's wives. Bourgeois marriage is, in reality, a system of wives in common and thus, at the most, what the Communists might possibly be reproached with is that they desire to introduce, in substitution for a hypocritically concealed, an openly legalised community of women.

> For the rest, it is self-evident that the abolition of the present system of production must bring with it the abolition of the community of women springing from that system, i.e., of prostitution both public and private.

Note the phraseology: the 'hypocritically concealed' pool of 'wives in common' will be turned into an 'openly legalised' community of women which, they assert, had existed, '... almost from time immemorial' In this remarkable rant, dripping with sarcastic indignation, Marx and Engels display a deep contempt for those whom they call 'bourgeois': the middle-class owners of capital and business whom they sought to overthrow by undermining marriage. Declaring it to be a morally corrupt, singularly bourgeois institution, Engels in particular argued that women had been a separate group from time immemorial who only shared possessions, resources, responsibilities, work, income and decision-making with men in a non-hierarchical, loosely bonded, sexually uncommitted social arrangement, where children were the property of the community, not of their biological parents in nuclear families.

He elaborated on this, saying that the marriages of the bourgeois were, '... a conjugal partnership of leaden boredom, known as domestic bliss' called individual family units, in which women were trapped —induced into being merely workers in the process of reproduction and cut off from being agents in the process of economic production. This was a theme that was to return much later in Betty Friedan's book *The Feminine Mystique*, when she argued that women were trapped in the strictures of affluent, middle-class marriages, and it is the underpinning presumption that led to widespread divorce during the feminist era. (I shall return to this in detail later.) In an essay entitled *Marxism and the Women's Movement*, included in the compilation of essays *Women in Russia*,[118] Professor Alfred Meyer describes how Engels saw the primeval sexual couplings of men and women as each doing a different job of work in the production of children, and how this led to a source of inequality between them in the allocation of economic work and enjoyment. Meyer comments thus:

> One must marvel at the nonchalance with which he [Engels] makes this statement. For all their lives, he and Marx had argued, with considerable heat, that society must be understood as a mechanism for production, and that the determinant driving force of all historic change was to be found in the development of the means of production. Suddenly, now, the production of

means for survival and the production of children are mentioned as equally basic activities. Suddenly the sex act is on a par with productive work, and that relations between male and female are as significant as those between capitalists and proletarians.

At the stroke of a pen, and with astonishing 'nonchalance,' therefore, Engels forges a conceptual link between natural procreation and economic production, which has never been broken in Marxist/feminist thinking ever since. We heard this expressed clearly by Jaqueline Ceballos at the Town Hall event when she said women should be paid wages for being wives. However, in another neat conflation of two ideas, Engels also declared the natural dichotomy between the sexes to be the same as the dichotomy between the bourgeois and the proletariat and, therefore, part of the class struggle. Thus was the revolutionary spark that kindled the wildfire of Women's Liberation 120 years later, and the philosophical underpinning of the gender class war that now rages among us. Meyer continues::

> Just as Engels regarded matriarchy as a male-female relationship functional to early communism, so he posited the oppression of women as linked to class oppression. The first class antagonism, he wrote, coincided with the development of the antagonism between men and women; and in this antagonism it was the men who established their supremacy. Class antagonism arises simultaneously with the defeat of the female sex. Slavery and monogamy appear at the same time.

Engels clearly and quite deliberately conflated monogamy with slavery. For him, women were the slaves of men in monogamous marriage. Such an emotive idea would naturally carry enormous significance for women and, of course, it does to this day for feminists, for whom it is a basic tenet of their doctrine. It can be heard time and again in their narratives, where it is assumed as a given, and it is poisonous as far as marriage is concerned because it informs the idea of the domination of women by men through patriarchy, and the woman as eternal victim, in need of liberation. Engels's own words, taken from his book *The Origin of the Family, Private Property, and the State* sum all this up:

> The overthrow of mother right was the world historic defeat of the female sex. The man took command in the home also; the woman was degraded and reduced to servitude; she became the slave of his lust and a mere instrument

for the production of children... In order to make certain of the wife's fidelity and therefore the paternity of his children, she is delivered over unconditionally into the power of the husband; if he kills her, he is only exercising his rights.

What is worth taking note of is that at the time Engels concocted these ideas, he was a highly precocious 24-year-old, described by Tristram Hunt[119] in his introduction to *The Origin of the Family, Private Property, and the State*,[120] as a raffish, Bohemian, counter-cultural young man who seems to have had a remarkably ambivalent relationship with his own political theorising, not least because he was himself a capitalist Manchester cotton-mill owner - by inheritance.[121] Hunt describes him as having a 'penchant for females' who, '... displayed few reservations about the exploited place of prostitutes within the capitalist mode of production,' and that the evidence for this comes from a letter Engels wrote in 1846 from Paris, to Karl Marx, in which he said:

> It is absolutely essential that you get out of boring Brussels for once and come to Paris, and I for my part have a great desire to go carousing with you. If I had an income of 5000 francs I would do nothing but work and amuse myself with women until I went to pieces. If there were no Frenchwomen, life wouldn't be worth living. But so long as there are grisettes [prostitutes], well and good!

In his theorising about marriage, Engels argued for 'sex love': a virtuous model of sexual relations between men and women, far removed from his idea of marriage as the conjugal partnership of leaden boredom. For him, there was, '...no point in marriage without love'. In his utopian, communist world men and women would only marry for mutual affection, not social security, property, or social betterment, and if sex love were to die or become supplanted by a new passionate love, the contract should be terminated painlessly without the couple, 'having to wade through the useless mire of divorce proceedings'. 'Separation is a benefit for both partners as well as society,' this 24-year-old declared. This, of course, is the current social narrative about marriage. It is the reason millions of people live in easily dissolvable 'free love' arrangements as 'partners', not spouses, and why millions of children suffer the unwanted trauma of the break-up of their parents.

Taken as a whole, Engels's arguments are the reason for the gender warfare in which society is now embroiled, and why women are in high dudgeon about men's alleged control of them in their relationships, and in broader society. We hear this in the endless social memes of domestic violence against women, alleged to be exclusively perpetrated by men, the idea that women are being routinely murdered by their husbands and partners, and the moral panic about rape, even though these are all gross and culpable distortions of reality. Nothing, it seems, will assuage the anger of the modern Marxist, Engelist, feminists who are unstoppable in making their case against men, and all of it is based on the unproven hypotheses of two young men, both in their twenties, who sat and conspired together in a window seat in Chetham's Library, Manchester, in the middle of the nineteenth century, and dreamed up the idea of Communism.

Lewis Henry Morgan

One of the key drivers of the development of the communists' ideas about the role of women in society was a narrow strand of anthropology followed by one man. Lewis Henry Morgan (1818-1881) was something of a darling of the early socialist movement, even though his firm allegiance was to the commercial and industrial class and its achievements. Engels in particular made extensive use of Morgan's anthropological studies when formulating his theories of class, the state, and the rise of the nuclear family. What attracted him was Morgan's understanding of the development of human social organisation in the Iroquois people of North America, whose system of kinship organisation, Morgan believed, represented the model of primitive societies, and gave anthropologists a glimpse into the way things were in the past.

In his 1877 book *Ancient Society, or Researches in the Lines of Human Progress from Savagery through Barbarism to Civilization*, Morgan developed the theory of 'Cultural Evolution,' which Engels borrowed. The theory goes that man's socio-economic development was the result of increased agricultural efficiency, and as society progressed from a hunting and gathering stage (which Morgan termed 'savagery') to a settled agriculture stage ('barbarism'), the increasing use of farming technology led to surpluses of food beyond those needed for the community's basic subsistence. This, Morgan argued, was the principal factor in the ultimate development of society to an urban model (which he called 'civilisation'), and it correlated with the move from sexual promiscuity, through various forms of family life, and ultimately to exclusive monogamy.

This was the idea that attracted the attention of Marx and Engels in the light of the social changes they were witnessing in Manchester in its chaotic development during the second surge of the Industrial Revolution from 1830. Engels saw that Morgan's theory could explain the uneven distribution of wealth, and the class system based on feudalism, which was a feature of the times, and he saw this as analogous to the way ancient societies' surpluses were allegedly unevenly shared, coming to the conclusion that no one individual or group should accumulate its own surpluses, and they should be shared out for the commonwealth. Following this argument to its end, Engels then believed that the capitalist obtained his wealth, and therefore his power, by immoral means.

Basing his arguments almost entirely on Morgan's views, Engels argued that the strictly monogamous pairing of men and women with their own offspring was unknown in ancient proto-society. Instead, people lived in sanguineous groups (blood relatives) in conditions of relative equality with one another. Meyer (op. cit.) points to Engels's assertion that, '…the farther back we go into history or prehistory; the more important kinship becomes the organising matrix of society. It is only in civilised societies that production relations and class structure become primary'. Using this to justify the argument for Communism, Engels argued that a shift toward more productive agriculture in ancient societies had led to an increased need for children to work in the fields, and that in turn had led to a demand on women to maximise their childbearing.

Thus, women became units of reproduction confined to a central role in the home, and men gained power over them through the accumulation of surpluses, which became wealth passed on to future generations through fathers favouring their own children. Meyer (op cit.) analyses this astutely:

> In the book itself, Engels seeks to link this changing balance between productive and reproductive activities and the subjection of women by asserting that the earliest human societies were matriarchies, in which women were highly respected and carried out important tasks… Throughout the book, Engels conveys the impression that matriarchy was preferable to male domination and that it corresponded to a nobler and more humane way of life. Matriarchy reigned in a communistic, propertyless [Sic] community blessed with equality, sexual freedom, general self-respect, and respect for others.

So, Engels' argument goes, women's roles changed with the development of private property and private wealth; as production moved away from the house and home, women lost their economic role and became essentially only valuable as producers of children, *ergo* they became sex slaves. The traditional order of inheritance, which, he alleges, was from the mother in early societies, was overthrown by men, who created wealthy property-owning families, and became the first ruling class, eventually spreading this model far and wide to the rest of society, which became constructed around men and men's dominant power.

'Big Men' and patriarchy

Engels justified this alleged patriarchal takeover by referring to the Latin root of the word 'family', which, he said, only came into use in Roman times to describe the total number of slaves a man owned (his *familia*) over whom he had the rights of life and death vested in him by the Roman State. The Marxist/feminist apologist Chris Harman explains this more clearly in his paper *Engels and the Origins of Human Society:*[122]

> … the divergent forms under which class society emerged must not make us forget the enormous similarities from society to society. Everywhere there was, in the beginning, primitive communism. Everywhere, once settled agricultural societies were formed, some lineages, lineage elders or 'big men' could begin to gain prestige through their role in undertaking the redistribution of the little surplus that existed in the interests of the group as a whole. Everywhere, as the surplus grew, this small section of society came to control a greater share of the social wealth, putting it in a position where it could begin to crystallize out into a social class.

So, with the emergence of 'Big Men,' men took over, and women's relationship to society became dependent on class and the amassing of private property. Women's economic role in proto-society was abandoned, and a wholly male-dominated class system emerged. Patriarchy, that eternal *bête noir* of feminism, prevailed. Adding fuel to this was Morgan's conclusion that Iroquois women had no small degree of authority in their communities, and lived in relative equality with men. Female elders, he said, sat on tribal decision-making councils exercising 'a negative power' (probably better thought of as a veto) over declarations of war. Thus women in the community acted as peacemakers, interposing themselves to break deadlock between warring tribes.[123] We hear this idea expressed in almost identical form in the alleged benefit of having women in the boardroom, or in Parliament, which is a current powerful feminist narrative.

However, it was Morgan's reports of contacts between seventeenth and eighteenth century Jesuit missionaries with the Innu (also known as the Montagnais or Naskapi), the Algonquian nomadic peoples from the subarctic and boreal regions of Northern Quebec and Labrador, that provided the inspiration for Communism, and especially the relationship of children to their parents and the state in that system. According to Morgan, the missionaries had apparently expressed surprise at the amount of sexual freedom the Innu practised, prompting one of them to comment to a native that it was not honourable for a woman to love anyone except her husband, and it was an evil that the man himself was not sure that his son was actually his. The man replied, 'Thou hast no sense. You French people love only your own children, but we love all the children of our tribe'. In communist societies, children are considered to be held in common for society, rather than being the total responsibility of their natural parents, and this has uncomfortable parallels with our society today.

An argument from Ignorance

The only problem with all of this is that there has never been a matriarchal society. No social arrangement has ever been known that even approached the notional model that underpins the communist-feminist model. The weakness of Engels's argument is that the period in which all this is alleged to have happened was before history as we know it. No one can know for sure whether early societies were matriarchal, matrilineal, or whether 'big men' emerged to dominate. To assert such things with safety, you would need evidence - and there isn't any. It is all supposition, with no historical record to support it at all. Indeed, Engels is now the subject of comprehensive negative commentary by scholars today. As Tristram Hunt, to whom I referred earlier, in his commentary to Engels's *The Origin of the Family, Private Property, and the State*, says in the following:

> In academic commentary today, The Origin of the Family, Private Property and the State is widely dismissed on account of its flawed anthropological foundations. For example, modern scholars suggest there is little evidence of any substantive system of equality between the sexes predominating within primitive communities or for the prevalence of group marriage and extensive promiscuity... In fact, women often carried out far more labour in hunter/gatherer societies than any supposed 'natural' division of labour (i.e., that dictated by human reproductive biology) sanctioned... There is also

considerable scepticism over Engels's claims for a powerful matriarchal component within 'savage' and 'barbarian' societies, with the particular example of the Iroquois being unscientifically recast as part of a much wider history…

Engels is accused of generally displaying a far too rosy view of the state of women in pre-modern communities with his eulogy for the 'naïve, primeval character' of 'old traditional sexual relations'… most damaging of all have been the ongoing researches of the Cambridge Group for the History of Population and Social Structure into European demography. In contrast to the vague assertions of Marx and Engels, their rigorous archival work has pointed to the remarkable longevity – through various modes of production – of the nuclear family in human society. Marion Levy has argued that this structure constituted the dominant form 'in all known societies in world history for well over 50e societies'… the eminent social historian Peter Laslett felt able to conclude that, 'It is not true that most of our ancestors lived in extended families. It is not true that industrialization brought the simple nuclear family with it.'

The bottom line here is that what Marx, Engels, or feminists say amounts to nothing more than an elaborately constructed set of assertions based on flimsy circumstantial evidence, apparently underpinned by academic research when it is not, plus a lot of imagination. Yet, an entire political theory has been constructed around it. Like the assertions of Communism, feminism's assertions are based on myths intended to justify a political proposition and they are built on a foundation of sand. Engels talked in utopian terms, and so did the early women's liberationists. He postulated a pre-class, matriarchal, proto-society that never existed, and the feminists such as Shulamith Firestone, Elizabeth Mann Borghese, Marge Piercy, Charlotte Perkins Gilman et al. also dreamed of a future state of living along similar lines. Like Alfred Meyer, one has to marvel at the sheer chutzpah of it all. Even Morgan's theories, as academically valid as they undoubtedly are, cannot be taken to be true of the development of all societies. They are just views and theories, based on his observations, and interpretations of the ways of a sample of one native North American tribe, and in any case Morgan is not universally accepted by modern anthropologists or sociologists, who argue that the groups he studied are only part of a much richer picture of mankind's social development. For example, Steven Goldberg says this:[124]

There has never been a matriarchy or 'Amazonian Society'. There have been a very few tiny societies with relatively little hierarchy, but in all such societies an informal male dominance played a role similar to that of patriarchy...there are many societies in which women work harder and longer outside the home - objectively doing more important economic work - than do men... [But] these never include primary responsibility for hierarchical position...assuming there were matriarchies just because there are myths about matriarchies makes as much sense as assuming that there were cyclopses just because there were myths about cyclopses.

Nobody can point to a shred of evidence that men usurped women's rights to property, or built wealth from surpluses in food. To accept the entire thrust of what Marx and Engels said about early communist proto-societies, indeed in order to accept feminism, which is indisputably founded on their arguments, you have to accept what they said as an act of faith, whilst at the same time ignoring the indisputable absence of evidence. John Locke, considered one of the most influential thinkers of the seventeenth century Enlightenment said, 'Another way that men ordinarily use to drive others, and force them to submit [to] their judgments, and receive their opinion in debate, is to require the adversary to admit what they allege as a proof, or assign a better. And this I call *Argumentum ad Ignorantiam* (an argument from ignorance), and Bertrand Russell, the twentieth century philosopher and logician, addressing the issue of people's belief in God, summed it up in his famous 'Tea Pot' analogy:

> Many orthodox people speak as though it were the business of sceptics to disprove received dogmas rather than of dogmatists to prove them. This is, of course, a mistake. If I were to suggest that between the Earth and Mars there is a china teapot revolving about the sun in an elliptical orbit, nobody would be able to disprove my assertion, provided I were careful to add that the teapot is too small to be revealed even by our most powerful telescopes. But if I were to go on to say that, since my assertion cannot be disproved, it is intolerable presumption on the part of human reason to doubt it, I should rightly be thought to be talking nonsense. If, however, the existence of such a teapot were affirmed in ancient books, taught as the sacred truth every Sunday, and instilled into the minds of children at school, hesitation to believe in its existence would become a mark of eccentricity and entitle the doubter to the attentions of the psychiatrist in an enlightened age or of the Inquisitor in an earlier time.

When we consider the degree to which feminism is believed almost religiously by its advocates, when we see the degree to which its mantras are religiously repeated by its followers, and the extent to which they are affirmed daily in the media and universities' 'Gender Studies' programmes; when we see the intolerance and the blind bigotry that permeates feminist's activities, we see how frighteningly close feminism is to a false doctrine, and a religious belief system.

Charles Fourier

Charles Fourier (1772-1837) is credited with the first use of the word 'Feminism', in 1837.[125] He had become very wealthy at a very young age (11 years old) through a substantial inheritance from his father that led him to live a somewhat dissolute adult life, spent travelling and odd-jobbing through Europe. During this time, it seems, he developed a deep contempt for 'modern' (eighteenth and early nineteenth century) society, particularly the trading practices of the era. Fourier saw civilisation as a depraved order and always referred to it in pejorative terms, using phrases such as, 'the knavery of merchants'. He was particularly dismissive of Jews, whom he called the 'sources of all evil,' and was an early socialist thinker and a strong supporter of women's rights.

Like the later Engels, he believed that all important work should be open to women, who should be judged purely on the basis of their skill and aptitude, and that a time existed in the distant past when humankind lived in a simpler state in perfect happiness and fulfilment - in instinctive harmony with one another, and with nature. He held up the original hunter-gatherer societies as models of perfect existence, and far from them being always at the edge of starvation and in danger of attack, he argued that these societies provided for people's needs in abundance because those needs were few, and people's desires were limited. He also believed that marriage damaged women's rights and as a matter of principle he never married.

Fourier was a 'Utopian'. He believed that people's concern for each other and their cooperation with each other in common purpose were the secrets of social success, and he wrote extensively about creating communes, which he called 'Phalanxes'. In these ideal communities workers would be paid according to their contribution through work assigned to them on the basis of their interests and individual desires, and jobs that were less desirable would receive higher pay for those who volunteered for them. In particular, he believed that relationships between the sexes in these phalanxes would be loosely tied, and that casual sexual encounters would be the predominant form of interaction between men and women. Yet again we see this idea widespread in modern Western nations.

In Fourier's ideal world, there was no war or oppression because no one had any motive for them, and his ideas found resonance in the Paris communes of the 1848 revolution. They also inspired a number of communes across America in the nineteenth century, not least one called 'Utopia', a settlement on the northern bank of the Ohio River in Clermont County, southwest Ohio. Founded in 1844, it failed within four years after a flooding disaster led to unresolved internecine conflict. The demise of the other experiments in communal living followed soon after, mainly because they had no meaningful social order or means of resolving differences between people.

The idea of utopianism did not die, however. Little more than a century later, in 1966, Marshall Sahlins presented a paper entitled *Man the Hunter* at a Chicago symposium, arguing that hunter-gatherer societies actually had a refined mode of subsistence that, despite a degree of deprivation, nevertheless were able to provide for and readily satisfy their people's needs and wants. Sahlins argued that you could achieve affluence by desiring little, and his Socialist principles were firmly nailed to the door when he presented his ideas as standing in stark contrast to the 'Galbraithean Way,' referring to the ideas of economist Kenneth Galbraith, which by then were gathering pace in the post Second World War economies of the developed world. Galbraith was the arch exponent of the idea that where man's wants are high or even infinite, and there was a gap between means and ends, that gap could only be bridged by increasing industrial productivity. These views were completely out of fashion, however, in the utopian, hippy-influenced social mood prevailing in the 1960s, in which 'make love, not war' was the prevailing ethos.

August Bebel

Marx and Engels laid the political framework for Communism, and Fourier defined its idealistic form, but it was Ferdinand August Bebel (1840-1913), the German Marxist politician, writer and orator, who brought a much clearer focus to the outworking of feminism under Marxism. In his 1879 book *Die Frau und der Sozialismus* ('Woman under socialism'), and with remarkable prescience, he says this:

The woman of future society is socially and economically independent; she is no longer subject to even a vestige of dominion and exploitation; she is free, the peer of man, mistress of her lot. Her education is the same as that of man, with such exceptions as the difference of sex and biological function demand. Living under natural conditions, she is able to unfold and exercise her mental powers and faculties. For her occupation, she chooses those fields that correspond with her wishes, inclinations, and natural abilities, and she works under the same conditions as man. Even if she is engaged as a practical working-woman in some field or another, she may be an educator, teacher, or nurse in the second part of her day; she may practice some type of art, or cultivate some branch of science in the third part; and she may fill some administrative function in the fourth. She joins in studies, completes chores, enjoys pleasures and social intercourse with either her sisters or with men – as she pleases or as occasion serves. In choosing love, she is, like man, free and unhampered. She woos or is wooed, and seals the bond out of no consideration other than her own inclination. This bond is a private contract, celebrated without the intervention of any functionary – just as marriage was a private contract until well into the Middle Ages. Socialism creates nothing new here: it merely restores, at a higher level of civilization and under new social forms, that which prevailed at a more primitive social stage before private property began to rule society.

What an astonishingly accurate description this is of modern society! All of it has come about through feminism - that pure expression of 'woman under socialism' described by Bebel who said, 'Women must not wait for men to help them out of this condition, just as workers do not wait for help from the bourgeoisie,' and all reiterated 100 years later by Germaine Greer in her open exhortation to the Marxist Women's Liberationists to 'get on with it.'[126] This is precisely what they did around 1970, with their plotting in loft apartments in Greenwich Village, and their burning of bras in 'Freedom Trash Cans' outside the Miss World Pageant in Atlantic City, chanting '...don't be a clown, take women seriously!' In the Bebel-defined ideal for *Woman under Socialism*, women today have entered into a Faustian pact with the Marxist-Engelist-Fourierist-Bebelist theorising that has destroyed marriage as a lifelong covenant, the family as the stable social unit in which children are brought up to be successful adults, and has turned women into the agents whereby their own children are being damaged and deprived of their rightful inheritance. Far from being idealistic dreaming, by buying into the Communist ideal, we have created a social nightmare.

Ernest Belfort Bax

Ernest Belfort Bax (1854-1926), the Socialist philosopher and commentator, whose commentaries I have cited in numerous places in this book, provides us with the final link that ties modern feminism to Marxism. This is what he said in one of his papers from 1912:[127]

> We may trace the origin of modern Feminism in a fairly continuous line back to the eighteenth century – to protagonists in revolutionary and pre-revolutionary literature – notably to Mary Wollstonecraft and William Godwin. From that time onward the Feminist question has always been present, though it only became prominent during the second half of the nineteenth century. It was about the end of the sixties [1860s] that the Woman's Suffrage plank first made its appearance in the modern Socialist movement, in the original International, at the instance of Michael Bakunin and his followers, and was one of the few proposals emanating from that quarter that was accepted by the Marx party. But for a long time the question remained in the background, being hardly referred to at all in the earlier programmes of the Continental parties. In fact, in the German party the 'Woman Question,' as apart from the general Social question, first received serious attention in 1883 in Bebel's book, the first edition of which was issued under the title of *Woman in the Past, Present, and Future*, contained very much Woman and very little Socialism. (In the later editions, under the title *Woman and Socialism*, it is only fair to say, the proportions have been altered.) In this work, Bebel, who virtually admits in his preface that the bulk of the party at that time was against him, maintained the dogma of the equal capacity of woman with man, with its corollary, the right of women to occupy all positions and exercise all functions hitherto controlled by men. In France, Lafargue was active on the Feminist side during the early eighties. Since then the Feminist dogma has found much favour with Socialists everywhere, and the demand for Female Suffrage has been officially embodied among the planks in the immediate political platform of the Social Democratic party. At the same time, it has been sought to exercise a pressure within the party to prevent dissentient Social Democrats from expressing an adverse opinion.

It is worth dwelling a little on this summary. Bax is considered to be one of Marxism's key philosophers. His voluminous correspondence on a wide range of Marxist-Socialist issues can be found proudly displayed to this day on the

Marxist web site. Yet, here he casts somewhat jaundiced views on 'the dogma of the equal capacity of woman with man, with its corollary, the right of women to occupy all positions and exercise all functions hitherto controlled by men'. One might note a somewhat serendipitous connection between this early stirring of feminism within Socialism and its emergence with a vengeance 100 years later, around 1970, but there was clearly more to this re-emergence, this so-called Second Wave Feminism, than just chance. The gang of revolutionary women's liberationists who seized their moment in those turbulent times were steeped in Marxist ideology, which undoubtedly did shape their thinking. These women were from an angry generation that was searching for a political framework in which to bed its anger, and Marxist Socialism fitted the bill very well indeed.

Erich Fromm and the Frankfurt School

There is one final piece of the jigsaw that needs to be put in place that links feminism inextricably to Marxism. The Institute for Social Research (ISR), which originally comprised a group of dissident Marxists, was located within the Goethe University, Frankfurt, Germany, and out of it emerged what became called The Frankfurt School. This was not a specific institution in itself, rather a group of neo-Marxist thinkers within the ISR who had come together because they believed that Marxism as it was being practiced in Communist Russia was too narrowly concerned with repeating a particular selection of Marx's ideas in defence of orthodox communist parties. Crucially, the Frankfurt School had come to the view that traditional Marxist theory was unable to explain the unexpected burgeoning of capitalism in the twentieth century, and its clear ascendancy over Communism, so it sought alternative paths to social development by integrating other schools of thought. Principal among these was 'Antipositivist Sociology,' which argued that society cannot be investigated by using the same research methods as used for studying the natural world, and the Frankfurt School rejected empiricism and the standard scientific method in favour of trying to understand and interpret the social actions of people being studied.[128] The Frankfurt School took inputs from psychoanalysis and existential philosophy, which became the core philosophy of feminism through Jean Paul Sartre and Simone de Beauvoir, who said that philosophical thought must begin with the presumption that the individual exists in an apparently meaningless and absurd world and in a state of confusion and disorientation. Søren Kierkegaard had aired this idea before Sartre but the latter was the first to self-identify as an existentialist philosopher.

One of the most important thinkers in this context was Erich Fromm (1900-1980), a German psychologist and sociologist whose theories anticipated much of later feminism and especially its ideas about socially-constructed gender. According to Douglas Kellner, Professor of Philosophy at the University of Texas at Austin, 'Eric Fromm [Sic] is one of the few members of the Frankfurt School who seriously engaged himself with theorizing the problems of gender and the differences between men and women'.[129] However, Fromm broke away from the Frankfurt School after receiving widespread criticism and dismissive responses from his colleagues for holding these views. In fact, according to Kellner, he was rejected out of hand by them, observing that whilst Fromm's gender analysis contained 'anticipations of contemporary feminist perspectives', it also had its 'moments of sexism and essentialism,' and was 'highly uneven and even contradictory'.

Kellner says that Fromm believed, 'The family is the medium through which the society or the social class stamps its specific structure on the child' (cited in Kellner, op. cit.) but 'this leads to the socialization of people into accepting bourgeois society as the norm, thus illicitly normalizing it' (Kellner). We can see here the seeds of Simone de Beauvoir's thinking and, later, that of Betty Friedan. We can also see the recurring theme of the overturning of the nuclear family in Marxist thought, and why feminism has sought to destroy it. Kellner goes on to say that Fromm argued that this meant 'ignoring the intrinsically historical nature of all social formations, institutions, practices, and human life', which, of course, is pure Engelist thought, and that, 'bourgeois society produced a character in people that was more concerned with parsimoniousness, discipline, and thrift...', which characteristics Fromm associated with patriarchy, '...rather than love, sensual pleasure, and kindness', which he associated with matriarchy, just as Engels had almost 100 years earlier. This exactly follows Fourier's ideas about utopianism and is later echoed in the fanciful writings of Charlotte Perkins Gilman, Elizabeth Mann Borghese, Shulamith Firestone, Marge Piercy, and Mary Gentle, those seminal feminist writers to whom I referred earlier. Kellner further comments that Fromm emphasised the positive qualities of women and the negative qualities of patriarchy, thus establishing 'a close kinship with the ideals of socialism'. Crucially, however, Kellner quotes Fromm as follows:

Aside from the fact that the theory of matriarchy underlined the relativity of the bourgeois social structure, its very special content could not but win the sympathy of Marxists. First of all, it had discovered a period when woman had been the authority and focal point of society, rather than the slave of man and an object for barter; this lent important support to the struggle for woman's political and social emancipation. The great battle of the eighteenth century had to be picked up afresh by those who were fighting for a classless society (Fromm [1932] 1970, p. 123).

Here, we see the inspiration for the re-emergence of feminism as Women's Liberation in the late 1960s and early 1970s. Fromm was the intellectual and ideological link for feminism's underpinning ideology that spanned the 100 years between its first expressions in Marx and Engels, and its outbreak around 1970 in Women's Liberation. Interestingly, Kellner goes on to refer to his own doubts about the idea of historical matriarchy; thus:

> While Fromm provides a positive analysis of the matricentric principles valorized by Bachofen and a critique of patriarchal values, it is not certain that his use of the myth of matriarchy is the best conceptual device to valorize the qualities of women. There is widespread skepticism today whether matriarchical societies actually existed and Bachofen's romanticization of mothering and matricentric values creates a prescribed normative role for women to fulfill, thus restricting their freedom to choose modes of existence at variance with social norms. Many women today are trying to escape from their definition as mothers, which the matriarchy myth uses to define women's essential functions. There are also questions concerning the anthropological and ideological value of Bachofen's work that need to be thought through.

A little note about Johann Jakob Bachofen (1815-1887), whom Kellner cites, seems appropriate here. He was a Swiss jurist and anthropologist whose main research interest was ancient tombs. Bachofen was a major contributor to modern social anthropology, especially in his exploration of the family as a social institution. However, in the last twenty years of his life, he increasingly adopted the views of Lewis Henry Morgan that had so influenced Engels, to which he added a distinct romanticisation of women's qualities, as Kellner observes. We see this in the title of his 1861 book *Das Mutterecht* ('Mother Right'), which echoes Engels's own terms, and we also see even more of the provenance of the ideas of ancient matriarchy, which were clearly much in favour in those days.

Fromm was undoubtedly influenced by sociologist Max Weber (1864-1920), whose ideas I refer to in the chapter 'On Patriarchy' and which were extant in Fromm's youth. Weber wrote extensively about authority within the family and, in 1936, Fromm published *Studien über Autorität und Familie* ('Studies on authority and family'), drawing on Weber's ideas and in which he also openly drew on the work of Sigmund Freud, especially his ideas of ego, super-ego,[130] and sado-masochism, to explain mechanisms of familial authority and submission. Kellner (op. cit.) explains it thus:

> Following Freud, Fromm presents the super-ego as the internalization of social authority, 'and specifically of the father in the patriarchal family of modern times...' Fromm then describes how the family is the key institution in the production of the super-ego and how development of a strong super-ego facilitates repression of rebellious impulses. Weak egos submit to super-ego authority, thus Fromm calls for the production of a stronger ego that will make possible more independent thought and action. This is particularly urgent since he believed that people's egos were becoming so weak that 'the masochistic character' appears almost 'normal'.

Fromm's book was the product of a five-year study he had carried out in collaboration with colleagues in the ISR, including Herbert Marcuse, the German-American philosopher, sociologist, and Marxist political theorist, often referred to as 'The Father of the New Left in the United States'. Marcuse undoubtedly had a strong influence on him. He is also known to have inspired many radical intellectuals and political activists in the 1960s and 1970s Beat generation, becoming the most influential theorist of the student movements of Germany, France, and the United States. In the early 1950s he was a teacher at Columbia University, the same time as the beatniks Jean-Louis 'Jack' Kerouac, John Clellon Holmes, and Allen Ginsberg were there, and he was also a close friend and inspirer of the French philosopher André Gorz, a strong supporter of Jean Paul Sartre in the French beatnik cluster.

In Fromm's work, we can see the essence of the rebellion of feminists against the patriarchy - the rule or authority of the father - and the father as head of the family. It is what underpins the feminist portrayal of women as submissive victims of men: first in the home, à la Betty Friedan in the 1950s, and today in the pronounced victim culture we see expressed everywhere, from the so-called rape culture, to the view that women are the victims of widespread domestic violence. Fromm provides the framework for this in his 1943 essay, *Sex and Character*, where he portrays sex as the basis for establishing the inherent vulnerability of women to men. In that essay, he argued, 'The woman's vulnerability…lies in her dependency on the man; the element of insecurity connected with her sexual function lies not in failing but in being "left alone," in being frustrated, in not having complete control over the process which leads to sexual satisfaction'.[131] Kellner comments as follows: 'Fromm suggests that in the battle of the sexes, the penis is a weapon with which men can sadistically dominate women…'[132] and directly quotes Fromm saying, 'Man's specific hostility is to overpower; women's is to undermine'.[133]

He goes on to say that the natural differences between men and women mean 'in fact and ideology, women are dependent on men',[134] and comments that this is a classic example of sociological conditioning, which sails very close to the wind of biological determinism when Fromm says, 'the craving for prestige and competitive success is found in men', and of the masculine character as '…having the qualities of penetration, guidance, activity, discipline, and adventurousness: the feminine character …the qualities of productive receptiveness, protection, realism, endurance, motherliness'.[135] As Kellner observes, Fromm's gender analysis was certainly 'highly uneven and even contradictory,'[136] but so is much of modern feminist theory.

More chillingly, however, Kellner reports a very dark sentiment in Fromm, expressed in an interview he had with him in 1975 (unreferenced by Kellner). When he asked Fromm to comment on the perception of the feminist movement as being, 'an open, violent fight against men', Fromm said this:

> One cannot understand the psychology of women, and for that matter the psychology of men, and one cannot understand the element of sadism, of hostility and destructiveness in men and women if one does not consider that there has been a war between the sexes going on in the last six thousand years. This war is a guerrila [Sic] war. Women have been defeated by patriarchalism six thousand years ago and society has been built upon the domination of men. Women were possessions and had to be grateful for every new concession that men made to them. But there is no domination of one part of mankind over another, of a social class, of a nation or of a sex over another, unless there is underneath rebellion, fury, hate and wish for revenge in those who are oppressed and exploited and fear and insecurity in those who do the exploiting and repressing (Fromm 1975, p. 59) … Women have been

so thoroughly oppressed that they have accepted unconsciously the role that the ruling sex, man, gave to them. They have even believed in male propaganda, which is very much the same as the propaganda in other wars, wars against colonial people, etc. Women have been considered to be naive: Freud said that they were narcissistic, unrealistic, cowardly, inferior to man anatomically, intellectually, morally. The fact is that women are less narcissistic than men, for the simple reason that there is almost nothing that man does which has not some purpose of making an impression. Women do many, many things without this motive and in fact what you might call women's vanity is only the necessity to please the victors. As far as the lack of realism in women is concerned, what should we say about male realism in an epoch in which all western governments, consisting of men, are spending their money building atomic bombs, instead of taking care of threatening famine, instead of avoiding the catastrophes which threaten the whole world? (Fromm 1975, pp. 59 and 94)

We should not forget that Fromm's ideas were initially met with a reserve that later developed into skepticism in his peers, who ultimately rejected him completely. Yet, what he said has been highly influential in the feminism we see today. His views form a significant part of the 'woman as the oppressed creature' narrative, which most people would instantly recognise as nonsense. Kellner again:

> Despite his movement towards the views held by Lewis Henry Morgan later in his life, as late as 1970 Fromm kept returning to the culturalist/feminist themes from his earlier writings. Returning to the theme of rebellion, in a very late book, For the Love of Life, Fromm says, women, like children, used to be regarded as objects, as the property of their husband. That has changed. They may still be at a disadvantage in a man's world, receiving less pay, for example, than a man does for the same work; but their overall position, their consciousness, is considerably stronger than it was. And all the signs would seem to indicate that the women's revolution will go forward, just as the revolution of children and young people will. They will continue to define, articulate, and stand up for their own rights. (Fromm 1986. Op cit,, p. 25).[137]

The most ridiculous of Fromm's assertions, however, is that women are less narcissistic than men. In fact, the feminist movement whose ideas Fromm and his like have inspired has produced the most narcissistic generation of women there has ever been. Their *idée fixe*, the false construct of objectification, is based on the Self-Other and social conditioning theories of Simone de Beauvoir, which many of them have learned in universities on gender studies programmes. We see this most visibly expressed in the *Everyday Sexism Project*,[138] wherein much of the rhetoric of objectification is endlessly expressed by thousands of young women subscribers who have clearly absorbed this and see objectification by men everywhere. These young, radicalised feminist activists will attack men at any opportunity for objectifying them, to the point where they have become dangerous to any man who compliments a woman on her looks, and this is inextricably bound up with a pronounced consciousness of self. Feminism is the agar in which narcissism has been cultured and it has grown into a monster. These young women, the 'selfie generation', have become radicalised - to the point of obsession with themselves. They have lost their *joie de vivre*, and have become a fear-ridden, 'rape culture', vindictive generation of professional grievance collectors.

Progress or regress?

In Erich Fromm, we have the final link in the chain that stretches across two centuries at least of social development since the Industrial Revolution. Like dye placed in a pool in the mountains to trace the source of a stream, we can see the passage of feminism's development from earliest thinkers, through Marx and Engels, and later sources throughout the twentieth century that finally led to the social revolution in the late 1960s that was Women's Liberation, and which today has become the flood of feminism that is engulfing us all.

Feminism does not have its roots in the Enlightenment ideals of equality of opportunity and the just distribution of social benefit, it is cultural Marxism. Feminism and Communism share identical DNA. They are inextricably bound together, and feminism's grip on modern thinking is dislocating our entire society, causing it to mutate into a communist hybrid, overturning centuries if not millennia of social development. In their *Communist Manifesto*, Marx and Engels unequivocally plead guilty to the accusation that communists want to end the marriages of the bourgeois and create what amounts to a separate community of women distinct from men, independent of men, detached from men in terms of their life's aims, and feminism has achieved that. They make it abundantly clear that this is part of a deliberate and self-conscious attempt to bring about the destruction of capitalist, class-based society, in order to cleanse it in preparation for the new communist order with an imposed equality, which pays only lip service to the real thing, and feminism has achieved that.

Feminism is becoming the new world order, the evidence is before us, and we must wake up to what is afoot before it is too late. Feminists hate the nuclear family and all it represents: they hate the home, marriage, commitment for life of a man and a woman to one another; they hate the role of housewife and mother, and they hate men for their social power. That is why they are systematically dividing the sexes, creating that 'legalised community of women' to which Marx referred, and all in the furtherance of their angry creed and its aims, which are not liberation for anyone, least of all women, but a form of social-political bondage to their overarching, overbearing, totalitarian ideology.

Yet, people still believe in the ideal of a marriage in which husband and wife are joined in common purpose for a better life, building wealth for themselves and legally passing that wealth on to their children. They believe in unions of equal dignity not equality, and I suggest that very few men are ever likely to see their wives as whores who only live with them out of economic necessity, and I suggest that most women would be appalled at the suggestion that they were selling their sexual services in return for the provision and the protection of a man. Many women, probably most these days, I suggest, would love to have the opportunity of being able to stay at home and bring up their children, fulfilling their natural desire of motherhood, but they cannot out of sheer economic necessity because successive governments have sold out to feminism and failed to uphold the dignity of motherhood, incentivising it through public policy. Instead even Conservative governments continue to throw vast amounts of tax-payers' money at child-care support, which serves only to reinforce the idea of women as economic units in the process of production and undermines women's inestimable contribution as mothers and wives to the social capital of society.

I further suggest that most men would be proud, if called to do so, to work hard for their families and would willingly provide for a wife who gave her full measure in the bringing up of their children. However, where are the women who are prepared to do that? It doesn't take much peeling back of the layers of our current social narrative to see the degree to which women have become sold-out to the Marxist/feminist worldview. Women in marriages truly want the feminist idea of equality. They want men to share the nurturing of children so they can go out to work and gain their self-fulfilment in career, rather than as full-time mothers. And that is what it is: *self*-fulfilment. They are happy to farm out their children to childcare, subsidised by the state, to whomever, rather than do the job themselves. They want to be equal earners with their husbands. They want to be part of a legalised community of women. They want their careers and their independent financial security, and they are using that in later life to free themselves from lifelong marriage and to re-marry or re-partner, which means they really are acting like wives held in common. This is the Marxist/feminist-constructed world in which we all now live.

The world now revolves around women and their needs, but it fails to recognise the needs of men, and it particularly fails to recognise those of children. Families are not simply economic units of production, consumption, and transaction as Marx, Engels and feminists would have us believe, they are there for the nurture of children, so we can produce the next generation of adequate, responsible, socially functional people. Neither are they the result of sex: animal gratification within a legalised construct called marriage or an informal contact of 'common law marriage' capable of being ended as soon as the fancy takes one or other of the partners. Families are a social institution in which higher feelings, values, and aspirations find their truest expression for men and for women who have found through centuries that these things need a covenant commitment for life if that expression is to find its truest form. I cannot believe for one minute that women in general find any satisfaction in a lifetime of casual sexual relationships without commitment, having children to men whom they don't respect, or with whom they have little or no emotional attachment. I do not believe that women are happier being single mothers, having children simply to leverage provision from the state, or are fulfilled by having a child to any man and bringing it up alone simply to satisfy their biologically-induced need to reproduce. Marx's and Engels's world is about as far away from their understanding of life as the Moon is from the Earth, but the outworking of their precepts are shockingly at work in our society today, through feminism.

Marxism is alive and well and living among us. It is ironic, however, that the ideology behind it, hatched beside those 'Dark Satanic Mills,' the icons of capitalism declared by Marx and Engels to be the root of all evil and the centre of injustice towards women and children, is actually causing that injustice in its spawn, which is feminism. For example, according to UNICEF, Britain is 14th out of 29 countries in a league of children's material well-being. One in six children live in poverty in the UK. Seventeen per cent of children live in homes where the income is substantially lower than the national average, and that rises to 29 per cent (3.5 million children) if you take subsidised housing costs into account. All manner of reasons are cited for this by our politicians, but it boils down to one thing - broken homes and one-parent families - all the product of Marxist-inspired feminism that has so radically changed modern society and motherhood. In espousing this angry creed with such alacrity, in buying into its precepts lock, stock, and barrel, we have shaken the entire edifice of our own society to its foundations, to the extent that it is becoming unstable, and to the point that it might come crashing down upon us.

We must look at feminism with a discerning, realistic eye before it is too late. We must critically examine what it is we are embracing, and we must do that informed by truth not dogma, by honesty, not weasel-word rhetoric. Women, as mothers, have a particular need to see what feminism is doing to their sons, and to the fathers of their children. Yes, and to their brothers and their own fathers too.

CHAPTER 8

THE PSYCHO-SOCIAL ASPECTS OF

FEMINISM

'To determine the true rulers of any society, all you must do is ask yourself this question: Who is it that I am not permitted to criticise?'

Kevin Alfred Strom (1956 -) Frequently mis-attributed to Voltaire

Feminism's fury

When Larry Summers, President of Harvard University, rose to give the keynote speech at a conference in 2005 on Diversifying the Science & Engineering Workforce, sponsored by the National Bureau of Economic Research, little did he realise that he was about to provoke a storm of feminist fury that would engulf him and bring his career at Harvard to an abrupt halt. Summers has a long and distinguished record of service to his country. He has made a significant contribution to economics in his work, serving as Chief Economist at the World Bank from 1991 to 1993. He is a man of supreme honesty, integrity, and intelligence, and yet he was destroyed by a vitriolic and sustained storm of hysteria mounted by the feminist lobby in the US, characterised by the headline, 'Not sexist Summers, Please' Such was the storm, President Obama declined to pursue his nomination for Chairman of the Federal Reserve. This is the degree to which feminists are prepared to go in defence of their brittle ideology. This is how afraid they are that it will be challenged.

But what did Summers say that was so damning? I do not propose to deal in depth with his entire speech, but suffice to say it addressed three hypotheses about why women appeared to be under-represented in university tenured professorial posts in engineering and science at top universities and research institutions. He talked about the different aptitudes between men and women and different social factors impacting on men and women in respect of their careers, especially as that seemed to influence women's choices in seeking high-powered jobs. Prefacing his address, Summers said this:[139]

I asked Richard, when he invited me to come here and speak, whether he wanted an institutional talk about Harvard's policies toward diversity or whether he wanted some questions asked and some attempts at provocation, because I was willing to do the second and didn't feel like doing the first. And so we have agreed that I am speaking unofficially and not using this as an occasion to lay out the many things we're doing at Harvard to promote the crucial objective of diversity.

There are many aspects of the problems you're discussing and it seems to me they're all very important from a national point of view. I'm going to confine myself to addressing one portion of the problem, or of the challenge we're discussing, which is the issue of women's representation in tenured positions in science and engineering at top universities and research institutions, not because that's necessarily the most important problem or the most interesting problem, but because it's the only one of these problems that I've made an effort to think in a very serious way about.

The other prefatory comment that I would make is that I am going to, until most of the way through, attempt to adopt an entirely positive, rather than normative approach, and just try to think about and offer some hypotheses as to why we observe what we observe without seeing this through the kind of judgmental tendency that inevitably is connected with all our common goals of equality. It is after all not the case that the role of women in science is the only example of a group that is significantly underrepresented in an important activity and whose underrepresentation contributes to a shortage of role models for others who are considering being in that group.

To take a set of diverse examples, the data will, I am confident, reveal that Catholics are substantially underrepresented in investment banking, which is an enormously high-paying profession in our society; that white men are very substantially underrepresented in the National Basketball Association; and that Jews are very substantially underrepresented in farming and in agriculture. These are all phenomena in which one observes underrepresentation, and I think it's important to try to think systematically and clinically about the reasons for underrepresentation.

Later, drawing his conclusions together, he said this:

So my best guess, to provoke you, of what's behind all of this is that the largest phenomenon, by far, is the general clash between people's legitimate family desires and employers' current desire for high power and high intensity, that in the special case of science and engineering, there are issues of intrinsic aptitude, and particularly of the variability of aptitude, and that those considerations are reinforced by what are in fact lesser factors involving socialization and continuing discrimination. I would like nothing better than to be proved wrong, because I would like nothing better than for these problems to be addressable simply by everybody understanding what they are, and working very hard to address them.

These words were what caused the storm of feminist protest to descend upon Summers. Feminists would rather defend their dogma than engage with the truth. The feminist's reaction to what he said is a classic example of hysteria and displays all the hallmarks of extreme mental stress caused by cognitive dissonance: the violent response of someone who is suffering when people have their most deeply held views challenged by rational thought and honest questioning. Anything that comes even close to questioning whether women are in all respects the absolute equal of men is immediately attacked and drowned in a storm of protest by feminists. It is as though these women cannot bear to hear the truth spoken, and one cannot but speculate that had this event happened just a few centuries ago, Summers would probably have been mobbed and strung up for his heresy by a screaming, fanatical, ravening hoard of women who would have danced as he convulsed on the rope.

Rejection of criticism

Professor Christina Hoff Sommers, who professes herself an 'Equity Feminist', recounts her experience of the reaction of extreme feminists to her challenges of them in her book *Who Stole Feminism?*[140] She too has been vilified by radical feminists and labelled along with Margaret Thatcher, as 'One of those female impersonators'. Here is what she says about the techniques feminists use to suppress dissent levelled against them:[141]

> Toni Mc Naron, professor of English at the University of Minnesota …
> reminds us that, 'proponents of Copernican theory were drummed out of
> their universities or, in extreme cases, excommunicated, jailed and even killed'.
> Acknowledging that contemporary feminists are not likely to suffer the more
> extreme retributions, she nevertheless warns of impending attacks. She
> exhorts feminist academics to 'stand and resist wherever possible the
> onslaughts' of those who find fault with the feminist agenda. Professor Mc
> Naron's remarks were brought to my attention because she mentions me as

one of the persecutors of the new Copernicans. By now, feminists have a well-deserved reputation for being good at dishing it out but completely unable to take it. Many know how to deal with opponents by *ad hominem* or *ad feminam* counterattacks: accusations of misogyny, racism, homophobia, or opposition to diversity or inclusiveness. Some would-be critics fear for their very jobs. In these circumstances a critic may find himself suddenly alone. Others, watching, learn to keep a low profile.

Almost 20 years after its publication, Hoff Sommers's book is a thoroughly balanced and thoughtful piece of scholarship, packed with examples in support of her claims, and that effectively has resulted in her and her fellow dissenters being ejected from the feminist movement. Her rejection is a classic example to the rejection of outside criticism that characterises groupthink, that phenomenon of 'in groups' who reject outside criticism because they believe they possess the truth. However, Hoff Sommers's experience is small beer when compared to Erin Pizzey's experience. Pizzey was an early women's activist who became famous for founding refuges for women in the early 1970s. Commenting on the way the movement conducted itself the early days, she said this about the 1968 women's liberation bra burning incident:

> There were very highly organised Marxist groups of women of one sort or another. I remember being horrified when I saw them storming the Miss World competition, thinking to myself, how can these women talk about liberation for women and women supporting each other and then go and bully a section of other women that they don't like because they are doing something they don't approve of. [142]

About another incident in London, she says this:

> And outside, and this is in the press cuttings, there was a huge demonstration with banners, and on the banners it said, 'All men are bastards'; 'All men are rapists'. And I went down and said to the police, 'If that was black men or Jews, you'd arrest those women, why don't you arrest them' and they just looked very uncomfortable and one of them said, 'We're frightened of them'. [143]

Because of this and other outspoken comments she made against the radical feminists who ultimately took over her movement, claiming it for themselves, Pizzey became the target of extreme venom:

> Over the 12 years that I was running the refuge, if I went to speak there were screaming feminists outside. I tried to publish a book called Prone To Violence, we finally did get it published, but I had to have a police escort all round England and there were death threats and bomb threats. And the final moment came for me, after struggling for all those years, when the bomb-disposal unit came to my house because there was a suspect package and so everything that came to me had to go to them first because they were concerned about my safety and the safety of my family. And that's when I left England and went into exile for something like 15 years. [144]

Taking the Larry Summers incident and this account by Erin Pizzey, and factoring in Christina Hoff Sommers's experience, it is clear that violent intimidation is the weapon of choice of feminists to both stop anyone criticising what they are trying to bring about and to help ensure that their views are embedded. There is no doubt that feminism is a totalitarian ideology that is intent on overcoming any opposition by fair means or foul, and there is equally no doubt that the mental state of feminists today, as in the past, amounts to a toxic mixture of psychological conditions to which I shall now turn. Some of these affect individuals, and some of them affect groups, but understanding what is going on helps us explain much of the work of feminism among us today.

Mind games

In my chapter on Feminism 101, I refer to Daphne Patai and Noretta Koertge, and their book, *Professing Feminism: Education and Indoctrination in Women's Studies*,[145] in which they talk of 'The sea of propaganda' that overwhelms the contemporary women's studies classroom, where 'sisterly sophistries' are peddled by hard-line feminists who seek to change the outlook of idealistic female students in their typical women's studies classes. Christina Hoff Sommers describes the same phenomenon thus: '...they turn these idealistic young women into relentless grievance collectors'. What is happening in our universities is brainwashing, it is not education. Young women are undoubtedly having their perceptions of men changed by tutors and mentors who are radical ideologues, and this is a process that has been ongoing for at least two generations since the early 1970s, but today we are seeing more and more young women being turned out from these courses, overly sensitised to see patterns in men's behaviour through the lens of feminism, and to make connections in their daily lives that reinforce feminist stereotypes of men and women.

The psychological mechanism at work in this is 'Apophenia' - the experience of seeing meaningful patterns or connections in random or meaningless data. It has been observed in gambling, in paranormal experiences, in religious manifestations, the New-Age idea of synchronicity, in divination - and in conspiracy theories. As Vaughan Bell, writing in The Guardian on 17 November 2013,[146] said, 'From seeing shapes in clouds to hearing Bing Crosby in a blizzard of static, we're all prone to finding things that aren't there. And there's a name for it: apophenia'. One of the unfortunate side effects of human cognitive architecture,[147] it pushes us to look for meaning where it seems least obvious, and Klaus Conrad,[148] who wrote about it in a monograph in 1958, has decisively associated it with the onset of schizophrenia. Dr. Michael Shermer, describing the same phenomenon, which he names 'Patternicity', points out that the brain is 'a belief engine' which, as soon as it takes in sensory data, immediately begins to look for and construct patterns, which it then infuses with meaning in a positive feedback loop of belief confirmation, which ensures that those beliefs are reinforced as truths and the sure knowledge that we are right that what we *think* is happening, really is happening. Summarising this, he says:

> We form our beliefs for a variety of subjective, personal, emotional, and psychological reasons in the context of environments created by family, friends, colleagues, culture, and society at large; after forming our beliefs we then defend, justify, and rationalize them with a host of intellectual reasons, cogent arguments, and rational explanations. Beliefs come first, explanations for beliefs follow.

Unfortunately, as Shermer also points out, our brains haven't developed a 'baloney-detection network' yet: a mechanism that allows us to distinguish between true and false patterns, and in his 2008 book *The Believing Brain* (2011),[149] he says that this process can lead to what he calls 'Agenticity'. Not only do we possess '... the tendency to infuse patterns with meaning and intention', we also infer agency behind those infused patterns. For example, we think a certain person's actions are done with knowing, deliberate intent. Added to this is the knowledge that the human brain is highly selective about the information it receives, which leads to confirmation, or 'my side', bias. In this selectivity, only those perspectives that fuel previously held views or perspectives tend to be selected, whilst the rest are ignored or dismissed. This is very apparent in people who seem unable to 'hear' others' opinions and see their points of view, however valid or factually grounded their opinions might be. Confirmation bias is stronger when the issues are emotionally charged. In that case, people tend to seek almost any evidence, however ambiguous, factoring it into their existing position.

One of the most dangerous effects of confirmation bias is the 'Backfire Effect,' a situation when individuals who are presented with evidence that directly contradicts what they believe become even more entrenched in their beliefs, placing greater emphasis on the earliest evidence that led them to those beliefs. Confirmation biases are also capable of perpetuating an 'Irrational Primacy Effect', where totally discredited beliefs continue to be held even when the primary evidence for them is negated or removed. The young women exposed to feminist indoctrination in our universities, feminist meetings, etc., are clearly sensitised to attribute intention to men's actions, which they see as somehow wrong, distasteful or dangerous. The most repeated example of this is the allegation that men are objectifying them, for instance when a man compliments them or they are whistled at in the street. This is then reinforced through social media.

The most glaring example of this is the *Everyday Sexism Project*, a web-based campaign based on a repository of young women's perceived grievances about men's behaviour towards them, which, they allege, are 'Sexist'. This is a neologism for the new social 'crime' of objectification, the theory inspired by Simone de Beauvoir, which denies men's expression of sexual attraction to women, behaviour which normal people would interpret as equally normal behaviour with no malintent. The accounts posted by young women to the site clearly display pronounced symptoms of apophenia, patternicity, and my side bias. The woman behind the web site and the campaign to stamp out everyday sexism is Laura Bates, a thirty-something feminist fanatic with an almost child-like quality about her, who has acquired a considerable following of similar women of her age and younger, all of whom believe they are being continually sexually harassed by any man who shows even the remotest sexual interest in them. Even a man who looks directly at one of them, say on public transport, immediately becomes sexist and in need of condemnation.

Bates presents herself as something of a *Jean d'Arc* at the head of a moral crusade, and speaks to large audiences of the faithful in sentences that amount to a series of feminism mantras strung together, presenting cherry-picked and wrongly interpreted official statistics as factoids in order to prove her case. Despite having the error of her factoids pointed out to her publicly, many times, she continues to use them, which makes her behaviour tantamount to culpable spreading of disinformation, and a clear example of backfire effect at work in her. Bates has clearly tapped into a nerve in already sensitised young women who are convinced that the age-old mechanism of male attraction for a young woman is a threat to them and their safety, and she has provided the means by which they can rally to their collective defence in solidarity, thus giving them the confidence to expose every occurrence of every day sexism. This, of course, feeds back to Bates, thus justifying her role as a social warrior and campaigner, even though most sensible people see the entire syndrome as highly infantile, hyper-sensitised young women whose activity is bordering on hysteria.

Groupthink

The deliberately induced tendency of feminists to seek solace and safety in their sisterhood leads us to another psychological manifestation of feminism. If the tendency towards conformity of any group becomes extreme, the phenomenon previously identified as 'groupthink' can manifest. Groups are especially vulnerable to groupthink when they comprise people of similar age, social and psychographic backgrounds, and especially where there are no clear rules for group conduct or collective decision-making. Professor Irving Janis first described the effect in 1972, after he had studied the aftermath of the Bay of Pigs invasion of Cuba, and other foreign policy disasters of the Kennedy cabinet in the early 1960s. In essence, groupthink leads to a group making faulty decisions because group pressures for conformity lead to deterioration of 'mental efficiency, reality testing, and moral judgment,' as Janis puts it. Groups so affected often ignore alternative paths to the resolution of issues upon which they have to decide, and are prone to engage in irrational actions. One of the most pronounced features of groupthink is the tendency to dehumanise other 'out groups'. Janis defined eight symptoms of groupthink, as follows:

1. An illusion of invulnerability that allows excessive risk taking.
2. Collective rationalisation. A refusal to listen to criticism and failure to reconsider assumptions when challenged.

3. Belief in inherent morality. A belief in the rightness of their cause to the extent that the ethical and moral consequences of decisions are ignored.

4. Stereotyped views of 'Out' groups. Negative views of 'the enemy' make effective responses to conflict seem unnecessary.

5. Direct pressure on dissenters. Group members are put under pressure not to express arguments against any of the group's views.

6. Self-censorship. Doubts and deviations from the perceived group consensus are either not expressed or covered up.

7. Illusion of unanimity. The majority view and judgments are assumed to be the unanimous opinion of the group.

8. Self-appointed 'Mindguards'. Certain members take it upon themselves to protect the group and the leader from information that is problematic or contradictory to the group's cohesiveness, views, and/or decisions.

I suggest that groupthink is at work in many of the social expressions of feminism today. For example, Mike Buchanan,[150] a prolific author on the subject of feminism, and leader of the political party Justice for Men and Boys (and the women who love them) persistently calls out vociferous feminists who falsely misrepresent research in support of their cause. In one notable case, he appeared before the House of Commons Business, Innovation and Skills Committee (20 June 2013) that was carrying out an enquiry entitled *Women in the Workplace*, along with Dr Heather McGregor, Managing Director of Taylor Bennett, an employment headhunting firm, a Guardian columnist and member of the steering committee of the 30% Club, an activist organisation that seeks to ensure more women are represented on UK corporate boards. McGregor refers to her Guardian readers as 'sisters' and it is a reasonable inference that she is a feminist.

Prior to their appearance, Buchanan emailed details of five longitudinal academic studies, a number of which were of companies in Norway where enforced quotas for women on corporate boards had been introduced. These studies showed that the increased presence of women on the boards of the respondent companies had a detrimental effect on their company's financial performance. Dr McGregor had acknowledged receipt of these studies before the hearing, through her PA, who said Dr McGregor had found the content of his email, 'very interesting'; however, when questioned at the inquiry, and asked if she had read the studies, Dr McGregor said:

I believe that Mr Buchanan is referring to a study in Norway, but I do not
know because he has not said so. The study in Norway, where they have had
quotas, Mr Chairman, shows that there has been no change in the financial
performance of companies, despite the fact that they now have 40% of
women on boards.

After the hearing Buchanan called McGregor out on this, enclosing the relevant
extract from the draft minutes provided by the Clerk to the Committee, which
laid what she had said out clearly, and reminded her of their email
correspondence before the hearing, which showed that the evidence she had
given was factually incorrect. This is a very serious matter. Knowingly giving
false evidence to the House of Commons, is not only legal contempt, but
perjury. The House of Commons is the supreme power in the land.

McGregor failed to respond, so Buchanan blogged about it, quoting the
House of Commons instruction to witnesses as follows:

The House of Commons has emphasised the obligations on witnesses to be
honest and open in the evidence, which they give to committees. Knowingly
to mislead a Committee is contempt of the House. If you have become aware
that you need to make corrections of any matters of fact or interpretation to
ensure that the final record of what you said to the Committee is accurate and
complete, you should submit a separate note, which will be appended to the
evidence either as a footnote or as a freestanding memorandum.

He invited her publicly to make a correction to her statement to the inquiry,
saying that unless he received an assurance to that effect, he would submit all
the evidence to the committee. Buchanan's second blog on the matter reads like
this:[151]

In the absence of a response [from Dr McGregor], I contacted the clerk to
the committee, asking that the matter be brought to the attention of the
inquiry's chairman. I don't know if Dr McGregor corrected the statement
voluntarily or after coming under pressure to do so, but the corrected report
has just been published...

He then goes on to publish the corrected minutes:

Chair: Have you read these longitudinal studies that Mike Buchanan has talked
about? If you have, have you any comment on them?

Original statement from draft minutes	**Statement from revised published minutes**
Dr McGregor: I believe that Mr Buchanan is referring to a study in Norway, but I do not know because he has not said so. The study in Norway, where they have had quotas, Mr Chairman, **shows that there has been no change in the financial performance of companies**, despite the fact that they now have 40% of women on boards.	Dr McGregor: I believe that Mr Buchanan is referring to a study in Norway, but I do not know because he has not said so. The study in Norway, where they have had quotas, Mr Chairman, **shows that there has been negative impact on financial performance due to the precipitous nature of the way quotas have been introduced in that country**.

Clearly this is a significant change, and one can only speculate as to why it came about. One might in fairness perhaps think that Dr McGregor had been so busy that she didn't have time to read the data Mr Buchanan had sent her in advance, although it has to be said a summons to appear before a House of Commons Committee is such an important event one would have thought she would have prepared thoroughly. Perhaps her PA's response was just a standard politeness and a put off, or maybe he or she did not consider it important enough to pass it on to Dr McGregor? Whatever the reason, it is reasonable to say that her original answer before the highest authority in the land was significantly corrected.

Could it be that Dr McGregor was suffering from groupthink? Was she so much under that illusion of invulnerability observed to be a symptom of the psychological mechanism at play between members of 'in' groups that she failed to recognise that empirical evidence was available that challenged her conviction? Could this be evidence of the collective rationalisation that feminists have in their rigidly constructed belief system that leads them to believe those beliefs are unimpeachable? Does Dr McGregor have such an inherent faith in feminism as a moral cause that she cannot see the ethical and moral consequences of her failure to factor in hard evidence that might show her cause not to be so morally just? In the light of this incident, I suggest these questions raise the very real possibility that feminists do suffer from groupthink.

Symbolic Convergence Theory

Symbolic Convergence Theory (SCT) is another robust and well-proven theory, recognised by the academic community for its elegant simplicity and practical utility, which informs other aspects of feminists' behaviour. Emory Griffin, Professor of Communication at Wheaton College, Illinois for 26 years and author of *A First Look at Communication Theory (1991)*,[152] says it has been used to study the emergence, development, decline and fall of social phenomena in a wide arc of experience, including the Puritans, American communism - and the women's movement. SCT is a theory of communication that explains why groups can become highly cohesive through shared emotions, shared motives and shared meanings, even though the members of the group may not necessarily know one another. The idea is that members of a group communicate by exchanging fantasies about their experiences of past events based on the emotions attached to the experience.

These fantasies might be about dreamed-of future events, as we saw in the small sample of delusional feminist writers whose literary outpourings about utopianism demonstrated complete detachment from reality, or they can be driven by the emotion of anger, which we saw in the vile utterances of Valerie Solanas and her *SCUM Manifesto* - that 'Society for Cutting Up Men'. Chillingly, SCT predicts how feminist in-group fantasies can lead to a chain-reaction within the group, fed by positive and energetic responses to the initial fantasy. Griffin (Ibid.) says this about it all:

> Through symbolic convergence, individuals build a sense of community or a group consciousness. As symbolic convergence ties a group together with cohesive bonds, a sense of togetherness is formed. Individual members begin using the words 'we' instead of 'I,' and 'us' instead of 'me'. Members may even become attached to each other, and sometimes, group conformity takes place... [Individuals] assume a joint venture.

Thus, the *Everyday Sexism Project* and the groupthink of the feminist sisterhood can be understood through SCT. Thus lesbianism can be seen as a key component of the 1970s feminist movement, just as it was in the Suffragette movement 100 years ago.

SCT also gives us an understanding of the development of groups such as feminism in four observable stages from inception to decline, as follows:

1. Emergence or creation
2. Consciousness raising
3. Consciousness sustaining
4. Vision declining
5. Terminus

Stage One is characterised by a dramatic event or series of events that lead to a feeling of uncertainty and the need to develop a rhetoric (a fantasy vision) in order to explain what is happening. So-called 'Fantasy Theme Artistry' develops the rhetoric in a way that makes the fantasy attractive, so members of the group share it, and integral to that process is the demonstration of an understanding of the issues people face by those who are promulgating the fantasy. In particular, this involves sharing stories common to the group, and using the stories to speak answers into the stories based on the developing group's rhetoric. This is always in favour of the rhetoric, never against it. This rhetoric-to-reality link seeks to chronicle an authentic account of the fantasy, and bind it to tangible evidence. The patriarchy myth of feminism is an excellent example of this process in action.

However, a shared group consciousness can only ever exist within the rhetorical community if the fantasy is to be able to develop into a saga. The telling and re-telling of the accomplishments and events in the lives of key players in the group, or the group *en masse*, develops a rhetoric which is packed with symbolism. This shared group consciousness then creates common ground on which develops mutual understanding, shared social reality, and a meeting of minds through empathetic communication. Once this stage is reached, the members have true group consciousness and no longer think in terms of 'I' or 'me' but in terms of 'us' and 'we'. Thus the group culture is formed, which reduces uncertainty in its members and that goes on to influence group norms, roles and future decision-making.

We can apply this easily to the emergence of feminism in the late 1960s, remembering the social upheaval that characterised that era, and it is easy to see how SCT must have been afoot in those turbulent times. In particular we can see the emergence of 'symbolic clues,' another SCT term that summarises the use of words, phrases, slogans and nonverbal signs or gestures, such as 'free love', 'women's liberation', 'male chauvinist pig', 'burn your bra', 'freedom trash cans,' etc. In SCT theory, these symbolic clues are believed to trigger previously shared fantasies and emotions, and their use heightens a group's cohesiveness, and there seems little doubt that they did.

In Stage Two of SCT, the fantasies begin to 'chain-out' into collectives of people sharing a common interest. The university campuses of west coast America, the hippy communities, and places like Greenwich Village in lower Manhattan in New York City, are historical examples of this process underway. Stage Two also involves the co-creation of a new vision that allows the participants to take on a new reality for their lives: a new meaning and new emotions that induce behavioural changes. We need only look to Betty Friedan's ideas that whipped up the discontent of women in the 1950s to see this at work in feminism. It is in this stage that ICT tells us the 'Principle of Critical Mass' emerges. Once the shared rhetorical vision is achieved, it starts a period of rapid growth that leads to a wider consciousness-raising. Crucial at this stage is the 'Principle of Dedication', in which members of the group have their consciousness raised even further through the use of planned events, which further inspire them by resonating with the key emotions present at the event. We could have no better example of this than the meeting that took place in Town Hall,[153] New York in 1971, as anyone who watches the video available on YouTube will see.

Stage Three in SCT is the 'Consciousness Sustaining' phase, where the focus is on maintaining the commitment of the people who share the rhetoric and its vision. Here, the 'Principle of Shielding' takes over, where the vision is defended against change by the quashing of counter messages. Then the 'Principle of Rededication' kicks in, where severe criticism of any counter-criticism is used to sustain the vision, assisted by the 'Principle of Reiteration,' which serves to sustain the rhetorical vision by restating the key fantasy themes through adapting them to the present reality, whilst framing any new information within the old rhetoric so as to maintain its explanatory power. In my submission, feminism has been in this phase for some years now.

SCT then says things can change suddenly. If the vision cannot adapt successfully, it will die. This is explained by the 'Principle of Explanatory Deficiency': when a rhetorical vision loses its explanatory power it declines. One of the key triggers for this is the 'Principle of Free Speech'. Feminism works hard at suppressing free speech through extreme political correctness and, often, sheer mob outcry at anything that speaks against it. However, sooner or later, free speech reasserts itself in a democratic society, and then a deluge of counter-rhetoric exposes the fantasy of the group's rhetorical vision, puncturing it like a balloon. Through the 'Principle of Resurfacing Competitive Rhetorical Visions', communication channels are opened up with the in-group, light dawns on some of its members, and that leads to a contradictory rhetoric invades from outside, which competes with the group rhetoric, finally overwhelming it.

The end of the rhetorical vision, (and specifically, I submit, the end of feminism, when that comes about) is Stage Five: Terminus. This final phase is when the 'Principle of Rapid Implosion' applies. It is rapid because the inflexible rhetorical vision means it cannot adapt. It is so brittle that it breaks under the increasing and eventually overwhelming pressure of the competitive rhetoric, with its contradictory aims and motives. This, I predict, is what will happen to feminism - one day - and the key trigger will be the degree to which contradictions to its rhetoric are articulated and pressed home by the opposing forces of men's rights advocates, which are building into a movement. This is happening now, and it is an irony that the originator of this complex but fascinating social theory, Ernest Bormann, is a former professor of communication at University of Minnesota, one of the hot-beds of feminism today.

The retreat of reason

According to Anthony Browne in his acclaimed book, *The Retreat of Reason*,[154] 'The easiest way to overcome the dissonance between what you believe and the evidence, is not to change what you believe, but to shut out the evidence and silence those who try to highlight it'. This is precisely what the Larry Summers episode was all about. Feminists metaphorically put their hands over their ears and said, 'La, la, la' when challenged about their ingrained prejudices. The truth no longer exists in objective reality in the feminist echo chamber, where only factoids and myth support pre-held beliefs. Rather than say, 'I disagree with what you say, but I would like to hear your side,' they say, 'you cannot say that. I disapprove of what you are saying'. Thus feminists seek to bring other people's thoughts and words under their moral jurisdiction, which is riding roughshod through people's right to freedom of thought and freedom to express those thoughts. As Baruch Spinosa said, '… in a free state every man may think what he likes, and say what he thinks.'[155] This feminist oppression is a flagrant denial of this principle.

Their ideology is so brittle that even flippant or humorous remarks will instantly be taken as heresy and reported in the media as though it was a crime to say such things. The 'perpetrator' (that much loved word in feminist rhetoric that condemns in its very expression) will then receive widespread opprobrium, which serves to dumb him down. Let me give an example of this in action, so as to illustrate the point. Under the headline, 'UKIP faces renewed accusations of sexism as Stuart Wheeler claims women are not as competitive as men...' here is what Nigel Morris, Deputy Political Editor of The Independent newspaper reported on 15th August 2013:

> For a party at pains to combat its reputation as a refuge for older men with views most kindly described as traditional, it was not the most helpful of comments... the UK Independence Party is facing renewed accusations of sexism after its treasurer suggested women should not be promoted to company boards because they were not as good as men at chess, bridge or poker... Mr Wheeler spoke his mind at a debate on whether 'gender quotas' should be imposed on companies to force them to appoint more women to senior positions. 'I would just like to challenge the idea that it is necessary to have a lot of women, or a particular number, on a board,' he said. 'Business is very, very competitive and you should take the performance of women in another competitive area, which is sport where [men] have no strength advantage. Chess, bridge, poker - women come absolutely nowhere. I think that just has to be borne in mind'.
>
> Clare Gerada, the chairman of the Royal College of General Practitioners, who was at the debate, immediately berated him for the 'disingenuous, sexist comment'. She said: 'My mother, at 83, is the biggest bridge champion and continues to be year on year. I think that is such a disingenuous, sexist comment'. Mr Bloom, who also attended the discussion on quotas, protested that women were sometimes given preferential treatment in the workplace. He joked that he and the party's leader, Nigel Farage, wanted an invitation to a 'bunga-bunga' party hosted by former Italian Prime Minister Silvio Berlusconi. UKIP, which has just conducted extensive testing of potential European election candidates to root out those with maverick views, played down the 'tongue-in-cheek' comments. But the Labour MP Alison McGovern said: 'These offensive and ignorant comments are yet more evidence that Ukip has become the laughing stock of British politics. Stuart Wheeler should apologise and he should try thinking before he opens his mouth, too'. Mr Wheeler later denied his comments were sexist. He said: 'All I was saying was there are areas were women are not as good as men, I'm sure there are areas men are not as good as women and therefore I don't think it's always essential to have a minimum number of either'.

A Ukip spokesman said: 'Mr Wheeler's comments were an anecdotal example to underline the point that quotas are not the way to appoint company boards. Companies, like any organisation, need the best they can get to ensure they survive in a competitive world. 'Meanwhile it was abundantly clear to every person in the room that the comments made about Berlusconi were a joke, something the media seem to have a huge problem wrapping their heads around'.

Clare Gerada's cry of 'disingenuous, sexist' is typical of the feminist response to criticism, and how it supplants reason, and it is astonishing that at the time she was Chair of the Council of the Royal College of General Practitioners, one of the most prominent and important positions anyone could hold in our society, that demands the highest level of professional expertise and balanced judgement. Yet the word 'sexist' sprung readily to her lips. For Gerada, her feminist ideology clearly takes precedence over her professional standing, to such a degree that she is prepared to use her high profile position to attack a man, also in public life but not in her sphere or within her remit, because he is making comments that challenge her ideology. Rather than engage constructively with what Wheeler said (which is what you might reasonably expect from a very senior doctor - the head of her profession), rather than try to counter his position with constructive arguments of her own and to win the intellectual debate with thoughtfulness, or, indeed, just keep out of something that isn't part of her remit, Gerada immediately jumped to the defence of feminism, hurling the term 'sexist' at Wheeler in breach of the basic 101 logical fallacy of the *ad hominem* attack.

These are the tactics of someone who has no counter-argument, or whose intellect is so low that they cannot assemble a counter-argument: they ill-befit Gerada's background, or her role as head of the Royal College of General Practitioners. Feminists do this, of course. They seem unable to understand that their allegation of sexism is in its very essence, sexist. They criticise their critics' behaviour, whilst engaging in the very thing they accuse others of doing, which is the hypocrisy of totalitarianism. Of course, it goes without saying that in order to be able to see one's own hypocrisy one needs an open mind to others' views (and a sense of humour), but sadly these attributes seem to be lacking in much of feminism's interaction with the world. Instead, its acolytes continue to throw insults and accusations of sexism at people, an approach which is all too normal, such is the degree to which the insidious ideology of feminism has penetrated all levels of the feminist psyche. And the sad thing is, it is working. Today, just about everyone in our land believes that sexism is a valid accusation, and that to be sexist is to hate women.

Political correctness

This is all about political correctness (PC), the spawn of feminism, which is used to such enormous effect to control free speech and silence dissent, and also to subvert democracy. As Brown (op. cit.) says, the first reaction of politicians when confronted with a set of policy options in any area is not to find the right answer, but to seek the PC answer, and gauge how it will play with the PC police. He avers that even when politicians know the right answer they choose the PC way in an effort to avoid controversy and not offend the powerful lobby behind it. This leads to difficult issues being fudged for fear of a backlash, and it applies to people in prominent positions in public life too.

The most obvious example of this is the business leaders who are being subjected to enormous pressure from feminists in government (many of them in Conservative party ranks, it has to be said) to raise the representation of women on corporate boards, and who are using artificial means to sidestep the issue. Rather than face the issue head on, which is simply that far less women than men seek such positions, they sidestep it by appointing women non-executive directors, paying them enormous sums of money out of shareholders' funds, in return for very little value. This cannot be in the interests of the shareholders whose firms they manage, and it represents a craven capitulation in the face of ideological pressure.

These businessmen (and, yes, they are mostly men) are using the age-old cop-out of doing things right rather than doing the right thing and acting in their shareholders' best interests, because they know that if they do that, they will attract the attention of the feminist mob as did Larry Summers. In fact, this amounts to a capitulation to a small but influential group of women who are using PC to their own advantage and securing sinecures that, by and large, they don't really deserve. PC and feminism are two sides of the same coin: a coin that is forged from the metal of Marxism. As Brown (op. cit.) says:

> Political correctness started as a study of cultural Marxism in 1920s Germany and was adopted by the counter-culture that emerged in the 1960s, which challenged conservative values that were the hallmark of that period... [and] spread its tentacles across the West.

William Lind, director of the Centre for Cultural Conservatism in the United States, agrees with this, and also describes PC as cultural Marxism, which he defines as Marxism translated from economic into cultural terms.[156] This is what he says about it:

> The cultural Marxism of political correctness, like economic Marxism, has a single-factor explanation of history. Economic Marxism says that all of history is determined by ownership of the means of production. Cultural Marxism, or political correctness, says that all history is determined by power, by which groups, defined in terms of race, sex, etc., have power over other groups and nothing else matters.

Richard Bernstein, culture correspondent of The New York Times, also developed the argument in his landmark article in 1990, where he said:[157]

> Central to pc-ness, which has its roots in 1960s radicalism, is the view that Western society has for centuries been dominated by what is often called 'the white male power structure' or 'patriarchal hegemony.' A related belief is that everybody but white heterosexual males has suffered some form of repression and been denied a cultural voice.

Here we see the link forged between feminism and PC and how it is used to great effect by feminists as a uniquely effective way of helping their ideology spread, unfettered by open dissent.

By the turn of the twenty-first century, PC had completed its short march to enslavement of people's tongues. In just 40 years or so, it had managed to install itself as the dominant and dominating culture of the universities and public institutions in the US, Canada, and Britain, where it remains, embroiling them in its web, tying people's tongues for fear of being off message, installing its anti-male rhetoric, the ideas of patriarchy and women's inherent oppression by men, and the supporting mechanism of the sisterhood. Not only is feminism the day-to-day culture on campus now, it is in lecture theatres, the tutorial rooms, and the offices and boardrooms of university authorities, which are now largely populated by feminists and their fellow travellers. This cultural Marxism is now embedded in the very soul of these institutions and PC is the means by which it is maintained.

What is more, these institutions have turned the entire ideology into an academic discipline, complete with faculties with professorial chairs, PhD candidates and masters' students (all of them populated by women, of course), as any Google search of the term 'gender studies' will reveal. The extent to which this is happening throughout the developed world is astonishing, with Ivy League universities, such as Harvard, Stanford, Yale, Princeton, Oxford, and Cambridge in the lead. In fact, it is hard to find universities that do not have gender studies faculties or offer courses in feminism. They amount to factories of feminism, annually churning out tens of thousands of young women who are filled to the brim with a belief that women's rights and women's equality are the driving issues of the era.

However, the equality and liberation they are being taught are not the true liberal enlightenment values of equality of opportunity exercised in a free democratic society, those admirable aims of the Enlightenment. What these young women are learning is the enforced equality of the communist collective, that system in which everyone is reduced to being the same as everyone else, and brought under uniform social control; where the rights and opportunities of the individual to find his or her own level in any walk of life are dumbed down to mean equality *qua* sameness, equality *qua* parity of numbers, etc. From doctors' surgeries to hospitals, from local government to national government, from universities to colleges and schools, from major corporations to the police, the church, and the media, feminist PC is now the embedded, dominant culture, which is tying the tongues of people who have a right to freely disagree with it, and it is installing an inbuilt antipathy to Western cultural values. The US commentator, Paul Weyrich, President of the Free Congress Foundation in America, confirms this when he says:[158]

> The United States is very close to becoming a state totally dominated by an alien ideology, an ideology bitterly hostile to Western culture. Even now, for the first time in their lives, people have to be afraid of what they say. This has never been true in the history of our country. Yet today, if you say the 'wrong thing', you suddenly have legal problems, political problems, you might even lose your job or be expelled from college. Certain topics are forbidden. You can't approach the truth about a lot of different subjects. If you do, you are immediately branded as 'racist,' 'sexist,' 'homophobic,' 'insensitive,' or 'judgmental'.

For Britain, the moment of total capitulation to PC came when Tony Blair's 'New Labour' won a landslide victory in 1997. As Browne (op. cit.) says, 'In

1997, Britain became governed for the first time by a government largely controlled by politically correct ideology,' and the feminist credentials of New Labour are well known, starting with 'Blair's Babes', the 101 women MPs, many of them elected from women-only candidate short lists in a flagrant denial of democracy, who were paraded to the press days after his landslide election in 1997. Amongst these women were some extreme feminist ideologues, such as Harriet Harman, one of the most radical feminists ever to get her hands on the levers of power: she was appointed by Blair as the first ever Minister for Women; and Yvette Cooper who said, '… our F-word is feminism' in her speech to Labour's National Women's Conference in September 2012.

PC is the technique of choice of feminists who are intent on exercising their social control to reshape society to their ideology. Using it, they define and dictate the terms and parameters of our social debate, and modify any social utterance that challenges them before it is even formed on a dissenter's lips. Using PC, this powerful elite of women maintains women's needs at the forefront of the social agenda, ensuring that they trump any other social issue such as poverty, immigration, the disabled, the old, the young, and so on. All must stand in line behind the feminism test. We must never forget that the operative term here is '*political* correctness', the means by which totalitarian communist/fascist/Nazi regimes have traditionally controlled people under their thrall, thereby ensuring that they maintain 'correct' positions on matters of doctrine and dogma. Neither must we forget that it is nakedly borrowed from Marxist communism, to which it is inextricably linked, just as Norman Mailer spotted as long ago as 1971 at that pivotal meeting in Town Hall, Manhattan.

Games feminists play

It is all a bait and switch process, of course, that works in the same way as radical religious or group identity in drug or alcohol rehabilitation programmes. There is comfort to be obtained from having a difficult or hurtful experience put in a clear, comforting context, accompanied by a clear explanation of why things are as they are, and shared with others going through the same experience. Then, when a solution to the problem is placed on offer, people will grab it like a drowning man will grab a lifebelt. From there it is easy to engender a common belief and a common purpose, and this is what feminism does. PC plays straight to the hurts and emotions of women, especially in their difficulties with men, or at a time in their lives when they are forming their views of the world and life ahead of them, but it is a deception because it takes those personal difficulties and offers a political answer. It makes the personal political, and the political in this case is a Marxist ideology that ultimately seeks to control people by organising them into the collective, where they are conformed to what amounts to communism. It is radicalisation pure and simple, and it is at work today in our young: for example, the *Everyday Sexism Project* mentioned earlier, and in how it is feeding off this new breed of radicalised young women.

The entire exercise is the outworking of a well understood psychological game, 'Rapo', as defined by Dr Eric Berne, the creator of Transactional Analysis (TA), which is now a mainstream psychological therapy, and which uncovers the dynamics of human relationships, defining them in terms of the 'Games People Play'.[159] Berne said, these games comprise '... an ongoing series of complementary ulterior transactions progressing to a well-defined, predictable outcome... a recurring set of transactions... with a concealed motivation'. The *Everyday Sexism Project* is perfect evidence of this process in action amongst a certain type of young woman today. First degree Rapo, also known as the 'Kiss off' or 'Mock indignation' game, is a mild flirtation game often played out in public. At this level of the game, a woman signals that she is sexually available, gaining pleasure when a man responds and pursues her. As soon as the man becomes committed, she calls time on the game, often ending it abruptly, and moves on to the next conquest, leaving the man to make more complicated manoeuvres if he wishes to follow her and press his suit. This, of course, is the normal flirtation process between women and men, but nowadays, young radicalised feminist women, obsessed by the feminist idea of objectification, are twisting it to turn the natural advances of a man into something that is offensive to them.

Even a cursory glance at the *Everyday Sexism Project's* website reveals endless accounts by young women that confirm this. However, there is now clear evidence that Second degree Rapo is being played by some young feminists. This is where a woman obtains greater satisfaction from her rejection of a man's advances than she does from receiving them. Berne explains this version of the game as a woman who leads a man into a more serious commitment or expression of attraction to her, which she then repulses openly, thus gaining her satisfaction from his discomfiture. One of the most notable examples of this came on 9th July 2015, when a 27-year-old barrister, Charlotte Proudman, made an unsolicited approach to a leading legal aid solicitor, Alexander Carter-

Silk, on the professional networking website LinkedIn, inviting him to connect with her - ostensibly, it seems, so she could expand her network of potential providers of legal briefs. Carter-Silk graciously accepted her invitation on 7th September as follows:

> Charlotte. Delighted to connect, I appreciate that this is probably horrendously politically incorrect but that is a stunning picture!!! You definitely win the prize for the best Linked in [Sic] picture I have ever seen. Always interested to understand people's skills anyhow we might work together.

To which Ms Proudman replied:

> Alex. I find your message offensive. I am on linked-in [*sic*] for business purposes not to be approached about my physical appearance or to be objectified by sexist men. The eroticisation of women's physical appearance is a way of exercising power over women. It silences women's professional attributes as their physical appearance becomes the subject. Unacceptable and misogynistic behaviour. Think twice before sending another woman (half your age) such a sexist message. Charlotte

One might regard this as not exactly the perfect way for a young and inexperienced barrister to treat such an influential potential provider of work, but her private comments pale into insignificance in light of the fact that she took the amazing step of publishing the exchange on her Twitter account, as follows:

> How many women @Linkedin are contacted re physical appearance rather than prof skills? @Jessica_Asato @ObjectUpdate

This was favourited 40 times and retweeted 58 times. It was picked up by the press and social media, and resulted in a storm of articles and contradictory exchanges - both in support and against - most of which questioned Ms Proudman's motives, suggesting that she was doing a very good job of destroying her future career.[160] In fact, her motives can be very well explained in terms of Second degree Rapo. Third degree Rapo is a much more serious matter, and it is becoming more and more apparent in so-called 'third wave' feminists, who are becoming increasingly obsessive in their pursuit of their angry creed. At this level, a woman will lead a man into a compromising physical contact with her, then claim he has assaulted her and caused her irreparable damage, thus gaining enormous power over him. However, in its most cynical and serious form, Fourth degree Rapo, the woman might even allow the man to complete the sexual act with her, then make an allegation of rape, thus gaining total power over him.

This is where the current sexual climate of alleged everyday sexism is leading us. The thousands of reports by over-sensitised young women are evidence of a social-sexual time-bomb waiting to go off. These are the professional 'grievance collectors' described by Christina Hoff Sommers, who are pumped up on feminist ideology, which sensitises them to see sexism everywhere, and they follow a known psychological game-playing pattern. Like Charlotte Proudman, they are often highly educated, clever young women, just like their counterparts in the 1960s and 1970s (and, indeed, like Christabel Pankhurst). They are often graduates who have been imbued with feminism in the foetid culture of our universities, from which they emerge articulate, passionate, focussed, blogging and tweeting incessantly, repeating and embedding what they have learned. The most prominent amongst them are courted by the media to write polemical articles so as to whip up controversy and attract readership (in some of the most respected newspapers, it has to be said). They appear constantly on television current affairs programmes whenever an issue about women in society comes up, and all this adds to the intensity of chatter about feminism, which becomes a self-reinforcing, self-building, self-feeding frenzy that plays directly into a well understood psychology.

Western society is now acutely aware of the dangers posed by the radicalisation of the young by extreme Islam. However, it seems unable to understand that our young are being radicalised by a set of radical academics who are possibly just as dangerous to society. These 'clerics' don't wear eye patches, or have hooks for a hand, they wear blue stockings and they occupy professorial chairs in just about all of our universities, from which they are influencing our young to accept their radical ideology through so-called 'gender studies'.

A martyr for the cause?

Another current young women's feminist icon is Caroline Criado-Perez, the feminist activist, who campaigned to get Jane Austen's image on the Bank of

England £10 note. Ms Criado-Perez chose her moment well, just when Mark Carney became the new Governor of The Bank of England and, being a Canadian, a country where feminism is absolutely rampant, was keen to be seen ingratiating himself with feminists. Perez, described as 'a low-rent journalist', is a flagrant self-publicist in pursuit of her radical feminist views, even to the extent that she is willing, with her mother, to lay out her damaged background for the world to see. No doubt she is seeking to emulate her role models from the past, learned about in her post-graduate master's gender studies course, which she openly declares she is studying. Under the title 'Independent Women: Ali and Caroline,' she uploaded an intimate conversation between her and her mother Alison ('Ali'), as part of the BBC Radio 4 Listening Project, which was broadcast in October 2013 on BBC Radio Leicester, and it is now placed in the British Library Sound Archive, so it is legitimate material from which to draw to illustrate my points. Here is a relevant extract:

> [Presenter:] Ally is 64 and a mother of three. She was married to a businessman who moved from country to country. She and the family followed him wherever he went. But, they got divorced and her daughter Caroline wanted to talk a bit about that time…
>
> [Caroline Criado-Perez: talking to her mother] 'My two memories, sort of traumatic, I suppose memories of you after the divorce were, ones that I heard of actually, rather than I saw. I remember, I don't know if you told me about you going and lying down in the snow and just crying and crying and crying. And then the other one; you were in Battersea Park up a tree or something or you were up a pagoda or something and crying and crying and some nice man came and talked you down…
>
> [Ali Criado-Perez: the mother] That's right, yes. I know. I'm sorry that you had to hear those stories…
>
> [Caroline] Well they're very, very vivid to me, but to have been in that position, to be so unhappy and lost and empty and desolate…
>
> [Ally] Oh dear! That's awful…
>
> [Caroline] Yeah.
>
> [Ali] I really never knew until this minute that's how you felt, I'm really s… about things like that
>
> [Caroline] Well yeah. It was really horrible actually
>
> [Ally] Well hopefully it was a positive experience for you when I picked myself up.
>
> [Caroline] I was influenced both negatively and positively. As in negatively by seeing how unhappy you were, knowing that I could never ever put myself

in the position you put yourself in or ended up in, with dad and, positively, in that seeing how happy and fulfilled you've become since you've started living a life in which you have autonomy, in which you get to decide what it is that you do and where you go, and you can make those decisions for yourself.

[Ally] Oh dear. But I don't want you to have ended up thinking that you cannot be happy in a relationship, because you can have relationships where it's like, as I've said, the Khalil Gibran thing of two trees growing up side by side

[Caroline] Obviously the other thing that's affected me negatively in terms of relationships is the very difficult relationship I had where I was very badly damaged by it, and I think that, you know, these negative experiences are good in a way because they do make you stronger. It's a cliché but that's a cliché for a reason, they do make you stronger. Watching my mother being incredibly unhappy has made me realise I need to be autonomous and independent and, having experienced a relationship where I had that taken away from me, has made me even more determined to never let that happen to me again. And you know I sort of fell into that and want a break up again.

[Ally] I was so impressed with you because you have so much more strength, emotional strength, than I do and that you could see a relationship was bad for you and you broke it off and you've become the strong, independent woman that you are at the moment.

[Caroline] The idea of relying on anybody else outside circumstances terrifies me.

[Ally] Mmm … (reflecting)

[Caroline] I can't imagine why anyone willingly would put themselves in that position…

This might move some people. As the presenter said when introducing the piece, 'We heard a bit about the echoes of divorce that still resound in their lives', and yes, it is sad when a child suffers from the divorce of her parents. After all, she didn't ask for it, nor did she have any part in it, other than purely as the victims of circumstance. However, you can almost see the hand held in anguish, its back to the forehead of the female presenter. Here is the badly-treated mother who, despite the pain and upset caused to her by the father of her child, nevertheless sees her daughter win through and become, 'the strong, independent woman': almost a heroine, who is getting on with life despite the vicissitudes of a hegemonic male-dominated world, with which she has to contend daily, and in which she finds support from her mother who has suffered so much. Frankly, these messages are beginning to sound like an old record, stuck in its groove.

Rational people, who nevertheless are compassionate, might see this entire exercise as a form of exhibitionism. They might take the view that for someone to place such an intimate insight into private lives on public display suggests a psychological motivation for doing so. More cynical people, perhaps psychologists, might see it as narcissism. What is clear is that this is intended to show, yet again, how women who become emotionally damaged by men resort to rationalising their experience in the framework of feminism, from which they obtain a strategy for future life, and I am left wondering whether women like Ms Criado-Perez (and her mother for that matter) really see the pattern that clearly exists in their behaviour? In their subjective angst, I wonder if they are able to see the degree to which they are exposing their psychological state to the world? What is the psychology behind such deeply personal nakedness, I wonder? Do they see themselves as heroines forged in adversity prepared to lay themselves down for the cause in a just struggle?

Caroline Criado-Perez was subjected to a tirade of abuse on her Twitter stream at the time of the announcement of her success in getting Jane Austen's image on a bank note. She was besieged for days on end by internet trolls who made the most vile comments about her, and even threatened her with rape and murder, and she expressed herself as being very afraid. Feminist sisters everywhere supported her, not least Jenni Murray of BBC Woman's Hour, who tweeted her support, and the press was hugely sympathetic. However, she was no shrinking violet. An accomplished user of Twitter herself, she defiantly fought back using choice language worthy of any barrack room. She was just as aggressive as the trolls. Yet, one would have thought that the most sensible thing for her to do was to be quiet and protect herself. The irony of it all was that the most extreme threat came from a woman in the North East of England, who was finally caught by the police and later imprisoned for her crime (along with a hapless and rather inadequate young man). And what is stranger than that, Ms Perez took on the forgiving martyr role and defended her publicly on television, saying that she had acted out of patriarchal conditioning. That is the degree to which these young feminists are steeped in their creed, and it shows the degree to which they are radicalised into the belief that it is all men's fault.

I speculate that feminism is now reaching such dangerous levels of indoctrination that a martyr for the cause could easily emerge. Any monitoring of their Twitter streams and their chatrooms will show that there is a rising sense amongst them that the movement has become stalled, and a new energy is needed, which is why, of course, they pull their publicity stunts to keep their message (and themselves) firmly in the public eye. The narcissistic need and the emotional atmosphere surrounding feminism is now reaching such dangerous heights that it is getting dangerously close to a syndrome in which a young woman will see it as worthy of laying down her life for the cause. After all, it took the passionate young Emily Davison running out in front of King George V's horse Anmer at the Epsom Derby on 4th June 1913, to galvanise the Women's Suffragette movement and project it firmly into the public gaze. Most people believe Davidson tried to kill herself for the Suffragette cause, even though recent analysis of what she did strongly indicates that what she was doing was trying to grab the jockey's reins so she could stick a banner on the horse, demanding votes for women. Davison was engaging in a stunt for women's suffrage that went horribly wrong when she was knocked to the ground like a waif by the massive animal in full gallop. In fact the only suicide in that incident was the jockey, who took his own life some years later by putting his head in a gas oven.

Whether suicide or accident, however, the Suffragettes turned Davidson into a martyr for the cause. Rather than being laid to rest by her family quietly and with dignity in the country churchyard in rural Northumberland where her remains rest, the Pankhursts and the Women's Social and Political Union staged a lavish funeral in central London, with thousands of Suffragettes accompanying the coffin, and tens of thousands of members of the public turned out to see them, lining the route of the cortege 10 deep. Thus, public opinion that had been shifting against these strident, law-breaking women was swayed back to them and their cause. It was a wholly cynical publicity stunt perpetrated on the back of a tragedy, and I suggest feminists today would not be reluctant to embrace another martyr for their cause. Could it be that another radicalised, extremist young woman, full of hysterical zeal, and whipped up by a passionate hatred of patriarchy, will become a martyr for the cause? God forbid that anything so serious happens, but the possibility of such a thing is very real in the current foetid feminist atmosphere.

The 'herstory' of hysteria

On 2nd December 2013, a violent, taunting, screaming mob of pro-abortion feminist women[161] confronted a line of praying priests in front of the cathedral in Buenos Aires in Argentina. In what amounted to a sustained bout of hysteria, these women displayed a level of violence and sheer unrestrained anger against the priests, which knew no bounds. Some of the men were clearly seen to be weeping as they held the line against this baying mob, but none of them made any retaliation against the abuses heaped on them. LifeSiteNews reported the incident as follows:

> The women, many of them topless, spray-painted the men's crotches and
> faces and swastikas on their chests and foreheads, using markers to paint their
> faces with Hitler-like moustaches. They also performed obscene sexual acts in
> front of them and pushed their breasts onto their faces, all the while shouting
> 'get your rosaries out of our ovaries'.

According to the *InfoCatolica* web site, some of the women chanted a song, with the lyrics: 'To the Roman Catholic Apostolic Church, who wants to get between our sheets, we say that we want to be whores, travesties [Sic][162] and lesbians. Legal abortion in every hospital!'

The authoritative source of information about mental disorders, the *Diagnostic and Statistical Manual of Mental Disorders* (DSM), published by the American Psychiatric Association since 1952, is relied upon worldwide by psychologists, psychiatrists, clinicians, researchers, drug regulation agencies, pharmaceutical companies, policy makers, and the legal system. It is where experts go for reliable information about mental illness. No longer, it seems. Hysterical Neurosis, as hysteria is technically known, was listed within its lexicon of psychological disorders but it was removed in 1980. Why? You might well ask.

The answer is that feminists within the profession of psychology saw to it that it was written out of history. This psychosomatic, peculiarly female condition, has been recognised and well documented for over 3,000 years as being associated with disturbances of the uterus, but feminists had it deleted because it was no longer politically correct. The evidence for this claim comes from a simple comment posted by a Dr Charles G. Sanderson on an article entitled, *In Defense of Hysteria*,[163] written by David Kronemyer and published by him on 18th January 2010. Here is the comment:

> Great article in the spirit of Mark Michale's work. The recent DSM changes
> were uncritical and subject to the criteria of being 'politically correct.'

Both Kronemyer's article and Sanderson's comment are but a tiny whisper in psychology circles today, because the subject of women's hysteria is taboo: it just isn't allowed anymore. Here is what Kronemyer says in the opening paragraph of his article:

> It now is fashionable to dismiss early psychologists like Jean-Martin Charcot, director of the Salpêtrière Hospital in the late nineteenth century and the modern inventor of hysteria. Charcot had plenty of raw materials to work with; Salpêtrière housed over 5,000 female patients, many of who [sic] were insane, demented, destitute or deemed 'incurable'... It [Hysteria] was applied predominantly to women and thought to be caused by disturbances of the uterus.

Hippocrates believed that too - around 2,400 years ago. He is one of history's outstanding historical figures. The founder of the Hippocratic School of Medicine, he is considered the father of modern western medicine and his oath, the Hippocratic Oath, underpins medical practice to this day: 'first, do no harm', and 'I will not give to a woman an abortive remedy'. The Greeks gave us the word 'hysteria'. It comes from hystera, which means uterus (as in hysterectomy - the removal of the uterus), but its understanding was hoary with age by the time Hippocrates' came on the scene. Nevertheless, feminist activism succeeded in expunging not just the word but the entire condition from existence just a few decades ago. Kronemyer (Ibid.) lays this action bare:

> There came a time when hysteria became an unpopular diagnosis. The Mental Disorders Diagnostic Manual (precursor of the DSM) deleted hysteria, institutionalizing its disappearance. Hysteria also has gone almost completely missing from current psychiatric literature. Diagnoses (such as hysteria), 'disappear as time elapses or even cease existence under the influence of certain social developments, while other, new entities take their place' (Libbrecht, p. 170). Various explanations for this have been offered. The most popular one is that, from a post-modern standpoint, gender relations became absorbed in medical discourse; when women are the doctors and the theorizers, rather than the patients, the narratives of hysteria change (Showalter et al., 1993).

Kronemeyer's words cannot be misunderstood. Women doctors saw to it that gender relations became the overriding consideration and this caused hysteria to be expunged as a psychosomatic condition of women. This is a truly amazing thing. A political ideology has re-written history and changed the narrative about the sort of activity I described earlier. The Argentinian outrage is only the tip of a very large iceberg, but feminist bigots have seen to it that what it really is, hysteria, is not politically correct. This is worthy of George Orwell's novel *Nineteen Eighty-Four*,[164] in which his principal character, Winston Smith, is employed re-writing history so that The Party's policies are always coherent - even when the policy changes. However, the sanitisation from the medical books of a long-known condition cannot fully succeed in removing it from reality. Kronemyer again:

> Hysteria carries a 'resonance' for commentators because of its 'textual tradition'. It is a 'powerful, descriptive trope' even in non-medical domains, including poetry, fiction, theater, social thought, political criticism and the arts. In this way it sheds light on the history of disease in general (Micale, 1994).

History might be re-written by totalitarian ideologues, books might be burned, documents shredded, and computer records deleted, but some things are so much part of the common understanding that they cannot be expunged. It is one thing interfering with the current official medical documentation, but it is entirely another when it comes to the plethora of references to hysteria in poetry, theatre, politics, the arts and so on burned into folk memory. Although the diagnosis of hysteria has a long history, much of it abandoned today, these 'powerful, descriptive tropes' are recorded in so many different ways and at so many different times that it is impossible to wipe them from the historical slate. So what really is hysteria? What are its manifestations? In what circumstances does it occur?

In a comprehensive paper on the subject, Tasca, Rapetti, Carta and Fadda[165] say that as far back as the second millennium BCE, the Ancient Egyptians recognised it as a peculiarly female psychological disturbance that manifested as a depressive syndrome and could involve seizures and a sense of suffocation or imminent death (Freud later called these *globes istericus*). The *Kahun Papyri*,[166] dated to around 1825 BCE, identify the cause of hysterical disorders as the spontaneous movement of a woman's uterus, and the *Eber Papyrus*[167] from 1600 BCE describes various therapeutic measures for remedial treatment of the condition, all aimed at adjusting the position of the uterus. They point also to the ancient Greeks recognising hysteria. (Tasca et al.):

The Argonaut Melampus, a physician, is considered its founder: he placated the revolt of Argo's virgins who refused to honor the phallus and fled to the mountains, their behavior being taken for madness. Melampus cured these women with hellebore and then urged them to join carnally with young and strong men. They were healed and recovered their wits. Melampus spoke of the women's madness as derived from their uterus being poisoned by venomous humors, due to a lack of orgasms and 'uterine melancholy' Thus arose the idea of a female madness related to the lack of a normal sexual life: Plato, in Timaeus, argues that the uterus is sad and unfortunate when it does not join with the male and does not give rise to a new birth, and Aristotle and Hippocrates were of the same opinion.

Thus, the ancient Greeks not only made the connection between hysteria and the uterus, but also found a cure for it - sex. When women 'who refused to honor the phallus' took on a form of madness, they were urged to have sex with lusty young men and 'they were healed and recovered their wits', and we cannot escape the remarkable connection here with the widespread lesbian anger of radical feminists, not least those women in the episode in Argentina. Hippocrates was the first to use the term 'hysteria',[168] describing it more technically, as follows:

The Greek physician provides a good description of hysteria, which is clearly distinguished from epilepsy. He emphasizes the difference between the compulsive movements of epilepsy, caused by a disorder of the brain, and those of hysteria due to the abnormal movements of the uterus in the body. Then, he resumes the idea of a restless and migratory uterus and identifies the cause of the indisposition as poisonous stagnant humors, which, due to an inadequate sexual life, have never been expelled. He asserts that a woman's body is physiologically cold and wet and hence prone to putrefaction of the humors (as opposed to the dry and warm male body). For this reason, the uterus is prone to get sick, especially if it is deprived of the benefits arising from sex and procreation, which, widening a woman's canals, promote the cleansing of the body. And he goes further; especially in virgins, widows, single, or sterile women, this 'bad' uterus — since it is not satisfied - not only produces toxic fumes but also takes to wandering around the body, causing various kinds of disorders such as anxiety, sense of suffocation, tremors, sometimes even convulsions and paralysis. For this reason, he suggests that even widows and unmarried women should get married and live a satisfactory sexual life within the bounds of marriage. However, when the disease is recognized, affected women are advised not only to partake in sexual activity, but also to cure themselves with acrid or fragrant fumigation of the face and genitals, to push the uterus back to its natural place inside the body.

So, the lack of a healthy sex-life in young women, 'within the bounds of marriage', is being inextricably bound up with the hysterical condition - and with its cure. Hippocrates recommended unmarried women should get married. Put as lightly and as delicately as possible, regular sex does much to keep the uterus from moving out of position, and prevents toxicity building up in a woman's body that can lead to psychological disturbance.

Aulus Cornelius Celsus (1st century BCE), in ancient Rome, also described hysterical symptoms, and Claudius Galen (2nd century CE) wrote about it in very similar terms to those used by Hippocrates. Galen said, 'I have examined many hysterical women, some stuporous, others with anxiety attacks ... the disease manifests itself with different symptoms, but always refers to the uterus'. Galen's treatments (which were used by medics until modern times) included purges, administrations of hellebore,[169] mint, laudanum, belladonna extract, valerian and other herbs, repressing stimuli that could excite a young woman - and he, too, advised getting married as beneficial.

Throughout the Middle Ages, we see repeated references to hysteria, all described with the same symptoms (and with the same causes), thus proving it was the same condition being described. Constantine the African described women who had what he called *amor herocycus*: 'the madness of love,' by which he meant unfulfilled sexual desire. In the 11th century, Tortula de Ruggiero, a woman physician from Salerno, Italy, and a known expert in women's disorders (she was called *Sanatrix Salernitana*: 'the woman healer of Salerno'), refers to hysteria being a woman's problem, and gives advice on how to deal with it: by placating sexual desire and using sedative remedies including musk oil and mint. Tortula also refers to sexual abstinence as a cause of this female illness.

Inevitably, during this time, bearing in mind the religiosity of the period, the hysteria becomes bound up in the religio-political milieu. Hysteria becomes associated with evil and sin. For example, Hildegard of Bingen (1098-1179), a German abbess and mystic, talked of 'slender and minute women, unable to fix a thought,' who were infertile because of a weak and fragile uterus. She attributed this to the dogma of original sin. Tasca et al. (Ibid.), with interesting flavours of the events in Argentina quoted earlier, flesh out the picture thus:

From the thirteenth century onwards, the struggle with heresy assumes a political connotation: the Church aims at unifying Europe under its banner, so breviaries become manuals of the Inquisition and many manifestations of mental illness are seen as obscene bonds between women and the Devil. 'Hysterical' women are subjected to exorcism: the cause of their problem is found in a demonic presence. If in early Christianity, exorcism was considered a cure but not a punishment, in the late Middle Ages it becomes a punishment and hysteria is confused with sorcery… But what has this to do with women's health? It is quite simple: if a physician cannot identify the cause of a disease, it means that it is procured by the Devil. The inquisitor finds sin in mental illness because, he says, the devil is a great expert of human nature and may interfere more effectively with a person susceptible to melancholy or hysteria. Hysteria is considered a woman's disease, and who more than women are prone to melancholy? This disease is the basis of female delirium: the woman feels persecuted and the devil himself is the cause of this 'mal de vivre', which deprives the women of confession and forgiveness, leading them to commit suicide.

After the Renaissance, we have a record of the physician and theologian Giovan Battista Codronchi (1547-1628) criticising the medical therapy for hysteria used at the time. Apparently, to put it as delicately as possible, midwives took care of hysterical women by introducing their fingers into the women's genital organs to stimulate orgasm, and by the time we get to the eve of the Modern Era, Thomas Willis (1621-1675) introduces a new set of causes of hysteria, which he no longer attributes to the uterus, but to the brain and the nervous system. Then, in 1680, another English physician, Thomas Sydenham (1624-1689), fluctuates between a somatic and a psychological explanation of hysteria. His work opposes religious-historical prejudices, especially the theory of 'uterine fury' which, by then, was firmly established, and which later became known as nymphomania.

There were several such outbreaks of hysteria in the seventeenth century, the most famous of which (or infamous, depending on how you look at it) was in the village of Salem, Massachusetts where, in 1692, a number of young, unmarried girls became 'possessed'. Nineteen of them were hanged as witches and a hundred more were detained in mental sanitoria. Marion Starkey, writing in the 1940s, compared these events to contemporary times, and concluded that they were classical hysteria manifesting in puritanically repressed young women, aggravated by the intervention of dogmatic pastors. We cannot escape another similarity with modern times in the conduct of young women on our university campuses who engage in anti-rape demonstrations and slut walks. They have left home with all its strictures on behaviour, much of that the result of the natural tension between parents (and fathers in particular - assuming they have one) and pubescent teenagers going up to university with their new-found freedoms, and being subjected to the 'dogmatic pastors' of radical feminists in their faculties and the 'rape culture' that is common parlance there.

Just 50 years or so after Salem, Joseph Raulin published a work in which he coined the term *affection vaporeuse* for certain symptoms in women that undoubtedly were those more commonly called hysteria. He believed this condition came about as a result of poor quality air in big cities, and an unruly social life. Echoing this, Pierre Roussel and Jean-Jaques Rousseau developed the idea of 'the excesses of civilisation' preventing the fulfilment of a woman's natural maternal purpose and that this was a causal factor in the imbalance of women's moral and physiological balance, resulting in hysteria. As Tasca et al. say, 'The incident [Salem] proves thus that hysteria could be seen as a consequence of social conflicts'.

We now take a leap to the late nineteenth and early twentieth century, and to Sigmund Freud, who reversed the paradigm. He saw hysteria as a disorder caused by the lack of libidinal evolution, rather than it being due to a lack of motherhood and sexual expression (all linked, of course, to his Oedipal Conflict theories). In Freud's analysis, the symptoms of hysteria become the 'primary benefit' that allowed the discharge of the libidinal urge. This release of libidinal energy, he argued, remained associated with sexual desire, and the woman uses this to manipulate the environment to serve her needs. The failure to conceive of women caught in this syndrome becomes the result and not the cause of the condition, according to Freud, who asserts that women use their libidinal energy to manipulate their environment, so as to serve their needs. It is easy to see why Freud is now declared *persona non grata* in many feminist circles, because this is precisely what feminists are doing in broader society. The evidence is all around us: the united sisterhood is running rampage, invading male institutions and male social spaces, colonising campuses, conspiring to bring about all-women prospective Parliamentary shortlists, pressing for more women on the boards of our commercial corporations - the list is endless.

As the twentieth century progressed, an inverse relationship emerged between the diagnosis of hysteria and the diagnosis of depression, probably because of the social and socio-economic changes precipitated by two world wars, an intervening economic depression, and increasing social pressures on people, which caused a general lowering of people's spirits. The same symptoms of hysteria, self-blame, low self-esteem and feelings of helplessness in women now became located in a depressive diagnosis. Tasca et al. point to an example in Africa during a period of increasing westernisation, during which disruptive economic development over highly compressed timescales overturned long-standing, traditional patterns of life and resulted in communities having to move from a subsistence economy to one in which people, particularly women, had to strive for economic individualism in a consumer economy, but without the support of a close-knit community. Their lives were no longer determined by fate but by a harsh responsibility for self and one's own future. To illustrate this, Tasca et al. cite a study carried out amongst the Namwera area in Malawi during such a social transformation. Following a popular referendum, which resulted in a multi-party democracy, an 'emotional earthquake' occurred in the people, who were suddenly forced to choose between innovation and tradition. In fact, the situation developed into 'a full-blown epidemic of hysteria among young women,' which prompted the study in which three age-matched groups of women were chosen: dressmakers, farmers/housewives (traditional role), and a group of nurses and obstetricians, who represented the innovative roles women were increasingly playing. Amongst other things, the study measured the degree of satisfaction the respondents had with their jobs, their married lives and other 'social inventory variables'. Innovative occupations were found to be the source of greatest satisfaction for the women. Housewives and dressmakers in particular were more dissatisfied with their situation than nurses, for example, but all showed increased psychopathological symptoms, and these were found to be due to a significant increase in interpersonal and couple conflicts, all the result of the changes in relationships brought about by the women's new roles (Tasca et al. Ibid.):

> The number of depressed subjects diagnosed according to DSM-IIIR was higher. Housewives also experienced an increased frequency of psychosomatic symptoms, such as headache, excessive fatigue, feelings of worthlessness, and often reported suffering from the conviction that people did not recognize the importance of their role, and that someone could affect their health, which is interpretable as an external localization of the source of their distress.

It has been said that the outbreak of feminism in the late nineteenth century was due to social tension caused by, on the one hand, acute social inequality in which many women were little more than baby factories and, on the other, middle-class women's growing boredom in a burgeoning economy in which rapid social and economic changes caused women to feel worthless on both sides of the social divide. The women's suffrage movement was a classic example of this sense of worthlessness in these Edwardian women who were the products of their era: that time when society was enjoying '… a period of pleasure between the enormous achievements of the Victorian age and the abyss of a half-century of war'. These women were basking in the wealth of a prosperity created by the Industrial Revolution, but that same phenomenon had created enormous poverty and social pressure for the working classes, and substantial shifts in political power were underway. Worker-power, egged on by Marxism and the Labour Party, was rising and the no doubt guilt-ridden middle-class Pankhursts sought to change the role of women in society on the back of that, using radical activism, very similar to the Argentinian episode I described earlier (albeit in a somewhat more constrained social context).

We must never forget the Suffragettes' angry anti-social behaviour: their illegal activities, which would not even be tolerated even today, and their histrionics. A number of them undoubtedly were hysterical young women who even went on hunger strike and had to be force-fed by the authorities to keep them alive. If ever there was a demonstration of a pronounced lack of self-worth this undoubtedly was it. And we must remember that many of these women were almost certainly lesbians. Emmeline Pankhurst, the mother and founder of the Women's Social and Political Union, whose activists were known as Suffragettes, had a close relationship with the known lesbian composer Ethel Smyth for many years, following the death of Emmeline's husband, who had been 28 years her senior, and Christabel Pankhurst, her firebrand daughter, was almost certainly a lesbian, having had an intimate relationship with Annie Kenney, a working class activist in the movement. Christabel never married, although she adopted a daughter, Betty, in California, where she died, alone, in 1958. All of these behaviours fit into the pattern of hysterical behaviour, known for millennia.

By the 1950s and 1960s, after another seismic social upheaval, this time caused by World War II, and in the settling down period following it, we saw the emergence of another form of hysteria in women, who were both privileged and at the same time unfulfilled and unsettled. Just as in the pre-Suffragette days, this was a time of growing prosperity that meant women (in America at least) effectively became birds trapped in a gilded cage of affluent domesticity and child rearing. Betty Friedan exemplified this in her 1963 book, *The Feminine Mystique*, in which she railed against her mother's metaphorical imprisonment in 1950s suburban conformity. Friedan's book was the spark that lit the mass outbreak of hysteria we call feminism today, and this, in turn, has led to a further breakdown in relationships between women and men - the break-up of countless marriages, and increased domestic friction, all of which form a feedback loop, making the entire problem become worse and worse.

Today we see more expressions of feminist hysteria. Slutwalks: women dressed as sluts, marching and protesting against what they call a rape culture in society today, followed by speakers' meetings, live music, receptions and parties, sign-making sessions for the next event, chanting, martial arts practice, and open microphone sessions in which women describe their experiences of rape. This phenomenon began in Canada after Constable Michael Sanguinetti, a Toronto Police officer, suggested that 'women should avoid dressing like sluts' as a precaution against sexual assault. *Wise words indeed.* However, that prompted feminist activist women to take to the streets taunting men to rape them. Is anyone going to suggest this is normal, balanced behaviour? It is as hysterical as the women in Argentina demanding 'get your rosaries out of our ovaries'.

These are all unmistakable manifestations of hysteria, no different from Salem. All the social upheaval of the last 40 years, the increased dissatisfaction of women with their lot, the increased interpersonal discord between women and men, the increased couple-conflicts, and divorce: all of these are the cause and effect of a condition in women that has been known for at least 3,000 years. Hysteria, that woman's condition, caused by dysfunctional sex lives, that has been known throughout the history of mankind, is alive and well in feminism, just as is the political correctness that is working to suppress the truth about what is going on, which is hysteria. By way of reinforcing this, allow me to return to where I began, to David Kronemyer and his *Defense of Hysteria* article:

> In my opinion the current disapproved state of hysteria results from historical revisionism and medico-cultural imperialism. Women around the turn of the last century who were thought to be suffering from hysteria actually were suffering from hysteria. Even though this diagnosis now may be

incomprehensible to us it defined and structured the then-prevailing symptomatology. In this respect hysteria is like many of the other culturally-deficient aspects of the DSM (Regier et al., 2009). In this respect I am in substantial sympathy with the views of Paul Feyerabend (1975) regarding the incommensurability of scientific theories.

If it walks like a duck and quacks like a duck, then it's a duck! Hysteria might have been wiped from the medical lexicon, but that doesn't wipe it from existence, and we need to recognise that hysteria is playing a significant part in modern feminism. If I might paraphrase Betty Friedan, it is 'the problem that has no name,' because it has been subjected to feminist revisionism.

Feminists might have declared hysteria to be non-PC, and have seen to it that the part it plays in their activities, from as long ago as the Suffragettes, has been redacted from the official diagnostic authority; they might have declared that knowledge of what is really going on is now taboo, but that doesn't stop us seeing the pronounced psychosocial outworking of hysteria in feminism, which is being used as a means of social manipulation. Feminism is a system of lies, built on lies, and promulgated by lies, and it is being used to whip up a mighty head of steam in susceptible young women today, by playing to their innate susceptibility to this psychophysical condition. Feminists might complain (as they do) that men have expunged women's achievements from history, and some of them might even go so far as to say that 'history' should be 'her-story'. Well, I suggest 'her-story' has hysteria running through it like a sliver thread.

CHAPTER 9

INSTITUTIONALISED FEMINISM

'People crushed by law, have no hopes but from power. If laws are their enemies, they will be enemies to laws; and those who have much to hope and nothing to lose, will always be dangerous.'

Edmund Burke

Domestic politics

All political parties today have feminists within their ranks, such is the degree to which this ideology has come to dominate the political process. Despite its extreme left-wing origins, feminism has displayed an almost unique ability to transcend traditional political leanings, and insert itself into political thinking right across the political spectrum. In Britain, the British Labour Party is the nurturing parent of feminism (for obvious reasons: Marxism is its pulsing heart), and it has been so since its inception in 1900. Whenever Labour gained sufficient political power with a strong enough majority, it implemented radical socialist agendas. It did so between 1945-1951 under Clement Attlee, who implemented social security and health initiatives, and it did it again in 1997-2007 under Tony Blair. But this time the socialist agenda was feminism.

Because it was formed from a coalition of left-wing interests represented by seventy different organisations, mostly trade unions, the British Labour Party has always had a strong tradition of Marxist solidarity. After all, its very *raison d'être* is the political representation of Marx's proletariat - organised labour, united against the bourgeois capitalist system. However, because it is a coalition, one of its principle weaknesses has been infighting, and that has always cost it dear at the polls in general elections. The Attlee government lost massive support in only five years because of internal disunity over policy and it was plunged back into opposition for 13 years. In fact, in the 100 years or so of its existence, Labour has only held office for 23 of those years and, with two significant exceptions, 1945 and 1997, it mostly struggled with inhibiting, narrow majorities. The rest of the time it has spent as the official opposition, unable to constrain its inherent progressive radicalism, its anti-capitalist elements, and, lately, its feminists. All of these factions have consistently worked behind the scenes to spread their particular doctrines and influence the party to their narrower political aims.

Labour has always had a strong female spirit within its ranks. (The 'sisterhood' of feminism reflects the 'brotherhood' of Marxist organised labour. Feminism is to all intents and purposes a trade union of women.) The idea of solidarity of men and women being equal comrades, living in peace and harmony - that classic communist principle - finds a resonance in socialist women, as does the ideal and the spirit of togetherness that Labour professes (although consistently fails to practice). Women have always been solidly behind Labour's left-wing aims, and many of them have been firebrand Marxists who have agitated for social change and shaped Labour's agendas, policies and tactics from within its ranks for most of the century of its existence. Today, Labour has more than its fair share of such women in Parliament, and they are almost exclusively feminists. (This is a form of entryism, a topic to which I shall return.) Their breakthrough came under Tony Blair and his reinvention of the Labour Party to New Labour, which resulted in his landslide victory at the polls in 1997, and a full 10 years of power between 1997 and 2007. In that time, he and his feminist colleagues unleashed unrestrained feminism upon Britain.

New Labour

When Tony Blair was elected in 1997 he had 101 women MPs, whom he and his wily press officer, Alastair Campbell, presented to the world as 'Blair's Babes,' parading them to the media for the entire world to see. Blair, of course, was at centre stage on the photographs and footage. This was the gloss, the spin, but behind it feminism was well and truly on the political agenda. 'Blair's Babes' demonstrated to the world the degree to which Tony Blair had changed the traditionally male working man's party into a party whose main focus was the women's vote. Blair and his New Labour architects had seized on feminism as the road to power and they had it at the centre of their broader political agenda. In fact, rather than rename the party New Labour, it would have been much better named the Feminist Party, for that is what it really was.

I do not propose to recount the feminist credentials of all 101 of these women MPs; just two or three of them are sufficient to give the flavour of the extent to which fundamental feminism was a driving agenda in this and subsequent Blair governments, but before I do so, let us take a look at Cherie Booth, the arch-feminist to whom Blair is married. Like Blair, Booth is a barrister. She is a Baby Boomer, born in 1954, and she fits the profile of pretty-well all of the founders of modern feminism born at that time. Her life career path reflects the social mobility of that generation. Cherie Booth was born into a working-class family in Liverpool. Her father was Anthony Booth, the famous TV actor whose character Mike Rawlings in *Till Death Us Do Part*, one of the most successful BBC TV sitcoms ever, that ran from 1965 to 1975, was a layabout socialist husband of Rita, whose father, Alf Garnett, was an anti-socialist, white, racist, ignorant, bullying, dyed-in-the-wool patriarch.

Anthony Booth, it seems, was well cast, for he abandoned Cherie and her mother when Cherie was little, leaving her mother to work in a fish and chip shop on the Liverpool docks so she could provide for her daughters' support and upbringing. Booth went on to marry three more times, siring six more daughters, and becoming the famous TV actor. This experience no doubt equipped Cherie with that classic credential of radical feminist women of her time - a latent hatred and mistrust of men, especially fathers. In her autobiography, *Speaking for Myself*, she recounts how she was the first in her family to go to university, where she took a first class honours degree in Law, before going on to come top of her year's Bar Exams - 'Beating the male élite' as she puts it. She says this about her childhood:[170] 'You know my story: I had opportunities that my mother and grandmother didn't have. I was a beneficiary of the time'. Cherie Blair is now a QC and judge, and founder of an international foundation mentoring young women and girls in the Middle East, Asia and Africa, and she has a strong feminist agenda. During the Blair years at 10 Downing Street she undoubtedly wielded enormous political power behind the scenes. By way of illustration of this, we have an interesting and somewhat humorous account from an insider's viewpoint. Under the headline 'Inside Blair's nest of vipers: Tony was delusional, and Prescott a bully - but the power of Cherie was not to be underestimated, reveals former Labour MP',[171] Bob Marshall-Andrews MP recounts the story of his first encounter with Cherie Blair soon after his election:

> Without a single pleasantry, she fixed me with a beady eye and enquired acidly: 'Where is your wife?' I answered cheerfully: 'Not invited'. 'Not invited?' hissed my hostess. 'Not invited? Didn't you get the directions?' I confessed I had not applied for the directions which, presumably, had included instructions to bring my wife. Cherie's lips set in something approaching a bloodline before she said: 'You will go to the bottom of the list'. There was something in the way she said, 'bottom' which left no doubt that no living thing, however

pestilential or foul, would be likely to inhabit the space beneath that to which I had been consigned. Cherie uttered a sound that would have sent primitive man scuttling to his cave, turned on her heel and disappeared. No one, I realised, should underestimate the power of the Prime Minister's wife. As the newly elected MP for Medway, it was an early lesson in New Labour's instinct for authoritarian control and intolerance of dissent. It was a lesson that would be repeated throughout my 13 years in the Commons.

Cherie has now lost the power of her husband's office to further her agenda, but she remains enormously influential in keeping the feminist cause high on the world stage. Speaking at the 'Women on Boards' debate in London on 5th September 2012, she stated that despite some progress in narrowing the gender gap on FTSE 250 boards, much more needed to be done. 'If anyone in this room thinks everything is all right for women in the UK,' she said, 'I'm afraid they are sadly misguided… I don't want to be depressing about this because there has been huge progress but still there is a persistent gender pay gap. We still have the glass ceiling'. One has to say, perhaps it is Cherie Booth/Blair who is misguided, but back to Blair's Babes.

If I were to write a thousand words about Harriet Harman (b. 1950) and her feminist credentials, nothing could sum them up better than the title she claims on her UK Parliamentary website, where she is listed as the 'Rt Hon Ms Harriet Harman'. Clearly for Harman, 'Ms' ranks up there with the title 'Right Honourable', but what is more telling is her use of Harman, because she is married to Jack Dromey. What is more, they have three children (two boys and a girl): the boys take their father's surname but their daughter takes Harman. It seems political correctness knows no limits in Harman's life. Currently in her sixties, therefore a Baby Boomer, she gained her degree in politics and then trained to become a solicitor. In her early career, she worked for Brent Law Centre in London and then became the legal officer for the National Council for Civil Liberties (NCCL) where, during her time there, she was found in contempt of court by a judge, although she successfully appealed this to the European Court of Human Rights on the grounds that the prosecution had breached her human rights. This experience and her professional probity notwithstanding, in 2004, having been given the post of Solicitor General in the Blair government, she became further embroiled in yet another contempt of court issue when her sister, also a lawyer, who was acting in a family court case, disclosed legally-privileged papers to Harman in her official government capacity. Joshua Rosenberg, the renowned legal affairs journalist, writing in The Telegraph newspaper on 24th March 2004, reports the matter as follows:

> Mr Justice Munby said it was, on the face of it, contempt of court for Sarah Harman, a solicitor based in Canterbury, to have given the documents to her sister in January… A Government department has no right to see a family court file and needs leave from a judge to do so. I do not see how any competent lawyer who had considered [recent case law] could come to any other view.

In this second incident, Harman was cleared of wrongdoing by the Attorney General's office, whose spokesman is reported to have said that she had 'acted in good faith'. However, Dominic Grieve, then Shadow Attorney General, her political opposition counterpart, said he believed the episode was an obvious error that no lawyer should make, and it therefore called into question Ms Harman's ability to run her department. In the Telegraph report he says, 'I would have thought that the law was very clear on this, the documents are confidential, it's as simple as that'. Once again, however, Harman survived her transgression, and she remained the MP for Camberwell and Peckham. First elected to Parliament in 1982, she has been Shadow Minister for Social Services (1984-87), Spokeswoman for Health (1987-92), Shadow Chief Secretary to the Treasury (1992-94), Shadow Employment Secretary (1994-95), Shadow Health Secretary (1995-96) and Shadow Secretary of State for Social Security (1996-97), and deputy leader of the Labour Party.

When Tony Blair took power in 1997, he made her Social Security Secretary and Minister for Women, ignoring completely any imperative for equality for men. In this high office of state, one of Harman's first acts was to skew the newly introduced winter fuel payments for the elderly in favour of women. In a remarkable interpretation of equality, elderly men, who were just as vulnerable to cold, had to wait five years longer to get the benefit under rules she devised. (This was later overturned by the European Union on the grounds that it breached sex discrimination laws.) During her time in office, Harman campaigned hard for the Sex Discrimination (Election Candidates) Act 2002, which allowed political parties to draw up all-women shortlists for prospective Parliamentary candidates, which was the first ever example of affirmative action in the United Kingdom and a naked example of positive discrimination in favour of women. Even within Harman's own party there were deep concerns about these all-women candidate lists; witness the words of Sundip Meghani, a Labour councillor in Leicester, who said this in the run-up to the 2010 general election:

> Dear Labour leadership candidates,
>
> As an ordinary Labour Party member I sometimes feel frustrated and excluded by the party that I have been committed to for the last 10 years. What I joined up to as a movement for the protection of the rights of working people, has in recent years begun to evolve into a top-down London-centric bureaucracy, with procedures and protocols so convoluted that only a complete jobsworth can properly understand them. This, of course, means that any actual control or sense of belonging to the Labour cause rests paradoxically not with the many but with the few; not with ordinary Labour Party members and activists like myself, but with those who either work for the party nationally and regionally, or those who don't work at all and can afford to get wrapped up in minutiae.
>
> It also seems clear to me and countless others that whilst we preach equality to the outside world, we practice discrimination within our own party, particularly when it comes to selecting candidates for election, or even choosing constituency delegates to attend the party's annual conference, to name but two examples. Positive discrimination for some means negative (or 'reverse') discrimination for others, and the reality is that whole swathes of our party membership are treated less favourably, simply because of their gender or their race. As a lawyer, if a client said to me that they only wanted a female barrister or one who was from an Asian background, I would be obliged to either try to modify their instructions, or ultimately cease to act for them. If I did not, I would fall foul of the law myself, because it is quite rightly illegal to discriminate on the grounds of gender or race. All-women shortlists in this country would also be illegal, were it not for the persistence of Harriet Harman, et al., [Sic] who vehemently campaigned for the Sex Discrimination (Election Candidates) Act in 2002, which made the process of selecting Parliamentary candidates exempt from Sex Discrimination laws.
>
> We need to avoid short-term, undemocratic, tokenistic [Sic] practices and focus instead on empowering people from underrepresented social groups. We need to create fair, balanced shortlists for candidates seeking election, and promote individuals not on the colour of their skin or the gender of their body, but because of their extraordinary talents and intellect, their life and work experience, and their ability to advance the needs and solve the problems of their prospective constituents.
>
> Regards, Sundip

Bearing in mind Mr Meghani's background, the irony of the precedence of female discrimination over racial discrimination in Harman's scheme of things cannot go unremarked. Nor can the wider discomfiture of Parliament at what she was up to. During the debate on the Bill, MPs inserted a 'sunset clause', limiting her measures until 2015, so as to avoid any long-term effect of what it said was a kick-start policy to encourage more women MPs. However, on 26 June 2008, having by now achieved the post of Minister for Women and Equalities, Harman ensured the will of Parliament was frustrated by simply announcing an extension of the time limit to 2030 during an oral statement to members setting out key proposals for the forthcoming Equality Bill. (This later became The Equality Act 2010,[172] passed by the Conservative/Liberal Democrat coalition soon after it took power from Labour.) At a stroke, with a simple statement, Harman secured a doubling of what, by any measure, is downright manipulation of democracy. Presumably the end justifies the means, which is a cry often uttered by extremists., And not content with that, Harman set another target to see that 40 per cent of the Parliamentary Labour party are women.

However, her passion for positive discrimination has its limits when it comes to furthering her husband's career. In 2010, as deputy leader of the Labour Party, Harman was unexpectedly absent from a key meeting in the Birmingham Erdington constituency, a traditional Labour seat with a rock-solid majority of 10,000, when a decision about all-women short lists was about to be taken. Her absence meant no weight was put behind her own policy at the meeting, which rejected the proposal. Her husband Jack Dromey was duly nominated, adopted and subsequently elected as a Member of Parliament. An article in *The Express* newspaper on 8th February 2010 entitled, 'Harriet Harman accused of double standards over shortlist,' says this:

> … Labour's deputy leader, 59, is said to have failed to lend her support at a
> key meeting to decide whether to impose an all-women shortlist. One critic
> said: 'Harriet is obsessed with all-women candidate lists, insisting that
> winnable seats should go to the sisterhood, but suddenly she goes missing so
> that Jack can join her in the House'.

This leads to another aspect of Harman's feminist politics: her attack on the family. She has remained unequivocally anti-family and anti-father in her public utterances for decades. In a May 2008 interview she gave to Civitas, the right wing think tank, she insisted that there was, 'No ideal type of household in which to bring up children'. This was a repeat of her views expressed 18 years earlier, when in the 1990 Institute for Public Policy Research (IPPC) report, *The Family Way*, which Harman co-authored, she said, 'It cannot be assumed that men are bound to be an asset to family life or that the presence of fathers in families is necessarily a means to social cohesion'. Erin Pizzey, the early women's activist, famous for founding refuges for women in the early 1970s, who became seriously disenchanted with feminists after they colonised her movement and took it over in order to leverage the enormous sums of government money being channelled towards it, severely criticised Harman over this. Writing in the Daily Mail, she said Harman's views were, 'a staggering attack on men and their role in modern life'. Little wonder, therefore, that Harman has acquired the epithet 'Harm-man' amongst her most adamant critics.

Harman's attitude to the family, which as we know is pure Marxist-feminist doctrine, is set in stark contrast by the report Breakdown Britain (2006), produced by the Social Justice Policy Group a decade after Harman and her colleagues' tender ministrations of our social policy in respect of families. Commissioned by David Cameron, then leader of the Conservative opposition and chaired by Iain Duncan Smith MP, former leader of the Conservative party, the report says this: 'Children whose fathers are absent in their youth experience far greater problems in adulthood'. The report goes on to say:

> The family is where the vast majority of us learn the fundamental skills for life; physically, emotionally and socially it is the context from which the rest of life flows. However, family life in Britain is changing such that adults and children today are increasingly faced with the challenges of dysfunctional, fractured, or fatherless families. This is especially the case in the least advantaged sections of society but these trends also profoundly affect people across the socioeconomic spectrum... We have adopted an inclusive use of the term 'family breakdown' which can be summed up in three key words: dissolution, dysfunction and 'dad-lessness'. Our interest is not narrowly restricted to what happens when parents separate or divorce, partly because solo parenthood (usually solo motherhood) is a growing family type in this country. 15% of all babies are born and grow up without a resident biological father... We have concluded on the basis of the extensive evidence that both family structure and family process matter. The statistics indicate that

marriages are far more likely to provide a stable environment for adults and children than cohabitation and are more resilient when the family is facing a crisis or stressful life event such as childbearing. Importantly we also conclude that family process matters and that families work best and thrive when conflict is low… Central to this argument is the robust evidence that the dissolution of cohabiting partnerships is the main driver behind lone parent family formation in the UK (see B4). Nearly one in two cohabiting parents split up before their child's fifth birthday compared to one in twelve married parents. Three quarters of family breakdown affecting young children now involves unmarried parents. A new study commissioned for this policy group looked at family breakdown amongst the Millennium Cohort Study of 15,000 mothers with three-year-olds. Cohabiting parents with young children were more than twice as likely as married parents to split up, regardless of age, income and other socio-economic background factors.

Despite all this, however, ideologically driven women such as Harman have consistently and persistently built up a case that marriage is unimportant and that men's only value is to provide monetary support so children can be born and reared by mothers alone (or in homosexual/bisexual and transgender situations). In other words, men are redundant as fathers and women can be supported by the State if necessary - allegedly perfectly successfully. In the last 50 years, influenced by feminism, politicians like Harman have progressively removed tax incentives to married couples, they have introduced so called 'no-blame' divorce, and put in place a raft of policies that effectively replace fathers as the main provider for families, turning a blind eye to the iniquitous activity of the family courts, populated by judges who make judgments without wisdom, in a system that prevents decent loving men from having access to their children after divorce. And all of this has sent a strong negative signal about the value of marriage to women, and society at large.

Radical left-wing extremism in a skirt, like Harriet Harman, has devastated the building block of society: marriage and the importance of patriarchy - the rule or authority of the father. It has resulted in an explosion of single motherhood, the ejection of men from fatherhood and serious damage to children, and that Harman has been one of the feminist forces behind all this can be seen from the incident in June 2008, when two members of Fathers4Justice, a fathers' rights organisation founded in 2002, staged a protest on the roof of her house in south east London. Their banner read, 'A father is for life, not just conception'. The police arrested them for a public order offence after they climbed down from the roof. However, complaining that Harman had contemptuously refused to meet them, they did it again in July of the same year; this time with a banner that said, 'Stop war on dads'. Harman denied she had received any request to meet Fathers4Justice.

Ms Harman has been involved in even more questionable issues. As we saw earlier, when she was a newly qualified in 1978, she was the legal officer for the National Council for Civil Liberties (now known just as Liberty). Amongst a number of groups affiliated to the NCCL was the Paedophile Information Exchange (PIE), to which I referred in my chapter about Simone de Beauvoir. Like de Beauvoir, PIE's members argued openly for the abolition of the age of consent for sex and, in its official response to proposed legislation, aimed at reforming sex laws, the NCCL made proposals that argued, 'childhood sexual experiences, willingly engaged in, with an adult result in no identifiable damage'. Harman has denied any association with these views, but it is reported in the press that she signed this document for and on behalf of the NCCL, and her denials notwithstanding, revelations some 30 years later cast further doubt on about the entire issue. On 9th March 2009, Martin Beckford, Social Affairs Correspondent for *The Telegraph* newspaper, published an article entitled, 'Harriet Harman under attack over bid to water down child pornography law' in which he said this:

> The Leader of the House of Commons and Minister for Women and Equality, who also sits on a Cabinet committee on young people's welfare, is being touted as a possible successor to Gordon Brown, but she faces fresh criticism from Opposition MPs and campaign groups after The Daily Telegraph obtained documents showing that she called on ministers to make sexually explicit photographs or films of children legal unless there was evidence that the subject had been harmed. At the time she made the official submission, she was a senior figure in a civil liberties organisation that wanted the age of consent to be lowered to 14 and incest decriminalised. It also defended self-confessed paedophiles in the press and allowed them to attend its meetings. Last night Tim Loughton, the Shadow Children's Minister, said: 'Clearly there is a serious conflict of interest with the committees she sits on, who might want urgently to clarify her position on the exploitation of children for the sexual gratification of adults. 'It's a shame that Miss Harman's zeal for positive discrimination and all things politically correct among adults does not extend to the exploitation of children. Any child who is used for the sexual gratification of adults counts as an abused child and needs protecting'.

Then, five years later, on 18th February 2014, the MailOnline published another article, this time by Guy Adams, entitled, 'How three of the party's most senior figures campaigned for a vile paedophile group now being probed by police for "abusing children on an industrial scale"'. Adams named Harman along with her husband Jack Dromey and another senior labour figure, Patricia Hewitt MP, all of whom had held senior positions at the NCCL during the period in question. Indeed, Hewitt was the NCCL's General Secretary throughout the time in question, again leaving her job to become one of 'Blair's Babes' and ultimately Secretary of State for Health before quitting politics. (She now sits on boards at British Telecom (BT) and the British United Provident Association (BUPA), one of the leading private health insurance providers.) Following the disclosure of her involvement in the affair, Hewitt openly apologised, saying she and NCCL 'got it wrong', but Harman's response has, perhaps characteristically, been rather less than forthcoming; indeed, she launched a counter-attack on *The Daily Mail*, accusing it of condoning the use of child imagery in its pages.

The entire Harman story can be viewed in the round simply by making a Google search, but what is clear is that there is substantial irrefutable circumstantial evidence that points directly to Harman and others being involved in something rather unpleasant in the 1970s, and it is reasonable to infer from that and her subsequent handling of the matter that she has been rather less than candid about it. At the time of writing, Harriet Harman has stood down as Deputy Leader of the Labour Party, and all the indications are that her Parliamentary career is approaching its end. There are many men (and, perhaps, no small number of women) who will not mourn her career passing. And there is another radical feminist in the Labour Party whose political career, one speculates, might be at a cross-roads.

Yvette Cooper (b. 1969), is another feminist close to the seat of power, whose utterances speak for her ideology. She is right out of the mould of a stereotypical feminist. She gained a first class honours degree in Philosophy, Politics and Economics from Oxford University, then went on to study at Harvard University on the back of a Kennedy Scholarship, finally gaining an MSc in Economics at the London School of Economics. One of 'Blair's Babes', she was elected as MP for Pontefract and Castleford in the 1997 General Election and later became Shadow Minister for Women and Equalities in 2010. Cooper is married to Ed Balls, former Shadow Chancellor of the

Exchequer, who lost his seat in the 2015 general election, and she has recently lost her bid to become leader of the Labour Party, coming third out of four candidates. Cooper is an outspoken, combative feminist who has remained in strong alliance with Harriet Harman and other feminist women in Labour. Here is a short extract from her speech to the Labour Party's National Women's conference in September 2012 to give a flavour of where she is coming from, and in which she helpfully lists the names of her fellow feminists currently active in the Labour Party (Note that she mentions Liz Kendall and Andy Burnham, both contenders for the 2015 Labour leadership race, which they all lost. Burnham beat her by a small margin, and Kendall came last by a long way.):

> Conference. It's good to be back in Manchester. The city we held our first September women's conference at Harriet's [Harman] suggestion two years ago. The city, where in 1905, Christabel Pankhurst and Annie Kenney asked Winston Churchill if he supported votes for women, and became amongst the first suffragettes to be arrested as a result. And the city where in six weeks' time, we will make sure the first ever woman MP for Manchester Central will be elected, Lucy Powell.
>
> 2012 is the year we got our first ever female General Secretary of the TUC, the fantastic Frances O'Grady. It's also a special thirtieth anniversary – for the woman who has done so much for equality and who was elected to Parliament in December 1982 - we pay tribute to our Deputy Leader Harriet Harman.
>
> And we'll never forget the summer of 2012 – our summer – an amazing spectacular of international sport that united our nation – without a Labour woman it would never have happened and we thank Tessa Jowell. And how amazing were those women role models. From Katharine Grainger to Ellie Simmonds, Sarah Storey to Laura Trott, Hannah Cockcroft to Nicola Adams, Jade Jones to Jessica Ennis.
>
> Perhaps most amazing of all to finally see them on the telly. A summer in which women's sport finally got equal status. But lest we ever assume battles are won, I checked out today's TV schedule. There's around 13 hours of sport on terrestrial television today. Men's football. Men's golf. More men's football. Men's motorcycling. More men's golf. Some racing – where the majority of the jockeys are men. And more men's football. Over 90 per cent of the sports coverage men-only.
>
> A lesson to us: Never to take our eye off the ball. Never to assume the clock won't be turned back. All the warm words from the TV executives and

editors are not enough. They need to act. We want women's sport back on TV where it belongs.

And campaigning is what Labour women have been doing this year. Keeping up the pressure to support women across the country:

- A new law to criminalise stalking as we called for last year, pushed through by Labour's Jan Royall in the Lords

- Clare's law and Jane's law – more protection and information for women at risk – backed by Hazel Blears and Helen Goodman now on the statute book

- And Kate Green, as our fantastic Shadow Equalities Minister, with Glenys Thornton, Seema Malhotra and Yvonne Fovarge, who are working in Parliament to keep the pressure on the Government.

Because sadly under this Tory-Liberal Government there has been much to fight against. Time and again, women are being heavily hit. Women's unemployment has gone up much faster than men's since the election. Long term unemployment has increased by over 100,000 since the election – but a shocking 80 per cent of that increase is among women.

Cuts to child care and social care leave women taking more of the strain. Refuges under threat of closure. Half a million street lights switched off, leaving women worried about walking home from the bus stop through the estate after dark. Women paying twice as much to bring the deficit down, even though they still earn less and own less than men.

That means Kath, a working mum and USDAW member here in the North West. She works 22 hours in a local shop. Can't get any regular overtime. Her husband had lost his job and struggled to get a new one because he had had a stroke. In April, the Government took away her working tax credit. They now struggle to pay their mortgage. They would be better off if she gave up work. David Cameron's priority is to give £40,000 to millionaires in the Cabinet and to take £3,000 from families like Kath's, who struggle to make ends meet. So much for David Cameron's attempt to be women-friendly.

Remember 12 months ago, that Number 10 memo? The one that admitted the Government had a problem with women and promised a new communications campaign to turn things around? It hasn't worked. And it's not hard to see why. Take one of the key recommendations. To 'focus on more visible women leaders'. Since then David Cameron has cut the number of women in cabinet posts. Five Government Departments with not a woman minister in sight. Sacked junior male ministers getting gongs. Sacked senior female ministers have been ignored.

And David Cameron even told Caroline Spelman, the Environment

Secretary that she was too old to do the job, aged 54. Who was the replacement? 56-year-old Owen Paterson. To top it all he stood up in the House of Commons and called for politicians to be more 'butch'. And let's not let Nick Clegg off the hook. Only six out of 25 Lib Dem Ministers are women and as research by Girlguiding [sic] UK, out next week, shows women are more likely than men to be put off by high tuition fees too. So perhaps next time they say sorry, they should sing a duet.

Last year, David Cameron's response to women was 'calm down dear'. But women won't. It's not just working mums who are getting cross and angry about what the Tories are doing, women of all ages and backgrounds are getting angry and active, determined to do more for women's equality. And yes that means it's time for us to use the f word again. And for Andrew Mitchell's benefit we'd perhaps better point out – our f-word is feminism.

And it is going to get worse. Tory Ministers backing reports that would stop women working for small companies getting maternity leave. A new child care Minister who is happy to cut the quality of care. A new minister for women and equalities who voted for restrictions on women's right to choose.

And the Universal Credit – designed around a traditional male breadwinner with no allowance for a second earner. So part time working mums lose out. And even worse.

Child tax credits and family support will no longer be paid to the main carer. All the support will be bundled together into one payment, often to the man. Money will go from the purse to the wallet – hitting women's financial independence too.

But as Harriet said this morning, this is not just about how we campaign to stop the Tories turning the clock back. We don't just want to protect the status quo. Our sights are set much higher. We have a vision of equality that goes much further. We won't just lie back and think of opposition. We are debating key areas where, we in the Labour Party, want to go further and faster to improve women's lives.

Ed Miliband has said we need an economy that works for working people. For working women and men. And that means changing services and the economy so that both women and men can balance work and family life – for the sake of their families, but also for the sake of our prosperity too.

In Government we did much to expand child care. But we know it still isn't flexible enough, affordable enough or extensive enough. That's why Labour has set up a Child Care Commission to draw up plans for our next manifesto. Child care needs to change. But let's be clear, work needs to change too. And this is about fathers, not just mothers, and the work and parenting responsibilities they share.

But family responsibilities no longer just mean children. Many women – especially older women – have found themselves forced to give up work to care for elderly relatives, especially as social care has been cut. Women worrying because their Dad's meals on wheels have been cut or they can't find support for their Mum who lives miles away.

That's why Liz Kendall and Andy Burnham's work on social care reform is so crucial to rebuilding our economy. And thanks to work by Barbara Keeley, Salford Labour Council has now agreed to pilot a new Social Care Information Service, to provide immediate practical help for families who need to find support.

But there's a wider problem here for women in their fifties and sixties. Losing most from Government pension changes. A 30 per cent increase in unemployment since the election – compared to 5 per cent for everyone else. Facing the toxic combination of ageism and sexism in the workplace. Pulled in all directions – helping their children financially, minding grandchildren, or caring for elderly parents too. Not just the squeezed middle but the stretched middle generation.

As Fiona MacTaggart has argued so strongly in Parliament, Labour must become the voice for the women in the middle. That is why we are launching our new Older Women's Commission, chaired by Harriet Harman. For the generation who fought for equal pay and child care, broke barriers, challenged prejudices now campaigning again, to whom younger generations owe so much, leading the way again now.

We also need new action on violence against women and girls. In Government we did much – from specialist courts to independent advisors, from housing help, to changing the law. But let's be honest, there's a complacency around. Because we worked hard to tackle the problem, most people assume everything possible is being done. Yet the reality is that, every day of the week, women are failed by the system that is supposed to protect them.

Still less than 6 per cent of rape offences reported end in conviction.

And the level of violence tolerated and ignored against young women and girls is deeply disturbing. In Rochdale vulnerable girls aged 12 to 18 were ignored and described as prostitutes by the authorities who were supposed to protect them. And we had a girl as young as nine, Imogen, who came to give evidence to the Women's Safety Commission to explain how uncomfortable she felt about the comments boys made about her body, and how she wanted a safe space in the playground.

It's not good enough. That's why we will consult over the coming months on new plans for stronger action against domestic and sexual violence. Next

February – on Valentine's Day – people not just across Britain but across the world will join the campaign to stand up against violence against women. An international campaign for One Billion Rising.

Already the brilliant work done by Stella Creasy means hundreds of women have joined workshops and events to see how they can get involved. See how you can too. We in the Labour Party believe in equality for women.

We believe in wider opportunities for women and girls, in challenging prejudices and discrimination, fighting against injustice. And it's more important now than ever. The Tories and the Liberal Democrats are failing women again. Failing women because their leaders just don't get it. Failing women because David Cameron just has a massive problem with women. And failing women because their party ideologies hold them back.

Our challenge now is standing up for women across the country, but also raising our sights to the future. Building Labour's feminism, which is welcoming and inclusive not narrow or divisive. A feminism which welcomes young and old, men and women, that listens to the varied voices and supports the different choices women make. Across generations, across genders, across the country.

That's what Labour women do.

Cooper uses her speech to press all the feminist buttons: the Suffragettes; Mary Kenney; the London Olympic Games; men and their interests such as football that allegedly excludes women's sports. She then turns to stirring up fear in women, such as stalking, violence against women (implicitly, by men of course), women's long-term unemployment (i.e., the implicit male patriarchy at work); that only 6 per cent of rape allegations result in convictions (without recognising that due process has been exercised in one of the fairest nations in the world); how women are 'failed by the system' - the list goes on. Cooper's attempt at associating the Labour Party with the Suffragettes is bizarre. The Pankhursts were no heroines of Labour. In fact the firebrand Christabel Pankhurst turned her back on the Labour Party, standing as a Women's Party candidate in 1918. In fact, she only narrowly lost to the Labour Party candidate, John Davison. The Pankhurst's political alliance was with the Lloyd George/ Conservative coalition, and they were in favour of abolishing the trades unions, a fact they announced publicly in *Britannia*,[173] their official Suffragette newspaper. She is also somewhat cavalier with her use of statistics in her desire to get over her message of discrimination against women. For example, her reference to there being only six out of 25 Lib Dem ministers is, frankly, mendacious, bearing in mind the coalition nature of the government after the 2010 election. In fact, eight women were elected as Lib Dem MPs in that election, out of a total of 57 MPs. That is 14 per cent, yet six were appointed ministers out of a total of 25 in the cabinet. That is 24 per cent, which is massively skewed in women's favour. No one could say this is negative discrimination, but Cooper deviously implies it. In this speech, she transparently reveals the subtext of the feminist subversion of politics. Her remarks about her sights, and those of Harman and the other active feminists in the Labour Party, being set much higher than just 'protecting the status quo of women' but having 'a vision of equality that goes much further… to go further and faster to improve women's lives' shows that Cooper is a fully paid-up member of the party that is within the Labour Party: that movement within the Labour movement - feminism. And, no doubt, she speaks for all those fellow travellers of hers whom she mentions in her speech. Through people like Cooper and Harman, feminism is undoubtedly at work in the party that allegedly stands for social justice, fairness and equality. But their version of equality is different. As she correctly emphasises, 'Our f-word is feminism'.

'Social-ism'

In 1997, Anthony Charles Lynton Blair ('Tony' Blair, a Baby Boomer, born in 1953) led the British Labour Party to a landslide victory, after 18 years of opposition. He secured a 418 seat majority: the most the party had ever held before, or since. (He then went on to win two more elections, in 2001 and 2005, but with massively reduced majorities, finally handing over the reins of power to Gordon Brown in 2007, who lost the 2010 general election.) From first becoming leader in 1994, Blair had recognised that Labour was virtually unelectable as the party of the working man, so he and others, such as Gordon Brown and Peter Mandelson, set about reinventing it. In fact, the working man as an economic social concept had all but disappeared by then, in the seismic economic shift to a service economy, coupled with massive strides forward in manufacturing technology, such as robotics in the motor industry, that had shifted the emphasis from manual labour to technical know-how. In what was a staggering move at the time, he managed to persuade the party of organised labour to abandon its principle to Marxist policy:

> To secure for the workers by hand or by brain the full fruits of their industry
> and the most equitable distribution thereof that may be possible upon the

basis of the common ownership of the means of production, distribution and exchange, and the best obtainable system of popular administration and control of each industry or service.

This was an amazing *volte face*. Clause 4 of Labour's constitution was part of its DNA. It had always been the party of class struggle and resistance to capitalism but Blair, a barrister by profession, used the classic guile of the politician to pull off this amazing coup. He gave the hardliners of the party a *quid pro quo* in the form of John Prescott, a former ship's steward, trade union activist and political bruiser, whom he appointed as his Deputy Prime Minister, and he went about transforming the 100 year old Marxist party, steeped in the capital-vs-labour paradigm, and populated with hard line left wingers, into a party led by progressive middle-class professionals, in which feminist women were to figure highly so as to secure the women's vote.

Blair openly redefined socialism to what he called 'Social-ism' (his own term, and a masterly piece of spin), which he defined as a set of constant socialist values adapted to a changing society, arguing that this was a necessary part of the process of making Labour electable again, and he pulled it off, putting clear water between New Labour and the old Labour Party. In 2002, long after she had left office, and by then in her seventies, Margaret Thatcher was asked what her greatest achievement was. She replied, 'Tony Blair and New Labour. We forced our opponents to change their minds'. I suggest there is a very strong case to be made that rather than Labour changing its mind, it simply changed its strategy. Blair ditched the blue collars and overalls of the working man and his aspiration to ownership of the means of production, and replaced it with the skinny latte and the skirt. Through Alastair Campbell, his formidable press secretary, Blair manipulated the news agenda in his favour and spun the New Labour message in terms of equal worth and equal opportunity for all citizens, but which really meant the feminist version of women's equality. Tony Blair and his New Labour collaborators were an entryist group that hijacked a traditional party of the working man and used it to install its own version of Marxism.

The nationalisation of childhood

In 2006, Jill Kirby from The Centre for Policy Studies published a paper entitled The Nationalisation of Childhood,[174] which amounted to a scathing attack on the Blair New Labour government's plans to introduce a system of universal child care by merging child protection services and the education system, putting all children's identities into a national computer database, ostensibly to monitor their use of services on a 'dawn to dusk' basis. Quoting Prime Minister Tony Blair, who had announced New Labour's plans as '… a new frontier for the Welfare State,' Kirby said this about what she saw was actually happening:

> In the guise of a caring, child-centred administration, this Government is effecting a radical change in the balance of authority between parents, children and the state. It is nationalising the upbringing of children.

Kirby was sounding a loud warning bell about Blair's motives and it went unnoticed. These astonishing measures met little opposition from the other parties at the time. Some members of Her Majesty's Opposition, the Conservatives, expressed unease at the government's direction of travel, and concerns were raised by the Liberal Democrats about minor details in the measures, such as the child database and its potential to become an identity card system by stealth. The newspapers on both the left and the right of politics expressed varied degrees of scepticism about the effectiveness of merging children's services and education, but no one questioned the naked political chicanery that was going on. As Kirby puts it:

> During the Blair years, New Labour has given the appearance of abandoning old-fashioned socialism. Embracing the language of the free market, acknowledging the importance of choice and talking of the need to 'personalise' public services, it has put on a good show of being a modern, post-Thatcher government of the centre ground. Yet under the skin, this Government's socialist heart beats strong. Nowhere is this more apparent than in its programme for raising children, a programme which displays a remarkable confidence in the ability of the state to regulate the lives of its citizens and to control their destinies… This 'new frontier' bears a remarkable similarity to the Marxist concept in which the collectivisation of childcare was considered essential to achieve an equal society with full productivity. Marx recognised that, 'you cannot abolish the family; you have to replace it'. As Leon Trotsky later explained, 'the functions of the family' were to be absorbed by the 'institutions of the socialist society.' The Marxist doctrine was brought up to date by Anthony Giddens, one of the architects of New Labour, in 1998. In The Third Way, Giddens explained how the 'democratisation' of the family demands that responsibility for childcare be

shared not only between men and women but also between parents and nonparents. [sic] Giddens also proposed that in the democratic family, parents would have to 'negotiate' for authority over their children... As this language demonstrates, the strategy is intended to create a direct relationship between child and state, with objectives determined by Government, not by parents. The role of parents would, in effect, be subsidiary to the state... In the guise of a caring, child-centred administration, constantly proclaiming its desire to support parents and reduce inequality, this Government is effecting a radical change in the balance of authority between parents, children and the state. The nationalisation of childhood is no longer a Marxist dream; it is becoming a British reality.

The prophetic words of Germaine Greer, who as long ago as 1970 openly said that through the women's revolution, 'Marx will have come true willy nilly, so let's get on with it,' were coming true.

Entryism

Despite its desperate efforts to remain cohesive and inclusive, the Labour Party is by its very nature highly susceptible to entryism, the process whereby a group that has a stronger affinity with its own ideological stance than with that of the larger organisation infiltrates its host, gradually populates its bases of power, imposing its own direction, and finally takes over control. This can be an overt process, in which case it appears a legitimate part of the political process: lobbying, cajoling and persuading brings others to the entryist point of view; or it can be a covert process - so called *sui generis* entryism (of its own kind) - which passes off a set of ideas expressed in innocent terms whilst underneath introducing a new ideology. During the 1950s a Trotskyist group called 'The Club' sought covertly to take over Labour, and in the 1970s and early 1980s, 'Militant Tendency', another Trotskyist group, attempted another similar infiltration. Militant had a long-term plan to infiltrate the Labour movement by gaining control of sub-groups within it, such as the Young Socialists. It then gained political control of Liverpool City Council, from where it sought to exercise political influence on Labour nationally. Ultimately, the Labour Party woke up to what was happening and expelled Militant's members, declaring their activities contrary to Clause II, Section C of the party's constitution (principally the requirement that all party units promote the broad aims and values of the party), which stress the need for common endeavour and living together in a spirit of solidarity, tolerance and respect.

This clause reflects the inherent instability of the Labour Party and the Labour movement as a whole. It has always suffered from an inherent tension between full-blown Marxist Socialism and social democracy, summed up perfectly in the obfuscatory wording of its aims and values:

Clause IV. Aims and values

The Labour Party is a democratic socialist party. It believes that by the strength of our common endeavour we achieve more than we achieve alone, so as to create for each of us the means to realise our true potential and for all of us a community in which power, wealth and opportunity are in the hands of the many not the few; where the rights we enjoy reflect the duties we owe and where we live together freely, in a spirit of solidarity, tolerance and respect.

This is what allows entryist groups to infiltrate it and seek to control it for its own purposes. No sooner had Militant Tendency been eradicated, Blair and his group 'Progress' emerged. Indeed, in 1996, just before Blair became Prime Minister, the General and Municipal Boilermakers Union accused Progress of behind the scenes activity seeking to influence Labour's front bench to support wage restraint, and also of undermining support for Ken Livingstone in his campaign to be re-elected Mayor of London.

What Blair did in the 1990s was classic entryism. He clandestinely prosecuted his agenda for change, drawing together his new elite, which included women such as Harriet Harman and Patricia Hewitt, both with a track record of radical feminist activity, and both the products of the 1970s women's liberation revolution. With Blair at the front, and his passionately feminist wife beside him, he triumphantly paraded his 101 'Blair's Babes' to the world, and a new era had begun, not just for Labour, but for the nation. This was the moment cultural Marxism, which is what progressive politics is all about, took control of the levers of power and unleashed a decade of unrestrained feminism on Britain. Prosecuted with alacrity by Harman, Hewitt, Yvette Cooper and their like, feminists re-engineered the welfare state to favour women over men, they undermined the family as an institution by extending child-care to bring more women into the workforce, they denigrated fatherhood and vilified men as habitual perpetrators of domestic violence, and they created the most toxic legal environment imaginable in the area of rape and sexual offences, overturning some of the most basic principles of criminal law to install their feminist ideology.

The Blair years in Britain changed it irrevocably, and massively for the worse, and it is interesting to see what happened to New Labour after he left in 2007 to pursue a massively lucrative career in international politics and religion, amassing a vast personal fortune. New Labour limped on for another three years under Gordon Brown, then imploded after a massive defeat at the 2010 general election. It then elected Ed Miliband, a non-Blairite, who was backed by the trades unions in the belief that he represented a return to old Labour values, but turned out to be a clone of his political contemporaries, Conservative David Cameron and Liberal Democrat Nick Clegg, leading the party to an even more crushing defeat in 2015. Then it elected an extreme left-wing Marxist, Jeremy Corbyn, in what commentators called 'A primal scream of pain'. Len McCluskey, leader of the Unite trade union, declared that the unions had got their party back. That is a claim that remains to be seen.

PC legislation

One of the most striking examples of the influence Harman, Cooper et al, had on the feminist-dominated Blair government is the passing into law of the Equality Act 2010. This brought numerous pieces of pre-existing anti-discrimination legislation together under one umbrella, following a number of EU Equal Treatment Directives, which required equality of access to employment in both private and public service. In fact, the act was a PC charter against women's alleged harassment in the workplace. It defined certain protected categories, including sex, but hidden within it is a declaration that everyone should be treated with dignity and respect at work, and it created a legal right in the workplace not to be harassed by third parties, which on the face of it can be seen as a good thing. All well and good, you might say. How could anybody argue with that? However, although it is couched in gender-neutral language, it is clear that this law is a feminist-inspired attempt to reengineer the culture of the workplace to facilitate the introduction of a feminist defined working environment.

The act defines harassment in the workplace as:

> Unwanted conduct related to a relevant protected characteristic, which has the purpose or effect of violating an individual's dignity or creating an intimidating, hostile, degrading, humiliating or offensive environment for that individual.

Again, all well and good. However, this statement is qualified by an explanation to be found later in the definition as follows:

> Harassment at work in includes 'unwelcome sexual advances – touching, standing too close, the display of offensive materials, asking for sexual favours, making decisions on the basis of sexual advances being accepted or rejected'.

This is feminist-speak. It is totally about women. Nobody could read any gender neutrality in this at all. Don't get me wrong, I am neither attacking this law, nor defending it, but you can't get away from the reality that this definition is aimed at protecting women from men. It is not only divisive, it carries implications for all of us that are far more serious than initially meet the eye. Frank Furedi, sociologist, commentator and author, identifies the issue in his essay, *So when is sex appropriate?*[175] In this article, he cites the policy statement of the East London NHS Trust in response to the Equality Act 2010, which defines its own interpretation of what harassment means, in practice, for them, under the act:

> Harassment is defined as what is offensive to the recipient and so is based on their **perceptions and feelings** rather than on the intent of the person who has displayed the behaviour. It will, therefore, be for **the recipient to determine what is inappropriate behaviour** – if it offends them, it is harassment. [Author's emphases]

The emphases tell the story. Harassment at work in the East London NHS Trust is entirely based on 'perceptions and feelings', and it is 'for the recipient to determine what is inappropriate behaviour'. But, as Furedi says, where are the objective criteria for judging harrassment? There aren't any, of course, it is all based on perceptions and feelings. How can an allegation be tested and refuted when the criteria underpinning it are so subjective? It cannot, of course. To reinforce the point, Furedi says this:

> The ambiguity of the language of harassment can be seen in the numerous workplace codes of conducts drawn up to regulate interpersonal behaviour. Many stress that it is the person who makes an allegation who gets to decide if what they experienced was harassment. These codes insist that the act of harassment is defined by its impact on the recipient rather than by the

intention of the alleged harasser. Definitions of sexual harassment are not remotely objective. They say that whether or not an act constitutes harassment depends on how it is perceived. This grotesquely arbitrary and subjective definition makes no attempt to distinguish between a simple act of miscommunication and an explicit attempt to coerce and humiliate another person. Some policy documents go so far as to state that harassment can be either 'deliberate or unintentional'. In doing so, they merely highlight the fact that, these days, the distinction between deliberate acts and unintentional hurtful gestures is of little significance.

And, he goes on to make this key point:

The researchers Wendy Hollway and Tony Jefferson have argued that highly subjective definitions of sexual harassment threaten natural justice. They questioned a definition of harassment used by the University of Sheffield, which was based on the 'impact and not the intention of the action'. Such a definition 'subverts two central tenets of natural justice simultaneously', they argued. First, by 'privileging absolutely the perception of the harassed, it removes any *mens rea* requirement [the necessity of proving a guilty or blameable state of mind in the accused] and hence any defence hinging on innocent intention'; and second, 'by making the test of what constitutes harassment wholly subjective… the nature of the offence is neither clear nor knowable in advance'.

If you cannot possibly know the nature of your offence before committing it, how can you know how to avoid committing it? The most important underpinning principle of our criminal law is that you must knowingly break it if you are to be declared a criminal, and this principle is enshrined in our legal system, going back to the Common Law of England, that system of natural justice that has been around since time immemorial. It stands on a commonly held understanding of what is right and wrong. It demands that the accuser must prove *mens rea*, a 'guilty or blameable state of mind' in the person accused. The act itself (*actus reus*) is not enough for proof of criminality under common law. However, PC feminists have seen to it that this fundamental principle of jurisprudence has been overturned in the modern statute law governing harassment, and enacted by feminists. It is a minefield of uncertainty, especially for men, at whom it is clearly aimed, and it prevents any form of personal attraction between men and women at work being expressed at work. As Furedi says:

> Any form of sexual approach or signalling of desire can be redefined as
> harassment these days, which means pretty much anyone or any organisation
> can be accused… From this viewpoint, the behaviour of an inept and anxious
> would-be suitor and the actions of a sexual predator are morally equivalent.

This is how PC feminism is being embedded into our daily lives. It is a classic
case of totalitarianism installed in our public sector, and it is spreading to the
private and third sectors too because they cannot avoid it for fear of breaching
the law. Examples of it can be found in all types of organisation, as a simple
Google search will show. Not only is the right of free speech being curtailed,
but the right of freedom of action under the law is now severely curtailed by an
ideology alien to our normal way of life. It is a form of social censorship that
curbs freedoms: particularly the freedom of men to express a genuinely held
view of women, and it has succeeded in replacing reason and objective truth
with subjective feeling, a particularly female characteristic.

Press & broadcast media

It is not just politics that has been infiltrated by feminists. They have colonised
the press and broadcast media, controlling the news agenda and filtering it
through their world view. Almost every edition of newspapers, news
programmes on radio and television, and news websites contain at least one
piece about women who have heroically succeeded in a society that is stacked
against them. Girls who get the best grades in exams, women who achieve the
top positions in our corporations, female athletes who gain medals, all are given
special emphasis and featured as important news. Then there is the endless
reinforcement of the standard feminist canards: how women continue to suffer
from lower pay, how they are being barred from the boardroom, how mothers
struggle to cope with career and family obligations and need more help, how
girls need protection from paedophiles/rapists/sexual abusers (even though
boys have probably been the greatest number of victims of paedophilia down
the decades), not to mention the relentless insinuations against men: their rapist
tendencies, their habitual violence in domestic abuse, their anti-social
behaviour, their everyday sexism, etc. All these are the warp and weft of the
daily news agenda that plays to the plight of women and never to the plight of
men and boys, who can just go hang as far as the feminist-dominated media is
concerned. Their suffering isn't news.

The organs of communication of our state have become controlled by feminists who endlessly pursue their agenda, and are so powerful in manipulating public opinion. Erin Pizzey made this clear when she said,

> The most successful part of it is, at that point in the 70s if you think about it, the majority of woman that [sic] were journalists internationally, were very heavy radical feminists and they had the women's pages, and of course, male journalists and male editors, seeing it as 'a woman's problem', left it to them. And very quickly there was a savage kind of censorship and anybody who dared argue, was in very serious trouble.

The author and journalist George Monbiot is also very clear about this. He argues that a Marxist group influenced by 'Living Marxism,' a magazine that pursued an agenda of entryism into scientific and media organisations in Britain from the late 1990s, is undoubtedly at work today in our media. In June 2013, for example, 42-year-old Tim Haries criminally vandalised the portrait of the Queen in Westminster Abbey, and the media duly reported it with headlines such as 'A man has been arrested' and, 'Queen's portrait defaced in Abbey,' etc. The reaction of the artist was reported, stories were written about what could be done to repair the painting and about its reinstallation after restoration, but nothing ever mentioned about the man's reasons for doing what he did.

No journalist, in that time-honoured principle of journalism, sought the human interest dimension, explored Haries' background or his motivation for what he did. Nothing. Even *Christian Today* reported the incident without compassion, choosing instead to use the term 'vandal' about Haries. In short, the media just buried the story under the bare minimum of journalistic obligation to report the facts. However, Haries was no mindless vandal, no anti-social recidivist, or even an anti-monarchist. Neither was he a Banksy creating a work of alternative art, he was just a man in pain who resorted to vandalism in the face of a societal deafness to what he later described at his trial as 'the social issue of our time'. He got six months in jail for spray-painting just one word onto the Queen's portrait, 'Help'. And he did it as Father's Day approached. Haries had reached the point where he didn't care any longer about his reputation or his freedom. All he wanted to do was bring attention to the plight of the legion of men who are being denied access to their children after divorce.

That is the real story behind Tim Haries, but it never got reported, such is the degree of *de facto* (and it might be deliberate) censorship to which activist feminists and their fellow-travellers in the media are prepared to go to suppress anything that might put men in a better light. These men are citizens of a civilised nation, yet they are having their human rights systematically abused, as are those of their children, who in the real world need a relationship with their father. These men are hurting and they are desperate. And who cares? Certainly not the press. And why? Because for them to have reported the human interest side of the Haries incident would have meant them recognising that men are being systematically and disgracefully disadvantaged. It is an ongoing human tragedy of gigantic proportions being played out daily, yet it is being suppressed by the feminist media for whom it is off limits because it exposes the damage their espoused ideology is doing to us all. These ideologically obsessed people will go to any lengths to keep what is going on under wraps, because theirs is a train whose destination is the total feminisation of society. The evidence of this is before us, hidden in plain sight.

One of the most egregious examples of this media bias was the approach the BBC took to a complaint of feminist bias made by the political party, Justice for Men and Boys (and the women who love them) (J4MB), about an item broadcast on 7th January 2014 on their flagship current affairs programme, *Newsnight*. In a 12 minute discussion (which involved Polly Neate on behalf of Women's Aid), not one mention was made of women also being perpetrators of violence. Mike Buchanan, leader of J4MB and a persistent campaigner, pointed out over fifty breaches of the BBC's two hundred and fifteen page editorial guidelines[176] in the broadcast, and received the following response:

Dear Mr Buchanan
Reference CAS-2526463-VBBJ6H

Thanks for your contact regarding 'Newsnight' on 7 January. We took your concerns to the Assistant Editor of Newsnight, who thanked them for their feedback. He added that the Newsnight team, as well as the wider editorial staff at BBC News, are aware that there are many male victims of domestic abuse and he appreciates you taking the time to contact us on this issue.

He disagrees, however, that the report was misleading and is confident that it did not breach our editorial guidelines. The fact that this particular film and discussion focussed on female victims of domestic abuse should not be taken as a denial that men too can be victims.

This is an issue that we have covered, for example: http://www.bbc.co.uk/news/uk-england-25038695, which actually links to the Mankind campaign, http://www.bbc.co.uk/news/uk-23876948 and http://www.bbc.co.uk/news/uk-12126783.

However, we have taken on board your comments. Thanks again for taking the time to contact us.

Kind Regards
<name redacted>
BBC Complaints

As Buchanan points out in one of his blog posts, this is a 'Bed Bug Letter,'[177] and says, 'Once you realise how corrupt the mainstream media are when reporting on gender-related matters, the world can never quite seem the same again'.

European Union

Feminist ideologues have deeply penetrated the European Union. Catherine Hakim, to whom I shall refer later when discussing her Preference Theory of women's choices in work and elsewhere, describes how the European Commission has adopted a policy of seeking to eliminate gender-based segregation and the 'stubbornly stable' 10-20 per cent difference in average earnings: the so-called 'pay gap'. It appears the Commission is intent on achieving 70 per cent employment of women despite a dramatic collapse of fertility rates in Europe, convinced that the differences in labour markets for men and women are due to sex discrimination. And what is the outworking of this blind social engineering policy? The Commission set up a European Institute for Gender Equality to actively campaign on equality issues, based on the premise that what they call 'occupational segregation' in all its forms, is an injustice which must be eliminated because it is the reason why there are earnings differences between men and women. (I shoot this idea down in flames in the next chapter.)

As Hakim says:[178]

> The European Commission has adopted the feminist, ideological position rather than the evidence-based, scholarly perspective. It assumes that it is purely a social accident that certain careers, some of them well paid, are male-

dominated and do not tolerate motherhood, long parental leaves, part-time hours of work, and family-friendly arrangements. It has adopted as major policy goals the elimination of gender-based occupational segregation and the stubbornly stable 10-20% difference in average earnings (the 'pay gap') between men and women in the workforce, and it insists on achieving a 70% employment rate among women despite the dramatic collapse of fertility rates in Europe. It attributes these and all other sex differences in labour market outcomes to sex discrimination, and is setting up a European Institute for Gender Equality to campaign on equality issues.

The weasel-word argument the European Commission offers is that occupational segregation restricts people's (for which read 'women's') choice of career, especially in the crucial early years of an adult's working life. (For which read 'a young woman's life'.) This is a well-rehearsed feminist claim. An even more well-rehearsed claim is that a 50:50 male to female split in job allocations must be the target. (Note: 'equality' now means parity of numbers of men and women in all walks of life, not equality of opportunity, based on merit, skill, ability, etc.). The Commission has made it known publicly that it is prepared to impose positive discrimination quotas in order to achieve this, despite the fact that the European Court of Justice has ruled quotas illegal. One wonders how long that will hold against the increasing pressure of gender politics.

The Church of England

Returning to the heart of England, the Established Church of England,[179] that institution integral to the very fabric of the English constitution, going back deep into history, has been ravaged by the cultural Marxism of feminism. For more than four centuries it has upheld the patriarchal values of patrimonial kingship, the right of kinship, marriage, inheritance and succession through families, and kept them locked into English society as models of our way of life. Even though it is true that fewer than one in ten Britons attend a church service regularly, most English people at least still see themselves as being 'Church of England,' as UK censuses continue to show. The census data are generally regarded as showing a historical expression of national cultural identity but one thing is sure, the institution that is the Church of England is inextricably interwoven with the very fabric of the nation as a whole.

For feminists, however, attacking and toppling patriarchy wherever it is found is an article of feminist faith, and the 400 years old Church of England is patriarchy incarnate. This is what is behind the issue of women priests and bishops: a struggle of titanic proportions within the community of believers in the church that has rocked it to its very foundations. When it is all juiced down, this has been the wresting of power from men in the church hierarchy (which, incidentally means literally 'the rule of the priest'). Why? Because they can, and because it is now politically correct. Through feminism, the politics of Marx and his views on religion[180] have triumphed, and it is easy to see why. Undermining and disrupting the Established Church serves two purposes of Marxism: attacking the heart of one of the solid pillars of our capitalist society; and mocking and diminishing its core religion. And what better way to do this than use feminism to overturn centuries of tradition? In the 1844 introduction to his proposed work, *A Contribution to the Critique of Hegel's Philosophy of Right*, he said this:

> [Religion]… is the fantastic realisation of the human essence since the human essence has not acquired any true reality. The struggle against religion is, therefore, indirectly the struggle against that world whose spiritual aroma is religion. Religious suffering is, at one and the same time, the expression of real suffering and a protest against real suffering. Religion is the sigh of the oppressed creature, the heart of a heartless world, and the soul of soulless conditions. It is the opium of the people. The abolition of religion as the illusory happiness of the people is the demand for their real happiness.

Embedded deep in the foundations of the Church of England lies the bedrock of Christian understanding: that the man is head of the woman in marriage, and the family in which children, the fruit of that union, are born and brought up to be fully formed, fully functioning adults, and valuable members of society. Yet, women of faith, who no doubt consider themselves servants of the Church, and women of integrity and learning, have risen up against this principle in the name of a form of equality espoused by a divisive, revolutionary Marxist ideology such as feminism, which stands implacably opposed to all their church stands for. Frankly, these women are either deeply deluded or they are feminists. It is hard to see any other interpretation of their actions.

The women in the Church (and the men too) who are the driving force behind women as priests and bishops are being remarkably selective in their Scriptural interpretation and its teaching on Church structure and governance, to the extent that it must cast doubt. They must know that what they are doing is a radical departure from everything the Church has held dear for centuries. As educated people, they must know that being militant for the cause of women in the Church amounts to a divisive disruption of centuries of tradition and an open rebellion against it. What they are driving at in this particular area is not Christianity as it has been known for at least 17 centuries, which has held men to be the leaders of its communities, and the dispensers of its liturgies, etc., as *primus inter pares* - 'first amongst equals'. Christianity teaches that all members of the church are equal anyway. Saul of Tarsus (St. Paul), the founder of the first church communities said, '… in Christ Jesus you are all children of God through faith, or all of you who were baptised into Christ have clothed yourselves with Christ. There is neither Jew nor Gentile, neither slave nor free, nor is there male and female, for you are all one in Christ Jesus.'[181] In other words, there is no inequality between men and women in Christianity, even though women and men have different roles to play in its church.

St Paul's teaching is very clear about roles men and women should play in the churches of the first century. He taught that in marriage the man is the head of the team of a man and a woman in a family, with responsibilities in how he discharges that leadership role. Here are some examples of what he said, to illustrate the point:

> Wives, submit yourselves unto your own husbands, as unto the Lord…
> Nevertheless let every one of you in particular so love his wife even as
> himself; and the wife [see] that she reverence [her] husband. (Letter to the
> church in Ephesus)… [to avoid] fornication, let every man have his own wife,
> and let every woman have her own husband. Let the husband render unto the
> wife due benevolence: and likewise also the wife unto the husband. The wife
> hath not power of her own body, but the husband: and likewise also the
> husband hath not power of his own body, but the wife. (First letter to the
> church at Corinth.) Let the woman learn in silence with all subjection. (Paul's
> first letter to his protégé, Timothy, who was active in leading the church in
> Ephesus) Marriage [is] honourable in all, and the bed undefiled: but
> whoremongers and adulterers God will judge. (Letter to the Hebrews)

Many people might not agree with this. That is their right. I might even agree with them. I am not quoting these passages as a Christian apologist, nor as an advocate for one form or another of the role of women in society. That is not the point. The point is, these are fundamental propositions in the Christian church and they have been flaunted by Christian women in the Church of

England who are undoubtedly asserting a 40-year-old ideology against at least a 400-year-old tradition, and they are creating a new set of values, which mirror those of society, which has itself been changed by feminism.

They are compromised by a secular world view whose questionable principles of equality they have bought into - lock, stock and barrel. So successful has feminism been in broader society, it is clear that women in the Church want a piece of the action - even at the expense of overturning the most fundamental tenets of the Church to which they belong. Their hypocrisy of this is astonishing, and what none of them seem to recognise is that the term 'woman priest' is an oxymoron. The word priest comes from the Greek *presbuteros*, meaning elder or old man. (The elders of Israel were the men who assisted Moses to lead the Children of Israel to The Promised Land.) *Presbuteros* became presbyter, then prester, then priest and it is a male noun. That notwithstanding, a relentless march towards women taking part in the priesthood began in 1974 when a number of male American Episcopalian bishops in the USA appointed 11 women priests (known as 'The Philadelphia Eleven') in what they called an act of 'prophetic disobedience' against the canon law of the Anglican Church, with which the American Episcopalian Church is in communion. This led to 32 women being ordained as Church of England priests in March 1994, and ultimately to the appointment of women as bishops, when the irresistible force overcame the immovable object. On 26th January 2015, 48-year-old Reverend Libby Lane, a mother of two, was consecrated at York Minster.

As Archbishop of York John Sentamu asked the congregation if it was their will that Mrs Lane should be ordained bishop, a vicar, Reverend Paul Williamson shouted: 'No! Not in my name. It is not in the Bible. With respect, your grace, I ask to speak on this absolute impediment, please.' Sentamu ignored him and carried on. Writing in the Daily Telegraph on the day, John Bingham, their religious affairs editor, said of Bishop Lane, '...she is part of a generation of women who grew up believing, as she puts it, that, "all things are possible".' Mrs Lane said, 'I am very conscious of all those who have gone before me, women and men, who for decades have looked forward to this moment. But most of all I am thankful to God'. One can only speculate if Bishop Lane's god is a she.

Whether the ordination of women bishops in The Church of England is a storm in a teacup: whether it is generally felt to be irrelevant to the ordinary non-religious individual, the issue of women bishops amounts to feminist

Christians saying they are prepared to promote worldly values, indeed Marxist values, above those of their church's traditional values. They might produce finely finessed arguments, couched in Christian terms, that seek to provide justification for what they are doing, but it is really just that women in the Church, as in broader society, do not want to be in subjection to men, both in principle, and *on* principle. This is an ideology that neither compromises, nor seeks appeasement, and it will have a profound impact on the Church of England. All the statistics show that women are becoming the overwhelming group of members of the Church of England. In 2010, they were 65 per cent of the confirmations,[182] and women comprise by far the biggest proportion of attendees at services. In the Church of England the ratio is 55 to 45,[183] but what is more important is the reality that the number of men attending services is declining. Writing in the Daily Telegraph on 19th December 2013, Jemima Thackray observes:

> Increasingly, however, the lack of men in the Church has been attributed to the rise of women in its public roles. The increasing 'feminisation', particularly of the Church of England since the first women were ordained as priests in 1994, is said to be off-putting for men. One former Anglican Bishop, Keith Newton, defected to the [Roman] Catholic Church in order to stay true to his traditionalist views, one of which was his belief that, 'the Church becoming more feminine could be a problem... I have seen research that says if you want children to go to Church, dad needs to go with mum. And we've got a real problem with dad not going'. Similar objections have been made more recently in the debate over women bishops who, some argue, would only further feminise an institution, which is already struggling to appear sufficiently manly. Not many have been brave enough to say publicly what this supposed 'feminisation' consists of. A few though have pointed to what they perceive as the increasingly emotional interpretation of Church practise in the hands of women – their sense that the Christian life has become a bit too touchy-feely – and that men are being repelled by the lack of engagement with masculine themes. I have even heard it argued that women have a sentimentalised concept of God who is increasingly described as 'loving' rather than 'just', 'tender' rather than 'righteous,' not to mention the fact that He occasionally becomes a She.

When it is all over, what is left of the Church of England will be a church of women, run by women, and whatever men are left in it will have been both spiritually and organisationally emasculated. It will become an institution that will increasingly cater for the needs of female congregants and pay disproportionate attention to catering for women's needs, rather than the needs of their congregations as a whole. In other words, the entire edifice will become self-serving - which really means women-serving. For Britain as a nation, it would amount to the toppling of one of its principal social and historical pillars.

CHAPTER 10

THE SOCIAL OUTCOMES OF FEMINISM

'A community that allows a large number of men to grow up in broken families, dominated by women, never acquiring any stable relationship to male authority, never acquiring any set of rational expectations about the future - that community asks for and gets chaos. Crime, violence, unrest, disorder - most particularly the furious, unrestrained lashing out at the whole social structure - that is not only to be expected; it is very near to inevitable. And it is richly deserved.'

Daniel Patrick Moynihan (1927 - 2003).
Four-term U.S. Senator, ambassador, administration official, and academic.

Lads and ladettes

I had an early flight from my local airport recently, and called a taxi for 04:30. On the journey, I noticed a woman's high-heeled platform shoe, silvered and sequinned, lying on the floor in the passenger seat well. My driver was an Asian guy and I said to him, joking, 'I guess that's not yours then?' He gave me a wry look and said he had just dropped off a young woman at her home and she had been so drunk she couldn't walk or even stand. He had had to wake her up on arriving because she was almost comatose, and manhandle her out of his taxi and up to her front door, finding her key in her handbag to let her in. She hadn't paid his fare and when I asked him what he was going to do about it he said he would have to go back to her address later that day and make sure he got his money. This was a regular occurrence apparently, as regular as having these women vomit in his cab. He seemed a really decent sort of chap, probably a Muslim with a wife and a family, trying to make an honest living by working unsocial hours, and it occurred to me that the woman in question had been very lucky. By happenstance, she had got a driver who was a decent man with good values; she might not have been so lucky. She might easily have been fleeced for an exorbitant fare by another driver, or sexually molested in her drunken incapacitation. She might even have been raped, and never really known about it. Feminists might say rape is rape and the woman is never responsible, but this young woman was irresponsibly placing herself in extreme danger. She is, of course, liberated.

I invite my reader to take a look around. What do you see in society today? Look in the bars and restaurants, the social spaces where people congregate, especially young people, and what do you see? I see groups of young men, drinking heavily, being loud and laddish as they enjoy themselves 'having a laugh'. On the other hand, I see women doing exactly the same thing - only worse - getting, 'off their faces' on low-cost treble-measures of spirits and cheap cocktails in 'happy hours,' after having 'pre-loaded' on cheap vodka from the supermarket before heading off to an evening of binge drinking and then a night of clubbing, after which they will leave half-way through the night, stagger to a taxi, hardly knowing where they are, and trusting the driver to get them home safely. This is the lad and ladette culture: the young women in particular vying with the men in drinking, loudness and sheer stupidity - and putting themselves into the most dangerous of situations into the bargain.

And it is not just the young. Take another look around that trendy bar and you will see the same pattern in older men and women, mostly 40-50 somethings, or even women in their 60s, also socialising within their gender groups, on 'girls' nights out', which they regard as their right even if they are married, or mothers (or even grandmothers), when their mothers would never have even contemplated doing what they do. They enjoy the female chatter - free of men. They're 'getting a life' before it's too late. Some of them are, no doubt, emulating the character Mrs. Robinson from the 1960s movie *The Graduate*, on the lookout for a toy boy if they get the chance. Then there are the 'Cougars', women 'of a certain age', almost certainly divorced, probably more than once. They are likely to have high-powered careers and have eschewed family for fame and power, and are on the lookout for a younger virile man as a trophy. Then there are the men: mostly divorced, often less than solvent, often on the lookout for easy sex, which is all too easily available, even with women on their girls' night out. Rarely do you see husbands and wives or boyfriends and girlfriends enjoying a night out with each other, almost never do you see a boy and girl lost in each other's company, in love and oblivious to the world around them. It is a sordid scene, and I suggest that it is the evidence that society is becoming gender polarised. Men and women have become separated, one might even say torn apart by women's liberation, which has liberated them - from men. It is now the norm for women to operate in single social autonomy, and not to be seen as a couple, with a man to whom they are permanently committed as their goal. Feminism has caused women unilaterally to renegotiate their side of the social contract, causing men, who realise that nothing they do or say will change things, to regroup into their common circles. When the Boers of South Africa were under attack in the Boer War, they would draw their armoured vehicles and wagons into a defensive circle called a *laager*.[184] Maybe men today have metaphorically done the same thing? Defensively withdrawing into their own groups in a culture based on *lager* and acting 'like boors'. Maybe the epithet 'lager lout' isn't so far from the truth?

There is a serious message here. The young strident feminists today, who constantly complain about men's sexist behaviour, citing the 'lad culture' as the worst example of maleness, would do well to stop and reflect for a moment that it is they and their ideological agenda who are driving the very social phenomenon which they condemn. When Karl Marx declared the communists' intention of creating a 'legalised community of women' little did anyone realise it would all come to pass in our modern capitalist societies - least of all in the way it has. Men today, particularly the young, are undoubtedly becoming boorish hedonists, and it is because women got there first. These men are hardly good husband and father material, but then neither are the women good mother and wife material. What goes around comes around. Feminism started a process in our society 40 or so years ago that has brought social havoc, and it will get worse - much worse - before it gets better. Men have returned to their tribal groups, and they will be essentially untameable by marriage and fatherhood.

The divorce revolution

It is fair to say that since those days in the early 1970s when Jacqueline Ceballos spoke at the packed Town Hall meeting in Manhattan and talked, as she did, about women's intention to renegotiate the idea of marriage, this once dominant institution has taken a heck of a hammering. If anyone is in any doubt about this they need only look at the figures for divorce. This former social taboo, once considered out of the question for all but the most serious of circumstances, is now so commonplace it is hard to find any adult who hasn't been divorced. Indeed it is almost expected that a man and woman who marry will not spend the rest of their lives together. This is what the UK Office for National Statistics says about marriage today:[185]

> Assuming that divorce rates and mortality rates remain unchanged from 2005, around 10 per cent of those marrying in 2005 will celebrate their Diamond Wedding Anniversary (the 60th). If current divorce rates continue, 45 per cent of marriages will end in divorce... This analysis suggests that around half of divorces occur within the first decade of marriage.

Figures for divorce are available as far back as the mid nineteenth century, and they show that for more than 100 years the number of divorces remained vanishingly small. Then came the 1960s and marriages started to fall like ninepins, as the following graph illustrates:

U.K. ALL DIVORCES 1858 - 2011
SOURCE: HM Office for National Statistics

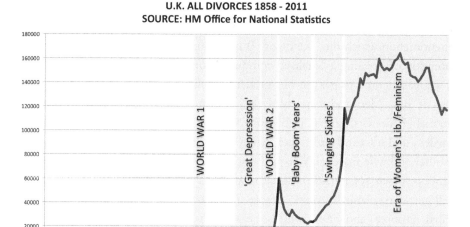

The brief spike in divorces at the end of World War II was probably due to servicemen and women returning home to find their spouses had found other loves, their relationships irreparably damaged after five years of enforced separation, which is the inevitable damage of war. However, the stratospheric rise of divorce in 1969 was for entirely different reasons. In that year a Labour government passed the Divorce Reform Act 1969 into law, which made no fault divorce available after two or five years separation, depending on whether both parties agreed or not. The Wilson government of 1964-1970 was in its second term, the period during which governments always implement their deeper ideological policies, having spent the first term overturning what their predecessors have built up, and there is no doubt that it had some pretty radical Marxists in its ranks who made it much easier for women to unshackle themselves from marriage and form the legalised community of women, which Marx had promised. The relaxation of divorce played right into the hands of the women's liberationists who were preaching that to be a wife was to be little more than a prostitute, which is Marxist dogma.

It was a false message, of course, but it was a powerful one, and it resonated profoundly with the spirit of the age. Women *en masse* began to break the covenant with men: and with monogamy, fidelity and the two-parent family. The destruction of bourgeois marriage was well underway. Divorce surged, reaching its peak in the mid 1990s, and if we separate the figures according to sex, we find that women drove this social tsunami. By the time we reached the 1990s, women were petitioning for divorce at almost three times the rate of men, and although the peak is past, they remain around twice the rate of men today. What is striking from these data is that after the initial 1969 spurt, men's petitions levelled off dramatically, remaining broadly the same ever since. Viz.:

U.K. FACT PROVEN DIVORCES MEN -vs- WOMEN 1898-2011
SOURCE: HM Office for National Statistics

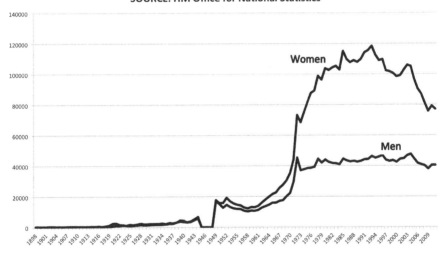

(Note: the flat line around 1946 is because of a gap in the records of the time.)

This is not the whole story, however. When we go deeper into the figures,[186] we find that divorces by mutual consent of both parties after either two years separation, or unilaterally after five years, have remained broadly unchanged since 1974, but 'fact proven' petitions on the grounds of adultery have actually declined: by 40 per cent in men, and by 59 per cent in women. Counterintuitively, considering the sexual revolution, sexual misconduct is not the major cause of failing marriages. Neither is desertion of the marriage by one party or another. Petitions on those grounds have dropped by 93 per cent for men and 88 per cent for women in the same period. Divorces granted to women on the grounds of their husbands' unreasonable behaviour (one of the grounds for divorce introduced into the 1969 divorce legislation) have also declined by 75 per cent, which is contrary to the current domestic violence and abuse narrative (of which more later). Men, it seems, are behaving themselves more appropriately in marriage. So what is driving the unprecedented divorce rate?

The primary reason given in both parties' petitions is 'unreasonable behaviour'. However, whilst women's petitions on these grounds in the period 1974-2011 have increased by 75 per cent, men's have increased by a massive 574 per cent. The way it looks is that both parties are saying they are not prepared to work at preserving their marriages, and men are getting increasingly fed up with the attitude of their wives. The shift to citing 'unreasonable behaviour' might be just an expedient, of course. It might just be being seen as the least contentious way for both parties to end the marriage. However, that does not explain the remarkable surge in men's accusations of women's unreasonable behaviour.

There are more statistics that paint an even more dismal picture. According to ONS figures,[187] the median length of a marriage today is just 11 years. If that seems like a difficult figure to accept, note that it is the median - the exact middle number in the data set. The mean or 'average' length of current marriages is 32 years, but that is being statistically pulled high by outliers: a relatively small number of long-lasting marriages, so the statisticians use the median as being more representative of the actuality, which is corroborated by the fact that one third of children[188] now experience their parents' divorce by the time they reach the age of 16. The astonishing reality is that the official statistics show that the most likely time for a marriage to end is between the 4th and 8th anniversary.[189] Divorce rates are declining, but this should not be taken as meaning that the institution of marriage is being restored, in fact it probably means the opposite. Fewer people are marrying. It is just as simple as that. Adults today who experienced their parents' divorce are alienated from marriage and its inevitable pain and suffering. Mature men in particular have woken up to the unbelievable cost of divorce, which lies on their shoulders, and that is not just financial, but emotional, especially the wrench of losing influence over the upbringing of their children, and in far too many cases the loss of them altogether. And the loss is the children's too.

'Losing the plot'

On 1st September 2013, after 22 years in office as Chief Rabbi, Lord Jonathon Sacks retired. In his final comments in a BBC Radio 4 programme, *Sunday*, broadcast on 25th August 2013, he said that in his opinion society is losing the plot:

> When trust breaks down, you see institutions break down. I think we're losing the plot actually, I think we haven't really noticed what is happening in Britain... I think a situation where children grow up in stable association with the parents who brought them into being is probably the biggest influence on the eventual shape of a society... If people work for the maximum possible benefit for themselves, then we will not have trust in industry, in economics, in financial institutions, we will not see marriages last... It's not the fault of one government or another, and it's not even the fault of government... It's the fault of what we call culture, which is society talking to itself.

Marriage is the bedrock of human experience that provides the framework in which children can be born and brought up to be responsible future contributors to the commonwealth and in which men and women can find true contentment and happiness. It is the ultimate expression of trust between a man and a woman, and it has always been the primary institution of our society. If we fail to value marriage as an institution, we fail to value society itself. If our society is talking to itself today, it is talking feminism, a culture that is intent on destroying marriage. It is talking about women's rights, needs and demands trumping everything, to the detriment of everyone, including women. This is the cultural conversation in Britain, America, Canada and a host of other developed nations, where feminism stands completely and directly opposed to marriage and the *status quo ante* of women, girls and motherhood. Its narrative, which is society's current narrative, is being totally driven by and shaped by Marx's openly declared desire to bring down marriage and create a legalised community of women. Feminism has undoubtedly inspired much of the political rhetoric in the last 20-30 years in the capitalist developed world, and it remains in a super-dominant position from where it continues to wreak untold damage on us all. If anyone is in any doubt about this, they need only read the findings of Civitas: The Institute for the Study of Civil Society, whose report, *Experiments in living: the fatherless family*[190] tells a sorry tale. Here are some headline facts from that report:

- Lone mothers are poorer.
- Non-resident biological fathers are at risk of losing contact with their children altogether
- Children living without their biological fathers are more likely to live in poverty and deprivation
- Teenagers living without their biological fathers:
    - Are more likely to experience problems with sexual health
    - Are more likely to offend
    - Are more likely to smoke
    - Are more likely to drink alcohol
    - Are more likely to take drugs
    - Are more likely to play truant from school
    - Are more likely to leave school at 16
- Young adults who grew up not living with their biological fathers:
    - Are less likely to attain qualifications
    - Are more likely to experience unemployment
    - Are more likely to have low incomes
    - Are more likely be on income support
    - Are more likely to offend and go to jail
    - Are more likely to suffer from long-term emotional and psychological problems
    - Are more likely to have children outside marriage or outside any partnership

This depressing litany of serious social problems, all of which are visible in society today, show us why destroying marriage and fatherhood is sheer social destruction. Marriage, and sticking at marriage through thick and thin, has always been 'for the sake of the children'. It is society's way of bonding fathers who form the weakest bond to young children, to mothers who form the strongest, and, by declaring it to be 'the voluntary union for life of one man and one woman to the exclusion of all others… for the procreation of children' as the church service has always said it is, it is the sanctuary in which children can be brought up in families who pass on not only inherited wealth, but a broader inheritance of family values, cultures and mores. Marriage is the means by which the legal legitimacy of children is achieved, who are recognised by their biological father so they can legally become heirs to all of this. That is what legitimacy means.

Family breakdown tears all this apart. Divorce causes fatherlessness not motherlessness, and that breaks the chain of family inheritance. The elimination of fathers and fatherhood, which is patriarchy, from children's lives creates a gross injustice to children. In our modern society, where the state has replaced fathers, substituting tax-payers' money in the form of subsidised welfare and child-support enforcement in place of the father's loving, ever-present support, children are being systematically deprived of their financial inheritance, which is called patrimony, and all because of the political hegemony of an extreme left-wing ideology, feminism, dressed up in the garb of equality for women, whose real intent is to bring all this about.

In its conversation with itself, society today must ask itself, father's rights apart, what about the equality and rights of the children? That is the deepest question. As Nicholas Langford[191] says:

> The divorce revolution has been devastating to the institution of the family, leading to huge increases in single motherhood and social pathology. Divorce and its fallout have led to a massive growth of the state and in the numbers of state officials who have a vested interest in encouraging divorce and societal breakdown. Nowhere is this more apparent than in the family courts and the domestic violence, child protection and child support industries. The primary function of many of these officials is to remove the father and let in the state. This creates a wide range of further dysfunctions, which the state can address through further expansion. These fathers are then criminalised and can be arrested for sending their children birthday cards or unintentionally bumping into their children in a public place. Fatherhood is 'encouraged' through the further state intervention of government initiatives, contact centres, and phony fathers' groups. Divorce has become an offensive weapon to politicise and criminalise fatherhood and justify a huge expansion of state bureaucracy. In this grand battle between the family and the state the family is losing. Without marriage there are no fathers. The institution of marriage exists to bind fathers to their families; in return it guarantees them legitimate heirs. Motherhood is a biological inevitability, but fatherhood is a social construct; marriage breakdown leads to fatherlessness, not to motherlessness. By pursuing policies which militate against marriage governments promote family breakdown and fatherlessness.

There is one thing upon which I beg to disagree with the honourable and thoughtful Lord Sacks. When he says governments are not at fault, I think he is in error. I believe all the evidence is that governments have had a lot to do with our current situation. Certainly left-wing, Marxist-inspired governments, but also governments from the right of politics, whose tradition is reaction. They too have colluded with feminism to the extent that they have abandoned their reactionary influence on creeping, overbearing socialism. They too have become infiltrated and colonised by radical feminists, many of them men, and are as much the cause of the problem.

Children: the true victims of feminism

The United Kingdom has proportionally more children in poverty than most rich countries in the world. UNICEF places it 14th out of 29 countries in a league table of children's material wellbeing, and the UK Department of Work and Pensions (DWP) reports that in 2011-12, 2.3 million children (20 per cent) lived in homes with incomes substantially below the average income in the UK (this rises to 3.2 million - 27 per cent - after housing costs are factored in). Yet politicians and other concerned bodies struggle to find the answer. For example, Beverley Hughes, New Labour Minister for Children, Young People and Families from 2005 to 2009, blamed the economic climate, saying, 'It is very difficult to model the impact of the recession on child poverty,' and Iain Duncan Smith, the Work and Pensions Secretary in the 2010-15 coalition government, said, 'While this government is committed to eradicating child poverty, we want to take a new approach by finding the source of the problem and tackling that.'[192] The Joseph Rowntree Foundation says, 'Ending child poverty requires action in a wide range of policy areas including childcare; skills; the availability, quality and flexibility of jobs; families and parenting; and benefits and tax credits'. These leaders of our society are struggling to find the answer because they don't understand the problem, even though it is staring them in the face.

In 2012, Sir Paul Coleridge,[193] retired senior judge of the Family Courts Division, reported that almost one-third of children in Britain were currently caught up in the Family Courts system because of their parents' divorce. Given that there are around 12 million children (under the age of 16 years) in the United Kingdom as a whole, that means 3.5 million children, after making allowance for those children in the Scottish and Northern Irish courts system,[194] which is outside his jurisdiction. This figure is very close to the 3.2 million children living in poverty, as estimated by the government DWP. Can there be any doubt that a substantial part of the problem is widespread divorce and broken homes? These figures suggest around 90 per cent of children who are caught up in divorce are immediately plunged into poverty, no doubt because of the cost of divorce, the cost of setting up and running two homes, and the single parenthood that, at least for a time afterwards, inevitably results.

And whilst all this is going on, politicians and concerned agencies dance around the problem, describing its symptoms whilst ignoring the elephant in the room, which is that our children are being sacrificed on the altar of the belief that women have a right to their autonomy, free of a husband and the strictures of conventional family life. We are besotted with the false idea that there is 'no ideal type of household in which to bring up children,' and the feminist sophistries that say children can come through family breakdown unscathed and still grow up to be successful adults, even though it is patently untrue. And all this is held enshrined and unassailable because no one, least of all our politicians, has the courage to speak out and risk the fury that descends upon them if they say anything that even hints at transgression of the feminist party line, which is all too often their own party's line.

We are throwing our babies out with the bathwater. There is no doubt about it, children are being made to pay a price for our systematic destruction of marriage as the institution it was intended to be: 'for the procreation of children to be brought up'[195] by both their biological parents in stability and unconditional love. Children, vulnerable human beings, are now just a possession to be passed like a parcel in widespread family breakdown; their care and upbringing often parcelled out between warring ex-spouses, and at least temporarily thrust into single parent families, invariably their mothers, to live in relative poverty and deprivation. When their parents re-marry or re-partner they then unwittingly, and often unwillingly, find themselves in so-called 'blended families': a jumble of step-parents, half-brothers and sisters and assorted non-blood relatives, and all too often they are permanently deprived of their biological fathers and their father's kin.

The cost of this to children is enormous. The current young generation, 'Generation Y', has been largely brought up in homes without fathers, by mothers who have struggled to cope, and the boys in that generation in particular have become de-motivated, neutered, and cowed, often retreating into their male spaces and becoming tribal. Many of them have resorted to their X-Boxes and PlayStations, losing themselves in a virtual world where the rules of engagement are clear cut, and releasing their sexual needs in that other virtual world of online pornography, which is readily available at the click of a mouse button. Far too many of them are giving up altogether and taking their own lives. According to the latest available figures from the ONS,[196] of 6,233 suicides in the UK in 2013, 4,858 of them, that is 4/5ths were men (78 per cent), the majority of those, a quarter (24 per cent), being in the age-group 20-34; with another spike between the ages of 35-49 (13 per cent), which is the age at which most divorce happens. Overall, the male suicide rate is 3.53:1 compared to women's, and it has more than doubled since 1982.

Political prudery

There is another area in which feminists are waging the fight against patriarchy: in what they call the sex-exploitation industry. Prostitution, pornography and the campaign against 'Page Three' pinups are now the latest impediment to sex equality, they argue; on the grounds that women's sexuality is being made available to men, who lay exclusive claim to it and regulate it on their terms in, for example, marriage under patriarchy in which the traditional role of a wife becomes legitimised. These arguments are just another version of the alleged objectification of women based on the self-other ideas of Simone de Beauvoir - to which are added the demand for sexual freedom for women in a looser social framework of absolute equals, the abolition of marriage as a sacramental institution and the covenant relationship between a man and a woman.

Then there is the added ingredient of the victim culture, which has emerged in feminism with a vengeance. This goes back deep into the theories of Friedrich Engels who, as Tristram Hunt[197] puts it in his Introduction to *The Origin of the Family, Private Property and the State*,[198] sees women as passive instruments of a class-based society, denied agency by patriarchal men. This translates directly into the idea that women today who engage in sexual activity of whatever kind have no moral agency in what they do: no responsibility for their own actions; are always the passive victims of men's hegemony over them, and are being exploited. Engel's ideas are very much at work in feminism's attitude to prostitution. Hunt goes on to say, 'By the time Engels came to write *The Origin of the Family*, he regarded prostitution and adultery more as products of the unnatural demands of monogamous marriage and the inequitable power relations it incorporated…' Thus, feminists are against prostitution because it undermines their desire to see bourgeois marriage destroyed, and, as Hunt puts it, '… a new kingdom of freedom would flourish in sexual relations: marriage for love, not money; communal living and child-rearing; an ability to change partners at will', would lead to, '… the eventual dying-out of prostitution.'

However much feminists purvey the idea of women as the eternal victims of men, that all sex is rape, that prostitution is all men's fault, the stark reality for them is that, like countless women down millennia, women who engage in prostitution are knowingly using their bodies for gain; they are cynically satisfying the biological drive in men that has always been there, and always will be there. It is true that some women are forced into 'turning tricks' through *force majeur* because they have no other means of making a living and need some quick money, or because they are feeding a drug habit; most sex workers see themselves as offering a legitimate service in return for payment. Indeed, most legitimate sex workers are deeply antagonistic toward feminists, whom they regard as interfering, controlling, petty moralists who have no right to tell them what they can and cannot do. They are not interested in ideology and totalitarianism.

No one who has any semblance of common sense can sensibly say that women who engage in prostitution are devoid of moral agency and that men are the cause of their 'downfall'. Prostitution is the 'oldest profession in the world', and whilst some women who do it are in some sense victims, they and the vast majority of professional prostitutes are not. The feminist narrative about prostitution is just another attempt to cast women as victims of men, while the truth is that most women who model for Page Three, or engage in any variety of sex work, are truly liberated and do not consider themselves victims in any shape or form. Indeed, many of them clearly choose to do what they do and they enjoy their way of life, making a lot of money by exploiting their natural attributes. Many of them build careers and become celebrities out of it, yet feminists continue to trot out their Marxist-Engelist mantras, which run like lava beneath the crust of rock, and are never too far from the surface.

One of the undermining errors feminists make in all of this is that their starting position is that all men are basically animals driven by their natures - and that men *need* sex because it is their nature. Nothing could be further from the truth. It cannot sensibly be said that men in general will use the services of a prostitute, or that they will attend lap dancing clubs, or even read Page-Three type newspapers. Neither is it true that men habitually use pornography, or even agree with any of it; least of all that they see sex as an expression of control over women. Even to imply this is insulting to men who, like women, are human beings with higher feelings, moral values - and self-respect.

If the sex industry is a social issue at all, it needs to be addressed by society as a whole, not blamed on men. Society needs to decide if it is a problem and deal with it, not because feminists say it is so, according to their own convoluted doctrines of men's alleged control of women. Yet, those doctrines have penetrated to the very heart of societies such as Sweden, whose laws follow the Nordic Model of prostitution. In 1999 the Swedish government enacted laws that decriminalised women who solicited for prostitution (selling sex has never been a criminal act in Britain, only soliciting, pimping, and kerb-crawling) and turned the tables by criminalising men for purchasing sex from them. Yet, this inversion of invented culpability contains within it an astonishing paradox. Does a free woman not have the ability to choose with whom she has sex? Does she not have the right to determine what she does with her own body? Can she not choose what line of work she wishes? This is the test of the feminist line on prostitution, etc., which exposes its true intention, which is, yet again, to attack men. But that is not the end of it. At 11.30 at night on 13th January 2015, the Human Trafficking and Exploitation (Criminal Justice and Support for Victims) Act (Northern Ireland) 2015 was enacted, making it illegal to pay for sex in Northern Ireland, thus bringing the Nordic Model into law in that Protestant province of the United Kingdom, whose fundamental culture, which is in favour of marriage and the family, is the antithesis of all that Marx and Engels stood for. The Bill was passed with cross party support, and had an overwhelming majority of 81 to 10. This is yet another example of the mesmerising effect feminism has on otherwise sensible people.

Legalised subjection of men

Martin Mears was the first solicitor to be elected by the entire solicitors' profession as President of the Law Society of the United Kingdom. He is a well-known legal journalist and author whose book Institutional Injustice: The Family Courts at Work,[199] is a tour de force, analysing cases from the official reports of the Family Division of the High Court of the United Kingdom, in which he shows the degree to which the family justice system is institutionally biased against men. In particular, he exposes how the judiciary flies in the face of the legal guidance given to them, to the effect that the courts' overriding duty is to give 'first consideration' to the welfare of any children in divorce proceedings. Mears states unequivocally that, in practice, this guidance is flagrantly and repeatedly ignored by judges who have taken 'first consideration' to mean, 'almost unlimited discretion' in making orders for custody, access and maintenance. He calls this 'The Law According to Denning'.

Lord Justice Denning was Master of the Rolls (in effect President of the Court of Appeal) for almost 20 years: from 1963 until 1982; and was considered by younger lawyers in his time as enlightened, radical, homely and very much lacking in the traditional pomposity of the judiciary. However, as Mears puts it, 'Denning's radicalism amounted to little more than an itch to legislate, to "interpret" rules in the way he thought they should have been made,' and that led to him taking delight in interpreting Acts of Parliament and trying to second guess the intent of Parliamentary legislators. According to Mears, Denning was undoubtedly a judge for his time. He would intervene, and create some pretty controversial case law when other judges would shrink from any form of innovative decision-making and leave it to Parliament to deal with unsatisfactory law. Crucially, however, Mears says this:

> For judges like Lord Denning's generation, women were weak, put-upon creatures ever in need of the active protection of chivalrous courts. This assumption went hand in hand with the notion that traditional male/female roles were part of the natural and inevitable order of things... In the 1990s the judiciary's paternalistic attitudes were supplemented by the impact of feminism and the Bench/Bar code doctrine that any kind of gender 'discrimination' was the worst of all evils. In practice, this meant that virtually every one of the courts' frequent 'reinterpretations' of the law represented a diminution in the position of husbands and an aggrandisement in that of wives... it is undeniable that they occurred... In children disputes, the attitudes of the courts were even more wife/mother biased... Bias and wrong headedness is... the strand running through the decisions of the senior family judges during the past 20 years. One consequence of this is that mature and responsible people, no matter how thoroughly and well advised, are not permitted to conclude their own binding prenuptial agreement or divorce settlement. The court insists on its right to set the agreement/settlement aside and to substitute its own. That Parliament should continue to permit this judicial arrogance is puzzling.

Mears suggests that the first signs of Denning's enormous influence in the corridors of the Judiciary came to the fore in the mid-1980s when positions of power and authority were being occupied by 'people, then in their middle-age, whose notions, prejudices and outlook had been acquired in the radical 60s and 70s'. Mears argues that this led to the appointment of a new type of judge: one far removed from the conservative reactionaries who were their predecessors. 'The new breed of High Court Judge,' Mears observes, '... might harbour a sentimental regard for Mr Scargill,[200] or pass an evening strumming the guitar acquired during his student days'. And the result of this? The entire Bar became infected with political correctness: '... a quasi religion in its assumption that there is a right and a wrong way of looking at the world...obsessed with discrimination, whether race, gender, sexual orientation or otherwise. The modern legal establishment shares and promotes this obsession'. Pointing out that three Bar Chairmen were overt Labour supporters who went to the House of Lords as Labour Peers under Tony Blair, Mears avers they too exerted considerable influence over legislation - but along party-political lines. He points to the Bar Council's Equality Code, issued in 1995, which is '... a model of its kind. It gives examples of the way in which the unwary might unwittingly fall into sin'. In particular, he singles out the following example of feminist-speak in all its glory, commenting that it could have been issued without amendment by any of the loony left local authorities of the 1980s:

> The document goes on to warn against asking women about their marital status or plans to have children. Such questions would stem from 'a stereotypical view of a woman's role in marriage'. It is even dangerous to ask a candidate about his/her outside activities as 'this could have an indirectly discriminatory impact on applicants with family responsibilities of an ethnic minority applicant, whose outside activities may conform to an unfamiliar set of cultural norms'. 'Informal methods of recruitment' are taboo as savouring of old boy networks. In interviewing an applicant you must not assume the sex of an interviewee's partner and a list is given of questions to avoid. These include the following: 'What are your plans for a family?', 'What does your spouse do?', 'Do you think you will be able to fit in?', 'Would you defend someone accused of homophobic harassment or attack?' [Mears, rather impishly, adds that it is not clear what the 'correct' answer to this last question is: Author]

Having dealt with the issues in The Bar, Mears turns to his own profession:

> ... [It] started out on the road to political correctness a lot earlier than the Bar. Most recently, the society has ruled that no-one can take his place as an elected member of its ruling council until he has undergone compulsory "equality and diversity" training, i.e., orthodoxy indoctrination... the catchphrase "celebrating equality and diversity" conceals the fact that, in the scale of the liberal orthodoxy, some groups count more equal than others and not all diversity is equally worthy of celebration.

Pointing out that the district judges who deal with the day-to-day workload of the family courts aren't barristers but solicitors, he candidly says they,

> ... are the products of the current orthodoxies. They too have read their Bench Book and undergone their equality and diversity indoctrination. They, no less than any of us, carry their own baggage of cultural conditioning, prejudices and preconceptions. Moreover, they are far from leaving this baggage outside the courtroom when they sit in judgement... In the exercise of his discretion, a District Judge can deprive a party of his/her home, or half his/her pension. He can order the transfer of assets representing a lifetime's work. He can impose a crippling and continuing maintenance obligation. He can, in short, impose sanctions (albeit not described as such) considerably more burdensome than a sentence of a criminal court. Who are the King Solomons vested with this draconian jurisdiction? The answer is that the typical District Judge is a very average solicitor who has achieved very moderate success in private practice. For him his appointment will usually represent a significant increment both in salary and status.

The Bench Book, issued by the Judicial Studies Board as guidance to judges, is, according to Mears, a document of 'impeccable liberal orthodoxy running to hundreds of pages,' and which, like the Bar Code '... could be issued without amendment by any of the official or semi-official organs of the discrimination industry'. This is the background, he says, which has produced the increasing flow of 'right-on judges' in the family courts who, although part of the establishment, 'will conform to the prevailing culture, whatever this happens to be,' and that is why the overriding characteristic of family law under these judges is an institutional bias in favour of wives, especially mothers, and against husbands and especially fathers. This, he says, derives originally from an old-fashioned paternalistic approach of the likes of Lord Denning and his brothers on the bench of the senior judiciary. Mears is very clear that the way the family courts have dealt with, and continue to deal with, financial and child access disputes in divorce represents '... an institutional injustice' against men, and comments that in view of the pro-wife bias of English courts it is surprising that any rich man marries at all. Mears is adamant that all is not well. 'The stream of anecdotal evidence about the injustices routinely inflicted on fathers and children has been flowing too strongly to be disregarded in the old complacent manner', he says, and, referring to the organisation 'Families Need Fathers,' which has been campaigning against this injustice for years, circulating literature, lobbying judges and MPs, writing to the newspapers, and so on, he says, 'All their efforts... got them nowhere at all. The left/liberal press sneered at them... [and] the judges continued to insist that all was well...' Turning to 'Fathers 4 Justice' a much more radical pressure group that turned to direct action, attracting much media attention over the years through stunts such as dressing up as Batman, occupying court rooms, and maintaining noisy vigils outside the homes of Family Division judges, Mears says:

> The fathers who have behaved in this way have attracted scant sympathy from the left-liberal press. On the contrary, they have been denounced as infantile exhibitionists whose alleged concern for their children was probably not genuine in any case. More probably, what we are seeing is desperate men behaving like desperate men.

'Desperate men behaving like desperate men'. What a simple statement of truth, but why does the press behave like this? The answer is because it has been colonised and compromised by feminists, who are so convinced they are right that they are operating a tacit conspiracy to suppress any dissent to their tainted beliefs about family and fatherhood. The press simply cannot see this human tragedy that is being worked out daily among us because men's feelings don't matter, they are already privileged enough, you see? Men are expendable, and anyway they are fathers - in other words, they are the hated patriarchy. There are some chinks of light in the judiciary, however. Touchingly, Mears recounts how Mr Justice Munby, a well-known family judge, said this about a case that had come before him in 2003:

> On 11 November 2003 a wholly deserving father left my court in tears having been driven to abandon his battle for contact with his seven-year-old daughter... Those who are critical of our family justice system may well see this case as exemplifying everything that is wrong with the system... There is much wrong with our system and the time has come for us to recognise that fact and to face up to it honestly. If we do not we risk forfeiting public confidence. The newspapers - and I mean newspapers generally, for this is a theme taken up with increasing emphasis by all sectors of the press - make uncomfortable reading for us. They suggest that confidence is already ebbing away. We delude ourselves if we dismiss the views of journalists as unrepresentative of public opinion.

This last comment is very interesting. Justice Mundy's sentiments are welcome,[201] but what is he saying about the press? Is he saying it represents public opinion? Either he is either being utterly naïve, or disingenuous, which is inconceivable for a judge of his seniority and experience, or he is grossly out of touch with what the press is doing. *Plus ça change, plus c'est la même chose!*

Inequality of sentencing

No discussion of the degree to which men have become the victims of society under feminism can take place without highlighting the gross imbalance in criminal sentencing that exists between men and women, which few people are aware of. Philip Davies, the Conservative Member of Parliament for Shipley, United Kingdom, has been a valiant exposer of this inequality for some time: it would seem to little avail. He is a former senior marketing manager for ASDA, one of the UK's major supermarket chains, elected to Parliament in 2005 on a slim majority of only 422, which he increased to 9,944 in 2010, maintaining it at that level in the 2015 general election. Clearly Mr Davies has impressed his constituents and enjoys their substantial and increasing support. Amongst other activities, Davies is the Parliamentary spokesman for the *Campaign Against Political Correctness*, and one of his principal interests is the sentencing of offenders in the criminal justice system.

Davies is a remarkably articulate man with a clear mind and a depth of integrity that shines through everything he says. Nowhere was this clearer than his speech in a debate at the report stage of proposed measures about women offenders and their sentencing in Westminster Hall on 16th October 2012. One of his Parliamentary colleagues said about him that he, '… stunned the Chamber into complete silence' when he painted the most remarkable picture of gender injustice in Britain today. Here is what he said,[202] with minor redactions for the sake of continuity of argument:

> 2.30 pm 16 Oct 2012. Sentencing (Female Offenders) [Sandra Osborne in the Chair]
> 'Philip Davies (Shipley) (Con): I am grateful for the opportunity to bring this debate to the House today. One of the starkest examples of how politically correct this country has become is the issue of women in the justice system and, more specifically for this debate, women in prisons and in courts. About 5% of the prison population at any one time in recent history has been female. The other 95% has been male, yet much time, effort, concentration

and brow-beating has taken place over the very small number of women in prison. There are countless groups and organisations calling for the number to be reduced. Far too many politicians - male as well as female - are willing to trot out politically correct nonsense on the subject, repeating facts that do not bear any scrutiny at all, and there are far too many calls for something to be done about a problem that, by anybody's standards, is hard to see exists, based on the actual evidence.

Let us imagine that the male population in prison represented just 5% of the total and that women made up the remaining 95%. Would there be an outcry on behalf of the men at the expense of the women? Of course not. There is absolutely no chance on earth that that would happen, so why is there all this concern over 5% of the prison population? How can normally thoughtful, intelligent people have taken such leave of their senses over the issue? The answer is simple. It is all about being politically correct, and not many people in public life like to challenge it, but I do, Mrs Osborne, and today I want to take the opportunity to scotch some myths about all types of sentencing for women. I want to bust five particular myths.

There is an old political maxim that if someone tells a lie often enough, people will believe that it is true. I can only conclude that has happened in this case. I heard the lie that women are more likely to be sent to prison than men and that they are treated much more harshly by the courts, and I was taken in by it. I presumed it was true, because I had heard it so often, and I thought it was an absolute outrage. I was so outraged by the inequality in sentencing that I decided to do some research into it. As many people know, I spend a lot of time researching matters to do with prisons, sentencing and justice, and I wanted to get to the bottom of why women were being treated so badly.

Imagine my surprise when, having looked at all the evidence, I found it was not the case that women are treated more harshly by the courts. The unequivocal evidence is that the courts treat women far more favourably than men when it comes to sentencing. I want to expose five myths today.

The first myth is simple: women are very likely to be sent to prison and are more likely than men to be given a custodial sentence. That is simply untrue. Everyone I have spoken to who is involved with the justice system confirms anecdotally that it is not the case, but let us not just take their word for it. Let us look at the facts. I asked the Library to provide evidence that more women than men were being sent to prison, as I had been told. Not only did it not provide that information, but it confirmed that the exact opposite is true. The Library stated:

'The published statistics show that a higher proportion of men are given a sentence of immediate custody than women, irrespective of age of offender (juveniles, young adults or adult) and type of court (magistrates or Crown). This has been the case in each year between 1999 and 2009 ... For each offence group, a higher proportion of males are sentenced to custody than females ... In 2009 58% of male offenders who entered a guilty plea for an indictable offence were given an immediate custodial sentence compared to only 34% of women.'

Seema Malhotra[203] (Female) (Feltham and Heston) (Lab/Co-op): Will the hon. gentleman clarify whether the information he received from the Library also looked at statistics by type of offence?

Philip Davies: Absolutely. It looked at every category of offence. For every single category, women are less likely than men to be sent to prison.

Kate Green[204] (Stretford and Urmston) (Lab): I congratulate the hon. gentleman on securing this important debate. I hope that at the end of it we will not be peddling myths, but facts. Will he comment on the fact that although 70% of men are in prison for a non-violent offence, 81% of women are, which suggests that although some statistics may favour women, that one most certainly does not.

Philip Davies: It does not mean that at all. The figures that the hon. lady quotes, which groups are fond of quoting, show the exact opposite of what they think the figures show. They show that women are treated more favourably by the courts. If she will let me continue with the speech, that will become evident to her, I hope. If she still has queries towards the end, and if the figures do not make sense, I will happily give way to her again. I am sure that the figures will make perfect sense, even to the hon. lady. I will continue with the quote from the Library:

'In 2009 58% of male offenders who entered a guilty plea for an indictable offence were given an immediate custodial sentence compared to 34% of women. For each offence group a higher proportion of males pleading guilty were sentenced to immediate custody than females.'

The Ministry of Justice's publication, 'Statistics on Women and the Criminal Justice System', published in November 2010—it is produced to ensure there is no sex discrimination in the system—states:

'Of sentenced first-time offenders (7,320 females and 25,936 males), a greater percentage of males were sentenced to immediate custody than females (29% compared with 17%), which has been the case in each year since 2005.'

People have had a briefing from the Prison Reform Trust, which tries to persuade them that women with no previous convictions are more likely to be sent to prison than men, but that is categorically not the case, as the Ministry of Justice's own publication makes abundantly clear.

Jenny Chapman[205] (Darlington) (Lab): I congratulate the hon. gentleman for providing us with an opportunity to help him understand the issue. Women convicted of a first offence—the same offence as a man—are more likely to receive a custodial sentence. I do not think he has the figures for that.

Philip Davies: No, they are not. That is the whole point. For every category of offence, men are more likely to be sent to prison than women. According to the Ministry of Justice's own publication, of first-time offenders, men are much more likely—not just slightly—to be sent to prison. That is a fact.

Jenny Chapman: May I explain again? I am talking about the first offence and the same offence. The hon. gentleman has figures for first-time offending overall and for different categories of offence. However, if we take the same offence for men and for women—the first conviction—women are more likely to get a custodial sentence.

Philip Davies: No, they are not. For the benefit of the hon. lady, I have every single category of offence. I have figures for the likelihood of men and women being sent to prison for exactly the same offence. What she is saying is simply not the case.

The Home Office undertook statistical research some years ago to try to ascertain the best comparison for similar situations. Home Office Research Study 170, 'Understanding the sentencing of women', edited by Carol Hedderman and Loraine Gelsthorpe, looked at 13,000 cases and concluded:

'Women shoplifters were less likely than comparable males to receive a prison sentence ... among repeat offenders women were less likely to receive a custodial sentence. Women first offenders were significantly less likely than equivalent men to receive a prison sentence for a drug offence.'

The Ministry of Justice publication I mentioned earlier also covers the issue of pre-sentence reports and their recommendations for sentences in the courts. It says:

'In 2009, a lower proportion of women who had a pre-sentence report that recommended immediate custody went on to receive this sentence than men (83% compared with 90% for males). For all other sentence options recommended in pre-sentence reports (Suspended Sentence Order, all community sentences or fines), a higher proportion of males received custodial sentences than females.'

Even probation officers, and we all know how soft on sentencing they are, recommend a higher number of custodial sentences than are actually given, and women again are on the receiving end of that particular benefit.

Guy Opperman (Hexham) (Con): I congratulate my hon. friend on securing the debate. I am not sure, however, that I agree with the entire thrust of what he is saying. What he is driving at, and the argument behind his thesis, is that women are being treated more preferentially, but would he accept at the very least that one of the reasons why women should be treated more preferentially is that, as mothers, they are in the position of having to look after those who might, if their mothers are not present to support them, lapse into the criminal justice system? I am sure that that is one thing with which he would wish to agree.

Philip Davies: I will come to the issue of women looking after children. As it happens, a large number of mothers who are sent to prison are no longer looking after their children when they are sent to prison. None the less, my hon. friend makes a reasonable point. There may well be good reasons for women to be treated more favourably in the criminal justice system in the courts than men. That is a perfectly legitimate argument to follow. If people want to use the facts to prove that women are treated more favourably than men and then actually give reasons why that should be the case, I am perfectly content for them to do so. What I cannot allow to happen is for the myth to perpetuate that women are treated more harshly in the sentencing regime than men, because that palpably is not the case. If we can start having a debate along the lines that my hon. friend suggests, I would be perfectly happy, but we are a long way from even getting to that particular point.

In addition to the undeniable evidence that women are less likely to be sent to prison than men is the fact that their average sentence length is shorter than that of men, too. Again, I refer to the Ministry of Justice's own published figures of November 2010. 'Statistics on Women and the Criminal Justice System':

'In 2009, women given an immediate custodial sentence for indictable offences received shorter average sentence lengths than men (11.0 months compared to 17.0 months for males)'.

That is not a minor difference. The figures show that the average male prison sentence is over 50% more than the average female prison sentence. That is something that those who allege to be so keen on equality should think about.

Kate Green: It is important to understand some of the factors behind those figures. For example, a substantially higher proportion of women in prison are first-time offenders—29% compared with 12% of men. Naturally, therefore, we would expect the sentencing for first-time offenders to be set at a lower level than for those with a pattern of offending behaviour. I am not suggesting that that explains all the difference in the figures, but it is important that the hon. gentleman gives us the full analysis and not just the headlines.

Philip Davies: It is equally important that the hon. lady listens to what I am saying rather than wrapping herself in her brief from the Prison Reform Trust. We have all heard it once but I will repeat it for her benefit. The Ministry of Justice's own publication, 'Statistics on Women and the Criminal Justice System' says:

'Of sentenced first-time offenders (7,320 females and 25,936 males), a greater percentage of males were sentenced to immediate custody than females (29% compared with 17%), which has been the case in each year since 2005.'

To suggest that more female first-time offenders are more likely to be sent to prison than men is not the case. The hon. lady says that a higher proportion of women in prison are first-time offenders, but that is because they are less likely to be sent to prison unless they commit particularly serious offences and leave the courts no option but to send them to prison. It is a complete distortion of the facts, and the Ministry of Justice publication makes that perfectly clear.

The Parliamentary Under-Secretary of State for Justice (Mrs Helen Grant): Will my hon. friend clarify whether all those statistics take into account the type and gravity of offence, previous offending history and all relevant mitigating factors, which sentencers are required to consider? It would be an unjust system if they failed to do that.

Philip Davies: Yes, they do. I will happily supply the Minister with the relevant information from the House of Commons Library, which goes to show, beyond all doubt - I am sure that she trusts the figures from her own Department - that for every single category of offence, for all ages and in all types of court, men are more likely to be sent to prison than women. There is not one blip anywhere. For every single offence, for every age and in every type of court, women are less likely to be sent to prison than men.

Mr David Nuttall (Bury North) (Con): The point raised by the Minister is important. Surely these other factors that have to be taken into account on sentencing would not affect the statistics, because they would be taken into account whether it was male or female. In fact, one assumes that they would be taken into account for both sexes, so they will not affect the statistics.

Philip Davies: My hon. friend makes a good point and he is right. Not only are women less likely to be sent to prison than men, and more likely to be sentenced to a lesser term than their male counterparts, but they are also more likely to serve less of the sentence they are given in prison. In its offender management statistics, the Ministry of Justice says:

'Those discharged from determinate sentences in the quarter ending December 2011 had served 53 per cent of their sentence in custody (including time on remand). On average, males served a greater proportion of their sentence in custody – 53 per cent compared to 48 per cent for females in the quarter ending December 2011. This gender difference is consistent over time, and partly reflects the higher proportion of females who are released on Home Detention Curfew'.

Seema Malhotra: To what extent are family circumstances, especially circumstances of children, taken into account in sentencing? Every year, 18,000 children see their mothers go to prison and only 5% of those children stay in their homes during that sentence. There are also statistics to suggest that a third of women in prison are lone parents, and it is more likely that their children will lose their homes or be placed in care as a consequence of their mothers' custody.

Philip Davies: The hon. lady is right. That is a fact that is given in the courts, which is why women are less likely to be sent to prison than men. That was a point that my hon. friend the Member for Hexham (Guy Opperman) made earlier. Let me emphasise my point with a case from earlier this year. Rebecca Bernard, who had 51 previous convictions for crimes including violence and threatening behaviour, led an all-girl gang that brought terror to her town. She has been the subject of two antisocial behaviour orders for making the lives of her elderly neighbours a misery. When this 23-year-old attacked two innocent men in a night club with a champagne bottle, it was thought that a custodial sentence was inevitable. However, she walked free from court after a judge decided that she was a good mother to her three young children. Bernard had smashed a bottle over one victim's head and then stabbed the other in the arm with its jagged neck. A court heard that she had launched the attack because she believed wrongly that the men were laughing at her. Quite clearly, those factors are taken into account by the courts, which explains why someone such as Bernard, who clearly should have been sent to prison, and who, if she had been a male, would definitely have been sent to prison, was not sent to prison. That is the explanation. I am perfectly content for the hon. lady to say that that should be the case, but at least let us argue from the facts, because then we will be acknowledging that men are more likely to be sent to prison than women.

Guy Opperman: I understand the basis on which my hon. friend is making his case. Will he address the nature of the sentence for female offenders and the degree to which they are required to work, take literacy lessons and address drug and alcohol addiction as part of the offending management programme?

Philip Davies: No, I will not, because that is a debate for another day. These are all important issues, but this particular debate is about the sentencing of female offenders, and I am concentrating on the likelihood of people being sent to prison. If my hon. friend was listening carefully at the start of the debate, he would know that the myth that I am currently exposing is that women are more likely to be sent to prison than men. As the figures that I have just quoted show, that is palpably not the case. I will go through other myths as we go through the debate, but there may not be time to go through every aspect of the criminal justice system at the moment.

Mrs Grant: It is important to clarify something. Regarding mitigation, does my hon. friend not accept that there may be some factors that are more relevant to women than to men and hence the difference—for example, domestic violence, self-harm, mental ill-health and caring responsibilities?

Philip Davies: I will come on to some of those points later. However, as the Minister will know from her Department's own figures, quite a lot of victims of domestic violence are men. In fact, for certain ages—I think that it is between 20 and 30 - there are more male victims of domestic violence than female victims. The point is that all the things that apply -

[Mrs Grant indicated dissent.]

Philip Davies: The Minister shakes her head. I know that she has not been in her post for long, but I advise her to go and look at the figures from the Ministry of Justice on domestic violence for different age ranges, because they were the figures that the MOJ quoted to me in a Parliamentary answer about three or four years ago. They may well have changed, but I urge her at least to go and look at them before she shakes her head.

Andrew Stephenson (Pendle) (Con): I secured a 90-minute debate on domestic violence here in Westminster Hall just before the recess, which a number of Members contributed to. I completely agree that there are many men who are victims of domestic violence. However, a number of studies have shown that as many as half of all the women in jail at the moment - I think that is the figure - have been victims of domestic violence and almost a third of all female prisoners have been victims of sexual abuse, so those factors are very relevant. I do not want to get into a statistical argument with my hon. friend, but I hope that this debate will broaden to discuss some of the other challenges faced by female prisoners and some of the factors that must be taken into account in sentencing.

Philip Davies: I am elated, because we now appear to have a consensus in Westminster Hall, which is an acceptance at last that men are more likely than women to be sent to prison. What we are now hearing from a variety of people are reasons why that should be the case. Those reasons may well be true - that is a debate for another day - but at least we are getting to the nub of the purpose of this particular debate that I have secured, which was to show that men are more likely than women to be sent to prison.

I will come on to discuss the women who are in prison and perhaps my hon. friend might like to explain which of the women in prison he would like to see released; perhaps other Members could do the same. However, that is the second myth; I will just finish off on the first myth that I am discussing.

All other MOJ figures confirm that men are treated more harshly by the courts than women, and that there is quite a disparity. In the past few years for which the figures are published, women had 50% more chance than men of being released from prison early on home detention curfew. So it is perfectly clear that on the likelihood of being sent to prison, on the length of sentence being handed out and on the proportion of sentence served, women are treated more favourably than men, and that applies to all ages and all categories of offences, in Crown courts and magistrates courts. At least we have made that particular point clear.

The second myth that I want to discuss, and my hon. friend the Member for Pendle (Andrew Stephenson) may well be interested in hearing about it, is that most women are in prison for petty or non-violent offences, and are serving short sentences. Many campaigners say that far too many women are in prison and should not be there; that instead, they should be serving their sentences in the community.

We can take a snapshot of the sentenced female prison population at a moment in time. The last figures that I have are for June 2010. Let us just look at the detail of all these 'poor women' who are serving prison sentences and who - apparently - should be out and about. Which of these women prisoners do those who advocate reducing the female prison sentence want to let out? Frances Crook, the director of the Howard League for Penal Reform, was quoted in The Guardian in 2007 as saying that

'For women who offend, prison simply doesn't work. It is time to end the use of traditional prisons for women.'

Perhaps she might explain which of these particular women she would like to see out and about, and not serving a prison sentence. Maybe it is the 211 women serving sentences for murder; maybe it is the 135 women in prison for manslaughter or attempted homicide; maybe it is the 352 women convicted of wounding; maybe it is the 142 women convicted of serious assault or other violence against the person; maybe it is the 58 women imprisoned for cruelty to children; it could be the 83 women who are in for rape, gross indecency with children or other sexual offences; maybe it is the 272 women who are in for violent robbery, or the 151 women who are in for burglary; or maybe it is the 398 female drug dealers who should not be in prison. The total of those figures is about 1,800, which is a figure often bandied around as the target for women offenders in prison. Maybe people would say, 'Those people should be in prison; it is the others who shouldn't be in prison'. As I have indicated, there are some people who say that no women should be in prison at all, but that argument is just so ridiculous that I hope nobody here is in favour of it.

Kate Green: I am sure that the hon. gentleman will agree that prison serves a number of purposes. One is the protection of the public. Another, though, is of course to rehabilitate offenders and prevent reoffending. It is pretty clear that prison is not doing a very good job at those things - for all sorts of reasons - both for women and for men. And the protection of the public could be better achieved through dedicated secure units for women rather than putting them into a system that is predominantly designed for a male lifestyle and male behaviours, and therefore incarcerates them in masculine-led regimes.

Philip Davies: These women are in women's prisons, which are not 'masculine regimes'. They are in female prisons, for goodness' sake.

Guy Opperman: Everybody accepts that those women are in women's prisons, but at the same time we cannot ignore a statistic that says that upwards of 70% of offenders - male or female - reoffend. Therefore, does my hon. friend accept that we have to look at a different approach, not only to sentencing male offenders - both Governments in the last five to 10 years have tried to do that - but to sentencing and dealing with female offenders.

Philip Davies: My hon. friend might be right if it was not the case that according to the MOJ - so I am sure it is true - the longer people spend in prison the less likely they are to reoffend, and quite markedly. The high rates of reoffending that he mentions only relate to people who spend short periods of time in prison. The longer people spend in prison, the less likely they are to reoffend. The figures are something like this: for those sentenced for up to 12 months, 61% of people reoffend; for one to two years, the figure goes down to about 47%; for two to four years, it is about 37%; and for more than four years, it is down to about 17%. So the longer that people spend in prison, the less likely they are to reoffend. If my hon. friend and other people are suggesting that -

Guy Opperman: Will my hon. friend give way?

Philip Davies: Hold on, hold on. If my hon. friend and other people are suggesting that the 5,442 women who are sent to prison each year for up to six months should not be in prison, presumably they must also be saying that the 51,588 males who are sent to prison each year for less than six months also should not be in prison.

[Kate Green indicated dissent.]

Philip Davies: The hon. lady may well send me a copy of her election address at the general election. If she would like to go round her constituency emblazoning the message that those who are sentenced to up to a year in prison - that is 70,000 people each year - should not be sent to prison, I will look forward to her issuing a leaflet to that effect. If she will not do that, I may well do it for her.

Kate Green: As the hon. gentleman knows, I represent a Manchester constituency where we have been piloting intensive alternatives to custody. In other words, those people who would otherwise meet the custody threshold and receive a short prison sentence of less than six months are diverted to community penalties. I must tell him that not only is that approach producing lower reoffending rates but it is very popular in Manchester, so he should not make a simplistic assumption that my constituents are not prepared to look at the deeper arguments about when custody works.

Philip Davies: I will make an offer to the hon. lady today: I am happy to go to Manchester and debate sentencing with her, any time that she wants to fix up a debate, and we will see what the majority of her constituents think. I think that the point that she makes is nonsense, but if she wants to argue it, that is perfectly fair. However, the point is that those things apply to men more than women, so this argument that this is all about women is complete nonsense. All of these issues relate to men just as much as they do to women.

[Author's Redaction: There follows an exchange about the length of sentences, not strictly relevant to the point at hand.]

Philip Davies: With respect, that is not the point that people are making, because it applies equally to men as to women. In debates and in questions we hear all this thing about women being treated more harshly than men. It is no good talking about these things, because they apply equally to men and women. No one, as yet, has been able to identify where women are treated more harshly in the criminal justice system, and that is the whole point of my debate.

Perhaps we are coming down to the other numbers. Perhaps it is the two dozen who are in for perjury...

[3.03 pm Sitting suspended for a Division in the House.]

[3.18 pm. On resuming-]

Philip Davies: No one has yet been able to tell us which of those people should not be in prison, so I presume that we can conclude only that all of them should be in prison. Therefore, we do not really have a problem.

I want to decouple one other thing. The number of women who receive short sentences in any one year is a completely different figure from the female prison population at any one time. Looking at recent figures as an example, just under 16% of female prisoners are serving sentences of less than six months, which is clearly a minority. If that is not classed as a short sentence, a further 6% are in prison for up to one year, so 22% of female prisoners are in custody for up to 12 months, which covers all cases heard in magistrates courts and some cases heard in Crown courts. All other female offenders are serving sentences of more than one year, which means their offences were so serious that they had to be dealt with by a Crown court. Those women, 78% of the total female prison population, are not serving short sentences for not-so-serious offences, as people would have us believe, but are serving much longer sentences for the most serious crimes. The figure of 78% of the female prison population comprises 34% serving between one and four years, 28% serving sentences of four years to life and 11% serving indeterminate sentences. A further 5% of offenders are in prison because after previously being released, they have either reoffended or breached their licence conditions. That is the second myth: women are imprisoned for short sentences and not very serious offences.

The third myth is that women are often remanded in custody but then are not sentenced to custody. I have heard the misuse of many statistics over the issue of remand and female offenders, so I want to introduce the House to the facts. The Ministry of Justice's own figures show that women are more likely than men to get bail. The figures are in 'Statistics on Women and the Criminal Justice System' of November 2010:

'In 2009 80% of females were bailed, compared with 62% of males; 20% were remanded in custody compared with 38% of males. The percentage remanded for both males and females is at a five-year low.'

Those figures yet again back up the fact that more men than women are sentenced to custody. The document goes on:

'Of those remanded in custody, 66% of females were then sentenced to immediate custody in comparison with 75% of males.'

When people complain about women being more likely to be remanded in custody and then not sent to prison, it is solely due to women being treated more favourably when they are sentenced. It is not that they are more harshly treated when the decision is made to remand them in custody or give them bail. The figures are perfectly clear—it is yet another deliberate myth.

The fourth myth is that prison separates mothers from their children, which unfairly punishes them. It is said that 17,000 children are separated from their mothers and that 60% of women in custody have children under the age of 18. It is also suggested that about 700 of more than 4,000 women are in prisons more than 100 miles away from their children. Let us take that in stages. First, it is not the system that separates any mother from her children. It is that individual's actions in breaking the law that have led to prison and that is almost certainly 100% their fault and their responsibility alone. As we already know from the evidence, they are less likely than men to go to prison. In addition, recently updated sentencing guidelines also incorporate consideration of the effect that custody would have on others, when the defendant is the primary carer for another. That again is likely to benefit further more women than men when they are sentenced.

If we are so concerned about the children of women offenders, what about the estimated 180,000 children who are separated from their fathers who are in prison? In this age of equality, what about that much higher figure? Should we not be more, or at least equally, outraged about that? If not, why not? Some women may be further away from their children than others in prison, but let us turn to the main point about all those women who are allegedly being so unfairly dragged away from their poor children by over-harsh magistrates and judges. That is another big myth.

My understanding is that a senior civil servant at the Ministry of Justice has helpfully confirmed recently that two thirds of the mothers sent to prison who have children were not even looking after them at the time. She apparently said of the women being sent to prison:

'Two-thirds of them didn't have their kids living with them when they went to prison.'

Why on earth is there such a huge outcry about separating mothers from their children, when most of the mothers in prison were not being mothers to their children anyway?

Jenny Chapman: I congratulate the hon. gentleman; he marshals his argument well. He makes good use of statistics up to a point. However, on this I must differ. Only 5% of children with a mother in custody are able to stay in their own home. That is not the case for men. What does the hon. gentleman think about that? What is the effect? We know that people who have parents in custody are much more likely to commit offences in future. We are trying desperately hard to break that pattern of offending, so it seems an obvious step to try to keep those relationships alive. We know that, especially with women, that is one of the single most important factors in preventing their reoffending.

Philip Davies: My point is that men are parents as well as women. The problems that the hon. lady articulates apply to men as well as women. The argument goes that this is all about women; it is not all about women. Let us not focus just on the very small proportion of women who are in prison. Let us also think about all the men, too. The whole point of the debate is to make people aware that where there are issues they apply equally to men, and that some of the issues are not even issues at all because the facts do not back them up.

Mrs Grant: On mother and baby units, it is not, with the greatest respect, all about the mother. The principal criterion for entering a mother and baby unit is that it must be in the best interests of the child. That is the most important criterion. Does my hon. friend not accept that?

Philip Davies: The point is that 66% of women sent to prison who have children are not actually looking after their children when they are sent to prison. That is the point I am making, so I am not entirely sure why we are all pulling our hair out about people who are not even looking after their children. Those children have probably either been put into care or are being looked after by other family members, probably because the mother is considered unfit to look after the children. Why should the courts treat her less harshly when the children have already been removed from her? It is a completely spurious argument.

When it comes to the minority who are looking after their children, we should not assume that they are all fantastic mothers and role models for their children. Many will be persistent offenders with chaotic lifestyles. Some will end up dragging their children into their criminal lifestyles and some will scar their children for life along the way. We presume it is in the children's best interest to stay with those mothers. It may not be in the best interest of the child for the mother to be released. It may be in their best interests for their mother to go to prison in some cases.

Others will have committed very serious offences. The same official from the Ministry of Justice said recently of women offenders:

'They can be very damaged and also very damaging.'

That is absolutely right. Sarah Salmon of Action for Prisoners' Families said:

'For some families the mother going into prison is a relief because she has been causing merry hell.'

That is another worthy point we should consider. Let us, finally, not forget those who are in prison for being cruel to their children—for abusing their own children.

The final myth is that women are generally treated more harshly than men in the justice system. It is clear that women are less likely than men to be sent to prison. Therefore, we need to look at other court disposals to see if they are then treated more harshly than men in other areas. If they are not being sent to prison as frequently as men they are presumably being sentenced at the next level down—a community order. They are not. The Ministry of Justice's figures yet again show that men are more likely than women to receive a community order: 10% of women sentenced are given a community order compared with 16% of men. The Ministry of Justice goes on to confirm that 'these patterns were broadly consistent in each of the last five years.'

Women are less likely than men to go to prison and less likely to be given a community order. That is not all. Of those who are given a community order the ones given to men are likely to be much harsher. The Ministry of Justice says:

'The average length of all community sentences for men was longer than for women...For women receiving a community order, the largest proportion had one requirement, whereas the largest proportion of men had two requirements.'

I do not want to veer into the realms of domestic violence that my hon. friend the Member for Pendle tried to go down; that is a debate for another day. However, one thing worth noting about sentencing is that despite all the evidence that shows women as the perpetrators of domestic violence in far more cases than some would like us to think, the community requirement imposed on those who commit an offence in a domestic setting is imposed only on men and cannot be handed down to women. As usual, this shows that the whole issue of equality works only one way, even when we are dealing with exactly the same offence.

Given the more severe sentences for men at the higher end of the sentencing spectrum, it is unsurprising that women are more likely to receive low levels of punishment at courts. It is a fact that a higher proportion of female defendants receive fines. All of that shows that throughout the court sentencing regime men are on average treated more severely than women.

Before I conclude there is another interesting statistic that is worth sharing. There is even an imbalance in the number of women reaching court compared with men, as more females than men were issued with pre-court sanctions. That has been consistently the case in recent years according to the Ministry of Justice. That is the evidence.

All the hysteria surrounding women in the justice system is completely without foundation, yet people want to be seen to be doing something about the so-called problem. We have the Together Women project, women-only groups for community sentences, a criminal justice women's strategy unit, women's centres, a proposal for women-only courts and, just the other day in Manchester, the right hon. member for Tooting (Sadiq Khan) proposed a women's justice board. That is all on top of the Corston report, which looked at the whole issue of female offenders and came up with even more suggestions.

Looking at the evidence, there appears to be sex discrimination in the sentencing of offenders, but the people being discriminated against are men not women. Women cannot have it both ways. They cannot expect to be treated equally in everything in society except when it comes to being sentenced by the courts for the crimes that they commit. People may want to argue that it is reasonable for women to be given lighter sentences than men, and that it is right that fewer women are sent to prison than men. That is an argument for another day, but at least when we have these debates about sentencing for men and women let us stick to the facts as they are and not what we would like them to be. Men are treated more harshly by the courts than women. If we can at least have debates that flow from that, based on the facts, we will have made a good start today.

[There then follows further political to-ing and fro-ing about minor points, redacted for the avoidance of tedium.]

This is a spirited exchange. The most vociferous opposition is almost exclusively from feminist women politicians, who make repeated attempts to waylay Davies's arguments. They try the sugar and spice argument, which is the standard feminist party line, asserting that men commit vastly more crimes than women. But that really doesn't hold water. Men and women might commit more of one type of crime and women another, but all stand equal before the law, and in any case, culpability must be the test, not classification. When that argument flounders, they revert to arguing that putting certain offences under the same generic heading hides the fact that men commit the more serious versions, and women the less. Again, that is still not the answer, as the statistics about the current UK prison population illustrate:

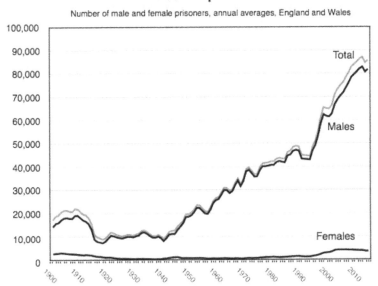

Prison Population

Number of male and female prisoners, annual averages, England and Wales

SOURCE: Ministry of Justice offender management statistics, annual to 2014.
Data supplied by Full Fact

These data strongly show two things about criminal sentencing: that after due process has taken its course, if you are a woman you will increasingly receive leniency and if you are a man you will increasingly get a prison sentence; and that these apparently unstoppable trends started in the 1960s. Taken with Davies's message that this applies for the same category of offences, there is something very wrong indeed happening in our criminal justice system. Whichever way you cut it: whatever the humanitarian considerations, or even the gallant, Denning-like view of how women should be treated in a civilised society, the extreme (one might reasonably say obscene) disparity between how women and men are receiving prison sentences for the same offences speaks of a systemic maltreatment of men,[206] and in a civilised society that constantly talks about equality, that is deeply suspicious. Women are either equal with men, and stand equal before the law with them, or they are not. Feminists cannot have their cake and eat it.

Who is John Galt?

In the autumn of 2013, the US teetered on the brink of a major fiscal crisis over a massive stand-off between Democrat President Obama and the predominantly Republican US Congress over Obama's signing into law of

'Obamacare', the Patient Protection and Affordable Care Act. This was a pure left wing-right wing tussle that nearly ended in chaos. Commenting on the crisis in an interview with BBC Radio 4's flagship morning news programme, *Today*,[207] former US Federal Reserve Chairman Alan Greenspan said he had not seen another situation in Washington where compromise seemed so far away. This is what he said:

> I actually agree with a goodly part of what the American Tea Party tries to do and I wholly disagree with their tactics. Largely because, I think which is an important issue here is that in a democratic society, people who choose to live together in the same physical location, you have to have certain fundamental things in common or you cannot obviously live together. In the United States, it's largely an agreement on our Bill of Rights, very particularly: freedom of speech and freedom of the press. Everyone agrees with that. These are principles which cannot be abrogated. But everything beyond that has to be compromised and negotiated. And what has been happening in the United States is the proportion of un-discussable issues, issues that cannot be discussed for compromise - the proportion of those issues are rising. I don't know where the key issue is but it has a very fundamentally debilitating effect on society, but there is such a level and when you get there, you run into very serious trouble. What concerns me most is that we're close to that level. I've never seen anything in my experience with Washington, and indeed before that, [where] compromise is such a small part of the discussion. Now, I don't know where we're going from here. I think that is precisely the problem. We haven't confronted the major issue, which is essentially this question: that is, it is perfectly conceivable to me that we will end up in three months, or again in six or nine months, precisely where we are now. And that is inadmissible. You cannot run a society in that respect.

Alan Greenspan towered over American fiscal policy for almost 20 years. He, better than many, knows what can happen if the normal democratic process is not adhered to, and people are left with no alternatives. He knows what happens to a society when rational mindfulness is removed, and whether you agree with Obamacare or not, a significant caucus within American politics is now very close to bringing the country to a major crisis because it believes the proportion of 'un-discussable issues' is too high. Should that happen, the normal political process will lose cohesion and people will become unable to negotiate with one another.

This, I believe, is close to a reality for men and women in our society under the relentless feminisation that is taking place in it. When any movement takes such a hold as feminism has, and seeks supremacy of its agenda over all others; when it brooks no criticism and entertains no debate from those who protest and relentlessly continues furthering its cause without due regard for the effect it is having on society as a whole; when those rational voices who speak against it are victimised and dumbed down and deprived of a meaningful voice in opposition; when debate is disbarred; when issues become 'un-discussable'; when no rational negotiation is possible; when those who dissent believe they are not being heard and cannot be heard; when the fight is futile or taboo (as in men being unable to fight women because of their deep social programming) there inevitably comes a time when they disengage and withdraw.

As a young man, Greenspan was part of the inner circle of philosopher Ayn Rand (1905-1982), a Russian émigré to the United States. Rand had lived through the Russian Revolution, witnessing the first shots in 1917, and, after graduating in philosophy in Petrograd in 1925, emigrated to the US, where she eventually rose to prominence in New York at the same time as the Beat Generation was beginning to have its influence on popular culture (although her ideas were diametrically opposed to theirs). Rand's philosophy was 'objectivism' (not to be confused with her contemporary Simone de Beauvoir's 'objectification'), which she explained, was, 'a philosophy for living on earth'. She held that there is a 'virtue in selfishness', by which she meant 'concern with one's own interests' and protecting them against those of the social collective mindset. In 1957, she published *Atlas Shrugged*, her fourth novel, which, despite receiving negative reviews, caught the American imagination and became an international best-seller. Forty-five years later, in 1991, a joint survey by the US Library of Congress and The Book of the Month Club placed *Atlas Shrugged* second only to *The Bible* as the most influential book among American readers.

Rand's ideas resonated with the spirit of independence of mind, and freedom from tyranny enshrined in the American psyche, and they still do. They underpin much of the emerging phenomenon known generically as the Tea Party movement, a conservative/libertarian political force whose principal objective is limiting the power of federal government and which draws its inspiration from the legendary Boston Tea Party, a non-violent political protest in Boston, Massachusetts in 1773 in which the 'Sons of Liberty' destroyed an entire shipment of tea sent by the East India Company in defiance of an American boycott of tea that carried an unauthorised tax. The Boston Tea Party triggered a series of events that resulted in the American War of

Independence just two years later, and today there is a mood afoot in America that socialism is being flirted with rather too much. State spending on social initiatives and interference in people's lives is going too far for the American taste, and the Tea Party movement sees this as a challenge to the precious core of the freedom to life, liberty and the pursuit of happiness, which are the founding principles of its way of life.

Rand started *Atlas Shrugged* in 1946 after World War II, when she saw the threat of communism spreading all over the world oppressing people under its collectivist heel, brutally suppressing the individual's human spirit and conforming people to the centralist political will in just the same way as the other extremists, the Nazis, had done. The West had achieved the victory over the Nazis, but Rand believed communism was the greater threat, bringing millions under centralised authoritarianism: suppressing the rights of the individual through moral and legal coercion, creating classless, moneyless and stateless societies, based on common ownership of the means of production, and imposing social, political and economic conformity. *Atlas Shrugged* makes a powerful defence of the freedom of man's mind and presciently presents the antithetical philosophical argument against feminism. As it unfolds, we see that without the independent mind, unstifled by totalitarianism, society will not progress but will collapse into a form of primitive savagery.

The novel portrays a time when America's twentieth century flirtation with socialist ideals goes awry; a time when most of the world is subsisting in abject poverty, having succumbed to communism, and American freedoms have been curtailed. What limited economic freedom remains in the US is being whittled away by a form of collectivism, which is causing the nation's prosperity to decline. The US government has forced the nation's inventors to give up their patents and intellectual property rights to the public so that all manufacturers can benefit from them; productive enterprises are being broken up and their markets shared out to weaker, less efficient competitors, and all this has led to corrupt business-men manipulating equally corrupt politicians for mutual personal gain. As the story progresses, the US Government annuls the rights of citizens to self-determination within a free democratic society, and America, the last bastion of liberty and capitalism on earth, succumbs to a surrogate form of fascist/communist dictatorship dressed in the clothes of democracy.

From the beginning of this enormous novel Rand has a number of her characters ask 'Who is John Galt?', enigmatically leaving the question hanging unanswered until the last third of the novel, when his identity is revealed. John

Galt is the leader of a group of independent-minded entrepreneurs, academics, inventors, scientists, and medical specialists who have refused to submit to the tyranny. They have chosen to defend their liberty in the only way possible, by withdrawing their services to the corrupt society and withdrawing from society itself, choosing to live their lives in a self-sufficient, inaccessible mountain community, which they have created for themselves, living off the fruits of their own talents and sharing them with no one else. Towards the end of the novel, John Galt goes on public radio and explains his reasoning for what he and his group have done. This is the beginning of that speech:

> For twelve years, you have been asking: Who is John Galt? This is John Galt speaking. I am the man who loves his life. I am the man who does not sacrifice his love or his values. I am the man who has deprived you of victims and thus has destroyed your world, and if you wish to know why you are perishing you - who dread knowledge - I am the man who will now tell you...
>
> You have heard it said that this is an age of moral crisis. You have said it yourself, half in fear, half in hope, that the words had no meaning. You have cried that man's sins are destroying the world and you have cursed human nature for its unwillingness to practice the virtues you demanded.
>
> Since virtue, to you, consists of sacrifice, you have demanded more sacrifices at every successive disaster. In the name of a return to morality, you have sacrificed all those evils which you held as the cause of your plight. You have sacrificed justice to mercy. You have sacrificed independence to unity. You have sacrificed reason to faith. You have sacrificed wealth to need. You have sacrificed self esteem to self denial. You have sacrificed happiness to duty.
>
> You have destroyed all that which you held to be evil and achieved all that which you held to be good. Why, then, do you shrink in horror from the sight of the world around you? That world is not the product of your sins, it is the product and the image of your virtues. It is your moral ideal brought into reality in its full and final perfection. You have fought for it, you have dreamed of it, and you have wished it, and I am the man who has granted you your wish.
>
> Your ideal had an implacable enemy, which your code of morality was designed to destroy. I have withdrawn that enemy. I have taken it out of your way and out of your reach. I have removed the source of all those evils you were sacrificing one by one. I have ended your battle. I have stopped your motor. I have deprived your world of man's mind.
>
> Men do not live by the mind, you say? I have withdrawn those who do.

The mind is impotent, you say? I have withdrawn those whose mind isn't. There are values higher than the mind, you say? I have withdrawn those for whom there aren't.

While you were dragging to your sacrificial altars the men of justice, of independence, of reason, of wealth, of self-esteem I beat you to it, I reached them first. I told them the nature of the game you were playing and the nature of that moral code of yours, which they had been too innocently generous to grasp. I showed them the way to live by another morality - mine. It is mine that they chose to follow.

All the men who have vanished, the men you hated, yet dreaded to lose, it is I who have taken them away from you. Do not attempt to find us. We do not choose to be found. Do not cry that it is our duty to serve you. We do not recognize such duty. Do not cry that you need us. We do not consider need a claim. Do not cry that you own us. You don't. Do not beg us to return. We are on strike, we, the men of the mind. We are on strike against self-immolation. We are on strike against the creed of unearned rewards and unrewarded duties. We are on strike against the dogma that the pursuit of one's happiness is evil. We are on strike against the doctrine that life is guilt.

There is a difference between our strike and all those you've practiced for centuries: our strike consists, not of making demands, but of granting them. We are evil, according to your morality. We have chosen not to harm you any longer. We are useless, according to your economics. We have chosen not to exploit you any longer. We are dangerous and to be shackled, according to your politics. We have chosen not to endanger you, nor to wear the shackles any longer. We are only an illusion, according to your philosophy. We have chosen not to blind you any longer and have left you free to face reality the reality you wanted - the world as you see it now, a world without mind. We have granted you everything you demanded of us, we who had always been the givers, but have only now understood it. We have no demands to present to you, no terms to bargain about, no compromise to reach. You have nothing to offer us. We do not need you.

Are you now crying: No, this was not what you wanted? A mindless world of ruins was not your goal? You did not want us to leave you? You moral cannibals, I know that you've always known what it was that you wanted. But your game is up, because now we know it, too. Through centuries of scourges and disasters, brought about by your code of morality, you have cried that your code had been broken, that the scourges were punishment for breaking it, that men were too weak and too selfish to spill all the blood it required. You damned man, you damned existence, you damned this earth, but never dared to question your code. Your victims took the blame and struggled on, with your curses as reward for their martyrdom - while you went on crying that your code was noble, but human nature was not good enough to practice it. And no one rose to ask the question: Good?: by what standard?

You wanted to know John Galt's identity. I am the man who has asked that question.

Yes, this is an age of moral crisis. Yes, you are bearing punishment for your evil. But it is not man who is now on trial and it is not human nature that will take the blame. It is your moral code that's through, this time. Your moral code has reached its climax, the blind alley at the end of its course. And if you wish to go on living, what you now need is not to return to morality - you who have never known any - but to discover it.

Today, more and more men are *Going Galt*. They are realising that disengaging altogether from women is becoming a viable strategy for living in a world where neither governments, nor those who are pushing feminism so hard, are listening to what they are saying about what feminism is doing to them and their lives, their freedoms, and their families. They are becoming resentful at the enactment of laws that are dangerous to them and eschewing the lies and gross overstatement of the women's case that permeates every news broadcast, every newspaper, every political utterance, by political parties, irrespective of their original ethos. They are becoming tired of the abusive rhetoric that is being levelled against them, the denigration of whom they are, and their value to society, and they are becoming resentful of being deprived of their liberty to speak and act freely. Using the imagery of Ayn Rand's Atlas, they are like Atlas shrugging it all off, and doing what men are uniquely equipped to do, which is find their own lives, free of all the cant. In precisely the same way that women have liberated themselves from men, men are doing the reverse - freeing themselves from women, declaring a plague on them and their ways, and this is becoming an increasing trend.

In America, it already has a name: *Men going their own way* (MGTOW), and it is taking hold in Britain and other parts of the developed world too. The blogs and chat rooms are buzzing with it, and groups of men are forming, demonstrating - resisting the increasingly anti-male stance of women, institutions, and governments. They have given up on relationships with women, or they are treating them with extreme caution, and they are studiously avoiding commitment of any kind with women, because they see it as a trap. These men know that intimate relationships have become corrupted by the ideology that women now almost universally espouse. They see women's approach to relationships as transactional, characterised by a struggle for power, and they know that they have become so regulated by law and dogma, that they are now sanitised of warmth and love. They also know women are very dangerous, sexually.

They know that the rape culture is out to get them, that they are pre-labelled as potential wife and girlfriend beaters, and that even an uncorroborated accusation is sufficient to get them arraigned. Far too many of these men have been cleaned out, both financially and emotionally, in divorce, or they will have seen other men - their fathers, their uncles, their work mates, their mentors - experiencing the deprivation of their children's love by women who have gamed the feminist-corrupted system[208] that passes itself off as a family courts' justice. They are eschewing taking on other men's children, which has become the norm in relationships nowadays, because widespread divorce and family breakdown have left so many women as a package, with other men's children in tow. Above all, they have become turned off by assertive, self-reliant women, who have abandoned the one thing that turns men on: the presentation of female vulnerability, that age-old femaleness that elicits a protective, caring response in men, and tames them to fatherhood and responsibility for their families.

Has feminism liberated men?

Writing in *Spiked*, online, on 3rd March 2015 about the 'chick flick' *Fifty Shades of Grey* - that red rag to feminists everywhere - Stephanie Gutmann said this:

> I'm not the only female who's had it up to here with politically correct men. A writer named Heather Robinson went to a Manhattan movie theatre and interviewed youngish professional women who were there in throngs to see the *Fifty Shades* movie on the eve of Valentine's Day. Manhattan dentist Alina, 33, explained that: 'The excitement of the whole thing was the seduction… [protagonist Anastasia Steele] is attracted to the fact he [Christian Grey] takes control.' Robinson wrote that: 'Many female filmgoers spoke about how refreshing it would be, in an age saturated by cyber dating and online porn, to meet more men who can step away from their computers to boldly and creatively pursue real-life women.' Robinson speculated that 'maybe the kink is just the "edgy" excuse… that gives women cover to respond to the story's true appeal. Namely, Grey's character embodies at least one old-fashioned ideal of manhood: he knows whom and what he wants, and he pursues his desires decisively.'

It seems, therefore, that sex in the city is not what it used to be. Gutmann goes on:

> ... what women have always longed for, at least in fantasy, is the alpha male (actually he doesn't even have to be that alpha, just attractive) who will pursue them and then sweep them off their delicate feet. After nearly 50 years of the systematic bludgeoning of male aggressiveness in every form by feminism, women under the age of 50 have had very little contact in their actual lives with men who pursue, who grasp, who dominate. Still, many women have a vague, inchoate sense that this might be very pleasant. I am, as they say, 'in touch with these feelings' and am able to say the unsayable because I had a tantalising taste of the world pre-feminism – before the lamps went out. It was in my preteens. Feminism was beginning its march, but it hadn't yet completely colonised every major institution of American life. It was still possible to be electrified and terrified by boys and men who showed their seemingly volcanic levels of interest, with behaviour which is now labelled 'sexist' and 'objectifying'. They did terrible things to me at the restaurant where I worked, like staring wolfishly or even walking over and saying things like 'you look so cute in your waitress uniform'. That's sexual harassment in the workplace now. Fast forward to my thirties – the age at which most women, sexually, are finally ready to really rock and roll – and to New York City. Instead of sex in the city, I found depressed, beaten men – cautious and passive around women. They were, in other words, products of Ivy League universities. They were alpha, demographically, but they sure didn't act alpha. They were coy; they sat on beds waiting for you to make the first move, they even waited for you to ask them for their phone number.

Quoting Heather Robinson, a New York writer, she continues:

> [I] went to a Manhattan movie theatre and interviewed youngish professional women who were there in throngs to see the Fifty Shades movie on the eve of Valentine's Day. Manhattan dentist Alina, 33, explained that: 'The excitement of the whole thing was the seduction... [protagonist Anastasia Steele] is attracted to the fact he [Christian Grey] takes control.' Robinson wrote that: 'Many female filmgoers spoke about how refreshing it would be, in an age saturated by cyberdating and online porn, to meet more men who can step away from their computers to boldly and creatively pursue real-life women.' Robinson speculated that 'maybe the kink is just the "edgy" excuse... that gives women cover to respond to the story's true appeal...

This is heresy indeed in our feminist age. Some women, no doubt women who have called themselves feminists in the past, or at least believers in feminism as being about women's equality, show that through their experiences in society, nothing happens in a vacuum. Every cause has its effect. Every action has a reaction, and any ideology that sweeps through a society as feminism has will produce unintended consequences for women whom, it seems, are now seeing what feminism has done for them. In the constant prattle about sexism, objectification, and professed false offence from and by women who are steeped in the rhetoric and culture of feminism, men as a class no longer dare proposition women for, you know, sex, let alone propose to women that they spend their lives together. This is the new reality. This is what is now happening in the home of sex in the city of New York, which, as we know, has been the crucible of social change for at least half a century: a place where you heard it here first. Is this a bellwether of a new zeitgeist that is going to backfire on women? Are men now so cowed by fear of relationships with women - indeed, fear of women since 'the lights went out' - that they have just switched off from it all?

Let us zoom across the world to Tokyo, Japan, where we find another manifestation of this same phenomenon. In a 2009 article entitled *Japan's 'grass eaters' turn their backs on macho ways* in *The Guardian*,[209] their Tokyo correspondent, Justin McCurry, describes an emerging breed of young professional men, estimated to be around 60% of the male population between 20 and 34, called *soshokukei danshi* - 'herbivorous boys', or *ojo*-men - 'lady-men' - who have eschewed traditional notions of masculinity and have adopted a subdued, more feminine persona in their appearance and attitude. McCurry says this:

> The typical herbivore cares, sometimes a little too much, about his appearance, eats sparingly, prefers afternoon tea with female friends to an evening spent drinking and shows little interest in the obsession that consumes so many of his peers: sex.

These young men spend their time shopping and dining out, and personal grooming: activities once the preserve of young women. They are the antithesis of the traditional, dominant Japanese male stereotype: the soldier and corporate warrior. The Grass Eaters represent a quiet social revolution in Japanese men directed against the Baby Boomer generation, 'whose lives revolved around company, colleagues and, a distant third, their wives and children' as McCurry puts it. What is even more striking about them is their attitude to life. Megumi Ushikubo, author of *The Herbivorous Ladylike Men Are Changing Japan*, says:

> They don't have the material aspirations of previous generations, they have no appetite for food, or sex. You ask them what they want out of life and they say, 'Nothing much'.

Ushikubo attributes this to young men having suffered a crisis of confidence towards the end of the 1990s, a time that coincided with the economic downturn in Japan that left the young feeling that things would never improve. However, Ushikubo points out that this lack of confidence has resulted in young men suppressing their carnal instincts because of an overdeveloped fear of rejection, which has translated into an aversion to relationship commitment. McCurry reports one herbivore respondent as saying:

> I have lots of female friends I'm attracted to, but you weigh up the risks and benefits and come to the conclusion that things are best left as they are. I'm lucky to work in an industry where there's no stigma attached to being single and no pressure to get involved with someone.

And Paul Krugman of the New York Times says, 'We're well on our way to doing similar or worse damage to ourselves.' This is the harvest we are sowing by tolerating the obscene over-feminisation of our society. Feminism is creating an entire generation of demoralised and disorientated young men.

'They died at their posts like men'

In Southampton, England, there is a memorial to those members of the ship's band who played to the end on that dark night in 1912, as RMS Titanic sank beneath the cold ocean. Cast in bronze and set in granite, it reads 'They Died at Their Posts Like Men', and the accompanying citation poignantly adds the verse from John 15:13: 'Greater love hath no man than this, that a man lay down his life for a friend'. In *Southampton: Gateway to the British Empire*,[210] Miles Taylor says this:

> These memorials serve as precursors to the kinds of public memorials that would become all too common in Britain during and immediately after the First World War when the listing of the names of the dead functioned as a

way to recognise ordinary people who had performed their duty in extraordinary circumstances. Rather than heroic deeds, these types of memorials commemorated those who 'stayed at their post' in the face of grave danger, much as many members of the Titanic's crew had done. They do not celebrate 'service beyond the call of duty, but rather [. . .] faithful performance of an allotted role'. These memorials are inherently democratic... naming the dead served as a recognition that they had 'all been equally valuable members of [the] community, because they had performed their allotted tasks to the extremity of death'... all were equally worthy of honour, 'great and lowly, peer and peasant, rich and poor, learned and ignorant, raised to one supreme level in death by common sacrifice for a common cause.'

Of the 434 women on board Titanic that night, 103 of them died, but 75% survived. Of the 2,226 men passengers, 1,357 died and only 19 per cent survived - a ratio in favour of women of over 13:1. On that fateful night in the North Atlantic Ocean, when it became clear that the ship was doomed, the traditional order 'Women and children first' was given and men dutifully complied. No longer, it seems. In her book *Men on Strike: Why Men Are Boycotting Marriage, Fatherhood, and the American Dream - and Why It Matters,*[211] Dr Helen Smith supports this view when she points out that in the Costa Concordia disaster in January 2012, men were no longer prepared to die in place of women, or children.

She quotes Rich Lowry, writing in the National Review,[212] who contrasts the disaster with that of the Titanic, saying that the men aboard the Costa Concordia had made sure the age of chivalry was dead. He cites reports of an Australian mother and her daughter who experienced men pushing women aside to get to the lifeboats, and a grandmother who had men banging into her and other women near the lifeboats as evidence.

However, Smith comments on Lowry's report by saying:

> Lowry seems to be blaming the men for what happened in the Concordia by saying that the guys aboard made sure that chivalry is good and dead, but he misses the point. The guys' behaviour is a culmination that has been years in the making. Our society, the media, the government, women, white knights and Uncle Tims have regulated and demanded that any incentives men have for acting like men be taken away ... Now they are seeing the result. Men have been listening to what society has been saying about them for more than forty

years... [And] Men got the message... As you sow, so shall you reap... Men are opting out, bailing out and going on strike in response ... a society can't spend more than forty years tearing down almost half of the population and expect them to respond 'give me another' forever. Pretty soon, a lot more men will be taking Captain Schettino's lead and jumping ship - only it will be on a lot larger scale than a boatload of people. The war on men is suicidal for our society in so many ways, and treating men like the enemy is dangerous, both to men and the society that needs their positive participation as fathers, role models and leaders.

She goes on:

I look around every day at the wonder of men, how many of them are the building blocks of our society, quietly going about their day around my office planting trees and doing the landscaping, or mowing lawns, running businesses that hire people, working as doctors to help people get better, or just making society a better place by their perseverance and abilities. But mainly what our society focuses on now is the negative traits that they perceive men to have. Misandry is so common that no one even questions it.

When I think back to the long list of men in who died in operations like Enduring Freedom in Afghanistan, Desert Storm in Iraq, the Falklands War, Vietnam, Normandy, Flanders, giving their lives and losing their limbs to protect our way of life, I ask myself: could I have done what they did? And then I realise that I would have had no choice. Men are expected to defend their country in times of war. That's just the way it is. Then I reflect on women's attitude to men these days: men who are the men's sons, grandsons and great grandsons of those who fought and died to keep us free, and I contrast their noble sacrifice with the naked hatred being practiced by those men's daughters, grand-daughters, and great grand-daughters today. Down the centuries, men have fought and died for the freedom of their women and children to have the rights women worry about so much today. They heroically rose to the challenge of those who would have taken those rights away, and they were maimed and they died so that freedom could be enjoyed by men and women alike. For as long as society has existed, men's sacrifice has preserved it. It is men who have made it possible for women, living in freedom, to be able to exercise the ability to worry about their rights in the first place, yet so many women - young and old - are on men's case today in what amounts to a study in hate-filled politicised narcissism. The sheer hypocrisy of the feminist position should make the insides of all of us heave with deep anger. Yet, even despite that, men just quietly carry on being the backbone of society, soldiering on, doing their duty, staying at their posts in faithful performance of their allotted role as fathers, protectors, and providers, acting in common sacrifice for a common cause - society.

Men like these, and many more like them, in all walks of life across the developed world, don't deserve to have to walk from a court of the land they stand up to serve and defend with their bodies, in tears, having had to abandon their battle for contact with their seven-year-old daughter because they can't beat a system that asks them to give their lives for it, and then so seriously reneges on the moral promise of equality for all. Our country doesn't deserve these men when it institutionally exercises bias in favour of women in criminal sentencing; the way it doesn't give a damn about men being the overwhelming majority of street homeless, or that men are dying of prostate cancer and there is no programme of screening or care anywhere near like that for breast or cervical cancer. The memory alone of the men who fought, were maimed, and died to allow us to have the society we have created for ourselves deserves better than the hateful rhetoric of feminism. These Atlases need to shrug, turn and refuse to give the sanction of the victim, simply saying, 'No, I refuse to fight and die for such a society'. In MGTOW we are seeing the first signs of this happening. Men are going on strike, and society will suffer as a result, of that there is no doubt. The time is here when every one of us needs to wake up to the stark possibility that in a time of national crisis, all we will have to stand between us and those who would destroy us will be a generation of young men who are demoralised, ineffectual grass eaters, or MGTOWs who don't believe in the society they might be asked to fight for.

'What our mothers didn't tell us'

In her thoughtful and revealing book, *What Our Mothers Didn't Tell Us*[213], Danielle Crittenden (b. 1963) says that feminists have a lot to answer for. Former journalist and now managing editor of blogs on the *Huffington Post*, Canada, Crittenden was described in the November, 1999 edition of *Vanity Fair* as 'one of the most important new thinkers about women and family'. She says that the general beliefs and assumptions that modern women have grown up with have led them into an entrapment: having to go to a job every day that they don't find fulfilling, and trying to be mothers in the evening in 'compressed time' as she puts it. She describes women as being at the mercy of a 'sea of demand and failing both ways', and states openly that feminism has misled the younger generation, and failed it miserably.

Women's lives, she says, are the most privileged in history, especially in the United States and Canada, and they have more opportunities than they have ever had. Yet they are as trapped and unhappy as that other generation Betty Friedan described in the *Feminine Mystique* way back in the 1950s. This, Crittenden argues, comes from the women's movement that tells women they should put everything into their career and postpone marriage and children as long as possible: that they should not lean on a man for support, or trust that men will support them, and that men discriminate against them. She counters these propositions by posing the hypothetical example of a 30-year-old man (whether married or not, whether he has children or not) and a 30-year-old childless woman: who, she asks, is an employer going to choose for promotion? It doesn't matter how many artificial legal mechanisms are put in place to avoid the obvious: women have children, and they have to interrupt their careers to do so. Putting off having children solves nothing. It is not making things easier for women. In fact, it is creating more potential for discrimination against them.

It is one thing to be equal before the law, says Crittenden, but women should not be pursuing equality if that means having the same life as a man: taking on the role of men; having the same jobs and the same career patterns as men. Yes, she admits, there are women out there who want a career, and they can have it if they pay the price of not having children, but most women basically want marriage and children, and that doesn't mean they lose their identity. The two are not mutually exclusive concepts. Crittenden unashamedly restates what her mother told her, 'Never forget, there is nothing like being a mother, and nothing more important than having a good marriage. These are the two most important things you can do as a woman', and she argues that the time for a woman to marry and have children is in her 20s, not only because she has the physical strength and resilience to cope with the demands of babies and youngsters, but also because it means she is still young when her children are grown up.

Admitting that these are strong ideas for today, she says that feminism's dogma have backfired on women in many ways. She argues that young women are getting the fallout from the 1960s feminist revolution because their mothers fell into a trap created by radical feminists. They did one thing, she says, whilst teaching their daughters to do another, and all in the name of liberation, an idea that has gone round in circles ever since, feeding on itself in a seemingly unbreakable iteration that has no meaningful solution. Real freedom for women, she argues, is not the same as the sort of equality she sees being practiced today. Women are being induced to demand freedom to pursue their careers, but the very pursuit of that freedom is creating more problems for them than it solves. Indeed, far from feminism raising women up, it is reducing their status: women are no longer respected in their role as mothers and wives.

These noble, satisfying things for a woman have been downgraded far too much because of feminism's doctrines, which, she argues, go unnaturally against women's feelings because most women have a need for motherhood, and careers are a poor substitute for what women really are there to do. Crucially, she goes on to say that women are the real losers in the sexual revolution. It used to be that a woman took time out of her career and willingly lost out on it, knowing that the payback would come in her husband's earning power later, from which she would benefit in a stable, lasting marriage. That was the deal: economic protection in return for motherhood. Yet women now assume that a marriage will not last so they have this need for a career on which to fall back when it does. However, women still have a need to marry and have their children at the appropriate time, which, interestingly, she argues, would have the added social benefit of dealing with the sexual drink-laden jungle out there.

Commenting on the effect on women of their rejection of men as economic providers, she observes that men have become re-socialised to such an extent that they don't date or buy women dinner anymore, and far too many of them are taking licence to walk away from responsibility.[214] Romance is gone from courtship, which has been abandoned in favour of men going out in gangs with each other, whilst women do the same. Even accomplished, eligible women in their 30s, who have put everything into their careers and are ready to have a family, cannot find a man who will commit to them anymore, and, she asks rhetorically, why should men commit to such a woman when they can get a younger woman for sex who doesn't want commitment? She even points to 50-year-old women leaving their husbands for 20-year-old men for the thrill, but with no hope of a long-term relationship, and they are stupidly foregoing emotional security to get a thrill, which is against women's deeper natures. She says that women are blinded not only to the social effects on women that feminism has induced, but also to the personal effects. She restates the obvious, that women are sexually different from men, and that they undermine themselves through promiscuity because it coarsens them inside.

Crucially, she reinforces the point that feminism is and always has been a highly ideological, political movement with utopian ideas about how the sexes should be, and that is why it has failed women. She points out that feminists are very hostile to criticism, and they won't brook any challenges to their ideology, but deep down the radical feminists' weakness is that they are hateful of, and towards, men. As she puts it in her own words:

> The institutionalised feminist message, according to their world view, is if you're a woman, the only way you can gain any self-respect is to join some isolationist female community and have a cat and become a lesbian; they don't want anything to do with men. They hate men. They hate little boys. They hate the whole thing and it is a very hate-filled movement.

Christina Hoff Sommers reflects similar sentiments. In her talk at Toledo Law School[215] (op. cit.), she says this:

> You've seen the play, the Vagina Monologues ... you can reduce it to a single phrase, 'Women are from Venus, men are from hell'. Most of the males, almost all of them are villains and the women are not, and it paints just a very, very grim view; it makes a woman's body look like just a site where crimes are committed ... you wouldn't know if a woman had any happiness, or pleasure, or tenderness with a man. It's so harsh...

Both Crittenden and Hoff Sommers are women with gentle voices in a shrieking jungle of feminist propaganda that always seems to have the biggest voice. One can only hope that through these women and their like, reason will prevail amongst women in general. One day, perhaps, in our torn-apart society, men and women might painstakingly be able to put their natural relationships back together again. One day, men and women might reunite in real harness with each other, not be opposed as separate political classes, vying for social power and privilege. Perhaps, one day, women will wake up to the futility of being opposed to men, whilst at the same time trying to emulate men. Perhaps they will come to realise that demanding unrighteous rights, and living out their lives as a separate community of women is not the way to life, liberty and the pursuit of happiness. One day, perhaps, the crazy competitiveness that women have launched against men might subside, and the term 'feminist' might become a pejorative term. I guess you could say, 'I have a dream' about that.

Has feminism liberated women?

Has feminism liberated women? It doesn't look like it from my perspective. What I see is a vast number of women from their 20s to their 60s who, in different ways, are more enslaved than free. No doubt, women today truly believe they are liberated, but the deep question is: liberated from what, and into what? Let us look at a few examples. First, the 20-something single professional woman, the obvious perfect beneficiary of feminism. She has a cocky self-confidence about her, a click in her high heels as she walks, and an outlook on life that gives her an air of unassailable independence, with not a hint of vulnerability. She is probably a trainee accountant, or lawyer, almost certainly from a middle-class background. She has been to university where she might have picked up a bit of gender studies on the way to her degree. At the very least, she will have been exposed for three years to feminist rhetoric through her students' union, and countless discussion groups and seminars in which political correctness rules. At work she is diligent and increasingly confident. She works really long hours, and you will see her mid evening in the mini-supermarket in bedsit land, still power-dressed and buying a cook-chill meal and a bottle of wine, which she will take back to her flat and consume before crashing out, ready for another early start next morning.

Her career is important to her. It is her security, which is her right to have. She learned that at school, from the media, and on campus, and she is utterly convinced about patriarchy and men's privilege in the world. She also probably agrees that everyday sexism is the norm and that this is because men objectify women. She might even have placed her experience of this on the everyday sexism website, and she sees Laura Bates as a heroine of the struggle for women. She will probably be in fear of being raped and will almost certainly be constantly wary of men, especially on the subway or the train. She will be convinced that domestic violence is at an all-time high, if not at epidemic proportions, and that it is always men who do it to women. That makes her even more wary of marriage and relationships with men, which probably actually aren't even on her radar. She is young and has the world at her feet - a world in which women will rule: where society will become conformed to the women's way, and all these ills will be fixed by feminism one day.

So is this young woman liberated? Does she have true liberty? Does she have a life that equips her to pursue happiness? You might well ask, especially when you see her counterparts who are 10 years older. These 30-something women are by now settled into their careers and are thoroughly middle-class singletons, still working hard and probably earning the same, if not more, than their male counterparts. She is competing successfully against them on the promotion ladder, using every ounce of her employer's efforts to be gender compliant, and be seen to be meeting all the diversity criteria. She takes advantage of that without conscience because she knows women have been oppressed for centuries, and this is her chance to overturn all that. So she will be getting ahead of many of the men in her peer group, displaying all their competitiveness, and more. She will be working even harder than her younger counterparts, and probably playing harder too.

However, her social circles will be her female peer group. She will go to a wine bar straight after work, where she will share a bottle of Chardonnay with her colleagues whilst they unwind and pull the men they work with, especially their bosses, to bits. Then, perhaps after a cocktail, or two, she will move on to an expensive restaurant where, with six or eight other women of her exact type will arrange a table for all of them and then enjoy good food, which they can well afford, and go on drinking. This woman is very much a member of legalised community of women that Marx promised her. However, her male peers are all off in their peer groups doing the same thing, so an eligible man isn't easy to find, especially one who will buy-in to her values and *her* desires for *her* life. At her age, her biological clock will be ticking and perhaps 'settling down' might be in her plans someday. However, not for her are the housewifely things, the dedicated motherhood, reliance on her husband for financial support, giving her husband and kids their breakfasts, driving them to school before returning to clean the house, spending a few hours on *Mumsnet*, then picking them up afterwards and preparing a family meal while they do their homework before sharing it with them and her husband when he returns from a heavy day at the office.

For her, the ideal husband is a man who will accept her feminist model of the modern woman in the modern marriage. She wants Marriage 2.0. One in which her husband will respect her right to continue her career: he will share equally in all the baby stuff, including changing nappies, and he will cook meals too, while she works late. She might even find the perfect man who wants to stay at home and be a house-husband so she can build up her career even further, and then be the primary wage earner. Why not? That is progress, isn't it? Why can't the roles be reversed? Feminism has changed the paradigm after all. The trouble is, although there are plenty of men around her because she is attractive, witty, sassy, and well off, they only want to sleep with her and leave the next morning. Then she either doesn't hear from them for ages, or they never come back. They just don't seem interested in commitment, and certainly not marriage. All the men who could be candidates for what she has on offer really don't want to know. They too are making money, they've got their freedom and they're out with their mates every night. Who wants to be tied down, they say. So she carries on with her wide circle of women friends in the same wine bars and restaurants, drinking with colleagues after work, and so on, but their conversation is limited to women's talk. She has no male perspective in her life. She laughs a lot but there is no dry male humour in her life.

Deep down she is becoming increasingly a loner, and lonely, and her inbuilt biological need to get pregnant starts driving her. She knows that having a child by any man is a possibility; don't many women do that these days? In fact, some women in her peer group have already done it, and at least two of them she knows never even told the father of their child. She knows she can support one, easily. She also fully believes she could pursue her career right to the top with a child in tow because all her feminist role models have assured her that she too can be a superwoman who can 'lean in' and 'have it all'. She can certainly afford to pay for child minding whilst she works long hours. In fact, the state will subsidise it. However, her background and personal values tell her she would much prefer to bring a child into the world in a proper marriage, as long as it is a marriage of equals. Anything else is unthinkable, especially the type of marriage her mother or grandmother had. That would just not fit with her ideology, or her status.

She might think about living with a man. Indeed most of her peers have been doing that since they were in their mid-20s. Few, if any, will be married though. They will be living as partners because partners are equals, see? They are definitely not wives in any shape or form because wives are chattels aren't they? Feminism has told them so. As time goes by, she starts to panic and might 'settle down' with the first likely candidate who comes along. Possibly he has resurfaced after a brief encounter one night at a night club, although they never had a second date. She might go and live with him in his flat, renting hers out, or vice versa because her flat is bigger and better furnished. However, children are not really possible because there isn't enough room for a family where they live, and in any case he doesn't want kids because he doesn't want to commit any more than he already has. She agrees, in a way. After all, he could split at any time (and so could she if a better prospect comes along) and she always has the security of her career and her own property, which she still enjoys. Nevertheless, the biological clock keeps ticking, and ticking. By now she is 40-something and resigned to not having children. She is truly married to her career, mature, poised, still good-looking, and still having a really good life. Lots of holidays and good company in far-away places. Many of her peers have done the same thing and they go away together, and have a ball. 'After all,' she rationalises, 'if women are to get to the top they have to make some serious choices. Career civil servants, the old-style matrons in hospitals never married or had children. Neither did the blue-stocking academics who rose to become professors. There is nothing new in that.' Indeed there isn't. However, what is new is the number of women who are doing that these days. Professional women are independent and rightly proud of their achievements. They have their future before them, but what does that future hold? Another 30 years of full-time and gruelling career-building and childlessness? Maybe having a child in a late, desperate marriage or cohabitation, or even without that, and still hammering on, climbing their way to the top of the professional or corporate ladder, and becoming a company director or senior partner in a leading law firm? Always fighting to stay up there with the men in terms of achievement and earnings?

Then what? Wealthy retirement, possibly with no children to produce grandchildren or to offer care and support in old age? Or having to care for an elderly and increasingly infirm parent, probably a mother because women live longer than men? No doubt some women live fulfilled lives despite all this, but many more don't, and there is little doubt that the feminist rhetoric is full of holes when it comes to these basic realities of life for many women of this type. Their perceived need to build a career for personal independence has significant implications for them. The security they build in a lifetime dedicated to career is tangible, but is it the sort of security that is real? And what about the cost of foregoing children, or not having them earlier in life? Down countless generations, women have had their children in their late 'teens and 20s, when they were strong and able to deal with the sometimes overwhelming physical demands that children bring: like the loss of sleep when they are being weaned, and endless washing of clothes, often worn only once by a naturally exuberant child, sometimes for only a few minutes. Having children at this normal time means the woman is still young when her children become independent; and not so old that she can't enjoy her grandchildren, when they come along. All of these things are stymied by delaying children. Then there is the increased risk of complications in pregnancy for older mothers, absent the risk to the child. Down's syndrome is a significant probability factor for mothers over 40.

There is another type of woman for whom things are very different. She will have foregone her career path and settled down in a much more conventional way, having found a decent man she can trust (very likely to happen if she is a middle-class professional). Indeed, 20 per cent of women do that, as I shall show in the chapter dealing with the pay gap. She will have married at age 29 or 30,[216] and her children are likely to get a good home and a stable upbringing (research is showing that almost 80 per cent of children born to middle class, professional couples will have a stable upbringing with two parents in a settled relationship). Once they are at school, she will likely return to work, which will be part-time, with hours adjusted to home life demands. However, she runs a near 50:50 risk of divorce,[217] her marriage ending possibly after only 11.5 years (the median figure given by the United Kingdom Office for National Statistics),[218] when she is in her early 40s, and she is most likely to be the petitioner, citing unreasonable behaviour on the part of her husband.[219] ONS data also tell us that divorces peak for women in the 40-44 years age group,[220] and this is also the age group in which most domestic violence and partner homicide occurs, no doubt because of the trauma and tensions of the break up.[221]

Then there is a third type of modern woman. She might be from the same socio-economic group, or perhaps a slightly lower one. She has also married in her late 20s, but after having each of her children, she has returned to work at the end of her statutory maternity leave (or even earlier). She will find, however, that her career path has stalled, and she is unable to pick up where she left off because even with the legal obligation on her employer to keep her job open, things have changed in the year or so since she left to have her child. The organisation has moved on, it has adapted to her absence, and in most cases she is obliged to take up an adapted role, (which is likely to be part-time because she will be having to balance work with the demands of children). In short, what used to be a career becomes just a job. However, with the feminist message in her head, she is told she should resent this because men create glass ceilings for women in the workplace that prevent them continuing in their careers to the very top. Feminist rhetoric still keeps telling her she can have it all: she can 'change the trajectory of women';[222] that she is entitled to better pay, more advancement, higher seniority because that is her right. But is it her right? What about if this is just being part of being a woman who recognises that her children have a right to her time and attention? A woman who recognises that her husband has rights also - to her care, love and companionship? The ship of feminist rhetoric is packed to the gunnels with women's rights, yet we hear little about the responsibilities that women undoubtedly have to their families.

So, she is in a dilemma. It is likely she will be paying out as much for childcare as she earns: in effect sub-contracting her mother's role to a stranger, and having to fit motherhood into her spare time, gleaned from a long and exhausting working day. That doesn't look like liberation to me: it looks more like slavery. And all because she has been led to believe by fanatical feminists that she is a 'modern woman' who can 'get a life'; and that motherhood and being a wife supported by a man (and not just financially but emotionally too) is not the real deal: only liberation is. Marriage and the nuclear family are a trap that stifles her, demeans her and makes her a chattel of a man, even though that man loves her. So she continues burning the candle at both ends, failing to do full justice to either career or motherhood. And she is stressed, harassed and perhaps her marriage suffers because her husband is just doing one job, albeit one that gives him no more time for family life than she has. This is the paradigm for around two-thirds of women in Britain today.

Then there is the group of women at the lower end of the socio-economic spectrum. It is almost certain that she will have several children, the first of whom will have been born during her mid to late teenage years. It is possible that some, if not all, of her children have different fathers, who may not be around or not. She is now in her 20s, and bringing up her children on her own. Her income is provided entirely by the state, comprising a cocktail of social benefits because the feminists have ensured she can exist and bring up her children without a man to provide for them. In order to maximise her benefits, it is likely she will not have disclosed the identity of her children's father(s). This woman is living in 'bureaugamy'[223] - she is married to the state, which provides for her and her children's needs in place of a father and husband. She has enough income, possibly, to make ends meet, but she never has more because the state is no substitute for a husband, it doesn't share the daily load. Her whole waking day is spent in service to her children and their needs: their clothing, eating, schooling, etc. The family remains permanently at or below the poverty line, and she never has a moment to herself for her own wellbeing, or for relationships. There might be a man somewhere in her life - perhaps he comes and stays from time to time, but never permanently because that would affect her state benefits, and, in any case, he is unlikely to want much more than sex. He certainly doesn't want to be a father to another man's children. So he acts neither like a husband to her or a father to her children.

That doesn't look like liberation to me either. It looks more like drudgery and slavery, with no prospect of any remission for at least 20 years, after which the children will have left home and started their own lives, and she will have nothing to fall back on because her family benefits will have ceased. By then she will be so worn out and her looks will have suffered so much, she is even less likely to find a relationship that gives her economic stability and true social security. She will have no work skills, nor the prospect of finding meaningful decently paid employment, and she will be forced into work for the national minimum wage in a menial job. Perhaps as a supermarket shelf-stacker on a minimum hours contract, or in the black economy as a cleaner for less than the national minimum wage, and without the prospect of a decent pension. Of course, feminists have told all these women that they are liberated. That men are superfluous to them, and they can go it alone, right? I leave it to my reader to reflect whether these descriptive stereotypes of modern women in a feminist society betray upon whose neck feminism's heel is firmly placed. None of these women, it seems to me, have benefitted from feminism. None of them are liberated in any meaningful sense of the word - at least the sort of liberation that goes with life and the pursuit of happiness. All women have done in their quest for equality and freedom is to throw away the inestimable benefits of interdependence with a man in a stable, secure, and rewarding marriage. One wonders when women will finally wake up to what they have done to themselves.

CHAPTER 11

THE FEMINIST FIFTH COLUMN

A Chapter in Three Parts

Fifth column: a clandestine group or faction of subversive agents who attempt to undermine a nation's solidarity by any means at their disposal. The term is credited to Emilio Mola Vidal, a Nationalist general during the Spanish Civil War (1936–39). As four of his army columns moved on Madrid, the general referred to his militant supporters within the capital as his 'fifth column,' intent on undermining the loyalist government from within.

Encyclopaedia Britannica

PART I

RAPE CULTURE

FEMINIST BELIEF:

'Whatever they may be in public life, whatever their relations with men, in their relations with women, all men are rapists, and that's all they are. They rape us with their eyes, their laws, and their codes.'

Marilyn French,[224] Feminist. *The Women's Room* (1977)

The anti-rape bandwagon

As I write it is autumn. The students are going back up to their universities, and the campus rape awareness bandwagon is getting itself into gear again, as it does every year. Predictably, BBC Radio's *Woman's Hour* has broadcast an item about it,[225] which presenter Jane Garvey opened by saying, 'We start with campaigns to raise awareness of rape, which is certainly not new, but tactics do seem to be changing: Is it possible to tackle and change attitudes and avoid the accusation that such campaigns inevitably lead to that age-old get-out, blaming the victim for being drunk, or for just being there?' In these opening comments, once again we hear the classic rhetoric of feminists and their regular trick of predicating their position on a begged question - in this case, two begged questions: the assumption that the attitude of society is that blaming the victim is real and needs changing, and that awareness about rape needs to be raised. Both of these propositions are highly debatable in their own right. It was all scripted to fit the programme's feminist narrative, of course. *Woman's Hour* long ago ceased to be about women's interests and current affairs seen from women's perspectives. Today, it is little more than a feminist apologetic, broadcast daily with a top-up on Saturdays (in case that isn't enough), on the formerly scrupulously unbiased and professional public broadcasting service, which continues to be paid for through a licence fee, levied on men as well as women, and enforced by the criminal law.[226]

Gone is the balance and fair-mindedness. No longer is any attempt made to tell life as it is: that time-honoured axiom of journalism. *Women's Hour*, with arch feminist Jenni Murray as its lead presenter, portrays feminism and women's interests as synonymous. That said, Ms Garvey's preamble was right on one thing: rape awareness campaigns are certainly not new. Neither is blaming the

302

victim. These are all standard soapbox sophistries for feminism. Following Ms Garvey's introduction, Rhiannon Hedge, Women's Officer for Wales of the National Union of Students (NUS), and a feminist, naturally, came on for interview. Apparently she had made four films for the NUS's Reclaim the Campus campaign, using funds made available to her by the Welsh government under its Right to be Safe policy, part of its overall aim of ending violence against women. When asked how and why she had made the films, Ms. Hedge said this:

> It was a campaign aimed at ending sexual violence towards women students and it was a campaign that creatively really wanted to tackle some of the issues, making sure we weren't blaming victims; that we were tackling perpetrators' attitudes and misconceptions about sexual violence against women… We made sure that the messaging was very much aimed at people who would or were committing the crime. We had one around the issue of consent, which was very much aimed at informing the perpetrator where the lines were, what the law was, and that it was their responsibility not to cross that line. And we had one around domestic abuse where we wanted to tackle misconceptions that physical violence was the only form of domestic abuse, so we included elements of psychological abuse, financial abuse and emotional abuse. Messages like that really… I think it's incredibly foolish to base anti-rape awareness campaigns around alcohol and that kind of consumption. I think if there's one common denominator in every single rape case, it's a rapist and if you're going to deal with a crime, you're going to look at the common denominator and that's not always alcohol. Nobody asks to be raped, whether they're drunk or wearing revealing clothing, nothing like that… I think with the students as well, particularly this drinking culture that everyone kind of attributes to students and think, well of course these things are happening, they're all getting drunk, but it is absolutely foolish to look at rape in any context other than, you know, male violence and patriarchy, in my view.

This is about as perfect an example of the party line of feminism on rape as you are ever going to get. Note the weasel words. Rape on campus is an ongoing, serious issue. Notice, '… the messaging was very much aimed at people who would or were committing the crime…' (For people, read men, of course.) Notice the *fait accompli* nature of the presentation that leaves the listener with no doubt that women are regularly being raped on our university campuses. Note the standard feminist terminology: 'perpetrator', and 'anti-rape' (as though anyone could be *for* rape?), and Ms Hedge's final sentence, '…it is absolutely foolish to look at rape in any context other than, you know, male violence and patriarchy, in my view,' thus making the neat conflation that male violence' and 'patriarchy' are one and the same thing.

This is the feminist's worldview. However, is campus rape and sexual violence against women on campus as prevalent as Hedge and *Woman's Hour* would have us believe? It doesn't take erudite scholarship to do a simple Google search for 'rapes on campus in Wales', which is what I did that morning, to reveal - well, not very much really. Such events in Wales, or even in the UK, are conspicuous by their absence. It took me quite a bit of searching to find a BBC News report of two rapes at the University of Glamorgan, which happened in the early hours of Saturday, 26th September 2009. The first was in a university residential block in Treforest, Pontypridd, and the second, on the same night, in another residential block nearby (although, strangely, the complainant didn't report it until a week later. Presumably she came forward following publicity about the first case.) As far as can be discerned from different local media sources, these offences appear to have been related. They were committed on the same night, in two closely connected halls of residence, and the attacker used the same *modus operandi*. These were clearly stranger rape incidents, committed by the same man. Only the first incident received a pretty standard piece of journalism from a local reporter who obtained the official response from the university, as follows:

> Vice chancellor Professor David Halton said full support was being offered to the victim. He said: 'Although **the campus has an excellent reputation as a safe, friendly campus,** in light of this incident we are reminding all students to follow basic safety advice such as keeping all windows and doors locked at night, stay in groups when walking around the campus late at night and to report any suspicious activity to security staff or the police. **Police said there was little crime on the campus of any description normally…** [Author's emphases]

Later in the report, he obtained a comment from the student body:

> Helen Wakeford, 23, president of the university students' union, said **it was an extremely rare incident**. 'The security on campus is excellent - there's 24-hour security and numerous cameras on campus. **To my knowledge this has never happened before,'** she said. 'The feeling at the moment [among

students] is they're trying to get on with their studies but feel deeply sympathetic to the victim. 'It's devastating to know this has happened'. [Author's emphases]

And the BBC News website report said, 'Police said there was little crime on the campus of any description normally.'

It is truly upsetting to hear of young women being attacked in their beds at night like this. In the first instance, apparently, the six foot tall rapist woke the student up as she slept in a friend's bedroom. He then threatened her at knifepoint. This must have been a terrifying experience. No doubt, it will remain with those women for the rest of their lives. But where are the reports of widespread campus rape? Surely if what Ms Hedge was saying on prime-time radio was real we would be being made aware of incident after incident, monthly, weekly, daily, wouldn't we? There would be a firestorm of protest not just on mainstream media, but social media too. Especially from the feminist lobby. But no, nothing. How does this reconcile with the absence of reports at all, let alone the comments from the university authorities, the student representative and the police, I wonder? Furthermore, how does it reconcile with the NUS's report *Hidden Marks: A Study of Women Students' Experiences of Harassment, Stalking, Violence and Sexual Assault*,[227] produced about a year after these incidents? This document, which amounts to little more than a superficial, self-styled literature review of the findings from a national online survey of 2,058 women students, amounts to a smorgasbord of comments interpreted by the NUS to show '... that harassment, stalking, violence and sexual assault are all prevalent in students' lives, and that the overwhelming majority of perpetrators were fellow students.'

In her Foreword, Olivia Bailey, NUS National Women's Officer says:

> The picture that we have revealed is disturbing. 14 per cent have experienced serious physical or sexual assault. 68 per cent have been subject to verbal or physical sexual harassment. Nearly one in four has experienced unwanted sexual contact...Very few students reported their experiences, either to their institution or to the police. In the category of serious sexual assault only 10 per cent reported it to the police, and more than four in ten told no one about the attack.

However, one cannot help being left with the conclusion that the hidden marks about all this must be truly hidden, especially in the light of the absence of corroboration from other sources, not least the comments of the police, the university vice-chancellor, and even the then president of the campus branch of the NUS in the University of Glamorgan. Were these people lying? Were they spinning and covering the truth? Or is the real truth that the feminists in the NUS are engaged in a propaganda exercise designed to whip up fear? Any reading of *Hidden Marks* will show it is no work of scholarship, nor is it research by any stretch of meaning of that word. It amounts to little more than an online survey whose questions are all about feelings and perceptions of the respondents, collected without any seeming research rigour. *Hidden Marks* amounts to little more than an assemblage of ad hoc surveys passed off as something more worthwhile; and all intended to prove an already held view: that rape on campus is widespread when it is clearly not.

It even includes reports from some respondents that relate to financial and other forms of alleged control by their parents, using their financial power to influence their children's choice of study course, and their proposed living arrangements when at university, all standard stuff for young people fresh from the parental strictures. And guess who we find adding her comments about this report on the *Aber Student Media* blog? Rhiannon Hedge, of course. This is the relevant extract:

> Rhiannon Hedge, the Women's Officer for NUS Wales, has spoken out against the misogynistic culture prevalent on many university campuses. In a statement on the Reclaim the Campus campaign, she said that; 'Educational institutions have a responsibility to create a culture that is safe for their women students – not by telling women what to wear or drink or how to behave to protect themselves from violence and abuse, but by promoting a culture that pro-actively challenges the attitudes that accept and normalise violence'.

This is the reality of our campuses today, which are intensely misandrist, and that should be of deep concern to parents of boys. It is natural that parents will be concerned about their children's choice of course and living arrangements, but those issues pale into insignificance when compared to what their sons are walking into as freshers in our universities. They are leaving home full of hope and excitement and walking into a miasma of feminism on campus, even from their own representative student body, which is working hard to install feminist dogma everywhere it can, even by making and showing propaganda films.

What is the value of making films about sexual consent, rape awareness, and DVA from the perspective of patriarchy? The answer is obvious to anyone with a discerning eye. The NUS, like many of its counterpart feminist groups, is trying to embed its party line in young people at the very earliest opportunity: as soon as they are away from home and forming their ideas for adulthood. What better time to condition them to the awfulness of men and offer the universal panacea of feminism? I suggest parents ought to be even more worried about the fact that feminists in our universities are out to either get their sons, or convert them to an ideology that plots their own downfall as men and fathers, and that these once august institutions, respected as seats of free inquiry and free expression are, to all intents and purposes, now madrassas of feminism that are turning out cohort after cohort of radicalised young people into the world, of both sexes, fully equipped with politically correct prose and feminist factoids that amount to nonsense passed off as scholarship, and never a contra argument even aired, let alone put.

This is all part of the in-depth infiltration of our universities by radical feminists who are shaping the world view of our young people, and it is being irresponsibly tolerated by university authorities who are either too stupid, too weak, too afraid, or too compromised to do anything about it. I wonder if those parents of girls from decent homes and good backgrounds, who are flexing their independence for the first time, are sanguine about their daughters being exposed to a politically-charged campus culture that says it is all right to get as drunk as they like, and dress as provocatively as they like, and if, God forbid, something awful were to happen to them, none of it would be their fault? I wonder if the parents of young men from the same backgrounds are happy to think that if, in their naïvety and inexperience, in their youthful hormonal rush, they misread signals from a drunken girl and end up in bed with her in a mutually drunken fumble, that turns out to be construed as rape or sexual assault? Even if subsequently unproven, such a charge would ruin both those young people's lives - for good. If I were the father of a son or a daughter going to university for the first time now, I think I would be very worried about their welfare indeed.

The 'f*ckrapeculture' culture

Caroline Kitchens, a researcher at the American Enterprise Institute, writing in *US News*, the online news blog, describes what it is like on US campuses these days. Under the title *The Rape 'Epidemic' Doesn't Actually Exist*,[228] she gives us an alarming insight of what is coming to the UK :

> A group of 100 protesters – including many topless women – recently
> marched the streets of Athens, Ohio chanting, 'Blame the system, not the
> victim' and 'Two, four, six, eight, stop the violence, stop the rape'. Organized
> by an Ohio University student organization called 'F*ckrapeculture,' the
> protest was designed to bring attention to what the founders believe is a toxic
> culture of sexism and sexual violence infecting their campus. F*ckrapeculture
> cofounder Claire Chadwick explained to the campus newspaper, 'The name
> of our organization and the statements that we've made are loud. But it's
> because we need to be heard'.

However, as Kitchens rightly points out, saying something loudly does not
make it true or just. As universities re-examine their sexual assault policies, she
says, administrators should be wary of the demands of these rape culture
activists, and how they condition university cultures. Bolstered by inflated
statistics and alarmist depictions of campus rape, the rape culture activists have
been remarkably successful in getting university authorities to change their
policies in order to make campuses safer places for women, but in so doing
they have made those same campuses treacherous places for falsely-accused
young men, as Kitchens illustrates with this harrowing story of Caleb Warner:

> In January 2010, University of North Dakota student Caleb Warner was
> accused of sexually assaulting a fellow student. A UND tribunal determined
> that Warner was guilty of misconduct, and he was swiftly suspended from
> school and banned from setting foot on campus for three years. Yet the police
> – presented with the same evidence – were so unconvinced of Warner's guilt
> that they refused to bring criminal charges against him. Instead, they charged
> his accuser with filing a false report and issued a warrant for her arrest.
> Warner's accuser fled town and failed to appear to answer the charges. Despite
> these developments, the university repeatedly rejected Warner's requests for a
> rehearing. Finally, a year and a half later, UND reexamined [*sic*] Warner's case
> and determined that their finding of guilt was 'not substantiated' – but only
> after the civil liberties group FIRE intervened and launched a national
> campaign on Warner's behalf.

Kitchens goes on to point out that Caleb Warner is not an isolated example.
Across America, male students are being accused of sexual assault and tried
before campus committees of as few as three people: students, faculty
members or administrators, all of whom are infiltrated by feminists and

influenced by feminist thinking, or are simply afraid of being out of step with the culture that has been created by feminism in universities. As Kitchens says:

> Such a panel is far more likely to yield gender violence activists than impartial fact finders. In a court of law, we rely on procedural safeguards to ensure unbiased jury selection and due process. But on the college campus, these safeguards have vanished. This means that if a majority of committee members believe it is just slightly more likely than not that a sexual assault occurred, they must side with the accuser... as universities re-examine their sexual assault policies, administrators should be wary of the demands of these 'rape culture' activists. Not only is their movement built on a foundation of dubious statistics and a distorted view of masculinity, but it has already led to policies that have proved devastating to those who have been falsely accused... advocates for due process, rules of evidence, basic justice and true gender equality need to speak louder than the 'F*ckrapeculture' alarmists.

These 'campus judiciaries', as she describes them, operate under dangerously low standards of proof as a result of federal mandates that, since 2011 have required institutions to consider their decisions under the 'preponderance of evidence' rather than the 'clear and convincing' standard that had prevailed hitherto. This is America today. It will be Britain tomorrow if the case of Ben Sullivan is a bellwether. At 05.30 on 7th May 2014, Sullivan, aged 21, the son of a banker and a former pupil of St Paul's school, one of the most prestigious private schools in Britain, was in bed in his room at Christ Church College, Oxford University when the police knocked at his door and arrested him. They held him in custody for 12 hours on an allegation of rape made by a fellow student, whose name he was not told. Furthermore, the case could not be reported because, although the accuser admitted making a false accusation almost a year after the encounter, after reigniting an older relationship with a former boyfriend, and had given as her reason that she had felt guilty at having had sex with Sullivan whilst drunk, she was legally allowed to remain anonymous, whilst Sullivan's name was dragged through the dirt by Sarah Pine, another student union official, who orchestrated a campaign of hate against Sullivan, who was president of the Oxford Union.

Pine brought pressure to bear on prominent people to refuse to speak at the Oxford Union, and, amazingly, Nobel Peace prize winner Tawakkol Karman, a leading human rights activist, acquiesced, as did David Mepham, the UK director of Human Rights Watch, Interpol secretary-general Robert Noble, and US entrepreneur Julie Meyer, investor, business adviser and Dragon's Den panellist. After Sullivan was told no further action would be taken against him, Pine appeared on the BBC flagship current affairs programme *Newsnight*, saying she stood by her campaign. No other interpretation can be drawn about this than that it is another example of the sheer blind feminist determination to continue stoking the fire of rape culture on our campuses with its vile message that young men are potential rapists. The entire exercise was utterly lacking in fair-mindedness and common sense, and it is sickening. Yet the activities of women such as Pine and Rhiannon Hedge are only brief examples of what can happen when the F*ckrapeculture alarmists are given a forum in which their insane ideas are treated as normal when they are not, on mainstream media, such as the BBC.

Widespread rape on campus isn't happening. There is no rape culture, only an anti-rape culture based on lies and hysteria, and that is just the tip of the iceberg of a general mass hysteria being whipped up amongst us by feminists. These malignant women, aided and abetted by the media, are deliberately and systematically trying to induce a moral panic about rape because they want to keep their ideology boiling and fomenting their deliberate calumny on men. The physical attraction men and women feel for each other: beauty, desire, and appreciation of the physical, and yes, love and tenderness, are being debased and corrupted by this insidious feminist cant, which is replacing decency with indecency. Feminist bigots are turning sexual relations, that natural, normal aspect of human behaviour into a political battleground; insidiously and relentlessly declaring men to be the enemy of women, and turning women's bodies into potential scenes of crime.

Real rape

Most people would think of rape as the example I quoted at University of Glamorgan, where a man, probably a stranger, attacks a woman for his own perverted sexual pleasure. People imagine a young attractive woman walking home alone at night being grabbed from behind, dragged into a field or a dark alley, and subjected to forced sex against her persistent protestations and sustained physical resistance. The overwhelming majority of men - good, decent men - would find such an act utterly abhorrent. There is little satisfaction for a man with a balanced sexual nature forcibly taking a woman and ravishing her against her will. For most men the real joy is the willing consent of a woman to sex, but there are some men who gain a perverted pleasure in raping women. The word rape comes from the Latin *rapere*, which means 'to seize, to carry off by force, to abduct,' and this idea was embodied in the Common Law of England as, 'The carnal knowledge of a woman forcibly and against her will'. The traditional view of carnal knowledge was that rape violated a woman's sexual purity - her virtue - a word that comes from the Latin *virtus*, in turn derived from the Greek *arete*, which means moral excellence. Virtue implies a trait or quality in women that is deemed to be morally good (the opposite word to virtue is vice). A woman's virtue, therefore, is an expression of her human dignity, and rape has always been considered not just a vile intrusion into a woman's body and a violation of her very integrity as a woman, but as the destruction of her moral good standing.

A number of basic assumptions underpinned these principles. The first was the belief that a woman who was otherwise healthy in mind and body would actively defend herself against her attacker should she be of sound mind and conscious, sufficient to cause him to use force sufficient to overcome her resistance. A continued state of physical resistance, therefore, was helpful to a woman's case in an allegation of rape. Second, it was universally believed that a woman defending her virtue would be indignant enough to make her accusation immediately and openly, and seek public redress for the alleged crime committed against her. Third, if a woman had been promiscuous, she was deemed to be without virtue, which made the proof of rape much more difficult. That is why, up until just a few decades ago, a woman's sexual history was considered important evidence by a jury of her peers trying a man she had accused of raping her. Finally, it was always considered axiomatic that an allegation of rape is the easiest thing to make and the most difficult thing to refute. However, today, that is not the case in our law, thanks to feminist activists in our political system. Rape is now nowhere near as clear cut as it used to be; indeed, the entire area of law on sexual relations between men and women has become so complex that it amounts to a mantrap. The offence of rape as most people understand it has become a series of technical rules, the infringement of any one of which convicts a man. A woman's virtue no longer has any relevance, and neither does her resistance. Indeed, a woman can now engage in the most licentious sexual activity with a man, or men, and still be deemed to have been raped, such is the technical nature of the offence today. Her allegation no longer must be made immediately, and a woman now enjoys complete anonymity throughout, whilst the man she accuses is publicly named even before his trial and the evaluation of evidence by a jury. Consent by the women must now be 'enthusiastic consent'; anything less, such as demure acquiescence to a man's advances, is likely to be deemed rape, and the man is expected to prove what steps, if any, he took to obtain the woman's consent, which is now deemed impossible to be given if the women is intoxicated with alcohol or social drugs to any degree at all. The entire burden of proof - the presumption of innocence until proved guilty - held sacrosanct for centuries in our common law, has been turned around and placed on men accused of rape.

85,000 women raped every year?

The feminists' focus on rape is, as usual, accompanied by the creation and dissemination of false information, peppered with cherry-picked incendiary statistics taken from reliable sources but cast in terms that are misleading. As we saw in the DVA debate, this is so widespread the errors become virtually immune to correction. When it comes to the difficult area of rape, two of the most widely used - and abused - examples of false statistics are the '1 in 5' factoid - that one in five women have experienced some form of sexual violence since the age of 16 - and the '85,000 women are raped each year' lie. These two falsehoods crop up time and again in the media, in official reports, and in a plethora of propaganda issued by feminist pressure groups such as *RAPECRISIS* England and Wales, whose website has a section entitled 'Myths and facts about rape and sexual violence'. In the opening paragraph *RAPECRISIS* says this:

> Government statistics released in January 2013 estimated that 85,000 women are raped on average in England and Wales every year, that over 400,000 women are sexually assaulted annually, and that 1 in 5 women (aged 16 - 59) has experienced some form of sexual violence since the age of 16. The same study reported that 28% of women who are victims of the most serious sexual offences never tell anyone about it, and we know from our experience within the Rape Crisis movement that only around 15% of women and girls who experience sexual violence ever report it to the police.

There are four statements here with which issue can be taken: 'that 85,000 women are raped on average in England and Wales every year'; that 'over 400,000 women are sexually assaulted annually'; 'that 1 in 5 women (aged 16 - 59) has experienced some form of sexual violence since the age of 16'; and 'that 28% of women who are victims of the most serious sexual offences never tell anyone about it'. First, let me point my reader to the source of these figures,

Table 2.2 given on page 13 of An Overview of Sexual Offending in England and Wales (2013),[229] which is the source to which *RAPECRISIS* hyperlinks on its website. It is a collation of data from the *Crime Survey of England and Wales* (CSEW), data from the Ministry of Justice, and a range of other official statistics from across the criminal justice system, such as police-recorded crime. Its purpose is to assemble as accurate a picture as possible of the pattern of sexual offending in England and Wales. Here is Table 2.2:

Table 2.2 – Estimated numbers of victims of sexual offences in the last 12 months among adults aged 16 to 59, average of 2009/10, 2010/11 and 2011/12 CSEW

Persons aged 16 to 59
England and Wales — Number of victims per year (thousands) [1]

Offence	Males Estimate	Males Range[2]	Females Estimate	Females Range[2]	All Estimate	All Range[2]
Any sexual offence (including attempts)[1]	72	54 - 90	404	366 - 442	473	430 - 517
Most serious sexual offences (including attempts	12	5 - 19	85	68 - 103	97	77 - 116
Rape (including attempts)	9	3 - 15	69	54 - 85	78	60 - 95
Assault by penetration (including attempts)	4	0 - 8	31	20 - 41	34	23 - 46
Most serious sexual offences (excluding attempt	9	3 15	62	47 77	70	54 87
Rape (excluding attempts)	6	1 - 11	52	39 - 66	58	43 - 73
Assault by penetration (excluding attempts)	4	0 - 8	21	12 - 30	25	15 - 34
Other sexual offences	68	51 - 85	369	333 - 406	436	395 - 477
Unweighted base [3]	20,692		24,203		44,895	

(1) Subcategory figures will not add up to the figures above them because respondents may have been victims of separate incidents of different types of sexual offence.

(2) The ranges presented in this table have been calculated using a 95 per cent confidence interval.

(3) The bases given are for any sexual offence the bases for the other measures presented will be similar.

Two 85,000 figures can be found in Table 2.2. The first is in the third column, three lines down, and the second is on the same line, but in column four. As anyone can see, the first figure relates to 'All serious sexual offences (including attempts)'. This clearly includes rape, but it also includes 'Assault by penetration (including attempts)'. So, neither of the figures relate solely to rape, and both include attempted rape and assault by penetration. The second occurrence of the 85,000 figure is the uppermost limit of a range of error induced by the sampling methods used, and it includes *attempted* rapes. Therefore it simply cannot be said that, 'Government statistics released in January 2013 estimated that *85,000* women *are* raped on average in England and Wales every year…' [Author's italicisation]

Why *RAPECRISIS* has used these figures is inexplicable, especially when Table 2.2 actually gives the number of estimated rapes as 52,000 (found in column three, line six). A similar situation applies to their claim that over 400,000 women are sexually assaulted annually. This is clearly derived from the figure 404,000, found in line one, column three. (It might also be the figure of 442,000 given in line one, column four, although that seems less likely, so I shall give *RAPECRISIS* the benefit of the doubt on that.) This figure applies to 'Any sexual offence (including attempts),' which, yet again, disallows their statement that, '…over 400,000 women *are* sexually assaulted annually,' unless they believe that attempts constitute actual assaults, which is nonsense, both legally and because attempts are classified as separate offences in their own right. Neither can it be said that, '… 85,000 women are raped *on average* in England and Wales *every year*. The title of the table clearly states that the data are an average of only three years (in fact, 2009/10 was the first ever year these data were collected), and even then the average (the arithmetic mean) is unrepresentative due to the fact that the number of respondents in each year varied widely. In the first year, only 11,000 respondents took part and that had only risen to 46,031 in the 2011/12 survey[230] - and the response varied widely. That is why the three-year average was used: to give some sort of a feel for the underlying picture. But that is by no means the full story. We must realise that these are estimated figures taken from a survey of a tiny proportion of the overall population of the UK: in fact just 0.07 per cent (calculated using 63 million as the UK population at the time), extrapolated statistically to give an estimate for the population as a whole, calculated to a 95 per cent level of statistical confidence. These are not hard data; they are not real statistics which prove their case.

Now, it might be that the people at *RAPECRISIS* are, shall we say, 'statistically challenged'? Perhaps they are not *au fait* with the use of statistics as perhaps one might reasonably expect them to be. Maybe they don't really understand the process of statistical inference? Or perhaps, which is more likely, they are simply parroting the 85,000 feminist factoid, which has become 'the truth' in the feminist echo-chamber through countless iterations, even though it is egregiously wrong. That said, surely it is reasonable to say that those charged with the responsibility of writing this organisation's propaganda (for that is what it is), can actually read, and are capable of understanding that saying 85,000 women *are* raped is not just stretching things a little too far, it is blatant lying. Whatever the truth, *RAPECRISIS* is skating on very thin ethical ice in promulgating this factoid. This is not just a matter of 'lies, damnable lies and statistics', these people are misusing a figure arbitrarily plucked from an official survey, and using it to build a case about rape that is, to say the least, highly exaggerated, and whose effect can be no other than to create misperceptions in the minds of the general public.

The extent to which the 85,000 lying factoid has become the common currency of feminists in positions of power in their desire to build their case about alleged widespread rape is well illustrated in the case of Vera Baird QC, formerly a New Labour Solicitor General, and now Police and Crime Commissioner for Northumbria. She used this feminist factoid in what was undoubtedly an ideologically-driven poster campaign on public transport in the North East of England, a conurbation of some 2.6 million people. Her posters boldly stated that, '*Over* 85,000 women *are* raped in the UK *every* year'. [Author's italicisation.] Not content, it seems, with just using the 85,000 figure, Ms Baird went totally over the top with it, saying that *over* 85,000 women are raped, and she didn't even say her figure was the estimate it is, or the average it is. She just nailed her colours firmly to the mast, adding embroidery, and sought to pass this off as a fact to millions of people. However, a member of the public apparently spotted her deceit and referred her to the Advertising Standards Authority (ASA) under their Code of Advertising Practice (the CAP Code), which requires advertising to be 'Legal, decent, honest, truthful'. The ASA upheld the complaint and Ms Baird was instructed to remove the advertising, which had cost the police authority (taxpayer's money) £15,729. This all came to light when the political party Justice for Men and Boys (and the women who love them) - J4MB - lodged a Freedom of Information Request (FoI)[231] with Ms Baird's office. When all was revealed, given the substantial sums of tax payer's money involved, J4MB called for Ms Baird's resignation in an open letter.[232] Viz.

> Using a FoI [Freedom if Information] request of your office, we obtained
> disclosure of the correspondence you had with the ASA. This indisputably
> shows that you defended your conduct robustly throughout, seeking all
> manner of excuses as to why the data were correct, when they were not, and
> you only capitulated when the ASA made it clear that their adjudication would
> be against you. Then you accepted ASA adjudication in an informal
> settlement, agreeing to withdraw the advertising in return for the ASA's
> undertaking not to make their adjudication public on their website.

Naturally, she ignored it with the usual chutzpah of feminists who are caught out in their lying propaganda. Yet this is culpable misuse of false information intended to deceive the general public, and I will leave the final comment on the issue to Professor Christina Hoff Sommers from her speech to the law school at Toledo University in March 2012:

> Now look, reasonable people can disagree about statistical findings. I don't want to get bogged down with that, but what I will tell you is that women's studies textbooks and factsheets really aren't interested in debate. It's not as if the textbook will say, 'Well some people say this and some say that, and here's what...' No, they find the most lurid, incendiary statistics and those are reported. They can be counted on to ignore studies that show low rates of victimisation or low rates of injustice for American women, no matter how rigorous or fair-minded the study may be. And they can be counted on just the same to embrace those that show high levels of victimisation or injustice, no matter how bogus the study may be... you may say that all text books have mistakes. There're bound to be some errors. Folks, I'm not talking about a few errors. I am talking about a body of false information that is at the heart of the modern women's movement. Egregiously false information, which appears to be immune to correction. And when you try to correct it, people think that you're insensitive to the problem. I'm not insensitive to the problem...I think it so heinous it drives me mad to encounter it or see evidence of it and it's because it's so serious and hateful that I think those women deserve good research: solid information, not hype, hysteria, hyperbole...

Amen to that is what I say.

The infamous 1 in 5 'statistic'

Even though it is not specifically about rape, I shall deal briefly with the claim that, '1 in 5 women has experienced some form of sexual violence since the age of 16,' because it is another false factoid that bounces around the feminist echo chamber and it is misleading people into believing sexual violence is at epidemic levels when it is not. In the 2011/12 CSEW (and remember, these are not actual figures from the entire population of England and Wales, they are an estimate, based on a sample of less than 50,000 respondents at best), the female respondents were asked to report about incidents that involved their vagina, anus or mouth being penetrated by a man's penis, even if only slightly, plus attempts to do so. These were classified into the most serious category of sexual offence, short of rape or attempted rape. In fact, 1 in 20 (five per cent) women reported that they had been the victim of the most serious sexual offences since the age of 16, not 1 in 5.

So how can *RAPECRISIS* make such a claim? It comes from the way sexual offences are categorised for the purposes of the CSEW. Only when you add 'unwanted touching' and indecent exposure does the *reported* incidence - over a lifetime - reach 1 in 5. Let us be clear about what this all means. *RAPECRISIS* calls these events 'violence', i.e., '1 in 5 women has experienced some form of sexual *violence* since the age of 16'. I do not believe any reasonable person would call indecent exposure an act of violence, nor, I suggest, would a lot of people call unwanted touching violent either. At the very most unwanted touching is likely to be construed in law as a common assault (or battery in American jurisprudence).[233] It could be something as simple as an inadvertent (or even opportunistic) contact by a man to a woman, and it could range from a brushing contact in an elevator (and, yes, even an inappropriate pat on a woman's bottom, which is definitely creepy, and which no decent man would even think of doing) to a lecherous man 'touching up' a woman in a full-blown sexual assault. All of these would be recorded in the Crime Survey of England and Wales. Whether all of these acts are generically violent is something I leave my reader to judge.

There is another element to all this. In 2012 (the latest year in which data were collected for Table 2.2), it is perfectly possible that mature women were reporting incidents from their youth. For example, taking the most extreme case, women of 59 might have reported incidents from their late teenage years or their twenties - 40 or more years ago - when they were perhaps being sexually experimental, playing courting games with boys and men, and perhaps attracting them as potential suitors. In the days prior to the era of feminism, a light pat on the posterior, or a touch of the hair by a man (or even a stolen kiss), were considered compliments by many women; today they are classed as 'unwanted touching' or assault. Now, in the narrow feminist world in which we now live, it is all 'violence'. Of course, indecent exposure - commonly called 'flashing' - might be considered intimidating or threatening by a girl or very young woman. That is right and proper. A man intimidating a girl like that deserves legal retribution. But surely mature women are able to deal with it? Before the dark ages of feminism descended, grown-up women who were 'flashed at' brushed it off and got on with their day, and their lives. In fact, most thought it was laughable. Now it is considered an unforgivable offence.

The new rape

There has always been a clear understanding of what rape is, and a clear context in which sexual intercourse was legal and illegal. Now it is not that simple. In modern rape law, a woman is deemed to have no responsibility at all, even for her own self-protection. In a sexual situation, the man is deemed to have total responsibility both for himself and the woman. Men must be in no doubt about this. This is the situation that feminists working in government have succeeded in bringing about. In the new legal regime, rape is no longer the premeditated (or at least knowingly executed) attack that forces intercourse with a woman against her defiant and repeated protestations. Now the law is so technically crafted that a man who has an ill-advised sexual encounter with a woman who has been drinking, or has taken drugs, and later alleges rape, becomes a culpable rapist, even though he has no guilty intent to violate the woman against her will, and even if his own capacity is similarly impaired through drink or drugs.

Of course some might say that our legal framework must move with the times, but what has happened in the case of rape is that it has moved as a result of pressure brought to bear by an all-pervading political totalitarianism called feminism. Feminists working behind the scenes in politics, in advisory roles, and through feminist rape lobby groups have seen to that. Since the advent of the feminist revolution in the 1970s, the legal definition of rape has been changed three times. The Sexual Offences (Amendment) Act 1976, passed by a Labour government, changed the focus from a violent attack to a non-consent model of rape; and it abolished the use of a woman's sexual history in evidence. This Act also protected the anonymity of the complainant and the accused, although this latter protection was removed in 1988 as a result of sustained pressure from feminist lobby groups, who claimed it would have a detrimental effect on justice. It was not until 2012 that Conservative Prime Minister David Cameron in the coalition government reviewed it but failed to change it on the advice of 'experts and advisers'. Cameron told *Heart FM Wales* radio: 'It's something we've looked at in the past, and there are some real issues with it. So I think it needs very careful thought before going down that road'.[234] There can be little doubt that the issues to which Cameron were referring was the potential backlash from the now massively powerful feminist lobby, led by vociferous academics who now fill the ranks of government experts and advisers.

In 1994, the Criminal Justice and Public Order Act, enacted by a Conservative government, re-defined rape as penetration of the vagina or anus by a penis without consent, thus narrowing the definition of rape considerably. It also included extended rape to include anal sex without consent, which also brought male homosexual rape under the law. Then came the feminist jewel in the crown, the Sexual Offences Act 2003 (SOA 2003), which Jeremy Corbyn, the newly elected leader of the Labour Party, acknowledged in his inaugural speech at the party's conference in 2015 as a triumph for Harriet Harman. This Act extended the 1994 definition to include penetration of the mouth by a penis without consent, and introduced a new category of offence generically entitled 'assault by penetration,' which brought what most people would call 'heavy petting' into the category of serious sexual offences, should a woman complain it was against her will. The SOA 2003 also created the offence of 'sexual assault by touching,' whereby if a person intentionally touches another person sexually without reasonable belief in the other's consent, he or she becomes guilty of a criminal offence. Therefore, the offence of rape is now part of a panoply of serious sexual offences far beyond the conventional idea of vagina-penis intercourse committed under duress on a woman.

Shifting burden of responsibility

The SOA 2003 is a legal minefield through which sexually active men - and only men - must tread with extreme care. It was specifically intended to make it easier for sexual offences, particularly rape, to be proved, and it overturned a defence to rape that had stood the test of time. In 1975, in Director of Public Prosecutions vs Morgan, there was a bizarre case whereby three men were invited by a woman's husband to have sex with her, saying she would put up a token resistance but enjoyed being overpowered in the sex act. Together with the husband, the men forcibly overcame the wife's resistance and each one had intercourse with her without her consent. At their trial, the men offered not guilty pleas on the grounds that they honestly believed the woman had consented, and the trial judge directed the jury that this was a defence in law. Nevertheless, the jury convicted the men and the case was heard on appeal by the House of Lords who upheld the conviction (on the grounds that no reasonable jury would have done anything other than find them guilty anyway), but found that the trial judge's direction, that a genuine and honest belief in consent was a valid defence, and that there was no requirement in law that required that belief to be reasonable.

This decision created legal precedent, which could only be overturned by an Act of Parliament, which is precisely what New Labour did in the SOA 2003. They negated the case law on consent in rape cases and put in place a much more codified set or rules about rape and sexual offences, introducing what is called the 'Consent Model,' which diametrically opposes the earlier genuine belief of consent defence. The proof of rape now hinges around whether a woman actively, indeed enthusiastically, consents to sex, and a man must prove that there was positive agreement on the woman's part at each stage of the sexual encounter, right up to intercourse (and even during it). Rape, therefore, is no longer about a woman defending her virtue, using whatever strength she has to prevent being violated. Least of all does she need to demonstrate the use of force by her assailant. All of these commonly held views about rape no longer apply. The issues of violence apart, a man can no longer rely on a woman's acquiescence to her seduction, to what used to be understood as a woman demurely succumbing to a man's advances. Unless an intimate encounter between a man and a woman is accompanied by that woman's enthusiastic consent, the man is at serious risk of being tried and convicted of rape should a woman so accuse him. Under the feminist-inspired New Labour SOA 2003, a clumsy, perhaps drunken, sexual encounter between a man and a woman, where both are acting stupidly, thoughtlessly and perhaps in lust: where a man may misread the woman's consent in the heat of passion, or press his sexual attention on her, to which she ultimately passively submits but later regrets, can result in that man being accused of rape with at least a very much weakened defence, and possibly one that is non-existent.

A boy at university who, in a bout of heavy petting with a girl, can easily become a rapist if the girl later alleges that what he did to her was unwanted, and any man who has had sex with a women without her enthusiastic consent at each stage is technically a rapist. How many men have had an early morning, lazy, sleepy sexual encounter with a woman, possibly their wife or partner? This is now the domain in which the feminist regime of rape is stalking. It has long been the law that a husband can rape his wife, but in their attempt to prevent blurred lines, feminists have now crafted a definition of consent that is so precisely crafted, the boundaries so easily crossed, and the context so irrelevant, that men can be rapists without even realising it. A man accused of rape is in serious difficulty if he has sex with a woman and he cannot demonstrate that he took all reasonable steps to check whether or not she was consenting to sex, and that her consent was enthusiastic. And as though that wasn't enough, the man must now show that the women had the capacity to give consent. According to the SOA 2003, a woman's consent to sex must be reasonable, '… having regard to all the circumstances', and '… a person consents if he [she] agrees by choice, and has the freedom and capacity to make that choice'. This means that a woman's consent to sex is deemed invalid in law if she has consumed alcohol or drugs sufficient to impair her judgement, even if she is far from being incapacitated in the popular meaning of that word (for example, if she is unconscious or in an alcoholic or drug-induced sleep - or even comatose - which most people would rightly regard as a rape situation). This is the degree to which sex between men and women has come under feminist regulation.

Now, some people might just say that this is all perfectly in line with modern thinking and modern sexual mores in a changing, modern world, but actually it is pure feminist doctrine, and the proof of that can be found in an essay Germaine Greer published in Playboy magazine in 1973:

> Morally, those of us who have a high opinion of sex cannot accept the idea of passive consent sanctioning all kinds of carnal communication; rather than rely on the negative criterion that absence of resistance justifies sexual congress, we must insist that evidence of positive desire alone dignifies sexual intercourse and makes it joyful. From a proud and passionate woman's point of view, anything less is rape.

The SOA 2003 is the epitome of feminist social engineering. It shows how far the law has now gone in obeying the feminist narrative. Not only have feminists succeeded in shaping social thinking about rape over decades, they have even succeeded in creating a legal regime for their doctrines and tenets. And not content with that, they are now trying to control the number of prosecutions for rape, which is a point to which I shall now turn.

An enlightened regime?

Jennifer Temkin (b. 1948) is described in an article in *The Guardian* as a 'Women's advocate'[235] who says that the London School of Economics (LSE), where she first studied, was a 'hotbed of revolutionary politics,' and, 'I was an observer of the phenomenon from the sidelines'. Ms Temkin is now a Professor of Law at City Law School, a prolific writer on the law of rape and the so-called 'justice gap' (the alleged disconnect between the changes in rape law and the number of prosecutions that have resulted from it). According to her City Law School web page, she has been a member of the Expert Group on Rape and Sexual Assault, Victims of Violence and Abuse Prevention Programme between 2005 and 2007 for the Department of Health, under the Blair Labour government, and in 2010 she acted as a Peer Reviewer for the Labour Ministry of Justice research report entitled 'Providing Anonymity to Rape Defendants: An Assessment of Evidence'.[236]

Professor Temkin is one of the many influential feminist academics who hover on the periphery of politics, from where, behind the scenes, they drive their feminist agenda, working tirelessly to pollute political perceptions about rape and nudge public policy towards the feminist narrative. This became clear when, in 1999, the then New Labour administration set up The Sex Offences Review, billed as part of an overall strategy to bring more criminals to justice, and Professor Temkin and another feminist activist academic, Liz Kelly, currently Professor of Sexualised Violence at London Metropolitan University, were appointed as members of the review steering group.[237] Both of these women are described as 'established feminist academics' in a footnote to a 2004 working paper[238] discussing rape law reform in England and Wales, published by Nicole Westmarland, a former taxi driver turned doctoral student at the School of Policy Studies, University of Bath, who is now a Professor of Criminology at the University of Durham and Director of the Durham Centre for Research into Violence and Abuse, and is an active advocate of universities circumventing the criminal justice system and dispensing their own summary judgement on young men accused of rape on campus.[239] Crucially, elsewhere in her working paper, Westmarland says, 'Intentionally or unintentionally, the [New Labour Sex Offences] review was therefore guided by a strong feminist influence'.[240] Professor Temkin's particular campaign is focussed on what she calls the 'Justice Gap,' which she describes as, 'a yawning chasm between the number of rapes reported, and the number of convictions'. In support of this claim, she says:

> Only 5.6 per cent of British women who take their complaint to the police see their assailant convicted. Many more decide to keep quiet rather than go through the humiliation of being interrogated in the dock.

This is the standard feminist party line of course, but it is an astonishing statement. Apart from the obvious emotive twisting of terms such as her reference to women being 'interrogated in the dock,' when complainants are questioned in the witness box (it is impossible to believe that as a professor she is not aware of the difference between the dock and the witness box), what she is implying simply beggars belief. How can she justify her assertion that, 'many more [women] decide to keep quiet, etc.'?

Professor Temkin's figures are right, of course. The latest statistics issued by the UK ONS for England and Wales available at the time of writing are for 2012-13, and these clearly state that in that year, 15,670 rapes were reported to the police. Of those, 2,910 cases were sent for trial by the Crown Prosecution Service (CPS) and that resulted in 1,070 convictions. By my calculation that is 6.8 per cent (rounded), which is more than her 5.6 per cent, but close enough for broad agreement. What is disturbing about her approach, however, is the lack of cool rationality, which stands in stark contrast to other women academics, such as Helen Reece, a qualified barrister and Reader in Law at Ms Temkin's *alma mater*, the LSE, who challenges Temkin's view head-on. Reece's main research interest is in probing the contemporary feminist approach to violence against women, and she is particularly concerned about what she describes as the trend towards 'the regulation of intimacy' in our feminist dominated society, and asking, 'why has the feminist approach permeated the development of the law in this area?' In an insightful paper entitled, *Rape Myths: Is Élite Opinion Right and Popular Opinion Wrong?*[241] Reece challenges the feminist commentators who complain of a lack of convictions for rape, despite the changes in the law, which were clearly intended to bring that about. Observing that 'While increasing the number of rape convictions has been, without doubt, a primary aim of rape law reform,'[242] and agreeing that an eight-fold increase (800 per cent) in the number of recorded rapes in the last 26 years has resulted in an increase in convictions of only some 2.35 times (235 per cent), she questions the feminist's line that this is due to failures in the administration of the criminal justice system. Quoting Ministry of Justice, Home Office and the Office for National Statistics, she says:

> In 2011–12 there were 14,767 recorded female rapes; with 1,842 in 1985, this represents an increase of eight times in the last 26 years. In 1985, there were 450 rape convictions; as of 2011, despite all the efforts noted above, this number was a little more than double (235%), reaching 1,058 convictions for rape of a female.

The 'efforts noted above' to which Reece refers are the efforts of various agencies and lobbies to increase the number of convictions for rape in line with the number of recorded allegations. However, as Reece points out, the rates for convictions for rape in 2013 (at seven per cent, according to her figures) were the same for burglary - also at seven per cent, and she expands on this as follows:

> The conviction rate, taken as the proportion of completed Crown Court trials for female rape that ended in a conviction, was 51.1% in 2011, a percentage which, like the attrition rate, is not out of line with other serious offences.

So, the administration of justice in rape cases is 'not out of line with other serious offences'. So much for the alleged Justice Gap, which simply doesn't exist, except in the febrile feminist imagination. And what reply does Professor Temkin have to this? In a speech she gave at a debate held on 30th October 2013 at the LSE entitled, 'Is rape different?',[243] at which Dr. Reece also spoke, she said this:

> Are conviction rates lower than for other offences? Helen says rates for burglars are the same. However, burglars are often unknown, whereas the identity of a rapist is known in 90% of cases. They could be prosecuted but they are not. Also, you cannot compare statistics for different crime groups because they are compiled differently.

The feminist premises in these words just don't bear rational scrutiny. What is Professor Temkin saying here? Because alleged rapists are known to their victims, more of them should be convicted? What nonsense is this? A conviction will only occur if an offender is detected, charged, tried by a jury of his peers who try the evidence and arrive at a conclusion of guilt. It is called due process of law. That puts accused rapists on the same footing as accused burglars, or accused murderers, or any other category of criminal offence. Whether the victim knows the offender or not has nothing to do with it. Ms Temkin might just as well be saying that people who drive dangerously and cause the death of a passenger in their car should have a higher conviction rate than if they cause the death of a pedestrian in the same circumstances, just because they are known to their victim. Her point is nonsense, frankly - as much nonsense as her allegation that you cannot compare different crime groups because 'they' (I presume by this she means the statistics), are compiled differently. It is incorrect to say that different methods of data collection mean crime data cannot be compared. The whole point of statistics is to allow comparison. This is a remarkably weak argument for a learned professor to put forward, and it amounts to one of the oldest logical fallacies in the book: the Red Herring.

The truth is, when an incident is reported to the police it is first assigned an incident number and then a crime number if, on initial investigation, it is believed that a crime has been committed. That becomes a recorded crime, and part of the statistics. If, after investigation, the crime is solved and an offender is arrested and submitted to due process, it becomes a recorded prosecution in court records. If it results in a conviction, it becomes a recorded conviction. All of these are hard data, and their method of collection makes them comparable across crime groups. What is so hard to understand? Frankly, Professor Temkin is advocating for more alleged rapists - men, naturally - to be convicted. For her and her like, rape really is different; therefore, it requires its own special treatment: its own draconian legal regime, one that is devised by feminists whom, as we have seen, believe all men are potential rapists. It really is just as simple as that.

Feminist groups in broader society have succeeded in creating a tidal wave of complaints, using incessant propaganda that encourages women to make complaints, and supporting them through every stage of the process. The police, also now significantly populated by women in detective positions, have rolled over and bowed to the propaganda that rape complainants must be believed implicitly, not treated with circumspection as most complainants of crime are (and should be, to avoid false accusations). Radical feminists in power have succeeded in bringing about a radical change in the law that redefines rape in ways that make it close to a technical offence, based on a burden of proof that has been shifted to the accused, who is rendered effectively incapable of defending himself because it is almost impossible to prove he had the woman's 'enthusiastic consent' at each stage of the encounter. They have also rigged the law to put the accused man (who is innocent until proven guilty) firmly on trial in the court of public opinion, by allowing him to be named as soon as he is charged when his accuser is guaranteed anonymity for life, irrespective of the trial's outcome. Through its use of emotive terminology, the feminist press has seen to it that an accused man is named as a 'perpetrator' long before his trial, and the anonymous woman, who technically remains his accuser, becomes his 'victim', thus effectively convicting him long before his trial. And yet none of this has resulted in an increased conviction rate for rape. It remains, as it should, broadly in line with the conviction rate for other crimes. The criminal justice system is still working. It is still winnowing the wheat from the chaff, and feminists don't like it. All these efforts to get more men imprisoned for rape have come to nothing, so they are trying to move the goalposts. Their next ploy is to try to nobble juries, an issue to which I shall now turn.

Rape myths and the assault on justice

The law on the statute books is one thing, but, as the conviction rates tell us, the decision of the man or woman in the jury room remains the means by which common-sense justice is still being delivered in rape trials. Despite the behind-the-scenes fifth-columnists who are actively seeking to impose their own form of justice, when all their froth about rape and rape statistics is scraped from the top of the brew, we are left with the decision of the common man and woman behind those locked doors that represent a bastion for justice. The ordinary man and woman in the street still knows that an allegation of rape is the easiest thing to make and the most difficult thing to refute: they still know what real rape is, and they carry that into the jury room when shouldering the enormous responsibility of deciding the guilt or innocence of a man accused of rape. Feminists are aware of this, of course, and, predictably, in their endless quest to spread their narrow, elitist views, they are now alleging that juries are the subjects of what they call 'Rape Myths', of which radical feminist activists such as Ms Temkin say they need to be disabused. They need to have their thinking straightened by the feminist progressive elite, because, obviously, they are getting it wrong. This is an interesting line to take for an ideology that itself uses myths to further its political aims, but I pass over that. So, what are these alleged rape myths? They fall into three main categories:

1. The 'real rape' myth, the belief that rape truly is a, 'violent attack in a dark alleyway';[244]
2. The 'women cry rape' myth, whereby a woman cries rape after a regretted sexual encounter;
3. The 'coffee as consent' myth, whereby a woman who invites a man into her home for a cup of coffee after an evening out on a date, is deemed to be 'asking for it'.

There are other variants, but in essence these are the alleged rape myths that feminists say are major impediments to increasing the number of convictions for rape. In as perfect an example of totalitarianism as you could imagine, they say juries should not harbour these myths because they, 'serve to deny, downplay or justify sexual violence that men commit against women'.[245] Not only that, but they cite their own research, which allegedly exposes how people are harbouring these wrong thoughts. It was carried out in 2007 using an analysis tool called 'The Acceptance of Myths About Sexual Aggression Scale' (AMMSA)[246] - developed by a group of academics: Heike Gerger, Hanna Kley, Gerd Bohner and Frank Siebler - that purports to validate rape myths by measuring them. This is what the Measurement Instrument Database for the Social Sciences (MIDSS)[247] says about AMMSA:

> Although the construct was introduced during the era of second wave feminism, it was not until 1980 that Martha Burt published the first social scientific examination of rape myth acceptance. This scale design began with the standard definition that rape myths are 'descriptive or prescriptive beliefs about rape ... that serve to deny, downplay or justify sexual violence that men commit against women' In rape myth methodology prior to the Acceptance of Modern Myths about Sexual Aggression (AMMSA), a minimum stipulation was that rape myths needed to be demonstrably false. Significantly however, the AMMSA and others move away from this: for their purposes, 'it would be more expedient to define rape myths not as false, but rather as "wrong" in an ethical sense.'

So, according to the feminist world view, ordinary people on juries are incapable of reaching the right conclusions based on the evidence laid before them, *ergo* they are exercising myths, *ergo* they must be 'wrong' and failing to dispense justice appropriately. And who is the arbiter of appropriateness of juries' decisions? Feminists, of course, in their almost unbelievable arrogance. The likes of Temkin and her sisters in feminism are setting themselves in judgement over all of us. This is not about justice, it is prejudice. Helen Reece also comments on AMMSA, as follows:

> In rape myth methodology prior to AMMSA, a minimum stipulation was that rape myths needed to be demonstrably false. Significantly however, Gerger and others move away from this: for their purposes, 'it would be more expedient to define rape myths not as false, but rather as 'wrong' in an ethical sense'. The weight of this admission is not always acknowledged, with some

describing the attitudes reported by using the AMMSA scale as inaccurate or subjective, when these attitudes are by the devisers' own definition not necessarily either: indeed, these attitudes may on occasions be accurate and objective.

Here we see exposed the arrogance of the feminist rape activists. Reece and her colleagues at MIDSS are clearly uncomfortable with their approach, and so should we all be. In using this highly questionable research tool, the researchers to whom Reece refers are demonstrating massive prejudice, evident in their very phraseology, viz. '... it would be more expedient to define rape myths, not as false, but rather as 'wrong' in an ethical sense'. Wrong by whose judgement? That is the question. For researchers to start with the premise that beliefs about rape serve to, 'deny, downplay or justify sexual violence that men commit against women,' is to reveal their agenda, which is naked, unashamed, arrogant feminist elitism. It is a prime example of how academic institutions are being used for political purposes, and it is never challenged. This is advocacy, not research, and it is dangerous because it is being used to manipulate juries' thinking: effectively it is an attempt at brainwashing people into making ideologically biased decisions rather than evaluating the evidence placed before them in the light of their own experience. Prejudices and all. Reece underlines this point when she says:

> This blurring of the unethical and the inaccurate carries over into the jury research. According to Temkin and Krahé, where juries believe inaccurate rape myths, they will not make decisions based on the case in hand.

The real question is: are the alleged rape myths firmly bedded in reality, and are they reasonable beliefs in the light of people's experience? As I have already shown, most people actually still believe that rape is a violent act. They know that human nature being what it is, women have claimed rape after a regretted sexual encounter, or when found out in adultery, and that most women are well aware that acceptance of a late night coffee in a man's flat after an evening out is a precursor to possible sexual activity, which might be what she wants too.

Is rape different?

Feminists believe rape is different from other criminal offences. In a strange hark back to Victorian times, during which, they argue, patriarchy was rampant, feminists would have us believe that rape truly is a fate worse than death. It is nonsense, of course. A woman might never get over the horrific experience of rape but life is life and she still draws breath, and that surely must be the most important consideration? It is the same with a soldier who, in the prime of his life, has his limbs blown away by an enemy's improvised explosive device, and has to get on with his life with fortitude.

Rape is vile. It is a despicable, cruel violation of a woman, and society has always condemned it in the strongest possible terms, but it is no different from other serious offences against the person, and it falls far short of the legal variants of homicide. That notwithstanding, as I have already mentioned, the LSE asked the question, Is rape different? in a seminar by the same name held on 30th October 2013. As well as Professor Temkin and Dr Reece, the platform was also shared by Nazir Afzal, Chief Crown Prosecutor in the North West of England, and Barbara Hewson, a practicing barrister from Hardwicke Chambers and forthright commentator on current issues in rape and sexual offences.

Dr. Reece opened the proceedings by expressing her views about rape myths and Professor Temkin followed her, saying this:

> So what then is Helen's agenda? She would like to turn the clock back. She doesn't like judges warning juries about making false assumptions about rape, based on myths and folklore. She thinks that the judges have been influenced by a malign elite. But seeking justice for rape victims is not elitist. Most people are in favour of this, including the popular press. It would be an outrage to turn the clock back on rape, as Helen would wish us to do. And what incredibly bad timing. Think of the Rochdale rapes, the Savile rapes, the Oxford rapes, the multiple rapes by Catholic clergymen, to name but a few scandals. The very idea that we should be making it more difficult now to bring successful prosecutions for rape simply beggars belief.

Professor Temkin is a mistress of rhetoric - and of basic logical fallacy.[248] In this one short opening, she runs the gamut of them. She opens with an *ad hominem* attack on her academic colleague, alleging she has an 'agenda', which is rich when you think about it. She questions Reece's motives, and she puts up a 'Straw Man' argument ('turning the clock back'), thus creating a false proposition and putting words into Reece's mouth. She lays a claim to the moral high ground in the, '…seeking justice for rape victims is not élitist…' argument. Then, she brings in the *argumentum ad populum* - the 'most people are in favour of this…' argument, without a shred of evidence to prove that assertion (and, of course, she adds '...including the popular press', as though they were the arbiters of balanced public opinion, which they are not). Finally, she throws in the *argumentum ad misericordiam* - the appeal to pity - citing the 'Rochdale rapes, the Savile rapes, the Oxford rapes, the multiple rapes by Catholic clergymen...', notwithstanding the rather obvious fact that in the case of Jimmy Savile there has been no trial, no objective evaluation of the evidence - and no conviction.

Ms Temkin uses all these tricks to keep her narrative uppermost, yet she holds a professorial chair in a major Law School, where her *raison d'être* is the pursuit of truth using logic not emotion: fact not fallacy. She is expected to be accurate and seek truth by enquiry, not engage in logical fallacy and polemic. She talks about Dr. Reece's agenda, yet she lays bare her own in the process. Jennifer Temkin is a good example of the elite group of feminist women who are out to install their ideological worldview wherever they can. In this case that means attempting to stoke a fire of fear about rape and sexual violence, and she knows others are on to her agenda. That is why she seeks to deflect attention by accusing those who don't agree with her of themselves being an elite with an agenda. Her words amount to nothing less than a deliberate muddying of the waters in the interests of pressing her ideologically constructed case, which is nothing to do with justice: this is a numbers game. She and her like are determined to get as many women as possible to make complaints of rape against men, and to see as many of those men convicted as she can. This is not about justice, either for men or women, and it certainly isn't in society's best interests. Using this and the false factoids that 85,000 women are raped and one in five suffers sexual violence in their lifetimes, feminist rhetoric is seeking to manipulate our criminal justice system by steadily, inexorably modifying public opinion to the extent that people cannot see what is really going on.

This is an elitist group who have installed themselves in positions of social power and influence from where they are shaping society, softening public opinion with platitudes and high sounding rhetoric, disseminated by their counterparts in the media and in politics, and they are relentlessly conditioning public opinion to accept what is really outlandishly radical social change. There is no doubt that this elite is trying to re-model our criminal justice system according to their dogma, and they and their fellow-travelling sympathisers are working hard to whip up a moral panic about rape in order to bring that about. As far back as the eighteenth century, Hegel described the dynamic behind this process: first create or sponsor an event or events that unleashes a fear in the population; as the fear spreads and a fear-reaction sets in, the public becomes ready for something to be done to protect it from the recurring events. Politicians and academics then offer their ideological answers, seeking power or extra powers to deal with the threat, and then legislating or using executive action to implement their purported remedies, which they offer under the guise of protecting the people from that which they fear. The people willingly grant them all the power they want, rationalising their loss of freedom by saying it is in their best interests. That is what the communist regimes of the 20th century did, for example, in North Korea, where a fear of the West - and particularly the US - continues to be whipped up there on a daily basis through the broadcast media; it is what Adolf Hitler did by inducing a fear and loathing of the Communists and the Jews, denigrating the latter group everywhere in newspapers, cinema newsreels and rousing speeches, and the feminist elite is doing precisely the same thing now in the fear that women naturally have of rape. What is worse, they have succeeded in harnessing the state prosecution apparatus to that end, as we shall now see.

Public servants, or Robin Hoods?

One of the key positions in any society is the office of state prosecutor, a post held by another panellist in the LSE debate - Nazir Afzal, whose contribution was, to say the least, extremely interesting. He opened his speech by saying:

> I totally agree with what Professor Temkin says. I want to give you some thoughts on the basis of my experience in dealing with such cases. The vast majority of all sexual offences that I've seen take place either in the family, either online - any indent photograph of a child is a crime scene - thirdly, they happen in institutions, places where women have generally not had a voice in the past, and fourthly they happen on the street. These are the grooming types of cases we have been dealing with in the last year or so. In relation to all of those environments, much of that has been hidden in plain sight. People knew what was happening.

By way of background, as soon as he took up his appointment as Chief Crown Prosecutor for the North West of England, Afzal controversially reopened a case about systematic sexual grooming and rape of young white girls by a group of men of Asian ethnicity in Rochdale that had been dropped by his predecessor. As a man of Asian background himself, he clearly felt this was wrong, and he brought the offenders to court and successfully prosecuted them for their heinous crimes. As he said,

> I think Rochdale was a classic case in point. People knew what was
> happening but nobody seemed to do anything about it. Victims were often
> ashamed to report and I have said it before, I will say it again, it was not their
> failure, it was mine. It was a failure of the criminal justice system as to why
> they didn't feel confident about reporting what happened.

What we ought to find disturbing, however, is what Afzal said next:

> In every instance, it wasn't the sex, it was the fact that they were in control.
> This is about men controlling women, and wanting to control women on a
> regular basis. It's about men making the rules that women have to obey. It's
> about women being brought up to think that men are the answer, when in fact
> men even aren't one of the questions… Abroad rape is being used as a
> weapon because it will subjugate, it will oppress… In the Rochdale case, the
> men were using rape as a weapon to show how superior they were to the
> normal white community and these women in question… The police are not
> sceptical about normal crimes, but they are in rape. Why should that be?
> That's my point… One of the reasons why rape is different is because
> historically we have been so bad at dealing with it…Another part of the
> difference is the court experience. Every part of your life is dissected. We
> traumatise them. Every part of the court process traumatises them… What do
> we know about rape? It has a prolonged psychological impact. I can't think of
> any other crime to be honest that is so beset by myths and stereotypes…

I could forensically dissect these statements at length, pointing out the degree
to which Afzal has absorbed the entire feminist case about rape, but I am sure
that by now my reader is well able to see this. Suffice to say that he is reiterating
a gendered theory of rape that closely resembles the thinking behind the
Duluth model of domestic violence, which asserts that men's behaviour
towards women arises from patriarchy, and which leads men to believe they are
privileged. This becomes clear in Afzal's subsequent comments:

> A lot of the questions about the Rochdale case is, they came to me and said,
> 'These are all Asian men who were the perpetrators, and they said, Nazir, how
> do you feel about prosecuting people from your own community,' and I said I
> don't really feel bad about prosecuting these other men. They need to bring it
> down to what it is - about male power and whether it's Patriarchy or not, it's

simply about men trying to control women's behaviour... One of the police officers dealing with rape victims for thirty years told me that of all the cases she had dealt with, rape is the worst violation that any human being can endure. That's her view, she knows it from her own experience.

It would be too easy to hear these words in the purely Asian context. Afzal is very much a man for the area of Britain over which he was appointed to preside. He was undoubtedly using wry humour about the pressure he must clearly have felt from people of his own ethnic origin to lay off them, but he exhibited clever deflection of that by showing that he viewed the Rochdale case as being a mixture of the two: race and gender. For him, rape is an expression of patriarchy, simple as that. However, he is a public prosecutor in a state prosecution system, charged with a heavy responsibility to see that the criminal justice system is administered in a non-partisan, dispassionate way and without his personal views clouding the issues. Afzal is entitled to hold views as an individual citizen, but he is ideologically partisan, and he makes that abundantly clear here. This must influence the decisions he makes.

Afzal undoubtedly righted a wrong in the Rochdale case, we must not lose sight of that. However, when his views cross the ethnic cultural divide and spill into attitudes toward men in general, that is dangerous because it must influence him in the just and appropriate application of the state's prosecution apparatus. The just defence of women who are truly abused must be balanced against the right of men to be treated fairly and equally before the law. That must be the watchword. In a just society, everyone stands equal before the law, and the state prosecutor, who acts for us all, must apply that principle without fear or favour. It is far too small a step to go from Asian men taking a controlling attitude towards women because of their ethnic culture and practice, to that principle being applied to all men, especially when it is based on the false construct of patriarchy. That is a feminist argument, and it has no place in a public prosecutor's vocabulary, especially in the current legal regime I have been describing, and that now so tightly regulates intimacy between men and women. It gets worse, however. Here is another extract from what he said:

99.99% of rape victims are women; 99.99% of men that are raped are also raped by men. So, from our perspective, there's the issue, it's about men and their desires or their needs, and being fulfilled in some way. It's a point that has been made many times already, it's not the drink, the rape is the rapist, and why should a woman have to not go to a nightclub once a week? Why should she dress up and put a chastity belt on or something? The point is, men need to take responsibility...

This last comment was met with enthusiastic support from the audience, but it is totally out of order. Apart from the fact that women are not 99.99 per cent of rape victims, anymore than only 0.01 per cent of men who are raped are the victims of men,[249] a public prosecutor of Afzal's status and power should not be taking such an ideological partisan position. He is entitled to hold personal views, but it is axiomatic that he must not allow those views to influence his vital role as state prosecutor because he is the guardian of the power of the state to deal with those who offend its laws. It is implicit that he must exercise unimpeachable even-handedness in the vicarious execution of that power - yet there is this massive question mark over that even-handedness in Nazir Afzal. It is also astonishing that he feels so free to express his views in a public forum, although the reason for that is pretty clear: feminism is now the unquestioned power in the land. It has become the operating system of society - a given. Afzal's words, 'So, from *our* perspective...' ought to give us cause for grave concern also. To whose perspective is he referring? Does he mean his and Jennifer Temkin's, in the context of the panel debate, or is he really saying this is the corporate culture of the Crown Prosecution Service of England and Wales? If the latter is the case, this key organ of state must be sold out to feminist dogma too, and this concern seems to be confirmed by Afzal's response to a question from the audience about the recent increase in prosecutions for sexual offences by the CPS, and his office in particular:

> In the point you made really as to why we bring these cases and whether we are doing people a disservice or not: in the last year, we've had a significant increase in our conviction rates, we've had a significant increase in the cases which we actually prosecute, which previously we didn't, so they're linked up. The reality is you can deal with these cases in front of a jury. You can talk to the jury about these issues in your opening speech. He or she might have been drinking, but the drink is not the rapist. You can say these things, which previously some of our lawyers didn't say those things, and previously some of the lawyers when they were considering whether to bring a case in the first place, didn't allow those cases to go to court because they applied their own myths and stereotypes, OK, those that are understood to be myths and stereotypes before those cases come to court, so from my perspective, the proof of the pudding is in the eating. Our conviction rates are going up, our

cases are proceeding at some speed now and getting better and better and better and, therefore, we must be applying the right tests.

Afzal clearly believes he is doing a good job, and is ethically and morally on the right track. But is he? His last phrase speaks volumes. Who is the judge of the rightness of the tests to which Afzal refers? The people? The CPS? The feminist elite? This is all the proof we could ever need of the CPS's capitulation to feminist dogma. Their test is increased convictions for rape: that overly simplistic, ideologically blind tool that takes no account whatsoever of better justice - for everyone.

It is truly astonishing that a public prosecutor should be aiming to increase conviction rates for any offence. That is partisanship. It is the misuse of public office. The job of the public prosecutor is to lay the facts plainly and clearly before a court and leave the justice system to take its proper course. His job is not to fight a corner, that is the work of the defence. Criminal justice is about creating a just society, not the individual views of its state prosecution service engaged in a numbers game. What has a mission to increase convictions in any offence, let alone rape, by the state prosecutor got to do with that? Now, of course, it is always possible that Afzal might be somewhat unique within the CPS, but what he has openly said in these recorded exchanges reveals a need for some very serious questions about what is currently going on in the administration of our criminal justice system. Any man who finds himself at the end of a rape accusation in the North West of England should be very concerned indeed about the motives behind him being prosecuted. From all appearances, the CPS in that region is out to get its figures up to achieve a higher than normal number of convictions for rape than other offences: and all of it driven by a feminist chief prosecutor.

Another comment from the floor revealed another agenda currently at work in the CPS. The questioner is not identifiable from the video, but he is audibly clear:

> Nazir, if I could ask you to clarify something because you actually said that the law in the past had dealt with victims very badly and that it was time that we made amends for past faults, and that is the way we have to deal with things now. Well that sounded more like a moral crusade than the law. And, forgive me, but I do worry if you start to use the law to make amends for some past CPS guilt or some bad boys in the police. That is not a correct use of the law; it is a dangerous, in fact, use of the law, and can only lead to, in

fact, an assault on justice.

And you also mentioned that women, you said, 'victims', and I think it is right that we say complainants because we do have to remember that people are innocent until they're proven guilty; that is an important thing that I at least do not want to lose in all of this. But it does seem to me that if it's the case that for women to be cross-examined and to have accused someone of rape, their intimate details are dragged before the courts, and you think this is inappropriate and horrible and terrible, you have to recognise, I would hope, that somebody who is accused of rape also has their intimate details dragged before the court and accused of the most heinous of crimes, and, somehow that we are not allowed to mention that without somehow being, you know - or you didn't mention it, let's put it this way, it's unpleasant to have your intimate details dragged before the court on either side of that; it's unpleasant and nasty, but in the cause of finding out whether somebody is guilty or innocent, when you as the CPS have the right to take their liberty away

I think it is important that things are tested [interrupted by the chair complaining that is two questions]. Alright ...' [Cut off again by chair who directs Afzal to answer]

This is what Afzal said in reply:

I don't recall saying that because of past things we needed to make amends. This is not about making amends. My point was that we treated these victims badly in the past, historically we have, for all the reasons that Jennifer [Temkin] outlined in terms of previous ways we've dealt with cases in the past, we now have very good guidance, we have now a good specialist prosecutor dealing with this case, specialist police investigators: it's about getting it right; that's all we are trying to do now and hopefully you will now see the benefits of that as we move forward...

This is really astonishing. This very senior CPS lawyer, who holds the power to decide who is prosecuted and who is not, clearly doesn't understand the rebuke being levelled at him. He is being challenged with some very basic legal principles from a position of reason about what appears to be a change of stance in the CPS: from the intended social justice basis of our criminal justice system to what appears to be a focus on the victim, and he seems so steeped in the now obvious CPS feminist culture that he cannot see how biased he is being. Afzal is concerned about 'getting it right,' which is fine, but his measure of that is in itself biased. He seems unable to see any other position than that being advocated by the likes of Jennifer Temkin (plus the entire feminist propaganda machine).

The last straw, however, comes towards the end of the proceedings. In response to another question from the floor, Afzal says this:

> ... I gave the example earlier on about Frances Andrade, what happened to her happened in 1979 to 1981; she tried to harm herself pretty much every year since. She needed justice: she deserved - justice. Our job, surely, is to give her justice...

But that is not right. The individual has no right to justice; that right resides with society as a whole. The job of the state prosecutor is to operate a state prosecution apparatus within a state's criminal justice system whose aim is to obtain justice for society in courts according to the law. It is not to obtain justice for individual victims. In other words, justice belongs to society, not to the individual. It is both done, and seen to be done, and it operates with two implicit justifications: the punishment of criminal wrongdoing, i.e., 'Desert,' the idea of exacting punishment in proportion to the action (as in 'He got his just deserts'); and, 'Utility,' the socially useful accomplishment of the control of crime. In turn, Utility is based on two principles: first, the proportional incapacitation of offenders against the peace through the use of imprisonment or curtailment of freedom (such as tagging, etc.), financial incapacitation by way of fines, etc.; and, second, the rehabilitation of offenders back into society. Justice, therefore, operates in the public interest, for the greater good, not the interests of the individual. For these reasons, the criminal justice system must be run by dispassionate civil servants, not moral crusaders. Their work must have nothing to do with payback for people who are wronged, and I suspect Nazir Afzal's questioner had his finger on the pulse of what is going on in our CPS today. This very senior prosecutor is indisputably sold-out to the current feminist rhetoric about rape, and he is light-years away from the impartiality and even-mindedness his office demands. Rather than seek the dispassionate, objective dispensation of justice through the criminal justice system, of which he is a servant not a master, he appears to be a man on a mission, seeking to right wrongs in society according to his own set of beliefs and constructs, and re-defining the role of public prosecutor to accommodate that. He is more like a Robin Hood character, or a knight in shining armour, than an obedient public servant administering justice dispassionately in a sophisticated, modern democracy with a very high level of lawfulness.

If he is representative of the service of which he is a high-ranking example, I believe that is serious cause for concern because it was Afzal's office that, in May 2013, instituted legal process against William Roache, aged 81, the lifetime star of Coronation Street, the longest running and most viewed UK television soap opera of all time. Roache was charged with two counts of rape and five counts of indecent assault allegedly committed some 45 years earlier against five women who were aged 14-16 at the time. A number of the complainants had only come forward when Roache's first arrest was made public, and the CPS lumped them all together in one composite case, rather than ensuring each complaint was tried separately. This is now commonplace in cases of alleged sexual offending when it would have been frowned upon just a few years ago, because it has long been held that one allegation of wrongdoing cannot reasonably be used to support another. As Daniel Finkelstein, writing in *The Times Opinion*[250] column observed:

> It was an explicit and implicit part of the case against William Roache that he was being charged with more than one crime at the same time. Explicit, because the prosecution asked the jury whether all the women could really have been lying. Implicit because clearly the prosecuting authorities felt the weight of making numerous allegations would cover up the weakness of individual cases... It is obvious that trying someone for more than one alleged crime at the same time prejudices the jury. Common sense suggests it must. And often it's meant to... William Roache, thankfully, is a wealthy man of good standing who can pay a top QC to fight for his reputation. What about the care worker or the teacher who can't?

Roache was acquitted on all counts by the jury, comprising eight women and four men, which was unanimous in its decision after one complainant admitted she had 'no actual memory' of the alleged incident, another changed her mind about how old she was at the time of the alleged offence, and another changed her story about being warned by an acting colleague about Roache, when it turned out the colleague wasn't in the show at the time she alleged. In fact the entire case was a fiasco. An 81-year-old man, hardly any threat as a sexual predator, was put through public humiliation and no doubt untold stress. He was able to afford the £100,000 legal costs but, as Finkelstein says, what about the care worker or the teacher who, placed in the same situation, cannot? And what was Nazir Afzal's response to it all? As Finkelstein again reports:

Nazir Afzal, the Chief Crown Prosecutor for North West England, was inappropriately bullish after the acquittal, saying he wasn't shy and he followed the evidence. Yet one of the charges against Mr Roache had to be dismissed during the trial because the woman concerned said she could only vaguely remember the incident… On the day of the Roache acquittal, Nazir Afzal said: 'The case was treated like any other.' I'm sure it was. That is what I'm worried about.

Finkelstein was rather reservedly expressing an increasing concern at what the CPS is up to, and we should all share that concern. Apart from the crippling financial cost of defending a case such as this, and the extraordinary emotional cost to a man accused of rape and sexual offending, a man suffers the destruction of his reputation in full public gaze, whilst his accuser enjoys legally enforced anonymity. That cannot be right by any standard of fairness, and is horribly reminiscent of that infamous feminist-inspired utterance of Catherine Comins in 2001 in a Time Magazine article,[251] who said:

> Men who are unjustly accused of rape can sometimes gain from the experience. They have a lot of pain, but it is not a pain that I would necessarily have spared them. I think it ideally initiates a process of self-exploration.

This unbalanced, unfeeling, frankly outrageous comment is typical of the degree to which the foul creed of feminism is prepared to go in its crusade about rape.

The voice of reason

It goes without saying that the issues surrounding rape are not as one-sided, nor as narrowly focussed as feminists would have us believe. This was further underlined by Barbara Hewson, the fourth contributor to the LSE proceedings. Hewson is a barrister with a clear lawyer's mind and, clearly, nobody's fool. This is what she said in her contribution to the proceedings:

> There is a Home Office study which points out that one of the biggest risk factors now for women who are assaulted is going to a nightclub once a week. So, in terms of what you do, the situations you are in can increase your vulnerability to certain types of crime. It seems to me we need to make a

distinction here between legal responsibility and moral responsibility.

The law does not attribute any responsibility now to the victim of rape, whereas, traditionally, we know judges would say when it came to sentence, well she was contributorily negligent - or something like that. But it seems to me that in terms of personal morality, bearing in mind that we are a very diverse society, I think it is wholly unrealistic to assume that there is only one moral approach to this.

And equally, it seems to me, simply factually we all know that if you are drunk you are far more likely to have accidents. So if you fall off a bar stool and hit your head, and have a serious brain injury because you are drunk, people are going to say, well, you chose to get drunk. So it does seem to me that there is something a little sanitised about the idea that we cannot even have a discussion about the moral responsibility, whatever people want to say about the legal responsibility.

Here is the voice of reason, not the narrow, distorted feminist view of rape and sexual offending. Hewson's cool and clear mind is taking in the entire picture, and it goes without saying, this is a woman saying it with womanly sense. Yes, of course women are responsible for the situations they get themselves into, just as men are. The portrayal of women as pure victims demeans them by infantilising them. Sexual interactions between men and women are a rich, multicoloured tapestry, yet feminists see things only in black and white, which is their weakness, and the weakness of the law, which they sponsored and nurtured into existence. All feminists can see, despite the evidence laid before them by other women like Helen Reece and Barbara Hewson, is the need to increase conviction rates for rape, because they are consumed by their ideological bigotry. Indeed, their malign intent in passing the SOA 2003 is hinted at by Hewson, as follows:

I think there is a problem with the Sexual Offences Act [2003], because what it did was to water-down the notion of consent. It was expressly done in order to make it easier to get a conviction for rape; it wanted to do away with the Morgan approach, whereby if a man honestly believed that a woman was consenting, he didn't have the necessary *mens rea* for the offence to be committed, although it was for the jury to decide whether they really believed him or not.

We're now getting into a rather strange area whereby consent has been redefined by feminists as not just consent, but, quotes, enthusiastic consent, unquotes, and Wadham College in Oxford now has compulsory courses for freshers whereby they must go to these courses and be told that consent to sex is the Antioch College definition of consent, where consent must be enthusiastic and active, and every single phase of the sexual encounter must have its own 'consent moment'.

This is another smoking gun for feminism. The Consent Model embodied in an Act of the UK Parliament is the product of feminist dogma, which is inimical to all that English Law stands for. Today, in the current social climate of rampant feminism, any sexual encounter is dangerous for men, especially when high-ranking CPS lawyers, who are clearly feminists, and who are using a deeply questionable feminist-inspired law, are prepared, gung-ho, to wield their power to initiate prosecutions against men - young or even very old - for alleged crimes that are now even easier to allege and even harder to rebut. The purpose of a criminal justice system is to prosecute, not to persecute, but persecution is what is happening in Britain today, there can be little doubt about it.

The truth about rape

So, I ask, is rape so widespread? And is it at such a crisis point that it needs students' women's officers standing guard over our university campuses to pre-empt it, influential academics pressing for more convictions rather than better justice, and our CPS on a crusade to stamp it out? Do we really need social institutions such as *RAPECRISIS* operating under charitable status purveying their services and spreading disinformation to justify their existence? Let me end this chapter with some hard facts about rape. These are not factoids, or inferences from surveys, they are real, hard figures obtained from police crime records (both of offences reported to them and those upon which they act), and court records of the prosecution of alleged offenders and their ultimate conviction or acquittal.

For balance, what I am about to say assumes that all the victims of rape were women and that all the perpetrators were men, even though it is obvious that the figures will include same-sex rape between men. The worst effect of this will be to slightly over-exaggerate the apparent incidence of rape of women, but for the sake of getting a clear picture, I consider that an acceptable err on the safer side of the argument. I have also chosen to use figures for the year 2011-12, to ensure a direct comparison between the actual figures and those claimed by *RAPECRISIS*, who use the CSEW as their source, and would ask my reader to accept what is likely to be a very small additional error caused by the difference between the age band used in the CSEW (16-59) and those used in the 2011 UK national census, which is 16-64. There is no way of knowing how many women aged between 59 and 64 years of age were raped in that year, but I believe it is reasonable to assume the figure will be small, if not non-existent, especially bearing in mind that the bulk of rapes are perpetrated on young women. Give or take timing differences in the collection of the different sets of data, and recognising the small overlap in age groups to which I have referred, in 2011-12 there were 18.2 million women in England and Wales in the target age band, and 15,670 complained of rape to the police. That is 0.09 per cent (rounded) of all women, which is a vanishingly small figure, far removed from the alarmist 1 in 5 feminist factoid, and hardly symptomatic of a rape crisis. If we then compare these 15,670 *actual* reported rapes to the 52,000 *estimated* rapes taken from the CSEW (as shown in the summary of Table 2.2, line 6, column 3, to which I referred earlier in this chapter, and which I reproduce here in summary for ease of reference), reported rapes are 30 per cent of the estimated rapes in the CSEW.

Estimated numbers of female victims of rape and assault by penetration

(From: Overview of Sexual Offending in England and Wales. Table 2.2 – Estimated numbers of victims of sexual offences in the last 12 months among adults aged 16 to 59, average of 2009/10, 2010/11 and 2011/12 CSEW. Ministry of Justice, Home Office & the Office for National Statistics Statistics bulletin. Published 10 January 2013)

	Females aged 16 to 59 Number of victims per year: England and Wales			
		Range		
(Including attempts)	**Officially estimated figure**	Lowest estimate	Highest estimate	Spread of estimate
Rape	**69,000**	54,000	85,000	31,000
Assault by penetration	**31,000**	20,000	41,000	21,000
(Excluding attempts)				
Rape	**52,000**	39,000	66,000	27,000
Assault by penetration	**21,000**	12,000	30,000	18,000

So what is going on? We don't know. We can only speculate. Part of the reason might be that most women don't believe that the legal definition of rape under the 'enlightened regime' is actually what happened to them. Part might be that they thought it was not something they wanted to report to the police. And part might be that there is a big difference between answering questions on a laptop computer that are couched in such terms that the respondents gave inaccurate answers. Maybe the women who completed the surveys know that no one is going to challenge what they are saying? Maybe they believe the so-called rape myths? Or maybe, in the current hothouse F*ckrapeculture culture that is British society today, women are being induced to report something they imagined or made up.

That is why it is dangerous to rely on the CSEW as being representative of the truth, let alone take its findings and use them as though they were gospel truth. Feminists rage against the system that lets men get away with rape. They lobby incessantly and furiously, besieging the authorities, alleging that society is letting women down; screaming that 85,000 women *are* being raped every year and that there is a crisis of rape, but their claims are not borne out by the facts, and that means serious questions need to be asked not only about their claims, but their motives. After all, the easiest way to secure more convictions of men for rape and sexual offences is to get society on the back foot: to create a moral panic about rape and induce more women to believe they have been raped.

Of course, reported rapes are only part of the picture. Of the 15,670 cases of reported rape, 2,910 (18.6 per cent) reached trial, despite the CPS's alacrity to prosecute. Of those trials, 1,070 resulted in a guilty verdict. That is a 37 per cent conviction rate after trial, and an almost exact seven per cent conviction rate from allegations, which vindicates Dr Helen Reece's assertion that this is in line with other criminal conviction rates. Seven per cent of 15,670 allegations of rape is 1,097, an almost identical figure to the actual number of convictions.

These results also tell us that only 0.006 per cent of the entire male population were convicted of rape in 2011-12 (assuming the jury who tried them arrived at the correct conclusion, of course), which hardly points to all men being potential rapists. But what is worse, these data tell us that almost 2,000 men in 2011-12 suffered the stress and expense of a trial for rape on a charge which didn't stand forensic scrutiny. Discounting the possibility of wrong verdicts being handed down due to the inadequacies of the jury system, a very substantial number of these allegations were found to be false.

In view of the CPS's attitude to increasing convictions for rape, and their approach to cobbling together cases against celebrities, one cannot but speculate that 2,000 men in 2011-12 went through the best part of two years of hell awaiting trial, incurring enormous legal costs, and enduring the agonising moment of the jury's decision, in order to prove their innocence all along. A one in two conviction rate would be bad enough - that would be equivalent to tossing a coin - but a one in three raises serious questions about the quality of the cases being brought by the CPS. But, of course, men who are unjustly accused of rape can gain from the experience, can't they? Somehow, I don't think so.

Creating pressure for women to report rape that they do not think is rape is wrong, very wrong. Over-exaggerating the true picture and deliberately misusing official data to overhype such a serious matter as rape is even more wrong. What it amounts to is getting at men through their genitals, and betrays the viciousness and narrowness of feminist thinking in this most difficult area. The truth is, there is no epidemic of rape, only an epidemic of panic, driven by people who are trying to whip up fear and over-sensitivity in the public's mind for their own political purposes. These deeply bigoted sophists are cynically playing to the hysterical susceptibility of women, about their deepest fear - the 'fate worse than death' - and they are succeeding in causing a moral panic, the outcome of which is entirely unpredictable, and very dangerous to society.

Fearmongering

Do ordinary women (or men for that matter) really believe the feminist versions of rape? Do they even understand how their basic understanding of what is undoubtedly a heinous crime has been overturned, to be replaced by an eye-watering miasma of misunderstanding so that feminists can install their twisted dogma about rape into their lives? We gain an insight into the degree to which this is at work by returning to the 2004 Walby and Allen[252] report, to which I referred earlier in the discussion on domestic violence. This is what the authors said:

> The vocabulary around rape is very difficult, not least in that few who have suffered this want to use the term 'rape'. This is probably partly because the term refers to a status that is typically regarded as degraded and few would wish to associate themselves with this, and partly because the image or indeed stereotype of rape in newspapers and popular culture is much narrower than that allowed for by the law. There have also been recent changes in the definitions used in law (such as the legal recognition of rape in marriage and inclusion of anus alongside vagina) that may have created further ambiguity. The traditional legal definition of rape involved the penetration of the vagina by a penis without the consent of the woman. This was revised in 1994 so as to include penetration of the anus, thus allowing for the category of rape of a

man as well as a woman (henceforth 1994 rape). The Home Office Recorded Crime convention in relation to attempts is to include them in the crime totals, so this is followed here. However, because this may be an additional source of ambiguity in popular definitions, it is separated out in some of the tables below. [The tables given in the report are not reproduced here.] Women who had been subject to serious sexual assault, that is, actual and attempted penetration of the body (vagina, anus or mouth) without consent, that is rape and other forced penetration, were asked how they would describe what had happened to them on the worst incident. Less than a third (29 per cent) selected the option of 'rape', with almost as many selecting 'sexual assault' (25 per cent), followed by substantial minorities selecting 'forced sex' (16 per cent) and 'sexual abuse' (16 per cent), while 14 per cent rejected all these options. There is no consensus among those who have suffered penetrative forms of sexual assault on the terminology to describe their experiences. When the perpetrator of the worst incident was a current or ex-intimate, 20 per cent of women called the incident sexual assault, 18 per cent sexual abuse, 23 per cent forced sex, 28 per cent rape, and 12 per cent 'something else'... If there was a physical injury additional to that of the rape, then women were more likely to describe the event as one of rape, although even then, 38 per cent did not so describe the incident. Where there was no physical injury additional to the rape, the women were almost as likely to describe the event as 'forced sex' as they were 'rape'. Women were less likely to describe an act that meets the legal definition of rape (excluding attempts) as rape if the rapist were an intimate or former intimate. In this case only one-third (31 per cent) described the incident as rape.

From this, it is clear that the centuries-old understanding of real rape, held by the common man and woman, has been reworked in the age of feminism to become something it isn't. People don't see rape like feminists see it, which is why feminists are attacking the so-called rape myths. Clearly the public steadfastly remains of the opinion that rape is a violent taking of a woman against her will and repeated protestations, and probably her physical resistance, overcome by an attacker through physical force, or the threat of it. For feminists, of course, all heterosexual sex is rape and a contest of power in a gender-based society in which patriarchy holds sway. We know this because the lesbians Kate Millett and Andrea Dworkin told us so in their pathological utterances. *RAPECRISIS* and its fellow feminist apologists are pressing this narrative at every opportunity, and they have the ear of politicians and the key organ of state prosecution the CPS, as witness the openness by which the CPS declares it is in constant consultation with them. One cannot escape the chilling possibility that the state prosecution apparatus of the United Kingdom has been compromised by a powerful lobby group intent on ensuring the implementation of legislation driven by feminists in Parliament.

However, it is not working: neither in the minds of the general public, nor in practice, as witness the endless assertions (without a shred of evidence other than assertion it has to be said) that most women who are raped don't report it. As *RAPECRISIS* says:

> … The same study reported that 28% of women who are victims of the most serious sexual offences never tell anyone about it, and we know from our experience within the Rape Crisis movement that only around 15% of women and girls who experience sexual violence ever report it to the police.

Even though it seems men and women in general recognise instinctively what real rape is, to the feminist mind, this is a problem that needs addressing. *RAPECRISIS's* real problem is that women are not reporting their version of rape, as defined by feminists in their 'enlightened regime'. Even to call it an underreporting issue is to put a wrong construct on it. As the UK Home Office observes:[253]

> Females who had reported being victims of the most serious sexual offences in the last year were asked, regarding the most recent incident, whether or not they had reported the incident to the police. Only 15 per cent of victims of such offences said that they had done so. Frequently cited reasons for not reporting the crime were that it was 'embarrassing', they 'didn't think the police could do much to help', that the incident was 'too trivial or not worth reporting', or that they saw it as a 'private/family matter and not police business'.

Taking a different look at what this is saying: 15 per cent of victims reporting a serious sexual offence to the police means that 85 per cent of feminism's so-called 'victims' took the view that what is alleged to have happened to them was either not serious enough to report it, it was just embarrassing, or they thought it just wasn't the business of the state, the police, or anyone else for that matter. It is also saying that the legal definitions of rape and sexual offences contained in the SOA 2003, an act introduced by the feminist New Labour Blair government by Harriet Harman (then Solicitor General for England and

Wales), who had been leading a drive against men for years,[254] doesn't reflect the voice of the people. If women don't report sexual offences, as defined by a law that goes against their own intuition, it seems pretty obvious that they don't agree with the law, and who are the feminists to seek to bring sustained campaigning pressure to women to change that view? Who are they to interfere with what goes on in people's lives? This amounts to nothing less than an attempt at gross interference with individual liberty and freedom.

Of course, that is what cultural Marxism is all about. Marxists seek state interference in people's lives, and to direct them as to how they should live. The failed socialist-communist experiments of the twentieth century showed this through their policies, pressures, and interventions, which ensured that the state crossed the boundary of the individual's freedom: to act; to think; to speak, and feminism's thought police, such as Jennifer Temkin, Nazir Afzal, *RAPECRISIS*, and a host of others, are seeking to do just that - even to the extent of standing in judgement on people's alleged prejudices, calling them rape myths.

These ideologues are the stalkers of people's freedoms, and they are using fear as their weapon of choice. In the Walby and Allen report[255] we see the real effect they are having on our society. Under the subheading, 'Rape is the most feared crime' they say this:

> Women fear rape more than any other crime, according to their responses to the BCS. Latest results show that for 2002/03, 23 per cent of women were 'very worried' about being raped, as opposed to 5 per cent of men.

Is there any wonder there is widespread fear in women today about rape, when they have organisations like *RAPECRISIS*, whose very name implies urgency, and a plethora of similar bandwagon organisations endlessly stoking that fear? Playing to women's deepest vulnerabilities? Stoking up fear that feeds on itself and becomes a wildfire of mistrust and allegation? These people, hopelessly lost in their own rhetoric, are fearmongering. They are creating a moral panic, which is dangerous: to men, and women; especially young men and young women, who are being induced to believe that men are dangerous creatures from whom women must be given sanctuary. And they are doing it in furtherance of a totalitarian ideology, called feminism, whose stated aim is equality, but whose real aim is to further drive a wedge between women and men, so women can become the dominant sex.

PART II

THE GENDER PAY GAP

FEMINIST BELIEF:

'If anyone in this room thinks everything is all right for women in the UK, I'm afraid they are sadly misguided... I don't want to be depressing about this because there has been huge progress but still there is a persistent gender pay gap. We still have the glass ceiling.'

Cherie Blair. Feminist.
(Speaking at the 'Women on Boards' debate in London, 5th September 2012)

Equal pay: where next?

In 2010, Ceri Goddard, CEO of the left-wing think tank the Fawcett Society, along with Sarah Veale, CBE, Head of Equality and Employment Rights at the Trades Union Congress (TUC), Dr Jean Irvine, OBE, Business Commissioner for the Equality and Human Rights Commission, and Dave Prentis, General Secretary of UNISON, a public sector union, and one of the UK's largest unions with 1.3 million public sector workers as its members, put their names to a report entitled *Equal Pay: Where Next?*[256] In the foreword to the document, they said this:

> Even though legislation on implementing equal pay has been in place for 40 years, the gender pay gap in Britain remains among the highest in the European Union. We still have a shocking gender pay gap of 16.4% that hurts women, society and the economy... Women in the United Kingdom still earn and own less than men. 64% of the lowest paid workers are women, contributing not only to women's poverty but to the poverty of their children... Ultimately, while the debate on equal pay grinds on, women continue to be unlawfully paid less than men for work of equal value.

UNISON and the Fawcett society claim that the pay gap is shocking, but what is really shocking is the sheer mendacity behind every word of this statement. The only thing they say that is true is that 64 per cent of the lowest paid workers are women, the rest is mendacious rubbish. Are they really saying that 40 years after legislation was passed that guaranteed equal pay for women as men for the same work, employers are systematically refusing to comply with it? If so, where are the prosecutions? How is it that the industrial courts are not

348

being run off their feet? Where are the strikes, and why aren't the media up in arms about it? We need to unpick this piece of politicised spin and show it in its true colours, because it is weasel words. Widespread law-breaking is not taking place. Women do not 'unlawfully' continue to be *paid* less than men, the reality is that, overall, they *earn* less than men, for reasons that will become clear as this chapter unfolds.

The key to understanding what is going on lies in grasping that equal pay and the gender pay gap are not the same thing. They represent a false conflation of two separate issues that amount to a deception, which is exposed in the key phrase 'work of equal value'. These words reveal a feminist concept that goes back into Engels's arguments, and which have been rich picking for labour trades unions for more than 40 years, since the Ford Dagenham women machinists' pay strike in 1968 that led to the then Labour government passing the Equal Pay Act 1970 (later repealed, its precepts becoming absorbed into the Equality Act 2010), which guaranteed equal pay for men and women - for the *same* work.

This celebrated strike - hailed as a triumph for feminism in the fight for equal pay - followed a re-grading exercise by Ford, who had classified women's work, sewing seat covers for cars, as less skilled than the jobs being carried out by men on the production lines. This meant that the women were being paid 15 per cent less per hour, so they came out on strike. It was finally resolved by the employer awarding an eight per cent uplift, and the case being referred to the courts under the Industrial Courts Act 1919 by Barbara Castle, an ardent Labour firebrand Secretary of State for Employment and Productivity. In the outcome, the court ruled against the women's case, but ever since the trades unions have made an industry out of looking for ways to compare women's work with that of men when formulating pay claims. For example, school dinner ladies' work has been compared to that of male council refuse collectors, putting them on the same pay grade, and several celebrated cases have been brought before the courts on these lines. The gender pay gap argument is firmly rooted in this milieu.

However, it is not just trades unionists and feminist propagandists who have bought in to the gender pay gap narrative. And it is not exclusively a UK narrative. Even the President of the United States of America, Barack Obama, cited it in an election broadcast in his second term bid in 2012, no doubt to appease the feminist lobbies and garner the women's vote. Amongst a number of utterances about it, this is what an election advert for his re-election campaign said:[257]

> 'The son of a single mom, proud father of two daughters, President Obama knows that women being paid 77 cents on the dollar for doing the same work as men isn't just unfair, it hurts families. So the first law he signed was the Lilly Ledbetter Fair Pay Act to help ensure that women are paid the same as men for doing the exact same work. Because President Obama knows that fairness for women means a stronger middle class for America.'

Notice the difference between this and the UNISON/Fawcett line. Rather than 'work of equal value', Obama is talking about equal pay for 'the exact same work', yet over 50 years ago, his predecessor President John F. Kennedy signed off the Equal Pay Act 1963 as part of his *New Frontier Program*, and President Obama's own US Department of Labor explained the gender pay gap in 2009, just one year after he was first elected president, in its report entitled, *An Analysis of the Reasons for the Disparity in Wages Between Men and Women - Final Report,*[258] which said this:

> … the raw wage gap [between men and women] continues to be used in misleading ways to advance public policy agendas without fully explaining the reasons behind the gap. The purpose of this report is to identify the reasons that explain the wage gap in order to more fully inform policymakers and the public. The following report prepared by the CONSAD Research Corporation presents the results of a detailed statistical analysis of the attributes that contribute to the wage gap and a synopsis of the economic research that has been conducted on the issue. The major findings are:
>
> • There are observable differences in the attributes of men and women that account for most of the wage gap. Statistical analysis that includes those variables has produced results that collectively account for between 65.1 and 76.4 per cent of a raw gender wage gap of 20.4 per cent, and thereby leave an adjusted gender wage gap that is between 4.8 and 7.1 per cent. These variables include:
>
> • A greater percentage of women than men tend to work part-time. Part-time work tends to pay less than full-time work.
>
> • A greater percentage of women than men tend to leave the labor force for child birth, child care and elder care. Some of the wage gap is explained by the percentage of women who were not in the labor force during previous years, the age of women, and the number of children in the home.
>
> • Women, especially working mothers, tend to value 'family friendly'

workplace policies more than men. Some of the wage gap is explained by industry and occupation, particularly, the percentage of women who work in the industry and occupation.

Obama must know what he is saying is untrue - his words cannot be interpreted any other way than as pure ideological cant - and it seems clear that he is just riding the feminist political bandwagon for all it is worth. So, given that the idea of the gender pay gap is widespread political currency, despite evidence to the contrary from authoritative sources, let us go on to explore the issue further in order to elicit the full truth.

'Ms-information'

The Fawcett Society claims a 'shocking' gender pay gap of 16.4 per cent that hurts women, society and the economy. But does it? And can the figure they give be justified? Let me deal with the second question first. As Mark Twain said in *Chapters from My Autobiography*,[259] 'Figures often beguile me, particularly when I have the arranging of them myself...' and, in the 16.4 per cent claim, Ms Goddard and her sisters at Fawcett are obviously playing this game for all it is worth. They claim the provenance of their figures as the UK Office for National Statistics 2009 *Annual Survey of Hours and Earnings*.[260] However, when we examine those data, we find that the government statisticians focus on the *median* (the precise middle number in the dataset), which is the most representative of the central tendency of pay rates, not the *average*, which is not. The ONS people know that a small number of extremely high and utterly unrepresentative pay rates - for senior executives for example - skew the picture. Yet, when we look at the Fawcett Society's web site, we see they deliberately use the mean, not the median.

Anna Bird, Fawcett's acting CEO at the time of writing, is very open about this, saying, 'For every hundred pounds men take home, women *on average* take home around £85' [Author's emphasis] and she openly admits using the average so as to take account of the high pay of the unrepresentative pay rates of high-earning men. Well, she would, wouldn't she? No doubt, my reader will see where all this is going. The *average* pay gap is 16.7 per cent, but the median figure is 12.2 per cent. This is still a significant difference, of course, but it is only three quarters the headline figure being promoted by Fawcett, and there can be no other interpretation of this than that she and her society are deliberately trying to 'gild the lily'. It is all smoke and mirrors. Ms. Bird and her colleagues are the purveyors of political 'Ms-information'. They assert that the pay gap is 'shocking', and it hurts women, etc., but the question we should all ask is: do feminist pressure groups such as the Fawcett Society hurt women, the economy and society even more with their hyperbolic spin?

Now let us go further. If we look at the ONS figures for the distribution of earnings, we can see that childless women in the initial phase of their careers are actually out-earning men, but when they get older and settle down with families, a pay gap emerges, and for most women this carries on for the rest of their lives. Young working women in their 20s earn more on average than their male counterparts,[261] but marriage and motherhood changes everything and a woman's success in the earnings stakes is sacrificed when that happens. Motherhood means that some women give up work altogether. Others take career breaks. Some switch to family-friendly work whilst their children are young, often abandoning the work they did in earlier life. Some go back to their original careers but on a part time basis, and only a very small number, the so-called 'superwomen,' who can afford the necessary servants and support systems needed when they choose to 'lean in' and carry on (and whose earnings pull the average high, incidentally). That is their choice, but the overwhelming majority of women choose differently. If you took the total amount of earnings in an average woman's life, and the total amount of earnings in an average man's life, the man's would be greater. Why? Because men are generally full-time, whole of life workers, and women have babies. It is as simple as that.

The market for labour

Most women have very little room to make the choices available to the elite, or the superwomen. For the vast majority of single mothers, or those in low-income families, their options are very much more limited. These women are forced into work that is of a low skill and of such a low level of required dedication in order to give them the flexibility they need to meet their family commitments, and that means lower pay levels, lower overall earnings, and for far too many a poverty trap. It also usually means part-time work, of which more anon, but first let us look at the market for labour and the effect the flood of women into the workforce has had in the last 40 or so years. During that time, women have been progressively displacing men from the pool of available work in the economy. The statistics show this very clearly:

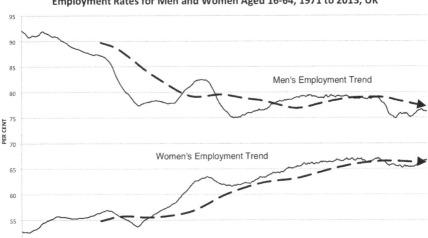

Employment Rates for Men and Women Aged 16-64, 1971 to 2013, UK

However, the picture isn't uniform. When you look in more detail at the work chosen by men and women across the board, roughly two-thirds of public sector workers are women, and two-thirds of those in the private sector are men. Women have colonised the public sector, the third (or voluntary) sector and those parts of the private sector that provide low-wage, low skill, repetitive work, and service work. Women are much less found populating value-adding activities of industry. We see this trend reflected in jobs such as school cleaners, dinner ladies, supermarket checkout assistants and shelf-stackers, shop assistants, local government office workers etc., and it is very prevalent in the charity sector too. Now, this is not to say that women's work is unimportant, or that all of it is low-skilled compared to men. Obviously that is not true. Neither is it to say that only men engage in value-added operations, or that they are cleverer or better trained, or that their work is more intrinsically valuable than women's, etc. That is not my point. My point is that the sheer volume of unskilled women in many areas of our economy cannot do anything other than suppress women's wage rates. The jobs market is a market: the price of labour varies according to supply and demand.

The public sector (and to a smaller extent retail and sales) is where it is all at for women because when they have family commitments, especially as mothers, they need work that is flexible, accommodating, and less all-consuming than, for example, a demanding professional career, and they have flocked to it. But apart from the supply and demand issue, the public sector is never going to produce high wages. Unlike the private sector, where individuals generally are able to bargain for more pay through higher skill acquisition, better loyalty, better productivity, etc., people who work in the public sector have close to zero bargaining power, irrespective of the individual's skill and ability. Except at the very highest levels, the public sector is bureaucratic. It has fixed job definitions, clearly defined pay-responsibility requirements, and a much more clearly defined pecking order for promotion than the private sector does. As Max Weber put it in 1922,[262] bureaucracies seek 'Precision, speed, unambiguity, knowledge of files, continuity, discretion, unity, strict subordination, reduction of friction and of material and personal costs'; 'these,' he said, '... are raised to the optimum point in the strictly bureaucratic administration'. Therefore, within narrow limits, the public sector has no need to offer higher hourly rates to attract better candidates because, by and large, they are set centrally and don't vary much. That is why the trades unions are now strong in the public sector. They seek always to enhance their members' pay through collective bargaining arrangements, and are constantly looking for ways to find similarities in 'work of equal value'. If we factor all these things into the equation, it is easy to see why the public sector is never going to be a source of high pay and advancement, but we can also see how its safety, security and steadiness is attractive to women.

However, there is a downside to this: a constant downward pressure on wage and salaries in the public sector because, by and large, the employer is the state, spending tax-payers' money. The same is true of the private sector. Clerks and back-office functions are, for the most part, a cost, not a part of the value-adding functions of the business. They are an overhead paid out of profits, and that means there will always be a similar downward pressure on wages as in the public sector, which is why public sector unions such as UNISON have their counterparts in the private sector who work to ensure pay stays at least in line with the cost of living. It is easy to see, therefore, why private employers try to circumvent this, and remove pressure on them to pay more than they can get away with in the labour market, even to the extent of enforcing zero-hours contracts, or paying the national minimum wage as the floor rate.

The same constraints apply in the third or voluntary sector, where wages and salaries are never high anyway because of the sector's essentially altruistic nature. The third sector comprises organisations that rely on time-limited funding from government or EU sources and sporadic and unreliable income streams. This puts them in very much the same position as the public sector, but without the reliability of that sector. Local government, for example, is always going to be there. Many third sector organisations are out-and-out charities funded only by voluntary donations whose value is enhanced by taxation relaxation. They too suffer relentless downward pressure on staff costs. To offset this, the voluntary sector is usually highly accommodating of its employees, which translates into an extremely flexible approach to their needs - working mothers for example - as well as providing a softer, more female culture than does business. The Fawcett Society argues that the gender pay gap '… hurts women, society and the economy', and whilst that may be true in a literal sense, we need to understand that it is women who are trying to fulfil a socio-economic role in the economy who are precipitated into lower pay by the economics of supply and demand. Women could earn more if society chose to spend more taxation on wages in the public sector, which brings us back to the left-wing agenda at the heart of this argument and the heart of feminism. Fawcett's, and UNISON's, and the TUC's and the Equality and Human Rights Commission's approach, is pure socialism. They are agitating for a political cause. You might agree with it or you might be a free-marketeer, but whichever way you choose, the gender pay gap argument comes down to 'robbing Peter to pay Paul': moving state income from taxation from one pot to another, so that women can be economic agents who are independent of men as husbands and fathers.

Ordinary women

One of the gems of unvarnished truth in the Fawcett/UNISON *Equal Pay: Where Next?* report (op. cit.) is the statement that, 'the lowest paid workers are women'. That is undoubtedly a fact. In April 2001, the then New Labour Minister for Employment, Tessa Jowell, announced that she had appointed Denise Kingsmill CBE, Deputy Chairman of the Competition Commission, to head up a review into women's employment and pay with the intention of examining women's participation in the labour market and to recommend ways of reducing the pay gap between men and women. Kingsmill was asked to identify how employees' skills and experience could be better used, and what measures needed to be taken to contribute to the development and promotion of higher awareness and good employer practice in equality. However, the entire exercise backfired somewhat when referring to women, when she said:

… Women are more likely than men to be on low pay. They are also much more likely to be working part-time, often in jobs that are only available for a limited number of hours per week. The concentration of women in poorly paid part-time work is a significant factor in the scale and persistence of the gender pay gap in Britain… The concentration of women in part-time work appears to arise primarily from pressure to combine work with home responsibilities. These pressures and the limited availability of part-time employment across the full range of occupations and skill levels mean that many women are unable to find employment in which their skills and potential are properly utilised.

Quod erat demonstrandum. It is amazing that we need an expensive government-commissioned report to tell us what we already know: that the low pay of women is due to women having to choose low paid, low skilled part-time work in order to try to balance the pressures they now have when trying to combine work and home responsibilities - often without a man to share the load. In the gigantic social experiment of feminism, women are being forced to try and balance their role in economic production with their role in reproduction, and the effect of this is not equality but inequality, especially for women. Women who are in stable relationships with intact families (and who have control over their fertility), have access to an abundance of work opportunities, which allows them to supplement their families' incomes; however, there is a very significant proportion of women today who are deprived of that freedom of choice. They and their children are trapped in a cycle of poverty by an ideologically-driven feminist elite that preaches equality and liberation for women.

The evidence for this is clearly laid out in the Kingsmill report itself (p 19), which states that of the overall 69 per cent of working-age women in employment, 60 per cent of them work in just 10 occupations (out of a total of 77). Women's employment is highly concentrated into:

Sales assistants and checkout operators	10.2%
Other sales and services	7.5%
Numerical clerks	6.8%
Secretaries, personal assistants, typists	6.3%
Health related occupations	6.0%
Teaching professionals	5.8%
Health associated professionals	5.4%
Clerks not classified elsewhere	4.7%

Childcare and related occupations	4.2%
Catering occupations	3.6%
TOTAL	60.5%

These are the types of work to which ordinary women with children and family commitments flock, because it allows them the choice they need to run their lives, and the high demand this creates means competition for wages and therefore low earning power, and a low wage bargaining power. This crush, combined with the nature of the employers (predominantly the state) and their needs ensures women's wage rates will always be kept low. It is a matter of supply and demand in a capitalist system, which can only be changed by taking a communistic approach, which is effectively what is behind the unions' and the feminists' gender pay gap agenda.

More part-time work is not the answer

After the 2010 *Equal Pay: Where Next?* Report, Fawcett produced another report, in 2013, entitled *The changing labour market: delivering for women, delivering for growth*,[263] where Ceri Goddard lays bare the feminist Socialist progressive agenda:

> … more must be done to encourage progressive working practices – particularly as competition for quality part-time work is fiercer than ever – women make up three-quarters of those in part-time work…A recent survey of women returning to work after taking maternity leave found that almost 2 in 5 of all women polled were refused the right to part time [Sic] hours (17.5%). Moreover, of the 40% of women who saw changes to their job on their return to work, more than a quarter had their request for flexible working arrangements refused (26%).

Once again, the point about competition for work in certain sectors is made, especially in part-time, i.e., family friendly work, where women are three quarters of the part-time workforce. In Fawcett's world, women have 'the right to part time hours', which is advanced as being 'progressive working practice'. Progressivism, of course, is New Labour Blairite feminist Socialism, and these statements once again betray the degree to which feminist social engineering is underway in our society. Society must support women to go back to work as soon as possible after having their children, thus endorsing the cultural Marxism that is forcing women into becoming working mothers, and employers must change their entire way of operating to accommodate this by creating flexible working arrangements to enable women to do this.

Increasing part-time work might be a boon to working women, but it is not a boon to the economy. In fact, increasing the availability of part-time work simply to favour feminism's political aspirations is economically destructive. Apart from the fact that it is more expensive to employ part-time workers who need the same HR services, the same buildings and resources (which can become under-used relative to utilisation levels by a full-time work force, or even over-used by virtue of more workers than their full-time equivalents using their facilities), and a host of other establishment costs and implications, part-time workers are nowhere near as productive as full-time, whole of life workers. A part-time worker is never going to be able to offer the same value for money to an employer as a full-time one. To believe otherwise is utter naiveté. By definition, part-timers are sharing their lives between work and the rest of their lives, which they are also doing part-time. There are only so many hours in the day. That means their dedication to an employer and to their work is not as much as it would be in a full-time worker. It takes no genius to work out that any sector that has a significant part-time workforce is never going to be as productive as one with a full-time, dedicated workforce. Full-time workers are undoubtedly more individually productive, as well as being more loyal and more dedicated to their employer, probably because the job will be his or her sole source of income and breadwinning. Thus, to increase part-time workers in an organisation means that the value-adding potential of that organisation must be decreased - and that is damaging to the economy.

Although, obviously, there are benefits to some employers in allowing part-time work and job sharing arrangements (such as tapping in to more experience in workers who have had full-time careers and have developed skills that are really useful), it is ridiculously simplistic to think that organisations of any type can generally run as efficiently on part-time workers as with full-time ones. There are times when part-time workers become more valuable to an employer, as in the situation where the employer's business model has a specific need for maximum flexibility. Hence the rise of zero-hours contracts, annual-hours contracts, agency work and other similar commitment-avoiding devices, which are for the employer's benefit, not the workers. The extreme flexibility they offer employers is an extension of the idea of the inverted doughnut metaphor,[264] in which the core dedicated workforce is surrounded by peripheral workers who can be called on as needed to cope with demand fluctuations, such as in supermarkets when they are taking deliveries and need a lot of shelves to be stacked, and retail stores at Christmas time. This is only for the employers' benefit, not the employees'. Is there any doubt that the rise of these types of contracts is only because of the rise of women in the workforce who need flexible employment and low dedication? Can no one see that the ideology that is driving this is the same ideology that offers women liberation and equality, yet it is the source of women's exploitation?

Zero-hours contracts are the ultimate reflection of low dedication by the employer, who is taking advantage of women's needs, and the blame for that can be laid firmly at the feet of feminism and the consequences of the social re-engineering in which it is engaged. Women flooding into the workforce means they are forced into certain types of work in which they can be exploited and used as little more than a hired pair of hands, subject to being hired and fired as and when needed, and encouraging more part-time work is not the answer. Women who have families and then take up part-time work are always going to get lower quality jobs, poorer working contracts and lower rates of pay than their full-time counterparts, irrespective of their ability, and the idealism that says employers need to change their working practices to accommodate them. Part-time workers will always be outside the mainstream for higher-paying employers, who mostly need involved, wholly dedicated, increasingly experienced people who allow them to guarantee continuity in their operations. They need people who will play their full part in helping the organisation become more competitive in its markets (or more efficient if they are in the public or non-profit-making sectors).

Now, of course, some people might argue that part-time workers give better value in the fewer hours they work, and that the amount of time actually spent in productive work by full-time workers is often only a fraction of the time they spend at work. That might be true in the bureaucracies of the public sector, but it is certainly not true in value-adding operations. The modern production line, for example, is a highly regulated workplace designed to extract the last ounce of efficiency from its workforce, who now work with high levels of production automation. The issue is not one of efficiency, it is one of attitude, expressed as loyalty and employee dedication, which enhances or diminishes productivity. A part-time culture militates against teamwork: that phenomenon that occurs in organisations where people working together move from being just a group to a unit whose output is greater than the sum of its component parts.

Key to this is the unwritten psychological contract that says the employer of full-time staff offers security in return for loyalty, and this is implicitly not the case for part-time workers. Nowhere is this made clearer than in the UK 2011 *Annual Survey of Hours and Earnings*,[265] which showed that 22.8 per cent of men worked overtime, whereas only 11.5 per cent of women did, and, on average, men worked three times longer overtime (1.5 hours) than women (0.5 hours). It is plain that women are not as dedicated as men, which must lead to lower productivity. (Unless you are prepared to argue that women work smarter than men, which is unmitigated feminist nonsense.) The truth is, for all the reasons we have seen, women simply don't want to work long hours generally, and cannot if they have a family and child commitments. As Catherine Hakim says:[266]

> One reason is that many full-time workers are not doing an 8-hour working day, in comparison with the part-time worker's 3-6-hour day. Many full-time workers are actually on the job, mentally or physically, for almost 24 hours a day. Their work takes priority over family life and social life, so they build up a momentum, knowledge, fitness and experience that can never be achieved by a part-time worker.

Furthermore, it is universally the case that women lose more hours from work than men through sickness and other absences. This is especially true in the public sector. The ONS report *Sickness Absence in the Labour Market* (April 2012)[267] confirms this:

> On average, women have more sickness absence than men and the public sector employs a higher proportion of female workers... looking at differences between men and women in the two sectors, women in the public sector lost the highest percentage of their hours in 2011 at 3.0 per cent. Men in the private sector lost the fewest at 1.5 per cent.

The predominance of lost hours due to women's sickness and absence is why they flock into the public sector (or, indeed, the voluntary sector). It is because that sector has a culture of tolerance far greater than the private, commercial sector, which demands a higher level of commitment and obedience, and is far less tolerant of employees who don't give full measure all the time. Women are less productive than men, because they are women. On balance, women make different work-life balance decisions than men. In fact, far from seeking to diminish the gender pay gap, there is a good case for saying that men should be paid more than women for their greater contribution to the economy.

The experience penalty

There is another multiplying effect on the gender pay gap. A worker who works fewer hours, whether male or female, will lose out on experience, and that makes him or her less valuable in the labour market. The more experience a person gains, the better they become at their job and the more economically valuable they become to an employer. That is why people get pay rises, and why experience counts in job interviews. Interrupt that process and there will be consequences, especially financial ones. Women who take career breaks to have children forego this experience premium. They may be just as qualified as their male counterparts, they may be every bit as clever and technically capable, but all other things being equal, employers pay more for more overall know-how, and up-to-date working practice, and that only comes with uninterrupted experience. Men don't take the career breaks most women do, and that makes them increasingly better qualified and better paid, and another reason why men earn more in the long run. Feminists can rant as much as they like about whether this is right or wrong, but if women choose to become mothers, enhancing their social capital by producing the next generation, they will diminish their economic capital as a result.

It is easy to see how women's economic value in part-time work is vastly lower than that of full-time, whole of life workers, like most men are. Women in this situation are having to weigh their economic and biological values in a balance, and the occupations which they seek are not the sort that need significant amounts of skill, training and continuing professional development (or even high-level qualifications in the first place). Women who work part-time cannot expect to get the same level of training and development as a full-time worker, and employers generally have little or no incentive to train part-time workers beyond a level strictly necessary to do the job, as Kingsmill (op. cit.) observes:

> There is evidence that women who work part-time have, on average, fewer qualifications and are less likely than those employed full-time to receive training from their employers.

Why should an employer invest in part-time workers unless they have a vested interest in doing so? Especially when there is a ready supply of candidates from whom they can take their pick of experience and prior qualifications. People who work more hours get more training and development, and that brings more pay. It is just a dynamic of capitalist society, and no amount of complaining or alleging discrimination is going to change that. It is tilting at windmills. Training and development is a major cost for an employer and simple economics demands that there has to be a return on the investment. Employers will inevitably want to direct their human resource development expenditures to those workers who are their core resource, largely because they are more economically valuable as a result of more hours worked and increased loyalty. A high churn in workers is an enormous cost to an organisation in terms of re-recruitment, training and induction, and part-time workers are frequently footloose, which means employers will not invest in them. There is no incentive to train their part-timers beyond a level strictly necessary to do the job; therefore, the employee will progressively lose out on better qualifications that might lead to higher pay. In summary, therefore, higher qualifications mean higher human economic value, which equals higher earning power. To all intents and purposes, part-time workers, who are mainly women, become little more than a hired pair of hands, and the work they need will always be at the lower end of the job quality spectrum unless there are other factors at play, such as in the professions, where qualifications, not the hands, and the bodies, are the job. But, not all women are as privileged as this.

Élite women

So far, I have focussed on ordinary women: the vast rank and file to whom feminists offer equality and liberation, but which is really a poisoned chalice. This is the most deceitful trick. The truth is, feminists aren't really interested in women's equality, they are only interested in favouring themselves. These elitist ideologues are standing by watching their sisters struggle on in the society they have created so they can further their own. If there is one group of women who are the perfect example of this elite, it is women doctors: specifically general practitioners (GPs) in the UK National Health Service. Since 2001, the proportion of women entering general medicine has increased by 50 per cent in Britain. For the first time in history, UK women GPs are expected to outnumber their male colleagues in the profession and the most up-to-date figures from the General Medical Council available at the time of writing show that the proportion of female medical students is currently 56 per cent (albeit down from 61 per cent in 2003).

This looks like a massive breakthrough for equality; however, what it amounts to is a massive grab for advantage by a feminist elite. It is naked advantage-seeking at the expense of society, which has been suppressed by feminists using their number one weapon of choice: shouting down dissent. In June 2013 in the House of Commons, for example, Conservative MP Anne McIntosh, Minister for Health, claimed that the proportion of women entering medicine is currently 70 per cent, and reported that these women are, '... well-educated and well-qualified, but when they go into practice, many marry and have children ... and they then often want to work part-time'.[268] She went on to say that it costs the state almost £250,000 to train a doctor, and this is not only failing the taxpayer, it is placing a disproportionate strain on the UK National Health Service. Predictably, of course, she came under the feminist backlash in the guise of Dr Clare Gerada, head of the Royal College of GPs, who accused her of causing, '... the biggest guilt trip of all when it comes to flexible working'. Gerada is something of a feminist Jack in the Box, who pops up at every opportunity to defend the feminist position. Using the classic obfuscation tactics of the elite of feminists of whom she is one, Gerada whinged 'that women doctors are being blamed for problems in the NHS', but she neatly missed the obvious: that this is one of those problems.

Melanie Philips, respected for her common sense, reported all this, as follows:[269]

> In a Commons debate last week on the deficiencies of the new 111 emergency service, a Tory MP, Anne McIntosh, suggested one reason why there were too few GPs to answer urgent calls. Since some 70 per cent of medical students were now women, she said, the fact that many of them wanted to have children and then go part-time meant a 'tremendous burden' on the NHS if it effectively had to train two GPs to do the work of one. In reply the junior Health Minister Anna Soubry said: 'You make a very important point when you talk about, rightly, the good number of women who are training to be doctors, but the unintended consequences ...' She didn't actually finish her sentence, but left the thought of 'the unintended consequences' hanging in the air. For these three words, she was instantly jumped upon and metaphorically beaten up by a steady procession of angry women. Yet others heaped withering scorn upon the hapless Health Minister. Didn't she understand that women had babies? So of course women doctors wanted to work part-time. Duh! And because it suited women to do so, there

couldn't possibly be any problem with that. It was obviously the perfect
solution for absolutely everyone. End of argument. No awareness whatever
of the total absence of logic in such claims — not to mention the failure to
acknowledge the interests of anyone other than women doctors.

Yes, £250,000 invested by the taxpayer to train you and then you run the show
the way you want. This is a serious matter for the people of Britain whose
taxpayer money is being used - indeed abused - by privileged women who are
cynically taking the country for a ride for their own personal benefit. It is
astonishing that even the head of the august and deeply respected Royal
College of General Practitioners could have the sheer chutzpah to defend what
is really an indefensible position, let alone turn it into an alleged attempt to
create a guilt trip for women doctors who are taking the country for a ride, but
feminists know no conscience when it comes to furthering their selfish aims.
They are now firmly installed in key positions in society and they are using their
power to soften the public to accept their dogma.

Working part-time as a general practitioner will pay between £30-45,000
per year for a few half-days, which is nice work if you can get it, and lest there
be any doubt in my reader's mind that this is what is happening, I found this
interesting little snippet entitled 'Spotlight: The salaried GP', which can be
found on the web site medicalprotection.org:

> Dr Linda Anne Jeffreys is a salaried GP in Yorkshire and a member of the
> sessional GPs subcommittee. She said: 'One of the big pluses of working as a
> salaried GP is that it's very flexible and you can dictate the hours. Your hours
> are circumscribed, you have approximate start and finish times and you don't
> have to attend evening meetings. It's a good way of getting back into work, as
> you spend more time seeing patients, so it can be a good choice if you are
> returning to work after being ill, or after having a child… Dr Beth McCarron-
> Nash is a GP in Cornwall, and has worked as both a partner and locum. Now
> working four clinical sessions a week, she was the first female UK GPC
> negotiator to be elected since 1991. 'If you're a GP the world is your oyster,
> and that's what I love about it'.

Call me a cynic if you like, but 'the world is your oyster' doesn't sound like a
particularly responsible attitude to have when you have been the beneficiary of
a massive state investment in your career by the taxpayer of a nation that
expects you to give back in full measure. It sounds more like an elite women's

gravy-train, brought about by, and powerfully defended by their elite sisters in high places, and paid for through the nose by the British men who contribute 72 per cent of all income tax to the central exchequer and now are finding it increasingly difficult to find a male GP in whom they can confide in their doctor's surgeries, which are struggling to recruit sufficient doctors at all, let alone male GPs.

MBAs

There is another dimension to the dynamic at work amongst highly educated professional women that undermines the arguments about the gender pay gap. Women's choices of career actually militate against the sort of gender equality for which feminists argue. In 2009, the same year that the US Department of Labor Report that explained all this was published, Marianne Bertrand at the Booth School of Business, Chicago University, together with Claudia Goldin of the Department of Economics at Harvard University, and Lawrence Katz, also from the Department of Economics at Harvard, published their findings from a 16-year study[270] of the careers of MBA graduates from the Booth School of Business, considered one of the top business schools in the US. The respondent group had all graduated between 1990 and 2006, and the researchers had followed their progress afterwards. In particular, Bertrand et al. wanted to know whether gender had any influence on career outcomes of people who to all intents and purposes started on a completely level playing field.[271]

In the preamble to their published findings, the researchers referred to the variety of current views as to why women apparently under-perform financially in their lifetimes. They were especially interested in the gender pay gap in the corporate and financial sectors, and they acknowledged the commonly held view that women may be subject to implicit or explicit gender discrimination in that world. They also had in mind other factors that might militate against women's earning power, such as them being less willing to negotiate aggressively for pay and promotion in a highly competitive masculine working environment, being unable to gain recognition in predominantly male-dominated workplaces, and being denied the most high-powered jobs in finance, banking and similar corporate careers. What they found confounded all these commonly held feminist myths. The results of their research show beyond any shadow of doubt that the training and education choices women make at the beginning of their careers, combined with subsequent career discontinuity, are the predominant reasons for the gender pay gap. Here is the abstract from the research paper, which succinctly sums up their findings:

> The careers of MBAs from a top U.S. business school are studied to understand how career dynamics differ by gender. Although male and female MBAs have nearly identical earnings at the outset of their careers, their earnings soon diverge, with the male earnings advantage reaching almost 60 log points a decade after MBA completion. Three proximate factors account for the large and rising gender gap in earnings: differences in training prior to MBA graduation, differences in career interruptions, and differences in weekly hours. The greater career discontinuity and shorter work hours for female MBAs are largely associated with motherhood.

So even MBA women, who in all other respects are absolutely equally qualified as their male counterparts, fall behind in their careers largely because of career interruptions caused by their motherhood commitments. Starting from a level playing field, women progressively fall behind in the earnings stakes because they have children and make work-life balance decisions that interfere with their career continuity, or even terminate it. Bertrand et al. go on to say:

> The share of female MBAs not employed also rises substantially in the decade following MBA completion, with 13 per cent of the women not working at all at nine years after MBA completion as compared with one per cent of the men.

Not only do high-powered, highly-qualified women experience career discontinuity due to motherhood, they are also prepared to write off a massive investment in career training, such as an MBA, to change life direction and seek the support of their husbands or partners to make a family. In fact this is made more likely if their husband is a high earner himself, a point that is driven home hard by Bertrand et al.:

> The dynamic impact of a first birth on women as labor market outcomes greatly depends on spousal income. New MBA mothers with higher-earnings spouses reduce their labor supply considerably more than mothers with lower-earnings spouses. In fact, the first birth has only a modest and temporary impact on earnings for MBA women with lower-earnings spouses.

Even high-powered women give up work to be full-time mothers, and it is a choice they naturally and willingly make because they are women. This is not a sexist issue or an issue of discrimination. Even demonstrably able and equally qualified women cannot escape the inevitable choices they have to make if they want to have children. And that means lower lifetime earnings.

Preference theory

Taking a broader view, Dr Catherine Hakim shows us how less high-powered women make choices about their lives. According to her public profile, Hakim is a prominent British sociologist, adviser to the British government, and an acknowledged expert on women's employment and other women's issues. She has published well over 100 articles in academic journals on labour market topics, women's employment, sex discrimination, social and family issues, plus over a dozen books, and she regularly engages in research for well-respected institutions such as the Centre for Policy Studies. Her Preference Theory[272] about women's choices in work penetrates deep into the rhetoric of both the pay gap and the so-called glass ceiling, to which I shall refer later.

Hakim tested her theory in two national surveys: one in Britain and the other in Spain, and the results showed that women's personal preferences strongly predicted their employment decisions and their decisions about fertility. She explains that in a society where women have control over contraception and where there are abundant secondary-earner opportunities under flexible contracts in white collar and service work, part-time work, homework, telework, etc., women have relative freedom to choose their own lifestyle, and they do so to actively create a balance between paid work and family life. She showed that her respondents were neither influenced in their life style choices by societal sex-role attitudes, nor by alleged social conditioning into gender roles. Indeed, she found that these things had virtually no impact on women's personal choices or behaviour.

Even more crucially, she found that women's attitudes to life choices were not caused by unexpected changes in their personal circumstances, such as unexpectedly becoming pregnant and having to settle down into family life, but that '...the majority of working women seek a large degree of work-life balance, certainly more than men do. Women are more likely to ask for shorter work hours than to ask for higher pay or promotion'.[273] In other words, career preferences were not *post hoc* rationalisations made for serendipitous reasons, but active choices women make about their life's pattern. In particular, Hakim found: that only about 20 per cent of women adopt a work-centred lifestyle, prioritising their careers and achievement, and remaining childless in order to do so; another 20 per cent give up work altogether to prioritise family life and share values with their husbands, adopting a family-centred lifestyle and having a number of children; and the remaining 60 per cent adapt and seek to combine the best of both worlds, content to take lower earnings in order to achieve what they want for themselves. As Hakim puts it:

> The great majority of women who transfer to part-time work after they have children are adaptive women, who seek to devote as much time and effort to their family work as to their paid jobs.

This is the key to understanding the complexity of the gender pay gap, which the simplistic use of statistics simply doesn't reveal.

Whose hegemony?

There is another logical knot that feminism has got itself into. We hear endless calls for 'family friendly' work: for work to be changed to conform to women's needs, but it is fallacious to assume that this will lead to equality and the eradication of the gender pay gap. Most well-paid occupations cannot be made family friendly. Modern work cannot be shoehorned to conform to domestic family arrangements, as Hakim further explains:[274]

> Some occupations and activities involve an enormous amount of travel, sometimes for long periods, often at short notice. This is obviously the case with occupations providing an on-site service of some sort (including professions like accountancy and architecture, as well as crafts such as plumbing repairs), and occupations that involve selling goods or services to a widely dispersed business clientele. Less obviously, many senior-level management jobs also involve vast amounts of travel, sometimes long distance, frequently on an unpredictable time-table, and periodically for extended periods of time away from the home base. Extensive amounts of travel are intrinsic to certain occupations, such as investment banking, news reporting, the airline and travel industries. Such occupations, and the careers based on them, are never going to be family friendly. Attempts to organise family friendly segments within them will be difficult, or the 'sedentary' versions of the job will never accumulate the same experience as the 'mobile' versions. Inevitably, the mobile worker will be promoted over the sedentary worker in such occupations and careers, because they have much wider experience and take greater responsibility.

Feminists talk about the hegemony of patriarchy, but if we are talking hegemony, a demanding career is inherently hegemonic. It is all-dominating and all-demanding and it militates against personal and family life. Children have to be taken to school and picked up. They need feeding and looking after. These things can be shared, at least in part by men, but men are the most likely to have a demanding career because they are inherently full-time, whole of life workers, and women revert to a partnership role in which they subordinate their career potential. As Hakim points out, around one-fifth of women actively make this their personal career choice out of an instinctive desire for their personal fulfilment, and around two-thirds do this on an adaptive basis.

Most women with child or family commitments do not wish to continue pursuing a career, let alone rise to the top. They are not interested in 'leaning in' and 'having it all'. They simply don't want to give the degree of dedication to the job that a successful career demands and that a man is able to (or for that matter, a woman if she remains childless). Work that needs continuous attention: that demands long hours to be devoted to it, with a high level of mental commitment, in almost total dedication of time and energy, comes at the cost of family life, even for a man, and if a woman chooses this (and, it has to be said, most women don't), she consciously pays a price in her earning potential which, for most women, is a price well worth paying.

The myth of the superwoman

I shall now turn to perhaps the most egregious examples of the feminist elite and its quest for advantage for itself in the name of equality for women. The so-called 'glass ceiling,' an alleged form of discrimination against women that prevents them rising to the top of organisations, is based on the idea that patriarchy either overtly or tacitly conspires to hold women back. This is the most naked and egregious lie. It is just blind, unreasoning feminism doing what feminism always does: deny the obvious to further advance its dogmatic demands. Today, there is nothing barring a woman from pursuing a career to the top to whatever degree she wishes, especially if she is middle class, educated, and she chooses not to have children. In those circumstances, a woman can be self-fulfilled and succeed, limited only by her own ability. Indeed, such is the degree to which society now favours women, there is a form of positive discrimination operating, as we shall see in the next section. If a woman chooses to work full-time, whole of life, she can go into the job/career market, compete on her own ability with anyone, and succeed. And good luck to her. No one, least of all this author, would argue with the right of every woman to achieve her dreams, and have equality of opportunity, based on merit. Indeed, historically, at least since the turn of the twentieth century, this has always been the case. Before that, as we have seen, society was different and different attitudes prevailed: not least amongst women themselves.

Women can be every bit as able as men in most forms of work and organisational life, and have just as much energy and resilience; they can be as qualified in terms of pieces of paper, but the work-life balance issues a woman faces in seeking top jobs causes conflicts for them. If a woman chooses to have children, as most women do, she is precipitated into a different world for all the reasons I have been exploring. She might try and 'lean in' and be a superwoman, thinking she can do both motherhood and career, and perhaps there are some women who can do that. They are not the norm, however, by any means. Even if a woman has the energy, the ability, and the opportunity, there can be no doubt that her children pay a price for her absence from their lives, often at the most critical part of their lives, and it must be said, such women are placing their own self-actualisation ahead of their children's needs. Career comes at a price for children and most women know that instinctively, notwithstanding the pressure of the feminist narrative. The reason women are numerically under-represented at the top of corporations, and the professions, and in public life, is because they choose not to be. Only about 20 per of women prioritise their careers and pursue achievement this way.[275] That is why there are few women in top executive positions, and in Parliament. The foot-stamping furore over the 'glass ceiling' is political chicanery: a canard.

The truth is, those women who spread the lie of the glass ceiling don't want to be conventional wives and mothers. They have made that choice. They have put themselves in competition with men and they want the same position, power, success, and money as men, and they know they can get that by whipping up a furore, based on a false premise - patriarchy. However, ideology will never win over nature. Children need their mother's nurture, yet these bigoted ideologues try to convince us that men can take over this role, (and should do) but, as everyone knows deep down, that is nonsense advanced in the pursuit of a selfish goal. There is no worm hole from pregnancy to the boardroom. No tele-transportation, career-wise, from a pre-child career state to a post-child one for a woman, and if a woman tries to do that she is not only depriving her child, she is placing herself in quantitative role overload: a situation well understood in the field of organisational behaviour, which leads to loss of a sense of control, burnout, and stress-related illness. In its extreme form, it can even lead to death. In Japan, for example, they have even named it *Karoshi*, 'death from overwork'.

However, there is a much more insidious form of overload for women who place themselves in this position - qualitative role overload - that which comes from having more than one demanding role at the same time, like parent and professional, or a job position with many weighty responsibilities,[276] which neither women nor men can sustain without damage to their health. Where women are parachuted into Parliamentary constituencies, or fast tracked to the boardroom without having completed the necessary experiential learning curve, they are highly vulnerable to qualitative role overload, and that results in, at best, low performance, and at worst the need to break away and change one's lifestyle. In January 2014, for instance, Jessica Lee MP, a Commons Aide to Dominic Grieve, the Attorney General, said she was stepping down from politics after considering her 'personal circumstances and responsibilities'. Lee will be the fourth of the female Conservative MPs elected for the first time in 2010 to leave Parliament, and David Cameron, Prime Minister, and advocate of more women in politics, has expressed his frustration about this. He even attacked his own Conservative Associations for their reluctance to pick more women to fight the 2015 general election, but is there any wonder, if their selected candidates only stay for one Parliamentary term? Like many feminists, Cameron is only seeing things through the doctrinaire lens. It is a fact that most women who have reached cabinet level have been childless, and that is not counting the stress caused by inexperience that women who are parachuted (or rocketed depending on your taste in metaphor) into top jobs suffer. Despite all the attempts made by feminist MPs[277] to make the House of Commons a more 'family friendly' place, for example by limiting late night lobby divisions and starting business earlier in the day, being an MP militates against anything like a normal family life, and even superwomen have their limitations, not just physically, but ethically, for women who instinctively put their children first.

Nature, not society, takes women on a different path to men; and, for centuries, society has evolved to adapt to that - until now. This is a truth fundamentally denied by feminism, whose propaganda has caused women to believe they can do it all when they cannot. And that means a lack of career continuity, which causes a woman to lose out on experience and career progression. Men don't have babies. They don't take career breaks and that is why men are at the top of our corporations, politics and most forms of public life. They got there through skill, talent, and good attendance. This was sensibly and bravely explained by Nigel Farage, leader of the United Kingdom Independence Party (UKIP), and a former commodities broker. On 20th January 2014, under the headline, 'Farage: Women must sacrifice family life to succeed in City,' the BBC News website reported him as follows:

> Women prepared to sacrifice family life can do as well as male colleagues in financial firms, if not better, UKIP leader Nigel Farage has said. Mr Farage, who worked in finance before politics, told an audience in the City that women make 'different choices' to men for 'biological reasons'.
>
> Those taking time off to have children were less valuable to employers on their return, he said. But discrimination against women in the City was a thing of the past, he added. Brokers are 'as valuable as the client base that sticks with you and will move with you', he explained. 'In many, many cases, women make different choices in life to the ones that men make simply for biological reasons,' he said. 'If a woman has a client base and has a child and takes two or three years off work, she is worth far less to the employer when she comes back than when she goes away because her client base cannot be stuck rigidly to her'. When he first started work in the City, it was a 'deeply sexist' place, he added. 'Very detrimental' 'I don't believe that in the big banks and brokerage houses and Lloyds of London and everyone else in the City, I do not believe there is any discrimination against women at all. 'I think that young, able women who are prepared to sacrifice the family life and stick with their careers do as well, if not better, than men'. Mr Farage elaborated on BBC Radio 4's The World at One: 'People who bring in commission business are people who've worked very closely with clients, over years and years and years. 'If you have children and take nine months, or a year, or maybe more off, you tend to lose some of that business. 'I think the reality for women in the City is that if they have children, it has a very detrimental effect on their future pay prospects'. He was asked whether it should it be this way. 'I can't change biology,' he replied.

It is evident from the way this article is written that the author is putting a lot of distance between himself or herself and Farage's comments, and I suggest this is because what Farage said is heresy in our current social climate. In fact, the 'Twittersphere' erupted over what he said. But what did he say except the truth based on common sense? Women who make it to the top of their careers pay a price. Either they forego having children and a family life (which is their choice) and get on with their uninterrupted career, or they start a family and lose out on their value as employees. It really is just as simple as that. Yet the feminist mob rule was, predictably, unleashed upon him in all its fury.

The furore over the lack of women in top jobs being whipped up by the feminists is nothing more than stupidity based on anger and borne of the fact that these people know there is a motherhood penalty to be paid for career success, but they want society to do something about that, even though it can't. Feminists lobby endlessly for governments to increase their spend of taxpayer's money to create ever more childcare, and for men to 'take more of their share' when what that really means is men taking over women's nature-allotted share of motherhood. Who says that childcare is legitimately a man's role, except feminists and those who have bought in to their dogma? Again, they are selling us a pup using logical fallacies - in this case, the *petitio principia*, 'Begging the question'. They are posing a question whose underlying premise is itself questionable and open to debate - and it is all part of the general technique of feminists to cloud issues in order to re-express them through their own dogma and hide their true purpose, which is to put an elite of women on top in society and bring men to a place of social subjection. Right from the outset: from the earliest agitators such as Millicent Fawcett, the Pankhursts, Betty Friedan, Kate Millett, and Germaine Greer, up to their latest counterparts, we see this elite of extremist women intent on only one thing - the advancement of their own kind - based on an ideological belief that now amounts to a religion for the masses.

The golden skirts

One of the best examples of feminism's futile aim of achieving parity of women in top jobs comes from Norway, the first country in the world to introduce legislated quotas for women on corporate boards. In 2003, the Norwegian Parliament passed a law forcing stock-exchange listed companies to appoint at least 40 per cent of women to boardroom positions by 2008, and head-hunters scoured Europe to get any women they could find. Even half-suitable women were approached, such was the scramble to fill the legal quotas by the due date. In Norway itself, some women took on so many directorships they came to be called 'Golden Skirts', and feminists hailed the whole exercise as a major success. However, it was a workaround: a fix. Those women were appointed as non-executive directors and this easy-fix solution came with a seriously heavy corporate price tag, as no less than five *bona fide* longitudinal studies carried out since show. Three of the studies come from the Norwegian experience and two from the United States and Germany, and collectively they paint a dismal picture of the outcome of legally-imposed gender quotas on the boards of corporations. Two common themes run through them: first, the reduction in the overall experience level of boards with artificially high proportions of women and, second, the lack of decisiveness in corporate decision making. Both of these factors resulted in a decline in corporate value for shareholders, although no doubt enhancing the personal bank accounts of Norway's Golden Skirts and their hangers-on from the rest of Europe.

Here is a summary of each study, compiled by Campaign for Merit in Business[278] (along with their emphases), to illustrate the point:

The Changing of the Boards: The Impact on Firm Valuation of Mandated Female Board Representation (2011)[279]
Professor Kenneth R. Ahern (University of Southern California, Marshall School of Business), Professor Amy K. Dittmar (University of Michigan, Stephen M. Ross School of Business).
Abstract:

'In 2003, a new law required that 40 per cent of Norwegian firms' directors be women – at the time only 9 per cent of directors were women. We use the pre-quota cross-sectional variation in female board representation to instrument for exogenous changes to corporate boards following the quota. We find that the constraint imposed by the quota caused a significant drop in the stock price at the announcement of the law and a large decline in Tobin's Q over the following years, consistent with the idea that firms choose boards to maximise value. **The quota led to younger and less experienced boards, increases in leverage and acquisitions, and deterioration in operating performance, consistent with less capable boards'**.

Governance and Politics: Regulating Independence and Diversity in the Board Room (2010)[280]
Professor Øyvind Bøhren (Norwegian School of Management),
Professor R Øystein Strøm (Oslo and Akershus University College).
Abstract:

'This paper analyses the economic rationale for board regulation in place and for introducing new regulation in the future. We relate the value of the firm to the use of employee directors, board independence, directors with multiple seats, and to gender diversity. Our evidence shows that the firm creates more value for its owners when the board has no employee directors, when its directors have strong links to other boards, **and when gender**

diversity is low. We find no relationship between firm performance and board independence. These characteristics of value-creating boards support neither popular opinion nor the current politics of corporate governance'.

A Female Style in Corporate Leadership? Evidence from Quotas (2011)[281]
Professor David A Matsa (Northwestern University, Kellogg School of Management), Professor Amalia R Miller (University of Virginia).
Abstract:

'This paper studies the impact of gender quotas for corporate board seats on corporate policy decisions. We examine the introduction of Norway's 2006 quota, comparing affected firms to other Scandinavian companies, public and private, that were unaffected by the rule. Based on differences-in-differences and triple-difference models, we find that firms affected by the quota undertook fewer workforce reductions than comparison firms, increasing relative labour costs and employment levels **and reducing short-term profits**. The effects are strongest among firms that had no female board members before the quota was introduced and present even for boards with older and more experienced members. The boards appear to be affecting corporate strategy in part by selecting like-minded executives'.

Women in the Boardroom and Their Impact on Governance and Performance (2008)[282]
Professor Daniel Ferreira (London School of Economics), Renée B. Adams (University of New South Wales). The paper's full abstract:

'We show that female directors have a significant impact on board inputs and firm outcomes. In a sample of US firms, we find that female directors have better attendance records than male directors, male directors have fewer attendance problems the more gender-diverse the board is, and women are more likely to join monitoring committees. These results suggest that gender-diverse boards allocate more effort to monitoring. Accordingly, we find that CEO turnover is more sensitive to stock performance and directors receive more equity-based compensation in firms with more gender-diverse boards. However, **the average effect of gender diversity on firm performance is negative**. This negative effect is driven by companies with fewer takeover defences. Our results suggest that mandating gender quotas for directors can reduce firm value for well-governed firms'.

Executive Board Composition and Bank Risk Taking (2012)[283]
(Deutsche Bundesbank Discussion Paper, 03/2012)
Professor Allen N. Berger (University of South Carolina, Wharton

Financial Institutions Center and Tilburg University), Thomas Kick (Deutsche Bundesbank), Professor Klaus Schaeck (Bangor University). The researchers studied German banks over 1994-2010.

Abstract:

'Little is known about how socio-economic characteristics of executive teams affect corporate governance in banking. Exploiting a unique dataset, we show how age, gender, and education composition of executive teams affect risk taking of financial institutions. First, we establish that age, gender, and education jointly affect the variability of bank performance. Second, we use difference-in-difference estimations that focus exclusively on mandatory executive retirements and find that younger executive teams increase risk taking, **as do board changes that result in a higher proportion of female executives**. In contrast, if board changes increase the representation of executives holding Ph.D. degrees, risk taking declines'.

Now, playing devil's advocate, some might say that this is simply an inexperience effect, which is temporary, and will eventually wash out of the system as more experienced women become available to fill these posts. The flaw in this argument is obvious, however. Where are these experienced women going to come from? To get the experience needed, they would have had to have risen through the ranks. They would have needed to be on the career ladder, from its bottom rungs to the top; never stepping off - always competing in the rat race. Women who have the experience and ability have every right to rise to the top, but only on their merit, and that means they would have had to be full-time, whole of life workers, and we know that the number of women who do that is vanishingly small. The sort of experience needed for top corporate governance is unavailable to women in general, for all the reasons I have been eliciting. Thus, we come back to the elitist argument, most advanced by those who are going to benefit from it.

True equality is equality of opportunity, and true diversity lies in everyone finding their own place in an organisation based on merit and skills, not on the possession of privilege and a golden skirt. The elite feminists in government and their fellow travellers who are driving the politics of this will, no doubt, take their places on the corporate boards in due course in order to finance their post-political retirements, and they are simply feathering their own nests. They are using feminism and the traction it has gained so they can generate even more privilege for themselves. As I said elsewhere: nice work if you can get it. The glass ceiling falsehood is a ruse to dupe public opinion into accepting the most obscene grab for power and privilege by an ideologically driven elite who are actively at work re-engineering society for their own benefit, and trying to create the very privilege they accuse men of having. What has the glass ceiling got to do with most normal women's lives? Can they afford the nannies and the child-minders to free them to gallivant across the globe, earning in one day more than the average working mother's monthly income? The blatant hypocrisy of this is nauseating. How can that be about women's equality?

Role models

What is worse, successful career women like the Golden Skirts are being lauded as role models for young women and girls. They are endlessly rolled out on the broadcast media and at schools and universities to speak to young women, being offered as perfect models of female aspiration, but are they? I suggest they are setting a false standard for political purposes, and that is irresponsible. What these women represent is an aspiration that is as immoral as it is unreal. Highly successful women are a self-selecting tiny minority who are able to do what they do because they eschew a full commitment to motherhood; is that really a good model of womanhood to girls? The real role models for girls are those women who, behind the scenes, and even in the face of the strident feminist rhetoric, quietly and diligently get on with life as it is, and fulfil their own aspirations, based on the role nature has given them to play. This is not to say that women with children should not be working, or that women can become fulfilled in work and achievement, or that all women should have children. But it is to say that there are times in women's lives when childbearing and rearing must come over career progression.

Feminists are skewing girls' aspirations and that is deeply wrong. The successful women role model narrative is part of a wider one that implicitly says full-time marriage, homemaking and motherhood are inferior and demeaning for women. It is trying to fit all women into a narrow elitist idea, and that is totalitarianism. It is also inherently contradictory. Women who make it in the corporate world, or in politics, disprove the very point feminists are trying to make. Far from successful women showing that men and women are equal, or that there are no god-given roles to play for each, the very act of emulating men by eschewing their nature-given motherhood responsibilities, only demonstrates that a natural role for women really does exist. Think about that for a moment. If people's social roles are not naturally conceived, but falsely socialised into us by a man-shaped society, why are feminists trying to socialise women into a new role: a man's role; as in the film *The Devil Wears Prada*? This is just another piece of non-logic: another knot that feminism frequently gets itself into in its blind rage for equality.

The caricaturist's aim is always to reveal the truth by grotesquely exaggerating those characteristics of their targets, and *The Devil Wears Prada* is such a caricature. Women who make it to the top, particularly in the corporate world, are often caricatures of the men they seek to outwit. They are often dominating, super-aggressive, ruthless, selfish, and frequently very difficult to work for, or with. These women are often more driven than the men whom they take such pride in beating. And by the way, there are hundreds of millions of men in Britain, America and other parts of the developed world for whom the likelihood of achieving high-powered jobs such as those to which these women aspire is as vanishingly small as it is for most women.

Blind (and blinding) equality

It is a lie that women are paid less than men. The truth is, they *earn* less than men over their lifetimes. Lower paid, less educated, less privileged women are trapped in a low pay syndrome from which they cannot escape, and which has been largely created by feminism's destruction of the nuclear family, with a man as its provider. The pay gap for privileged, educated women is caused by their early training choices, which leads them to certain careers, career discontinuity due to children and family commitments and the overall choices women make about career types, which on balance pay less than those chosen by men. There is no pay gap for women in their 20s, or for very high-powered women who make their careers their life. For some women, such as women GPs and the Golden Skirts, positive discrimination has given them a nice little earner and they ride it for all it is worth.

When women take career breaks and have children, and then work part-time, they sacrifice experience and career progression, which lowers their economic value to employers. This has a multiplying effect, which leads to most women earning cumulatively less than men in a working life. Women also switch careers when they go back to work after children, and that adds to the effect. Even highly educated women frequently abandon their earlier careers altogether and devote themselves to their families, as we saw in the MBA studies in Chicago, which also illustrated the career choices issue compared to men. This was confirmed in 2015 by a joint study between Cambridge University in England and Harvard University in the US,[284] which used the anonymised tax data and student loan records of 260,000 students who graduated between 1998 and 2011; the study revealed that 10 years after graduation the top 10 per cent of women earners took home just 78 per cent of their male counterparts pay: a 22 per cent pay gap; and for the top one per cent of earners, the pay gap was 40 per cent.[285] Just 10 years from graduation, women's earnings do fall behind men's, because they choose careers that pay less, and that is precisely the time (around age 30) when women marry and have children. Interestingly, this study also underlined the fact that feminism is nothing for ordinary women working in the public sector and those areas of the private sector that wax and wane according to economic fluctuation. Viz.:[286]

> … most of the lowest paid are nongraduate [Sic] females. Second, women were more negatively impacted by the recession. Although higher earning men increased their earnings during and after the recession period but not as much as previous cohorts and women saw a real decline in earnings over the period, some of which is attributable to the recession.

One of the most revealing results of the Cambridge/Harvard research is that women graduates earn three times more than non-graduate women (the ratio for men is two-to-one). That is a staggering difference, and it makes the alleged 16.4 per cent gender pay gap between men and women pale into insignificance. In their drive for privilege, feminists are creating an intra-gender pay gap of massive proportions. Far from creating equality, feminists are fomenting inequality, amongst women. Truly all animals are equal: but some are more equal than others, it seems.

The endless argument about how work is valued for ordinary women, about the need for equal numbers of women in the boardroom, or Parliament, must be recognised for what it is: extreme left-wing political socialism. Only in a Socialist-Communist society is equality interpreted as parity of numbers, only there can men's and women's pay be equalised precisely, and that is the direction of travel of feminism, let us be in no doubt about that. People who believe that the fight over the gender pay gap is all about equality and fairness: that women earning less than men is somehow morally wrong and society must do something about it, are either politically motivated, or they are dupes who have bought the specious Marxist party line. In a free market economy, which like it or not is the template for the developed world, the market pays for labour value, just like all markets do, and if we assume equal ability between women and men (and there is absolutely no reason not to), women who want parity of hourly pay with men must adopt the same employment and work patterns as men; otherwise they will lose out. In its very essence that is what the gender pay gap is all about.

However, women cannot avoid their biological destiny. Women bear the children who are the next generation and those children need their mother's nurture, especially in their most vital early years. Women also naturally fall to being homemakers, feminism's sophistries notwithstanding. Most women are fulfilled by marriage and motherhood, and tending to their own families, and they make work-life balance decisions to achieve that. Women willingly sacrifice their economic capital in favour of their social capital as mothers and homemakers, and no amount of ideological politicising is going to change that. That is what makes the entire argument about the gender pay gap sterile and futile. All it does is drive men and women further apart, and that is not good for them or society.

From each according to his ability...

So, we must ask, given that there is a rational explanation for the gender pay gap, and given that the great and the good, such as the President of the United States and a host of other world leaders, continue to make it their political policy, why on earth are they doing so? The answer is simple. We need only go back to that day on 30th April 1971 and the meeting in Town Hall, New York, when Jaqueline Ceballos, speaking on behalf of the National Organisation for Women said, '… women are underpaid and overworked, and there is no chance for advancement anywhere. If women are to be married in a society that pushes them towards marriage, they should be paid for the work that they do.' This is simply an expression based on the Marxist Engelist ideological principle that, 'the bourgeois [man] sees in his wife a mere instrument of production,' which is spelled out clearly in the *Communist Manifesto*, 1848, and Engels's idea that the primeval sexual couplings of men and women are a source of inequality between them when it comes to the allocation of economic work and enjoyment because each does a different job of work in the production of children.

This is the ideological direction of travel behind the spurious, illogical, easily disproved rhetoric of those who promote the gender pay gap lies. The real intention is to increase working mothers' part-time pay to such an extent that their income (not their pay) becomes equal to that of men. Thus, wealth in society will be redistributed 'from each according to his ability, to each according to his [her] needs'. Women will finally be able to bear children free from any economic dependence on men. The nuclear family will be finished for good, men will be subjugated and forced to become 'new men'- their patriarchal power finally defeated - and the feminist's dream of the matriarchal society will be fulfilled. And no one seems to care about the children.

This process is already underway, as the most recent statistics released at the time of writing by the UK's Her Majesty's Revenue and Customs, show.[287] From 2011 to 2014, men paid an increasingly greater proportion of income tax than women, their share increasing from 72 per cent to 72.9 per cent, almost a full percentage point increase in just three years. Of the total income tax revenues in 2013-14, 17.4 million men paid £120 billion, an increase of £7 billion from 2011, while 13.0 million women paid £44.6 billion, an increase of just 0.6 billion. Put another way, men paid £69 billion more than women in 2011-12, and £75.4 billion in 2014-15. If we're talking about pay gaps, perhaps we should talk about taxation gaps too?

The feminist dream is fast becoming a nightmare, but for more reasons than these (and the obvious: that men will not be subjugated). Breaking the link between women's economic productivity and their pay is undermining the very system that gives women the opportunities being claimed for them by feminism, and it will fast send their pay rates into a downward spiral. According to the Bank of England's Quarter 1 report 2016,[288] entitled *Wages, productivity and the changing composition of the UK workforce*, which deals with the ever-increasing problem of low productivity in the British economy, 'Over the past 30 years the composition of UK employment has changed substantially [and] these changes have important implications for wage and productivity growth'. The report goes on:

> Wage growth is typically thought to be driven by three main factors: productivity, inflation expectations and labour market slack (that is, the level of hours worked relative to potential labour supply). In the long run, an individual's real wage should track their productivity - the value of what they produce over a given period measured in real terms… Productivity per worker is simply the total value of all output produced in the United Kingdom divided by the number of workers.
>
> Female participation in the workforce has also increased over time. The share of women in employment has gone up from 41% in the mid-1980s to

47% in 2015. Numerous economic studies show that there is a gender pay gap faced by women relative to men which is unexplained by socioeconomic factors like education and the industries in which they work.

The Bank of England says that the gender pay gap is unexplained by factors like education and the industries in which women work. It might be right about the former, but it certainly is not right about the latter, as we have seen, and it signally fails to name the elephant in the room. The real explanation for the so-called gender pay gap is the massive influx of women into the workforce, and the fact that very large numbers of them seek part-time work because they are wrestling with the work-life balances feminism has created for them. These women, no doubt full of divine discontent, are being used as cannon fodder in the ideological struggle for female supremacy that feminism really is.

Divine discontent

Many women are exercised about the alleged gender pay gap today. Some are harbouring a resentment about their perceived lack of equality, and they have a general sense that they are being disadvantaged by society (and, by implication, by men) in life, in work, and in pay. This unrest is being fomented by feminists who have a political axe to grind. Such is the falseness of their proposition, women are foregoing their natural roles and their natural desires in order to comply with the enormous memetic pressure, and that is diminishing them through its false message of elevating them. As Margaret Meade, cited by Carolyn Graglia in her book *Domestic Tranquility: A brief against Feminism*, said:[289]

> The recurrent problem of civilization is to define the male role satisfactorily enough … so that the male may in the course of his life reach a solid sense of irreversible achievement, of which his childhood knowledge of the satisfactions of child-bearing have given him a glimpse. In the case of women, it is only necessary that they be permitted by the given social arrangements to fulfil their biological role, to attain this sense of irreversible achievement. If women are to be restless and questing, even in the face of child-bearing, they must be made so through education.... Each culture--in its own way--has developed forms that will make men satisfied in their constructive activities without distorting their sure sense of their masculinity. Fewer cultures have yet found ways in which to give women a divine discontent that will demand other satisfactions than those of child-bearing.

The gender pay gap and the glass ceiling are all part of feminism's stirring up of a divine discontent in women, and it is destructive: for women, and society. It is the product of unstable reasoning, born of wild imaginings and musings of a dream of a world in which the fundamental biological function of motherhood doesn't exist, social-political idealising, and downright political chicanery that is causing women to undervalue themselves as women, and their vital role in society as wives and mothers. Feminists know this of course, which is why they keep up their relentless propaganda and incessantly try to ensure that women are always portrayed as being victimised and that men are responsible. It is nonsense but, as we saw in their DVA agenda, radical feminists cannot let the truth get in the way of their radical political dogma. Patriarchy must be destroyed and that is that.

Lower women's earnings is not discrimination. If the truth be known it is the product of the social re-engineering that feminism is creating for women in a world in which they must make choices between work and family. Women are never going to be able to earn the same as men in a lifetime. They will never be able to reconcile the conflicting demands of motherhood and a self-actualised career-orientated life, as advocated by a feminist elite, because the two propositions are mutually contradictory, and irreconcilable. The blind demand for more pay and the alleged discriminatory pay gap fed to us daily in the media is propaganda passed off as legitimate social comment by feminist pressure groups intent on grinding their axes and stirring up their sexual politics.

Those women who find themselves struggling to make ends meet as single mothers, having to find work in sectors that pay less, where they are unable to develop their skills and experience potential, and in which they are inevitably just a hired pair of hands, are just as much the victims of radical feminism as are their fathers and husbands. Women cannot have the best of both worlds, they can only ever settle for the worst of each if they submit to being fully functioning pawns in the Marxist feminist revolution, and it is high time they woke up and smelled the coffee about this.

PART III

DOMESTIC VIOLENCE

'Women are the only oppressed group in our society that lives in intimate association with their oppressors.'

Evelyn Cunningham. Feminist. American journalist.

Violence against women and girls worldwide

Violence against women and girls (VAWG) is undoubtedly seen as a worldwide problem. Ban Ki Moon, United Nations Secretary General, says this about it:

> Violence against women continues to persist as one of the most heinous, systematic and prevalent human rights abuses in the world. It is a threat to all women, and an obstacle to all our efforts for development, peace, and gender equality in all societies. Violence against women is always a violation of human rights; it is always a crime; and it is always unacceptable. Let us take this issue with the deadly seriousness that it deserves.

Indeed! Let us do just that. Before I do so, though, I want to make this abundantly clear: in my view, violence of any kind, against anyone, is an abomination, and that includes violence against women and girls as much as against men and boys. Terrorising people, victimising them, abusing them, or violating them in any way, especially in ways that involve the exploitation of their sex and their physical vulnerability is disgusting, and should rightly be condemned by civilised people. However, focussing only on violence against women and girls worldwide is yet another expression of international feminism. It is the outworking of international Marxist Socialism, whose intent is to install its world view in all nations, and which has infiltrated and taken over the United Nations, turning it into a tool of its ideological hegemony. Note the aspiration to achieve gender equality in all societies, presumably that is to be in the face of individual nations' cultures? Feminists have colonised the UN and compromised it, as witness another phrase used by its Secretary General: 'It [VAWG] is a threat to all women, and an obstacle to all our efforts for development, peace, and gender equality in all societies'.

Another thing we need to get clear is that the definition of VAWG being used is not just the application of physical battery. *The United Nations Declaration on the Elimination of Violence Against Women* (1993) provides us with its much wider definition, as follows:

> For the purposes of this Declaration, the term 'violence against women' means any act of gender-based violence that results in, or is likely to result in, physical, sexual or psychological harm or suffering to women, including threats of such acts, coercion or arbitrary deprivation of liberty, whether occurring in public or in private life. Violence against women shall be understood to encompass, but not be limited to, the following:
>
> (a) Physical, sexual and psychological violence occurring in the family, including battering, sexual abuse of female children in the household, dowry-related violence, marital rape, female genital mutilation and other traditional practices harmful to women, nonspousal [Sic] violence and violence related to exploitation;
>
> (b) Physical, sexual and psychological violence occurring within the general community, including rape, sexual abuse, sexual harassment and intimidation at work, in educational institutions and elsewhere, trafficking in women and forced prostitution
>
> (c) Physical, sexual and psychological violence perpetrated or condoned by the State, wherever it occurs.

The insertion of the political word 'gender' rather than the non-political word 'sex' is the key to understanding what is going on here. International VAWG is the standard feminist stance, pure and simple. The very fact that such a UN declaration exists only about women speaks volumes about what is behind it. By implication, worldwide, men are a threat to women and this implicit message causes all of us to be very concerned. Men and boys suffer violence and abuses of their human rights every bit as much as women do. In fact, probably more so, if the truth be known, but that doesn't matter because they are all potential rapists anyway.

However, men and boys are raped. Male infants have their genitals mutilated, and that is not just in third world countries: non-therapeutic circumcision performed on infants who cannot give their consent is routinely practiced in the US, Canada, Britain, and in other civilised nations across the world. It is illegal in the UK, under offences against the person legislation, but no one says anything about it, let alone against it. Men are falsely imprisoned for their beliefs, they suffer psychological violence condoned by the state, even in developed countries; they are lined up and shot in the head just because they are of a particular race, religion, or ethnic origin. They receive physical and psychological abuse from their wives and partners, and their mothers. Boys are systematically abused in institutions from Ireland to Australia by priests, and countless thousands of them are routinely forced into prostitution in many countries of the world, not least in Britain, where the trade in male prostitution among the overwhelmingly male homeless is a major problem, not counting the 'rent-boys' used by homosexual paedophiles. And yet there is no specific United Nations Declaration protecting men and boys.

What is more, women routinely perpetrate violence against girls: women are the major procurers of female genital mutilation. They also condone honour killings, collude in arranged forced marriages, and even offer their daughters as child prostitutes, trafficking them for money. (Aceh province, destroyed by the Boxing Day tsunami in 2004, was a known export point of trafficked boys and girls.) Even in Britain, we hear of these things. We are a nation embedded in the world, with permeable borders, and I suggest permeably cultural ones too. We heard recently of a gang of men of Asian ethnic origin in Rochdale and Bradford, British citizens, singling out white British girls and grooming them for organised and systematic rape. We know there are international and domestic paedophile rings who use the dark web to organise dissemination of child pornography and the systematic abuse of children, often boys; paedophilia is not just a man/girl child deviant activity. Such is the degree of this vile activity, the Child Exploitation and Online Protection agency (CEOP) had to be formed. We hear of people of both sexes trafficked from other parts of the world to become what amount to domestic slaves to wealthy foreigners living here.

And, yes, occasionally we hear of local, domestic violence, among ordinary families where a man has beaten up or murdered his wife or partner; his children, or his stepchildren - or where a woman has done exactly the same. The world truly is a violent and unpleasant place; there is no doubt about it. Mankind's inhumanity is neither woman-kind nor man-kind, and it can be breathtakingly repulsive. That is why we should see that a narrative focussed solely on women and girls is wrong. Anyone can be vulnerable to social violence, which is a violation of all human beings' rights. That is the real obstacle to worldwide peace and harmony. Yet women and girls continue to be singled out for special attention by international agencies such as the UN. The ever-widening woman centric culture, driven by feminism and its innate misandry is spreading its warped ideological views worldwide, casting women everywhere as victims of men, and men as the eternal aggressor, irrespective of whether they are men living in a civilised way in a civilised society. In its relentless drive to divide so it can rule, international feminism is spreading its gender agenda far and wide, politicising sex, and setting women against men everywhere it can find traction. And it is doing that under the specious banner of VAWG.

Domestic violence and abuse

International feminism is behind the drive against VAWG in the UN and in all developed nations. It is all part of the same divisive agenda we are experiencing at home. The fathers, husbands, sons, and brothers of those nations who are trying to live out their lives in a civilised way, under the rule of a civilised legal system, are being tarred with the same brush as the Taliban who shoot a girl in the head because she wants to go to school, or the rapists in the internecine wars in, say, sub-Saharan Africa, or the traffickers of children in Indonesia. It is all too easy to conflate these atrocities in the public mind with the atrocious idea that civilised men in civilised countries habitually beat up their wives and partners and murder them. Decent, honourable, civilised men are not like that. That is why they are civilised. Yet, feminists in their own countries are maliciously trying to associate these men with human rights abusers, and that is not right. The only thing that connects the male Taliban with a father and husband in Britain is the possession of a penis, yet Britain is currently being whipped up into a moral panic about domestic violence by deliberate association of the idea of controlling patriarchy.

If we listen to the inflammatory rhetoric of the deeply feminist women's groups who are offering help to women to stamp out what they purport to be an epidemic of domestic violence and abuse (DVA), and the politicians who are playing to the women's lobby for votes, we could easily be led to believe that the home is a seriously dangerous place for women and girls to be, rather than their sanctuary. Such is the degree of moral panic being whipped up, there is little doubt that people generally believe DVA is widespread, systematic - and that it is men who are doing it to women. None of these things are true, which I shall reveal as this chapter and its successors will show.

Using the standard technique of building a victim narrative for women on the back of the patriarchy narrative, feminists have been incredibly successful in creating an unhealthy and widespread belief, indeed a fixation, in society that men are habitual and inherent abusers in the home. This is a preposterous idea, but it is widespread. Feminist thinking is turning the home into a gender-political battleground and it is driving another wedge between men and women who otherwise love one another and who basically just want to get on with their lives together seeking happiness. Inasmuch as domestic violence is a problem, and it is, although nowhere near the level feminist activists would have us believe, my argument is that it is being blown up out of all proportion. Men - civilised men - are generally no more wife or child abusers than women are husband and child abusers, but men are being singled out and labelled the same as real abusers of human rights across the world by feminists, yet no one seems able to see that, in itself, this is abuse of men and victimisation on a grand scale. A rigid, vindictive, zero-tolerance culture about men who are just ordinary husbands, partners and fathers is being whipped up against them, and all of it is part of the strategy of destroying the family by toppling fatherhood, which is patriarchy, from its natural place in that family. This is the degree to which Marxist feminism is operating clandestinely to re-shape our societies.

Is it abuse or violence?

One of the key issues at the heart of the DVA/VAWG rhetoric is the misuse of terms: particularly 'violence' and 'abuse,' which are used both synonymously and interchangeably in the feminist rhetoric, where they dance and play, obfuscating the core issues. Obviously, the two terms are not the same. Violence is the physical application of battery with the intention of hurting, damaging or killing someone. Abuse, on the other hand, is the improper use of something to bad effect or for a bad purpose. In its most understood meaning, abuse is verbal or behavioural, and it may be sustained. Yet even in the official statistics, this interplay of terms can be found, and it is misleading. A good example is this list of bullet points taken from the UK Office for National Statistics (ONS) annual summary, *Focus on Violent Crime and Sexual Offences 2011/12*,[290] as follows,[291] with my emphases to illustrate my point:

> • Only a small proportion (5%) of respondents who reported being victims of **domestic abuse** in the self-completion module had reported that they were victims of **domestic violence** in face-to-face interviews, reflecting both the broader scope of **domestic abuse**, and the sensitivity and complexity of this topic
>> • … **violence** spans minor assaults, such as pushing and shoving that

result in no physical harm through to serious assault and murder… In half of incidents identified by the Crime Survey for England and Wales (50%), and offences recorded by the police, (56%), the violence resulted in no physical injury to the victim

• In the last year, 7.3% of women and 5.0% of men reported having experienced **domestic abuse**, equivalent to an estimated 1.2 million female victims and 800,000 male victims. There was no statistically significant change in the level of **domestic abuse** experienced in the last year between the 2010/11 and 2011/12 surveys

• In the last year, **non-sexual abuse** by a partner and stalking were the most common of the separate types of intimate violence:

• 4.2% of women and 3.0% of men reported having experienced non-sexual **partner abuse**

• 4.2% of women and 2.7% of men reported having experienced stalking.

• Three of the four main categories of **domestic abuse** (non-sexual **partner abuse**, non-sexual **family abuse** and stalking) have all shown statistically significant decreases between the 2004/05 and 2011/12 CSEW

• Women who were separated had the highest risk of any domestic abuse in the last year (21.0%) compared with all other groups by marital status. The pattern was slightly different for sexual assault, with single women (6.5%) and separated women (4.1%) being more likely to be a victim than those who were married (0.8%)

• Women aged between 16 and 19 or between 20 and 24 were more likely to be victims of any **domestic abuse** (13.7% and 12.6% respectively) or of stalking (7.9% and 7.3% respectively). Women aged between 16 and 19 were most likely to be victims of sexual assault (9.2%) (Table 4.08).

• Women with a degree or diploma were less likely than women with no qualifications or other qualifications to be a victim of any **domestic abuse** in the last year (5.6% of women with a degree or diploma compared with 7.9% of women with 'A level or equivalent qualifications' and 9.3% of those with 'GCSE or equivalent qualifications')

I invite my reader to note the constant interchange of the terms 'violence' and 'abuse' in these statements. The circumstances to which they relate are all accurate, but anyone reading them can easily fall into the trap of believing that they are synonymous terms and, as I shall go on show, this opens the door wide to their misuse. Not all of the situations, grouped generically as domestic abuse, are violent, as in actual applied physical battery. Of course, that is abuse, but 'abuse' is far more widely defined than simple applied physical battery. For example, the ONS refers to stalking, which is not violence. The common understanding of violence as the application of battery on a scale that can ultimately lead to injuries that put people into hospital, or even kill them, is not the true picture being painted here. The broad definition of DVA undoubtedly includes serious physical attacks such as stabbing, strangling and so on, but it also includes women slapping their partners' faces, and men grabbing their wives by the wrists to restrain them in a moment of heated exchange.

What is more, the broad DVA definitions cover behaviours by broader family members. DVA is not just a binary man-woman phenomenon. Yes, spouses and partners push and shove one another. They throw plates at one another and slap one another and, yes, they even punch one another too, but so do other family members, not least teenagers who push their parents aside, slam doors, scream and rant when they don't get their way. It is not like that all the time in all families, thank goodness, but it happens in most families from time to time, and it is included in the generic treatment of DVA. There is also a socio-economic aspect to DVA, which occurs more in certain groups than others, and it affects people in different personal circumstances at different times in their lives, such as during separation and divorce, when disputes, emotions and tensions are running high in both women and men.

These considerations are never brought out in the feminist rhetoric, however (as I shall demonstrate soon), and if we fail to recognise this and contextualise DVA in its wider contexts, not least normal family behaviour: if we will fail to distinguish the subtlety of what feminists are trying to do in this most difficult area of human interactions, which is to perpetrate a rhetorical trick on us, we will be drawn into their world, where all men are abusers and all women are victims. So let me unpack this a little further in order to distinguish the truth from the rhetoric, and discern the dogma behind the deceit. Before I do that, however, allow me to deal with some semantic points. The word 'force' as used in the definitions comes from *fortis* (Latin) meaning 'strong'. As a noun, it really means 'strength or energy', and contains the meaning of influence, possibly coercive influence as in 'a force to be reckoned with, but also as in 'a force for good'. Taken as a verb, however, it becomes determination, as in 'forcing a smile', and about manoeuvring, as in 'forcing someone's hand' when playing a card game. Force, therefore, can mean someone being physically made to do something against their will as in 'she was forced into retirement,' and it doesn't have to mean assault and battery.

So, returning to the argument, notice in the ONS definitions given earlier the predominant use of the term 'abuse' to include threats and the inclusion of emotional or financial factors within its compass. Notice also that stalking and indecent exposure are included, neither of which could be regarded as physical violence, even though they might be intimidating. Then notice that sexual threats are linked to sexual assault, as is unwanted touching. Clearly, the latter could technically be considered as the application of battery, but it is hardly what the man in the street would call physical violence. Notice also the absence of gender-specific language. The ONS is not saying domestic violence/abuse is focussed essentially on women, or that it is committed essentially by men, the real definition of domestic violence. The entire approach is gender neutral. Finally, notice that only the last category - stalking - has any reference to a pattern of behaviour. This is important in the light of how feminist organisations such as Women's Aid treat this in their institutional narrative of an ongoing pattern of behaviour in men who commit DVA.

Women's Aid

The group of charities spread around Great Britain called Women's Aid generically describe themselves as 'The key national charity working to end domestic violence against women and children,' and it is certainly highly influential. Its umbrella organisation lists among its patrons leading feminists such as Jenni Murray, the voice of feminism on *Woman's Hour*, broadcast daily on the BBC, Sarah Brown, wife of former British Prime Minister Gordon Brown, the internationally famous actors Julie Walters CBE and TV actor Kevin Whateley, star of a popular detective series, and even a famous TV chef, Gordon Ramsay, and his wife Tana.[292] Under the catch line, 'Until women are safe,' Women's Aid's one-sided aim is, '... to end violence against women and children,' and its public utterances reek of a feminist agenda. In its fact sheet of *Frequently Asked Questions* in 2009, we find the following statement (with my emphases to elucidate the point):

> Who is responsible for the violence? The abuser is - always. There is no
> excuse for domestic violence. The abuser has a choice to use violence for
> which **he** is responsible and for which **he** should be held accountable. Abusers
> do not have to use violence. They can choose, instead, to behave non-violently
> and foster a relationship built on trust, honesty, fairness and respect. The
> victim is never responsible for the abuser's behaviour.

In the midst of high-sounding rhetoric and a thinly-veiled attempt at gender neutrality, here we see Women's Aid's real agenda disclosed. The use of the male subject personal pronouns exposes the mendacity behind this ridiculous utterance. Notice also the intermixing of the terms 'violence' and 'abuse' (and, of course, the term, 'abuser'), then look at the last sentence, which is a blank denial of adult women's agency. In the context of intimate partner situations, which become violent, how can the abuser always be responsible, and the victim never so? And who is the abuser anyway? Often abuse begets abuse in the tense dynamic of intimate relationships. And what do we mean by 'responsible'? If someone gets drunk and falls over into the path of an oncoming car, is the driver responsible - always? I think not. What about a man who verbally abuses another man, squares up to him and waves his fists, and the other man responds by assaulting him? Does the first man not at least share the responsibility for what happens to him? I think he does. Certainly, the law thinks so because if the assault were made pre-emptively, in the genuine belief by the second man that the first was about to attack him, he would be able to claim self-defence. Even if that wasn't upheld, and he was held criminally responsible, the actions of the first man would almost certainly be considered mitigation by a judge when sentencing him.

However, in Women's Aid's world, and its false constructs, only men can be abusers and women their victims in domestic strife, which means that men, in thrall to their animal instincts and barely able to control themselves, must carry total responsibility for the relationship and its ups and downs, whilst women are utterly innocent; without agency, and exempted from their personal responsibility for their part in it all. And what is Women's Aid's prescription for dealing with this concocted syndrome? If only men would act like women, creating 'trust, honesty, and fairness' in their relationship difficulties, then all would be well - allegedly. This entire approach is an insult to any intelligent person's understanding of life, and it reeks of the feminist agenda which is rampant throughout the entire DVA industry. Women's Aid is promulgating a feminist apologetic, let no one be in any doubt about that, and the smoking gun can be found in its published core thesis about DVA (with my emphases again):

> **What is the cause of domestic violence?** Domestic violence against
> women by men is 'caused' [Sic.] by the misuse of power and control within a
> context of **male privilege. Male privilege** operates on an individual and

societal level to maintain a situation of **male dominance**, where **men have power** over women and children. Perpetrators of domestic violence choose to behave abusively **to get what they want and gain control**. Their behaviour often originates from **a sense of entitlement**, which is often supported by sexist, racist, homophobic and other discriminatory attitudes. In this way, **domestic violence by men against women** can be seen as **a consequence of the inequalities between men and women**, rooted in **patriarchal traditions** that encourage men to believe they are **entitled to power and control over their partners**.

Here is the old feminist canard of the hegemony of patriarchy writ large. Notice also the peppering of feminist terms such as 'entitlement,' 'privilege,' 'dominance,' 'power,' 'control,' 'sexist,' etc. They come straight from the feminist lexicon and are used to support the rigid feminist stereotypes of 'men bad, women good,' to which is added the cry, 'if only men were more like women...,' 'if only men would change their natures'. This stylised feminist solution to what has always been a cross-gender problem is taken straight from the little red book of feminism, and it reeks of the unhinged ravings of the early feminists of the 1970s like Andrea Dworkin, and Valerie Solanas, and her Society for Cutting Up Men and *SCUM Manifesto*, whose pages teem with hatred and disgust for men, maleness, and manhood. No doubt, these radical feminists' theories and mantras, no doubt learned in gender studies' classes, permeate the offices and corridors of Women's Aid in all its myriad incarnations across the length and breadth of the land. It is a gender-political organisation furthering a one-sided radical feminist worldview. Its depiction of men and women in what has always been called 'domestic disputes' but is now DVA, is both stylised and utterly divorced from the reality of how men and women really are, and this becomes even more extreme in the next example of its utterances on the subject:

> 'Blaming the victim' is something that abusers will often do to make excuses for their behaviour. This is part of the pattern and is in itself abusive. Sometimes abusers manage to convince their victims that they are to blame for the abuser's behaviour. Blaming **his** behaviour on someone or something else - the relationship, **his** childhood, ill health, alcohol or drug addiction - is an abuser's way of avoiding personal responsibility for **his** behaviour.

Note, again, the specious attempt at gender neutrality betrayed by only one word, '... blaming **his** behaviour,' but also note the attempt to pathologise male behaviour in DVA. Men are being depicted in relationship disputes as seeking to blame their behaviour 'on someone or something else,' offering excuses to avoid personal responsibility. These are lies, as anyone with common sense knows. They amount to the creation of a straw-man argument, one that is set up to be shot down, and they are pure propaganda, typical of totalitarianism down the centuries whose tactics have been consistent: declare an 'in' group as victims, an 'out' group as victimisers, then step in and offer a solution based on a totalitarian ideology. The oxygen of Women's Aid rhetoric is radical feminism, an ideology that seeks to politicise and then regulate relationships between men and women, so it can overturn the alleged control of women by men, and all based on the false allegation that men are somehow inherently controlling creatures. It is all lies, dressed up in innuendo and propaganda, and it is intended to set up Women's Aid as the answer to an artificially created problem.

To portray women as hapless, helpless victims of men in DVA is to deny women both their integrity and their autonomy, and it is doublespeak of the highest order, worthy of the Orwellian world in which this feminist bigotry is now the dominant culture. Women have choices. They can choose to extricate themselves from dangerous situations, and from toxic relationships. An independent woman living in a feminist age can choose whether to get into such a situation in the first place. In fact, men are often more locked into toxic relationships than women because they know they will be victimised in the financial consequences of divorce, which rewards women and punishes men, and they face the constant fear of losing contact with their children, a threat that is all too often offered by irresponsible women who know they are backed by agencies such as Women's Aid, who will encourage them in their victimhood, and reinforce them in the narcissistic view that they are unimpeachable. This is reinforced by the feminist-biased courts' system, effectively run by feminists and presided over by fellow-travelling junior judges who routinely hand down unjust judgements about child access and custody because they are craven in the face of political correctness.

Perhaps the celebrities and other fellow travellers: the actors, chefs, and wives of former politicians who appear in the ranks of those who lend their names to Women's Aid would do well to consider all this? Could it be that they have simply taken Women's Aid's 'right-on' message, so glossily and expensively produced as it is, rather too much at face value? Have they become dazzled by the tens of millions of pounds of taxpayers' money which is being thrown annually at this organisation by central and local government and the National Lottery Heritage Fund? Perhaps they were beguiled by the fawning attention Women's Aid receives from governments of all political hues, and at whose table it has a guaranteed seat when policy about DVA is being decided? Or are they convinced of its *bona fides* when they see how embedded it is in the Crown Prosecution Service, who openly quotes Women's Aid's inputs into its policy formulation in its publicity material?

Maybe these celebrities and the great and the good would do well to reflect that perhaps they have taken Women's Aid a little too much at face value? That what they are lending their celebrity to is actually a feminist-inspired, anti-male, anti-society, socially-divisive organisation, whose *raison d'etre* is to conjure up a false narrative, which feeds a moral panic about DVA, and looks to the state for funding to solve the 'problem'? Women's Aid is an ideologically driven political pressure group that is working under the shelter of charitable status and is pursuing an agenda that is far from philanthropy. It is as rich as Croesus from funds channelled from the public purse, and it is using that to engage in what is now called sock-puppetry: nakedly lobbying to influence social policy to further its own continued existence and its ideological political agenda. Women's Aid sits at the centre of a gigantic and very clever feedback mechanism that guarantees its continued existence, yet it is a giant with ideological feet of clay. Women's Aid is doing nothing to reconcile men and women in domestic disputes. In fact, through its shelters and advocacy of only women in the legal family industry, it is serving only to divide people further.

Perhaps the celebrities who support it might do well to consider all this and hasten back to their chef's kitchens and actors' film sets to consider whether in lending their name to such a socially divisive organisation they are doing such a good thing after all? Neither their careers nor society at large are going to be helped by aiding and abetting the stoking of a false fire in such a sensitive area as the difficulties men and women face in their interpersonal relationships. Nor is the quality of life for any of us going to be improved by key figures in society lending their support to the activities of an organisation which has such a skewed understanding of the issues in which it purports to have expertise, and which is succeeding in causing us all to get the entire DVA situation so much out of proportion. Taking such a one-sided view of DVA is to feed off the misery and human frailty of others, and it behoves those amongst us who have celebrity to consider whether helping to further the aims of a massive empire that has feminism as its beating heart - an intentionally family-destroying

Marxist ideology that is seeking to divide society so it can rule it - is such a good thing after all?

The Duluth model

Women's Aid's philosophy about DVA, which is the common view in most feminist-inspired social institutions and government departments, is built on what is called 'The Duluth Model'. Created in Duluth, Minnesota, in 1993, following a serious domestic violence homicide, it is a gendered theory formulated entirely on feminist principles and beliefs. The Duluth Model asserts that men's alleged abusive behaviour towards women arises from patriarchy, which socialises men to believe they are privileged, and breeds in them an innate sense of entitlement. This, the theory goes, leads to a power dynamic in men's and women's relationships, which *ergo* oppresses women and results in a tendency for men to be violent with their female partners. The 'cure' for this alleged male pathology is for 'abusers' to undergo 'batterer intervention programmes,' which amounts to them being educated in feminism. This is explained clearly on the 'Knowledge for Growth' applied psychology website,[293] where we find this:

> The goal of treatment is to educate men about gender roles, and how
> behaviours and values identified as 'masculine' have been shaped by societal
> messages and attitudes that reinforce patriarchal privilege and unhealthy ways
> of relating with [*sic*] women... The 'Duluth Model' represents the dominant
> treatment approach aligned with feminist theory. This model was created
> following a serious domestic violence homicide that took place in Duluth,
> Minnesota (Pence & Paymar, 1993). Community and government officials
> wanted to address the problem of domestic violence, but did not know where
> to begin. They wanted to create a treatment approach that involved the courts,
> police services, and 'human services'.

Whilst the Duluth model recognises that men can be victims of DVA too, it couches that in terms of their inherent slavery to their own natures, from which they need rescuing. This is a classic Catch 22, worthy of the most bigoted feminist thinking. In simple terms, men cannot be real men unless they capitulate to feminist ideology and be subjected to retraining. It is nothing less than a naked attempt at brainwashing by a totalitarian ideology that will not accept that women can also be aggressors of men. It is also the silver bullet for women who act violently towards men and then try and turn the tables, knowing they will receive the benefit of the doubt. Erin Pizzey[294] describes this as:

> A particular trait of women abusers when confronted with their behaviour, for example by the police, is to turn the tables on their victim by claiming to be the victim themselves. This is a common behaviour characteristic and is known as DARVO (Deny, Attack, and Reverse Victim and Offender)

But why, in the light of such overwhelming evidence and even practical common sense, does Women's Aid continue to promulgate this deeply reprehensible model and its deceitful propaganda? The answer is very simple. It is peddling a lucrative brand: one that has a ready market.

Women's Aid comprises well over 400 individual companies and affiliates, spread throughout the United Kingdom. Many of these are small companies that fall below the small companies' reporting threshold, which makes data about their activities difficult to obtain; however, an analysis of 171 Women's Aid companies[295] for the period 2011-15 shows that in 2015 they had a combined turnover of circa £324M, employed almost 2,000 staff earning on average £24,000 per year, had a combined net worth of £44.3M, which was growing annually at a rate of over 3 per cent, and their combined cash reserves stood at £27.5M. The CEO earns more than the Prime Minister of the United Kingdom. Taking a sample of eight Women's Aid companies, spread across the UK,[296] the average amount being spent on refuges is about 11 per cent of income. From its annual statement for 2013/14, Women's Aid estimates that 9,500 women stayed in one of its refuges in that year, which equates to £34,100 per woman aided, although one Women's Aid company reported an average refuge stay was 22 weeks, which equates to £80,600 of income, per woman-year.

These are astonishing figures. Women's Aid is a massive hydra-like organisation of gigantic proportions, and it has an almost monopolistic grip on the state-funded DVA industry. Is there any wonder that it wants to protect its brand and its continued existence, and that it is using the panoply of brand development methods that are well known in the commercial world? It has secured the endorsement of the great and the good, it has set up a substantial lobbying base to petition leading politicians and their departments, and it is deeply embedded in other key organs of state, not least the UK Crown Prosecution Service (CPS). The extent of this penetration is astonishing, as the former Director of Public Prosecutions, Kier Starmer QC, made clear in his speech to the Women's Aid Annual Conference, on 11 July 2012. Under the heading 'Record year for convictions in Violence against Women and Girls,' the CPS reports him saying this:

Record year for convictions in Violence against Women and Girls
… Women's Aid has played an important ongoing role in the development of the CPS's approach to these crimes since becoming members of the first External Consultation Group on domestic violence more than ten years ago. Director of Public Prosecutions, Keir Starmer QC said today: 'The evidence is clear that ten years of progress is paying off and not only are the conviction rates steadily increasing, but our service to victims is also improving. These results send a powerful message to perpetrators that they are more likely than ever to be convicted for their crimes.

And this continues under Alison Saunders QC, Starmer's successor,[297] as witness the latest CPS report (25th June 2015), in which Polly Neate, Chief Executive of Women's Aid is featured:

Polly Neate, Chief Executive of Women's Aid, said: 'Today's annual Violence Against Women and Girls report from the Crown Prosecution Service demonstrates that significant progress has been made in taking more cases of domestic violence through the criminal justice system. This is positive. Nearly 18% more defendants for domestic abuse cases are being sanctioned for their crimes, sending a clear message that domestic violence will not be tolerated. This progress must continue until we have a system where women who experience domestic violence have exactly the same level of confidence as victims of other crimes, that they are heard and believed, the system works for them and protects their human right to live free from violence.

What Women's Aid has achieved with the CPS is astonishing. It is right at the centre of the state prosecution apparatus promulgating its feminist agenda and justifying its role as the 'go-to' source of information on DVA 'until women are safe,' which is likely to be a very long time, judging by the effect its underlying ideology is having on society. Women's Aid is lobbying for its own agenda, and it has got society and its policy makers entirely on the wrong track to solving it. And it doesn't stop there. Organisations like Women's Aid are clearly seeking to influence government policy, and they are being invited to do so. For example, between August and October 2014 the UK Coalition government instigated a consultation exercise entitled *Strengthening the Law on Domestic Abuse*, publishing the results in December of that year in the form of sample answers from 'various respondents'. The organisations are not named in the document, just given generic titles such as 'criminal justice agency' and a 'domestic abuse charity,' etc. Here is a pie chart showing the proportion of inputs from each category:

Strengthening the law on domestic abuse- Respondents' inputs

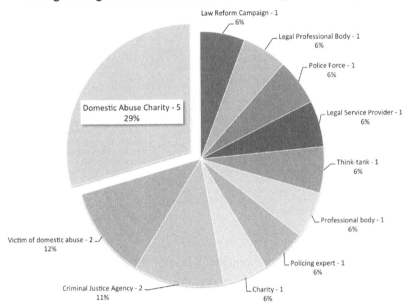

We can only speculate who these respondents are. It seems likely that the two victims of domestic abuse are different individuals, and one wonders how many Criminal Justice Agencies there are? But notice, five out of the seventeen (29%) are from the category 'Domestic Abuse Charity'. This is the degree to which the government is listening to this ideologically driven sector. Here are the domestic abuse charities' responses juxtaposed with the 'Criminal Justice Agency' responses, for comparison.:

QUESTION	'Domestic Abuse Charity'	'Criminal Justice Agency'
1) Does the current law adequately provide sufficient protection to victims of domestic abuse?	"…the key to improving protection and safety to victims is in the rigorous and effective implementation of the law. This means effective policing, successful prosecution, adequate accountable sentencing and effective offender management."	-
2) In what ways could the law be strengthened?	"Since only 17% victims who experience no physical abuse, but who suffer high levels of coercion and control, report to the police, it is essential to have a noncriminal justice route in order to address the situation of as many victims as possible…"	-
3) How would any changes you suggest be practically implemented?	"The law – existing or new – is not enough on its own to provide sufficient protection to victims of domestic abuse. Law must be implemented alongside prevention programmes, public awareness raising and ring-fenced resources for age and gender appropriate support services to adequately protect all victims of domestic abuse."	"…there would be evidential problems in proving this type of conduct as controlling or coercive, for example that someone has been denied access to finances or friends…"
4) Does the current law sufficiently capture the Government's non-statutory definition of domestic abuse?	Response No. 1: 'The law should be strengthened as suggested within intimate, but should include non-intimate relationships to capture the experiences of BME† women above the age of 16 within the extended family.' Response No. 2: 'The conflation of family violence with violence in intimate relationships in the definition does not recognise that coercive control is an aspect of the latter and not the former.'	"The proposals in the consultation and the non-statutory definition are based on a narrow understanding of domestic abuse – that it takes place between two people in an intimate relationship aged 16 +. There are, however, unique and complex features surrounding children and young people's involvement in domestic abuse."
	[Author's emphases.] † Taken to mean 'Black, Ethnic Minority'	

One might be excused for thinking that whoever these domestic abuse charities are, their responses bear a striking resemblance to Women's Aid-speak, and three of the four suggestions seem to be arguing for the government to set aside funding to resource non-governmental intervention in DVA. I am not for one minute suggesting this is Women's Aid, naturally.

Agency and culpability

Anyone who is or has been married, or who has cohabited with a member of the opposite sex, will know that men and women inevitably have difficulties in living intimately with one another, and that tensions sometimes boil over. This is, and always has been a fact of married life, even in civilised societies, and those societies have always seen it for what it is: mostly tit for tat squabbling. The general belief has always been that it is best left alone so the couple can sort out their differences between themselves behind closed doors and not 'wash their dirty linen in public'. The only time society would (and should) intervene is in the event of serious offending by one or the other, such as repeated serious assault, wounding or homicide (either actual or threatened). Now, however, DVA has become something in which society interferes. The state has assumed control of people's private lives. Indeed, DVA is a politically hot issue, stoked by feminists, who, cynically conflating the widespread systematic VAWG in the world with what goes on domestically, are inserting their ideology into hearth and home, driving the wedge even further between men and women and imposing their totalitarianism on them.

Physical violence by men against women happens. There is no doubt about it. It is reprehensible, and it is obscene if it is gratuitous or used as a means of control. The very thought of a man hitting a woman is one of the most deeply embedded cultural taboos for men, who consider it a dishonourable and cowardly thing to do. Boys are brought up to understand that a man's physique should not be used against the weaker sex, whatever the provocation; that a man who is truly a man must never hit a woman, least of all with full force, because it will assuredly cause her disproportionate harm than a man. Thus boys become socially conditioned to restrain themselves should violence with a woman occur, and if they lapse they suffer inner guilt and self-blame to which is added the censure of other men. In fact, the originators of this taboo are women. Mothers and wives perpetuate it in their sons and husbands, and they do so from their own deep social conditioning that ensures their self-preservation. However, women can and do abuse that. All too easily they use their womanhood as a cover for their own physical violence, knowing that a man cannot fight back on even terms. The classic male response to a slap on the face is to hold his hand to the slapped area and look bewildered, or ashamed. And women's abuse of men isn't limited to just a slap on the face; women stab men in domestic disputes, they scald them, they cut off their genitals, they poison them, they damage men's property: scratching car paintwork, ripping off wing mirrors, cutting up men's suits - that classic act of the wronged woman. As William Congreve wrote, 'Heav'n has no rage like love to hatred turn'd / Nor Hell a fury, like a woman scorn'd.'[298]

A woman can make a man very angry indeed with her words, knowing he cannot fight back: she might taunt him, belittle him in front of others, undermining his self-confidence; she might relentlessly nag him to get him to do what she wants. Women are not all 'sugar and spice and all things nice,' and they are certainly not the eternal victim of men's aggression who lack agency in their own misdemeanours, as feminists would have us believe. Far from men being routine perpetrators of violence in the home, most men when under physical attack from a wife or partner will withdraw, and if they can't they will try to restrain the woman rather than fight back as they would with a man. Men turn their backs on violent attacks from women, and that frequently leads to a hail of hammered fists or, worse, them being stabbed in the back or bludgeoned on the head with some heavy item. Feminist lies notwithstanding, most one-way domestic violence is woman to man,[299] not the other way round, and only 4 per cent of women report self-defence as a motivation for their violence against their partners, according to Dr Nicola Graham-Kevan,[300] reader in the psychology of aggression in the school of psychology at the University of Central Lancashire, United Kingdom.

Yet feminists portray women in DVA as inestimably precious creatures, helpless in their relationships with men, who are invariably controlling and potentially brutal, and, of course, this justifies their ideological stance that the man must always be held to account for his actions, whilst women must never be. The feminist philosophical position is that the woman, *qua* 'the victim', can never be really capable of, let alone be responsible for, violence against her by a man, *qua* 'the perpetrator'. Only the man must be responsible for his actions, which must be unconditionally condemned, whilst the woman must always be seen to be acting in justified self-defence. In their quest for ideological supremacy, feminists cut men no slack and miss no chance to embed their calumny against men. Even the terms they use - 'victim' and 'perpetrator' - are pregnant with implicit meaning. Rather than the correct terms 'complainant' and 'accused', these newspeak words have become the *lingua franca* in the press, the broadcast media, and even in the courts, thus implicitly convicting men and excusing women before proceedings start. It goes without saying that each and every one of us, man and woman alike, must be held responsible for our own actions. That is the principle of agency, that bedrock of society and of the law. But in feminism's DVA rhetoric, only the man is expected to exercise agency, never the woman. She can never be responsible in any way for what happens to her, whatever her contribution to the circumstances in which DVA happens. Even when women kill their partners in a planned and deliberate way, or intentionally mutilate them in cold blood, perhaps in jealousy or anger, the woman must always be given the benefit of the doubt in the new feminist world order, even if this flies in the face of the core idea of the liberated, autonomous, empowered woman - who actually does have full agency. Frankly, this is just bizarre.

Statistical assault and battery

If Women's Aid is really concerned about abuse, it should be concerned about its abuse of statistics in support of its cause. It would take another book to analyse and evaluate the mountainous case this organisation makes against men's alleged violence toward women, using dubiously attributed, cherry-picked figures, passing them off as statistics (which mostly they are not), which it promulgates as factoids[301] with irresponsible abandon. As Mark Twain once acidly observed, 'figures are beguiling, particularly when you arrange them yourself', and Women's Aid is very good at this. He also said, attributing the remark to Benjamin Disraeli, the twice elected Prime Minister of Great Britain during the Victorian era, who played a major role in the foundation of the modern Conservative Party, 'There are three kinds of lies: lies, damned lies and statistics!'

Before I expose the flagrant and iniquitous misuse by Women's Aid of 'statistics' about DVA, allow me a short digression for the sake of clarity. Statistics are data about the state - indeed, the word shares the same etymological root. Statistics are numbers upon which you should be able to hang your hat: cold, hard facts subjected to scientific collection and analysis, and designed for only one purpose, which is to discern the true picture. To take any other approach is to fall back on 'guesstimation', supposition, assertion, belief, impression, and false inference, none of which are bases upon which rational decisions can be made, or opinions reliably formed. There is nothing as helpful as real, hard numbers, as long as they are properly understood, and nothing as dangerous as fuzzy numbers, improperly understood and spread around as fact. If statistics are to have any value at all, therefore, they must be properly obtained, properly interpreted, and properly presented with the utmost integrity.

In the UK, as in most developed nations, we have the Office for National Statistics (ONS) that works tirelessly to provide good data that give as true a picture as possible about the state of society today. However, even the ONS is unable to provide hard data about DVA because there is no real way of measuring it. Try as you might, it is impossible to put your finger on any statistics for recorded incidents of domestic violence because there are no empirical numbers available anywhere that tell us precisely what is happening behind closed doors, and this is the statistical vacuum in which the falsifiers of factoids have a field day.

Organisations like Women's Aid scout around for odds and ends of data from a variety of sources, and turn them into items of unreliable information, taken out of context, and repeated so often that they become accepted as fact. Factoids are the weapon of choice of the women's movement, and Women's Aid is a veritable factoid factory, offering us all kinds (some, it has to be said, referenced to apparently reliable sources), which it fires, one after the other, as from a machine gun, strafing the reader, and felling anyone who might say, 'Hold on, this doesn't add up!' Penetrating this wall of lead is not easy because of its sheer volume and few people have the time or the ability to discern what an overwrought, egregiously skewed picture Women's Aid is painting about DVA and VAWG.

To make my point, allow me to take just a couple of representative examples from the 20-page document (including eight pages of apparently appropriate references), entitled *Statistics About Domestic Violence* (May 2013),[302] which Women's Aid publishes on its website. It states clearly at the top, 'There are no reliable national data on the general incidence of domestic violence in the UK,' thus making my earlier point. This at least is true. Undaunted, however, Women's Aid goes on with its headline factoid: 'Domestic violence is very common, with at least 1 in 4 women experiencing it in their lifetime and between 1 in 8 to 1 in 10 women experiencing it annually'.[303] This is the infamous, so-called, '1 in 4'factoid that endlessly echoes around in the feminist echo-chamber, being cut, and pasted over and over again, and which as Professor Christina Hoff Sommers says, 'is harder to kill than a vampire'.

This factoid seems absolutely unequivocal: a *quarter* of all women have experienced 'domestic violence' at some point in their lifetime, and around 1 in 10 experience it annually. But, dear reader, does that really sit comfortably with you? Does your own experience confirm this? Do you think that every fourth woman you know - at home, at work, socially, has suffered domestic violence in her lifetime? Has every tenth woman you know so suffered this year? Think about it, because if it is true, would that not be cause for serious concern? If you are a woman, it means either your husband or male partner, or one of only three other men in your family or social circle (perhaps your father, or your brother or your son?) has been violent to his wife or partner, or girlfriend at some time in her life - and probably this year. Does that sound right?

Women's Aid uses the term 'violence'. This is very specific. It leaves no doubt that women are currently being battered in very large numbers in the domestic situation. Surely that must mean that society is in uproar and close to breakdown? But is this really the case? (And remember, 'violence' is one of the shape-shifting words to which I referred earlier.) Of course it isn't. This is not just misinformation, it is deception being passed off as truth when it is not, and it is a trap for those who are, shall we say 'statistically-challenged'? Let us examine it and its provenance in more detail.

The 1 in 4 factoid

Where does the 1 in 4 factoid come from? Women's Aid cites its source as a report compiled for the UK Home Office in 2004[304] by Professor Sylvia Walby and her co-researcher Jonathon Allen (one presumes he is a doctoral student of hers). Professor Walby is the Distinguished UNESCO Chair of Gender Research at the University of Lancaster, Department of Sociology, and even the most cursory reading of her report shows that Women's Aid's quotation of her findings has been reworked. Now, I am not alleging deliberate mendacity on the part of Women's Aid here, or any of its employees or agents; my reader can draw his or her own conclusions about that, but it is incontrovertibly true that the Women's Aid's version of the '1 in 4' factoid, which it claims comes from Walby and Allen, is not the same as it appears in their findings, as juxtaposing of the two versions shows:

WOMEN'S AID'S VERSION

'**Domestic violence is very common** with at least 1 in 4 women experiencing it in their lifetime and between 1 in 8 to 1 in 10 women experiencing it annually.'

'An analysis of data from the Intimate Personal Violence (IPV) module British Crime Survey 2001 showed that **26% of women have experienced at least one incident of non-sexual domestic abuse** since they were 16.' (Note that these figures do not include sexual abuse, which, in many cases, is perpetrated by a partner, former partner or other family member).

'If sexual assault and stalking are included, then 45% of women **have experienced** at least one incident of inter-personal abuse in their lifetimes. (Walby and Allen, 2004).'

WALBY AND ALLEN VERSION (2004)

'The BCS [British Crime Survey] **estimates** that **one in four (26%) women and 17 per cent of men** aged 16 to 59 have experienced at least one incident of **non-sexual domestic abuse, threat or force** since they were 16.

If financial and emotional abuse are excluded,** limiting the violence to the use of **non-sexual threats or force,** then **21 per cent of women and 10 per cent of men** had experienced domestic violence since age 16.'

'Overall, 45 per cent of women and 26 per cent of men aged 16-59 **could recall being subject to** domestic violence (abuse, threats of force), sexual victimisation or stalking at least once in their lifetimes (domestic violence since 16; sexual victimisation or stalking at any point in a respondent's lifetime).'

A number of points arise from this comparison:

1. Women's Aid states as fact what Walby and Allen say is an estimate. Viz. Walby and Allen say '... the BCS estimates that one in four (26 per cent) women...,' whereas Women's Aid says '... [The] British Crime Survey 2001 showed that 26 per cent of women...,' etc. The BCS 'shows' nothing of the kind. No one in all conscience, acting with probity, can say that a survey 'shows' something to be true or false if it is an estimate based on a relatively small-sample survey. An estimate of something doesn't mean it is a fact.

2. Women's Aid has exchanged Walby and Allen's 'non-sexual domestic abuse, threat or force' with 'domestic violence'. These are absolutely not the same thing.

3. Note also, the opening term 'domestic violence' becomes 'domestic abuse' in the same statement.

4. Note also how Women's Aid uses only the figures that relate to women, and completely omits those relating to men that would dilute its message. There is no balance here: no attempt to correctly report the academic research. In fact it is cherry picking of the worst kind, and wholly inappropriate use of research findings.

5. The second claim: that including stalking, 45% of women have experienced 'interpersonal abuse at least once in their lifetimes' can hardly be justified. The definition of stalking includes written letters, sending nuisance or threatening material through the post, loitering near the workplace or across the street, and interfering with a person's property. The use of this term implies direct insulting language to a person's face. These are not occurrences of an interpersonal nature.

6. Then there is the issue of how Walby and Allen's 'sexual victimisation' becomes Women's Aid's 'sexual assault'. The two are entirely different things.

7. And we must ask, how does 'could recall' become 'have experienced'? An experience is a fact, whereas a recollection is - well - a recollection - of respondents across their entire lifetimes.[305] Lifetime memories of events in people's lives cannot be taken as fact. These data cannot in all conscience be used to indicate the present situation. Memory is fickle. A 17-year-old recollecting something that happened, say, in the last two or three years, is a much more reliable witness than a 59-year-old recalling some event from 40 years ago, and what is more, memory retention is mixed with emotion and a lot of factual infill based on

subsequent experience and other experiential conditioning. That is the nature of memory; it is well understood through research, and it is unreasonable for Women's Aid to pass such data off as being representative of the present situation.

Now, you might say Women's Aid is after all a women's organisation, and it naturally wants to justify its existence and make its case. You might even say it has a right to make its case any way that it chooses. I would say that it is how a case is made that matters. The selection and sanitisation of data out of context and using it in a way that fails to reflect the wholeness of those data, or creates a different reality, cannot be anything other than deceitful, and no one benefits from such behaviour except those trying to build the false case.

Women are not routinely suffering gratuitous or undeserved violence from their husbands, male partners or boyfriends. It is just not true. Neither is it true that it is all violence in the meaning that most normal people would understand that term. The truth is that most occurrences of DVA are non-violent, and they are often mutual. Men suffer from DVA too: in all categories of the definition, although the proportion between the sexes in each category varies. Women's Aid's interpretation of the Walby and Allen report data, which seeks to inform us of the true picture, presents neither a balanced nor a current view. What Women's Aid is saying is not what its cited source is saying. It is at least inaccurate and misleading, and could be seen as naked falsification. Walby and Allen are trying to give a balanced view, whereas Women's Aid is giving an unbalanced one that suits its case. To put it simply, this is spin that is intended to justify the claim that, 'Domestic violence is very common'. It is not, as we shall see, and no amount of cherry-picking of factoids in support of this self-justifying belief is going to change that.

The truth is, DVA is mostly 'kettles calling pots black'. There are exceptions, some of them egregious and serious - and, yes, some of those exceptions are perpetrated by men - but, by and large, DVA cuts both ways - and to suggest otherwise is highly questionable behaviour, especially if it is behaviour in pursuit of funding. As we have seen, Women's Aid is in receipt of very substantial ring-fenced funding from central government, but it is also a charity aided by tax relief for the purpose of acting philanthropically, a word that means acting out of the love of fellow men. The United Kingdom Charities Commission lays down guidelines for the operation of charities, and these include *inter alia* 'the advancement of citizenship or community development and the advancement of human rights, conflict resolution or reconciliation, or the promotion of religious or racial harmony or equality and diversity', and charities must operate in not just in the letter of this ruling, but also in its spirit.

In my submission, based on the evidence adduced so far, Women's Aid is in flagrant breach of both the letter and the spirit of its charitable requirements. It has adopted a biased, divisive approach to what it does, and its utterances undeniably vilify half the population - men - whilst signally failing to pay due regard to the balanced case about DVA. I suggest it is acting far outside its charitable social contract, which is the love of fellow men.

Teasing out the truth

Bearing in mind the feminism industry's clear intention to over-egg their pudding, the first thing we need to do is get the entire DVA issue into perspective. What is needed is a cold dispassionate review of what really is going on in DVA, not a biased, one-sided view intended to pursue an ideological viewpoint. So, let us start by revisiting Walby and Allen's analysis in order to get an idea of how widespread the DVA problem allegedly was in 2004 when they wrote their report:

> **Four per cent of women and two per cent of men were subject to domestic violence** (non-sexual domestic threats or force) during the last year. Extending the definition to include financial and emotional abuse increases these figures to six and five per cent respectively. If the definition of domestic violence is narrowed to non-sexual domestic force only, then three per cent of women and two per cent of men were affected.[306] [Author's emphasis]

Bear in mind these are old figures, but what they show is that just after the turn of the millennium, four per cent of women are said to have been suffering from DVA and two per cent of men. That is 1 in 25 women, based on the population at the time, not 1 in 4, and 1 in 20 men also suffered a DVA. Even by Walby and Allen's extended definition, which includes financial and emotional abuse, the figure is still around 1 in 17 women. I suggest this blows Women's Aid's claim that domestic violence is 'very common' out of the water. It is not. In fact, it is comparatively rare by any reasonable measure, and Women's Aid's own cited source proves this. Let us look at the word 'violence' because herein lies a rich source of misinformation. What does the word really mean? For that we need only look to the definition given by the United Kingdom Home Office, which defines it as follows:

> Any violence between current or former partners in an intimate relationship, wherever and whenever the violence occurs. **The violence may include physical, sexual, emotional or financial abuse.**

Immediately we can see that the official definition of violence is not exclusively the application of assault and battery, but a generic term covering activity that normal people would not regard as violent. For a fuller picture, we need to go to the definitions used in the *Intimate Violence Self-Completion Module* of the *Crime Survey of England and Wales* (CSEW), which is freely available online from the UK Data Service[307] archive.[308] This gives us the entire format of the survey, and, in Section 19, entitled *Self-Completion Module: Domestic Violence, Sexual Victimisation and Stalking Module* we find the questions asked of the respondents, and the categories of domestic violence that channel their responses:

Thinking about ANY relationships you have had since you were 16, has any PARTNER ever done any of the following things to you? By partner, we mean any boyfriend or girlfriend, as well as a husband, wife or civil partner.

1. Prevented you from having your fair share of the household money
2. Stopped you from seeing friends and relatives
3. Repeatedly belittled you to the extent that you felt worthless
4. Frightened you, by threatening to hurt you or someone close to you
5. Pushed you, held you down or slapped you
6. Kicked, bit, or hit you with a fist or something else, or threw something at you
7. Choked or tried to strangle you
8. Threatened you with a weapon, for example a stick or a knife
9. Threatened to kill you
10. Used a weapon against you, for example a stick or a knife
11. Used some other kind of force against you
12. None of these

With the possible exception of question 4, which is debatable as to whether it is actually a violent act, it is clear that items 1, 2, and 3 (and 12, of course), are emphatically not violent acts *per se*. So why does the government include them in the definition of violence? You might well ask. It seems inexplicable. Perhaps it has something to do with the fact that it is taking advice from Women's Aid, and senior academics in the field, who almost certainly are feminist women?

Women's Aid and feminist apologists in general are making an utterly one-sided, false case. They are entitled to their own opinions, but they are not entitled to their own facts. Here is a graph showing the gender split of DVA:

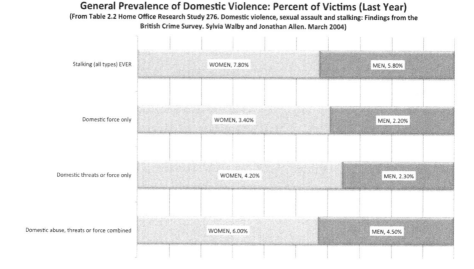

General Prevalence of Domestic Violence: Percent of Victims (Last Year)
(From Table 2.2 Home Office Research Study 276. Domestic violence, sexual assault and stalking: Findings from the British Crime Survey. Sylvia Walby and Jonathan Allen. March 2004)

Category	Women	Men
Stalking (all types) EVER	WOMEN, 7.80%	MEN, 5.80%
Domestic force only	WOMEN, 3.40%	MEN, 2.20%
Domestic threats or force only	WOMEN, 4.20%	MEN, 2.30%
Domestic abuse, threats or force combined	WOMEN, 6.00%	MEN, 4.50%

This undoubtedly shows that women are not the primary victims of DVA, and men are not its exclusive perpetrators. It is true that women appear to suffer more domestic 'violence' than men, and that in certain categories such as strangulation and being frightened they come off substantially worse than men, which is intuitive, bearing in mind men's generally greater strength than women's, and that women are inherently more easily frightened than men generally are. Notice, however, that there is broad parity in the categories involving the use of a weapon, kicking, hitting with a fist, throwing things, stopping a partner seeing friends, and withholding money. Given Women's Aid's declared aim of continuing 'until women are safe,' this has something of a hollow ring about it. I am reminded here of Betty Friedan's comment, 'My husband was not a wife-beater, and I was no passive victim of a wife-beater. We fought a lot, and he was bigger than me.'

So, given that only a very small proportion of women and men are suffering DVA, and given that not all 'violence' is violence, what is really going on? Who is doing what to whom? Let us go back to Walby and Allen's data[309] again, and think about each category. I have appended some comments in the right hand column as food for thought:

Detailed prevalence of domestic violence

(From Table 2.2 Home Office Research Study 276. Domestic violence, sexual assault and stalking: Findings from the British Crime Survey. Sylvia Walby and Jonathan Allen. March 2004)

NATURE OF DOMESTIC VIOLENCE	WOMEN	MEN	COMMENT
Non-sexual domestic violence	% Victims once or more (Last Year)		
Prevented you from having your fair share of household's money	1.5%	0.7%	*About half as many men (47%) as women* are prevented from having their fair share of the household's money
Stopped you from seeing friends of relatives	2.0%	2.1%	*More men (105%) than women* are stopped from seeing friends or relatives
Either prevented you from share of household money or stopped seeing friends/relatives	2.9%	2.6%	*Almost the same number of men (90%) as women* were prevented from having a share of household money or were stopped seeing friends/relatives
Domestic threats			
Frightened you by threatening to hurt you or someone close to you	2.0%	0.2%	*One tenth of men as women* were frightened by threats
Domestic force (minor)			
Pushed you, held you down or slapped you	2.6%	1.1%	*42% of men as women* suffered being held down or slapped
Domestic force (severe)			
Kicked, bit or hit you with a fist or threw something at you to hurt you	1.3%	1.2%	*Almost the same number of men (92%) as women* were kicked, bitten or hit with a fist or had something thrown at them
Choked or tried to strangle you	0.4%	<0.1%	*Up to a quarter of men as women* were choked or attempts made to strangle them
Threatened you with a weapon such as a stick or knife	0.2%	0.1%	*Half as many men as women* were threatened with a weapon
Threatened to kill you	0.5%	0.1%	*One fifth of men as women* had threats made to kill them
Used a weapon against you e.g. a knife	0.1%	0.1%	*The same number of men as women* had a weapon used against them
Used some other kind of force against you	0.6%	0.4%	*Two thirds of men as women* had some other kind of force used against them
Stalking			
Received a series (i.e. two or more) 'phone calls or written letters that were obscene, a significant nuisance or threatening or had been left obscene, offensive or disturbing material	4.9%	2.7%	*More than half as many men (55%) as women* received obscene, threatening calls or letters or had been left obscene, offensive or disturbing material
Someone loitered regularly outside my house/work place/ place I regularly visit or persistently followed me around (at least twice)	1.1%	0.4%	*More than a third as many men (36%) as women* have had someone loitering outside their house/work/regular place they visit at least twice
Someone deliberately interfered with/damaged my property on at least two occasions	2.5%	3.1%	*A quarter more men (124%) than women* had someone deliberately interfere with or damage their property on at least two occasions

Women's Aid is very clear in arguing that DVA against women is only the tip of the iceberg: that there is a big under-reporting issue, which is covering an even bigger problem than their distorted 'statistics' purport to show. Be that as it may, one thing we do know is that men's under-reporting is well known. Men do not generally admit that they are being bullied by their wives or partners nor, indeed, do they complain about it to the authorities, and there are sound reasons for that, as research conducted by Dr Nicola Graham-Kevan, reader in the Psychology of Aggression in the School of Psychology at the University of Central Lancashire, whom I cited earlier, shows. She has identified a raft of reasons why men don't leave abusive female partners, and using figures taken from a study by Hines & Douglas in 2012, she ranks those reasons as follows:

1. Concerned for the children – 89%
2. Marriage is for life – 81%
3. Love – 71%
4. Fears he may never see kids again – 68%
5. Thinks she'll change – 56%
6. Not enough money – 53%
7. Nowhere to go – 52%
8. Embarrassed – 52%
9. Doesn't want to take the kids away from her – 46%
10. She threatened to kill herself – 28%
11. Fears she'll kill him / someone he loves – 24%

These findings must surely bring a lump to the throat of any ordinary person who must also wonder how the feminist bigots who relentlessly attack men for being habitual wife abusers sleep peacefully in their beds.

There is a further dimension to all of this. Stephen Roe in Chapter 3 of the official *Home Office Statistical Bulletin, Homicides, Firearm Offences and Intimate Violence 2007/8* and, in particular Figure 3.4,[310] shows the socio-economic distribution of DVA:

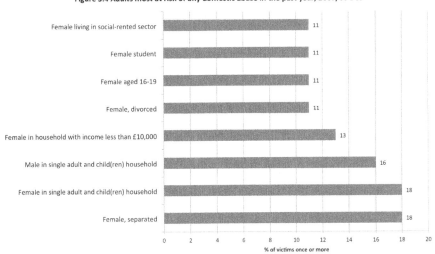

Figure 3.4 Adults most at risk of any domestic abuse in the past year, 2007/08 BCS

From these data we can see a pronounced socio-economic and relationship status skew. Those women most at risk of DVA in the year 2007/8 were those who were separated from their husbands or partner, those living as single mothers, those on low incomes, and divorced women. DVA is the product of jealousies and the tensions that happen between men and women in divorce and separation, and that is exacerbated by lower incomes and lower socio-economic status, as the report entitled *Domestic Violence: A Literature Review* produced by HM Inspectorate of Probation[311] observed in 2004:

> There are inter-linkages between several factors relating to a woman's socio-economic status and an increased risk of abuse, such as poverty, inequality between partners, relative isolation and unemployment (Walby & Myhill 2001b). Higher socio-economic status has generally been found to offer some protection against the risk of domestic violence [for women]. Internationally, studies indicate that women living in poverty are disproportionately affected (WHO 2002). In the UK, women in lower income households and/or living in council properties were found to be at significantly greater risk in both the 1996 and 2001 BCS. The low income-abuse link is confirmed in other national surveys and reviews (Hotaling & Sugarman 1986, Rodgers 1994, Bunge & Locke 2000). In a Finnish national study, Piispa (2002) found unemployed women on low incomes to be disproportionately represented amongst those who had experienced the fiercest, longstanding violence.

We cannot escape the multi-factor causation of DVA, not least its correlation

413

with poverty and broken homes, and single parenthood, which, of course, is predominantly women. All of these factors are inextricably linked to the feminists' attack on marriage and the widespread destruction of the nuclear family. DVA is the product of tensions wrought in broken families, between broken men's and women's relationships, and it produces broken children. People's emotional makeup is unable to cope with the radical reengineering of society that feminism has wrought, and they are overwrought by it all, and snap. Yet feminists place the blame firmly and squarely on men's shoulders, and offer condemnation of men as their answer. This is as ludicrous a solution as it is inhuman. In fact it is insane. It is a form of victim blaming, given that women are overwhelmingly likely to have initiated divorce or separation in the first place, and given the seemingly endless cases of men being denied access to their children by bitter women who use their children as pawns or even weapons with which to beat him. The man-fixated thrust of the feminist narrative about DVA, endlessly portrayed as a one-way dynamic: men toward women; and with men always presented as the perpetrator, is plainly wrong. All the evidence we have paints a different picture and points us in an entirely different direction. A line must be drawn against Women's Aid and their gender-politics, and their misandrist messages. They are so blatantly and egregiously promulgating a biased case, it amounts to a scandal. In fact, DVA is not even a gender issue, which is a topic to which I shall now turn.

Indisputable lies

Martin Fiebert has been professor of psychology at California State University since 1978 and in 2013 he published his latest study of 286 scholarly investigations comprising over 371,600 individual case studies worldwide, entitled *References Examining Assaults by Women on their Spouses or Male Partners: An Annotated Bibliography*.[312] The investigations primarily relate to the USA, but they include six papers from the UK, five from Australia, six from New Zealand, 14 from Canada, and a smattering from other countries (Finland, India, Russia, Ukraine, etc.) Here is the abstract from Fiebert's review study:

> This annotated bibliography describes 343 scholarly investigations (270 empirical studies and 73 reviews) **demonstrating that women are as physically aggressive as men (or more) in their relationships with their spouses or opposite-sex partners**. The aggregate sample size in the reviewed studies exceeds 440,850 people. [Author's emphasis]

It has to be acknowledged that the definitions of DVA used across the world do not accord precisely with definitions used in the British Crime Survey Crime Survey of England and Wales, but the differences do not hide the truth universally revealed. DVA is not exclusively, or even essentially, man on woman. The sheer volume of data drawn from respondents across the world indisputably gives the lie to this false assertion.

In another study, John Archer carried out a statistical meta-analysis on 82 intimate partner violence studies, seeking to identify patterns amongst their results. He concluded that '…women were slightly more likely than men to use one or more acts of physical aggression and to use such acts more frequently. Men were more likely to inflict an injury, and overall, 62% of those injured by a partner were women,'[313] and in 2013, the journal Partner Abuse published the Partner Abuse State of Knowledge Project (PASK),[314] the work of 42 academics in 20 universities in the UK over three years. This was the most comprehensive review of DVA ever conducted, and it concluded that, 'Women perpetrate physical and emotional abuse, as well as engage in controlling behaviours, at comparable rates to men'. Here is a summary of its key results:

-   Among large population samples, 57.9% of intimate partner violence (IPV) reported was bi-directional, 42.1% uni-directional

-   13.8% of the uni-directional violence was male to female and 28.3% was female to male

-   Among school and college samples, the percentage of bi-directional violence was 51.9%; of which 16.2% was male-to female and 31.9% was female to male

-   Male and female IPV was perpetrated for similar motives: Primarily to get back at a partner for emotional hurt caused by stress or jealousy; to express anger and other feelings that they could not put into words or communicate; and to get their partner's attention

-   Eight studies directly compared men and women in the power/control motive and subjected their findings to statistical analyses. Three reported no significant gender differences and one had mixed findings

-   One paper found that women were more motivated to perpetrate violence in order to gain power or control than were men, and three papers found that men were so motivated; however, the differences between the genders in this area were not pronounced

-   None of the studies reported that anger/retaliation was significantly more of a motive for men than for women; instead, two papers indicated that anger was more likely to be a motive for women's violence as compared to men's violence

- Jealousy/partner cheating seems to be a common motive for violence for both men and women

There is a further dimension to this. The Home Office Statistical Bulletin, *Homicides, Firearm Offences and Intimate Violence* 2008/09,[315] shows us that lesbian women are far more abusive to their partners than either homosexual or straight men are. Table 4 from that survey tells its own story:

Table 4: Domestic Abuse by Sexual Orientation, 2008/9

Category	Male Victims		Female Victims	
	Straight	Gay	Straight	Lesbian
All domestic abuse	4.1%	8.9%	5.9%	17.3%
Non-sexual partner abuse	3.3%	6.2%	4.3%	12.4%
Non-sexual family abuse	1.5%	3.3%	2.2%	8.5%
Sexual assault or attempts	0.3%	4.2%	2.6%	8.7%
Number of respondents	20,892	512	24,795	473

In percentage terms, for all domestic abuse, lesbians are twice as likely to be victims of their lesbian partners than homosexual men are of theirs, and three times more than heterosexual women are of their male partners. (It is interesting that 2008/9 was the last year the breakdown of DVA figures by sexual orientation was made available. The CSEW seems to have ceased the practice after that.)

Taken in the round, all of these findings sit entirely with normal people's experience and common sense, yet such is the power of feminist propaganda produced by the feminism industry that most people believe that men are the sole perpetrators of DVA, and this view even influences the formulation of public policy and legislation. As the political party Justice for Men and Boys (and the women who love them), in a 154 page submission[316] to the UK Home Office, in response to a consultation conducted by Theresa May, the current Home Secretary in October 2014, said in its Executive Summary:[317]

> ... this factual position is not matched by public perception, nor by provision of support for male victims, nor by the policies and practices of public bodies, as we'll outline. On the contrary, as we expose, women's refuge organisations minimise concern over male victims. As a result, the publicly funded provisions for male victims are vanishingly slight compared with those for female victims. All these bodies have produced documentary guidance

which focuses solely on violence against women and girls, effectively air-brushing away male victimisation. This review has failed to identify any rational reasons for the neglect of male victims. The continuing failure of public bodies to recognise the suffering of male victims of partner violence, and their failure to support these men at times of crisis, are long-standing scandals. One of the most solidly established facts in the social sciences is that the incidence and severity of domestic violence inflicted on men is comparable to that inflicted on women. This is not a recent finding. Researchers have known it for 40 years. Yet the narrative to which the public is exposed paints a very different picture, one in which domestic violence overwhelmingly involves female victims and male perpetrators. These contrasting perspectives are examined at length in this report. A consistent picture emerges of a level of male victimisation by partners, which is, on the crudest level of approximation, comparable to the level of female victimisation by partners. The consistency of this picture over time, between countries, and between studies, and the sheer volume of data and case studies available, mean that the reported extent of male victimisation by female partners is undeniable.

It is undeniable, but deny it is precisely what Theresa May did. On 3rd March 2015, only five months after the consultation, a bill having been drafted, having gone through the committee stage, and voted on in the House of Commons, the consultation measures were brought into law in a portfolio piece of legislation entitled *The Serious Crime Act 2015*, which introduced a new offence in marriage and intimate partnerships of 'controlling or coercive behaviour'.

In Section 2 of the Home Office document entitled *Controlling or Coercive Behaviour in an Intimate or Family Relationship, Statutory Guidance Framework*,[318] issued seven months later, in December 2014, we read the following:

> The offence closes a gap in the law around patterns of controlling or coercive behaviour that occurs during a relationship between intimate partners, former partners who still live together or family members. This offence sends a clear message that this form of domestic abuse can constitute a serious offence, particularly in light of the violation of trust it represents and will provide better protection to victims experiencing repeated or continuous abuse. It sets out the importance of recognising the harm caused by coercion or control, the cumulative impact on the victim and that a repeated pattern of abuse can be more injurious and harmful than a single incident of violence.

And highlighted in a text box beneath this statement was this quote:

> 'Not only is coercive control the most common context in which [women] are abused, it is also the most dangerous' Evan Stark (2007) Coercive Control. How Men Entrap Women in Personal Life. New York: Oxford University Press.

The document could well have been written by Women's Aid, so closely does it follow its narrative. It represents yet another insertion of the law into people's private lives, and it emanates from a conservative government. But what do you expect from a Home Secretary who wears a T-shirt emblazoned with 'This is what a feminist looks like'?

Domestic homicide: the crime of passion

Before ending this chapter on DVA, I would be remiss if I didn't address the concomitant issue of domestic homicide, especially as one of the most used feminist factoids is that, 'On average two women a week are killed by their partner or former partner.' It is there, naturally, on Women's Aid's 'fact sheet' entitled *Statistics About Domestic Violence. Incidence and prevalence of domestic violence: General, (Updated May 2013)*, where we see it plainly on Page 2 (In this case, the emphasis is Women's Aid's):

> **On average 2 women a week are killed by a male partner or former partner**: this constitutes around one-third of all female homicide victims.

Yet again, this is an emphatic statement of fact presented as a statistic; however, it is yet another example of the statistically-challenged world of feminist propaganda. According to the website *fullfact.org*, this claim has been around for many years, and it is not strictly true. Its provenance seems to be a statement made in a television interview by Sandra Horley, Chief Executive of Refuge, another major domestic abuse support group, when referring to the case of Maria Stubbings, a woman brutally murdered by her ex-partner in 2008. Horley related that terrible incident to the fact that in 2004-5, 105 women had died at the hands of their partners. She did a simple division sum based on one year, and arrived at, 'On average two women a week were killed, etc.,' thus creating a classic piece of feminist hyperbole for media consumption.

Anyone can play this numbers game, however. For example, using the same data source as Ms Horley and Women's Aid, the 2008 Home Office crime report[319] shows that 38 men were also killed by their partner or ex-partner in that year - that is not an 'average' of one man killed by his partner every nine days. In fact, the ONS tells us in their paper entitled *Chapter 2 - Homicide*,[320] released in 2014: 'Due to the relatively low numbers of homicides there can be considerable year-to-year variability' illustrating the point as follows:[321]

Figure 2.5: Number of homicide victims aged 16 and over killed by partner/ex-partner, by sex of victim 2002/4 to 2012/13(1,2)

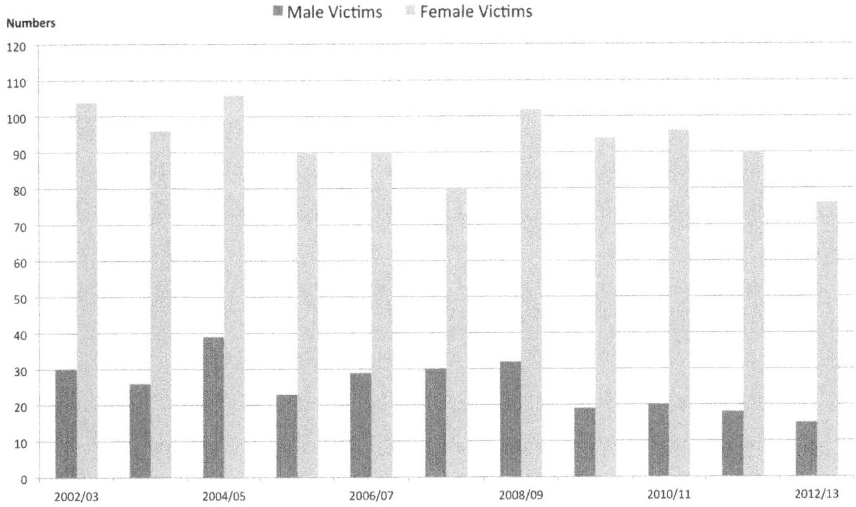

Notes:
1. Source: Homicide Index, Home Office

The numbers game is far too simplistic. It doesn't help us understand what is really going on in this most serious aspect of DVA. To do that, we need to start joining up some dots. In *Chapter 2 - Homicide*, which is a treasure-chest of useful data for those who are interested in the truth about domestic homicide, there is a section entitled *Focus on Partner/Ex-Partner Homicides*,[322] in which we find the following facts:

- 'In 2012/13, just over half (53%) of female victims,' [of domestic homicide, aged 16 or over] 'were killed by their partner/ex partner (76 offences)'.
- [Of the 76 homicides] '... all but one of the female partner/ex partner homicide victims was killed by a male suspect'.
- The definition of 76 women's assailants is given more precisely as their [male] 'spouse, cohabiting partner, boyfriend, ex-spouse or ex-cohabiting

partner, ex boyfriend.'

- 'Female victims of partner/ex partner homicides were younger than other female homicide victims (41 compared with 51 years)'.
- '... just over a half (52%, or 284 offences),' [of all homicide cases in 2012/13] 'resulted from a quarrel, a revenge attack or a loss of temper.'

So, there is no doubt that the overwhelming majority (75) of the 76 women who were killed in a domestic situation in 2012/13 were killed by a male partner. Only one woman's assailant appears to be a woman, who may or may not be a lesbian partner or another jealous woman, we simply do not know. There is also a pronounced age difference between women who are killed in a domestic homicide than that of women in other scenarios[323] (41 years -vs- 51 years), and the predominant motive is '... a quarrel, a revenge attack or a loss of temper'.

Now, let us revisit some figures I gave earlier in this book and factor them into this particular mix:

- Women in the UK typically marry for the first time at age 29[324]
- The median length of marriages ending in 2013 was 11.5 years[325]
- 45% of all marriages end in divorce[326]

The ONS Statistical Bulletin. Divorces in England and Wales 2011,[327] issued on 20th December 2012, tells us that women have been (and still are) initiating divorces between two and three times more frequently than men. From these data, we find that the main reason both parties cite for ending their marriages is 'unreasonable behaviour', and that men's petitions on these grounds have shot up by 574 per cent in the last 40 years (although still only about a third of women's petitions in total).

So, women are increasingly ending their marriages because of conflict with their spouses, who probably see them as being unreasonable. Typically this is happening at about 11 years of marriage, which puts them in their early 40s, having married about age 29, and this the time when women are most at risk of being killed by their partner or ex-partner in '... a quarrel, a revenge attack or a loss of temper.' Frankly, it isn't rocket science to figure out what is going on here. Female domestic homicide is clearly correlated with premature marriage failure, initiated mainly by women. This inevitably causes passions to rise in both partners, who snap and bad things happen. (And by reasonable inference, this must surely also apply to cohabitation arrangements.)

There is another twist in this sad tale. The ONS figures for partner/ex-partner homicide include the sub-categories 'spouse, cohabiting partner, boyfriend/girlfriend, ex-spouse/ex-cohabiting partner/ex-boyfriend/girlfriend, **adulterous relationship, lover's spouse or emotional rival,'** [Author's emphasis] which opens up the possibility that a number of the women killed in domestic homicide situations might have been involved in adulterous relationships and died at the hands of an emotional rival - defined as, 'those instances where two persons come to know or meet each other through their association or knowledge of a third person, and where their emotional or sexual interest in this third person brings them into direct conflict with each other' - who was not their husband, partner, ex-partner, etc.

Perhaps some of these women had already formed an association with another man who became their assailant in a *menage a trois* situation? (A lesbian scenario such as this is ruled out, as only one of those killings was at the hands of another woman.) Frustratingly, the ONS doesn't give us any actual figures for women's homicides at the hands of an emotional rival (although it does, interestingly, for men, as we shall see in a moment), so we cannot discern much more than that some of these tragic incidents might include contributory factors of the victim's own making, not least adulterous liaisons that backfire. It takes two to tango, as they say, and this is supported in the detailed figures we are given for men who are killed in domestic homicides.

The average number of men killed in this category each year in the three years 2010-13 was 19; and we are told that of those deaths, 14 of them were at the hands of '... the victim's lover's spouse or emotional rival.[328] The figures are clear. Three quarters (74%) of men who are the victims of domestic homicide meet their death at the hands of their spouse or emotional rival in the circumstances of a love triangle. Now, the immediate conclusion is that these homicides might be due to jealous gay men killing their wayward partners. However, it could also be where a woman meets a man through her husband, partner, boyfriend, etc. - say, at work or socially - and forms an adulterous relationship with him, thereby cuckolding her husband. The husband becomes an emotional rival to the woman's lover, and jealousies lead to the husband being killed in a fight, or even deliberately, by his wife's lover. The point is, even allowing for the real possibility that a proportion of these deaths might be male homosexual incidents, where women are involved, but are not the victims, it is possible they are still players in male domestic homicide. In other words, women are not always the passive victims of men's gratuitous violence that Women's Aid would have us believe.

As reprehensible as physical attacks by men on women are, as much as we as a society need to be concerned with violence of any kind, groups like Women's Aid is over-stating its case through the scurrilous misuse of figures, and we must ask how that is going to benefit anybody, least of all women? We cannot separate male domestic homicide from female domestic homicide. They are two sides of the same coin, and it is absolutely wrong to see this as a feminist-defined gender issue. Such a view is far too narrow and too full of errors to withstand anything more than cursory scrutiny. Spousal/partner homicide is a problem of relationships that are made difficult by the insidious polarisation of the sexes caused by feminism, and the major societal shifts we have seen in marriage and the family since it took its grip of our society.

CHAPTER 12

THE LINE, IT IS DRAWN

The line it is drawn, the curse it is cast,
The slow one now will later be fast.
As the present now will later be past,
The order is rapidly fadin'.
And the first one now will later be last
For the times they are a-changin'.

Bob Dylan, born Robert Allen Zimmerman, May 24, 1941.
American singer-songwriter, artist and writer.

Tides in the affairs of man

There are tides in the affairs of man[329] that ebb, surge and flow, and people with agendas have always been ready to ride these tides for their own political purposes. The Boomer generation was arguably the most privileged generation in history. It was the precious product of men and women who had fought a desperate world war, and had regained peace, and security at a heavy cost - and their parents had done almost exactly the same thing. The Boomer children grew up at a time of almost exponential economic growth. They had the best of everything that their parents and grandparents could give them: education, health, and freedom from oppression. Through fantastic social and economic progress after World War II their place in a new society in which they could flourish was assured. These children had all the opportunities a modern world could offer them, but, they squandered their birthright in hedonism, sexual liberty and wanton social wilfulness, led astray by a half-generation - an angry generation, with an angry creed - that had been born just a few years earlier than them.

Harvard psychologist Timothy Leary (b. 1920), then in his 40s, was urging the young to 'turn on, tune in, and drop out,' and his 'far out' ideas, plus the 'free love', the dyed shirts, flared trousers, mini-skirts, and the hippies' psychedelic 'trips' inspired the Boomers to reject everything that had gone before: the religion, the politics, and the guidance of their parents. The women, protected by Margaret Sanger's magic pill, made themselves promiscuously available, throwing away the sexual capital that had always been the measure of a woman's value, and the men threw off the male stereotypes of their fathers and grandfathers, grew their hair long, eschewed responsibility, and, basically screwed around, without conscience or consequence.

Leary was described by the *New York Times* as the, 'Pied Piper of the Psychedelic 60s',[330] but President Richard Nixon called him, 'the most dangerous man in America,' and so he proved to be. He and his like - the Beatniks - led the Boomers off, dancing, into a life of social turmoil. Carolyn Graglia[331] puts it like this:

> The 'Beats,' popularised in Jack Kerouak's *On The Road*, and the mimicking 'beatniks' continued the male revolt against family life through a rebellion that extended to the world of work and the consumer consumption work supported. Our media accorded these new rebels a visibility that further popularized men who, in Ehrenreich's words, 'refused to undertake the support of women and seemed to get away with it.' They also got away with something else equally inimical to women's interests: their obvious attachment to each other and to the male adventures that they found much more interesting than female companionship... the Beat had women but made clear that he neither needed nor enjoyed them much at all.

This was feminism's golden opportunity. This was the trigger for the Marxism-laced, lesbian-driven angry female uprising that was to become the Women's Liberation movement, which ultimately morphed into feminism. This Marxist-communist-utopian ideology caught the tide, the perfect peeling wave of social, economic, and philosophical change, and rode it right down the line; in the process undermining the fundamental, values of capitalist democracy, whose bastions had been marriage, the rule and authority of the father, and the sanctity of the nuclear family, and the Boomers bought the entire package, lock, stock and barrel, espousing it to themselves, making it their life's purpose.

The Boomers were the first generation to be truly liberated, yet in the name of a false version of equality - a communist version - their crusade tore into the very vitals of the society that had given them everything like a wrecking ball. Like a vector spreading a virus, they went out into the world to evangelise it, colonising the crucial nodes of society: the universities, the media, the key institutions, and, eventually, government, from where they subsequently imposed their utopian ideals on their nations when they assumed the mantle of power and influence, as each generation in its turn does. The 1960s saw a longing for alternative belief systems. The Beatles famously found eastern transcendentalism; the hippies found 'free love' and communal living, and the Boomer women found feminism, which they promulgated in furtherance of their narcissistic self-centred indulgence of the freedom that was theirs by birthright. As a generation, they will no doubt stand judged by history as useful idiots.

Ideological subversion

History has roundly condemned Senator Joseph McCarthy for his witch hunt of communists in 1950s America; however, there is no doubt that communists were at work in American society in those dangerous days after the cessation of the hot war and the beginning of the Cold War. There is no doubt, for example, that a cadre of communist sympathisers was at work in Hollywood, which was one of the foci of McCarthy's attentions. Mainly screenwriters, producers and directors, they were undoubtedly writing communist propaganda into their screenplays, and the 'Hollywood Ten', including Dalton Trumbo, the much awarded screen playwright, were held in contempt of Congress and imprisoned when they refused to answer questions about their activities. This resulted in them being blacklisted in Hollywood for many years afterwards, as the recently-released (2016) film *Trumbo* vividly depicts. Communism was undoubtedly infiltrating Western society in the 1950s by clandestine means, and although the Americans spotted it, and fought it, both internationally and at home, its re-branded form, feminism, succeeded in installing it culturally. Today, we see the same tactics being used in the plethora of TV sitcoms, advertising, and documentaries, which depict women as being the savvy, dominant sex, whilst men are shown as weak and ineffectual creatures always outwitted by their female partners.

In 1970, Yuri Alexandrovich Bezmenov (b. 1939), the son of a high-ranking Soviet Union army officer and former deputy chief of the Research and Propaganda Group, a secret department of the KGB attached to the Soviet embassy in New Delhi, dressed as a hippy and defected to the West, where he was eventually granted asylum in Canada. In 1984, he was interviewed by G. Edward Griffin about The Soviet Subversion of the Free World Press,[332] in which he made some startling revelations about the KGB's activities in the immediate post World War II period:

> GRIFFIN: When you spoke several times before about ideological subversion, that is a phrase that I'm afraid some Americans don't fully understand. When

the Soviets use the phrase 'ideological subversion,' what do they mean by it?

BEZMENOV: Ideological subversion is the process, which is legitimate, overt, and open: you can see it with your own eyes, all you have to do - all American mass-media has to do is to unplug their bananas from their ears, open up their eyes, and they can see there's no mystery. It has nothing to do with espionage.

I know that espionage - intelligence getting - looks more romantic, it sells more deodorant to the advertising, probably, that's why your Hollywood producers are so crazy about James Bond type of trailers. But in reality, the main emphasis of the KGB is not in the area of its intelligence at all. According to my opinion and [the] opinion of many defectors of my calibre, only about 15 per cent of time, money, and manpower is spent on espionage, as such. The other 85 per cent is a slow process, which we call either ideological subversion or active measures, *activitia perionachia*, a term in the language of the KGB - or psychological warfare. What it basically means is to change the perception of reality of every American to such an extent that, despite the abundance of information, no one is able to come to sensible conclusions in the interests of defending themselves, their families, their community, and their country.

It's a great brainwashing process, which goes very slow, and is divided into four basic stages: the first one being demoralisation. It takes from 15 to 20 years to demoralise the nation. Why that many years? Because this is the minimal number of years, which requires to educate one generation of students in the country of your enemy: expose [it] to the ideology of the enemy. In other words Marxist-Leninist ideology is being pumped into the soft heads of at least three generations of American students, without being challenged or counterbalanced by the basic values of Americanism – American patriotism. The result? The result you can see. Most of the people who graduated in the mid 60s: dropouts or half-baked intellectuals, are now occupying the positions of power in the government, civil service, business, mass media, [the] educational system. You are stuck with them you cannot get rid of them. They are contaminated. They are programmed to think and react to certain stimuli, in a certain pattern. You cannot change their minds even if you expose them to authentic information. Even if you prove that white is white and black is black, you still cannot change the basic perception and the logical behaviour. In other words, in these people, the process of demoralisation is complete and irreversible. To rid society of these people, you need another 20 or 15 years to educate a new generation of patriotically minded and common-sense people who would be acting in favour, and in the interests of [the] United States society.

GRIFFIN: And yet these people have been programmed and, as you say, in place, and are favourable to the Soviet concept: these are the very people who would be marked for extermination in this country?

BEZMENOV: Most of them, yes, simply because the psychological shock when they will see in future what the beautiful society of equality and social justice means in practice, obviously they will revolt. They will be very unhappy, frustrated people and the Marxist-Leninist regime does not tolerate these people. Obviously will join the leagues of dissenters – dissidents. Unlike in [the] present United States there will be no place for dissenters in future Marxist-Leninist America. Here, you can get popular like Daniel Ellsberg, and filthy rich like Jane Fonda, for being dissident, for criticising your Pentagon. In future these people will be simply squashed like cockroaches. Nobody is going to pay them nothing for their beautiful, noble ideas of equality. This, they don't understand, and it will be [the] greatest shock for them of course.

The demoralisation process in the United States is basically completed already. For the last 35 years, actually, over-fulfilled, because the demoralisation now reaches such areas where previously not even Comrade Andropov and all his experts would even dream of such a tremendous success. Most of this is done by Americans to Americans, thanks to [their] lack of moral standards. As I mentioned before, exposure to true information does not matter anymore. A person who is demoralised is unable to assess true information, the facts tell nothing to him. Even if I shower him with information: with the authentic truth, with documents, with pictures - even if I take him by force to the Soviet Union and show him concentration camps, he will refuse to believe it until he's going to receive a kick in his fat bottom. When the military boot crushes him: then he will understand, but not before that, that's the tragic [Sic] of the situation of demoralisation. So, basically, America is stuck with demoralisation and unless - even if you start right now: here, this minute - you start educating a new generation of Americans, it will still take you 15 to 20 years to turn the tide of ideological perception of reality back to normalcy and patriotism.

The next stage is destabilisation. This time, [the] subverter does not care about your ideas and the patterns of your consumption. Whether you use junk food and get fat and sloppy doesn't matter anymore. This time - and it takes only from two to five years to destabilise a nation - what matters is [Sic] essentials: economy, foreign relations, defence systems. And you can see it quite clearly in some areas – in such sensitive areas as defence and [the] economy, the influence of Marxist-Leninist ideas in the United States is absolutely fantastic. I could never believe it 14 years ago, when I landed in this part of the world, that the process will go that fast. The next stage, of course,

427

is crisis. It may take only up to six weeks to bring a country to the verge of crisis. You can see it in Central America now, and after crisis, with a violent change of power structure and economy, you have the so-called period of normalisation. It may last indefinitely. Normalisation is a cynical expression borrowed from Soviet propaganda. When the Soviet tanks moved into Czechoslovakia in '68, Comrade Brezhnev said, 'Now the situation in brotherly Czechoslovakia is normalised.'

This is what will happen in the United States if you allow all these schmucks to bring the country to crisis, to promise people all kinds of goodies and the paradise on Earth, to destabilise your economy, to eliminate the principle of free-market competition, and to put a big-brother government in Washington DC, with the benevolent dictators like Walter Mondale, who will promise loads of things, never mind whether the promises are fulfilled, or not. He will go to Moscow to kiss the bottoms of [a] new generation of Soviet assassins. Never mind, he will create false illusions that the situation is under control. [The] situation is not under control. [The] situation is disgustingly out of control. Most of the American politicians, media and [the] educational system trains another generation of people who think they are living at a peace time. False, the United States is in a state of war: undeclared, total, war against the basic principles and the foundations of this system. And the initiator of this war is not Comrade Andropov, of course, it's the system.

However ridiculous it may sound the world communist system ordered the world communist conspiracy. Whether that scares some people or not, I don't give a hoot. If you're not scared by now, nothing can scare you. But you don't have to be paranoid about it. What actually happens now [is] that, unlike myself, you have literally several years to live on. Unless [the] United States wake[s] up, the time bomb is ticking. With every second, the disaster is coming closer and closer. Unlike myself you will have nowhere to defect to, unless you want to live in Antarctica with penguins. This is it, this is the last country of freedom and possibility.

GRIFFIN: Okay, so what do we do? What is your recommendation to the American people?

BEZMENOV: Well, the immediate thing that comes to my mind is, of course, there must be a very strong national effort to educate people in the spirit of real patriotism. That is Number One. Number Two: to explain to them the real danger of socialist, communist, whatever, welfare state, big brother government. If people will fail to grasp the impending danger of that development, nothing ever can help [the] United States. You may kiss goodbye to your freedoms, including freedoms to homosexuals, to prison inmates; all those freedoms will evaporate in five seconds, including your precious lives. The second thing: at the moment at least part of the United States population is convinced that the danger is real. They have to force their government - and I'm not talking about sending letters, signing petitions and all this beautiful, noble activity – I am talking about forcing [the] United States government to stop aiding communism, because there is no other problem more burning and urgent than to stop the Soviet military industrial complex from destroying whatever is left of the free world.

And it is very easy to do: no credit, no technology, no money, no political or diplomatic recognition, and, of course, no such idiocies as grain deals to the USSR. The Soviet people, 270 million Soviets will be eternally thankful to you if you stop aiding a bunch of murderers who sit now in [the] Kremlin and whom President Reagan respectfully calls government. They do not govern anything, least of all such complexity as the Soviet economy. So, two very simple, maybe too simplistic, answers or solutions, but nevertheless they are the only solutions. Educate yourself; understand what's going on around you. You are not living at a time of peace, you are in a state of war, and you have precious little time to save yourself. You don't have much time, especially if you're talking about [the] young generation. There's not much time left for convulsions to the beautiful disco music. Very soon it will go, just overnight. If we are talking about capitalists or wealthy businessmen, I think they are selling the rope on which they will hang very soon. If they don't stop, if they cannot curb their insatiable desire for profit, and they keep on trading with the monster of the Soviet Communism, they're going to hang very soon. And they will pray to be killed. But unfortunately they will be sent to Alaska probably, to manage [the] industry of slaves.

It's simplistic. I know it sounds unpleasant. I know Americans don't like to listen to things, which are unpleasant, but I have defected not to tell you the stories about such idiocies as microfilms, James Bond type espionage. This is garbage. You don't need espionage anymore. I have come to talk about survival. It's a question of survival of this system. You may ask me what is it in for me? Survival; obviously. Because, as I said, I am now in your boat. If we sink together we will sink beautifully together, because there is no other place on this planet to defect to.

It has to be acknowledged that Bezmenov's account is uncorroborated personal testimony. He might just have been telling a good story. And, of course, neither he nor anyone else at the time anticipated the fall of the Berlin Wall only five years later, which signalled the fall of the USSR, so his stark warnings about the US being brought to a place of crisis and eventually coming under the heel of

Communism never came to pass. It is also possible that he had a grievance with his former political masters and was trying to discredit them. He might even have been trying to make a career for himself as a professional defector, earning substantial sums on the speaking circuit. However, he was extensively debriefed by the US authorities following his defection in 1970 and given a new identity in Canada, taking the name Tomas Schuman, and he didn't speak out until a decade later.

Perhaps he sensed that the Cold War had run its course, and maybe he felt safer. Perhaps he knew something most people didn't yet know: that something was afoot in the USSR, which resulted in Mikhail S. Gorbachev (1931-) being appointed general secretary of the Communist Party of the Soviet Union less than a year later, in March 1985. He set about taking the USSR on a new course with his twin ideas of *perestroika* (restructuring) and *glasnost* (openness), which initiated profound changes in the economic stance, internal affairs and the approach to international relations of the USSR, eventually removing the political and economic rivalry between the East and the West. Within five years, his revolutionary programme resulted in all the communist governments in Europe falling, and the Soviet Union being split into15 separate republics.

We cannot know the truth about what Bezmenov was saying; we can only speculate, and factor what he said into our own experience. However, placed into the context of what I have been saying in this book, what he recounts could all fit together, and could explain the emergence of feminism in the West in the post-World War II period. There is also quite a lot of corroboration. Ayn Rand allegorically predicted the same future for the US in her book *Atlas Shrugged*, and, of course, Senator McCarthy and the House Un-American Activities Committee did actually expose communist moles in key areas of American life. Then there is Allen Ginsberg, that key player in the Beat generation. He was on McCarthy's list, and he was very active in denouncing what he described as, 'the destructive forces of capitalism and conformity'. His mother was known to be a signed-up member of the Communist Party of America, and it is very possible that he was part of a cell of Soviet agitators active in Greenwich Village, feminism's ground-zero, and the home of the Beats during the 1950s and '60s. It is highly likely that Soviet infiltrators were harnessing the dissident spirit there, and stirring up social disruption.

We also know that capturing the hearts and minds of youth in the universities was a known tactic of the Soviet Union, as far back as the 1930s. The 'Cambridge Four', for example - Guy Burgess, Kim Philby, Donald

McClean, and Anthony Blunt - were recruited by the KGB during their undergraduate years at Cambridge University in England. Three of them rose to high rank in the UK diplomatic and intelligence services, passing countless defence secrets to the Soviet Union, from World War II to the time they were discovered and unmasked as Soviet spies in the 1960s. There was a fifth man, John Cairncross, who had been an MI5 mole. He was exposed as a spy by KGB colonel and double agent Oleg Gordievsky, who defected to the West in 1985, and many commentators believe that these were only the tip of an iceberg of Soviet infiltration into post-war Britain. Then, we have Mallory Millett's testimony about her sister Kate, with which this book opened. She was undoubtedly a prime mover in the Women's Liberation movement, and she lived on the edge of Greenwich Village, the ground zero of feminism. We can also surround her with a plethora of other feminist writers of the time who expressed overtly Marxist sentiments, such as Germaine Greer with her open advocacy for the fall of the patriarchal family, and her self-identification as 'an old anarchist', who reaffirmed her opposition to 'hierarchy and capitalism' on Australian radio, as recently as 2008. These are savvy women. It is difficult to see them just as useful idiots.

'The long march through the institutions'

It is no secret that Socialist beliefs are widespread among the intellectual elite of many developed nations. As early as 1949, Friedrich Hayek published his famous paper *The Intellectuals and Socialism*,[333] in which he said this:

> In every country that has moved toward socialism, the phase of the development in which socialism becomes a determining influence on politics has been preceded for many years by a period during which socialist ideals governed the thinking of the more active intellectuals. In Germany this stage had been reached toward the end of the last century; in England and France, about the time of the First World War. To the casual observer it would seem as if the United States had reached this phase after World War II and that the attraction of a planned and directed economic system is now as strong among the American intellectuals as it ever was among their German or English fellows. Experience suggests that, once this phase has been reached, it is merely a question of time until the views now held by the intellectuals become the governing force of politics.

Coining the famous term 'secondhand dealers in ideas,' Hayek went on to lend further credence to the argument, saying this about the intellectual class and their influence on society:

> The character of the process by which the views of the intellectuals influence the politics of tomorrow is therefore of much more than academic interest. Whether we merely wish to foresee or attempt to influence the course of events, it is a factor of much greater importance than is generally understood. What to the contemporary observer appears as the battle of conflicting interests has indeed often been decided long before in a clash of ideas confined to narrow circles. Paradoxically enough, however, in general only the parties of the Left have done most to spread the belief that it was the numerical strength of the opposing material interests which decided political issues, whereas in practice these same parties have regularly and successfully acted as if they understood the key position of the intellectuals. Whether by design or driven by the force of circumstances, they have always directed their main effort toward gaining the support of this 'elite,' while the more conservative groups have acted, as regularly but unsuccessfully, on a more naive view of mass democracy and have usually vainly tried directly to reach and to persuade the individual voter.
>
> The term 'intellectuals,' however, does not at once convey a true picture of the large class to which we refer, and the fact that we have no better name by which to describe what we have called the secondhand dealers in ideas is not the least of the reasons why their power is not understood. Even persons who use the word 'intellectual' mainly as a term of abuse are still inclined to withhold it from many who undoubtedly perform that characteristic function. This is neither that of the original thinker nor that of the scholar or expert in a particular field of thought. The typical intellectual need be neither: he need not possess special knowledge of anything in particular, nor need he even be particularly intelligent, to perform his role as intermediary in the spreading of ideas. What qualifies him for his job is the wide range of subjects on which he can readily talk and write, and a position or habits through which he becomes acquainted with new ideas sooner than those to whom he addresses himself.
>
> Until one begins to list all the professions and activities which belong to the class, it is difficult to realize how numerous it is, how the scope for activities constantly increases in modern society, and how dependent on it we all have become. The class does not consist of only journalists, teachers, ministers, lecturers, publicists, radio commentators, writers of fiction, cartoonists, and artists, all of whom may be masters of the technique of conveying ideas but are usually amateurs so far as the substance of what they convey is concerned. The class also includes many professional men and

technicians, such as scientists and doctors, who through their habitual intercourse with the printed word become carriers of new ideas outside their own fields and who, because of their expert knowledge of their own subjects, are listened with respect to most others. [Sic] There is little that the ordinary man of today learns about events or ideas except through the medium of this class; and outside our special fields of work we are in this respect almost all ordinary men, dependent for our information and instruction on those who make it their job to keep abreast of opinion. It is the intellectuals in this sense who decide what views and opinions are to reach us, which facts are important enough to be told to us, and in what form and from what angle they are to be presented. Whether we shall ever learn of the results of the work of the expert and the original thinker depends mainly on their decisions.

This left-leaning intellectual class almost certainly became the lecturers and professors into whose charge the Boomers were placed when they came of university age in the late 1960s, and they probably ensured that those youngsters were, as Bezmenov puts it, pumped full of Marxist-Leninist ideology before being sent out into the world filled with the 'beautiful, noble ideas of equality,' to which were added Hayek's ideas of 'half-baked intellectuals', such as Simone de Beauvoir and Jean Paul Sartre, who gave them a philosophical underpinning for their feminism.

In the 1960s, Rudi Dutschke, the communist leader of the German student movement, called for a 'long march through the institutions of power' in order to create radical change in Western society, from within. His metaphor was Mao Tse Tung's 'Long March', and the objective was to place communist-socialist thinking into the highest positions in society in the target nations. By placing people who thought like that into the machinery of society, they would influence policy and socially re-engineer it to conform to communist principles. Dutschke was a student of Antonio Gramsci, the leader of the Italian Communist Party in the 1930s, to whose ideas about cultural hegemony I referred earlier. Gramsci disagreed with Joseph Stalin's approach to spreading communism by confrontation, which he called a 'war of manoeuvre', and advocated a 'war of position' for communism to become a cultural hegemony. The process was one of gradual infiltration of schools, universities, courts, parliaments, newspapers and other media (latterly, of course, television channels), and this is what we find has happened through feminism, which is just an expression of Gramsci's cultural hegemony in operation.

Those of us who were youngsters in the 1960s, particularly those who went to university, are now grown up, and in high-ranking positions in government, the civil service, the law, business, the media, in think tanks, and the education system. These are the 'right-on', low-level judges described by Martin Mears in his book *Institutional Injustice: The Family Courts at Work*,[334] to whom I referred earlier, who routinely dispose of fathers from their children's lives, and they sit on the highest benches of the Family Division of the High Court of Justice, where their benchmark is political correctness, and the socialist-defined version of equality. 'Half-baked intellectuals', the 'secondhand dealers in ideas', now run gender studies departments in universities where they inculcate even more generations of 'soft-headed' youngsters into their Soviet-style feminist form of equality, and they sit on advisory boards for governments.

In 1992, in a commentary in *Feminisms: A reader*,[335] Frances Maher said this:

> From the first British Women's Studies course run by Juliet Mitchell at the Anti-University in 1968-9 and the first American courses at San Diego State University and the Free University of Chicago, Anglo-American women's studies has grown to over 30,000 courses. The 1970s and 1980s have seen an equally rapid growth in new forms of research and new teaching methods, any of which adopted consciousness-raising techniques from the Women's Movement. The American sociologist Marcia Westkott was one of the first critics to indicate how feminism might revolutionise the disciplines. She argues that a feminist perspective of education is not simply an academic view but an educational strategy for social change… Westkott argues that feminist research is *for* women rather than *about* women. [Maher's emphasis]

Today, according to a list published by the University of Maryland, Baltimore County,[336] in the US alone there are 777 out of an estimated 2,600 colleges and universities (30 per cent) offering every level of study in gender or women's studies, from university certificates to full doctorates. In the UK, there are 34 universities and higher education institutions out of an estimated 280 (36 per cent), doing the same. Interestingly, of the 333 universities and *Grand Écoles* in France, only five offer a gender studies course (0.3 per cent), and one of those is the American University in Paris. One cannot help but speculate that the French might know rather more about the true nature of *égalité*, and hold it in higher esteem than the Marxist political version. After all, French equality, which is built into their constitution, was born in the Modern Era, which started about the time of the fall of the Bastille in 1789, and it has strong Enlightenment credentials.

One thing is sure: the infiltration of our seats of learning has been a feminist strategy from the beginning. That is revealed by a rather chilling comment by Marcia Westkott (b. 1943),[337] writing in 1983, little more than a decade following the emergence of Women's Liberation:

> To have a woman-centred university (Rich, 1979) requires at the very least having women in the university, and beyond that, having women in positions of power to make changes for women. To criticize the culture, history, and procedures that undergird the institution through whose ranks we seek to advance, and to expect that our criticism will be accepted as a valid means to that advancement, is to have a tough problem, indeed… the goal of creating change for women guides us in our struggle.

This is how our universities have been turned into madrassas of Marxism masquerading as feminism, that now support a wide network of like-minded fellow travellers, both men and women, who are now distributed throughout society like yeast in dough, silently working to leaven. These feminist acolytes would almost certainly deny they were communists. Many of them might even call themselves conservatives - and some might even be members of the Conservative Party and ministers of the Crown, such is the degree to which feminism has slipped in under their radar. These are the political classes who now rule us, and they are useful idiots. They are the ruling Establishment, and there is increasing evidence that this class is positioning itself to be a worldwide ruling class.

International feminism

I referred earlier to Ban Ki Moon, Secretary General of the UN, and his utterances on violence against women and girls in *The United Nations Declaration on the Elimination of Violence Against Women* (1993). Twenty-five years ago he gave us a taste of how much the feminist agenda was being driven by the UN, and today, hidden in plain sight, we can see the same agenda at work, but massively magnified. On 9th October 2012, a man walked onto a school bus in Swat, the northwest district of Pakistan, and singled out one girl by threatening to kill all the children until one identified her, then he shot her in the head at point blank range. After being swiftly air-lifted to hospital in Pakistan, then transferred to the new Queen Elizabeth Hospital in Birmingham, United Kingdom, which has a trauma ward specialising in treating British personnel wounded in Afghanistan, Malala Yousafzai miraculously survived and she is now internationally famous. She was the youngest ever Nobel Laureate in 2014, when she was the co-recipient of the Nobel Peace Prize, and *Time Magazine* named her one of the '100 Most Influential People in the World' three years in succession. She was nominated for the World Children's Prize in Sweden and awarded the Sakharov Prize for Freedom of Thought by the European Union; the University of King's College, Nova Scotia, gave her an honorary doctorate, and Canada granted her honorary citizenship. Malala's attack was not a random act, however. She was targeted because of her activism for girl's education. Her family runs schools, and from the age of 11 she has activated for girls' education in her country, blogging about her life under the Taliban regime, and expressing clear views that attracted the attention of the Western press who pursued her for interviews. That led to her being nominated for the International Children's Peace Prize by Archbishop Desmond Tutu of South Africa, hence the assassination attempt on her by the Taliban. Malala has been embraced by the UN, whose general assembly she addressed[338] on 12th July 2014, her 16th birthday. Here is a small extract from what she said:

> Today I am focusing on women's rights and girls' education because they are suffering the most. There was a time when women activists asked men to stand up for their rights. But this time we will do it by ourselves. I am not telling men to step away from speaking for women's rights, but I am focusing on women to be independent and fight for themselves. So dear sisters and brothers, now it's time to speak up. So today, we call upon the world leaders to change their strategic policies in favor of peace and prosperity. We call upon the world leaders that all of these deals must protect women and children's rights.

Although, as late as 2014 (at the Forbes Under 30 Summit, held in Philadelphia, PA), Malala did not self-identify as a feminist, it was but a small step to take in the climate of Western adulation and political pressure that came upon her. She finally declared herself a feminist after hearing Emma Watson, the British actress, model and feminist activist speak at the UN on 20th September 2014 in support of the UN's 'HeForShe' campaign, part of its UN Women initiative. *HeForShe* was a call for one million men to advocate for gender equality by July 2015, and become 'agents for change' in order to bring about gender equality and women's rights worldwide.

Malala's story is touching for any right-minded person, but this single, tragic, feisty young woman has undoubtedly been taken over by international feminism and turned into an icon of female persecution by patriarchy, in the same way that Emily Davidson's death under the King's horse propelled the Suffragette movement to a form of legitimacy it never really had. Although not a martyr, Malala is even better. She is a 'survivor', the perfect example of the female victim of male oppression who survives and triumphs, to rise Madonna-like from the experience and be a potent role model for girls worldwide. Malala is now an international symbol of the women's struggle worldwide, lauded by, encouraged by, promoted by, and given credibility by the United Nations, in furtherance of its feminist aspirations that have been emerging progressively for at least the last 25 years. Today, we see how much the feminist agenda in that would-be world-governing body, situated so close to feminism's ground-zero in New York, has moved on. On 25th September 2015, the UN General Assembly adopted resolution A/RES/70/1[339] entitled, *Transforming Our World: The 2030 Agenda for Sustainable Development*, in which, amazingly, in the third paragraph of the Preamble, we read this:

> The 17 Sustainable Development Goals and 169 targets which we are announcing today demonstrate the scale and ambition of this new universal Agenda. They seek to build on the Millennium Development Goals and complete what they did not achieve. **They seek to realize the human rights of all and to achieve gender equality and the empowerment of all women and girls.** They are integrated and indivisible and balance the three dimensions of sustainable development: the economic, social and environmental. [Author's emphasis]

In this amazing resolution, gender equality and the empowerment of women and girls is being inextricably linked with the 'lasting protection of the planet and its natural resources'.[340] In paragraph eight, we read, 'A world in which every woman and girl enjoys full gender equality and all legal, social and economic barriers to their empowerment have been removed',[341] and in paragraph 14, 'Gender inequality remains a key challenge' to sustainable development. However, in paragraph 20,[342] we see the grand feminist plan spelled out:

> 20. **Realizing gender equality and the empowerment of women and girls will make a crucial contribution to progress across all the Goals and targets.** The achievement of full human potential and of sustainable

development is not possible if one half of humanity continues to be denied its full human rights and opportunities. Women and girls must enjoy equal access to quality education, economic resources and political participation as well as equal opportunities with men and boys for employment, leadership and decision-making at all levels. We will work for a significant increase in investments to close the gender gap and strengthen support for institutions in relation to gender equality and the empowerment of women at the global, regional and national levels. All forms of discrimination and violence against women and girls will be eliminated, including through the engagement of men and boys. The systematic mainstreaming of a gender perspective in the implementation of the Agenda is crucial. [Author's emphasis]

Then the apotheosis of this grand idea is to be found in Goal 5[343] (of 17), which is intended to be achieved by 2030:

Goal 5. Achieve gender equality and empower all women and girls

5.1 End all forms of discrimination against all women and girls everywhere

5.2 Eliminate all forms of violence against all women and girls in the public and private spheres, including trafficking and sexual and other types of exploitation

5.3 Eliminate all harmful practices, such as child, early and forced marriage and female genital mutilation

5.4 Recognize and value unpaid care and domestic work through the provision of public services, infrastructure and social protection policies and the promotion of shared responsibility within the household and the family as nationally appropriate

5.5 Ensure women's full and effective participation and equal opportunities for leadership at all levels of decision-making in political, economic and public life

5.6 Ensure universal access to sexual and reproductive health and reproductive rights, as agreed in accordance with the Programme of Action of the International Conference on Population and Development and the Beijing Platform for Action and the outcome documents of their review conferences

5.a [Sic] Undertake reforms to give women equal rights to economic resources, as well as access to ownership and control over land and other forms of property, financial services, inheritance and natural resources, in accordance with national laws

5.b [Sic] Enhance the use of enabling technology, in particular information and communications technology, to promote the empowerment of women

5.c [Sic] Adopt and strengthen sound policies and enforceable legislation for the promotion of gender equality and the empowerment of all women and girls at all levels

The gender bias of this document is astonishing. Men and boys as a specific group are mentioned only twice, and then only as a comparative group to whose apparently inherent advantage women and girls must be elevated. In fact, the word 'boys' is only mentioned three times, whereas 'girls' occurs 15 times, and then only in the context of describing children as girls and boys (and, yes, in that order). This resolution ought to give grave cause for concern in any right-minded person - man or woman. It shows the degree to which feminism is now internationally embedded, and how its agenda is being driven, but hidden in plain sight. It is as clear an example we can get of the long march through the institutions in action, and of the duplicity being used to further the ideology of Marxism worldwide, through feminism. The document reeks of utopianism. It is an echo of the hippy communes in the 1960s, and goes even further back to the Paris communes and the failed utopian experiments of Charles Fourier in early nineteenth century Ohio. It is also pure Engels, and his ideas for communism.

However, what this document tells us is far more than that. In it, we see how the climate change panic and feminism are becoming conflated and merged into one world movement by this once august organisation, once charged with the responsibility of ensuring that world war did not break out again. The UN is exporting Western cultural values across the entire world, overriding all other cultures which, without defending them or their values in any way, are mostly far more ancient than ours. One cannot but speculate that perhaps the violent backlash against the West by Islamic extremists is at least in part driven by all this. But that is another story.

The new establishment

From Karl Marx to Tony Blair, Marxist feminists have been at work, using underhand means to disrupt Western capitalist democracies, and installing a Soviet-style utopian form of matriarchal society. Feminism has increased its power by creating a discrete political class, even though the members of that class span the entire political spectrum. In Britain, even Conservative Prime Minister, David Cameron, is an openly declared feminist, and his Home Secretary, Theresa May is too, even advertising her allegiance to the feminist cause on her T-shirt. It is incomprehensible that these successors to Margaret Thatcher and Winston Churchill, two towering Conservative political leaders of modern times, who fought an uncompromising battle against National Socialism and then Communist Socialism should support feminism, an ideology that comes from the same stable as the latter, but that is the way it is. Using all the tactics of the latter to further its aims, feminism has succeeded in bewitching even Conservatives into destroying the family, marriage, and good parenting, the very things they nominally stand for.

In the US, the leading nation of the free world, one of the earliest members of the Boomer generation, Hillary Clinton (b. 1947), is currently Democratic presidential candidate in waiting, and she is a rabid feminist; she has been for 40 years. This is what she said to the *First Ladies' Conference on Domestic Violence* in San Salvador in November 1998:

> Women have always been the primary victims of war. Women lose their
> husbands, their fathers, their sons in combat. Women often have to flee from
> the only homes they have ever known. Women are often the refugees from
> conflict and sometimes, more frequently in today's warfare, victims. Women
> are often left with the responsibility, alone, of raising the children.

Women, the primary victims of war? One can almost hear the graves of the almost exclusively male war-dead of the United States (and indeed the rest of the world, up and down the centuries), heaving and turning at Clinton's unbelievable utterances. What about the sons, husbands, and fathers of America who went to Vietnam to fight against Communism, an ideology they probably didn't even understand? What about the boys who stormed the beaches of Normandy in 1944, their young, strong bodies mown down in defilade fire from German machine guns?

And their predecessors who went to the carnage in the trenches of Flanders, and died in abject fear and squalor - far too many of them lying in unmarked graves or their remains never found? When Charles De Gaulle, President of France in the 1960s, decided that the time had come that American troops should no longer remain on French soil, an angry President Johnson asked him whether he wanted the US to dig up its dead and remove them as well? These are the sons, the fathers, the brothers, and the husbands of the women who, in the name of feminism, Clinton so one-sidedly espouses, and whose cause is so fundamentally opposed to their men's interests. This is what is in store for America should it choose to elect this feminist as Commander in Chief of the United States' overwhelmingly male armed forces. Clinton's utterances and Cameron and his hench-women's attitudes stand implacably opposed to the very values of the nations they seek to lead: the values of justice and freedom, the sanctity of the family, and the importance of the institution of marriage, in which children are brought up to be competent, fully-rounded future members of society. In adopting feminism as their driving ideology, these partisan political leaders are embracing the wholesale destruction of the very fabric of the nations that gave them their values in the first place. This is the reality of the United States, Britain, Canada, Australia, the northern states of Europe, and it is spreading throughout the world.

Elitism

The feminist elite wants power. We see this in the universities, in the media, in business, and in the political arena, where the utterances and actions of women like Cherie Blair, Theresa May, Hillary Clinton, Angela Merkel, Christine Lagarde, and their ilk, reek of the creed of their youth: 1970s women's liberation. We see it in 'The Women's Power List', sponsored by the BBC *Woman's Hour* radio programme, that feminist propaganda machine broadcast daily on the most influential public broadcasting service in the world, and headed by a group of superannuated women's libbers, and we see it every time we hear a news report of yet another woman entrepreneur, a 'heroine' of the women's struggle, who has prevailed despite the patriarchal system, or who has become a successful and powerful sportswoman, and is heralded as a role model for girls. In the never-ending gender class war, these bigots try to enlist ordinary women to their cause by constantly inciting them with the repetition of invented historical grievances, reminding them of men's privilege, and how women are as good as men, even though women are downtrodden. It is like a record stuck in its groove, but it works. We see this in the plethora of privileged young women from these women's daughters' generation (or even their grand-daughters'), from sports to Hollywood, from everyday sexism to 'slutwalks' and campus 'Take back the night!' campaigns. These radical feminists are relentlessly at work puffing up women, massaging their egos, stoking the boilers of their resentment, and creating inequality for men in the pursuit of equality for women. Although small in number, this fantastically privileged and powerful group of left-wing matriarchs are working tirelessly to re-shape our world to their ways, and largely for their own ends. In truth, they care nothing about fairness for women. They care nothing about women, period. They only care about their narrow, bigoted aims - which are communist aims - and they are prepared to go to any lengths to see those aims achieved in our hitherto free democracies.

When it is all boiled down, all they are doing is creating more inequality for, and between, women. Rather than liberation, they have delivered something that approximates slavery - both ideologically and practically - for many of those whom they call sister. This is only too apparent at the other end of the social spectrum from the women's power lists. There, in true Engelian fashion, aimed at creating a matriarchy, we see women becoming the new heads of mother-only families, and men being excised from any authority at all in their children's lives; even from any meaningful social role, save only as sperm donors and cash machines. This isn't solving women's problems, it is increasing them. Ideologically indoctrinated feminist media pundits and their sisters in politics across the spectrum are seeing to it that the state makes these women dependent on it, not their husbands and the fathers of their children.

Today, in the UK, childcare is estimated to cost more than the average mortgage, which means mothers are having to work to pay someone else to bring up their children, because they can't do it themselves, and, in true communist fashion, our feminist-driven governments are ensuring more and more women are given financial provision for child care, and are even going so far as to ensure single mothers are granted allowances for food, clothing and rent in order to perpetuate this system. This is bizarre, but explainable if we understand feminism's grand matriarchal plan. Women, you see, have a right to a career, and motherhood is demeaning - but only for the elite. For the rest, who are the vast majority, that is not the way it is, or is wanted. Thus, feminists are creating poverty and hardship for their less privileged 'sisters', and all taken from central taxation of course, provided by hard-working men, who work diligently and provide seventy-two per cent of income tax revenues.[344] In the ideological struggle in which they are engaged, these bigots are prepared to see mothers who are not so privileged as them floundering, caught between the waterline of making ends meet and the engulfing tide of poverty, unable to cope with the pressures they are facing, and all they can keep saying is that women must 'lean in' because they can 'have it all'. The detachment from reality this represents is stupefying, just as is their inhumanity in declaring men *personae non grata* in families. By these means, these elitist feminists, who are able to indulge their ideological purity and their relative wealth sufficient to order their lives while they pursue their ambitions, have condemned tens of thousands of ordinary women to the trauma of broken marriages, broken homes, and often to a life of hopelessness as single mothers who struggle to bring up children in poverty without a man to share the load.

Then, as if that wasn't enough, these arrogant fools shame and vilify other women whose natural instinct is to be mothers and home-makers, and turn the beauty and basic humanity of that noble female aspiration into something shameful. Thus, they oppress other women, and seek to shame them into conformance with their ideology, just as the Marxist beatnik Simone deBeauvoir said: 'No woman should be authorised to stay at home to bring up her children. Society should be totally different. Women should not have that choice, precisely because if there is such a choice, too many women will make that one.' And what is this saying about these women? Why aren't they just calm and collected: coolly confident in their liberation? Why do they need to keep this pot boiling? I suggest that they are so steeped in their ideological beliefs about not being born a woman but being forced to become one in an alleged man's world, they are harbouring an inner rage, driven by a latent sense of inadequacy, which has all the hallmarks of hysteria. They must keep reminding themselves that they are the victims of discrimination, that the vicissitudes of life are a form of discrimination against them, and that men are their enemies.

This is another aspect of making the personal political and it all amounts to the root of their angry creed, which is so ingrained in them they simply cannot see why they are as they are. Feminists have lost sight of reality, in exactly the same way that the 1970s women's liberationists did, such as Kate Millett, Andrea Dworkin, Shulamith Firestone, and Valerie Solanas, and the earlier feminist writers, such as Charlotte Perkins Gilman, Elizabeth Mann Borghese, Mary Gentle, and Marje Piercy in their wild hysterical writings. I also suggest a more selfish motive. They are manipulating women because they are afraid they might lose traction on the lines upon which their gravy train runs, and see their undoubted social power diminished.

What feminists seem to be unable to discern is the inherent flaw in their logic (inasmuch as logic has anything to do with it). Carried to its conclusion, the aspiration of women's equality with men is really saying that men are the benchmark by which women must be measured: the ideal to which women must aspire. It is saying that women don't possess their own value, their own dignity, their own specialness and uniqueness, and the logical outcome of this is that men can be equalled but not surpassed. It is crazy, but that is what this is really saying. Under this form of totalitarian thinking, women might be equal to men, but they are not free to fulfil their own destiny, as women. They are being made to conform to men and men's *modi vivendi*, which is the very thing feminism seeks to challenge, and it only serves to underline how far women have actually fallen from their hitherto high status in society.

Yet feminists continue to wilfully tear society apart in order to try to achieve their false state of being, and are prepared to abrogate on behalf of all women that one part of the social contract which is vitally important to women: marriage to a husband for life, and a stable nuclear family, free of interference from outside - especially the state. By casting down these basics of civilised life, and forcing women to revert to a primitive form of coupling, a la Engels and Lewis Henry Morgan, feminism has thrown countless women into a state of living that is far less dignified than they had before. It has also created poverty, insecurity and heartache for them, and their children, from whom it has taken the only real path to physical and emotional security while they are growing up - the nurture of their mother and the love and protection of their natural father. This is what 45 years of feminism has wrought among us. This is what it continues to wreak. Feminism is damaging children - women's children, as well as men's. It is a monster that is inexorably eating up womankind as well as mankind, feeding its insatiable appetite for power and female supremacy, and that is continuing at an increasing pace, because in the gender race feminism has initiated, women must win, at any cost.

Common purpose

Today, most people call themselves feminists in the belief that it is about fairness for women. Nothing could be further from the truth. These ideas are just sops sown to appease broader society, whilst the real feminism is getting on with its political chicanery in order to bring about its desired social order. This process is now well underway, and rolling. Feminism is now so normal that most people see it as obviously just the right thing to do. But that is the warning sign. Since when did the belief of the majority represent the truth about anything? As Bertrand Russell said, 'The fact that an opinion has been widely held is no evidence that it is not utterly absurd; indeed, in view of the silliness of the majority of mankind, a widespread belief is more likely to be foolish than sensible'.[345] Even those who have a rudimentary knowledge of feminism's dogma and tenets fail completely to join up the dots and see the big picture, and just go with the flow. I constantly hear (from women in particular) who declare themselves to be feminists, that feminism is a 'broad church' with many different aspects to its expression, and feminists can't all be expected to see eye-to-eye with each other. Some feminists, for example, might say they disagree with the hard-liners who parade in their nakedness and depravity in 'Slutwalks', provoking anyone to say anything against their self-asserted right to dress as provocatively as they wish. They might be repulsed by the screaming of obscenities against men and patriarchal power, and the taunting of men by those women who deliberately provoke them so they can be labelled as potential rapists, but still believe it is justified because so many are actually being raped, aren't they? Some feminists might secretly think that 'Page three' pin-ups and prostitution are not that bad, but allow others the space to complain that it objectifies women and must be banned. 'After all' they might say, '…people can disagree about detail but it's all in a good cause, isn't it?'

But is it? I'm afraid this selective hypocrisy simply doesn't wash if you stack it up against reality. The sluts who walk the streets semi-naked, shouting vile obscenities, and accusing men of being rapists and objectifying women, and the women who take a stand against Page Three pin-ups are in common purpose. Theirs is a common cause: the disproportionate advancement of women's social and political power. They are in joint enterprise, and as culpable as those who seek to pervert democracy with all-women Parliamentary candidate short lists aimed at ensuring as many women as men in Parliaments, or those who corrupt equality of opportunity by seeking quotas for women on corporate boards. The truth is that there is no difference in principle, just in degrees of expression of feminism. It is all the same deep down. To say otherwise is to take an impossible ethical position. The same angry, rebellious creed that is setting women against men and dividing society is the overarching ethos of anyone who declares themselves to be a feminist, and they must stand by that. Feminists might think they are in a broad church, but it is the same religion acting in common cause in the crusade against patriarchy.

No one can legitimately pick and choose what they believe is good in feminism, and reject what is bad in it. The power-dressed 'devil who likes Prada' in the boardroom is fighting for the same thing as the undressed slut walker in the street. There is nowhere to hide from this stark truth for people who claim to be feminists. *If it walks like a duck, swims like a duck, and quacks like a duck, then it is a duck.* The common law principle of common purpose imputes culpable liability to any individual in a group for another member of that group who commits an unlawful act. No proof of intent is needed for joint venture, the only test is whether any member of the group could have reasonably foreseen that one of its members might commit a criminal act. If that test is met, all carry the guilt. For example, someone taking part in a riot knowing that other rioters are carrying firearms and are willing to use them is just as guilty as the actual perpetrators. Each carries the guilt as much as all carry the guilt. It applies in a military situation too. In a platoon of soldiers, if some loot, rape or murder innocent people, the rest are morally guilty because all are engaged in common purpose and joint venture. A similar principle applies in business. Where two or more parties in an unincorporated enterprise share the profits and losses, each carries joint and several responsibility for all the losses in the event of failure, and the creditors can pursue any of the partners, sequestering their personal assets to pay the partnership debt.

In Germany in the 1930s and 40s, some people didn't agree with Hitler and his anti-Semitic ranting, yet they remained members of his National Socialist Party. Some actually saw the movement as a cause for good, as people do with feminism. Some saw Hitler as a messiah of Germany after its humiliation in the aftermath of World War I, and they attended rallies and parades and shouted the slogans, whilst others avoided them and kept their heads down. We now know, of course, that all of them were deluded by a man who sold them a 'Big Lie'. The German people were duped by the NAZIs, who became the directing mind of a nation in whose midst truly evil things were done. Yet, they just went with the flow, to their nation's and their own destruction, and all of them, by their actions and inactions, were complicit in what eventually happened, and the collective guilt that appeared in the German post-war generation is the test of that reality. So those who say they are feminists yet seek to wash their hands of the extremist elements of feminism are being morally and ethically dishonest. They are deluding themselves if they think they are not responsible for the acts of others. The woman who takes advantage of an all-woman Parliamentary candidate short list and gets elected undemocratically is jointly and severally responsible for the destruction of marriage, the widespread breakdown of family life, and the disruption to children's lives that are the outcomes of feminism in our lives.

No one can reasonably say that there is good feminism and bad feminism; it is all feminism. It is cultural Marxism whose aim is to overturn the natural order of western democratic capitalist societies, and creating chaos. Right-minded people who espouse this angry creed would do well to wake up to this stark truth. What is happening today with feminism is a joint venture against

446

society as we know it; instigated by, and led by, an élite, and followed by far too many rank and file women (and far too many men, it has to be said) who are failing to question the reality of what it is they are part of. No one who calls herself or himself a feminist can escape this. Even those who are not card-carrying feminists must face the stark realisation that they are at least in common purpose, and likely in joint venture with extremists who are wreaking lasting damage on the conventional family, on men's and women's relationships, on legions of children who are suffering the close-to-total dismantling of the basic fabric of their societies, and that is as much their responsibility as it is the likes of Germaine Greer, Kate Millett, Andrea Dworkin, Valerie Solanas, Betty Friedan, and yes, even Emmeline and Christabel Pankhurst.

When Germaine Greer said in 1970, 'Women's liberation, if it abolishes the patriarchal family, will abolish a necessary substructure of the authoritarian state, and once that withers away Marx will have come true, willy nilly, so let's get on with it,' she was deadly serious. And so too were Harriet Harman and Patricia Hewitt who reinforced this in 1990, when they said, 'It cannot be assumed that men are bound to be an asset to family life or that the presence of fathers in families is necessarily a means to social cohesion', and later, in 2008, when Harman repeated that there is 'no ideal type of household in which to bring up children'. These and countless thousands of their like have taken a wrecking ball to the family, that 'substructure of the authoritarian state,' and they are still at work doing that: in politics, in the institutions, in universities, and in the streets, walking like sluts, or complaining of everyday sexism.

For the length of their lives, the children of today will bear the cost of their mother's espousal of the highly politically motivated, Marxist, partisan ideology that has in very large measure achieved what it set out to achieve among us. For the length of their lives, those children will suffer from the institutional dismantling of fatherhood and the disposal of fathers from their lives. They will suffer from the absence of their mothers during those crucial first years, that time when attachment is so important to their ability to carry on healthy adult relationships. And all because their mothers bought the lie that they had a right to a career and self-actualisation against all the evidence, and common sense based on custom and practice built up over millennia of social development. The widespread, blind, unreasoning belief in feminism we see around us today is already the cause of a lot of social misery, and those who believe in it will be jointly and severally responsible for that misery for generations to come. They cannot hide behind the idea that it is only the extremists' fault. A day will come when every person who espouses this socially destructive ideology will feel the pangs of guilt for what they have brought about in their joint venture with gender extremism.

Real equality and diversity

Our modern, capitalist, free-market economies have been under sustained attack by Marxism for the last 70 years, and vast swathes of people don't realise that they are its targets. Under the cover of the mesmerising ideological miasma called equality, Western capitalist democracies have opened the gates wide to a Trojan Horse, bearing its name that has hidden in its ideological belly, a political pollution that seeks to disrupt our way of life, restricting freedom - not least the freedom of speech - retarding social progress, and sapping the energy from people's lives in unnecessary and pointless gender antagonism. The most bigoted totalitarian ideology ever is leading us to abandon all that has made us who we are, and it is being implemented by a feminist fifth column that has penetrated deep among us, and is endlessly at work whipping up a one-sided gender class war in the name of equality.

Marxist feminism is tearing down the framework of ordinary people's lives, simply because as more and more people in modern Western democracies are (or aspire to be) essentially middle-class, and therefore bourgeois, they are its legitimate targets. Millions of people in the West are small-scale capitalists who own their homes. They own property for rent, or run small businesses, they are the exchangers of commodities and services in return for the money they earn in our modern system of monetary exchange - and that makes them bourgeois - that old ideological enemy of Marxist communism. Even if they are not consciously bourgeois, most people in Western developed societies reflect the political stance of the bourgeois and vote for the centre left or right, not the extreme left. Yet, they declare themselves to be feminists, so little do they understand the degree of the deception that has been perpetrated on them.

Capitalism, not communism, is what defines us in the West. It is a system with massive shortcomings. It is often ugly in many of its manifestations, but it remains the best system available to deliver wellbeing, wealth - and freedom - and it will continue to do this as far as anyone can see into the future. The owners of small businesses are the historical bourgeois. Most of them never seek to grow large businesses, preferring instead to keep them as reliable sources of income that will provide savings and pensions (which provide the capital for all this to happen) that see them through their last years in self-provided comfort. Then, they seek to pass on whatever wealth they have acquired to their children, something that communism prevents, and which is now fast becoming a reality in our Western democracies because of the feminists' destruction of families and father's patrimonial inheritances. Winston Churchill once said, 'Socialism is a philosophy of failure, the creed of ignorance, and the gospel of envy, its inherent virtue is the equal sharing of misery,' and the test of the wisdom of his words lies in the fact that all of the socialist/communist experiments that started in the twentieth century are either over, are changing to a capitalist footing, or are tottering on the brink of collapse. In Cuba, for example, ordinary people now run small businesses, which would have been illegal just a few years ago, and even Russia has succumbed to the inevitable and now has massively wealthy oligarchs. These entrepreneurs are the galvanising energy of these formerly communist societies, whose true essence is to be the agents whereby capital and labour are brought together to contract for opportunities.

Feminism is not progress, it is regress. Certainly, it is not there to benefit women, or advance them. In fact women are its fodder, made to work willy nilly, and become units in the means of economic production rather than curators of the social capital, which is children and families. That is not to say women cannot choose careers and success for themselves, based on their own merit, hard work and skill, but it is to say that mixing a lifetime of enforced work with bearing and bringing up children is giving neither the women themselves, their children, or their children's fathers a fair deal. Women are worth far more than feminism has to offer them. Those whose hands down the centuries have rocked the cradle and ruled the world, who bravely kept the home fires burning during existential threats to their nations, who buckled down to the struggle in the factories, who invented drugs and therapeutic treatments, went to far-flung places and founded institutions and hospitals, who embraced orphaned children and refugees, as well as their own offspring, have been turned into wage slaves or caricatures of unutterably selfish creatures, who endlessly issue a wail of victimhood, and accuse men of being the cause of all their perceived ills. This amounts to the most obscene display of selfish entitlement, demanding special treatment and unfair advantage, and it is sickening to see. None of what feminism has achieved edifies women, or womankind.

Free people don't want narrow ideologies that define them and enforce their precepts on them. That is what the Taliban do. Free people want equality of opportunity for everyone but based on merit, and the just distribution of social benefit; and they want that regardless of race, creed, or colour, or sex. Like men the world over, free women, dignified women, clever, brave, honest women, crave liberty and the pursuit of happiness, yet feminism delivers none of these things. The feminist argument is not about equality *for* women, but equality *of* women. It is socialism of the most extreme kind, and feminists are hard at work trying to bring that about in women's lives. Theirs is the communist-utopian definition of equality *qua* sameness: parity disconnected from achievement through merit and ability, and divorced from skills and attributes. And, like in the dystopian communities communism created, feminists are positioning themselves to be a powerful ruling elite who run society for their own benefit, building a gigantic gravy-train, only for themselves. We need only look to power-hungry women who are using this false form of equality to gain equal representation in the boardroom and in politics on no other merit than that they are female. We also see it in the shameless pursuit of positive discrimination in the all-women short lists for prospective parliamentary candidates, adopted by the Labour Party (*who else?*) in Britain, in the appointment of women bishops in the church of England, in vast numbers of women taking over command of the police and the armed forces, where feminists are now even demanding that women take up combat roles.

Feminists constantly use terms like diversity, but true diversity means difference, not conformity or sameness. It comes from social colour-blindness, discretion over disability, and normal self-selection by the sexes in different social and work activities, according to individual men's and women's personal preferences. True diversity is just people finding their own level, their own niche, their own way, without impediment or the direction of others. It cannot be engineered, or brought about by coercion intended to create artificial outcomes. Diversity and real equality of opportunity is about being free to choose for oneself according to one's own wishes, dreams, desires, skills, individual discrimination, and individual attributes, seizing opportunities as they come along and making one's own way in life, free of impediment or artificial aid. Therein lies the path to liberty and the pursuit of happiness, yet feminists seek to deny this, using their dubious (one might say devious) definition of diversity as a trick to bring about the fundamental social change they desire - which is, in its essence, communistic. This is social engineering, not equality of opportunity in the face of serendipity. It is the system that prevails in states such as China, Vietnam, North Korea, and Cuba today, and which we saw in Czechoslovakia, East Germany, and the USSR during the Cold War, all of which fell because of the spirit of freedom to choose their own lives and how they should live them, in the people themselves. Under the specious guise of liberal equality and fairness, feminists are leading otherwise liberal or conservative people by the nose to accept a re-engineered socialist society - a 'legalised community of women' - in which sex is politicised, gender-driven class-war is normalised, and society is divided along the fault line of a political construct called gender.

'It is poison'

The truth about feminism is that it is a gender war of a particularly pernicious kind, fomented and stirred-up by misfits, malcontents, and ideologically driven people who are intent on reshaping society to their own world view. Feminists lie about rape, they lie about the pay gap, they lie about domestic violence, they lie about families, and they lie about fathers. They lie about history, and they bully, threaten and hound anyone who speaks against their lies. For almost half a century, they have worked systematically to socially emasculate men, to strip men of their dignity, their self esteem, and their social value, and they have achieved remarkable success doing that.

Feminists have altered our politics and our law. They have commandeered our criminal justice system, conforming it to political correctness so it enforces their laws, and their angry creed now has unreasonable power in our land. Yet, no one will speak the truth about their power. Why? Basically because no one dare, and because they have compromised the press, the only agency that could and should speak truth unto power.[346] As Orwell showed us, when no challenge to totalitarianism is brooked, free thinking becomes thought crime, which leads to a dumbing-down of people who become mute and politically pliable. Even if they know the ideology is wrong and dangerous, they are prevented from speaking out in opposition, for fear, at the very least, of appearing out of sync with the general view, and at worst, of retribution. The popular view is that if you speak against feminism, you speak against women as a class. You then become labelled as a misogynist and cast into outer darkness, never to be rehabilitated. But that is not right, as Baruch Spinosa pointed out to us 300 years ago, '... in a free state every man may think what he likes, and say what he thinks,'[347] and as Salman Rushdie said, 'The moment you declare a set of ideas to be immune from criticism, satire, derision, or contempt, freedom of thought becomes impossible'.

This is what feminism has achieved in our society. Feminist dogma are now close to being held to be unquestionable, and to speak against them is seen almost as heresy, punishable by widespread condemnation and disapproval. Men and women are having their entire way of life changed and conformed to an elitist ideology, and they simply can't speak out against it. Is there any wonder that our nation is besotted with the ideas of equality, and the alleged rights of women, when people have these ideas thrown at them daily, like sweeties thrown to children who fight and squabble over them whilst those who throw the sweeties laugh and get on with their own agenda? In her outstanding analysis in her 1998 book *Domestic Tranquility: A Brief Against Feminism*, Carolyn Graglia gives us arguably the most accurate description of what feminism is really all about:[348]

> Since the late 1960s, feminists have very successfully waged war against the traditional family, in which husbands are the principal breadwinners and wives are primarily home-makers. This war's immediate purpose has been to undermine the homemaker's position in order to drive her into the work force. Its long-term goal is to create a society in which women behave as much like men as possible, devoting as much time and energy to the pursuit of a career as men do, so that women will eventually hold equal political and economic power with men... Feminists have used a variety of methods to achieve their goal. They have promoted a sexual revolution that encouraged women to mimic male sexual promiscuity. They have supported the enactment of no-fault divorce laws that have undermined housewives' social and economic security. And they obtained the application of affirmative action requirements to women, undermining the ability of men who are victimised by this discrimination to function as breadwinners. A crucial weapon in feminism's arsenal has been the status degradation of the housewife's role. From the journalistic attacks of Betty Friedan and Gloria Steinem to Jessie Bernard's sociological writings, all branches of families are united in the conviction that a woman can find identity and fulfilment only in a career. A housewife, feminists agree, was properly characterised by Simone de Beauvoir and Betty Friedan as a 'parasite,' a being something less than human, living her life without using her adult capability for intelligence, and lacking any real purpose in devoting herself to children, husband, and home... Operating on the twin assumptions that equality means sameness (that is, men and women cannot be equals unless they do the same things) and that most differences between the sexes are culturally imposed, contemporary feminism has

undertaken its own cultural impositions. Revealing their totalitarian belief that they know best how others should live and their totalitarian willingness to force others to conform to their dogma, feminists have sought to modify our social institutions in order to create an androgynous society in which male and female roles are as identical as possible. The results of the feminist juggernaut now engulf us. By almost all indicia of well-being, the institution of the American family has become significantly less healthy than it was 30 years ago.

No one should be in any doubt that a cultural revolution has been pulled off by feminists, and that it has been a conscious process. A determined band of ideologues has succeeded in turning our entire society into a communist-type social structure, in which women supposedly have a better status, but actually have had their entire social role degraded and changed, probably irrevocably. Feminism has taken us back to a model of proto-society where people lived in tribes not families; where marriage didn't exist; where sexual coupling only took place for uncommitted pleasure or the casual procreation of children, and where children were the property of the community, not that of the sanguineous family. Any thoughtful reading of our society today will see chilling echoes of these things, and I trust my reader will also be chilled by their implications, if for no other reason than for the sake of the children. Graglia[349] again:

> None but the limited number of the very best child care establishments (or the very best nannies) who, in fact, provide care which even remotely resembles care by professionals educated in the latest child rearing techniques. But even if this were not the case, the happiness and well-being of infants and young children depends very little on any specific knowledge or technique employed by a caregiver. They depend far more on responsiveness to need as undivided as possible and on a continuing, loving interaction with the person to whom this child is uniquely precious. In the eyes of such a person, what this child does is happening for the first time. And this child knows that what he does is comparatively important because this person thinks it so. Those of us who reject surrogate care for our children doubt that such response to our child is likely to come from any worker in a daycare centre or from an average nanny. It is a response that cannot be taught; and rarely can it be bought.

When the man-woman-child family as the primary unit of society ceases to be the norm, when marriage between heterosexual couples ceases to have any meaning, when men are excised from their rightful place as head of the nuclear family, when home life becomes redefined to a broader, boundary-less concept in which men and women are connected but do not necessarily live together; when a woman's sexual virtue has no meaning because she is not committed to one man, or to his support for his children; when women rely on the state as their support, when child-care is subsidised by the state, and is subcontracted to people hired to do the job, whilst mothers work; when the rights of the father to have access to his children are routinely negated in the courts, but his obligations are enforced with draconian vigour; when the right of the child to have access to its natural father, or even know his identity, are dispensed with; when the legal legitimacy of children that allows them to inherit from their father's line has no meaning, and men become reduced to being only a means by which children are sired; when the nuclear family ceases to be the basis of society at all, then the ideas of Marx and Engels have found their truest expression. A different form of society comes into being - one where the state becomes society and socialism (or even Tony Blair's variant: Social-ism) becomes its dominant ethos.

This is precisely what Margaret Thatcher warned against when she said:

> ...there is no such thing as society. There are individual men and women, and there are families. And no government can do anything except through people, and people must look to themselves first. It's our duty to look after ourselves and then, also to look after our neighbour. People have got the entitlements too much in mind, without the obligations, because there is no such thing as an entitlement unless someone has first met an obligation.[350]

She could see what was afoot in the deeply left-wing, totalitarian ideology that was always lurking, ready to pounce during her time in office, and she knew feminism for what it is: an ideology of the far left, and about as far removed from her politics as the moon. She well knew that a powerful minority of bigoted women, a politicised socialist-feminist elite, was at work changing her world, and despite her holding socialism at bay for over a decade, it finally burst upon Britain under Tony Blair, who raised feminism to be the 'ism above all 'isms. Mrs Thatcher is on record as having said, 'The feminists hate me, don't they? And I don't blame them. For I hate feminism. It is poison.'

Ideologies and 'isms

I hope that by now I have shown convincingly that feminism is the cultural expression of Marxism, complete with its anti-father (patriarchy), anti-marriage, anti-nuclear family stance, all aimed at creating equality *qua* sameness - equality of outcome, not of opportunity. I trust I have laid its socialist communist credentials bare. I hope I have shown that feminism is just another set of ideas that have caught the public imagination and become very deeply embedded through a sustained and clever manipulation of the popular psyche, and that it displays all the characteristics of countless ideologies down the centuries, most of which were based on myth and distortion of fact, and promulgated by a small group of influential people who played the long game to sway society to their ways. I trust my reader will also see that like a virus in a computer, feminism has changed the very operating system of the society in which we live.

Feminism is just another 'ism: a system of ideas and ideals that form the basis of an economic or political theory; it is no different to the 'isms of Communism, Fascism, National Socialism, Chartism, Separatism, etc. - and, yes, Conservatism, Liberalism, Republicanism, and so on. The list of 'isms is immense. The eighteenth, nineteenth, and twentieth centuries were full of them. Each had its own formula for the way things should be, and each sought to embed that formula in the popular imagination, so as to influence society according to its ways. So, let me say it again: feminism is just an 'ism - a set of ideological precepts, no different in principle to any other - and that is all it is. It is no more objectively valid, right, or true than any of the rest. The only thing that is valid, true, and right, is life, liberty, and the pursuit of happiness, for a people free from the cloying 'isms that would seek to control them, divert them, and place them in their own brand of ideological straight jacket. If there is one thing history has taught us about 'isms, it is that they automatically lead to schisms. In their most extreme form, they stereotype and idealise social groups: setting one against the other, creating 'in' and 'out' groups. That is what feminism has done. It has placed women and men into 'in' and 'out' groups - women good, men bad - and that has set women in direct political confrontation with men. When, like feminism, an 'ism takes hold in a nation state, and becomes embedded, it takes over established forms of thinking, forcing conformity to its dogma and precepts. Values, morals, rationalisations, behaviours, generally held beliefs, all become inexorably conformed to their particular set of rules. If an 'ism is really successful, it takes over as the dominating ideology of the state itself, as we saw in National Socialism and Communism in the twentieth century, and people become deprived of their freedom to speak, act, and assemble. Thus, the inherent aim of 'isms is totalitarianism, where everybody thinks the same - and, of course, that confers power on those who install them.

If women could but see the extent to which they are being sold a pup by feminism, they would rise up and overthrow its domination of them. Women are as worldly as men. They have as much common sense as men. They can think and act for themselves, just as men can. They don't need the sanctuary of the collective, or the sisterly sophistries of feminism to support them in their life's journey. Women can make their own decisions about how they live their lives, unbound by the straitjacket of other people's dogma, and if they could but see the extent to which feminism is conforming them to its own false stereotypes, casting them, and their daughters, as automata with no agency, framing them as eternal victims, etc., they would eschew the falseness of it all and cast off the cloying control over their lives that feminism really is exercising over them. If women used their mental faculties instead of slavishly toeing the feminist party line (and, it has to be said, for going along with it for personal gain), they would soon see how they are being denied their basic freedoms. If they were to question the false factoids that are being peddled by the feminism industry in their name, they would laugh at them and shrug them off. If women woke up to the lies, the deceit and the downright chicanery that feminists are up to, they would reject it all and reclaim their personal integrity. Then, they would be truly liberated. All of us who have the privilege of living in a free society under the rule of law, not under tyrants or tyrannical regimes, know that our freedom has been hard-won over the centuries since Magna Carta, and we should cherish it and preserve it, while trying always to extend it and protect it, particularly from governments that, despite their political labels, are all creeping ever closer to the left - to totalitarianism and elitism - always trying to be our masters not our servants, forever shifting from the true role of government - of the people, by the people, for the people.

The Common Law was the law of the people, not of kings, politicians, or ideologues with axes to grind. It was created in the courts; not by parliaments, committees, or cabinets (least of all by ideologically driven lobby groups or infiltrators), and it was based on the practical wisdom of the common people, not the ideological dogma of an elite who would seek to rule them. The Common Law was the friend of the people and the enemy of tyrants. Short of serious criminal activity, which the law covers anyway, no one has a right to dictate what goes on behind closed doors. What happens in people's private lives is their business - even if those lives are turbulent. The Englishman's home is his castle, and it is a bastion against the state: a redoubt against unwanted and unwarranted intrusion. It is where men and women have the inalienable right to keep out nuisance and interference - especially from an ideologically driven state that wishes to regulate intimacy, which is what we are seeing happen in the legislation about sexual offences and in the domestic arena. It is a statement of people who want the freedom to live their lives as they see fit, subject only to the rule of a just law, and feminism is creating both an unjust law and an unjust society.

Animal Farm revisited

Extremist movements have always tried to grab power without proper authority while the society they are infiltrating is otherwise engaged, distracted, asleep, or just comfortable in its own prosperity. This was George Orwell's message in his massively influential book, *Animal Farm*. It is widely believed that Orwell was allegorically warning us about the reality behind Stalin's Soviet Russia, but his tocsin sounds true and clear down the decades for the countries of the developed world that are now so consumed by feminism.

Adopting the Seven Commandments of Animalism, including 'all animals are equal,' Orwell portrays the farm's takeover by the animals from the drunken, self-absorbed, and otherwise-preoccupied farmer, renaming it 'Animal Farm'. The ordinary animals are sold the idea of equality for all, but this utopian idea unravels when the pigs opportunistically elevate themselves above the others and assert alleged rights to special food and consideration, asserting this was needed to keep them in especially good health. Soon, the pigs start emulating the humans, dressing like them, and ultimately becoming indistinguishable from them. In the final move, Napoleon, the chief pig, announces the renaming of Animal Farm to its original feudal system name, Manor Farm and holds a dinner for the humans during which he announces a rephrasing of the primary goal of the revolution to, 'All animals are equal *but some are more equal than others*'. After that, the farm returns to its original state, but under new management.

This is the message of feminism today. In the false name of equality, feminists are seeking a change of order where they become the power in society. They are demanding special consideration, and they are trying to emulate men in everything they do. Some, it has to be said, dress like men. Finn Mackay, for example, is a particularly driven and articulate lesbian feminist who is almost indistinguishable from a man. Feminists are doing precisely what Orwell predicted, and they are doing it now in Europe, Britain, America, Canada, and a host of other nations and societies where their creed has been planted. Feminism is undoubtedly a hegemonic, worldwide movement that has infiltrated almost every organ of state in the developed nations of the world: every institution, the media, the universities, and feminists now have their hands on the key levers of power in world agencies such as the UN. Working under most people's radar, feminists are relentlessly bringing everybody under their heel, in a new world order, in which men and their influence are being progressively subdued.

Feminists will continue relentlessly to cajole women to resist alleged male oppression everywhere. They will continue to promote the cause of women as victims, ensuring that women are kept in a state of latent fear of men - as pre-rapists, potential wife beaters, and would-be controllers of women. They will wheeler-deal in the media and in parliaments and legislatures. No quarter will be given to men: no room to live as men will go untouched, and they will endlessly drive men back from what social power they have left. They will use every tactic, every ruse, every lie they can until men reach the point where men are subdued and conformed to the feminist way, which is their overall objective because they want men's power for themselves. Feminists want 'the sisterhood' in control of society, and they will never relent from attacking men and maleness until that new order is achieved. This is the future for societies that embrace this angry creed, which is a parasite that will continue feeding on its host until either it dies, or the host dies.

The danger of a male backlash

For decades, men have been systematically and institutionally prevented from having access to their children. That is now a given, so widespread, almost everyone knows about it, and almost everyone has been touched by it, either personally or vicariously, through their families and friends. Men's social spaces have been needlessly invaded, their manhood has been mocked, their higher feelings derided, and men are now being forced to see their sons being conformed to feminist ways, and their daughters radicalised against men, as though men were some form of separate, dangerous species. The TV and film media are complicit in this, undermining boys' confidence, and making men out to be wimpish, useless, ineffectual creatures who need a savvy woman to show them how to function properly, and, of course, the formula for that is feminism.

Increasingly, men are being exhorted by the feminist propaganda machine to 'play their part,' to 'bear the load' of children, which really means giving up their primary role as breadwinner and protector in order to allow women to assume more of those roles. This is about the neatest switch from patriarchy to matriarchy ever to be pulled off, and the vast majority of men cannot see what is happening to them, so bemused are they by the false notion of 'equality,' the 'woman-as-victim,' and 'women's rights,' which are lollipops handed to them to suck - which they do with eagerness. Young men are being urged to 'man up', and rise to the challenge of the new world order in which women's power is a reality; the *HeForShe* initiative is a good example of this in action. This is as hypocritical as it is devious because if men willingly become as feminists would have them become, the way will be cleared for feminism to become the overarching ethos of society and the aim of female supremacy - the final overturning of patriarchy, replacing it with matriarchy - will be complete.

What is worse, in their relentless anger and sustained attack on men and maleness, the feminist elite, replete with its muddled messages, has gone so far as to attack boys, getting at them at school when they are at their most impressionable - and vulnerable - instigating programmes of political correctness in junior schools, pathologising boys' natural boisterousness as Attention Deficit Hyperactivity Disorder (ADHD), and even the drugging of these children with Ritalin to calm them down. All this morphs into an overall excuse to 're-educate' boys about their maleness, in other words to 'save' them from their own natures, which is child abuse, frankly; there is no other way to describe it. On the other hand, for decades, and with increasing intensity, feminist bigots have been falsely elevating the self-esteem of girls to unhealthy levels, using every form of psychological reinforcement possible, convincing them that girls are superior to boys in every way. They have even presented themselves as role models to falsely induce girls to believe that theirs is the best way to go in life, which is also child abuse. (It is also a flagrant inversion of the fundamental feminist principle of social indoctrination into a sex role, a la Simone de Beauvoir.)

We cannot escape the reality that men are being strategically marginalised in our society, and in far too many cases they are being removed from any influence at all. For example, men no longer teach young children for fear of being accused of sexual misconduct or paedophilia, which has turned all early years and junior education into the sole preserve of young women teachers, who have been radicalised to feminism in their universities. These young women are already ensuring that education is orientated to favour girls over boys. Even boys' later schooling is being rigged to favour girls' way of learning, and boys are missing out. Girls peak earlier than boys intellectually, and that is being used to create unfair advantage for them so they can enter universities in far greater numbers than boys, which is now a fact in the UK. If ever there was a time to reinstate single-sex schools to protect boys, then that time is now.

Then, when boys finally get to university, they are encountering an intimidating climate of fear that sees them as 'pre-rapists' who must be put through 'consent courses' in their fresher's week, so they are aware of how they should treat women. Young men on campus today are running the gauntlet of false rape accusations from female students, who are convinced they are in imminent danger from them. This hysterical rape culture is constantly being whipped up their student's unions, and tacitly allowed to run without check by university authorities, who sit on their hands because they are either compromised by feminists in their own ranks, or emasculated by their threats. We must be in no doubt that university campuses are being turned into no-go areas for men, so that more and more women can occupy campuses, and ultimately be the only ones who get a higher education. It is all part of the grand feminist plan.

I referred earlier to the call by feminists for men to re-visit their roles as men: to become 'new men': nurturing, caring, in touch with their feminine side; men who are happy to let a woman be the major earner, while they 'take their share' of child rearing. Well, this has already been tried, with disastrous results. In 1960, Fidel Castro promised to create a 'new man' in Cuba (*'un hombre nuevo'*), who would construct a new and prosperous socialist society for the benefit of all the people of Cuba. Within a year of gaining power, among a raft of communist policies, he made divorce little more than a rubber stamp affair (something that happened in the West only a handful of years later) and, of course, that unleashed a tidal wave of divorce, which moved women *en masse* into the workforce, which is a communist aim. However, it also created a mass of broken homes, and an underclass of ne'er-do-well men who became freed of the responsibilities men must discharge if they are to be contributing members of society. Forty-eight years later, on July 12th 2008, Raul Castro, Fidel's brother and successor as head of state, gave a speech to the Cuban parliament in which he mentioned a scarce will to work among Cuban men ('… *menciono tendencia general la escasa voluntad de trabajo existente entre los cubanos'*), mentioning in passing that in practice egalitarianism had amounted to the exploitation of the good worker by the lazy one ('… *esto es una forma de explotacion, la del buen trabajador por el que no lo es, por el vago.*').[351] Fidel's 'new man' had become Raoul's '*un vago*', a lazy, feckless, unmotivated human being, without a purpose and of little use to society.

Another way this strategic attack on men as boys has been pressed is through the almost complete destruction of the true meaning of marriage as a covenant for life for the procreation of children (and, by logical implication, their wellbeing). This has resulted in substantial parts of at least two generations of boys being brought up without the steadying influence of a father, with the result that boys have no role models for manhood. Far too many boys are 'failing to launch' and remain living at home, often retiring to their bedrooms and disappearing into an online virtual world where they don't have to deal with responsibility.[352] They are without social anchors and broken in spirit, and far too many of them are prematurely ending their own lives, as we have seen. I suggest that suicide is only the tip of the iceberg of an increasing and widespread male misery, yet we never hear a squeak about it because it is drowned in the shriek of female entitlement that engulfs us all. By trying to re-engineer manhood and men's true roles in our societies, we in the West are courting a disaster, and the signs are there for us to see.

Most men are dealing with the present situation by blanking it. They are just getting on with their lives, finding their social companionship with other men: in drinking, sports, and generally 'having a laugh'. Others are just keeping their heads down and avoiding what is going on as best they can, by-passing the pitfalls, rationalising their situation, and hoping it will all just go away, or somehow it will work itself out. It won't. What is the best way to boil a frog alive? Put it in cold water and gradually increase the temperature until it is too late for it to escape. Despite the myth created in the media today, that men are basically stupid, they are not. For many, the temperature is already too high. They know they are living in an increasingly toxic society, drunk on gynocentric feminist ideology that is marginalising them and weaving a complex and sticky web of dogma and false beliefs around them. They know they are being collectively labelled as potential or 'pre-rapists', or wife beaters, or as sexist misogynists. They know that the alleged rape culture, and the Violence Against Women and Girls (VAWG) agendas are false, and they are being framed for crimes they are not committing.

They know that feminists in power have created laws that are out to get them, and they are making rational decisions to quit early, getting out of the cauldron, and shifting their locus of responsibility back to themselves. These are the MGTOWs ('Men going their own way'), which is a new version of bachelordom. Young men and older men, good men, sensible, self-reliant men are going their own way, refusing to marry and even eschewing relationships with women altogether. They are especially avoiding fatherhood because they know the consequences, having seen what has happened to their fathers, their brothers, their friends, and, for some, even their grandfathers. These, they argue, are small prices to pay for their freedom and safety, and women must take note of this phenomenon, because it presages something unpleasant and possibly dangerous. Women in particular who espouse, practice and promulgate feminism need to beware of what they wish for, because it could all go horribly and irretrievably wrong for them.

In a free society, within the law, everyone has the liberty to act in any way he or she wishes until that liberty infringes the liberty of another. As the late US Supreme Court Justice Oliver Wendell Holmes, Jr., said, 'The right to swing my fist ends where the other man's nose begins'. Women can continue to assert their alleged rights, but they would do well to recognise that women's rights end where men's rights begin. There are only so many rights to go around. Rights don't exist in a vacuum, and if we as a society permit the continuation of the gross calumnies, the inequalities and the injustices that men and boys are experiencing, we will all pay a heavy price. Men's role is not to be subservient to women, any more than women's destiny is to be subservient to men. Men are not women's lap dogs or useful idiots, and neither are they destined to be just the cogs in the machine of a society run by women. Men built the machine and they keep it running, and if they are defeated, everyone will suffer, including women, who will actually be worse off.

The fight for women's so-called rights already comes with a heavy social price tag, but that price might become even heavier if men as a class finally work out what is really happening to them and put a stop to it. When the penny finally drops in enough men, there will be a backlash. When men refuse to be complicit in their own destruction, when they refuse to bow the knee to women, if they are forced to reassert their masculinity *in extremis*, they will do so with all their manly strength and determination, and it will be a sight to behold. Men will reclaim their manhood, and their basic human rights, and should that come about, women's equality will be worthless; their mantras meaningless. As long as the feminist attack on men continues; as long as the eternal quest for the rights of women goes on whilst ignoring the concomitant rights of men, as long as the only let-out for men is to disengage from society, something will give. That day is surely coming, and when it arrives it could well be tumultuous. Hot-headed, angry men could easily launch a counter-revolution and those who have walked away for the time being will join in - and it might not be pretty.

Crucial moment in history

We in the West live at a crucial moment in our history, and we must ask ourselves, can any good come out of the wanton onslaught on men, which is undoubtedly underway? Is the fabric of our civilised, democratic nations to be torn apart because one sex has risen up in defiance of the other? Are we going to allow our society to be reduced to an endless, grotesque struggle between men and women for jobs, for power, for wealth, for social spaces - for children? Do we really want men's and women's relationships to be a pitched battle, a war of attrition, which no one can win? Are we going to become a people amongst whom a form of gender apartheid develops, where each sex engages in its own separate development? Surely, each and every one of us is jointly and severally responsible for the society we create for ourselves, and for our children? The present social division along the fault line of gender is not the way to a better future. Men and women are not separate species, and women must not allow themselves to become locked in sisterly solidarity against them. All of us are in the same boat and we must stop rocking it, lest we all drown.

Short of two world wars in the twentieth century, the politicisation of gender has been the greatest tragedy ever to fall on the developed world. The idea of men and women as politically opposed classes is the most arrant, outrageous nonsense, but it is now a fact of life, and it is all designed to manoeuvre men into engaging in a political struggle with women with the intention to divide us and, therefore, rule us, depriving both sexes of their freedoms. I defy anybody to prove that women were ever specifically discriminated against as a class, least of all by men as a class, and I defy anybody to point to any male discrimination against women today. Even if women had been given a raw deal in the past, that still doesn't justify their rising up against men today. Two wrongs never made a right. Retribution is not restoration, and the past cannot be rectified by repeating its mistakes.

What is being perpetrated against men and the very essence of maleness in the name of feminism is dangerous and morally wrong, and anyone who considers it is a good thing needs to reappraise their view in the light of what I have been saying in this book. There never has been a hegemony of men over women. Men have never held women back - or down. Quite the reverse: men have revered and honoured women, and in any case, for most of history, ordinary men had neither the time, the freedom, nor the power to hold women down, they were too busy trying to survive and get a life for themselves and their families, whom they loved, and for whom they provided, protected - and died, in war, at work, and, all too often, prematurely. In any case, as any man knows, women cannot be dominated. They know precisely how to outmanoeuvre men, and get around them, if need be. Men have no more worked to shape society to suit themselves than the moon is made of blue cheese. In fact, if there is any hegemony over women at work in our society today, it is the hegemony of feminism, which seeks unreasonable and unjust social power over them.

Wherever you look in the developed world, you will see the bitter fruit of feminism at work. Women, especially young women, *are* locked into a struggle for power with men, based on the lie they have been sold, that men are an oppressing class. We *are* moving to a matriarchy, which is replacing patriarchy. Societies *are* being divided by gender, driven by an alien ideology that is using a classic divide and rule strategy. Children *are* being scattered to the winds in the fray, and the birth rate is plummeting because women are abrogating their biological responsibility to bear the next generation in favour of their own independence. This is a ticking time bomb, and the main question all of us must ask ourselves is: are we prepared as a society to see an unbridgeable rift between men and women come about, and for men and women to become permanently locked into a socially damaging power struggle?

What goes around comes around. Society doesn't exist in a vacuum, it is a dynamic system in which one person's rights end where another's begin, and if the basic human rights of one section of society are invaded, curtailed, or smashed-and-grabbed, that section will kick back and reassert its rights. The social seesaw will swing back, and that swing will be violent if the insanity isn't stopped, and stopped now, because men will one day draw a line in the sand and say enough is enough. Women in the West today are the most privileged and free women in history. But has feminism wrapped up its banners and turned off its rhetoric? Of course, it hasn't. That is because it has nothing to do with justice for women, it is a political struggle against capitalism, democracy, and liberal values. One's sex is one's sex, not one's 'gender'.

Ordinary, sensible folk need to wake up to this false feminist construct and see it for what it is: nonsense intended to deceive them into believing that men's and women's roles in society are socially constructed, therefore can be changed at will. They cannot.

The real aim of the cultural Marxism that masquerades as feminism is to re-engineer our middle-class, bourgeois, capitalist societies to make them conform to communist principles; to disrupt us from within in order to divide us, then to rule us. The process began with the *Communist Manifesto* of 1848, hatched by two young men sitting in a window seat in Chetham's Library in Manchester during the chaotic social upheaval of the second surge of the Industrial Revolution. Feminism is part of that conspiracy of the left. It is now an international movement that will not lie down, despite its patent failures during arguably the most turbulent and bloody centuries in history. Feminism is a conspiracy that is working to the four-phase formula described by Yuri Bezmenov: demoralise, destabilise, infiltrate, normalise. The first three phases of this clandestine struggle are all but complete. We are now in the normalisation phase, during which men will come under even more pressure to accept the new orthodoxy, and accept feminism as their pattern for living. This will happen mainly to our sons and grandsons, who are going to become hostages to female superiority. Eventually, men will be subjugated and removed from being the driving force of future society, and we see the evidence of that already underway in our schools where boys are being stigmatised and short-changed in their education. Thus, young men will be removed as a threat or counter force to the long march of feminism.

As youths they will be particularly susceptible to the feminist message, which will seduce them into believing they should be 'new men' (which really means neutered men) who can also be 'liberated' by feminism, and all too many of them will succumb to that siren call. Large numbers of these future men will be brought up only by their mothers in broken families. Other young men, like in the Grass Eaters of Japan, will come to reject men's work ethic and men's sacrificial stoicism in favour of narcissism and self-interest, and they will lose their manliness altogether. Some young men will free themselves of the strident rhetoric and the unreasonable expectation that a feminist society presents, and will move into male ghettoes: social spaces where they find the companionship only of other men - or their bedrooms and bedsits, where they will increasingly lose themselves in a computer-mediated world, satisfying their natural sexual drive with online pornography in isolation.

All this will lead to serious consequences, as Daniel Patrick Moynihan (1927 - 2003), four-term U.S. Senator, ambassador, administration official, and academic, said:

> A community that allows a large number of men to grow up in broken families, dominated by women, never acquiring any stable relationship to male authority, never acquiring any set of rational expectations about the future - that community asks for and gets chaos. Crime, violence, unrest, disorder - most particularly the furious, unrestrained lashing out at the whole social structure - that is not only to be expected; it is very near to inevitable. And it is richly deserved.

Men who become MGTOW are not sad, socially dysfunctional men, they are just men who have become resigned to the reality that normal, decent, exciting relationships with women are now legally dangerous, and near to impossible. MGTOW is men acting rationally, just giving up a fight they can't win, and walking away, shoulders slumped, hands in pockets, exiting the stage - doing what men are uniquely equipped to do, become self-reliant - and this is the dystopian future towards which we are all heading in the far from loving embrace of febrile feminism. In truth, MGTOW is a disaster for any society that needs reliable men to be fathers and providers, and it is all the result of the destructive rhetoric about men that has induced in women a foul attitude towards them. Many women today truly believe they are sleeping with the enemy, and if we are ever going to reunite women with men, it is going to take a long time - probably several generations.

That is why feminism must be resisted now, before it is too late. As Edmund Burke once wrote, 'When bad men combine, the good must associate; else they will fall one by one, an unpitied sacrifice in a contemptible struggle'. Some men, although far too few, have metaphorically swallowed the red pill and are standing up and being counted, refusing to be unpitied sacrifices of the women's liberation struggle. They are bravely speaking out with logic and reason against the tidal wave of lies and obfuscation emanating from the women's lobby, challenging the rhetoric that seeks to diminish and subdue them. But this is not enough. Too many of them have swallowed the blue pill and bought into the deal, selling their birthright for a mess of potage, or regular sex.

It therefore falls to sensible women to eschew this ideology, declaring they do not need it in their lives. Right-minded women must wake up to what feminism is doing to their children. Mothers must square up and take responsibility for the future - for their sons especially - of the doctrine of putting women first. We need female phalanxes metaphorically standing with their men, advancing arm in arm, resisting the oppression together. Both sexes must assume the mantle of joint recognition of the problem. It is true that some women are already seeing this and are rising to the cause. The so-called Honey Badgers are blogging and making YouTube videos, and telling the feminists where to get off, often in no uncertain terms. Some women journalists are putting their toes in the water, speaking about how feminism isn't for them, but they are too frightened by the backlash of the sisterhood and too enchanted by the privilege they enjoy because of feminism to dive in and make waves. Overall, however, the need to fight feminism has yet to capture the imagination of women in general.

I end this book by revisiting another verse from Bob Dylan's song *The Times They Are a Changin'*, because its final verse shows how revolutions can come a full circle:

> The line it is drawn, the curse it is cast,
> The slow one now will later be fast.
> As the present now will later be past,
> The order is rapidly fadin'.
> And the first one now will later be last
> For the times they are a-changin'.

The curse of feminism has been cast, and the line now needs to be drawn. This book is my contribution to that necessary and noble cause.

Endnotes and References

[1] FrontPage Magazine (also known as FrontPageMag.com) is an online political magazine, edited by David Horowitz and published by the David Horowitz Freedom Center (DHFC; formerly, the Center for the Study of Popular Culture), a non-profit organization in Los Angeles, California. Available from: http://www.frontpagemag.com/2014/mallorymillett/marxist-feminisms-ruined-lives/#comment-1575472425

[2] Paglia. C 1992, *Sex, Art and American Culture : New Essays*, NY: Vintage, p. 243. Citation taken from Wikipedia

[3] Mailer, N. 1971, *The Prisoner of Sex*. Little Brown. Boston

[4] The event was filmed and later made into a documentary entitled 'Town Bloody Hall,' which is freely available on You Tube (just Google 'Town Bloody Hall') and it provides us with first-hand insight into the forces and ideas that were driving the women's liberation movement at the time, later to become full-blown feminism.

[5] An arts and politics-oriented weekly newspaper distributed in Greenwich Village from 1955

[6] Crick and Watson won the 1962 Nobel Prize in Medicine, together with Maurice Wilkins, for their discovery of the structure of DNA. Maurice Wilkins and Rosalind Franklin, both working at King's College, London, were using X-ray diffraction to study DNA, and Crick and Watson used their findings in their own research into the molecular structure of DNA based on all its known features - the double helix. They published news of their discovery in April 1953 and, sadly, Franklin died in 1958. Her massive contribution to the entire project went unrecognised in the Nobel Prize, whose rules prevented posthumous inclusion.

[7] Graglia F. C. 1998, *Domestic Tranquility: A brief against feminism*. Spence Publishing Company. Dallas.

[8] Available at: http://www.pbs.org/wgbh/amex/pill/peopleevents/p_sanger.html

[9] Katherine Dexter McCormack's antecedents went straight back to the Mayflower. Unlike many women of her class, she was encouraged by her father

to pursue an education, and in 1904 she graduated in biology from the Massachusetts Institute of Technology. Once described 'as rich as Croesus' she acquired her fortune by marrying Stanley McCormick, heir to the International Harvester Company fortune. Two years into the marriage, however, her husband was diagnosed with schizophrenia and ultimately suffered dementia. She then turned her attention to philanthropy and feminist activism, including the Suffragette movement. She firmly believed it was a woman's right to control her own body as much as it was her right to vote. She met activist Margaret Sanger through the Suffragettes.

[10] Available at: http://www.bbc.co.uk/news/uk-15984258

[11] *How the contraceptive pill changed Britain.* Article on the BBC News website written by Rebecca Cafe on 4 December 2011 quoting Jane Falkingham's research on fertility. Available at: *http://www.bbc.co.uk/news/uk-15984258*

[12] Rebecca Cafe Ibid.

[13] Golden C. Katz L.F. 2000, 'Career and Marriage in the Age of the Pill', *The American Economic Review, Papers and Proceedings of the One Hundred Twelfth Annual Meeting of the American Economic Association* Vol. 90, No. 2, May, 2000, pp. 461-465 Available at: *http://www.jstor.org/stable/117269*

[14] 'Social Trends 40' 2010 edition. *United Kingdom Office for National Statistics.* Figure 2.16

[15] Little A. C. et al, 'Oral contraceptive use in women changes preferences for male facial masculinity and is associated with partner facial masculinity' *Psychoneuroendocrinology* , Volume 38 , Issue 9 , pp. 1777 - 1785

[16] 'Social Trends 40' ONS. Ibid.

[17] Beaujouan E Bhrolcháin M. N. 2011 Introduction to cohabitation and marriage in Britain'. *Population Trends* Np. 145 Autumn 2011 ESRC Centre for Population Change, University of Southampton

[18] Murphy M. 2000. 'The Evolution of Cohabitation in Britain, 1960-95', *Population Studies* 54: pp. 43-56.

[19] *The Equal Pay Act* of 1963 is a United States federal law amending the *Fair Labor Standards Act*, aimed at abolishing wage disparity based on sex (see Gender pay gap). It was signed into law on June 10, 1963, by John F. Kennedy as part of his New Frontier Program. SOURCE: Wikipedia

[20] Eventually, over 300 screenwriters, actors, directors, musicians, and other US entertainment professionals were blacklisted, effectively denying them work, because of their suspected Communist beliefs or associations with the

Communist Party of America.

[21] Although de-classified documents released many years later revealed the extent to which the Soviet Union had been involved in substantial espionage in post-war America. The USSR had undoubtedly funded the Communist Party of America and used it to recruit spies from within its public services.

[22] The evacuation of civilians in Britain during World War II was designed to save civilians, particularly children, from the risks associated with aerial bombing of cities by moving them to areas thought to be less at risk. Operation Pied Piper, which began on 1 September 1939, officially relocated more than 3.5 million. Further waves of official evacuation and re-evacuation occurred on the south and east coasts in June 1940, when a seaborne invasion was expected, and from affected cities after the Blitz began in September 1940. SOURCE: Wikipedia

[23] Battiscombe G. 1969. Queen Alexandra. London: Constable. p. 217. (Reference taken from Wikipedia.)

[24] *Bartleby, the Scrivener: A Story of Wall Street* is a short story by the American writer Herman Melville, first serialised anonymously in two parts in the November and December editions of Putnam's Magazine, and reprinted with minor textual alterations in his The Piazza Tales in 1856. SOURCE: Wikpedia

[25] Vendler, H, 1986 'Books: A Lifelong Poem Including History', *The New Yorker*, p. 81 Citation taken from Wikipedia.

[26] SOURCE: Wikipedia

[27] 'Bob Dylan, the Beat Generation, and Allen Ginsberg's America', The New Yorker. Available from: *http://www.newyorker.com/news/news-desk/bob-dylan-the-beat-generation-and-allen-ginsbergs-america*. Also quoted widely on the Internet in various publications.

[28] De Beauvoir. S. 1949 *Le Deuxieme Sexe*, Book 2, Part 4, Chapter 1: 'Childhood', p. 267

[29] Greer G. 1970 *The Female Eunuch*. Harper. Various editions. (Page 329, 1981 edition)

[30] Dworkin A. 1987 'Occupation/Collaboration', *Intercourse*. Basic Books; 20th Anniversary Ed edition (7 Nov. 2006) Page 175.

[31] Dworkin A. 1974 *Woman Hating*. Published by the Penguin Group worldwide. Page 184

[32] Dworkin A. 1974. Op. cit., 'Androgyny', Part 4.

[33] Dworkin A. 1974. Op. cit. Page 178

[34] Dworkin A. 1974. Op. cit., Page 180

[35] Dworkin A. 1974. Op. cit., Page 190

[36] John Stoltenberg, writer and editor who founded Men Against Pornography was the author of *Refusing to be a Man: Essays on Sex and Justice* (1990) and *The End of Manhood: A Book for Men of Conscience (1993)*

[37] Fahs, Breanne 2014. Valerie Solanas. The Feminist Press, p. 85, referenced in Wikipedia

[38] *Notes from the First Year* was produced in 1968, *Notes from the Second Year* in 1970, and *Notes from the Third Year* in 1971.

[39] Marx K., Engels F. (1848) The Communist Manifesto. Oxford: Oxford University Press, 1992. Chapter II. Proletarians and Communists. Available from: *https://www.marxists.org/archive/marx/works/1848/communist-manifesto/ch02.htm*

[40] Moore R. S. 2015 *Sex Trouble: Essays on Radical Feminism and the War Against Human Nature*, CreateSpace Independent Publishing Platform. Available from: http://theothermccain.com/2014/08/25/sex-trouble-feminism-mental-illness-and-the-pathetic-daughters-of-misfortune/

[41] Gilman, Charlotte Perkins, in *Feminist Theory* 2005 Eds. Kolmar and Bartkowski, eds. McGrawHil, Boston: P. 114. (Citation from Wikipedia.)

[42] Available from: *http://www.vfa.us/Jacqui%20Ceballos%20Bio.htm*

[43] My thanks go to Neil Lyndon for pointing to this and other material about Germaine Greer in his excellent book, *Sexual Impolitics: Heresies on sex, gender, and feminism.* Self-published. Available on Kindle. (Includes the original, uncensored text of his earlier book *No More Sex War: The Failures of Feminism*)

[44] Denton A. 2003 'Enough Rope' *ABC TV*, Retrieved 8 February 2007. (Source: Wikipedia)

[45] Lyndon, N. 2014. *Sexual Impolitics: heresies on sex, gender and feminism.* Amazon Digital Services, Inc.

[46] Available from: http://www.ljmaywatchwords.com/107744590

[47] Ginsberg L. 2000 'Ex-hubby fires back at feminist icon Betty,' *New York Post*, July 5, 2000. Reported in Wikipedia

[48] Available from: *http://www.theguardian.com/world/2006/feb/07/gender.bookscomment*

[49] *Encyclopaedia of Women's Social Reformers* (Vol 2.) p.p. 512-131 Ibid.

[50] *Encyclopaedia of Women's Social Reformers* (Vol 2.) Op. cit. p. 509

[51] *The Observer* Ibid.

[52] *Encyclopaedia of Women's Social Reformers* (Vol 2.) p. 509 Ibid.

[53] Professor Martin Pugh was Professor of British History at Newcastle University and Research Professor in History at Liverpool John Moores University. He is a Fellow of the Royal Historical Society, a member of the advisory panel of the BBC History Magazine, and the author of over twelve books on nineteenth- and twentieth-century history

[54] 'Diary reveals lesbian love trysts of suffragette leaders', *The Observer*, Sunday 11 June 2000

[55] *Purvis J. 2002* 'Pugh's book is full of errors' *Times Higher Education Supplement* 25 January. Purvis is professor of Women's and Gender History at the University of Portsmouth, and author of the book *Emmeline Pankhurst: A Biography.*

[56] *Encyclopaedia of Women's Social Reformers (Vol 2.)* Op. cit. p. 510.

[57] *Encyclopaedia of Women's Social Reformers (Vol 2.)* p. 509 Ibid.

[58] *Encyclopaedia of Women's Social Reformers (Vol 2.)* p. 511 Ibid.

[59] *Encyclopaedia of Women's Social Reformers (Vol 2.)* p.509 Ibid.

[60] Roger Fulford in the *Oxford Dictionary of National Biography*. Oxford University Press. Citation from Wikipedia.

[61] 'Make the personal, political' is a phrase widely attributed to Carol Hanisch, one of the early leaders in the Women's Liberation movement, but it was almost certainly coined by Shulamith Firestone, who was a co-editor, with Hanisch, of the early anthology of 1960s feminist writings entitled *Notes from (the First Year, the Second Year, and the Third Year): Women's Liberation*, passed around the movement 1970 in the US, which included a memo written by Hanisch, who uses the phrase. In 2006 Hamish gave a full explanation on her website, available from: *http://carolhanisch.org*

[62] 'Erin Pizzey on Feminism' *MWM Productions* 2011. SOURCE: YouTube

[63] 'Radfem Collective: Positively Revolting Women'. Available from: *https://web.archive.org/web/20150904155320/http://www.radfemcollective.org/news/2015/8/29/an-interview-with-julie-bindel*

[64] Hoff Sommers, C. 1994 *Who Stole Feminism?: How Women Have Betrayed Women*. New York: Simon & Schuster, 1994. p. 22. Footnote as follows: Sandra Lee Bartky, Femininity and Domination: Studies in the *Phenomenology of Oppression* (New York: Routledge, 1990), p. 50. Bartky is relying on the work of the feminist anthropologist Gayle Rubin, who was among the first to speak of the

'sex/gender system'.

[65] De Beauvoir. S. 1949 *Le Deuxieme Sexe,* Op. cit. p. 508

[66] Friedan. B. 1976 'A Dialogue with Simone de Beauvoir', *It Changed My Life: Writings on the Women's Movement.* Random House. New York. p.p. 311–12. (Cited in Wikipedia.)

[67] Lamblin B. 1994, *Mémoires d'une jeune fille dérangée.* Livre de Poche. Published in English as *A Disgraceful Affair.*

[68] Swaab D. F. (2014) *We Are Our Brains: A Neurobiography of the Brain, from the Womb to Alzheimer's.* Ed. Swaab DF. Spiegel & Grau, New York, NY, 2014

[69] Baron-Cohen S. (2003) *The Essential Difference: Men, Women and the Extreme Male Brain.* Penguin, London.

[70] Conellan J., Baren-Cohen S., Wheelright S., Batki A., Ahluwalia J. 2000 'Sex differences in neonatal social perception' in *Infant Behavior and Development 23* Elsevier Science Inc. p.p. 113-118

[71] Northrop, H.D. 1890 *Beautiful Gems of Thought and Sentiment,* The Colins-Patten Co., Boston, MA.

[72] 'An open letter to Suzanne Moore': Paris Lees responds to the furore surrounding an article in *The New Statesman* in which Moore quipped, 'women are expected to look like Brazilian trans women'. Available at: *www.divamag.co.uk* Sun, 13 Jan 2013

[73] Swaab D. F. 2014 *We Are Our Brains. Op. cit.* P. 78

[74] Donaldson M. 1993 *What Is Hegemonic Masculinity?* University of Wollongong

[75] R. Connell. 'Gender and Power: Society, the Person and Sexual Politics' (Sydney: Allen and Unwin. 1987), 107; Carrigan. Connell and Lee, 95. Cited in Donaldson M. Op. cit.

[76] Connell, 'Which Way is Up'; Connell. 'Gender and Power'; R. Connell, 'A Whole New World: Remaking Masculinity in the Context of the Environmental Movement', *Gender and Society* 4 (1990): 352-378: R. Connell. 'An Iron Man: The Body and Some Contradictions of Hegemonic Masculinity', in M. Messner and D. Sabo, editors, *Sport, Men and the Gender Order* (Champaign. Ill.: Human Kinetics Books, 1990): Connell, 'The State, Gender and Sexual Politics'; Carrigan, Connell and Lee, 86; R. Chapman. 'The Great Pretender: Variations in the New Man Theme' in R. Chapman and J.Rutherford. Eds.. *Male Order: Unwrapping Masculinity* (London: Lawrence and Wishart. 1988) 9-18; C. Cockburn. 'Masculinity, the Left and Feminism', in *Male Order.*103--329; P. Lichterman. 'Making a Politics of Masculinity', *Comparative Social Research* 11

(1989): 185-208; M. Messner 'The Meaning of Success: The Athletic Experience and the Development of Male Identity', in *The Making of Masculinities*:193-2 10; J. Rutherford. 'Who's That Man'?' in *Male Order*, 21-67. Cited in Donaldson M. Op. cit.

[77] Connell, 'Which Way is Up': 236, 255, 256. Cited in Donaldson M. Op. cit.

[78] Originally attributed to John Norris in 1707

[79] Kipling R. 1895. 'If you can hear the truth you've spoken twisted by knaves to make a trap for fools…' *IF*.

[80] Hoff Sommers, C. 1994 *Who Stole Feminism?: How Women Have Betrayed Women*, Simon & Schuster. New York.

[81] Hoff Sommers, C. 2000 *The War against Boys: How Misguided Feminism Is Harming Our Young Men*. Simon & Schuster. New York.

[82] Dr. Christina Hoff Sommers's lecture, 'Sex, Lies, and Feminism', was delivered on Wednesday, March 14, 2012, at the University of Toledo College of Law, as part of the Stranahan National Issues. Published on YouTube Aug 17, 2012. Available at: *http://youtu.be/fgpbDpXrEr4*

[83] Patai D. Koertge N. 2003 *Professing Feminism: Education and Indoctrination in Women's Studies*. Lexington Books; 2 Rev Ed.

[84] Hoff Sommers. C. 'Sex, Lies, and Feminism' Op. cit. P. 91

[85] Marx K., Engels F. 1848, 'Proletarians and Communists', *The Communist Manifesto*. Chapter II. Available at: *https://www.marxists.org/archive/marx/works/1848/communist-manifesto/ch02.htm*

[86] *Feminisms: A Reader*. Ed. Maggie Humm. First published in 1992 by Routledge

[87] Finn Mackay 2015 'The greatest threat to feminism? It's not just the patriarchy', *The Guardian*, 23rd March 2015.

[88] Charles Alexander Eastman, (born Hakadah and later named Ohíye S'a) was a Native American, writer, national lecturer, and reformer, educated at Boston University, who worked to improve the lives of youths, and founded thirty-two Native American chapters of the Young Men's Christian Association (YMCA). He also helped found the Boy Scouts of America, and is considered the first Native American author to write American history from the Native American point of view.

[89] Goldberg S. 1973 *The Inevitability of Patriarchy*. New York: William Morrow and Company.

[90] French, J. R. P., Jr., Raven, B. H. 1959. 'The Bases of Social Power', in *Studies in Social Power* D. Cartwright (Ed.) p.p. 150–167). Ann Arbor, MI: Institute for

Social Research.

[91] Proverbs 31:9-31 Lexham English Bible Translation

[92] Herodotus was an ancient Greek historian who was born in Halicarnassus, Caria (modern Bodrum, Turkey) in 484 BC and died in 425 BC

[93] Jones S. 2000 'Church for the New Millennium – What does the Bible say?' *Christianity + Renewal Magazine* March 2000 Edition. Ed. John Buckeridge. Published by CCP Ltd. London

[94] Deuteronomy 14:29. The Old Testament

[95] James 1:26-27. The New Testament

[96] 1 Timothy 5:16. The New Testament

[97] The word 'endow' is used in its verb form in the marriage service, and it means 'To pay for, provide for, subsidise, support financially'. It also means, 'To bestow', as in one who puts up the money to establish, found or set up an institute, which is the probable reason why marriage is commonly referred to as an institution.

[98] Schiffman L. 1998 (Ed.) *Texts and Traditions: A Source Reader for the Study of Second Temple and Rabbinic Judaism.*

[99] Reported in Bax E. B. 1908 'The Legal Subjection of Men', Twentieth century Press. Reprinted by New Age Press

[100] Bax B. E 1910 'Feminism and Female Suffrage', *New Age*, 30 May 1910, p. 88-89.

[101] In the US in the 1960s, a bank could require a husband to counter-sign a credit card application made by a married woman until The Equal Credit Opportunity Act 1974 in the US made it illegal to refuse to issue a credit card to a woman based on her sex.

[102] Bentham, J. 1843 'Radical parliamentary reform: Elementary arrangements in this edition of it - their necessity', *The Works of Jeremy Bentham*, Vol 3, 'Section V: Remedy in Detail: Usury', *Political Economy, Equity, Parliamentary Reform.*

[103] Bradford. R. 2014 'Universal Suffrage - The True History'. *Available* from: http://rickbradford.co.uk/UniversalSuffrage.pdf

[104] Mill J. S. 1869 *The Subjection of Women*. Mill. Longmans, Green, Reader, and Dyer. London. Available from: Project Gutenburg. *www.gutenburg.net*

[105] Mill J. S. 1859 *On Liberty,* The Walter Scott Publishing Co., Ltd. London and Felling-on-Tyne, New York and Melbourne. With an introduction by W. L. Courtney, LL.D.in 1901. Produced by Curtis Weyant, Martin Pettit and the

Online Distributed Proofreading Team. Available at: *http://www.pgdp.net*

[106] Bradford. N. 2014 'Universal Suffrage - The True History'. Op. cit.

[107] In *Paperspast*, an online resource of the national library of New Zealand. Available at: http://paperspast.natlib.govt.nz/cgi-bin/paperspast?a=d&d=EP19160605.2.16

[108] The White Feather campaign was originated by Admiral Charles Fitzgerald, who founded the Order of the White Feather, an organisation aimed to shame men into enlisting in the British Army by persuading women to present them with a white feather if they were not wearing a uniform. It was joined with alacrity by prominent feminists and suffragettes of the time, such as Emmeline Pankhurst and her daughter Christabel, who in addition lobbied to institute involuntary universal draft, which included men who lacked the right to vote because they were too young, or were not property owners. SOURCE: Wikipedia

[109] Reagan, G. 1992. *Military Anecdotes* p. 63 Guiness Publishing. (Story recounted. and author cited, in Wikipedia.)

[110] Regan 1992 Ibid..

[111] Available from: *http://www.marxists.org/archive/bax/1911/02/suffrage-symposium.htm*

[112] Adams J. 2005 *The Rule of the Father: patriarchy and Patrimonialism in Early Modern Europe.* Russell Sage Foundation. New York

[113] Weber M. 1922 *Wirtschaft und Gesellschaft* (Economy and Society), published posthumously.

[114] Hitler A. 1925 *Mein Kampf.* Vol 1, Ch X(1)

[115] *Hitler as His Associates Know Him* (OSS report, p.51) Cited in Wikipedia

[116] Professor Christina Hoff Sommers's talk to the Law Faculty of Toledo University, March 14, 2012. Available on YouTube: *https://youtu.be/fgpbDpXrEr4*

[117] Marx K. and Engels F. 1848 *The Communist Manifesto*

[118] Meyer A. G. 1997 'Marxism and the Women's Movement', *Women in Russia.* Editors: Dorothy Atkinson, Alexander Dallin, Gail Warshofsky Lapidus. Stanford University Press.

[119] Tristram Hunt is on of Britain's leading young historians. Educated at Cambridge and Chicago universities, he lectures in British history at Queen Mary, University of London, and is the author of *Building Jerusalem: The Rise and Fall of the Victorian City* and of *The Frock-Coated Communist: The Revolutionary Life*

of *Friedrich Engels.*

[120] Engels F. 1884 *The Origin of the Family, Private Property and the State*, 2010 editiion by Penguin Classics London.

[121] Engels was the wealthier of the two and he supported Marx financially most of his life.

[122] Harman C. 1994 'Engels and The Origins of Human Society', in *International Socialism 65*: Winter 1994, p. 84 Available from *http://www.marxists.org/archive/harman/1994/xx/engels.htm*

[123] We see this idea reflected in Aristophanes' play *Lysistrata* performed in Athens in 411BCE that tells the story of one woman's mission to end the Peloponnesian war by persuading the women of Athens to withhold sexual privileges from their husbands and lovers, as a means of forcing them to negotiate a peace settlement, which backfired when it inflamed a battle between the sexes in Athenian society and weakened it enormously. Perhaps this is a lesson we need to draw on when considering the socially divisive impact of feminism today?

[124] Goldberg S. 1973 *The Inevitability of Patriarchy*. Op. cit.

[125] Goldstein, L 1982. 'Early Feminist Themes in French Utopian Socialism: The St.-Simonians and Fourier', *Journal of the History of Ideas*, vol.43, No. 1.

[126] Greer G. 1970 *The Female Eunuch*. Harper. Various editions. (Page 329 1981 edition)

[127] Bax E. B.: 1912 *Problems of Mind and Morals* (Chap.8). Originally published by Grant Richards, London 1912. Reprinted by Grant Richards, London 1920

[128] SOURCE: Wikipedia

[129] Kellner D. 1998 'Erich Fromm, Feminism, and the Frankfurt School'. *Illuminations: The Critical Theory* Website. University of Texas at Austin.

[130] According to Freud, the superego acts to perfect and civilise our behaviour. It works to suppress all unacceptable urges of the id (which strives for immediate gratification of all desires, wants, and needs) and struggles to make the ego (the component of personality that is responsible for dealing with reality) act upon idealistic standards rather than upon realistic principles.

[131] Quoted in Kellner Op cit.

[132] For the sake of balance, he finishes this sentence by saying, '... though women can ridicule men and even make them impotent'.

[133] Quoted in Kellner Op. cit.

[134] Quoted in Kellner Op cit.

[135] Quoted in Kellner Op cit.

[136] Kellner Op cit.

[137] Kellner Op cit.

[138] 'The Everyday Sexism Project exists to catalogue instances of sexism experienced by women on a day to day basis. They might be serious or minor, outrageously offensive or so niggling and normalised that you don't even feel able to protest…By sharing your story you're showing the world that sexism does exist, it is faced by women everyday and it is a valid problem to discuss.' Available from: *http://everydaysexism.com/*

[139] Remarks at NBER *Conference on Diversifying the Science & Engineering Workforce*, Lawrence H. Summers, Cambridge, Mass., January 14, 2005. Archived at *The Wayback Machine*.

[140] Hoff Sommers C. 1994 *Who Stole Feminism?* Op.cit.

[141] Hoff Sommers C. 1994 *Who Stole Feminism?* Op. cit.

[142] 'Erin Pizzey on Feminism' *MWM Productions 2011*. Available from YouTube: *https://youtu.be/Ix5-jqQYU1M*

[143] 'Erin Pizzey on Feminism' *MWM Productions* 2011 Ibid.

[144] 'Erin Pizzey on Feminism' *MWM Productions* 2011 Ibid.

[145] Patai D. Koertge N. 2003 *Professing Feminism: Education and Indoctrination in Women's Studies*. Lexington Books; 2nd Rev. Ed.

[146] 'Why we can "see" the house that looks like Hitler'. Vaughan Bell. *The Guardian* 17 November 2013. Available at: *http://www.theguardian.com/science/2013/nov/17/why-we-see-hitler-house*

[147] Poulsen B. 2012 'Being Amused by Apophenia: Can we find pleasure and amusement in faulty reasoning?' in Reality Play, *Psychology Today*. July 31, 2012. Available at: *http://www.psychologytoday.com/blog/reality-play/201207/being-amused-apophenia*

[148] Conrad K. 1958 *Die beginnende Schizophrenie. Versuch einer Gestaltanalyse des Wahns* (in German). Stuttgart: Georg Thieme Verlag.

[149] Shermer, M. 2011. *The Believing Brain: From Ghosts and Gods to Politics and Conspiracies - How We Construct Beliefs and Reinforce Them as Truths*. Times Books; 1St Edition (May 24, 2011)

[150] Mike Buchanan leads the political party Justice for Men & Boys (and the women who love them) *http://j4mb.org.uk* and also leads two campaigns, the

Anti-Feminism League *http://fightingfeminism.wordpress.com* and Campaign for Merit in Business *http://c4mb.wordpress.com* – 'C4MB'. He is the author of *David and Goliatha: David Cameron – heir to Harman?* (2010), *The Glass Ceiling Delusion: the real reasons more women don't reach senior positions* (2011), and *Feminism: the ugly truth* (2012).

[151] Available at: https://c4mb.wordpress.com/2013/03/12/heather-mcgregor-corrects-the-misleading-statement-she-made-to-a-house-of-commons-inquiry/

[152] GRIFFIN, E. 1997, *A First Look at Communication Theory* (3rd ed.). New York: McGraw-Hill. Cited in Young D. 1998, *Bormann's Symbolic Convergence Theory*. Comm 3210: Human Communication Theory University of Colorado at Boulder. Spring 1998

[153] Available at: *http://youtu.be/Z8aHocOPGMQ*, or Google 'Town Bloody Hall'.

[154] Browne A. 2006 *The Retreat of Reason*. Civitas. London

[155] De Spinoza B 1670 *A Theological-Political Treatise*. Chapter XX

[156] Lind W. S. 1998 'The Origins of Political Correctness', address to the 13th Accuracy in Academia conference, George Washington University, 10th July 1998. Cited in Brown B, *The Retreat of Reason*.

[157] Bernstein R. 1990, 'The rising hegemony of the politically correct', *New York Times*, 29th October 1990. Cited in Brown B, *The Retreat of Reason*.

[158] Weyrich P. 1999, 'Open letter from Free Congress Foundations, Sixteenth February 1999', reported in the *Washington Post*, 18th February 1999, in an article entitled, 'Key Conservative Surrenders in Culture War'. Cited in Brown B, *The Retreat of Reason*.

[159] Berne. E. 1964 *Games People Play: The Psychology of Human Relationships*. Penguin. London. 'Games People Play' spent over 100 weeks in the New York Times Best Sellers list and was the best selling non-fiction book in the 1960s. Since its first publication, it has sold over 5,000,000 copies worldwide and continues to sell tens of thousands of copies annually. It is currently available in 20 languages.

[160] At the time of these events, Charlotte Proudman was an associate tenant at the Chambers of Michael Mansfield QC, a leading human rights lawyer, although on sabbatical from practice in order to complete a PhD in Political Sociology at the University of Cambridge. She is listed as being a member of the Society of Labour Lawyers and the Fabian Society.

[161] An uncensored video of this event can be viewed on YouTube under the title: *'Abortistas atacan a católicos que defendían la Catedral de San Juan'*.

[162] Taken to mean 'transvestites'

[163] Available at: *http://phenomenologicalpsychology.com/2010/01/in-defense-of-hysteria/*

[164] Orwell G. 1949, *Nineteen Eighty-Four*. The central character, Winston Smith, works in the 'Ministry of Truth', re-writing history according to 'The Party's' current interpretation of what is truth'.

[165] Tasca C., Rapetti M., Carta M. G., Fadda B. 2012 'Women And Hysteria In The History Of Mental Health' *Clin Pract Epidemiol Ment Health. 2012; 8: 110–119*. Published online 2012 October 19. doi: 10.2174/1745017901208010110

[166] The *Kahun Papyri* (KP) is a collection of ancient Egyptian texts discussing administrative, mathematical and medical topics. Their many fragments were discovered by Flinders Petrie in 1889 and are kept at the University College London. This collection is one of the largest ever found. Most of the texts are dated to c. 1825 BC, to the reign of Amenemhat III. In general the collection spans the Middle Kingdom of Egypt. SOURCE: Wikipedia

[167] The *Ebers Papyrus*, also known as *Papyrus Ebers*, is an Egyptian medical papyrus of herbal knowledge dating to c. 1550 BC. Among the oldest and most important medical papyri of ancient Egypt, it was purchased at Luxor (Thebes) in the winter of 1873–74 by Georg Ebers. It is currently kept at the library of the University of Leipzig, in Germany. SOURCE: Wikipedia

[168] Tasca et al. Ibid..

[169] Several legends surround the hellebore; in witchcraft it is believed to have ties to summoning demons. Helleborus niger is commonly called the Christmas rose, due to an old legend that it sprouted in the snow from the tears of a young girl who had no gift to give the Christ child in Bethlehem. In Greek mythology, Melampus of Pylos used hellebore to save the daughters of the king of Argos from a madness, induced by Dionysus, that caused them to run naked through the city, crying, weeping, and screaming. SOURCE: Wikipedia

[170] Cherie Blair: 'It's always been about women and girls'; Jane Martinson, *The Guardian*, Wednesday 19 December 2012

[171] *The Mail Online* (May 2011 edition)

[172] *The Equality Act* 2010 also provided for employers to discriminate in favour of female and ethnic minority applicants for jobs.

[173] In October 1915 the WSPU changed its newspaper's name from *The Suffragette* to *Britannia* with a new slogan: 'For King, for Country, for Freedom'.

[174] Kirby J. (2006), *The Nationalisation of Childhood*, Centre for Policy Studies. London. Available from: http://www.jillkirby.org/wp-content/uploads/

2011/11/the-nationalisation-of-childhood.pdf

[175] *Spiked Online*, 4 March 2013. *Spiked* is a British Internet magazine that focusses on politics, culture and society from a humanist and libertarian viewpoint, although it is worth bearing in mind that it is effectively an online resurrection of *Marxism Today*, a publication that was put out of business through losing a libel law suit.

[176] Available from: *http://www.bbc.co.uk/editorialguidelines/guidelines/*

[177] Years ago, the story goes, when people travelled in Pullman railway sleeping cars, a passenger found a bed bug in his berth. He wrote a letter to George M. Pullman, president of *Pullman's Palace Car Company*, informing him of this unhappy fact. By return, he received the following: 'The company has never heard of such a thing and as a result of your experience, all the sleeping cars are being pulled off the line and fumigated. The Pullman's Palace Car Company is committed to providing its customers with the highest level of service, and it will spare no expense in meeting that goal. Thank you for writing and if you ever have a similar problem, or any problem, do not hesitate to write to me again.' However, enclosed with this letter, by accident, was the passenger's original letter to Pullman, across the bottom of which the president had written a note to his secretary, 'Send this S.O.B. the standard bedbug letter!'

[178] Hakim C. 2006, 'Women, careers, and work-life preferences', *British Journal of Guidance and Counselling*, Vol. 34, No. 3, August 2006/ Page 280

[179] An established church is one that is officially endorsed by a state. It embodies the expression of the official religion of the state although it does not necessarily come under its control. The official sponsoring of religious cults is an ancient one, reaching into prehistory. The first recorded state-sponsored church was the *Armenian Apostolic Church*, founded in 301 CE.

[180] Karl Marx is often reported as saying, 'Religion is the opiate of the masses,' but the phrase originally used was *'Die Religion ... ist das Opium des Volkes'* in the 1844 introduction to his proposed work *A Contribution to the Critique of Hegel's Philosophy of Right*. He never completed it, but the introduction was published in 1844 in Marx's own journal *Deutsch-Französische Jahrbücher* (SOURCE: Wikipedia)

[181] 'Galatians' Chapter 3. V. 26-28 The New Testament

[182] TABLE 8: 'Confirmations'. *Church Statistics 2010/11: Parochial attendance, membership and finance statistics together with statistics of licensed ministers for the Church of England,* January to December. Archbishops' Council Research and Statistics,

Church House, Great Smith Street, London SW1P 3AZ

[183] Walter, T. 1990 'Why are Most Churchgoers Women? A Literature Review' *Vox Evangelica* 20 (1990): p.p. 73-90

[184] From the Afrikaans word laager, probably from German lager, camp, lair, from Middle High German leger, bed, lair, from Old High German legar; see legh- in Indo-European roots

[185] 'Divorces in England and Wales 2011', Statistical Bulletin, Office for National Statistics, United Kingdom. Issued 20th December 2012.

[186] 'Number of Divorces, Age at Divorce and Marital Status before Marriage'. 'Divorces in England and Wales 2011'. Statistical Bulletin, Office for National Statistics, United Kingdom. Available from: *http://www.ons.gov.uk/ons/search/ index.html?newquery=Number+of+divorces%2C+age+at+divorce+and+marital+status +before+marriage*

[187] Op cit.

[188] Op cit.

[189] Op cit.

[190] O'Neil. R. 2002, *Experiments in Living: the fatherless family*. CIVITAS – The Institute for the Study of Civil Society, London.

[191] Langford N. *An Exercise in Absolute Futility: Chapter One. Available from:* http://exinjuria.wordpress.com

[192] Reported by Angela Harrison, Social affairs correspondent for BBC News, on 13th June 2013

[193] Sir Paul Coleridge speaking at the launch of *UK Marriage Week* at the House of Commons, London, on 6th February 2012. Refers to 3.8M children caught up in the family justice system out of a total of around 12M children under 17 in Britain at that time. Available from: *http://www.marriagefoundation.org.uk/Web/ News/News.aspx?news=113&RedirectUrl=~/Web/Search/Default.aspx?Search=3.8m %20children*

[194] Estimated by finding the ratio of the 5.3 million population of Scotland, plus the 1.8 million population of Northern Ireland, taken from the national census in 2012, to the overall UK population of 63.7 million, i.e., 11.2 per cent, rounded ((7.1/63.7) x 100) per cent. Thus the estimated number of children in the family courts in England and Wales (excluding Scotland and Northern Ireland) is 4 million less 11.2 per cent, which equates to circa 3.55 million.

[195] From the *Common Book of Prayer Solemnization of Matrimony*, Church of England.

[196] 'Suicides in the United Kingdom 2013 Registrations.' Office for National Statistics Statistical Bulletin, February 2015.

[197] Ibid.

[198] Op cit.

[199] Mears M. 2005, *Institutional Injustice: The Family Courts at Work*. Civitas: Institute for the Study of Civil Society, London.

[200] The extreme left-wing miners' leader during their strike between 1984-85

[201] Sir James Lawrence Munby (b. 1948 -) became Britain's most senior family judge on 11th January 2013, having been appointed as President of the Family Division of the High Court of England and Wales.

[202] Reproduced verbatim under the Open Parliament Licence v1.0

[203] According to Wikpedia, Seema Mulhotra was the special adviser to Harriet Harman during her tenure as Leader of the Labour Party.

[204] According to her official web site, Kate Green is a member of *The Fawcett Society*, one of the most active organisations in Britain today, advancing a strident feminist apologetic.

[205] Chapman is Vice Chair of the Blairite organisation, 'Progress'.

[206] For an excellent, in-depth discussion of the entire sentencing disparity issue, go to William Collins' blog. Available from: *http://mra-uk.co.uk/?p=215*

[207] Broadcast Monday 21st October 2013 at 07.34 on BBC Radio 4.

[208] Gaming the system (also referred to as gaming the rules, bending the rules, abusing the system, cheating the system, milking the system, playing the system, or working the system) can be defined as using the rules and procedures meant to protect a system in order, instead, to manipulate the system for a desired outcome. Source: Wikipedia. Available at: *https://en.wikipedia.org/wiki/Gaming_the_system#cite_note-1*

[209] Mc Curry J. 2009. Available from: http://www.theguardian.com/world/2009/dec/27/japan-grass-eaters-salaryman-macho

[210] Tauris I. B. 2007, *Southampton: Gateway to the British Empire*. Ed. Miles Taylor.

[211] Smith H. 2013, *Men on Strike*. Encounter Books, USA

[212] Lowry R. 2012, 'Dude, Where's My Lifeboat?' In *The Italian cruise-ship disaster, another death knell for the age of chivalry*. Available from: http://www.nationalreview.com/article/288253/dude-wheres-my-lifeboat-rich-lowry

[213] Crittenden M. 1999 *What our mother's didn't tell us: why happiness eludes the modern woman*. Simon & Schuster, 1999, Touchstone 2000

[214] Smith H. 2013, *Men on Strike*. Encounter Books, USA. Helen Smith refers to this in her book *Men on Strike*, in which she observes that men are sensing that American society has become anti-male and they are consciously and unconsciously going on strike: dropping out of college, leaving the workforce and avoiding marriage and fatherhood at alarming rates.

[215] Professor Christina Hoff Sommers's talk to the law faculty of Toledo University March 14, 2012. Op. cit.

[216] Women in the UK typically marry for the first time at age 29 according to the UK Office for National Statistics, available from: *http:// webarchive.nationalarchives.gov.uk/20160105160709/http://www.ons.gov.uk/ons/ dcp171778_315549.pdf*. However, that appears to be rising - to 33,8 years - according to UK Office for National Statistics *Marriages in England and Wales (Provisional)*, 2011 available from: See also the *Daily Telegraph* article, 'Average age for women to marry hits 30 for first time', available from: *http:// www.telegraph.co.uk/news/8415852/Average-age-for-women-to-marry-hits-30-for-first-time.html*

[217] Divorces in England and Wales 2011

[218] 'Divorces in England and Wales 2011'. *UK Office for National Statistics Statistical Bulletin 2011*. Available at: *http://webarchive.nationalarchives.gov.uk/ 20160105160709/http://www.ons.gov.uk/ons/dcp171778_291750.pdf*

[219] 'Divorces in England and Wales: Number of Divorces, Age at Divorce and Marital Status before Marriage'. *UK Office for National Statistics*. Available at: *https://www.ons.gov.uk/peoplepopulationandcommunity/birthsdeathsandmarriages/ divorce/*

[220] 'Divorces in England and Wales: Number of Divorces, Age at Divorce and Marital Status before Marriage'. *UK Office for National Statistics*. Op. cit.

[221] Interpolating the ONS data for domestic homicide back to 2002, from 2013, we find that 270,000 or so women married in 2002 and that 76 women were killed by their husbands, partners etc. 11 years later in 2013.

[222] Sheryl Sandberg wrote the book *Lean In: Women, Work, and the Will to Lead*. Sandberg was the chief operating officer of *Facebook* and ranked on Fortune's list of the '50 Most Powerful Women in Business', and as one of *Time's* '100 Most Influential People in the World'. In 2010, she gave a TED Talk that has been viewed more than 2,000,000 times, in which she argued that women unintentionally hold themselves back in their careers and she encouraged them to 'sit at the table,' and seek challenges, take risks, and pursue their goals with

gusto.

[223] Lionel Tiger in his book *The Decline of Males* describes the so-called 'Welfare Queen', that icon of the modern welfare state, who keeps having children by different men but seeks support from the state – he coins the term 'bureaugamy' since she is really married to the state and its welfare bureaucracy.

[224] French M. (1977) *The Women's Room*. Book 5. Chapter 19

[225] BBC Woman's Hour. Monday 21st October 2013

[226] In the United Kingdom, it is a criminal offence not to pay the broadcast licence fee, punishable by a fine, which might lead to imprisonment if it is not paid. According to the campaign created by Caroline Levesque-Barlett, available from: *https://you.38degrees.org.uk/petitions/end-the-bbc-licence-fee.* in 2014 the BBC sent 52.8 million letters chasing alleged evaders, following them up with 3.8 million visits by TV licence enforcement officers. In 2012, more than 3,000 people were summoned to appear at magistrates' courts, accused of watching television without a licence, and licence fee evasion makes up around one ninth of all cases prosecuted in magistrate courts. Of the 204,018 prosecutions (or out of court disposals) in 2014, as many as 24,025 were unsuccessful, but 39 people were actually imprisoned in England and Wales, for an average of 20 days each.

[227] 'CCTV Examined after Campus Rape', 29th September 2009. *BBC News* website. Available from: http://www.nus.org.uk/Global/ NUS_hidden_marks_report_2nd_edition_web.pdf

[228] Kitchens C. 2013, 'The Rape "Epidemic" Doesn't Actually Exist', October 24, 2013. Available at: *http://USNews.com*

[229] *Overview of Sexual Offending in England and Wales.* Ministry of Justice, Home Office & the Office for National Statistics Statistical bulletin. Published 10 January 2013.

[230] A minimum of 1,000 interviewees in each police region were statistically selected as being demographically representative of the population as a whole, and that selection was statistically weighted to adjust for possible non-response bias.

[231] *Justice for Men and Boys (and the women who love them)* website. Available from: https://j4mb.wordpress.com/2015/01/28/a-renewed-call-for-vera-bairds-resignation-the-ideologically-driven-poster-campaign-cost-taxpayers-15729/

[232] Available from: https://j4mb.files.wordpress.com/2015/01/150102-vera-baird-challenge-final-v2.pdf

[233] Common Assault has been recognised in the common law of England from time immemorial and is now enshrined in the UK *Criminal Justice Act* 1988 (s. 39). An offence of 'common assault' is committed when a person either assaults another person or commits a battery. An assault is committed when a person intentionally or recklessly causes another to apprehend the immediate infliction of unlawful force. A battery is committed when a person intentionally and recklessly applies unlawful force to another. SOURCE: UK Crown Prosecution Service.

[234] Reported in the Daily Mail on 7th January 2015. Available from: http://www.dailymail.co.uk/wires/pa/article-2898550/No-action-against-rape-claim-MP.html#ixzz3SST9MiYC

[235] Arnot C. 'Jennifer Temkin: Women's advocate'. *The Guardian*. Tuesday 5 December 2006

[236] SOURCE: *The City of London Law School*, City University, London web site.

[237] The group also included representatives of the Campaign to End Rape, and RAPECRISIS.

[238] Westmarland N. 2004, *Rape Law Reform in England and Wales*, Working Paper No. 7, School for Policy Studies. University of Bath. Available from: *http://nicolewestmarland.pbworks.com/f/Rape+Law+Reform+in+England+and+Wales+-+Westmarland+2004.pdf*

[239] In a *Daily Telegraph* article from 20th January 2015, entitled 'Sexual assault: Our universities are a national embarrassment', Westmarland is quoted as follows: 'The criminal process can take months. If universities refuse to investigate or take action during this time, then the victim is forced to live and study alongside their attacker… Our students cannot be left to study in a culture of fear and misogyny. Due process just takes too damn long - much easier just to find the student guilty as charged and kick him out, right?' Available from: *http://www.telegraph.co.uk/women/womens-life/11354771/Sexual-assault-Our-univeristies-are-a-national-embarrassment.html*

[240] Westmarland N. op cit. p. 5

[241] Reece H. 2013 'Rape Myths: Is Elite Opinion Right and Popular Opinion Wrong?' *Oxford Journal of Legal Studies*, (2013), pp. 1–29

[242] Reece Op cit. p.p. 7-8

[243] A video of the entire event is available online from The London School of Economics and Political Science, web site here: *http://www.lse.ac.uk/newsAndMedia/videoAndAudio/channels/publicLecturesAndEvents/player.aspx?*

id=2081 Or Google 'Is Rape Different?'

[244] Krahe B and Berger A, 2009, 'A Social-Cognitive Perspective on Attrition Rates in Sexual Assault Cases' in ME Oswald, S Bieneck and J Hupfeld-Heinemann (eds), *Social Psychology of Punishment and Crime* (Wiley-Blackwell 2009): Cited in Reece, *op. cit.*

[245] Reece Op. cit., Page 9

[246] Gerger, H., Kley, H., Bohner G., Siebler, F. 2007. 'The Acceptance of Modern Myths About Sexual Aggression (AMMSA) scale'. *Development and validation in German and English. Aggressive Behavior*, 33, 422-440. The AMMSA is a measure of rape myth acceptance (RMA)

[247] The site is designed to be a repository for instruments that are used to collect data from across the social sciences. Available from: http://www.midss.org/content/acceptance-modern-myths-about-sexual-aggression-ammsa-scale

[248] A logical fallacy is a mistake combined with an error in reasoning. The idea goes back to Aristotle, the first formal logician who, in the 4th century BCE, codified the rules of correct thinking and catalogued the errors.

[249] In fact, Afzal is being technically correct, as under *The Sexual Offences Act* 2003, rape can now only be by a penis - women who force men to penetrate them, which is rape by any measure, are not criminalised under the present law

[250] 'These bundles of charges pose a real danger: William Roache was cleared, but gathering similar allegations into one prosecution will bring miscarriages of justice'. Daniel Finkelstein. 'Opinion'. *The Times*, London. 12th February 2014. Page 25

[251] Gibbs N. 2001, 'Cover Stories Behavior: When Is It RAPE?' *Time Magazine* Sunday, June 24, 2001. Available from: http://content.time.com/time/magazine/article/0,9171,1101910603-157165,00.html

[252] Allen J., Walby S., 'Domestic violence, sexual assault and stalking: Findings from the British Crime Survey'. *Home Office Research Study 276*. Home Office Research, Development and Statistics Directorate March 2004. Op. cit. pp 51-53

[253] Ministry of Justice, Home Office, and Office for National Statistics Statistical Bulletin *An Overview of Sexual Offending in England and Wales. Chapter 1: Executive Summary*. Page 6.

[254] Specifically, Harman had been leading a campaign against domestic violence since 2001, which resulted in The Domestic Violence Crime and Victims Act

2004 and a nationwide team of specialist prosecutors to ensure more effective prosecutions for domestic violence, plus a network of 60 specialist domestic violence courts across the land. One of the most controversial aspects of The Domestic Violence Crime and Victims Act 2004 is that, for the first time in centuries, bailiffs were empowered to forcibly enter private homes, overturning a fundamental principle of British life that, 'An Englishman's home is his castle,' confirmed by Semayne's Case of 1604 in which it was held that, '…the house of every one is to him as his castle and fortress, as well for his defence against injury and violence as for his repose'. William Blackstone in the eighteenth century said of the principle: 'For this reason no doors can in general be broken open to execute any civil process; though, in criminal cases, the public safety supersedes the private. Hence also in part arises the animadversion of the law upon eaves-droppers, nuisancers, and incendiaries: and to this principle it must be assigned, that a man may assemble people together lawfully without danger of raising a riot, rout, or unlawful assembly, in order to protect and defend his house; which he is not permitted to do in any other case'.

[255] Op. cit. Page 54

[256] 'Equal Pay: Where Next? A report of the discussions and conclusions from the 2010 Equal Pay conference, marking the 40th anniversary of the Equal Pay Act.' Available from: *www.fawcettsociety.org.uk*

[257] A YouTube video of the TV advertisement is available from: https://www.youtube.com/watch?v=ayILjfYs7xw&feature=player_embedded

[258] 'An Analysis of the Reasons for the Disparity in Wages Between Men and Women - Final Report'. Prepared for the U.S. Department of Labor Employment Standards Administration 200 Constitution Avenue N.W. Washington, DC 20210, by *CONSAD Research Corporation* 211 North Whitfield Street Pittsburgh, PA 15206. Under Contract Number GS-23F-02598 Task Order 2, Subtask 2B. January 12, 2009

[259] Twain M 1906, *Chapters from My Autobiography, North American Review*. Project Gutenberg. Retrieved 2007-05-23: Cited in Wikipedia

[260] 'Annual Survey of Hours and Earnings', *Office for National Statistics, Statistical Bulletin, 2009*, 12th November 2009.

[261] Wardrop M. 2012, 'Young women now earning more than men: Women in their 20s are now earning more than men of the same age, research indicates', *The Telegraph*. 3rd October 2011. Available from:

http://www.telegraph.co.uk/news/uknews/8803019/Young-women-now-earning-more-than-men.html

See also: Hardman I. 2014, 'Save the male! Britain's crisis of masculinity: It's not just that women are doing better. Men, on all sorts of measures, are beginning to fall behind'. *The Spectator*, 3rd May 2014. Available from: http://www.spectator.co.uk/features/9197481/the-descent-of-man/

[262] Weber M. 1922, *Wirtschaft und Gesellschaft* (Economy and Society), first published posthumously in 1922

[263] 'The changing labour market: delivering for women, delivering for growth', *The Fawcett Society*, April 2013 Page 34. Available from: http://www.fawcettsociety.org.uk/wp-content/uploads/2013/04/Fawcett-The-changing-labour-market.pdf

[264] Charles Handy's model of 'the inverted doughnut' comes from his book, *The Empty Raincoat*, and is a representation of how societies, organisations, and even individuals need to manage themselves in times of change. Unlike a real doughnut where the space is in the centre and the solid material around it, the inverted doughnut has the material at the core and the empty space around it. The core represents the essential requirements of the job while the space is the opportunity for initiative and creativity, going beyond what must be done, adding extra value. This model can be applied to relationships, jobs, change, products, and organisations themselves. SOURCE: http://www.managetrainlearn.com/page/charles-handy

[265] 'Annual Survey of Hours and Earnings (SOC 2000)' *Office for National Statistics Statistical Bulletin 2011*, issued 23rd November 2011. Page 31.

[266] Hakim C. 2006, 'Women, Careers, and Work-life Preferences', *British Journal of Guidance and Counselling*, Vol. 34, No. 3, August 2006, Op cit.

[267] 'Sickness and Absence in the Labour Market, April 2012'. *Office for National Statistics*, issued 15th May 2012

[268] 'Female doctors put NHS under "tremendous burden" because they get married, have children and want to work part-time.' Sophie Borland and Matt Chorley. *MailOnline*. 5 June 2013. Available from: *http://www.dailymail.co.uk/news/article-2336235/Female-doctors-NHS-tremendous-burden-married-children-want-work-time.html*

[269] 'Part-Time Women Doctors ARE a Real Problem'. Melanie Phillips. *Daily Mail*. 9th June 2013. Available from: http://www.dailymail.co.uk/debate/article-2338607/MELANIE-PHILLIPS-Part-time-women-doctors-ARE-real-

problem-Why-sexist-say-so.html

²⁷⁰ Bertrand M., Goldin C., Katz L. F. 2009 'Dynamics of the Gender Gap for Young Professionals in the Financial and Corporate Sectors'. *The National Bureau of Economic Research*, revised December 2009. Available from: *http://www.nber.org/papers/w14681*

²⁷¹ An MBA is the top qualification for a career in business and it equips anyone with it to look forward to high earnings and success in their subsequent careers, and it is arguably one of the most empowering, equalising qualification any woman can obtain.

²⁷² Hakim C. 2006 'Women, careers, and work-life preferences'. *British Journal of Guidance and Counselling, v*ol. 34, no. 3, August 2006

²⁷³ Hakim C. 2006, Op cit. Page 290

²⁷⁴ Hakim C. 2006, 'Women, careers, and work-life preferences'. Op cit.

²⁷⁵ Hakim 2006. Op cit.

²⁷⁶ Arora R. 2000. *Encyclopaedic Dictionary of Organization Behaviour*, vol 2, p. 388. Sarup and Sons. New Delhi

²⁷⁷ The All Party Parliamentary Group (APPG) for Women in Parliament was set up in 2010 and, predictably, of its 15 members, only two were men. Available from: http://appgimprovingParliamentreport.co.uk/download/APPG-Women-In-Parliament-Report-2014.pdf

²⁷⁸ My thanks to the Campaign for Merit in Business for having compiled these studies and making them available from: *https://c4mb.wordpress.com/improving-gender-diversity-on-boards-leads-to-a-decline-in-corporate-performance-the-evidence/*

²⁷⁹ Ahern, Kenneth R. and Dittmar, Amy K., 'The Changing of the Boards: The Impact on Firm Valuation of Mandated Female Board Representation' May 20, 2011 *Quarterly Journal of Economics*, 2012, vol. 127(1): 137-197. Available from SSRN: *http://ssrn.com/abstract=1364470*   or *http://dx.doi.org/10.2139/ssrn.1364470*

²⁸⁰ Bøhren, Øyvind and Strøm, R. Øystein, 'Governance and Politics: Regulating Independence and Diversity in the Board Room', *Journal of Business Finance & Accounting*, vol. 37, issue 9-10, pp. 1281-1308, 2010. Available from SSRN: *http://ssrn.com/abstract=1733385*   or *http://dx.doi.org/10.1111/j.1468-5957.2010.02222.x*

²⁸¹ Matsa, David A. and Miller, Amalia R., 'A Female Style in Corporate Leadership? Evidence from Quotas' (December 13, 2012). *American Economic Journal: Applied Economics, Forthcoming*. Available from SSRN:*http://ssrn.com/*

abstract=1636047 or *http://dx.doi.org/10.2139/ssrn.1636047*

[282] Adams, Renee B. and Ferreira, Daniel, 'Women in the Boardroom and Their Impact on Governance and Performance' (October 22, 2008). Available from SSRN: *http://ssrn.com/abstract=1107721* or *http://dx.doi.org/10.2139/ssrn.1107721*

[283] Berger A. N., Kick T., Scheack K, 'Executive board composition and risk taking. Discussion Paper. No. 032012', *Deutche Budesbank Editorial Board*: Klaus Dullman, Frank Heid, Heinz Herrmann. Available at: *http://www.econstor.eu/bitstream/10419/56024/1/688561233.pdf*

[284] Britton J, Shephard N., Vignoles A. 2015, 'Comparing sample survey measures of English earnings of graduates with administrative data during the Great Recession', *Institute for Studies Working Paper W15/28*. ISSN; 1742-0415

[285] Of the top 10 per cent, men earned £55,000 a year, whilst the women earned £43,000. In the top one per cent, the figures were £148,000 and £89,000 respectively.

[286] Op cit. pp 41-42

[287] 'Income and tax, by gender, region and country'. Part of: *Personal income by tax year and Personal income by tax year statistics*, published 1st March 2016. Available from: *https://www.gov.uk/government/statistics/income-and-tax-by-gender-region-and-country-2010-to-2011*

[288] 'Wages, productivity and the changing composition of the UK workforce'., *Bank of England Q1 Report 2016*. Available from: *http://www.bankofengland.co.uk/publications/Documents/quarterlybulletin/2016/q1pre.pdf*

[289] Cited in Graglia F. C. 1998, *Domestic Tranquility: A brief against Feminism*, p. 168-169

[290] Office for National Statistics. United Kingdom. *Statistical bulletin: Focus on: Violent Crime and Sexual Offences, 2011/12*. http://www.ons.gov.uk/ons/rel/crime-stats/crime-statistics/focus-on-violent-crime/stb-focus-on--violent-crime-and-sexual-offences-2011-12.html

[291] NOTE: The redactions are of references to sexual abuse/violence so as to keep to the present topic of domestic violence. I turn to the issues of sexual violence/abuse later.

[292] Tana Ramsay famously had a longstanding and acrimonious feud with her father who, she claimed, had systematically defrauded her husband whilst chief executive of his business. See: 'Tana Ramsay: my dominating father tore our family apart', *The Telegraph*. Friday 30th January 2015

[293] The Duluth Model is well explained by the *Knowledge for Growth* website. *http://knowledgeforgrowth.wordpress.com/2011/03/21/explaining-domestic-violence-using-feminist-theory/*

[294] Available from: *http://www.avoiceformen.com/women/working-with-violent-women/*

[295] My thanks go to William Collins for providing a multi-page analysis of Women's Aid, including a comprehensive spreadsheet of the financial data from 171 Women's Aid companies and satellite organisations

[296] Cardiff, Fife, North Kent, Foyle, Ipswich, Northampton, Salford, and Welsh WA.

[297] Keir Starmer left the CPS, gaining a Knighthood in the process, and is now the Member of Parliament for Holborn and St Pancras, a safe Labour seat with a 17,000+ majority.

[298] This is a line from *Mourning Bride*, a tragedy written by British playwright William Congreve, first performed in 1697 at Betterton's Co., Lincoln's Inn Fields. The play centers on Zara, a queen held captive by Manuel, King of Granada, and a web of love and deception which results in the mistaken murder of Manuel who is in disguise, and Zara's also mistaken suicide in response. SOURCE: Wikipedia

[299] *Intimate Partner Violence:The Gender Bias Against Men in England & Wales.* Published by Justice for Men and Boys (and the women who love them) pp 18-19https://j4mb.files.wordpress.com/2014/10/141026-submission-to-home-office-improved-layout.pdf The same is true worldwide according to the *Partner Abuse State of Knowledge Project* (PASK), summarised here: http://www.sciencevsfeminism.com/myth-of-oppression/violence-by-women/domestic-violence-partner-violence-statistics-worldwide/

[300] Bates, Elizabeth A., Graham-Kevan, Nicola and Archer, John (2013) 'Testing predictions from the male control theory of men's partner violence'. *Aggressive Behaviour*. ISSN 0096-140X

[301] A factoid is an item of unreliable information that is reported and repeated so often that it becomes accepted as fact.

[302] Available from *http://womensaid.org.uk*

[303] Women's Aid. Domestic Violence: Frequently Asked Questions Factsheet 2009. Page 3. Available as a pdf from: *http://womensaid.org.uk*

[304] Allen J., Walby S., 2004 *Domestic violence, sexual assault and stalking: Findings from the British Crime Survey.* Home Office Research Study 276. Home Office Research, Development and Statistics Directorate March 2004

[305] The ONS data do not differentiate between memories of long-gone events with recent ones.

[306] Walby and Allen (2004) Op cit. Page vi Summary

[307] The UK Data Service, established in 2012 by the Economic and Social Research Council (ESRC), is one of the seven Research Councils in the United Kingdom. It receives most of its funding from the UK Government Department for Business, Innovation and Skills, and provides funding and support for research and training work in social and economic issues, such as postgraduate degrees.

[308] UK Data Archive Study Number 7252 - *Crime Survey for England and Wales, 2011-2012*

[309] Walby and Allen (2004) Op cit. Page 16

[310] Figure 3.4 Page 63. Home Office Statistical Bulletin: *Homicides, Firearm Offences and Intimate Violence 2007/08* (Supplementary Volume 2 to Crime in England and Wales 2007/08) Third Edition David Povey (Ed.), Kathryn Coleman, Peter Kaiza and Stephen Roe 22 January 2009 02/09

[311] Barnish M. 2004, *Domestic Violence: A Literature Review*, Her Majesty's Inspectorate of Probation. UK

[312] Fiebert M. S. 2013, *References Examining Assaults by Women on their Spouses or Male Partners: An Annotated Bibliography* Earlier versions of this review have appeared in *Sexuality and Culture, 1997*, 1, 273-286, and *Sexuality and Culture, 2004*, 8, (No. 3-4), 140-177, and Sexuality and Culture, 2010, 14 (1), 49-91. It is currently available from: *http://www.csulb.edu/~mfiebert/assault.htm*

[313] Archer, John 2000. 'Sex Differences in Aggression between Heterosexual Partners: A Meta-Analytic Review', *Psychological Bulletin* 126 (5): 651. doi: 10.1037/0033-2909.126.5.651. PMID 10989615. Retrieved June 28, 2014. (Cited in Wikipedia)

[314] *The Partner Abuse State of Knowledge Project*, 2013, available from: http://www.prweb.com/releases/2013/5/prweb10741752.htm

[315] 'Homicides, Firearm Offences and Intimate Violence 2008/09': Supplementary Volume 2 to *Crime in England and Wales 2008/09 (Third Edition)*, Home Office Statistical Bulletin. See Table 3.07.

[316] Available from: https://j4mb.files.wordpress.com/2014/10/141026-submission-to-home-office-improved-layout.pdf

[317] Available from: https://j4mb.files.wordpress.com/2014/10/141015-j4mb-submission-first-of-two-to-the-home-office-consultation-on-strengthening-the-

law-on-domestic-abuse-final-draft.pdf

[318] Available from: *https://www.gov.uk/government/publications/statutory-guidance-framework-controlling-or-coercive-behaviour-in-an-intimate-or-family-relationship*

[319] 'Homicides, Firearm Offences and Intimate Violence 2007/08' (Supplementary Volume 2 to *Crime in England and Wales 2007/08*) Third Edition. David Povey (Ed.), Kathryn Coleman, Peter Kaiza and Stephen Roe. (See - Table 1.05)

[320] Office for National Statistics. *Chapter 2 - Homicide. Coverage: England and Wales.* 13th February 2014

[321] Op. cit. Page 11

[322] Ibid. Page 10

[323] The other 47% of women were killed by someone with whom they were acquainted such as a son or daughter, a parent, a friend or acquaintance, or another member of their family.

[324] 'Average age for women to marry hits 30 for the first time', Harry Wallop, *The Daily Telegraph*.30th March 2011. Available from: http://www.telegraph.co.uk/news/8415852/Average-age-for-women-to-marry-hits-30-for-first-time.html

[325] 'Divorces in England and Wales 2011'. *Office for National Statistics Statistical Bulletin 2011*

[326] Ibid..

[327] Available from: http://www.ons.gov.uk/ons/dcp171778_291750.pdf

[328] Op cit. Page 11

[329] Brutus: 'There is a tide in the affairs of men. Which, taken at the flood, leads on to fortune; Omitted, all the voyage of their life is bound in shallows and in miseries. On such a full sea are we now afloat, And we must take the current when it serves, Or lose our ventures'. William Shakespeare. *Julius Caesar*, Act 4, Scene 3, 218–224

[330] 'Timothy Leary, Pied Piper Of Psychedelic 60's, Dies at 75', by Laura Manserus. *New York Times*. June 1, 1996

[331] Graglia F. C. 1998, *Domestic Tranquility: A brief against feminism*. Op. cit.

[332] This interview is available on a number of mirrored sites on YouTube. Here is a link active at the time of writing: *https://youtu.be/bX3EZCVj2XA*

[333] Hayek F. A. 'The Intellectuals and Socialism'. *The University of Chicago Law Review*, (Spring 1949), pp. 417-420, 421-423, 425-433. The University of

Chicago Press; Ed. George B. de Huszar.

[334] Mears M. 2005, *Institutional Injustice: The Family Courts at Work*. Civitas: Institute for the Study of Civil Society

[335] Maher F. 1993 'Classroom Pedagogy and the New Scholarship on Women', in M. Culley and C Portuges (eds). Citation taken from 'Gendered Subjects: The Dynamics of Feminist Teaching', London. Routledge, in Humm M. (1992) *Feminisms: A Reader*, Harvester Wheatsheaf.

[336] *Women's Studies Programs, Departments, & Research Centers* University of Maryland, Baltimore County • 1000 Hilltop Circle • Baltimore, MD 21250. Available from: http://userpages.umbc.edu/~korenman/wmst/programs.html#outside

[337] Westkott M. 1983. 'Women's Studies as a Strategy for Change', in *Feminisms: A Reader* Ed. Humm M. (1992) Harvester Wheatsheaf.

[338] Malala Yousafzai:"Our books and our pens are the most powerful weapons', The Guardian. Friday 12th July 2013. http://www.theguardian.com/commentisfree/2013/jul/12/malala-yousafzai-united-nations-education-speech-text

[339] *Transforming our world: the 2030 Agenda for Sustainable Development*. Resolution A/RES/70/1, United Nations General Assembly, 25 September 2015. Available from: *http://www.un.org/en/ga/search/view_doc.asp?symbol=A/RES/70/1*

[340] Op. cit. Page 3/35

[341] Op. cit. Page 4/35

[342] Op. cit. Page 6/35

[343] Op. cit. Page 18/35

[344] Source: Table 3.3: 'Distribution of total income before and after tax by gender, 2011-12 – Taxpayers only', *Survey of Personal Incomes 2011-12*, updated January 2014. United Kingdom Office for National Statistics

[345] Bertrand Russell 1950, 'Christian Ethics' from *Marriage and Morals*, quoted from *2000 Years of Disbelief*, James A Haught, ed.

[346] According to Answers.com, the phrase 'to speak truth unto power' has long been associated with the British Civil Service in the context of giving honest and objective advice to ministers. It is particularly associated with the historian and academic Professor Peter Hennessy of Queen Mary College London, an avid 'Whitehall watcher', who used it on many occasions during his distinguished career. However, its provenance is widely attributed to the 1955

book, *Speak Truth to Power: A Quaker Search for an Alternative to Violence*, published by the American Friends Service Committee, of the Society of Friends, better known as Quakers.

[347] De Spinoza B 1670, *A Theologico-Political Treatise*. Chapter XX

[348] Graglia F. C. 1998 *Domestic Tranquility: A brief against feminism*. Spence Publishing Company. Dallas.

[349] Graglia F. C. (1998) *Domestic Tranquility: A brief against feminism*. Op cit.

[350] Taken from Wikipedia, this famous saying of Margaret Thatcher's is often misquoted and, indeed, this might be such a misquote, although it appears the best summary.

[351] Fernández G., 2009 *Cuba's Primer - Castro's Earring Economy*. Lulu self-publishing press.

[352] It cannot be denied that economic factors also have had a major influence on this social phenomenon, but these have also, at least in part, been the result of the significant social upheaval I have been discussing at length in this book.

Index